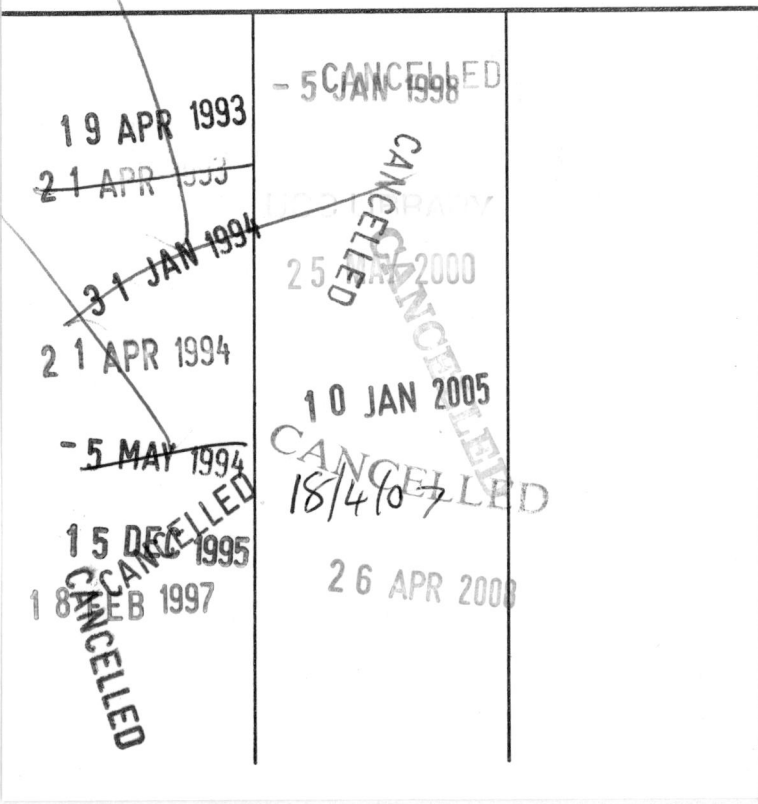

ISLAMIC HISTORY
A FRAMEWORK FOR INQUIRY

REVISED EDITION

R. STEPHEN HUMPHREYS

I.B. TAURIS & CO LTD
Publishers

LONDON • NEW YORK

Published in 1991 by
I.B. Tauris & Co Ltd
110 Gloucester Avenue London NW1 8JA

A CIP record for this book is available from the British Library

ISBN 1–85043–360–7

To John A. Petropulos

IN THANKS FOR HIS EXAMPLE

AS TEACHER AND SCHOLAR

CONTENTS

PREFACE AND ACKNOWLEDGMENTS

ISLAMIC HISTORY presents severe challenges even to an experienced specialist. Many of these are technical in nature—e.g., the multitude of languages needed to read both sources and modern scholarship, the vast number of major texts still in manuscript, the poor organization of libraries and archives. More important, however, is the difficulty of grasping the subject as a whole, of developing a clear sense of the broad themes and concepts through which this sprawling and underdeveloped field of study can be bound together. The first goal of this book, then, is to propose some of the lines of inquiry and research strategies which might be used to construct a persuasive and well-integrated synthesis of the Islamic past.

Even so, this is not a book only for experienced students of the Islamic world. I hope that those just entering the field will find here a practical guide to the bibliography and research skills required for productive work in this area. In addition, I have had very much in mind the needs of scholars in related fields, such as Byzantium, the Crusades, the medieval and early modern Mediterranean, the Ottoman Empire, and the modern Middle East. For them I hope this book will provide a useful overview of the current state of Islamic historical studies and a means of comparing its characteristic methods and problems with those of their own fields. For most historians even now, Islam does not really belong to the mainstream of historical inquiry. If I can help scholars in other fields to view Islamic history as an intelligible and rewarding field of study, I will feel that I have done something of real value.

In this book I focus on political and social history, in the broad sense of the patterns of behavior through which people structure their relations with one another, define common goals, and allocate resources. Within this framework, culture (the ways in which people express their values, attitudes, and beliefs) and religion (the ways in which people relate themselves to ultimate realities) will have an important place, but only insofar as they throw light on questions of social structure and political power.

The geographical and chronological boundaries of this survey are broad but carefully defined. I deal with what M.G.S. Hodgson calls the Central Islamic Lands, because these territories (the Nile-to-Oxus region, plus North Africa and Spain) were brought under Islamic political domination within a century of the *hijra* and remained the core area of Islamic political power and cultural development throughout the nine centuries covered here. I have chosen 600 and 1500 as terminal points for several reasons. The rationale for 600 is clear enough, since that date suggests the immediate historical milieu in which Islam emerged. On the other hand, 1500 marks a number of important changes in Islamic life and our knowledge of it. First, by this time Islam was developing major political and cultural centers far beyond the core established by the early conquests. Second, we must now take account of Europe, an increasingly prominent and disruptive presence in the evolution of Islamic society. Finally, after this date the Ottoman archives completely transform the character of our sources.

Even within these limits, however, the field before us in this book is vast, complex, and sometimes almost impenetrably obscure. Devising a survey of the sources and methods required to study it has thus been an extremely arduous task. Had I realized just how arduous and time-consuming it would be, I would surely never have taken it on. In any case, I have not attempted to add another bibliographic survey to the several good ones which we already have. Rather, I am concerned primarily with questions of method and approach, with ways in which we can use our resources to extend and deepen our knowledge of medieval Islamic history.

I have divided this book into two parts. Part I tries to give a comprehensive (though far from exhaustive) survey of the reference tools and sources available to historians of medieval Islam. In addition to identifying the main reference works, I have tried to evaluate them, to point out the many gaps which must be filled, and where necessary to explain how to use them. In regard to the sources, I make no effort to list them systematically. Rather, I have tried to find a clear and convenient way of classifying them. Within this framework I have reviewed the various repertories, catalogs, and specialized bibliographies which give one access to specific items. In addition, I have discussed the special problems connected with each class of source material and the skills needed to use it effectively.

Part II is made up of ten chapters, each one focused on a broadly defined research problem. These chapters make no pretense of "covering" the whole field of medieval Islamic history—an illusory goal utterly impossible of achievement in any case. Rather, they deal with a series of topics chosen to represent the concerns of modern historical studies generally, and at the same time to reflect the most important work which has been done or is in prospect in the Islamic field. Though every chapter proceeds according to its own plan, all of them are based upon a common agenda:

1. To point out the range of questions raised by the general problem discussed in the chapter. This book is in fact very centrally concerned with the issue of asking valid and productive questions, since these are the nucleus of historical knowledge.

2. To identify the sources (not only texts but material traces) available to us for answering these questions. In regard to textual sources, I pay special attention to those available in translation, not because I think that even the most skillful translation can be an adequate substitute for the original, but because I expect that many of my readers will not be practiced Arabists, Turcologists, etc. Moreover, even scholars competent in these languages will find translations useful in clarifying technical terms, throwing difficult passages into a fresh perspective, etc.

3. To explore the strategies through which these sources can most effectively be exploited. In many cases, this is best done by pursuing lines of inquiry worked out (or sometimes merely sketched) by Islamic specialists. In other cases, I draw on methods developed in other, more highly developed fields of history. Finally, it has sometimes seemed useful to propose new approaches which have not yet appeared in scholarly writing; these should be taken as suggestions, obviously, rather than as fully elaborated research designs.

4. To survey and evaluate the scholarly literature which pertains (often in a very broad sense) to the topic of the chapter. I have made a special effort to include important studies in Arabic, Persian, and Turkish, for these are seldom reviewed or indexed in Western publications.

Two general points must be made. First, no chapter includes all the sources and scholarly contributions which could be cited, and doubtless there are some unfortunate omissions. My goal is not exhaustive coverage, but rather a balanced evaluation of the state of the field, and this goal has compelled me to focus on those works which most clearly bring out the nature of the topics and problems being examined. Moreover, a persistent reader should be able to develop as thorough a bibliography as he desires simply by following up the footnotes and bibliographies of the works cited. Second, I have tried to take a constructive approach to the works of scholarship which I have cited, with the aim of building further on what they have achieved. Shortcomings are inevitable and must sometimes be pointed out, but I look at these not as failings so much as problems for future scholarship to resolve. Where it is a question of highly controversial work, I may seem a bit equivocal. However, I think it more useful in the present context to indicate where points of conflict lie, allowing my readers to make up their own minds, rather than to promulgate dogmatic judgments of my own.

The first five chapters in Part II deal primarily with politics in one form or another. Each chapter examines a different dimension of the subject and calls attention to a distinct body of materials. Chapter 3 is concerned with the problems created for modern researchers by the narrative tradition of early Islam, and asks how we can use this tradition to analyze questions of political cohesion and authority in the primitive Community. Chapter 4, on the Abbasid Revolution, focuses on modern scholarship and the conflicting interpretations of this paradigmatic event which it has produced. Chapter 5 returns to the narrative sources—in this case the court chronicle, a genre which is crucial for our knowledge of the politics of the Islamic world between the 10th and 15th centuries. By examining the analysis of military government presented by two very astute chroniclers, our discussion tries to define the conceptions of politics imbedded in writings of this kind. Chapter 6 turns to the symbolic dimension of politics with an account of the role of ideology in the inter-dynastic quarrels of Iran and Iraq during the 10th and 11th centuries. Of particular significance in this context is the synthesis of ideas proclaimed by the early Seljukids. Finally, Chapter 7 examines our sources for reconstructing the machinery of government in medieval Islam and for assessing the impact of this machinery on society as a whole. The admittedly favorable case of the Mamluk Empire (1250–1517) has been chosen, because this regime preserves at least fragments of every type of source, whether textual, documentary, or archaeological, which might be used for the study of medieval Islamic administration.

The next five chapters belong to the elusive domain of socio-economic history. Because this field includes almost everything we do in our daily lives, I have had to be ruthlessly selective. I am acutely aware that many fascinating and even vital topics are touched upon only in passing, if at all. Among those I most regret shortchanging are three: (a) tribalism—a crucial feature of Middle Eastern life in all periods, but perhaps most notably under the Umayyads, in post-Almohad North Africa, and in Il-Khanid and Timurid Iran; (b) the Sufi orders, which provided much of the Islamic world's social and cultural cohesion, not to mention its religious vitality, from the 7th/13th century down to modern times; (c) finally, the complex status and roles of women, a topic on which serious research is just beginning, but which already promises a major rethinking of the inner dynamics of medieval Islamic society. My readers no doubt will have regrets of their own. If there has been a single criterion favoring some topics rather than others, it has been my preference for those which have generated a substantial and reasonably sophisticated literature. Moreover, I believe that those who control the ideas and materials presented in these chapters will be in good shape to define and pursue their own areas of interest.

Chapter 8 looks at the social group which we know best, the *ʿulamāʾ*, and examines various ways of defining the characteristics and social roles of this group. This chapter also calls attention to the biographical dictionary, which is both our principal source for the *ʿulamāʾ* and the most distinctively Islamic of all literary genres. Chapter 9 examines the body of thought produced by the *ʿulamāʾ*—viz., *sharīʿa* jurisprudence—and asks how and to what extent this highly abstract, normative form of writing can be applied to the problems of social and economic history. Chapter 10 deals with urban history—both the conceptual problem of the "Islamic city," and the methodological issues presented by archaeology and topographical texts. As in many other chapters, this one tries to give substance to broad general problems by examining a specific time and place—here, Damascus between the 12th and 16th centuries. Chapters 11 and 12 both investigate social groups which were obviously crucial in real life but appear as very marginal actors in most of our texts: the non-Muslim communities (Chapter 11) and the peasantry (Chapter 12). Chapter 11 examines the most remarkable trove of documents to reach us from the medieval Middle East, the papers of the Cairo Geniza; in contrast, it also discusses the almost undocumentable process of conversion to Islam. Chapter 12 asks what techniques we can devise to penetrate into the lives of people who could not speak for themselves and who were almost ignored by the literate classes. In addition, it looks at issues of human ecology—at the challenges posed by a harsh physical environment, and the technologies and social systems which people have created to confront these challenges.

A final comment. I propose many interpretations of the subject matter discussed in these ten chapters, but I do not pretend that these are in any sense definitive statements. They are rather brief discourses, meant to suggest possible lines of inquiry and explanation. Nor do I frame rigid methodological models: I hope only to suggest the kinds of approaches which are (or ought to be) central to our field. On one level, then, these chapters describe the present stage of research in Islamic historical studies; but on another, they try to show how this field can be developed and even transformed, as it must be if the study of the Islamic past is ever to take its rightful place in the study of human societies and cultures.

. . . . .

A book of this kind is in every sense a collaborative effort. Many colleagues have generously read one or more chapters, providing me with a host of important criticisms, corrections, and references. I have benefited greatly from their suggestions, though limits of time and space did not permit me to incorporate all of these. In alphabetical order, my readers are William Brinner, Mark Cohen, Bruce Craig, Robert Dankoff, Fred M. Donner, Robert Frykenberg, Paul Hyams, Charles Issawi, Bernard Lewis, Maureen Mazzaoui, Roy P. Mottahedeh, Eric Ormsby, Carl Petry, Fazlur Rahman, Paula Sanders, Jan Vansina, and Jeanette Wakin.

I owe a great deal to all of these scholars, but I must say something more in regard to two of them. Bruce Craig originally suggested this book to me, and read and discussed with me the entire manuscript as it developed. He has also supplied, tactfully but firmly, the friendly pressure needed to see it through. Bernard Lewis shared not only his immense erudition but many items from his personal library; more important, he gave steadfast support and friendship at a troubled time.

I am also grateful for the help of three graduate students at the University of Wisconsin: Susan Grabler, Nurhan İsvan, and James Lindsay. They showed much skill and dedication in assisting me with several hateful chores—checking and correcting the bibliography, proofreading, and compiling the index. Several drafts of four chapters were typed by Kimberly Roach, and Sandra Heitzkey displayed her customary efficiency and great good humor in entering the Bibliographical Index on a word processor. All this made the final stages in preparing the manuscript go much faster than is normally the case.

I could never have finished at all without the research time and financial support generously provided by several institutions: the Institute for Advanced

Study, Princeton, N.J. (1980–81); the American Council of Learned Societies (spring, 1982); the Graduate School of the University of Wisconsin-Madison (summer, 1982 and 1983; autumn, 1984); the Joint Committee on the Near and Middle East of the Social Science Research Council and the American Council of Learned Societies (autumn, 1984), with funds provided by the National Endowment for the Humanities and the Ford Foundation; the Institute for Research in The Humanities, University of Wisconsin-Madison (spring, 1985).

I wish likewise to thank the following scholars and publishers for their kind cooperation: John E. Woods, for permission to quote from his unpublished translation of a segment of Abū al-Faḍl Bayhaqī's *Ta'rīkh-i Masʿūdī*; Bernard Lewis, for permission to use his translation of another brief passage from Bayhaqī as the heading to Part II, Chapter 5; the University of California Press, for permission to quote extended passages from Volume III of Ibn Taghrībirdī, *History of Egypt, 1382–1469 A.D.*, translated by William Popper (*University of California Publications in Semitic Philology*, xvii, 1957).

The text of this book is substantially the same as that of the original edition published in 1988. However, that version went to press in 1985; the field of Islamic history has changed somewhat during the intervening years, along with a number of my ideas about it. I have thus taken advantage of the opportunity to revise or clarify certain points, to correct errors, to add several recently published books and articles, and to delete items that are now plainly obsolete. All too predictably, these revisions took much longer than I had supposed. I wish to extend my warmest thanks to my editor, Margaret Case, for her calm patience and good counsel during this aggravating process.

Finally, a more personal note. I wrote this book largely while I was a member of the Department of History at the University of Wisconsin-Madison. I owe my colleagues at that splendid institution a profound debt of gratitude for the confidence which they have always shown in my work and for the supportive environment which they have provided. I have no way to express my thanks to my wife, but she knows how much her love, companionship, and unwavering loyalty over the past quarter-century have meant to me.

Madison, Wisconsin
June 1990

PART ONE

SOURCES AND RESEARCH TOOLS

INTRODUCTION

IT IS BEST to admit at the outset that no scholar can become the master of everything he needs to know. Even in a narrowly defined aspect of Islamic history, the erudition and technical skills required for a really adequate investigation may seem overwhelming. Thus, the administrative history of Umayyad Egypt calls for a thorough command of Greek, Arabic, and Coptic, of papyrology, numismatics, and archaeology, of early Islamic historiography, of late Roman and Islamic law and administrative practice. To deal with Syria in the age of the Crusades, one ought to control sources in at least eight languages (including Armenian and Syriac)—not only narrative texts, but administrative manuals, legal compendia, chancery correspondence, and poetry. And here too numismatics, epigraphy, and archaeology are vital. In short, a scholar who tries to master every research skill which he might reasonably want to use will never do anything else. A just sense of one's limits is not only salutory but absolutely necessary.

Even so, no one can afford to forgo a broad acquaintance with the tools of his craft. In this light, the two chapters which follow are the foundation for everything else in the book. They make no claim to be exhaustive surveys of their subject matter. Rather, they are intended to show how to use the main sources and reference works for Islamic history. In the case of reference works, this goal will require a fairly extended discussion of their aims and organizational idiosyncrasies—for many of them are far more mysterious than the Orient which they purport to explain. In addition, we will identify the major gaps (some of them really astonishing) in the set of tools at our disposal. Such an overview of reference works does have broader implications, to be sure. However elementary it may seem, it will suggest a picture of the development of Islamic historical studies, of the current state of the field, and of the directions which it might take in the future.

As to the sources, I have tried to develop a practical and convenient classification of them, so that even a newcomer can readily learn what kinds of materials we have and do not have. A survey of this kind serves two purposes. First, it establishes a common frame of reference for the specific source citations in later chapters. Second, by showing what resources we have at our disposal, it can suggest which problems and lines of inquiry in the field are likely to prove most productive, and what research skills one must acquire in order to pursue these effectively.

Chapter One

REFERENCE WORKS

A. General

THE MOST important and comprehensive reference tool for Islamic studies is the *Encyclopaedia of Islam*, an immense effort to deal with every aspect of Islamic civilization, conceived in the widest sense, from its origins down to the present. There are now three versions, as follows:

1. The first edition (*EI*^{1}): four volumes plus a supplement; in English, French, and German editions (1913–1938).
2. A new edition (*EI*^{2}): five volumes completed, with a sixth well along (letters A to Ma), and the fascicles for a supplement for Vols. I–III; French and English only. Begun in 1954, *EI*^{2} was originally intended to be a simple updating and modest expansion of the original, but it has grown in scope almost with each fascicle, and there are now no strict limits on the length of contributions.
3. *Shorter Encyclopaedia of Islam (SEI)*, ed. H.A.R. Gibb and J. H. Kramers (1953). This work contains the articles in *EI*^{1} specifically dealing with law and religion, together with additional bibliography and a few revisions. (German version: *Handwörterbuch des Islam*, ed. A. J. Wensinck and J. H. Kramers; 1941).

EI is no anonymous digest of received wisdom. Most of the articles are signed, and while some are hardly more than dictionary entries, others are true research pieces—in many cases the best available treatment of their subject. Each article contains a bibliography, sometimes rather elementary but often extraordinarily detailed. The articles are arranged alphabetically, but of course things are not that simple; with few exceptions entries are made under the relevant Arabic-Islamic technical term or indigenous name. "Fiḳh" instead of "Jurisprudence" is perhaps self-evident, but "Ḳabḳ" (for "Caucasus") is distinctly less obvious, and "Kitābāt" instead of "Inscriptions" verges on preciosity. For *EI*^{2} the problem will be somewhat alleviated by an index volume, of which a fascicle for Vols. I–III has already appeared.

EI's imposing apparatus can easily lead one to take its pronouncements for objective truth. But *EI*^{1} and *SEI* were produced almost entirely by European scholars, and they represent a specifically European interpretation of Islamic civilization. The point is not that this interpretation is "wrong," but that the questions addressed in these volumes often differ sharply from those which Muslims have traditionally asked about themselves. *EI*^{2} is a somewhat different matter. It began in much the same way as its predecessor, but a growing proportion of the articles now come from scholars of Muslim background. These persons do not represent the traditional learning of Qom and al-Azhar, to be sure; they have been trained in Western-style universities, and they share the methodology if not always the cultural values and attitudes of their Western colleagues. Even so, the change in tone is perceptible and significant.

The concern of Muslim scholars not to leave their own history in European hands has led to a number of adaptations of *EI*: Turkish, Persian, Arabic, Urdu. Of these the oldest and most important is the Turkish *İslam Ansiklopedisi* (abbrev., *IA*; 13 vols., 1945–1988). There are valuable additions (and of course some tendentious ones) even to items simply translated from *EI*, while the articles on Turkish subjects—a very broad category indeed—are original and often major contributions.

A very recent and potentially extremely important project is the *Encyclopaedia Iranica*, under the general editorship of Ehsan Yarshater. In format and approach it much resembles *EI*², though of course it ranges far beyond the Islamic era. Moreover, "Iran" is understood here in very broad terms indeed, as the whole zone of Iranian political-cultural influence, so that much of the medieval Islamic world is included at one point or another. *Encyclopaedia Iranica* is an ambitious venture; commencing publication in 1982, it has required more than two volumes (of 900 pages each!) to complete the letter A. Even halfway through Vol. III, only the earliest fascicles of "B" have appeared.

A reference very different in conception but likewise on a vast scale is the *Handbuch der Orientalistik*, ed. Bertold Spuler (abbrev., *HO*; 1952–in progress). *HO* originally intended to provide concise, authoritative synopses of the languages, literatures, religions, legal systems, and political history of Asia—i.e., the traditional Orientalist areas of concern. However, some volumes in the series are almost exhaustive treatments of their subjects, based on much original research (e.g., the works by Manfred Ullmann and Mary Boyce listed below).

HO is organized in an extremely complex manner, and its constituent volumes are normally catalogued as serials rather than by author and title. Briefly, *HO* is subdivided in descending order into *Abteilungen* (Divisions), *Bände* (Volumes), *Abschnitten* (Sections), and *Lieferungen* (Fascicles). For Islamic history the most significant categories are as follows:

Erste Abteilung: *Nahe und Mittlere Osten*

- III. Band: *Semitistik*
- IV. Band: *Iranistik*
- V. Band: *Altaistik*
- VI. Band: *Geschichte der Islamischen Länder*
- VII. Band: *Armenisch und Kaukasische Sprachen*
- VIII. Band: *Religion*
- *Ergänzungsbande*

Within these broad categories individual contributions are numbered according to a pre-arranged schema; the numerous apparent gaps simply represent units not yet published.

Several important titles are unfortunately not easily located within this framework; note in particular the following:

B. IV; 1. Abschn.; Lfg. 2: G. Morrison, ed., *History of Persian Literature from the Beginning of the Islamic Period to the Present Day* (1981)

B. IV; 2. Abschn.; Lfg. 1: *Literatur* (1968). See especially Bertold Spuler, "Die historische und geographische Literatur in persischer Sprache," pp. 100–167

B. V; 1. Abschn.: *Türkologie* (1963)

B. V; 5. Abschn.: *Geschichte Mittelasiens* (1966)

B. VI: *Geschichte der islamischen Länder*—the original German text has been replaced by B. Spuler *et al.*, *The Muslim World, a Historical Survey*, trans. F.R.C. Bagley (4 vols., 1968–81)

B. VI; 5. Abschn.: H. R. Idris and K.Rohrborn, *Regierung und Verwaltung des Vorderen Orients in islamischer Zeit*, (1977–in progress)

B. VI; 6. Abschn.: *Wirtschaftsgeschichte des Vorderen Orients in islamischer Zeit*, 1. Teil (1977); 2. Teil, in preparation

B. VIII; 1. Abschn.: Mary Boyce, *A History of Zoroastrianism* (1975–in progress)

B. VIII; 2. Abschn.: *Religionsgeschichte des Orients in der Zeit der Weltreligionen* (1961)

Ergbd. I; Heft 1: Walther Hinz, *Islamische Mässe und Gewichte umgerechnet ins metrische System* (1955; rev. ed., 1970)

Ergbd. II; 1. Halbband: Adolf Grohmann, *Arabische Chronologie; Arabische Papyruskunde* (1966)

Ergbd. III: *Orientalisches Recht* (1964)

Ergbd. VI; 1. Abschn.: Manfred Ullmann, *Die Medizin im Islam* (1970)

Ergbd. VI; 2. Abschn.: Manfred Ullmann, *Die Natur- und Geheimwissenschaften im Islam* (1972)

Ergbd. VII: Ibrahim Gomaa, *A Historical Chart of the Muslim World* (1972)

Ergbd. VIII: Hans-Jürgen Kornrumpf, *Osmanische Bibliographie mit besonderer Berücksichtigung der Türkei in Europa* (1973)

Zweite Abteilung: Indien; B. IV; 3. Abschn.: Annemarie Schimmel, *Islam in the Indian Subcontinent* (1980)

One last reference should be mentioned, though it is aimed at a more general audience than the works discussed above. This is the *Dictionary of the Middle Ages* (abbr. *DMA*; 13 vols., 1982–89). As its title implies, *DMA* deals with Latin Europe and Byzantium as well as the central Islamic lands. Its Islamic articles are often too brief to serve serious research purposes, and the bibliographies emphasize English titles. Even so, many contributions are significant interpretive essays, and in any case *DMA* provides useful background and introductory statements.

B. Bibliographic Tools

Bibliography has in the last two decades turned into one of the leading growth industries in Islamic studies. Indeed, the very profusion of such references has by now created a bibliographic problem in itself. Computer technology will certainly help to manage this; a scholar armed with a personal computer and a good program (e.g., *Pro-Cite*, produced by Personal Bibliographic Software, Inc., Ann Arbor, Michigan) should be able to control his own fields of interest far more effectively than in the past. But even in an electronic age, printed bibliographies serve a number of functions—allowing a scholar to check and confirm his own listings, providing ready access to new areas of inquiry, etc.—and in any case they represent the current reality of scholarly life. In the following discussion we will try to examine at least the indispensable references, since an exhaustive survey is hardly possible within reasonable limits.

The most systematic and comprehensive tool at our disposal is the *Index Islamicus*, edited by J. D. Pearson and his associates. It is meticulously and intelligently organized, but nothing is perfect, and there are inevitably errors, omissions, and oddly classified entries. In addition, the *Index* has serious gaps: until 1976 it did not include books and monographs; and except for an occasional Turkish title, it does not include listings in Oriental languages. (The failure of Western bibliographers to establish a regular, systematic survey of scholarly books and articles published in Arabic, Persian, Turkish, and Urdu is both a disgrace and a serious inconvenience; as things are, one learns about such titles only through a haphazard combination of oral tradition and scattered references, and much worthwhile research inevitably slips through the cracks.) Even with these shortcomings, however, *Index Islamicus* is invaluable, for it covers almost every article published on any aspect of Islamic studies, in every European language, between 1905 and the present. It surveys not only an immense array of scholarly journals but *Festschriften* and conference volumes as well. The main volume (1958) covers the years 1905–1955, while five-year supplements (currently, 1956–1960 to 1976–1980) deal with the period since. Since 1976, a *Quarterly Index Islamicus* has also been issued, with an annual table of contents and author index. Locating recent contributions can be a tiresome chore, obviously, but at least most things can now be found in one place.

Islamic studies did not emerge full-blown in 1905, of course; the centuries of European scholarship neglected by Pearson have been surveyed by Wolfgang Behn in *Index Islamicus, 1665–1905* (1989), which contains some 21,000 entries. Behn essentially follows Pearson's classification of topics, and he also adheres to the decision to omit books and monographs. Since 1982, Behn has also published an annual *Islamic Book Review Index*, which in some sense supplements the *Quarterly Index Islamicus*. Here he lists by author all relevant books which have received reviews during a given year; titles are entered under each year in which they have been reviewed, and new notices are cumulated with earlier ones for as long as eleven years. The project provides a very convenient means of assessing the quality and impact of recent scholarship, and one must hope that it will be sustained.

For the period before 1905 and for books and monographs published down through World War I, we have another valuable resource in Gustav Pfannmüller, *Handbuch der Islam-Literatur* (1923). Pfannmüller's scope was broad, including geography and ethnography as well as religion and politics (though religion did get 285 of the book's 420 pages); moreover, he not only listed titles but gave concise discussions of the more important items. In a sense, then, his work is a precis of European Orientalism at the close of its heroic age—the period of Nöldeke, Becker, Snouck Hurgronje, Goldziher, Wellhausen, van Berchem, and Caetani—and for this reason it still merits our attention.

The difficulty with an exhaustive bibliography like *Index Islamicus* is precisely that it is exhaustive, making no distinction between sound metal and dross, major studies and derivative ones. We can often get a better sense of the field from a good selective bibliography. There are now a number of these, but for the historian the best is still a work first issued in 1943. Jean Sauvaget's *Introduction à l'histoire de l'Orient musulman* was hastily cobbled up to support his war-time lectures at the Collège de France, but his erudition, methodological brilliance, and force of personality made it a very useful companion even for experienced scholars. It was drastically overhauled by Claude Cahen in 1961, and then translated into English (with some not always fortunate revisions) as *Introduction to the History of the Muslim East* (1965). It has now been revised again under a new title: Claude Cahen, *Introduction à l'histoire du monde musulman médiéval: viie–xve siècle* (1982). Much of value is omitted, and the bibliographic data is often excessively terse, but its historically oriented organization, concise evaluations of the items cited, and comments on methodology make Sauvaget-Cahen a most effective overview of Islamic historical studies.

Sauvaget-Cahen contains a good discussion of references and periodicals, but the best guide to this sort of thing is Gustav Meiseles, *Reference Literature to Arabic Studies: a Bibliographical Guide* (1978). Meiseles' survey gives titles only, without discussion or comment, but it is carefully organized and contains a wide array of Arabic as well as European-language works. Particularly useful are his extensive lists of Arabic biographical collections (both medieval and modern), dictionaries of every sort, and Qur'ān and Hadith research tools. The chapter on periodicals (with standard abbreviations) is also excellent. In contrast, his coverage of history, geography and art seems a bit spotty and arbitrary.

Meiseles can be supplemented with the *Arab Islamic Bibliography*, edited by Diana Grimwood-Jones, Derek Hopwood, and J. D. Pearson (1977). This represents a reworking of Giuseppe Gabrieli, *Manuale di bibliografia musulmana* (1916); it makes no attempt to survey the substantive aspects of Islamic history, but simply aims to outline the reference tools, sources, and main centers of study for the Islamic-Middle Eastern field. For Iranian subjects (including the pre-Islamic period), the most useful guide is probably L. P. Elwell-Sutton, ed., *Bibliographical Guide to Iran* (1983), which was explicitly prepared as a companion volume to the *Arab Islamic Bibliography*. It includes all fields of Iranian studies, and it gives concise but pointed comments on both general problems and specific titles.

Such bibliographic compendia codify the past, but they cannot serve the equally pressing need to keep track of recent publications. For many years, this function was served preeminently by *Abstracta Islamica*, an annual survey of monographs, text editions, and major articles in all fields of Islamic studies. *Abstracta Islamica* is published as part of the *Revue des études islamiques*, normally as a separate fascicle. Its coverage is very broad, albeit selective, and in contrast to *Index Islamicus* it does include scholarship in Arabic, Turkish, and Persian. Entries usually include a concise critical summary. *Abstracta Islamica* would be even more useful if it were published regularly, but very lengthy delays are unfortunately the rule. Its role may be filled to some degree by the admirable *Bulletin critique* of *Annales Islamologiques*, first published in vol. xx (1984). (Since 1986 it has been printed and bound separately.) The goal of the *Bulletin critique* is to present full-length reviews of all major publications in Islamic studies: Arabic language and literature, religion and philosophy, history down to 1945, history of science, art and archaeology. So far, at least, it has lived up to its promise.

Since *Annales Islamologiques* is published by the Institut Français d'Archéologie Orientale in Cairo, it will almost inevitably slight Turkic and Iranian topics. For these, fortunately, help is available. The *Türkologischer Anzeiger*, published as an annual supplement (though separately bound and paginated) to *WZKM*, gives a meticulous survey of all aspects of Turkish studies. It contains no abstracts or critiques of the works listed, however, and covers only Anatolia and the Balkans. For works published before 1974, see H.-J. Kornrumpf, *Osmanisches Bibliographie* (*HO*, Ergbd. VIII, 1973); the immense size of this compilation makes it cumbersome to use, and it shares *TA*'s narrow geographical focus and lack of commentary on titles listed. For Iran, see *Abstracta Iranica*, an annual supplement to *Studia Iranica* published since 1978 by the Institut Français d'Iranologie in Tehran. It includes works in Middle Eastern as well as European languages, translations and editions of texts as well as modern studies; each entry is followed by a critical summary.

Central Asia and ancient Iran both had an enormous impact on the evolution of Islamic civilization, but both fields fall outside the expertise of the majority of Islamists and are very difficult to control in any case. Here two titles are very helpful:

J. D. Pearson, ed. *A Bibliography of Pre-Islamic Persia* (1975).

Denis Sinor, *Introduction à l'étude de l'Eurasie Centrale* (1963).

Pearson's survey is well organized but simply lists titles without further comment; Sinor's is a bibliographical essay which somewhat resembles Sauvaget-Cahen.

Unpublished doctoral dissertations, even when they are little more than ill-digested compilations, bring out a rich fund of new data, and for some reason many of the best ones in the Islamic field are never published. In addition to the standard current reference for U.S. doctoral theses, *Dissertation Abstracts*, which is at times exceedingly frustrating to use, we now have a reliable and clearly organized three-volume series by George D. Selim:

1. *American Doctoral Dissertations on the Arab World, 1883-1974* (2nd ed., 1976).
2. *American Doctoral Dissertations on the Arab World, 1975-1981* (1983).
3. *American Doctoral Dissertations on the Arab World: Supplement, August 1981 - December 1987* (1989).

Regrettably there is nothing similar for the Irano-Turkic lands, which did play a certain role in medieval Islamic history. For British dissertations, see Peter Sluglett, *Theses on Islam, the Middle East, and North-West Africa 1880–1978, Accepted by Universities in the United Kingdom and Ireland* (1983). For German theses see the comprehensive listing compiled by Klaus Schwarz (1980), *Der Vordere Orient in den Hochschulen Deutschlands, Österreichs, und der Schweiz. Eine Bibliographie von Dissertationen und Habilitationsschriften (1885–1978)*. Schwarz gives the relevant bibliographic data, including altered titles, for theses which were later published—an uncommon and very useful feature.

There is no long-term compilation of this kind for French theses, but in 1982 the Association Française des Arabisants published *Dix ans de recherche universitaire française sur le monde arabe et islamique de 1968–9 à 1979*, which lists some 6000 theses (thèses de troisieme cycle as well as thèses d'état) undertaken or presented during this period. A cumulative listing of earlier titles is hardly called for, since the traditional system of doctoral studies mandated that theses be published. On the other hand, supplements at ten-year intervals would be most welcome. The organization is Gallic to the core: thesis titles are listed by university and director; only for completed theses are the authors named. Bibliographic data aside, this work also provides a very welcome outline of the exceedingly complex infrastructure (research centers, overseas institutes, etc.) of contemporary Islamic studies in France.

One item must be mentioned but cannot really be recommended. Maurice Saliba, *Arabic and Islamic Studies: Doctoral Dissertations and Graduate Theses in English, French, and German (1881–1981)* (1983), has too many errors and omissions to be relied upon, in spite of its promising title.

A comprehensive and regularly updated listing of Islamic texts translated into European languages would obviously be extremely useful. A good first step in this direction has been taken by Margaret Anderson, *Arabic Materials in English Translation: a Bibliography of Works from the Pre-Islamic Period to 1977* (1980), which includes, with brief comments, more than 1600 titles. Something of the kind is desperately needed for Persian and Turkish, and among other European languages the vast French translation literature should certainly have priority status.

One of the constantly recurring themes in this book will be the need for historians of medieval Islam to familiarize themselves with the theory, method, and substantive research of the social sciences, even if they choose to reject them in particular cases. Social scientists are fickle, to be sure. Leonard Binder, ed., *The Study of the Middle East: Research and Scholarship in the Humanities and Social Sciences* (1976), already shows signs of conceptual as well as bibliographic obsolescence. Ongoing changes and developments can be tracked through the "state of the field" articles which appear in the *Bulletin of the Middle East Studies Association.* A more personal but very wide-ranging survey is that of Dale Eickelman, *The Middle East: an Anthropological Approach* (1981; 2nd ed., 1989), which is really a critical assessment of our current understanding of Middle Eastern societies and cultures. Eickelman's focus is naturally on the contemporary, but he deals also with a number of medieval and early modern topics. The second edition contains an author index, which makes the fund of bibliographic data buried in his footnotes fairly accessible.

We have so far overlooked the bibliographies which are usually attached to scholarly monographs, but these are often the most useful resource at our disposal. A new study may be far from the best thing on its subject, but at least it ought to reflect the state of the literature. More than that, such bibliographies are sometimes remarkably comprehensive; incomparably the best bibliography on Islamic law, for example, is that provided by Joseph Schacht in *An Introduction to Islamic Law* (1964). In general, I believe that research should begin with the references cited in recent articles and monographs. In this way, one's reading is guided by a growing knowledge of the subject. Only when the main lines of scholarly debate have been explored does it make sense to undertake a systematic survey of bibliographic reference tools, with the aim of completing and correcting the body of titles already assembled.

C. Languages

In spite of the disheartening array of languages used in the medieval Islamic world—a veritable Babel—the great bulk of our sources were recorded in only three of them: Arabic, Persian, and Turkish. Among the plethora of grammars and dictionaries available for each of these, we will try to identify those which are particularly useful for the social/political historian.

HO (1. Abteilung) provides concise descriptions of them in the context of their broader linguistic families, along with surveys of their literatures: for Arabic, B. III, Abschn. 3; for Persian, B. IV, Abschn. 1–2; for Turkish, B. V, Abschn. 1. In addition, there are three major collective works devoted to Arabic, Iranian, and Turkish philology:

1. *Grundriss der Arabischen Philologie.* vol. I, *Sprachwissenschaft,* ed. by Wolfdietrich Fischer (1982); vol. II, *Literaturwissenschaft,* ed. by Helmut Gätje (1987).
2. *Grundriss der Iranischen Philologie,* ed. by Wilhelm Geiger and Ernst Kuhn: vol. I, *Sprachgeschichte* (1896); vol. II, *Literatur, Geschichte, und Kultur* (1904).
3. *Philologiae Turcicae Fundamenta* (2 vols., 1959–in progress).

Of these the *Grundriss der Iranischen Philologie* is the largest in scale, a real attempt at a summa. It is obviously antiquated, but some contributions retain much of their original value; Theodor Nöldeke's "Die iranische National-Epos" for example remains a classic study. The *Fundamenta,* begun by Jean Deny and supervised by a distinguished editorial committee, is of course more representative of current knowledge; vol. I (1959) is a survey of Turkic languages, while vol. II (1965) is devoted to their respective literatures. A third volume on history has been announced for many years, but to date only one small fascicle has appeared (1970)—an all too common fate for collective works in the Islamic/Middle Eastern field. The *Grundriss der Arabischen Philologie* is of course up-to-date and quite comprehensive. To a greater degree than the Iranian and Turkish works, it represents a precis of scholarship available elsewhere; even so, it is a sensible place to start.

Arabic was not only the first language of Islam, but was also the one which produced by far the largest number of texts during our period. Arabic occurs in many varieties, but for our purposes the most important form is the one called Classical Arabic—the language of the Qur'ān, the hadith, and the ancient poetry—which has also provided the grammatical and lexical framework for *formal* usage (both written and spoken) down to the present. Even by the 3rd/9th century, however, there were features in current usage which did not conform to Classical canons, and in the historical writing of the 7th/13th and later centuries we encounter a growing number of "colloquial" elements. Moreover, the practical demands of administration, commerce, and everyday life brought about the coinage of a host of terms which did not occur in the Classical texts. Since medieval Arabic grammar and lexicography were based almost entirely on such texts, however, the modern scholar is often left in the lurch precisely in those crucial passages where help is most desperately needed. As we must learn to expect in the Islamic field, progress towards an adequate set of linguistic research tools has been fitful and slow.

The dictionaries of Classical Arabic by G.F.W. Freytag, *Lexicon arabico-latinum* (4 vols., 1830–1837), and Albert de Biberstein-Kazimirski, *Dictionnaire arabe-français* (4 vols., 1860) are generally reliable, though both are antiquated by now. Freytag's definitions are drawn chiefly from two prestigious but concise medieval lexicons, by al-Jawharī and al-Fīrūzābādī. Biberstein-Kazimirski regrettably neither cites his sources nor makes any statement of method; he does include post-Classical and even some Maghribi colloquial words and definitions, however. The splendid achievement of Hans Wehr, *A Dictionary of Modern Written Arabic* (1st English ed., 1961; 4th ed., revised and much expanded, 1979) is surprisingly useful for later medieval texts in spite of its focus on 20th-century writing.

The great work in this field, however, is E. W. Lane, *An Arabic-English Lexicon* (8 vols., 1863–1893), a meticulous collation and translation of the vast resources of medieval Arabic lexicography. Lane is essential, but presents three serious problems: (1) he does not gloss texts directly, but only reproduces the data of the medieval dictionaries; (2) like his sources, he seldom cites post-Classical meanings, even though the great bulk of our historical sources are post-Classical; (3) he could not complete his work before his death, so that the eight letters *qāf-yā'* are represented only by fragmentary notes. For obvious reasons, no serious historian can avoid at least occasional reference to the compilations of medieval Arab lexicographers. A convenient introduction to their work is John A. Haywood, *Arabic Lexicography: its History and its Place in the General History of Lexicography* (1960; 2nd ed., 1965).

When it is completed, the standard lexicon for medieval Arabic will certainly be the *Wörterbuch der Klassischen Arabischen Sprache* (abbr., *WKAS*; 1957–in progress), published by the Deutsche Morgenländische Gesellschaft under the editorship of Manfred Ullmann. *WKAS* is based on the direct glossing of a vast array of texts written up to ca. 1500, and gives not only definitions (in both German and English) but brief textual citations. It is not a hasty affair. In order to fill the gaps in the last two volumes of Lane, the editors began with the letter *kāf*; as of this writing, the letter following (*lām*) has yet to be completed, and it is rare to produce more than one fascicle (ca. 65 pp.) per year.

Starting from the other end of the alphabet, the *Dictionnaire arabe-français-anglais* (4 vols., 1964–in progress), is inching along, and has now reached the middle of the letter *ḥā'*. Begun by the late Régis Blachère and continued by his colleagues in Paris, this work is also based on the direct glossing of texts (both medieval and modern), though it draws on a far more restricted repertory than does *WKAS* and adds little to what we already have.

The most valuable lexical tool for the historian at this point is R.P.A. Dozy, *Supplément aux dictionnaires arabes* (2 vols., 1881; repr. 1927, 1960). Dozy omits the Classical definitions given in Lane and Freytag, restricting his entries to non-Classical terms and usages. He has glossed an immense variety of texts, but since the bulk of these were written in Spain and the Maghrib, his definitions do not always fit writings from the Nile-to-Oxus region. It is an indispensable companion all the same. A roughly similar though much smaller work, especially useful for legal terminology, is Edmond Fagnan, *Additions aux dictionnaires arabes* (1923).

A very important additional resource can be found in the glossaries which are sometimes annexed to critical editions and translations. A few examples will suffice. In his remarkable translation of al-Maqrīzī's *Kitāb al-sulūk li-maʿrifat duwal al-mulūk* (*Histoire des sultans mameloukes*, 2 vols., 1845), E. Quatremère provided a series of extended lexical footnotes, which can be located through an index of technical terms at the end of vol. II. Old as they are, these notes are still an essential tool for deciphering Mamluk administrative and military terminology. More comprehensive are the glossaries provided by M. J. de Goeje in his classic textual editions; see for example the following:

a. *Annales quos scripsit ... at-Tabari* (15 vols., 1879-1901), vol. XIV, *Introductio, Glossarium, Addenda et Emendanda*, pp. ci–dlxxii.

b. *Bibliotheca Geographorum Arabicorum* (8 vols., 1870–1894); vol. IV, *Indices, Glossarium, Addenda et Emendanda ad Partes I-III*, pp. 175-380.

De Goeje's glossaries are in Latin, to be sure, which to some readers may seem hardly more accessible than Classical Arabic, but they can be used with a quite rudimentary knowledge of that language. Other examples of glossed texts will be cited as they arise in later chapters.

Although Turkish and Persian belong to two entirely different language families, it is useful to consider them together because of the enormous impact which each has had on the other. Before the 20th-century language reforms, some seventy percent of the Turkish lexicon is estimated to have been of Perso-Arabic origin, and the speech of educated persons was saturated with Persian grammatical structures. In the same way, from the 6th/12th century on Persian absorbed a vast quantity of Turkish expressions, especially in the areas of tribal-pastoral life and military-administrative institutions.

This interpenetration of the two languages is of course reflected in the standard dictionaries of Redhouse (Ottoman Turkish), Steingass, and Haim (both Persian). On a more detailed level, the absorption of Turkish into Persian can be studied through the great work of Gerhard Doerfer, *Türkische und Mongolische Elemente im Neupersischen* (4 vols., 1963–1975). Vol. I deals with words and expressions of Mongol origin, vols. II-IV with Turkish items; the contents in both sections are arranged in Arabic-alphabetical order.

The name "Turkish" represents a whole family of languages and dialects, of which several were used in the Islamic world from the 11th century on. For this reason a sound comparative-historical dictionary of the Turkic language group is a real necessity. Two works respond to this need:

1. Wilhelm Radloff, *Versuch eines Wörterbuchs der Türk-Dialekte* (4 vols., 1893–1911; repr. 1960). An essay in comparative lexicography, Radloff's compilation is based on a survey of living Turkish languages. Each entry is headed by a base word, transliterated into Cyrillic characters; this base word is then followed by definitions in Russian and German for each of the Turkish languages which use it or an obvious cognate. Words in use among Muslim peoples are given in Arabic letters as well.

2. Sir Gerard Clauson, *An Etymological Dictionary of Pre-Thirteenth Century Turkish* (1972). Clauson arranges his entries according to reconstructed "roots," and this feature makes his dictionary somewhat difficult to use. On the other hand, it is based on a very broad survey of ancient Turkic texts (to which exact references are given for each entry), and it attempts to bring together within a comparative framework all the Turkic dialects attested for its period. It is thus an invaluable resource for dealing with the earlier phases of the Turkish penetration of the Islamic world.

We come finally to a book which is both an invaluable research tool and one of the great monuments of medieval Islamic scholarship, the *Dīwān Lughāt al-Turk* of Maḥmūd al-Kāshgharī, a Turkish-Arabic lexicon composed in Baghdad in the late 11th century by a noble Turk from the Kashghar region (Sinkiang/Xinjiang). It focuses on the Qarluq dialect used by the Kara-Khanid dynasty of Transoxiana, but also includes data from two other groups who would have a decisive role in Islamic history—the Ghuzz/Oğuz (the ethnic core of the Seljukid and Ottoman states) and the Kıpçak (the political-military elite in the early Mamluk Empire). Although Kāshgharī gives his definitions in Arabic, he cites a wealth of Turkish verse and proverbs to support them; in this way he created not simply a dictionary but an anthology of ancient Turkish poetry and folklore. His compilation is not easy to use, for he (quite naturally) tried to fit Turkish into the rigid framework of Arabic morphology and lexicography. Thus words are listed by "root" (a very elusive concept in Turkish) and in rhyme-order—i.e., according to the final rather than the initial letter of the word. Obviously the *Dīwān Lughāt al-Turk* demands some time and patience before it can be put to use. Three printed versions are now available:

1. printed Arabic text: ed. Kilisli Muʿallim Rifʿat Bilge (3 vols., 1333–35/1917–19).

2. modern Turkish translation with facsimile Arabic text: ed. and trans. Besim Atalay (6 vols., 1939–1957. Vols. I–III, translation; vol. IV, facsimile text; vols. V–VI, indices).

3. critical English translation, *Compendium of the Turkic Dialects*, by Robert Dankoff and James Kelly (2 vols. 1982–84).

Among these Dankoff-Kelly, prefaced with a lengthy and very solid introduction, is the most reliable version. The Arabic portions of the text are translated into English, while the Turkic elements are left in the original language but scientifically transliterated into Roman characters.

D. Geography and Topography

Until very recently, historians of Islam had to contend with a dearth of good research atlases; there were indeed none at all. The situation is now beginning to improve, though it will certainly be many years (and most likely decades) before we have an adequate array of resources at our disposal.

By far the most important effort to fill this very frustrating gap is the *Tübinger Atlas des Vorderen Orients* (abbr., *TAVO*), which is being prepared under the supervision of the University of Tübingen, but draws on all the formidable resources of German Orientalist scholarship. The first maps were issued in 1977, and according to the prospectus the final count will surpass 380. The maps, which are issued unbound in sets (*Lieferungen*) of ten or so per year, are large (72×50 cm) and superbly produced. They deal not only with physical and political geography, but also with demography, economics, culture, etc., and cover the region from pre-historic to contemporary times. The following examples will give some sense of the project's scope:

A VIII 2: *Middle East—Population Distribution*
A VIII 3: *Middle East—Population Density*
A VIII 7: *Lebanon—Religions*
A IX 9.4: *Esfahan/Esfahan Bazar*
A X 12: *Pastoral Migration Systems—Examples (Zagros Region, Iran)*
B VII 3: *The Islamic Empire under ʿAbdalmalik (685–705)*
B VIII 16 to B VIII 18: *The Islamic Law Schools*

In addition to the maps, *TAVO* is issuing a series of *Beihefte*, research monographs intended to provide fresh documentation for those topics for which existing research does not permit reliable cartography. These are very often of extraordinary importance, as the numerous citations in later chapters will demonstrate. Here we need only note the German propensity for meticulous organization. The maps are issued in two series, A (Geography) and B (History). The *Beihefte* are likewise arranged in series A and B, but this time with an altered division of subjects: *Reihe A, Naturwissenschaften*, and *Reihe B, Geisteswissenschaften*.

Though there is nothing to match the scope and scientific rigor of *TAVO*, a few other cartographic references merit notice. *EI*² has issued *An Historical Atlas of Islam*, ed. W. B. Brice (1981). This is a work of folio size, very handsomely printed, with a number of unusual maps (e.g., the constellations as known to medieval Islamic geographers; the political evolution of Spain and Anatolia) and a good gazetteer. On the other hand, the political evolution of Iran and the Fertile Crescent is handled only in very general terms, not at all adequate for the needs of a research scholar; boundaries (dotted bands in red ink on a beige ground) are often hard to make out; and there is rather little on cultural, economic, and ethnographic topics—an odd failing for a geographer like Brice. A new work is Georgette Cornu, *Atlas du monde arabo-islamique à l'époque classique (ixᵉ-xᵉ siècles)* (1985), which attempts to analyze and record the data given by the medieval Muslim geographers. It contains twenty folding maps, plus a gazetteer keyed to the Arabic sources and selected modern references. Finally, two older atlases intended as pedagogical rather than research tools can often be useful. R. Roolvink *et al.*, *Historical Atlas of the Muslim Peoples* (1957) is broadly conceived, with attention to India and Southeast Asia as well as the Middle East, intelligently selective, and very attractively printed; unfortunately there is no index. H. W. Hazard, *Atlas of Islamic History* (1951), is crippled by its rigid century-by-century scheme and restricts itself entirely to political topics, but it does possess an adequate index.

TAVO deals only with the Nile-to-Oxus region; however, a second cartographic project (also based in Germany and superbly produced) addresses the need to deal with North Africa and the Bilād al-Sūdān: *Afrika-Kartenwerk*, ed. J. H. Schultze *et al.* (1976–in progress). This collection will apparently deal only with physical geography and contemporary topics, but it should still prove indispensable for the historian of medieval Islam.

In principle India and Pakistan lie outside the purview of the present book; however, Sind and the Punjab at least cannot be ignored, not merely because of their proximity to Iran but because of the intense and constant interaction (cultural, political, economic) between these regions from an early period. For the Subcontinent (including Afghanistan) we now have a major reference tool in Joseph E. Schwartzberg, ed., *A Historical Atlas of South Asia* (1978). The political maps before 1800 do not attempt to construct hard-and-fast boundaries between the region's multifarious political entities; this is undoubtedly honest, since such boundaries did not exist, but it does make these maps quite difficult to read. The most interesting maps, however, are those which deal with the cultural and economic geography of the late 19th and 20th centuries; used sensibly, these can do much to illuminate the conditions of earlier centuries. The value of Schwartzberg's atlas is greatly enhanced by its extensive explanatory texts and bibliographies.

A good historical gazetteer is very nearly as important a research tool as an atlas. No comprehensive work of this kind now exists, or is in prospect, for the central Islamic lands as a whole. However, we are not without resources, largely because medieval Muslim scholars felt the same need as we do. The most valuable single text is doubtless the *Muʿjam al-buldān*, compiled in the early 7th/13th century by the freedman Yāqūt b. ʿAbdallāh al-Rūmī al-Ḥamawī. Yāqūt travelled extensively throughout the eastern Islamic lands, and in addition he immersed himself in the enormous Arabic geographic literature of the Middle Ages (much of it since lost). He was thus able to give us a reliable compendium of everything known in his time about the regions and towns of the Islamic world. Place-names are entered in simple alphabetical order, with extracts or paraphrases of older texts (and some contemporary observation) pertaining to each locale. Though Yāqūt is comprehensive and easy to use, however, he makes no distinction between contemporary and purely antiquarian data. There are two printed versions of his work:

1. *Jacut's Geographisches Wörterbuch*, ed. F. Wüstenfeld (6 vols., 1866–1873).
2. *Muʿjam al-buldān* (5 vols., Beirut, 1955–1957).

For the 3rd/9th and 4th/10th centuries, Yāqūt's information can be supplemented and checked in the works of Ibn Khurdādhbeh, Ibn al-Faqīh, Ibn Rusta, al-Yaʿqūbī, al-Iṣṭakhrī, Ibn Ḥawqal, and al-Muqaddasī, which are collected in the *Bibliotheca Geographorum Arabicorum* (8 vols, 1870–1939; abbr., *BGA*). In the 6th/12th century, a valuable compendium of existing knowledge (with some original elements regarding the Muslim West and Europe) was written by the Sicilian al-Idrīsī, *Nuzhat al-mushtāq fī ikhtirāq al-āfāq*, ed. E. Cerulli et al. as *Opus geographicum* (issued in 9 fascicles, 1970–84). An annotated Italian translation is projected, which will replace the unreliable version of P. A. Jaubert, *Géographie d'Edrisi* (2 vols., 1836–1840). Meantime, there are good partial translations by M. J. de Goeje and R.P.A. Dozy, *Description de l'Afrique et de l'Espagne par Edrisi* (1866; repr. 1968); and by S. Maqbul Ahmad, *India and the Neighboring Territories* (1960). These writers, like Yāqūt, do not distinguish current from obsolete information; moreover, their organization (by region rather than alphabetical order) makes them difficult to use. An early Persian work, the anonymous *Ḥudūd al-ʿālam*, would be of value chiefly for Central Asia were it not for the remarkable commentary supplied by V. Minorsky with his translation: *The Regions of the World, a Persian Geography 372 A.H.–982 A.D.* (1937).

For the Fertile Crescent, Arabia, and Iran, the data of the medieval geographers is digested in two old but still useful books by Guy Le Strange: *Palestine under the Moslems* (1890), and *The Lands of the Eastern Caliphate* (1905)—both several times reprinted. For Iran, a much fuller compilation is Paul Schwarz, *Iran im Mittelalter nach den arabischen Geographen* (9 vols., 1896–1936). Far more concise and convenient is a classic synthesis by W. Barthold, *An Historical Geography of Iran*, trans. Svat Soucek (1984), bristling with its author's usual erudition and critical intelligence. For Syria, see the exhaustive survey of René Dussaud, *Topographie historique de la Syrie antique et médiévale* (1927); this work is based on a thorough command of Greek, Latin, and Arabic texts as well as a good direct knowledge of the terrain, but it focuses on the identification of toponyms rather than the broader issues of historical geography.

Among modern research tools, *EI*[2] has articles even on rather obscure places, but these vary in character; some are hardly more than sketches of the comings and goings of a succession of conquerors, while others—especially the more recent contributions—are superb pieces of cultural and historical geography. Two surveys of Afghanistan and Iran compiled by Ludwig W. Adamec have promising titles but are in fact of limited value to medievalists. These essentially reproduce the secret gazetteers prepared for the General Staff of British India between 1871 and 1918, to which Adamec has added additional material from survey maps, Iranian censuses, PRO and India Office files, etc. On balance, however, these volumes reflect conditions—or rather British knowledge of conditions—around 1900. Each entry (in both Roman and Arabic characters) is keyed to the set of maps placed at the end of the volume.

1. *Historical and Political Gazetteer of Afghanistan* (6 vols., 1972–1985).

2. *Historical Gazetteer of Iran*. Vol. I: *Tehran and Northwestern Iran* (1976). Vol. II: *Meshhed and Northeastern Iran* (1981). Vol. IV: *Zahidan and Southeastern Iran* (1988). (Vol. III will cover Khuzistan and Fars).

E. Chronology and Genealogy

Establishing the date and sequence of events in Islamic history is often an extremely frustrating chore. This is due less to the gaps in our information than to the many disparate calendars which confront us. The most important of these is of course the official Hijri calendar, established in the reign of the Caliph ʿUmar. This calendar is in general clear, consistent, and easy to use; we need go through none of the contortions inflicted on the historian of Rome and Byzantium, faced as he is with consulates, indictions, regnal years, etc. Because it is a lunar calendar, however, conversion to Julian/Gregorian dates is a complicated matter. And because the change of months was traditionally established by observation of the new moon (instead of a fixed number of days per month), Hijri-Christian correspondences cannot always be correctly generated by mathematical formula. Indeed, the use of observation means that discrepancies of a day or two will find their way into even the most accurate and exact texts.

Under these circumstances, conversion tables are almost a necessity. The most elaborate set is that of F. Wüstenfeld and E. Mahler, *Vergleichungs-Tabellen zur muslimischen und iranischen Zeitrechnung* (3rd ed., revised by J. Mayr and B. Spuler, 1961), which spells out month-by-month tables down to 1500/2076. Even here there are occasional problems, however; some useful rules for confirming or correcting the correspondences derived from such tables are given in W. B. Stevenson, *The Crusaders in the East* (1907), Appendix A, "The Chronology of the Arabic Historians," pp. 356–361. A less detailed but reliable presentation is given in G.S.P. Freeman-Grenville, *The Muslim and Christian Calendars* (1963), who also discusses the rationales governing the two systems and explains how to calculate conversions between them.

Medieval Muslims were unfortunately not content with only one calendar. Fiscal administration, based heavily on agricultural revenues, always had to rely on solar calendars, which varied to some degree according to the ancient practices of particular regions. Iran, Syria, and Egypt all had distinct systems. Luckily Wüstenfeld-Mahler contains many of these (including those of Eastern Christendom). Useful general information, though not detailed tables, can also be gotten from Adolf Grohmann, *Arabische Chronologie* (*HO*, Ergbd. II,1 [1966]). The several calendars in use among Christians can be studied through V. Grumel, *La chronologie* (Vol. I of *Traité d'études byzantins*, ed. Paul Lemerle, 1958), who also includes a Julian/Hijri table and detailed lists of rulers for those Islamic dynasties relevant to Byzantine history; for any scholar using Christian sources, then, Grumel is an essential tool.

Certain Persian works written after the Mongol invasions of the mid-7th/13th century use a Turkmen calendar based on the seasonal migration between summer and winter pastures. And occasionally we encounter texts employing the Mongol calendar, which was based on a cycle of twelve years named after animals. These problems are surveyed in H. Taqizadeh, "Various Eras and Calendars Used in the Countries of Islam, *BSOAS*, ix (1937–39), 903–922; x (1940–42), 107–132.

Whatever the problems caused by dating, they are as nothing compared to those raised by the stupefying succession of tribes and dynasties who parade through the nine centuries of medieval Islamic history. No one scholar can ever hope to control on his own this horde of caliphs, anti-caliphs, would-be kings and self-styled emperors. The reference tools at our disposal are not entirely adequate to the task, but they at least provide a provisional orientation. A good evaluation of these works (more or less in their order of publication) is given in C. E. Bosworth, *The Islamic Dynasties: a Chronological and Genealogical Handbook* (1967; rev. ed., 1980).

By far the most detailed and wide-ranging is Eduard von Zambaur, *Manuel de généalogie et de chronologie pour l'histoire de l'Islam* (1927). In spite of its general excellence, however, Zambaur contains numerous errors of detail, and of course there is now a vast corpus of source materials which he did not have. Anyone working in Islamic political history will start with Zambaur, but inevitably he will have to construct his own for the dynasties and families which he is studying. What we would ultimately like to have for every major dynasty is something like A. S. Alderson, *The Structure of the Ottoman Dynasty* (1956), which attempts to reconstruct and present in tabular form all the kinship and marriage ties which linked this vast clan together.

Whatever the faults of Zambaur, he does give precise dates, fairly full names and titles, and substantial genealogical data. Bosworth's handbook (cited above) gives only years, short names, and *no* genealogical information; for this reason, some scholars find Stanley Lane-Poole, *The Mohammedan Dynasties*

(1894; repr. 1965), to be a more satisfactory manual, though it is obviously antiquated in many respects.

F. The Scriptures of Islam: Qur'ān and Hadith

We cannot give here even a partial survey of Islamic religious writings which might prove relevant to social and political history. However, the twin foundations of Islam—Qurʾān and hadith—deeply pervade the texture of daily life and are commonly cited in every form of writing (including coins and monumental inscriptions). For purely practical reasons, any competent historian has to be able to identify such citations. On a more serious level, of course, a good scholar will from the outset try to immerse himself in these texts, since he must know the values and attitudes of medieval Muslims even if he cannot fully share them.

For a long time Western scholars used the edition of the Qurʾān by Gustav Flügel, *Corani Textus Arabicus* (1834; often reprinted), to which he also prepared a concordance, *Concordantiae Corani Arabicae* (1842; repr. 1898). Flügel's edition blends together the canonical "Seven Readings" of the Qurʾān so as to obtain a relatively smooth and easily intelligible text. Since this harmonization is mostly a matter of choosing among alternative ways of numbering the verses, it involves very little distortion of the verbal form of the text. Even so, it does differ in some degree from the textual tradition ascribed to Ḥafṣ b. ʿUmar, which has long been preferred among the majority of Muslims. This recension is the one enshrined in the official Egyptian edition, first issued in 1347/1928 and now generally standard. Users of the Egyptian edition also have an excellent concordance in M. F. ʿAbd al-Bāqī, *al-Muʿjam al-mufahras li-alfāẓ al-Qurʾān al-Karīm* (1364/1945).

The Qurʾān is for the most part direct and forceful, but some passages are very difficult; more than that, the meaning of this book for medieval Muslims—or rather, its complex layers of meaning—seldom emerge from the text itself. For both these reasons we must often have recourse to the commentaries. In view of the immense bulk of the *tafsīr* literature, I will mention only a few recent works in European languages. Rudi Paret, *Der Koran: Kommentar und Konkordanz* (1971) was written to accompany his excellent translation. Paret's goal was to grasp the original meaning of the text, as it was understood by Muhammad and his contemporaries, rather than to rely on the interpretations developed by later generations of Muslims. That is obviously an important and valid goal in itself, but a historian must also be acquainted with these later interpretations. The anthology of Helmut Gätje, *The Qurʾān and its Exegesis* (1976) is reliable but does not give a very adequate cross-section of this literature. J. Cooper has recently published the first volume (five are projected) of an abridged translation of al-Ṭabarī's famous *Jāmiʿ al-bayān* under the title of *The Commentary on the Qurʾān* (1987). When completed, this should be both a sound reference tool and a valuable overview of the early exegetical tradition. A projected multi-volume survey by Mahmoud M. Ayoub, *The Qurʾān and Its Interpreters*, provides extensive citations and paraphrases from both medieval and modern exegesis. Vol. I (1984) gives an overview of the principles and main works of *tafsīr* and examines the first two suras of the Qurʾān. Progress has been slow, and Ayoub's choice of material has been criticized, but even so this work promises to be a useful introduction to a very difficult subject. Among annotated translations of the Qurʾān, the scrupulous though hardly poetic effort of Régis Blachère, *Le Coran: traduction selon un essai de reclassement des sourates* (3 vols., 1947–1951) deserves special mention.

For medieval Muslims (and most modern ones as well), the hadiths which recounted the teachings and example of the Prophet were no less significant than the Qurʾān itself. As with the Qurʾān, it is essential for every historian to grasp both the role of hadith in Islamic culture and the principles which governed its study. And again, practical reasons demand that one be able to recognize hadith reports as they occur. Overall, the most useful introduction to the classical science of hadith is probably Fuat Sezgin, *Geschichte des arabischen Schrifttums*, vol. I (1967). His arguments in favor of the authenticity of this material are debatable, to be sure, but his analysis of the technical terminology and his meticulous survey of early authors and works (down to ca. 430/1040) are indispensable.

Because the hadith literature is so scattered and diffuse, it can be most challenging to identify and confirm particular citations. Certain collections of these narratives had a special prestige and authority, however, and all of these are available in reasonably reliable printed editions. First of all, there are the quasi-canonical "Six Books" of the Sunnis, by al-Bukhārī, Muslim, al-Tirmidhī, Ibn Māja, Abū Dāʾūd al-Sijistānī, and al-Nasāʾī—all scholars of the late 3rd/9th–early 10th century; second, the *Muwaṭṭaʾ* of Mālik b. Anas (d. 179/795); third, the vast *Musnad* of Aḥmad b. Ḥanbal (d. 241/855). The most prestigious of all these works, the *Ṣaḥīḥ* of al-Bukhārī, is available in a French translation by O. Houdas and W. Marçais, *Les traditions islamiques* (4 vols., 1903–1914). For this translation and the edition on which it is based, see the index by Oscar Rescher, *Sachindex zu Bokhari nach der Ausgabe Krehl-Juynboll und der Übersetzung Houdas-Marçais* (1923). Finally, an 8th/14th century compilation drew on the early collections named above to establish a sort of summa and was much esteemed by Muslim scholars: Walī al-Dīn al-Tibrīzī, *Mishkāt al-Maṣābīḥ*, trans. James Robson (4 vols., 1960–1965). As well as being a convenient reference, Robson gives us a very exact and highly readable translation of some 6,000 hadiths on every subject.

Hadith plays a more limited role in Shīʿī religious thought, but it came to be widely studied all the same. Four collections are especially revered: (1) al-Kulaynī (d. 329/941), *al-Kāfī*; (2) Shaykh al-Ṣadūq (also known as Ibn Bābawayh, d. 381/991), *Man lā yaḥḍuruhu al-faqīh*; (3) Muḥammad b. Ḥasan al-Ṭūsī (d. 460/1067), *al-Istibṣār* and (4) *Tahdhīb al-aḥkām*. In late Safavid times, al-Ḥurr al-ʿĀmilī (d. 1104/1692) produced a massive and highly regarded compilation entitled *Wasāʾil al-Shīʿa*.

Two invaluable tools provide ready access to the Sunni hadith collections. (There is nothing equivalent for the Shīʿīs.) The first is A. J. Wensinck, *A Handbook of Early Muhammadan Tradition, Alphabetically Arranged* (1927; repr., 1960, 1971). This is a subject index to all the topics (some under English headings, others under Arabic) touched on by the hadiths in every major collection. Far more ambitious in scope is the *Concordance et indices de la tradition musulmane*, ed. A. J. Wensinck et al. (8 vols., 1936–1988). In these vast folio tomes, every substantive term which occurs in the major hadith collections is listed in alphabetical order. Under each such heading, a "core" version of each of the different hadiths containing that term is given, together with exact references to the original texts. The *Concordance* is awkward to use, but it represents the surest way to track down any given hadith and to locate parallel versions of it.

G. Research Libraries and their Catalogs

Scholars who do not reside at places with comprehensive research collections often find it difficult to locate exact bibliographic citations or to survey the printed works of a particular author. The ordinary reference tool for these things is of course the *National Union Catalog* produced by the Library of Congress. But the massive size and numerous supplements of *NUC* make this a cumbersome task, enjoyable only by those who like to beat librarians at their own game. Moreover, *NUC* has numerous gaps for books printed in the Islamic world. Some of these problems will be mitigated by a new project, *The Near East National Union List*, which collects all the pre-1979 imprints in Middle Eastern languages registered in the Near East Section's card file. As of 1988, only Vol. I ("A") had been issued, however, so a degree of patience may be in order.

Under such circumstances, the photographed card catalogs of the Middle East collections in major research libraries can be very helpful. The more important of these would include the following:

1. University of Chicago. *Catalog of the Oriental Institute Library* (16 vols., 1970).

2. University of Chicago. *Catalog of the Middle East Collection. First Supplement* (1977).

3. New York Public Library, Reference Department. *Dictionary Catalog of the Oriental Collection* (16 vols., 1960).

4. New York Public Library, the Research Libraries. *Dictionary Catalog of the Oriental Collection. First Supplement* (8 vols., 1976).

5. Harvard University. *Catalogue of Arabic, Persian, and Ottoman Turkish Books* (5 vols., 1968).

6. Harvard University. *Catalog of the Arabic Collection* (6 vols., 1983).

7. School of Oriental and African Studies, University of London. *Library Catalogue* (28 vols., 1963). *First Supplement* (16 vols., 1968). *Second Supplement* (16 vols., 1973). *Third Supplement* (19 vols., 1979).

8. British Museum. *Catalogue of Arabic Printed Books in the British Museum* (3 vols., 1894–1901). *Supplementary Catalogue* (1926). *Second Supplementary Catalogue* (1959).

9. British Library. *Third Supplementary Catalogue of Arabic Printed Books in the British Library, 1958–1969* (4 vols., 1977).

10. British Museum. *A Catalogue of Persian Printed Books in the British Museum* (1922).

As computer technology and access improves, it is possible that such massive compilations will become obsolete. But until programmers devise adequate transliterations and record the mountain of existing bibliography, catalogs of this kind will remain an essential part of the scholar's repertory.

Chapter Two

THE SOURCES

AN ANALYTICAL SURVEY

ISLAMISTS like to complain about the state of their sources, but in fact what they have is extraordinarily rich and varied, far surpassing the miserable fragments which challenge the student of the late Roman Empire or early medieval Europe. The real problem is to use this patrimony effectively. To a large degree that is a matter of asking good questions, but good questions in turn depend on understanding the character of one's sources. The aim of this chapter, then, is to outline the materials at our disposal, and to suggest in general terms what kinds of questions these can and cannot answer. Ideally such a survey would be based on some rigorous and theoretically satisfying classification, and several historians have made valuable efforts in this direction. (An old but very good example is Ernst Bernheim, *Lehrbuch der historischen Methode* [5th–6th rev. ed., 1908], 255–259, 465–506.) In the end, however, I have found such classifications not rigorous but rigid, for any given system can reflect only one of many possible perspectives on the past. I have thus chosen to arrange my discussion simply according to the external features of the sources: written or non-written, paper or durable substances like metal and stone, literary or documentary in form. Whatever may be lost in theoretical sophistication will, I hope, be gained in clarity and flexibility.

A. Narrative and Literary Texts

Under this heading I include all those works which were written for general circulation among some broad and loosely defined group of interested persons, rather than composed as a direct instrument of business or administration. In the framework of this book, of course, the most important genre of such writings would be chronicles and biographical dictionaries. But this category includes many other things as well: administrative handbooks, anthologies of entertaining and edifying anecdotes, jurisprudence, lyric and satirical poetry, folklore, etc. It seems a very disparate lot, but material which has little to offer the student of politics may have much for a historian of social mores and values. In any case it is a grave error to exclude *a priori* any literary genre as a possible source of evidence whatever the nature of one's subject.

Obviously we cannot expect to achieve anything of value just by plunging into a pile of texts. On the most elementary level, it is essential to begin with a survey of all the sources which may pertain to the problem under investigation, and to determine the relationships (borrowings, common sources, etc.) among them. Moreover, since the interpretation of any text depends on an understanding of its conceptual structure and rhetoric, we need to acquire a broad overview of the scientific-literary tradition within which it was composed.

The introductions to Arabic, Persian, and Turkish philology discussed above (p. 12) can be a useful beginning for such tasks, but serious work rests on a series of bio-bibliographic works which survey in detail the whole range of literary production in the classical Islamic languages. None of these is or could be wholly adequate: all are afflicted with an inevitable quota of gaps and errors, and all are on the road to obsolescence the moment they are published. Even so they are the indispensable foundation for research in Islamic studies, a historian's most constant companions.

The most famous of these is certainly Carl Brockelmann, *Geschichte der arabischen Litteratur* (abbr. *GAL*). This is in fact not a "history" at all, but an annotated repertory of Arabic manuscripts, arranged by author and organized in a generally chronological order. For each author we are given a capsule biography, a short list of references (both sources and studies) for his life, and a bibliography of his extant works comprising both manuscripts and printed editions. *GAL* has a complex publication history and thus can be somewhat confusing and cumbersome to use: 2 vols., 1898–1902; 3 supplementary volumes, 1937–42; revised edition of the original Vols. I-II, 1943–49. The three supplementary volumes did not in any way replace the original two, but only added new materials—authors, works, or additional manuscripts. For any topic, then, both the original and supplementary volumes must be consulted. By the time the supplementary volumes had been published, there was still more material to be included, but this time it was done through a thorough revision of the original two volumes. The revised Vols. I-II were of course repaginated, but the *original* page numbers of the 1898–1902 edition were retained in the margins, so as to facilitate use of the indices and cross-references in the supplementary volumes. In scholarly usage, citations are always made to the original pagination of Vols. I-II, although everyone is in fact referring to the data of the revised edition.

The author and title indices for the entire set are located in Supplementband III. The alphabetization for the authors' names differs somewhat from normal usage, but Brockelmann explains his rules clearly. Authors can normally be located both under their "common" names (al-Ṭabarī) and their given names (Muḥammad b. Jarīr). The title index unfortunately gives titles without reference to their authors and without indicating different works using the same name or variant titles (which are very common) for a single work.

Beyond such mechanical difficulties, there are problems inherent in *GAL*'s organization and approach. *GAL* only includes authors and works for which we have catalogued manuscripts. As a result, Brockelmann's survey is radically incomplete, especially for the earlier phases of Arabic literature (down to the 4th/10th century or so). Many writers (including some of great historical importance) are not listed at all, and for those who are we have only a partial conspectus of their *oeuvre*. Nor can we let ourselves be misled by *GAL*'s organization, for each author is listed only once, under a single (albeit broadly defined) literary genre. This seems clear and simple enough, but it leads to numerous absurdities. Most authors cultivated several fields of learning, so that we constantly encounter cases like that of Ibn ʿUnayn, a noted 7th/13th century satirical poet listed under *Geschichte* on the strength of a single misunderstood title. Brockelmann's achievement is an imposing one, but a naive user will get little benefit from it.

An ambitious and largely successful attempt to supplant *GAL* is Fuat Sezgin, *Geschichte des arabischen Schrifttums* (abbr. *GAS*; 9 vols., 1967–in progress). The volumes so far issued cover only the period down to 430/1040, and even within these limits such major genres as geography, philosophy, and *belles-lettres* remain to be dealt with. How many tomes will be required to complete this vast enterprise is almost beyond calculation; fourteen are projected for the first period alone:

1. *Qur'anwissenschaften, Hadiṯ, Geschichte, Fiqh, Dogmatik, Mystik* (1967)
2. *Poesie* (1975)
3. *Medizin-Pharmazie, Zoologie-Tierheilkunde* (1971)
4. *Alchimie-Chemie, Botanik-Agrikultur* (1971)
5. *Mathematik* (1974)
6. *Astronomie* (1978)
7. *Astrologie-Meteorologie und Verwandtes* (1979)
8. *Lexicographie* (1982)
9. *Grammatik* (1984)

10–11. *Literatur (Literaturgeschichte, Literaturtheorie, Erbauungsliteratur, Kunstprosa)* (in preparation)

12. *Physik-Technik, Geographie, Musik* (in preparation)
13. *Philosophie, Logik, Ethik, Politik* (in preparation)
14. *Einführung in die Geschichte der arabisch-islamischen Wissenschaften* (in preparation)

Although Sezgin is by no means immune to ambiguity and error, his work surpasses its predecessor in many areas. First, it is based on a much broader survey of Arabic manuscripts. Sezgin has benefitted from the energetic efforts of Muslim scholars in recent decades to record the holdings in their countries' libraries and to collect new manuscripts. (In the latter regard the Arab League's collection of photographed manuscripts from all over the Muslim world, including many private collections, is especially noteworthy.) To this he can add his own unrivalled knowledge of the immense holdings of Turkish libraries, not only those of Istanbul but of many provincial centers as well. His survey is thus not only larger but far more representative than Brockelmann's. The scope of his efforts can be seen in the systematic repertory of libraries and manuscript collections given in Vol. I, and then again, thoroughly revised and updated, in Vol. VI.

Second, Sezgin's philological and historical commentary on each of the fields which he covers is much richer than Brockelmann's. His statements are at times controversial or overly self-assured, but they are significant all the same.

Finally, Sezgin's arrangement of his materials is for some purposes more rational than Brockelmann's, though it can be time-consuming to use. In Vol. I he sticks to Brockelmann's plan: each author, with all his extant writings, is listed once, under the heading of a single literary-scientific field. The later volumes, however, list each author separately within each of the fields which he cultivated. Thus, if we are interested in the medical writings of an author known also for philosophic and mathematical concerns, we can be reasonably confident of finding them in Vol. III. On the other hand, if we want to survey all the works of a given author or to define a broad intellectual tradition, the task is likely to prove profoundly frustrating.

Sezgin focuses on extant authors and works, and thus like Brockelmann he gives us only a partial survey of the Arabic literary universe. However, he also records writings which survive in substantial citations or are well attested by other authors; especially for the first two Islamic centuries, where so little has come down in its original form, this permits a far more adequate if sometimes more speculative picture than we had from *GAL*.

Several works can supplement *GAL* and *GAS*; of these we shall mention three.

1. ʿUmar Riḍā Kaḥḥāla, *Muʿjam al-muʾallifīn* (15 vols., 1957–61).

Kaḥḥāla gives capsule biographies (arranged in alphabetical order) of all authors, both medieval and modern, known to have written in Arabic, together with the titles of their major works. He lists no manuscripts but does give references to *GAL*. Though terse, his entries are based on a thorough knowledge of the Arabic biographical literature, including sources available only in manuscript.

2. Khayr al-Dīn al-Ziriklī, *al-Aʿlām* (1st ed., 1927–28; 2nd rev. ed., 11 vols. plus supplement, 1954–59; 3rd rev. ed., 8 vols., 1979).

A work similar to the preceding though more broadly focused, since it gives the lives of notable figures in Arab-Islamic history in general (including major Western Orientalists), not just writers. In Vols. 10–11, Ziriklī produces a great many facsimiles of autograph manuscripts, reader's certificates, etc. produced by the authors in his survey. Both Kaḥḥālah and Ziriklī include 20th-century figures.

3. Hajjī Khalīfa, *Kashf al-ẓunūn ʿan asāmī al-kutub wa'l-funūn*: ed. and trans. by Gustav Flügel as *Lexicon Bibliographicum et Encyclopaedicum* (7 vols., 1835–1858); Arabic text ed. from the author's autograph by Şerefettin Yaltkaya and Kilisli Rifat Bilge (2 vols., 1941–43).

The manuscript collections of Istanbul have never been adequately surveyed and catalogued, though important steps are now underway (see below, p. 38). For that reason this 11th/17th century compilation by an outstanding Ottoman scholar (on whom see "Kâtib Çelebi," *EI*², iv, 760–762) is still a very useful bibliographic tool. Ḥajjī Khalīfa lists in alphabetical order some 14,500 titles of works available in the Istanbul libraries in his day, each one with a capsule description of its author and contents. In addition, he includes a series of discourses (also arranged in alphabetical order) on the various Islamic sciences. The *Kashf al-ẓunūn* has no shelf-marks or locations, but it does tell us whether manuscripts of a particular work might be found in Istanbul (some have been lost since the author's day, and many others added). More than that, because it is based on a direct survey of the manuscripts, it is very helpful in verifying the authors and titles mentioned in the medieval biographical dictionaries. A supplement to Ḥajjī Khalīfa, which draws largely on libraries founded after his death, was written around the beginning of this century: Bağdatlı Ismāʿīl Paşa, *Īḍāḥ al-maknūn fī al-dhayl ʿalā kashf al-ẓunūn*, ed. Yaltkaya and Bilge (2 vols., 1945–47).

Impressive as these massive surveys are, they sometimes fail us, and then we must have recourse to the medieval Islamic biographical compilations. Here Paul Auchterlonie, *Arabic Biographical Dictionaries: a Summary Guide and Bibliography* (1987), can be helpful. Auchterlonie is very selective, but he is judicious and writes with the practical needs of librarians and researchers in mind.

Since the overwhelming majority of authors writing in Arabic were Muslims, it is natural that Brockelmann and Sezgin should focus on specifically Islamic sciences and literary genres. However, Arabic-speaking Christians composed a very considerable body of literature as well, and much of their work is of the highest importance for Islamic studies. It will suffice to mention the scientific translations from Greek and Syriac by the Nestorian Ḥunayn b. Isḥāq, or the chronicles of the Melkite Yaḥyā al-Anṭākī and the Copt Sawīrūs b. al-Muqaffaʿ. Some of this material can be found in *GAL* and *GAS*, but the most thorough survey is Georg Graf, *Geschichte der christlichen arabischen Literatur* (5 vols., 1944–53).

A related body of material is covered in Anton Baumstark, *Geschichte der syrischen Literatur, mit Ausschluss der christlich-palästinensischen Texte* (1922, reprinted 1968). Syriac writing, with its focus on theology, liturgy, and the miraculous lives of the saints, may seem marginal to the normal concerns of the Islamic historian, but for certain topics it is very important indeed. Syriac chronicles, such as those by the pseudo-Dionysius of Tell Mahré (fl. ca. 800), Michael the Syrian (d. 1199), and Bar Hebraeus (d. 1286), often add vital material to the accounts of Muslim historians. Especially for the earliest Islamic centuries, valuable information and perspectives can be extracted from hagiography, sermons, etc. Baumstark is more an integrated literary history than the other bio-bibliographic works reviewed above, but in the notes he gives complete manuscript references.

In regard to the other "Christian" languages of the medieval Near East (Greek, Armenian, and at certain points even Latin), by far the most important reference is Gyula Moravcsik, *Byzantino-Turcica* (2 vols.; orig. ed., 1942–43; 2nd rev. ed., 1958), which throws light on many aspects of medieval Turkish history and culture. Vol. I surveys the Byzantine sources which touch on Turkish history, while Vol. II treats the Turkish linguistic data yielded by Byzantine texts. Of particular value in Vol. II is the extensive glossary of Turkish words and proper names which occur in the Greek texts.

Among the languages of medieval Islam, Persian is second in importance only to Arabic. Beginning in the 5th/11th century, Persian became the chief literary tongue not only of Iran proper but also of Anatolia, Transoxiana, and North India; it is thus an essential tool for any scholar studying the lands east of the Tigris River or north of the Taurus Mountains.

In this light, it is unfortunate that we still have no real equivalent for Brockelmann and Sezgin. A serious beginning in this direction was made by C. A. Storey, *Persian Literature: a Bio-Bibliographic Survey* (3 vols., 1927–in progress) but this remains an unfinished if impressive torso. As it stands it consists of the following parts:

Vol. I, Part 1 (1927–39): Qur'anic Literature; History
Vol. I, Part 2 (1953): Biography; Additions and Corrections
Vol. II, Part 1 (1958): Mathematics; Weights and Measures; Astronomy and Astrology; Geography
Vol. II, Part 2 (1971): Medicine
Vol. II, Part 3 (1977): Encyclopaedias, Arts and Crafts, Science, Occult Arts
Vol. III, Part 1 (1984): Lexicography, Grammar, Prosody and Poetics

The gaps here are all too evident, especially the lack of a volume on poetry, the proudest achievement of medieval Persian letters.

Some of the problems in Storey are addressed in the Russian translation and revision by Yuri Bregel, *Persidskaia literatura: bio-bibliograficheskii obzor* (3 vols., 1972). Bregel was able to draw on the vast and still only partially catalogued Persian manuscript holdings in the Soviet Union, and claims that his version contains twice as much material as the equivalent parts of the English edition. However, only the contents of Volume I, somewhat rearranged, were actually translated, though for most historians this is admittedly the most important section.

For Turkish literature we have only partial surveys. In the context of the present book this may not seem a crucial problem, since Turkish emerged as a major literary language (in both the Ottoman and Timurid lands) only towards the end of the 9th/15th century. Even so, the relatively few earlier works which do exist are very important, and a complete bio-bibliographic survey is clearly badly needed. For the time being, a solid assessment of the situation can be found in Eleazar Birnbaum, "Turkish Manuscripts: Cataloguing since

1960 and Manuscripts Still Uncatalogued," *JAOS*, ciii (1983), 413–420, 515–532, 691–708; civ (1984), 303–314, 465–504.

For our purposes the most useful reference is doubtless Franz Babinger, *Die Geschichtsschreiber der Osmanen und ihre Werke* (1927). So old a work is by definition obsolete, obviously, but the slow progress of Ottoman manuscript and historiographic studies means that it has retained much of its value. For other fields of Ottoman literature there is nothing similar, but useful information can be gotten from Bursalı Mehmet Tahir, *Osmanlı Müellifleri* (3 vols., 1333–42, in Ottoman script; new ed., 1970–75, in modern Turkish).

For Eastern Turkish (Chaghatay) writing, a major survey is now in progress: H. F. Hofman, *Turkish Literature, a Bio-Bibliographical Survey*. Section III: *Moslim Central Asian Turkish Literature*. Part I: *Authors*. (6 vols., 1969). As Hofman notes, this work is a kind of annotated index, arranged alphabetically, to the authors mentioned in M. F. Köprülü's study, "Çağatay Edebiyatı," *İA*, iii, 270–323. However, the current volumes omit the work of the most famous and influential writer in this dialect, ʿAlī Shīr Nevāʾī, proposing to deal with him separately.

A few bio-bibliographic surveys deal with particular fields, though not nearly as many as one might expect. As one example of these, which could stand as a model for others, see Ismail K. Poonawala, *Biobibliography of Ismaili Literature* (1977). Poonawala arranges his material according to the sects which made up the Ismāʿīliyya, and then according to the authors within each sect. The known works of each, extant or not, are listed and concisely described. Anonymous works, which abound among the Ismāʿīlis, are given in a separate section. Poonawala includes all the relevant languages—not only Arabic and Persian, but Urdu and Gujarati as well. For any scholar dealing with Islamic religious history, and not just Ismāʿīli specialists, this is obviously an invaluable resource, and definitively supplants the older surveys of Massignon (1922), H. F. Hamdani (1933), and W. Ivanow (1933, 1963).

All the bio-bibliographic surveys we have examined share a confusing and often frustrating point of usage. When they refer to manuscripts listed in printed catalogs, they give only the catalog numbers; these are usually *not* the shelflist or accession numbers used by the libraries holding these manuscripts. Since librarians cannot find a volume without its shelfmark, and since scholarly monographs and articles almost always identify texts by shelfmark as well, one must go to the printed catalogs to get this number. (Catalog references in the bio-bibliographic works should always be checked out in any case, since even the best of them are full of errors.) Thus, *GAL* may refer to a manuscript as "Rieu 465"—i.e., no. 465 in C. Rieu, *Supplement to the Catalogue of the Arabic Manuscripts in the British Museum* (1894). Under no. 465, along with an identification and description of the volume, its shelfmark is given—in this case "Or. 4215" (e.g., Oriental Manuscripts, no. 4215). The usual reference in the scholarly literature would thus be "BM Or. 4215" (or since 1973, "BL" for British Library).

The bio-bibliographic works permit a reasonably efficient survey of our potential sources and a provisional selection of the texts to be examined. But they are of little help in the next stage, that of deciding which versions of these texts we will use. The great bulk of medieval Islamic book production is still in manuscript, and many printed editions are so poor that manuscripts must be consulted to establish reliable readings. In Islamic history, at least, textual criticism and palaeography are not a refuge for erudite drudges but an absolute requirement for effective research.

The study of medieval manuscripts should be founded on an exact knowledge of how books were made, distributed, and used. Though much remains to be done, we have an attractive and scholarly introduction to the subject in Johannes Pedersen, *The Arabic Book* (trans. Geoffrey French, 1984). This work was originally published in Danish in 1946, thus ensuring that most scholars could not use it when it was new, and by now substantial parts of it are of course obsolete. But Pedersen had a deep knowledge of Islamic religion and culture, and the notes and bibliography have been brought up to date in the translation. Altogether, this is still the best place to begin. Also very valuable, though more narrowly focused, is Franz Rosenthal, *The Technique and Approach of Muslim Scholarship* (1947), which analyzes the norms and practices which governed the copying of manuscripts.

Palaeography is obviously the one indispensable skill for the would-be reader of manuscripts. It is essential not so much because it enables one to decipher difficult scripts—some handwriting is beyond any science—but more importantly, because it provides criteria for estimating the age and provenance of undated and unsigned manuscripts.

For Arabic literary manuscripts there is unfortunately no real handbook of palaeography. For the scholar who simply needs to make out the text in front of him, however, the gap is not as crucial as it might seem. Literary manuscripts in Arabic, no matter where or when they were copied, are almost always written in some variant of a script called *naskhī*, which in principle at least is clear and precise. The major exceptions to this rule are two: (1) very early manuscripts, especially of the Qur'ān, are done in the much more difficult Kufic script; (2) the scribes of Andalus and North Africa evolved a very distinctive though easily learned Maghribi script which retains some archaic Kufic elements. In *naskhī* manuscripts, the main problems stem from the individual habits of the scribe—legibility and care, the use or neglect of vowels and diacritical points, etc. But no handbook is much help in equipping one to deal with personal idiosyncrasies of this kind; only experience and a solid knowledge of Arabic, such that one knows what words an author is using even when they cannot be deciphered, will turn the trick.

A good overview of the problems of Arabic palaeography is given by J. Sourdel-Thomine, "Khaṭṭ," *EI²*, iv, 1113–1122. The best presentation of the variety of hands which one can expect to encounter is probably Bernhard Moritz, *Arabic Palaeography: A Collection of Texts from the First Century of the Hijra till the Year 1000* (1905)—a munificently produced collection of plates in elephant folio format. Based almost entirely on the holdings of what was then the Khedivial Library in Cairo (now the Dār al-Kutub al-Miṣriyya), it contains 188 plates; there are however no transcriptions or notes. On a more modest scale are the following—also without transcriptions or annotation:

a. A. J. Arberry, *The Chester Beatty Library: A Handlist of the Arabic Manuscripts* (6 vols., 1955–66). Plates of selected manuscripts in this truly remarkable collection at the end of each volume.

b. A. J. Arberry, ed., *Specimens of Arabic and Persian Palaeography* (1939). Contains 48 examples, half in Arabic and half in Persian, from the India Office Library, London; almost all are 6th/12th century or later.

c. Ṣalāḥ al-Dīn al-Munajjid, *al-Kitāb al-ʿarabī al-makhṭūṭ ilā al-qarn al-ʿāshir al-hijrī.* Juz' 1, *al-Namādhij* (1960). An excellent collection in folio size of examples from the Arab League's Institute of Manuscripts, but many of the plates seem faint or out of focus.

d. Georges Vajda, *Album de paléographie arabe* (1958). Contains 94 plates drawn from manuscripts in the Bibliothèque Nationale, Paris, chosen expressly to illustrate the basic problems of Arabic palaeography. In general the most representative volume in this group, and save for the Chester Beatty catalogs the best produced.

A proposed summa by Adolf Grohmann, *Arabische Paläographie*, unfortunately remained unfinished at its author's death. Vol. I (1967) discusses writing materials, and Vol. II (1971), subtitled *Die Lapidarschrift*, deals essentially with Kufic letter-forms, which have only a limited significance for manuscripts.

Down to Timurid times at least, the scripts used in Persian and Turkish literary manuscripts are much the same as those used for Arabic. However, from the 10th/16th century, Persian and (to a lesser degree) Turkish scribes favored an elegant but often difficult hand called *nastaʿlīq*. A terse introduction to Perso-Turkish palaeography is Ali Alparslan, "Khaṭṭ," *EI*², iv, 1122–26, and examples of Persian script, mostly of Indian provenance, are given in Arberry, *Specimens*. The plates at the end of each volume in A. J. Arberry *et al.*, *The Chester Beatty Library. A Catalogue of the Persian Manuscripts and Miniatures* (3 vols., 1959–62), are very beautiful, but most of them focus on the illustrations of these manuscripts rather than the texts *per se*; Vol. I, dealing with the older items, has some important examples of Persian script, however.

The art of calligraphy, so highly esteemed among Muslims in modern as well as medieval times, really lies outside our concerns here. Even so, it can throw some light onto the criteria which governed ordinary scribal practice. A brief but attractive introduction to it is Annemarie Schimmel, *Islamic Calligraphy* (1970).

However correctly it may be read, a manuscript is not evidence for anything until its provenance, authenticity, and accuracy have been assessed. Since Islamists seldom enjoy the luxury of scientific critical editions, they have no choice but to learn the skills of textual criticism. An historian, unlike an editor or translator, is not called on to resolve every textual problem in the text before him, but he must be able to cope with any issue which substantively affects the questions he is pursuing. It is essential to know how to identify the significant manuscripts of a text, determine the affiliations among these manuscripts, choose among differing versions of the same passage, and emend a corrupt or unintelligible passage.

These skills, together with the principles underlying them, are discussed in many places. Sound general guidelines can be found in the classic European textbooks on historical method: E. Bernheim, *Lehrbuch der historischen Methode*, 330–464; and Ch. V. Langlois and Ch. Seignobos, *Introduction aux études historiques* (1898), 51–78; trans., G. G. Berry, *Introduction to the Study of History*, (1898), pp. 71–100. (The latter is certainly clear, but also far less nuanced and more dogmatic than Bernheim.) In addition, however, I would strongly urge two titles in Classical studies, which was the birthplace of textual criticism and is still the most sophisticated field in this regard. The most rigorous statement of method is Paul Maas, *Textkritik* (original ed., 1927; 4th rev. ed., 1960; English translation by Barbara Flower, *Textual Criticism*, 1958). An historical perspective is given by a solid and very approachable study of the transmission of Greek and Latin literature from Antiquity to early modern times: L. D. Reynolds and N. G. Wilson, *Scribes and Scholars* (1968). In a substantial appendix, the authors also present a perceptive critique of the underlying assumption of Maas' work—viz., that every manuscript tradition ultimately stems from a single authentic archetype.

The principles of textual criticism often emerge most vividly in the introductions to good scientific editions. We will glance at three particularly instructive examples. For the problems involved in confirming the authorship and assessing the contents of a single manuscript (a "unicum"), see Ibn ʿAqīl, *Kitāb al-funūn*, ed. by George Makdisi (Pt. I, 1970). A somewhat different case is represented by J. A. Bellamy's edition of Ibn Abī al-Dunyā, *Kitāb makārim al-akhlāq* (1973). Here the editor not only gives an astute and methodologically very conscious examination (based on a critical use of Maas) of the relationships between his two manuscripts and their hypothetical archetype, but also illuminates the transmission of a manuscript tradition in medieval Islamic culture. Finally, Franz Rosenthal's survey of the textual history of Ibn Khaldūn's *Muqaddima* (2nd. ed., 1967; Vol. I, pp. lxxxviii–cxv) is a model for the study of a text transmitted by numerous manuscripts representing several different recensions.

Written texts, especially those with high religious value, were very often transmitted orally through a process of formal recitation and dictation. These practices are discussed in their broad institutional context by George Makdisi, *The Rise of Colleges* (1981); see especially pp. 99–105, 140–146. Academic dictation is studied by Max Weisweiler, "Das Amt des Mustamli in der arabischen Wissenschaft," *Oriens*, iv (1951), 27–57. One element of this system was the "certificate of recitation" (*samāʿ*) inscribed on the title page of certain manuscripts; an important body of such certificates is analyzed by Georges Vajda in *Les certificats de lecture et de transmission dans les manuscrits arabes de la Bibliothèque Nationale de Paris* (1956). (They are not common, unfortunately; in a collection of some 7000 Arabic manuscripts, there are only seventy-two *samāʿāt*.) The whole system was rooted in the effort to establish rigorous standards for the transmission of Prophetic hadith, and so it is useful to develop some acquaintance with this science. In addition to Sezgin's discussion in *GAS* I (see above, p. 22), see two medieval Islamic texts on method:

1. al-Ḥakīm al-Naisābūrī, *An Introduction to the Science of Tradition*, trans. James Robson (1953).
2. W. Marçais, "Le *Taqrīb* de en-Nawawī," *JA*, ser. 9: no. xvi (1900), 315–346; no. xvii (1901), 101–149, 193–232, 524–540; no. xviii (1901), 61–146.

Al-Ḥakīm al-Naisābūrī's treatment is extremely terse, but it is one of our earliest treatments on hadith methodology and is easy to follow. Al-Nawawī's work is an abridgement of the standard treatise on the subject, the *ʿUlūm al-ḥadīth* of Ibn al-Ṣalāḥ al-Shahrazūrī (d. 643/1245).

Here we cannot deal in any systematic way with the problems of textual criticism, but a few general points which especially concern historians should be made.

In every case, the first step must be to establish the relationship between the manuscript we are using and the original work of which it claims to be a copy. Otherwise we cannot know if the statements before us are copyists' corruptions or even forgeries. Establishing the link between copy and original is no easy task: dated and signed colophons are rare, and authors' autographs or direct transmissions guaranteed by certificates of recitation are rarer still. To a large degree, one's judgment must be based on such elusive data as scripts, unusual errors shared by two or more manuscripts, etc.

Even in the case of a unicum with few external indications of date and provenance, however, we are not without resources. In the fields of history, biography, and jurisprudence in particular, medieval Muslim authors tended to absorb the work of their predecessors, either by direct quotation (not always attributed) or by extensive paraphrase. Thus the text of the vast chronicle of al-Ṭabarī (d. 310/923) often rests on a single manuscript, but the readings of these sections can be substantially confirmed by comparing them to Ibn al-Athīr (d. 630/1234), whose early volumes follow al-Ṭabarī very closely, albeit with some abridgement. Likewise, the one partial manuscript of ʿIzz al-Dīn b.

Shaddād's life of Sultan Baybars can be checked and completed by a chronicle written half a century later by al-Yūnīnī, who appears to have cited the bulk of Ibn Shaddād almost verbatim. Obviously this technique will not yield a completely secure text; on the other hand, we get some compensation by learning how a given work was used and understood within the scholarly tradition of medieval Islam.

In the happy event that we have two or more manuscripts of the same text, there are other pitfalls. In particular, the temptation to harmonize the contents of different manuscripts must be strenuously avoided, for this is likely to blot out significantly different recensions of the work being studied. If, for example, Ms. A represents a rough but detailed draft version of a given chronicle and Ms. B a polished but somewhat abridged reworking of it, every effort must be made to preserve the differences between them. A particularly clear case of this kind is the *Mirʾāt al-zamān fī taʾrīkh al-aʿyān* of Sibṭ ibn al-Jawzī (d. 654/1256), one of the most important and influential chronicles of the 7th/13th century, which still awaits an adequate edition; see the review by Claude Cahen of a partial edition, *Arabica*, iv (1957), 191–194, and the same author's general remarks in "Editing Arabic Chronicles: a Few Suggestions," *Islamic Studies* (1962), 1–25; reprinted in *Peuples musulmans*, 11–36. A second example, this time drawn from jurisprudence, would be the *Muwaṭṭaʾ* of Mālik ibn Anas, whose complex textual history can be followed in *SEI*, 321f.; *GAS*, I, 458–460; and Ignaz Goldziher, *Muslim Studies*, (trans. S. M. Stern and C. R. Barber, 1967–71), II, 204–209. In short, the definitive "original text" is most often a chimera; better to focus one's energies on doing justice to all the data than to try to capture such an elusive beast.

In an ideal world, with time and expense no object, we would examine directly all known manuscripts of any text we intended to use, and would make our choice of variants and recensions according to the standards of a good critical edition. Obviously this is seldom feasible, and even microfilms (which are no substitute for the real thing) are often extremely difficult to obtain, especially from Eastern Europe and Asia. In such circumstances, we must turn to the printed catalogs and handlists produced by most of the world's major manuscript repositories. In addition to authors, titles, and shelflist numbers, these normally give such data as the number of pages or folios in each volume, its size, the number of lines per page, a description of the binding, and (if known) the date it was copied. A few catalogs go much further, giving quite detailed summaries of the contents of each manuscript, analyses of its date, provenance, and transmission, and even references to related manuscripts in other collections. The outstanding achievement in this field is no doubt the magnificent survey of the Islamic manuscripts of Berlin made late in the last century, so thorough and exact that it almost constitutes a history of the three literatures:

Wilhelm Ahlwardt, *Verzeichnis der arabischen Handschriften der königlichen Bibliothek zu Berlin* (10 vols., 1887–1899).

Wilhelm Pertsch, *Verzeichnis der persischen Handschriften der königlichen Bibliothek zu Berlin* (1888); *Verzeichnis der türkischen Handschriften der königlichen Bibliothek zu Berlin* (1889).

Catalogs of similar quality, though on a smaller scale, were prepared for several other European libraries at about the same time, but the 20th century has seen the near-demise of such efforts, doubtless due to their immense cost and limited audience. There are happily some important exceptions. West Germany has mounted a sustained project to survey the country's Oriental manuscript resources: *Verzeichnis der orientalischen Handschriften in Deutschland* (abbr., *VOHD*; 1961–in progress). The work has been divided into thirty-two volumes (many of them in several parts), one for each of the languages to be covered. In addition, a separately numbered series of supplementary volumes, dealing with specific problems or manuscripts, is also being issued; to date twenty-six of these have appeared. Within *VOHD* three volumes are of central interest for Islamic history:

B. XIII. *Türkische Handschriften.* 5 Teile (1968-81)
B. XIV. *Persische Handschriften.* 2 Teile (1968-80)
B. XVII, Reihe A. *Materialien zur arabischen Literaturgeschichte.* 2 Teile (1976–87)
B. XVII, Reihe B. *Arabische Handschriften.* 1 Teil (1976)

VOHD can be supplemented by Fuat Sezgin, *Beiträge zur Erschliessung der arabischen Handschriften in deutschen Bibliotheken* (3 vols., 1987), which assembles a useful (albeit antiquated) set of studies describing German manuscript collections of the mid and late 19th century. Vols. II and III reprint the old catalogs for Munich and Tübingen respectively; the articles in Vol. I focus on a number of personal libraries (by Landberg, Hartmann, Sprenger, et al.) which became the very heart of the great public collections in Berlin and elsewhere.

The vast majority of printed catalogs do not begin to approach German standards. Perhaps worst-served of all is Turkey, the country which possesses by far the richest Islamic manuscript holdings in the world. For the libraries of Istanbul, which contain at least 125,000 volumes, scholars have had to make do with a series of handlists (a separate one for each of forty or so institutions) published at the turn of the century. These are obsolete, laconic, and riddled with errors. For many other major centers, such as Konya or Bursa, we do not have even this much. In view of this situation, Fuat Sezgin has performed a real service with his recent anthology of articles describing selected manuscripts in Istanbul and other Turkish libraries: *Beiträge zur Erschliessung der arabischen Handschriften in Istanbul und Anatolien* (4 vols., 1986). Vol. IV is an index to the manuscripts described in the first three, organized by library and shelflist number. The papers collected here were published between the late 19th century and 1961, and all are by German or Turkish scholars. There are unfortunate omissions—e.g., an important study of historical manuscripts in Istanbul by Claude Cahen, "Les chroniques arabes concernant la Syrie, l'Égypte, et la Mesopotamie de la conquête arabe à la conquête ottomane dans les bibliothèques d'Istanbul," *REI*, x (1936), 333–362. But Sezgin's initiative is a most useful one even so.

The situation has slowly begun to improve. F. E. Karatay, for example, did a competent set of catalogs for the Topkapı Sarayı Müzesi (7 vols., 1961–69), which for the first time made this great repository of some 12,000 manuscripts readily accessible to modern scholarship. The most crucial step, however, has been the decision of the Ministry of Culture in the mid-1970's to prepare a comprehensive union catalog of all the manuscripts in Turkey:

Türkiye Cumhuriyeti Kultur ve Turizm Bakanlığı, Kütüphaneler Genel Müdürlüğü. *Türkiye Yazmaları Toplu Kataloğu / The Union Catalogue of Manuscripts in Turkey* (11 vols., 1979–in progress; abbr., *TUYATOK*).

This immense campaign will inevitably stretch on for decades, and the initial volumes have tended to focus on small and hence relatively manageable collections. The entries are very terse, often without references to printed editions or the relevant bio-bibliographical sources. However, there are author and title indices for each collection, as well as full-page plates of selected manuscripts. And not least, the quality of the printing is quite high. The organization of the project is somewhat confusing. First, each volume is devoted to one or more of the collections in a given province (as defined by current boundaries). However, the provinces are not treated in sequences: Adana is covered in Vols. IX and XI, Istanbul (so far) in Vols. III and VIII. Second—in contrast to most European catalogs—*TUYATOK* deals with collections, not libraries per se. Thus, there will be no overall survey of the vast Süleymaniye Library in Istanbul; rather, each of the innumerable collections which make it up will be catalogued separately. For example, Vol. III is devoted to the collection of 425 mss assembled by Ali Nihat Tarlan, which happens to be housed at the Süleymaniye. In spite of such shortcomings, *TUYATOK* is an exciting venture and will surely have a profound impact.

A useful attempt to establish a union catalog of Persian manuscripts was undertaken by Aḥmad Munẓavī, *Fihrist-i Nuskhahā-i Khaṭṭī-i Fārsī* (6 vols., 1348–51/1969–72), under the sponsorship of the Regional Cultural Institute in Tehran. Munẓavī does not claim to add new materials, but simply abstracts the available printed catalogs; even so, these represent collections all over Europe, India, and the Middle East, and some 49,000 manuscripts are included.

We have already noted that articles dealing with selected manuscripts can help a scholar faced with non-existent or inadequate printed catalogs. In addi-

tion to the the two anthologies by Sezgin for Germany and Turkey, most of the important ones down to the mid-1970's can be found in the thorough survey of manuscript collections in *GAS* VI, 311–466. A superbly produced new journal devoted specifically to Islamic manuscripts made its appearance in 1986: *Manuscripts of the Middle East* (abbr., *MME*)—a very welcome addition indeed. For current European-language contributions, *Index Islamicus* is the best reference, albeit a somewhat cumbersome one. In addition, such articles appear regularly in a number of Middle Eastern journals which the *Index* does not survey:

a. *Majallat Maʿhad al-Makhṭūṭāt al-ʿArabiyya* (abbr., *MMMA*; Arab League, Cairo; since 1982 published in Kuwait, with volumes numbered in a new series)

b. *Mélanges de l'Institut Dominicain d'Études Orientales du Caire* (abbr., *MIDEO*)

c. *Majallat Majmaʿ al-Lugha al-ʿArabiyya bi-Dimashq/Révue de l'Académie Arabe de Damas* (abbr., *RAAD*)

d. *Majallat al-Majmaʿ al-ʿIlmī al-ʿIrāqī* (abbr., *MMII*; Baghdad)

e. *Nashriya-i Kitābkhāna-i Markazi-i Dānishgāh-i Tihrān dar barrā-i Nuskhahā-i Khaṭṭī* (University of Tehran; abbr., *Nuskhahā-i Khaṭṭī*)

The survey of Arabic manuscript collections in *GAS* VI has largely supplanted two older bibliographic works: A.J.W. Huisman, *Les manuscrits arabes dans le monde: une bibliographie des catalogues* (1967); and Georges Vajda, *Répertoire des catalogues et inventaires de manuscrits arabes* (1949). See also Kūrkīs ʿAwwād, *Fahāris al-makhṭūṭat al-ʿarabiyya fī al-ʿālam. Catalogues of the Arabic Manuscripts in the World* (2 vols. 1405/1984). ʿAwwād tries to be exhaustive, and provides brief evaluations of the catalogues he lists; in spite of numerous minor misprints, he is worth consulting. For Persian collections, in addition to Storey and Bregel, see the excellent though now obsolescent survey of Īrāj Afshār, *Bibliographie des catalogues des manuscrits persans* (1337/1958). For Turkish we seem to have nothing of this kind, though *VOHD* has announced that a repertory by G. Hazai is in preparation (Suppl. XXII); in the meantime, see E. Birnbaum, "Turkish Manuscripts" (mentioned above, pp. 30–31). A broad overview, going far beyond the limits of Islamic studies, is provided by J. D. Pearson, *Oriental Manuscripts in Europe and North America: a Survey* (1971). Pearson briefly describes and assesses each of the collections which he includes, and though he has omitted Turkey he does discuss the Soviet Union. His comments on the USSR (still terra incognita for most scholars) can be supplemented by R. D. McChesney, "A Guide to Orientalist Research in Soviet Central Asia," *MESA Bull.*, xii, no. 1 (1978), 13–25. On the United States and Canada, finally, see Thomas J. Martin, *North American Collections of Islamic Manuscripts* (1977).

The conclusions to be drawn from this discussion are daunting: medieval Islamic manuscripts are likely to be full of errors, written in barely legible

scripts, and scattered in unlikely and inaccessible locations. That is all perfectly true; as historians we are clearly better off when we have our sources in a critical printed edition. But it is also true that manuscripts are alive in a way that printed texts can never be. Manuscripts put us in immediate contact with the men and women whom we study; through them we ourselves become participants in a living scholarly and literary tradition. For this privilege, mere inconvenience is a small price to pay.

B. Archives and Documents

In medieval Islamic history we are poor in archives but rich in documents. For the most part we have only begun to identify and study these, let alone integrate them into the main stream of historical research, which still depends overwhelmingly on narrative and literary sources. But documentary materials are quickly moving from the periphery to the center of historical thinking in the Islamic field, and a serious historian can no longer avoid the hard job of learning how to use them effectively. As a consequence, documents and the problems surrounding them will often claim our attention in the pages which follow, and in three chapters in Part II (7, 9, 11) we will explore certain groups of them in considerable detail. For this reason the present analysis will be a general one, in order to provide a broad context for more concrete discussions later on.

Medieval Islamic documents are very unevenly distributed in space and time. For Egypt alone do we have a nearly continuous (though extremely disparate) sequence of them, and the overwhelming majority of our total corpus in fact comes from that country. Other countries are represented only by tantalizing fragments; and precious as these are, they are no adequate foundation for the study of broad problems or periods. Only near the end of the time-span covered in this book—i.e., the later 8th/14th and 9th/15th centuries—does the quantity of documents even for the most favored regions (Anatolia, northwestern Iran, Syria-Palestine) begin to approach a critical mass.

Down to the 6th/12th century, all the extant documents are loose items—i.e., they are not part of an ordered archival collection, though in a very few cases it has been possible through extraordinary labors to reconstruct a partial archive from scattered pieces. Even when the documents come from large troves, as do most of the papyri or the Geniza papers, these are just miscellaneous aggregations of material which commonly originated literally as trash heaps. Between the 6th/12th and 9th/15th centuries, the few archival collections which exist are small and fragmentary, though there is a substantial improvement for the last decades of this period. The 10th/16th century, however, marks a revolution, for from this point on the vast resources of the Ottoman archives lie before us. The Ottoman documents mostly postdate the limits of this book, but even so we shall refer to them at many points, since they often

throw a direct light on the later phases of some problem we are discussing, provide a valuable comparative perspective, or suggest a useful set of questions and approaches.

Many documents have come down to us not in their original form, but through citations (of varying accuracy and completeness) in the narrative sources or through inclusion in collections of model documents. Such collections, usually called *majmūʿāt* or *munshaʾāt*, were compiled to provide chancery officials with formularies to guide them in the composition of elegant and formally correct state documents. Where possible the compilers would draw on actual documents registered in the state archives, and for this reason these *inshāʾ*-collections are potentially very important. There are pitfalls, however; compilers were not above inventing documents, and in any event it was common to omit such vital data as dates and personal names. Even in the most scrupulously made collection, important elements like seals, registration marks, etc., are inevitably absent. (On these matters see "Inshāʾ," *EI*², iii, 1241–44.)

Documents, both official and private, were written on a variety of materials, but only three of these were widely used: papyrus, paper, and stone. The last of these of course pertains to inscriptions, which will be discussed under a separate heading. Papyrus (Ar., *qirṭās*), though produced only in Egypt, was used all over the ancient Mediterranean world down to early medieval times, and its import and sale was often a state monopoly. In Egypt, it continued to be used for both public and private business until the introduction of paper manufacture in that country in the early 5th/11th century. Since it was relatively cheap and common in Egypt, and since local soil conditions favored the survival of organic materials, it should be no surprise that almost all surviving papyrus documents have been discovered in that country, though Syria has also yielded a few pieces. As for paper (Ar., *kāghad*), it was introduced into Transoxania from China in the mid-2nd/8th century and was being manufactured in Baghdad some fifty years later. By the 5th/11th century it had become the principal writing material even in the conservative and relatively remote regions of Andalus and the Maghrib. The paper mills of medieval Islam produced an excellent product which remains strong and flexible for centuries, and so it is natural that paper documents form the bulk of what has come down to us. (On these topics see Grohmann, *Arabische Paläographie*, I, 66–117; "Kāghad," *EI*², iv, 419–420; "Ḳirṭās," *EI*², v, 173–174.)

The scripts used in Islamic documents can be most intimidating; to a far greater degree than literary manuscripts, their study demands careful palaeographic training. As to language, one must be prepared to confront extremes of style and usage: colloquial informality in private and business papers, almost impenetrably florid rhetoric in the chancery decrees and correspondence of later centuries. For at least some of these problems, fortunately, a number of useful titles are available.

Since the papyri represent the earliest body of Islamic documents (both official and private), we can begin with a handbook by Adolf Grohmann, *From the World of Arabic Papyri* (1952). This work was meant as an elementary introduction to the subject. Even so, it has useful chapters on script and language. It contains also a number of printed and translated sample documents, but the few accompanying facsimiles are unfortunately too poorly printed to be of much value. The author's statements on script and language are more fully developed in his *Einführung und Chrestomathie zur arabischen Papyruskunde* (1955), but this important study contains no texts at all. On the grammar of the papyri, which departs in significant and sometimes confusing ways from the norms of Classical Arabic, see the excellent analysis by Simon Hopkins, *Studies in the Grammar of Early Arabic, Based upon Papyri Datable to before A.H. 300/A.D. 912* (1984). Given the lack of a comprehensive handbook, the best recourse is probably to study papyri which have been published with good facsimiles, printed transcriptions, translations, and thorough annotation. For state documents, a good example would be Nabia Abbott, *The Ḳurrah Papyri from Aphrodito in the Oriental Institute* (1938). An important archive of private documents has recently been reconstructed by Yūsuf Rāghib, *Marchands d'étoffes du Fayyoum au iiiᵉ/ixᵉ siècle d'après leurs archives (actes et lettres); I, Les actes des Banū ᶜAbd al-Muʾmin* (1982). (Six fascicles altogether are projected in this series.) The largest published collection of papyri is still Adolf Grohmann, *Arabic Papyri in the Egyptian Museum* (6 vols., 1934–62); through it one can get a good idea of the sort of linguistic and palaeographic problems likely to occur in any of these documents. The skills required to handle papyri are precisely the same as those needed for paper documents, at least those of non-governmental provenance; papyrology is a science to be acquired by anyone who has to handle loose documents dug from the ground, often in tattered condition and written in illegible and ungrammatical prose.

Perhaps because so few original state documents in Arabic still survive, we have no full-length modern account of the chancery scripts used in these texts. Most of what is known is presented in the meticulous study of S. M. Stern, *Fatimid Decrees* (1964), which has small but clearly printed facsimiles of seven items from 6th/12th century Egypt. As his title implies, Stern deals only with documents from the caliphal chancery, and does not address the very different scripts and formats used in such quasi-official texts as deeds of *waqf* or minutes of judicial hearings.

In regard to Persian state documents we are somewhat better off. First of all, here we do have a general handbook: Lajos Fekete, *Einführung in die persische Paläographie: 101 persische Dokumente*, ed. G. Hazai (1977). This is an anthology of documents drawn up in chanceries throughout Iran, Anatolia, and Transoxiana between 1396 and 1702. Each piece is given in facsimile, printed transcription, and German translation, and there is also a lengthy introduction which discusses scripts, the format and structure of the documents, diction and rhetoric, etc. Unfortunately this book must be used with caution; the facsimiles are often hard to make out, and more important, it contains many significant errors of transcription and translation. A more reliable and convenient introduction to the arcana of Persian palaeography and diplomatics can be gotten from the fine study of Heribert Busse, *Untersuchungen zum islamischen Kanzleiwesen, an hand Türkmenischer und Safawidischer Urkunden* (1959). Busse's scale and approach rather resemble Stern's; he studies twenty-three documents dating from 1453 to 1717.

As already noted, the Ottoman archives contain materials of extraordinary importance even for periods before the 10th/16th century, not only for the the Mediterranean Basin but for Iran as well. This material is often extremely difficult to use, but by now a considerable technical literature has been generated; this is ably reviewed in Valery Stojanow, *Die Entstehung und Entwicklung der osmanisch-türkischen Paläographie und Diplomatik* (1983). A practical orientation to the decipherment of Ottoman state documents can be found in J. Reychman and A. Zajaczkowski, *Handbook of Ottoman-Turkish Diplomatics*, trans. A. S. Ehrenkreutz (1968). The chapter on palaeography is broadly applicable to Persian chancery usage as well, though of course there are significant differences in technical terminology, names of scripts, etc. The forbidding script used by the Ottoman financial bureaucracy is presented in Lajos Fekete, *Die Siyaqat-Schrift in der türkischen Finanzverwaltung* (1955), an important work which is far more satisfactory than the same author's *Einführung* discussed above.

Language and script are not the only problems which confront us. No less important is reconstructing the context of institutions and procedures within which these documents were produced, for without such a context they are meaningless and unintelligible. The relevant context will of course vary greatly according to the kind of document in question. Many items—business papers, minutes of court proceedings, deeds of *waqf*—call for a solid grounding in practical jurisprudence (*furūʿ al-fiqh*) and judicial procedure. (For further discussion of these issues, see Part II, Ch. 9.) State documents, in contrast, require an exact knowledge of the chanceries and finance bureaux of medieval Islam. These are in many cases still only poorly understood, however; not only were they complex organizations in themselves, but they varied greatly from one region and period to another. In recent decades, fortunately, a considerable number both modern studies and sources written by members of the Islamic bureaucracies have been published. These do not solve all difficulties, obviously, but they give us a working vocabulary and suggest some possible lines of analysis. In the following paragraphs, we will review briefly the basic texts and studies for several periods of Islamic history. A far more detailed examination for one polity (the Mamluk Empire in Egypt and Syria) will be presented in Part II, Ch. 7.

We begin, naturally enough, with a series of articles in *EI*[2]: "Diplomatic," ii, 301–316 (an overview of documents and how they were produced); "Daftar," ii, 77–81 (the file or register prepared by the finance bureaux); "Dīwān," ii, 323–337 (originally the muster-roll of soldiers entitled to stipends, but generally the term for a bureau or department); "Farmān," ii, 803–805 (the royal decree); "Kātib," iv, 754–760 (the official or secretary); "Khātam," iv, 1102–1105. In *EI*[1] certain articles are still of value: e.g., "Ṭughrā," iv, 822–826 (the royal signature in Turkish dynasties).

The roots of Islamic diplomatics and administration obviously lie in the usage of the Early and Marwanid Caliphates, but our knowledge of the institutions and procedures of these regimes remains uncertain. Under such circumstances, the best strategy is to begin with a few recent monographs and work back into the sources and studies cited by them. Early Islamic Egypt is by far the best-documented province, though the documents are hardly transparent. (A warning is in order here: Egypt is typical only of Egypt, and the urge to generalize must be staunchly resisted.) The most recent analysis is Kisei Morimoto, *The Fiscal Administration of Egypt in the Early Islamic Period* (1981), to be compared with the astute though polemical account of D. C. Dennett, *Conversion and the Poll Tax in Early Islam* (1950), pp. 3–13, 65–115. The forms used in the official papyri are treated in Grohmann, *Einführung*, pp. 107–130. For the crucial and innovative region of Iraq, a mass of data on every aspect of administration has been sifted from an impressive array of sources by M. G. Morony, *Iraq after the Muslim Conquest* (1984), pp. 27–164, although his general conclusions may need further study. On the origins and character of the fiscal system in this region, Dennett is again incisive though far from definitive.

The Abbasid dynasty has a special role in the development of Islamic government, not only because of its early grandeur, but even more because of its immense prestige, which made it a model of bureaucratic organization and administrative procedure for so many successor states in the Nile-to-Oxus region. In addition, the growing elaboration and self-consciousness of the bureaucracy led to the composition of numerous treatises on taxation, the art of the secretary, etc. The chancery and fiscal practices of the Abbasids and their early Iranian successors are summarized in the chapter on *kitāba* in al-Khwārizmī's *Mafātīḥ al-ʿulūm*, ed. G. van Vloten (4 vols., 1895; repr. 1968); this text is most conveniently studied through an extensively annotated translation by C. E. Bosworth, "Abū ʿAbdallāh al-Khwārizmī on the Technical Terms of the Secretary's Art," *JESHO*, xii (1969), 113–164. The general structure of Abbasid administration is traced in the formidable study of Dominique Sourdel, *Le vizirat abbaside de 749 à 936* (2 vols., 1959–60). Sourdel's work is exhaustively documented, but its real merit lies in its focus on the problem of change in the functions and political power of the *wazīrs*. The Egyptian papyri are still numerous in this period; their data is analyzed in the relevant chapter of Morimoto.

Since post-Abbasid Egypt and Syria are treated in considerable detail later on, it will be enough here to refer to a few works which between them sum up or give access to everything else. By far the most important literary source is the imposing summa of al-Qalqashandī, *Ṣubḥ al-aʿshā fī ṣināʿat al-inshāʾ* (14 vols., 1913–20; repr. 1964). The bulk of this vast compilation makes it difficult to approach, but it is summarized in Walther Björkman, *Beiträge zur Geschichte der Staatskanzlei im islamischen Ägypten* (1928). On chancery procedures, the crucial study is Stern's *Fatimid Decrees*. Finally, Hassanein Rabie, *The Financial Administration of Egypt, A.H. 564–741/A.D. 1169–1341* (1972) provides a wealth of data on his subject, though his interpretation of his material seems incompletely worked out and in any case is difficult to follow.

The 5th/11th century opens a new era in the evolution of Iranian administrative practice, for it is from this time that a separate and distinctive Persian-language chancery tradition begins to emerge. Although the Iranian chanceries have bequeathed us no comprehensive works like that of al-Qalqashandī, we do have a number of extremely valuable specialized treatises. On financial procedures, see ʿAbdallāh b. Muḥammad b. Kiyā Māzandarānī, *Risāla-i falakiyya dar ʿilm-i siyāqat*, ed. Walther Hinz (1952), the bulk of which consists of models of the various kinds of financial registers in use in the author's time (8th/14th cen.). This treatise has been analyzed by Hinz in a separate study: "Das Rechnungswesen orientalischer Reichsfinanzämter in Mittelalter," *Islam*, xxix (1950), 1–29, 113–141. From the end of the 11th/17th century we have an anonymous work entitled *Tadhkirat al-mulūk*, ed. and trans. V. Minorsky (1943), which gives a critical account of the administrative institutions of the decaying Safavid regime. In spite of the late date of this work, the editor's introduction and notes make it a significant resource even for far earlier periods. In Persian, see the general work of Jahāngīr Qāʾim-maqāmī, *Muqaddima-i bar shinakht-i asnād-i tārīkhī* (1350/1971).

Among modern studies of Iranian diplomatics, a sound general survey is given by H. Busse, "Persische Diplomatik in Überblick: Ergebnisse und Probleme," *Islam*, xxxvii (1961), 202–245, which can be studied in conjunction with the same scholar's *Untersuchungen zum islamischen Kanzleiwesen* (see above, p. 43). For the formative period of the Iranian tradition (5th/11th–7th/13th centuries) we have no extant documents in their original form, but must depend on the *inshāʾ*-collections. Several of these are studied in Heribert Horst, *Die Staatsverwaltung der Grosselǧūqen und Ḫorazmšāhs (1038–1231)* (1964). Horst's conception of administration is rather static and mechanical, and there are numerous errors in his summary translations from the documents, but he provides a useful orientation to the subject.

For the periods covered in this book, North Africa seems to have left us neither original documents nor systematic treatises on administration. Under the circumstances, we can probably do no better than to examine the relevant chapters in Ibn Khaldūn's *Muqaddima* (trans. Franz Rosenthal, Vol. II, pp. 3–48). As in the eastern Islamic lands, of course, numerous documents are transcribed (but how reliably?) in the chronicles, biographical dictionaries, and *majmūʿāt*.

It would be extremely useful to have accurate and complete calendars of Islamic documents, organized by period, region, and subject—the sort of thing that students in English history, for example, simply take for granted. But it will be a very long time before our field can achieve anything like this, and in the meantime historians of Islam will have to count on expending much time and effort just to determine what documents may be available. However, we do have a few reference tools, survey articles, and printed collections, and we will conclude this section by identifying the most important of these, insofar as they deal with original documents and not transcriptions in literary texts and *majmūʿāt*.

Certain European archives contain a number of Arabic documents—treaties, diplomatic correspondence, etc. Among these the most important published collections are the following:

a. M. A. Alarcón y Santón and R. G. de Linares, *Los documentos arabes diplomaticos del archivio de la Corona de Aragon* (1940)—162 documents, dealing with Granada, North Africa, and Egypt.

b. Michele Amari, *I diplomi arabi del R. Archivio Fiorentino* (1863).

c. Salvatore Cusa, *I diplomi greci ed arabi di Sicilia* (2 vols., 1868–1882)—mostly items from the Norman period.

Documents of a very different kind—marriage contracts, personal letters, household inventories—are presented in the meticulous collection of Wilhelm Hoenerbach, *Spanisch-Islamische Urkunden aus der Zeit der Nasriden und Moriscos* (1965).

The volume of published documents from Egypt is far too large for any adequate survey here. Unfortunately these publications are terribly scattered, and to date there is no general index for them. Under these circumstances, we shall restrict ourselves to identifying the most important groups of documents, together with those studies and surveys which best give access to them.

To the papyri we have already devoted considerable attention. An exhaustive inventory of find-sites, museum and library collections, and publications is given in Grohmann, *Einführung*, to be updated by the same author's *Arabische Papyruskunde*, *HO*, Ergbd. II, 1 (1966). A body of materials rather similar in character and provenance to the papyri, though later in date, are the so-called "Vienna papers"—many thousands of loose scraps of paper stored in uncatalogued boxes at the Österreichische Staatsbibliothek. Of these there is a brief but concrete description in H. Rabie, *The Financial System of Egypt*, pp. 3–6. (Much of the Vienna material is available on microfilm at a rather surprising location, the Hill Monastic Library of St. John's University, Collegeville, Minnesota.) New troves of documents are always being uncovered. For example, excavations during 1978 at the Red Sea port of Quṣayr revealed some 400 letters, bills of lading, etc., deposited by merchants residing there during Mamluk times.

No doubt the most remarkable corpus of documents from Egypt are the Geniza papers—a vast tumble of writings of all kinds discovered in a sealed storeroom of the Fusṭāṭ synagogue during renovations to that building in 1890. These will be discussed more fully in Part II, Ch. 11; here we need only note that the Geniza has yielded some 10,000 documents, dating from the late 4th/10th to the 9th/15th centuries. This hoard was broken up early on, so that Geniza materials are now scattered among collections all over Europe and Asia. The best introduction to this material and its extraordinary importance for Islamic and Mediterranean history is S. D. Goitein, *A Mediterranean Society: the Jewish Communities of the Arab World as Portrayed in the Documents of the Cairo Geniza* (5 vols., 1967–88); for a description of the Geniza finds see Vol. I, 1–28. Geniza publications and studies are voluminous; down to 1964 they have been recorded by Shaul Shaked, *A Tentative Bibliography of Geniza Documents* (1964), which remains useful in spite of the flood of new work over the past two decades. The first part gives a comprehensive list of Geniza texts, arranged according to the collections where they are now housed; the second part presents a bibliography of publications and studies.

Very few Egyptian state documents (decrees, official correspondence, cadastral surveys, etc.) from before the Ottoman conquest have come down to us. However, the archives do preserve nearly 900 deeds of *waqf*, contracts of sale, etc., drawn up on behalf of the sultan and other high officials. These have now been catalogued (with facsimiles and printed transcriptions of nine sample documents) by Muḥammad Amīn, *Catalogue des documents d'archives du Caire, de 239/853 à 922/1516* (1981, in Arabic)—a work which will surely have a strong impact on the study of social and economic life during the Mamluk period.

The only substantial series of chancery documents still extant is located at St. Catherine's Monastery on Mt. Sinai. These are available on microfilm at the Library of Congress, Washington, D.C., and have been catalogued (albeit in a very terse manner) by A. S. Atiya, *The Arabic Manuscripts of Mt. Sinai* (1955). Most of those relevant to our period have been published—the Fatimid and Ayyubid documents by S. M. Stern, the Mamluk items by Hans Ernst, *Die mamlukischen Sultansurkunden des Sinai-Klosters* (1960). An overview of this field is given by H. R. Roemer, "Arabische Herrscherurkunden aus Ägypten," *OLZ*, lxi (1966), 325–347.

In contrast to Egypt, the lands of the Fertile Crescent have pathetically few documents to offer; the bulk of these come from Jerusalem and Damascus. There are a few 3rd/9th century papyri published by Nabia Abbott, "Arabic Papyri of the Reign of Ǧaʿfar al-Mutawakkil ʿalā-llāh," *ZDMG*, xcii (1938), 88–135. In Istanbul, the Museum of Turkish and Islamic Art houses some remarkable fragments brought there from the Umayyad Mosque of Damascus after that building was gutted by a disastrous fire in 1893. These are described by J. Sourdel-Thomine and D. Sourdel in two articles: "Nouveaux documents sur l'histoire religieuse et sociale de Damas au Moyen Âge," *REI*, xxxii (1964), 1–25; À propos des documents de la grande mosquée de Damas conservés à Istanbul. Résultats de la seconde enquête," *REI*, xxxiii (1965), 73–85. Three of the oldest items were published by the Sourdels in "Trois actes de vente damascains du début du ive/xe siècle," *JESHO*, viii (1965), 164–185. Finally, we should mention an archival collection which is in some respects comparable to that of St. Catherine's, though on a markedly smaller scale. This is the body of documents held at the Franciscan Custodia Terrae Sanctae in Jerusalem. A series of royal decrees running from al-Ashraf Shaʿbān (764–778/1363–1376) to Khushqadam (865–872/1461–1467) were published in N. Risciani, *Documenti e firmani* (1931), and a summary catalog was provided by E. Castellani, *Catalogo dei firmani e altri documenti legali conservati nel'archivio della Custodia in Gerusalemme* (1922). Neither publication was ever put into general distribution, however, and both are almost impossible to find.

Far more important than any of the above collections is a trove of some 1000 documents of every kind—decrees and petitions, household inventories, acts of sale, etc.—from the Ḥaram al-Sharīf in Jerusalem, dating from the 7th/13th to the late 9th/15th centuries, with the great majority belonging to the 790s/1390s. These were first described by Linda S. Northrup and Amal Abul-Hajj, "A Collection of Medieval Arabic Documents in the Islamic Museum at the Ḥaram al-Šarīf," *Arabica*, xxv (1978), 282–291; see also Donald P. Little, "The Significance of the Ḥaram Documents for the Study of Medieval Islamic History," *Islam*, lvii (1980), 189–219. Little has published a detailed catalogue of this material, *A Catalogue of the Islamic Documents from al-Ḥaram as-Šarīf in Jerusalem* (1984). The documents are grouped according to their legal function (e.g., decrees, estate inventories, contracts), and an English abstract of each item is presented. There are regrettably no facsimiles or Arabic texts. Some of Little's readings have been criticized. (See for example the review by D. S. Richards in *BSOAS*, l [1987], 362–364.) However, the script of these documents is almost impenetrable in places, and whatever its flaws, Little's catalog is an invaluable resource for the student of Mamluk Syria. The few studies of the Ḥaram documents already published are enough to demonstrate their profound importance, especially if they can be used in conjunction with the Egyptian materials catalogued by Amin.

If only because of the bureaucratic needs and traditions of the Ottoman state, we might expect to find quite a number of Anatolian documents dating from the 7th/13th to the 9th/15th centuries. In fact such items seem to be rather sparse, though a careful survey of the provincial *sharīʿa*-court records might still turn up a great deal. In the meantime, see the bibliographical essay in Claude Cahen, *Pre-Ottoman Turkey* (1968), especially pp. 434–35. Documents belonging to the very end of our period are presented in Mehmet Şefik Keçik, *Briefe und Urkunden aus der Kanzlei Uzun-Hasans: ein Beitrag zur Geschichte Ost-Anatoliens im 15. Jahrhundert* (1975).

Iran is well served by a recent publication: Bert G. Fragner, *Repertorium persischer Herrscherurkunden: publizierte Originalurkunden (bis 1848)* (1980), which gives bibliographic data on 868 documents, the earliest dating from ca. 1200. Fragner includes only royal chancery documents, to be sure, and does not directly address unpublished materials. What may yet be found is suggested by a body of documents discovered in 1970 at the Safavid shrine in Ardebil. This collection numbers more than 500 items, dating from the 6th/12th to the 9th/15th century. It was first described by Gottfried Hermann, "Urkunden-funde in Āzarbayǧān, *AMI*, NF iv (1971), 250–262; see also the comments by Fragner, "Das Ardabiler Heiligtum in den Urkunden," *WZKM*, lxvii (1975), 171ff. Twenty-five of the earliest judicial and notarial documents of this group have been published and translated (with a detailed legal commentary) by Monika Gronke, *Arabische und persische Privaturkunden des 12. und 13. Jahrhunderts aus Ardabil (Aserbaidschan)* (1982).

The discovery and classification of documents will be urgent tasks for a very long time to come. Even as things stand, however, historians of Islamic society can begin to progress from collection and technical analysis towards the integration of documentary evidence into the mainstream of historical inquiry.

C. Numismatics and Metrology

The Arab Conquests irrupted into two highly monetized economies—the Roman-Byzantine and the Sassanian—and from the outset the new rulers attempted to integrate the established monetary systems into their own emerging fiscal and economic framework. In this effort they succeeded, and one of the salient features of Islamic history, in almost every period and region, is the primary role of coined metal (gold, silver, and copper) within its several monetary systems. Thus coins will inevitably have a large part to play in our efforts to reconstruct the political, social, and economic life of medieval Islam. Every coin is a direct and authentic reflection of the political and economic system which produced it; it is therefore perfect evidence for that system if only we can learn how to decode it.

To achieve this is of course no easy matter; even the finest numismatists will often find that the full significance of a coin escapes them. Even so, any competent Islamic historian must become familiar with the many ways in which coins can be both evaluated as objects in themselves and used to illuminate broader historical concerns. A good introduction to the special concerns and skills of numismatists will be found in the handbook of Philip Grierson, *Numismatics*, (1975). Grierson is certainly not oblivious to "Oriental" coinage; since he focuses on Classical and medieval European issues, however, some of what he says can be applied to the Islamic world only with reservations. A book more specifically concerned with method and technique is that of J. M.

Dentzer, P. Gauthier, and T. Hackens, eds., *Numismatique antique: problèmes et méthodes* (*Annales de l'Est*, mémoire 44; 1975).

Unfortunately no guide to numismatic method specifically addresses medieval Islam. This gap can be partly remedied, however, through an important series of articles by Michael L. Bates, "Islamic Numismatics," *MESA Bull.*, xii, no. 2 (May 1978), 1–16; xii, no. 3 (Dec. 1978), 2–18; xiii, no. 1 (July 1979), 3–21; xiii, no. 2 (Dec. 1979), 1–9. In a remarkably thorough and lucid manner, Bates surveys reference tools, collections and research facilities, the main problems of method and research in the Islamic field, and the major studies relating to specific periods, regions, and dynasties. His account permits us to restrict our attention here to a few basic or representative works.

A sound overview of Islamic coinage can be found in Stephen Album, ed., *Marsden's Numismata Orientalia Illustrata* (1977). This work reviews, dynasty by dynasty, all the major coin types issued by Islamic mints down to late Ottoman times. It is illustrated not by photographs but by line drawings, most of which are of excellent quality. It also has a concisely annotated bibliography giving the more important references to the numismatic literature for each dynasty. Album intended his book primarily for dealers and collectors, but it is a good place to start when one needs to identify a book or to compare it to other issues.

Far more systematic surveys will be found in two of the major museum catalogs:

Stanley Lane-Poole, *Catalogue of the Oriental Coins in the British Museum* (10 vols., 1875–1890).

Henri Lavoix, *Catalogue des monnaies musulmanes de la Bibliothèque Nationale* (3 vols., 1887–1891).

The post-Conquest and Umayyad issues in the British Museum were re-catalogued in two masterful volumes by John Walker, *A Catalogue of the Muhammadan Coins in the British Museum* (Vol. I: *Arab-Sassanian Coins*, 1941; Vol. II: *Arab-Byzantine and Post-reform Umaiyad Coins*, 1956). In Paris, Gilles Hennequin has taken up the unfinished work of Lavoix. Three volumes are projected, of which one has recently appeared: Vol. V, *Asie pré-mongole, les Salğūqs et leurs successeurs* (1985)—a massive compilation covering 2000 coins from thirty-five dynasties. Between these two great surveys, almost every type of coin issued by any Muslim dynasty is represented somewhere. Of course both Lane-Poole and Lavoix are seriously antiquated, and neither gives modern numismatists all the information they may seek, but there will be nothing to replace them in the foreseeable future.

A project which is both more limited and in some ways more useful than redoing comprehensive museum catalogs is the preparation of detailed dynastic surveys which bring together coins from many different collections. This approach permits a far more systematic view of all the coin-types produced within a given period and region than we can obtain from the holdings of a single museum. On the other hand, it can be cumbersome to compare the issues of different states, or to discern how a given coinage type evolved over a long period of time. Moreover, such dynastic surveys are extremely time-consuming and expensive to prepare, and because they require the cooperation of many institutions and collectors they are sometimes not feasible at all. In spite of such difficulties and shortcomings a few really outstanding dynastic surveys have been done. See for example two works by Paul Balog: (1) *The Coinage of the Mamluk Sultans of Egypt and Syria* (1964); (2) *The Coinage of the Ayyubids* (1980).

Islamic coins are usually (but not always) aniconographic—i.e., they bear no images. Instead, they are inscribed with a variety of names and phrases. Typically, a gold or silver coin will carry (1) the name and titles of the issuing ruler, (2) the name of the mint-city where it was issued, (3) the date of issue, (4) some religious legend, most commonly the *shahāda*. Since these words are often only half-legible at best, the assistance of several reference works may be needed to decipher them.

The most valuable of these (though it contains numerous errors and omissions) is doubtless Eduard von Zambaur, *Die Münzprägungen des Islams, zeitlich und örtlich geordnet*, ed. Peter Jaeckel (1968). This is an alphabetically arranged repertory of all the mint-cities of medieval Islam west of India. Each mint-city is briefly identified, then keyed to an extensive bibliography of sources and to all the published coins (arranged by dynasty and date of issue) which come from that place. We can thus identify any mint-city which we are likely to encounter, and in addition almost any coin can be placed within the context of other issues from the same place or time. To Zambaur's basic work the editor (Jaeckel) has added a valuable cross-reference by creating twenty-six tables which classify all known coins by date. There is no separate listing by dynasty (which is in fact the most common classification system in Islamic numismatics), but this is easy enough to establish for any given case from the data given here.

To confirm the names and titles of the issuing rulers, we can go to Zambaur's *Manuel de généalogie et de chronologie* and other reference works of the same kind (see above, pp. 20–21). For titles and honorifics only, there is a very helpful compilation by Ḥasan al-Bāshā, *al-Alqāb al-islāmiyya fī al-taʾrīkh wa'l-wathāʾiq wa'l-āthār* (1957), a work which is well documented from Arabic (but not Persian or Turkish) sources, such as inscriptions, chronicles and biographical dictionaries, and al-Qalqashandī's *Ṣubḥ al-aʿshā*. For each term the author presents both its literal meaning and its usage in formal protocol.

Religious legends and pious exclamations may have real political and ideological significance. For such expressions, the otherwise antiquated work of O. Codrington, *A Manual of Musalman Numismatics* (1904), contains a chapter which is still helpful.

As for dates, if they cannot be read then we are out of luck. To some degree a coin can be dated by its stylistic characteristics (script, ornament, etc.) but that is obviously a dangerous expedient.

Metrology is a crucial aspect of numismatic analysis and interpretation. Most of what we know in this field is summed up in two major references. The older is a classic compilation by Henri Sauvaire, "Matériaux pour servir à l'histoire de la numismatique et de la métrologie musulmanes," strewn throughout various issues of the *Journal Asiatique* published between 1879 and 1887. (For a detailed outline see the Bibliographic Index.) It is divided into four parts, dealing respectively with coinage, weights, volumes, and lengths. Within each part, Sauvaire lists all the terms used in the Islamic world to represent units of value, weight, etc.; under each term, he then cites in translation all the texts available to him which explain or illustrate it. In the final installment of the series (entitled "Complément"), he constructs price tables for the basic necessities of life, arranged by region and date, and a chronologically ordered price table for miscellaneous items which comes down to 1051 A.H. In the section on weights, he attempts to convert them to metric values, but this is best ignored. In spite of its age and confusing organization, it remains an invaluable contribution.

A second reference is much more compact, more reliable in its metric conversions, and easier to use: Walther Hinz, *Islamische Masse und Gewichte, umgerechnet ins metrische System*, (*HO*, Ergbd. 1, 1955; 2nd rev. ed., 1970). At the same time, it is not so rich a resource as Sauvaire, and where possible it is useful to consult the two works together.

In the crucial area of bibliography Islamic numismatics is quite well off. For contributions down to 1950 we have the exhaustive survey of L. A. Mayer, *Bibliography of Moslem Numismatics, India Excepted* (1954). Since 1947, the American Numismatic Society has published a semi-annual survey, *Numismatic Literature*—well-organized and easy to use but unfortunately never cumulated. Scholars must simply keep current and assemble their own files of potentially relevant items.

Many of the problems involved in dealing with coins are strictly technical in character—deciphering inscriptions, establishing frequency tables of weights, determining standards of fineness, etc.—and any properly trained numismatist should be able to do these things adequately. On the other hand, applying the results thus obtained, and in fact deciding what data to collect in the first place, is a matter not of technical skill but of historianship. There is no general essay on the roles which numismatics might play in Islamic historical studies; here as in many places models must be found in a few unusually imaginative studies. The problem is that numismatics has been applied with great sophistication to some aspects of Islamic studies, and only ineptly if at all to others—including precisely those topics where coins should be our prime resource.

Numismatics has undoubtedly made its greatest contribution in the fields of political and administrative history. Coins have provided invaluable evidence in determining the regnal dates of obscure princes and the territorial scope of their authority. They have done much to clarify the administrative status of numerous urban centers. Finally, they have been put to good use in defining the links which bound regional dynasts to the Caliphate. Many excellent studies which address such problems could be cited; among them those of George C. Miles are preeminent. As examples, see an early work, *The Numismatic History of Rayy* (1938), and his chapter "Numismatics" in the *Cambridge History of Iran* (1975), Vol. IV, 364–377. An early work of Oleg Grabar, *The Coinage of the Tulunids* (1957), can also be warmly recommended.

In the answering of political and administrative questions, however, numismatics can only have an ancillary role—i.e., we use it to address problems which have been defined by evidence of a different kind, usually textual. The field for which coins ought to be the principal source is the history of monetary systems in Islam. There have in fact been preparatory essays in this field (see in particular the numerous though scattered articles of A. S. Ehrenkreutz), but most have been narrowly "numismatic" in character—i.e., determining the standard of fineness, establishing die counts, etc. There have been efforts to define the circulation of precious metals, but most of this work has been rather speculative and hard to reconcile either with economic theory or with the little hard data which exists. In general, the progress of monetary history has been crippled by the failure of Islamists to evolve an adequate theory of the character and function of money in medieval Islamic society. This theoretical failure has been rather pointedly explored in a series of studies by Gilles Hennequin; among these, see (a) "Problèmes théoriques et pratiques de la monnaie antique et médiévale," *AI*, x (1972), 1–51; (b) "Nouveaux aperçus sur l'histoire monétaire de l'Égypte à la fin du Moyen-Âge," *AI*, xiii (1977), 179–215. Until this "theory gap" is bridged, we cannot expect numismatics to make its full contribution to Islamic history.

D. Epigraphy

Monumental inscriptions of remarkable documentary value were produced in great profusion in medieval Islam, but they have been badly neglected by historians, especially in Great Britain and America. It is true that inscriptions present a variety of technical problems, and these may account in part for the failure of scholars to make better use of them. First of all, they are written in an astonishing range of scripts, some very crude and others superbly calligraphic. In either case they can be extraordinarily difficult to decipher, and in the end the content may be so banal that it hardly seems to have been worth the effort. A second problem is that many, perhaps most, inscriptions have been badly damaged by man and climate over the centuries, and of course it is always the crucial phrase which has been effaced. Again, since inscriptions are often written on large blocks of fine stone, many have been carted away from their original locations to be reused in entirely unrelated buildings. Real as these problems are, however, they are hardly worse than those which affect the other categories of sources we have reviewed, and the rewards which inscriptions offer should be adequate compensation for the trouble.

We begin with a few general comments about the external characteristics of these texts. Historians normally deal with monumental inscriptions—i.e., texts attached to buildings as part of their structure or decor. However, some texts of historical interest occur in other contexts, such as ceramic and metal vessels, fine textiles, or wooden pulpits and sarcophagi. The majority of monumental inscriptions are engraved in stone, but we also find them carved in stucco or made of colored ceramic tiles (faience) or mosaic. However, inscriptions done in stucco, faience, or mosaic are almost invariably literary or religious in content (most commonly citations from the Qur'ān) rather than dated records concerning specific acts or persons.

Arabic is the language used in the overwhelming majority of inscriptions which fall within the purview of this book. Turkish first appears in the early 9th/15th century, and only becomes widely used in the 10th/16th. As to Persian epigraphy, we find the first examples at the end of the 5th/11th century. Though Persian came to be used in an increasingly broad array of contexts, it never entirely supplanted Arabic, which was always the preferred language for religious texts and founders' inscriptions.

We do not have room to deal with the scripts in any detail. Down through the 5th/11th century most are carved in some form of Kufic, and this script remained very popular in later periods for literary and religious texts because of its striking ornamental potentialities. The development of Kufic can best be followed in the richly documented and beautifully produced study of Adolf Grohmann, *Arabische Paläographie*, II, *Die Lapidarschrift* (1971), which contains a full bibliography up to the date of publication. On the specific problems connected with the lovely but appallingly difficult style called "floriated Kufic," see Grohmann, "The Origin and Early Development of Floriated Kufic," *Ars Orientalis*, ii (1957), 183–215. From the 6th/12th century on, various forms of *naskhī* came to be used almost universally for such information-conveying texts as epitaphs, decrees, notices of construction or restoration, etc., but this script is only beginning to attract serious study. In later centuries, Persian and Turkish inscriptions would make much use of such elegant scripts as *taʿlīq* and *nastaʿlīq*, but these need not concern us here.

There is no handbook of Islamic epigraphy, but a sound introduction to the field can be found in the article "Kitābāt," *EI*², V, 210–233, by various authors. The introductory section, by J. Sourdel-Thomine, is a wide-ranging statement on the development and general problems of Islamic epigraphy; the succeeding sections (by various authors) are each devoted to the inscriptions of a particular region, with an emphasis on the development of scripts. An overview of this kind is best followed up by the study of specific studies which can serve as models of epigraphic method. An excellent example would be Khālid Muʿādh and Solange Ory, *Inscriptions arabes de Damas: les stèles funéraires*; I, *Cimétière d'al-Bāb al-Ṣaghīr* (1977). This survey contains eighty inscriptions, dating from 439 to 935 A.H. Each inscription is presented in a plate of good quality (with additional line drawings in exceptionally difficult cases), printed transcription, and translation. In addition, each inscription is furnished with an analysis of its script and textual contents, a careful description, and a precise localization. Finally, the authors give us a general discussion of the scripts and formularies used in this body of inscriptions. This study of course does not meet every need of the novice epigrapher: epitaphs are a limited genre at best, and seldom carry the more florid scripts or more complex verbal formulae.

Although inscriptions were commonly used by the ancient Middle Eastern monarchies, including those of the Hellenistic and Roman period, to recount major political events (victories, coronations, etc.), they almost never serve this function in Islamic times. Perhaps the widespread availability of paper made the chronicle and the official letter a more effective means of achieving such self-glorification. However that may be, the contents of Islamic inscriptions may conveniently be grouped in four classes: (1) literary; (2) religious; (3) commemorative; (4) legal and administrative.

Literary texts are found only in two contexts: on palaces and on luxury objects such as metalwork and decorated ceramics. In the case of art objects, the inscription (incised or painted) is most often just a cliche or a piece of doggerel—e.g., "Glory and prosperity to the owner of this vessel." On the other hand, Iranian ateliers in particular did produce many pieces decorated with identifiable lines of verse. As for palaces, very few of these have survived, but two of them present inscriptional programs of remarkable significance, that of Masʿūd III (492–508/1099–1115) in Ghazna, and the Alhambra in Granada. On Masʿūd's palace see Alessio Bombaci, *The Kufic Inscription in Persian Verses in the Court of the Royal Palace of Masʿūd III at Ghaznī* (1966). The publications relevant to the Alhambra inscriptions can be traced through Oleg Grabar, *The Alhambra* (1978); see especially the notes to Ch. 2.

The religious texts used in monumental inscriptions are overwhelmingly taken from the Qurʾān. In the past it has been normal to consider such passages as banal and historically insignificant. In many cases this point of view is probably valid, for most mosques and madrasas draw their Qurʾanic inscriptions from a very limited repertory of verses. But we cannot take this for granted. For example, in his discussion of the mosaic inscription in the Dome of the Rock, Oleg Grabar (*The Formation of Islamic Art* [1973], pp. 48–67) argues for a very specific anti-Christian, anti-Byzantine message in that text.

Likewise, the Qur'anic passages carved on the Fatimid mosques and shrines of Cairo spell out (for those who know how to interpret them) crucial elements of Ismāʿīli ideology; see two studies by Caroline Williams: (1) "The Cult of Alid Saints in the Fatimid Monuments of Cairo, I: The Mosque of al-Aqmar," *Muqarnas*, I (1983), 37–52; "II: The Mausolea," *Muqarnas*, iii (1985), 39–60; (2) "The Qur'anic Inscriptions on the *Tābūt* of al-Ḥusayn," *Islamic Art*, ii (1987), 3–13. In general, we should work from the assumption that the Qur'anic inscriptions on a mosque or any other religious structure constitute a conscious program, and hence are a vital key to the intended meaning of that building. Qur'anic passages are often done in extremely ornate if not impenetrable scripts; in the many situations where only a few words can be made out with some confidence, a concordance like ʿAbd al-Bāqī's *al-Muʿjam al-mufahras* (see above, p. 21) is an indispensable aid.

Commemorative inscriptions fall into two sub-classes. Most common are epitaphs, which typically give a person's name, genealogy, official titles, a few pious slogans, and date of death. It seems a very thin body of data, but these few facts can be exploited to good effect. They can for example help us uncover the notable families of a district and some of the kinship links among these families, all the more since women as well as men are included. Epitaphs can establish or confirm the death and regnal dates of rulers, and supply official titulature.

The second class of commemorative inscriptions—foundation and restoration texts on public buildings—can be put to even broader use. Typically, inscriptions of this kind will contain the following data: the function embodied in the building (e.g., *masjid*, *jāmiʿ*, *mashhad*, *turba*, etc.); the kind of work done (original construction, restoration and repair, conversion); the name, genealogy, and titulature of the person at whose behest the work was done; sometimes, but not always, the names and titles of the officials who actually oversaw the work; the date on which the work was ordered or completed. The value of such information is manifold. By comparing the information given in the inscription with the monument on which it is located, historians of architecture can establish precise and valid correspondences between form and terminology. By using inscriptions to track down the most visible patrons of architecture within a given period and locality, key members of the socio-political elite can be identified, since the funding of major construction projects requires wealth, prestige, and power. Or finally, the titles of the men named in the inscriptions can clarify many details of local or provincial administration. Such examples of course only suggest a few of the possibilities offered by inscriptions.

For commemorative inscriptions to be used in these ways, however, they must be integrated into a broad archaeological and historical context, and only a few scholars have endeavored to do this in any systematic way. Among these the preeminent figure is Max van Berchem, whose *Matériaux pour un Corpus*

Inscriptionum Arabicarum (abbr., *CIA*), though sadly incomplete, remains one of the great monuments of Islamic studies and a model of what epigraphy in our field might achieve. Van Berchem not only gives critical transcriptions and translations of the texts, but extended discussions of the monuments on which they are found and the historical situations in which they were composed, together with lengthy and fascinating discourses on such matters as titulature, the evolution of administrative offices, etc. Obviously much of what he has to say is obsolete, but the sense of discovery in these volumes, as well as his capacity to suggest fruitful lines of inquiry, are still very vivid indeed. In addition to *CIA*, van Berchem did a great many other epigraphic studies, which were intended as preparatory studies for his *magnum opus*; these have been collected in his *Opera Minora* (2 vols., 1978). Finally, he made an extremely valuable collection of photographs, which have now been catalogued by Solange Ory, ed., *Archives Max van Berchem, I: Catalogue de la photothèque* (1975).

CIA was planned as a cooperative venture, and in fact several of his associates did contribute one or more volumes. Still, van Berchem was the heart and soul of the project, and his death in 1921 brought it effectively to an end. The volumes published after that time for the most part represent a picking up of loose ends, not fresh research. The following volumes have been published:

a. *Égypte, le Caire*: Max van Berchem, *MMAF*, xix (1896–1903); Gaston Wiet, *MIFAO*, lii (1930).

b. *Syrie du Sud, Jérusalem*: Max van Berchem, *MIFAO*, xliii (1922–23); xliv (1925–27); xlv (1920).

c. *Syrie du Nord, Tripoli*: Moritz Sobernheim, *MIFAO*, xxv (1909).

d. *Syrie du Nord, Alep*: Moritz Sobernheim and Ernst Herzfeld, ed. E. Combe, *MIFAO*, lxxvi–lxxvii (1954–56).

e. *Asie Mineure, Sivas et Divrigi*: Max van Berchem and Halil Edhem, *MIFAO*, xxix (1910–17).

f. *Arabie: La Mekke*: H. M. al-Hawary and N. Elisséeff, *MIFAO*, cix (1985).

For a long time Van Berchem had no real successors; many highly accomplished scholars shared his approach and concerns, to be sure, but only Gaston Wiet ever attempted a new volume, or even a thoroughgoing revision of an old one, in *CIA*. However, the recent contribution by Hawary and Elisséeff and a projected volume by Sheila Blair (for which see below) suggest a revived impetus to achieve at least part of van Berchem's vision.

In the intervening seventy years, important new material has come out from time to time; though we cannot give any adequate survey of titles here, certain scholars have made particularly substantial contributions in this field: Gaston Wiet, Jean Sauvaget, Nikita Elisséeff, Dominique Sourdel, Janine Sourdel-Thomine, Heinz Gaube. In Spain, a good initial corpus was published by E. Lévi-Provençal, *Inscriptions arabes de l'Espagne* (1931), and in recent years several scholars (most notably M. Ocaña Jimenez) have continued to build on this foundation. Two very important projects do deserve special notice. First, Moshe Sharon has announced a corpus of the Arabic inscriptions of Palestine: "Un nouveau corpus des inscriptions arabes de Palestine," *REI*, xlii, no. 1 (1974), 185–191. Second, the Sourdels have undertaken a critical re-edition, with a concise but valuable annotation, of the inscriptions of Damascus, which have heretofore been scattered among a myriad of extremely uneven publications. The first installment of this survey, covering twenty-one inscriptions dating from 444/1052 to 544/1149, has appeared as "Dossiers pour un *Corpus* des inscriptions arabes de Damas," *REI*, xlvii, no. 2 (1979), 119–171.

It is evident from our discussion so far that Syria and Egypt have been privileged territories. The crucial region of Iran in particular remains from an epigraphical point of view almost *terra incognita*, though an important initial step had been taken before the 1979 revolution, with the establishment of a *Corpus Inscriptionum Iranicarum*, devoted to the publication of Persian-language inscriptions from earliest antiquity down to Safavid times. So far, however, only two slender volumes have been devoted to the Islamic period: on Khurasan, ed. William Hanaway, (Vol. II, 1977); and Mazandaran, ed. A.D.H. Bivar and E. Yarshater (Vol. VI, 1978). These publications are unfortunately extremely concise, consisting only of plates and terse identifications, without the systematic transcriptions, translations, and annotation needed to elucidate these texts. Far more valuable will be a volume now in press by Sheila Blair, *A Corpus of Early Arabic Inscriptions from Iran and Transoxania (to A.H. 500)*, which adheres to *CIA*'s general approach in its presentation and analysis of seventy-six inscriptions.

Finally, we come to inscriptions of legal and administrative content. Under the Roman Empire it was very common for decrees to be "published" in the form of inscriptions on temple walls, triumphal arches, etc. This practice was far less widespread in the Islamic world, but it was occasionally followed. Jean Sauvaget published in exemplary fashion two collections of such material: (a) "Décrets mamelouks de Syrie," *BEO*, ii (1932), 1–52; iii (1933), 1–29; xii (1947–48), 5–60; (b) *Quatre décrets seldjoukides* (1947). Far more common than the official decree was another kind of document, the deed of *waqf*. When a school or mosque was built or given some additional endowment, the benefactor would often carve an inscription in a prominent spot on the building, identifying himself, the objects of his charity, the main properties which he had donated, and the date of the grant. Such inscriptions had no legal force in themselves, but were simply resumes of the official deed of *waqf* registered with the courts; even so, their value for the study of social and economic history should be obvious.

Obviously we do not have the kinds of reference and research tools that we need for a really effective use of inscriptions in historical research. However, we do have a most useful interim survey in the *Répertoire chronologique d'épigraphie arabe* (abbr., *RCEA*; 17 vols., in progress; 1931–1982). *RCEA* attempts to bring together all known Arabic inscriptions, both those previously published (whether well or badly) and also items collected but left unpublished by van Berchem, Sauvaget, Wiet, et al. It makes no effort to be critical; badly deciphered, duplicate, and spurious texts abound. It uses both a chronological and geographical framework—all the inscriptions for each year are brought together, and within each year citations begin with the westernmost sites and move toward the east. Each text is given in printed transcription and French translation only, without photographs. However, sources and places of publication are cited, so that there is at least this degree of control. There are no historical or archaeological notes; it is up to the reader to reconstruct the context in which these texts occur. *RCEA* still goes down only to 783/1381, so that a vast body of material remains untouched. Finally, the transliterations of the locales where the inscriptions were found are highly arbitrary—French imperial orthography at its worst—and cause much wasted time simply in tracking down place names, though the *Index géographique* (1975) for the first 16 volumes does ameliorate this problem. It should also be said that T. XVII, edited by Ludvik Kalus, shows a marked improvement in procedure and format.

In short, in spite of a series of major efforts throughout the 20th century, we still have nothing comparable to what Theodor Mommsen and his colleagues bequeathed to Roman history a hundred years ago, and there is little prospect that we ever will.

E. Art, Archaeology, and Technology

Because history is a verbal representation of human behavior, it is natural that it should rely most heavily on the evidence of words. However, such evidence can be highly misleading in regard to societies like those of medieval Islam, where the art of writing was the monopoly of a small cultural elite. And even in broadly literate societies, material artifacts are far more productive forms of evidence for many aspects of life than are "mere words." This statement applies not only to such obvious areas as technology or the apparatus of daily life, but in many cases even to social relations and to cultural symbols and values. Obviously no one object is usable evidence for every aspect of the society which produced it, but every artifact is multivalent and throws light on many areas of life. For example, glazed ceramics can be evidence for aesthetic values, for the technology which produced them, for the economic and commercial milieu in which they were made, and (if they have figurative decor) for widely used visual symbols of the period. An artifact of a very different kind, the layout of a city marketplace, can be a mine of information on business organization, class structure, etc. As an inquiry develops, then, even the most text-minded scholars need to make an effort to canvass and utilize the possible artistic and archaeological evidence for their subject.

It must be said that very few Islamic historians are trained to do this, in large part because until the late 1960s there were (at least in the United States and Canada) almost no art historians and archaeologists whose primary interest was the Islamic world. This gap is now well on the way to being rectified, but it will still be some time before the majority of social and political historians are in any position to use the work of art historians and archaeologists productively. Even when people are ready to look in that direction, caution and a degree of humility will be needed, for art history and archaeology are highly developed and self-conscious disciplines and neither can be mastered without a substantial apprenticeship. For this reason we shall not try to deal seriously with problems of method here. An overall assessment of the state of these fields—still largely valid—can be found in Oleg Grabar, "Islamic Art and Archaeology," in L. Binder, ed., *The Study of the Middle East* (1976), pp. 229–264. For archaeology, a critique of method through an analytic presentation of a case study is given in C. L. Redman, "Archaeology in a Medieval City of Islam," *MESA Bull.*, xiv, no. 2 (1980), 1–22. Many archeologists would disagree with Redman's stress on the scientific rather than cultural character of archaeology, but views like his are currently very influential.

There are still very few synthetic works which attempt to integrate the approaches and results of art history and archaeology within a broad interpretation of Islamic history. Two fairly recent works are successful in this endeavor, however, and in addition suggest many interesting lines of inquiry:

Dominique and Janine Sourdel, *La civilisation de l'Islam classique* (1968).

Oleg Grabar, *The Formation of Islamic Art* (1973; 2nd ed., 1987). (Has an excellent bibliographic essay covering topics down to ca. 900 A.D.)

For architecture—perhaps the single most important dimension of art for social and political history—there are now several good surveys, but historians might benefit most from a recent collective work edited by George Michell, *Architecture of the Islamic World; Its History and Social Meaning* (1978), which goes beyond the standard emphasis on great monuments to look at the social functions of architecture. Particularly significant are the chapters on marketplaces and ordinary private homes. The text is very general, as one would expect in this class of book, but an attentive reader will find many useful ideas to pursue.

For most of the periods and regions of medieval Islam, we still lack adequate repertories of monuments and objects, let alone the kind of detailed survey which provides a rigorous description of all the extant buildings or artifacts which fall within a defined area of interest. An early attempt at a general survey was made in Henri Saladin, Georges Marçais, and Gaston Migeon, *Manuel d'art musulman* (4 vols., 1907–1927), which covers both architecture and the plastic and industrial arts. Obviously it is now thoroughly obsolete; the best comprehensive overview currently available is probably Janine Sourdel-Thomine and Bertold Spuler, *Die Kunst des Islams* (1973), Vol. IV of the *Propylaen Kunstgeschichte*. It is both scholarly and beautifully produced, though its focus on individual masterpieces prevents it from dealing effectively with regional developments, broad cultural problems, etc.

In an ideal world, every region and every category of art would be covered by something like the monumental productions of K.A.C. Creswell:

Early Muslim Architecture (2 vols., 1938–40; 2nd revised ed. of Vol. I, in 2 parts, 1969).

The Muslim Architecture of Egypt (2 vols., 1952–59).

It is hard to think that we will ever again see anything like these magnificent volumes—in folio size, with meticulous descriptions, accurate measurements (otherwise almost unknown in the Islamic field!), and superb drawings and plates for every monument. *Early Muslim Architecture* covers all the central Islamic lands down to ca. 900 A.D., while the volumes on Egypt focus on the period from the Ikhshidids through the early Mamluks (939–1326). Creswell has his faults, to be sure, among which his tight focus on technical problems will be most apparent to new readers, but his work remains the foundation for all further progress. The well-documented later Mamluk period in Egypt has yet to be surveyed, but a number of palatial private homes from this and the early Ottoman period survive, and these can be studied in the admirable survey of J. Revault, B. Maury, and M. Zakariya, *Palais et maisons du Caire du xive au xviiie siècle* (4 vols., 1975–83). The results of their work on the Mamluk period have been placed in a broader architectural and social-historical context in a separate volume: J.-C. Garcin, B. Maury, J. Revault, M. Zakariya, *Palais et maisons du Caire, I: époque mamelouke* (1982). (Working with other collaborators, Revault has also produced similar surveys of late-medieval domestic architecture in the North African cities of Tunis and Fez.)

For other regions and genres, there is much less to work with, in spite of several meritorious surveys and a growing number of solid monographs. For Spain and North Africa, Georges Marçais, *L'architecture musulmane de l'Occident* (1954) is an excellent synthesis. At the other end of the medieval Islamic world, a splendid collective work dealing with all periods and genres was edited by A. U. Pope and Phyllis Ackerman, *A Survey of Persian Art* (6 vols., 1938–39; index vol. by T. Besterman, 1958; repr. in 14 vols., 1964–67). This work is very uneven and is now obsolescent, but its comprehensiveness and its superb plates continue to make it indispensable.

When we move from regional to genre-oriented surveys, a few works are particularly precise and wide-ranging. The development of early Islamic painting (down to the 8th/14th century, with a natural emphasis on manuscript illustration) is treated in the classic study of Richard Ettinghausen, *Arab Paint-*

ing (1962). The two volumes by Arthur Lane on ceramics are now old but remain a useful and reliable introduction to the subject: *Early Islamic Pottery* (1947); *Later Islamic Pottery* (1957). A new and lavishly produced book by Jean Soustiel, *La céramique islamique* (1985), supplants Lane in many respects. Like its predecessor it focuses on masterpieces, and in general addresses the interests of the collector and museum curator rather than the historian. (See the review essay by Oleg Grabar in *Muqarnas*, v [1988], 1–8.) The field of metalwork—one of the finest achievements of Islamic art—has at last received a reliable and well-documented overview from Eva Baer, *Metalwork in Medieval Islamic Art* (1983). She does omit certain classes of work from consideration (e.g., arms and armor), and the plates, while perfectly usable, are much less impressive than the text. The vast gaps in our coverage are all too apparent—textiles, glass, Persian painting in the post-Mongol era, the architecture of the Fertile Crescent and Iran in the Middle Periods (900–1500). Clearly it will be the work of decades to fill these in any adequate way.

Under these circumstances especially, museum and exhibition catalogs are often of enormous value. Unfortunately, very few museums have attempted to publish comprehensive catalogs of their Islamic collections. What can be done is illustrated by two of the volumes produced for the Museum of Islamic Art in Cairo by Gaston Wiet:

1. *Catalogue général du Musée Arabe du Caire: lampes et bouteilles en verre émaillé* (1929).
2. *Catalogue général du Musée Arabe du Caire: objets en cuivre* (1932).

Since Wiet's work, the only museum to undertake a catalogue on the same scale is the very important Benaki Museum of Athens, originally established as a private collection at the turn of the century by a Greek residing in Egypt, Anthony Benaki. As the first part of a proposed *Catalogue of Islamic Art in the Benaki Museum* under her general editorship, Helène Philon has recently produced a splendid volume, *Early Islamic Ceramics* (1980). Further volumes on later ceramics, woodwork, textiles, metalwork, jewelry, and tombstones have been announced, each to be done by a well-known specialist.

A different type of publication altogether is the exhibition catalog, which presents the objects gathered together for a particular occasion. The value of these of course depends heavily on the conception governing the exhibition in question and on the curator's skill in obtaining loans of the most appropriate pieces. A particularly fine recent example, on both the scholarly and aesthetic level, would be Esin Atıl, *Renaissance of Islam: Art of the Mamluks* (1981), which is unquestionably the best account we have of Syro-Egyptian art between the 7th/13th and 9th/15th centuries.

We usually think of art as a cultural and aesthetic phenomenon, but it is no less an embodiment of technology. Art undoubtedly expresses what was felt to be important or beautiful, but it also conveys the manufacturing skills available to a given society. For this reason, the full exploitation of art as evidence for political and social history requires a knowledge of the materials and techniques that produced it. The study of medieval and "traditional" Islamic technology is unfortunately still in its infancy. However, two very different works bring together most of what is known. In *Islamic Technology: an Illustrated History* (1986), A. Y. al-Hassan and D. R. Hill comb texts, manuscript illustrations, and artifacts to reconstruct a very impressive array of arts and manufactures: shipbuilding, textiles, irrigation, metallurgy, et al. Both authors are engineers as well as scholars, and that fact obviously enhances the value of their work. Hassan and Hill's historical study should be read in tandem with Hans E. Wulff's invaluable *The Traditional Crafts of Persia* (1966). Wulff's meticulous account is based on direct observation of artisans at work during his lengthy residence in Iran in the 1930s, and covers agriculture and building as well as industrial crafts. Finally, we now have an important work on architecture: Caʿfer Efendi, *Risāle-i Miʿmāriyye: an Early Seventeenth-Century Ottoman Treatise on Architecture*, annotated trans. by Howard Crane (1987). Works of this kind are extremely rare, since pre-modern Muslim architects hardly ever wrote about their craft. Medievalists must obviously use this text with caution, since Ottoman architecture is very distinctive and indeed unique. Even so, it gives us direct if partial access to the way in which Muslim builders understood their work.

The archaeological and art-historical literature is very scattered, and important contributions often crop up in very unlikely places. In this area, however, we are well provided for, at least for older publications: K.A.C. Creswell, *A Bibliography of the Architecture, Arts, and Crafts of Islam* (1961), to which the same author issued a *Supplement* going down to 1972. It is meticulously and logically organized. The original volume includes titles in Arabic and Persian, while the supplement adds Turkish and Russian. For some entries Creswell adds terse and typically acerbic comments. From 1972 on, we must fall back on the *Index Islamicus*.

Islamic archaeology is more obviously connected with the concerns of social and political historians than is art history, but it has not yet made the contributions to historical studies which we might hope for. There are many reasons for this. Until very recently, very few archaeologists had any interest in the Islamic period, and tended to regard the "Saracen layers" at their sites mostly as a nuisance. On the other hand, very few Islamists had any archaeological training, perhaps because so much material from medieval Islam is still above ground and even occupied. Yet even at the beginning of this century the work of Friedrich Sarre and Ernst Herzfeld at Samarra showed what could be gained from archaeology. Fortunately, during the last two decades the pace of excavation at the hands of serious archaeologists has picked up sharply, and at least until the troubles of the last decade work was being actively pursued throughout the central Islamic lands.

It would obviously be extremely useful to have a comprehensive survey of all the sites where significant archaeological work has been done, with summaries of the main data, general conclusions, critical bibliographies, etc. An excellent model for such a survey can be found in L. Vanden Berghe, *Archéologie de l'Iran ancien* (1959), and its (somewhat belated) companion volume, *Bibliographie analytique de l'archéologie de l'Iran ancien* (1979)—works which are obviously important for scholars of early Islamic Iran. A very important work on Afghanistan should also be noted: Warwick Ball and Jean-Claude Gardin, *Archaeological Gazetteer of Afghanistan* (2 vols., 1982). The authors survey some 1200 sites, beginning with the oldest remains known and coming down to the end of Timurid times. It is based wholly on published descriptions and reports, but obviously these are all we shall have for a long time to come.

Archaeology is no longer an affair of free-lance amateurs; legal excavations at least are always carried out either by national antiquities services or by officially recognized foreign research institutes. It will thus be useful to list those organizations which regularly sponsor work on the Islamic period, and which have well-established publications series in which the results of this work are likely to appear. We cannot cite every potentially relevant organization and journal, but those listed below are responsible for the bulk of published work in Islamic archaeology.

American Research Center in Egypt
Journal of the American Research Center in Egypt (abbr., *JARCE*)

British Institute of Archaeology at Ankara
Anatolian Studies

British Institute of Persian Studies
Iran

British School of Archaeology in Iraq
Iraq
(Note that all three of the British journals publish annual reviews of current excavations within their respective countries of interest.)

Centre National de la Recherche Scientifique (Paris) (abbr., CNRS)
Archéologie mediterranéenne (abbr., *Arch. med.*)

Deutsches Archaologisches Institut, Abteilung Kairo (abbr., DAI)
Mitteilungen (annual; abbr., *DAI (Kairo), Mitt.*); *Abhandlungen, Islamische Reihe* (occasional; abbr., *DAI (Kairo), Abh.*)

DAI, Abt. Istanbul
Istanbuler Mitteilungen (annual; abbr., *Ist. Mitt.*); *Istanbuler Forschungen* (occasional; abbr., *Ist. Forsch.*)

DAI, Abt. Teheran
Archäologische Mitteilungen aus Iran (annual; abbr., *AMI*); *Teheraner Forschungen* (occasional; abbr., *Teh. Forsch.*)

Délégation Archéologique Française en Iran
Cahiers (abbr., *CDAFI*); *Mémoires* (occasional; abbr., *MDAFI*)
Institut Français d'Archéologie Orientale au Caire (successor to the Mission Archéologique Française au Caire)
Mémoires de la Mission Archéologique Française au Caire (abbr., *MMAF*); *Mémoires publiés par les membres de l'Institut Français d'Archéologie Orientale au Caire* (abbr., *MIFAO*); *Bulletin de l'Institut Français d'Archéologie Orientale au Caire* (abbr., *BIFAO*); *Annales Islamologiques* (abbr., *AI*).
Institut Français d'Études Arabes a Damas
Bulletin d'études orientales (*BEO*)
Iraq, Directorate General of Antiquities
Sumer
Nederlands Historisch-Archaeologisch Instituut te Istanbul
Anatolica (annual); *Uitgaven* (occasional; abbr., *Ist. Uitgaven*)
Saudi Arabia, Department of Antiquities
al-Aṭlāl
Syria, Direction generale des Antiquites et des Musees
Annales archéologiques de Syrie (since 1969, *Annales archéologiques syriennes*; abbr., *AAS*)

There are many important archaeological journals not listed here—e.g., *Syrie*, *Berytus*, *Israel Exploration Journal*—but these almost never deal with Islamic topics and it seems best to exclude them. In any case, there is obviously a rich and rapidly growing fund of archaeological data and interpretation for those historians who are prepared to learn how to use it.

PART TWO

PROBLEMS IN ISLAMIC HISTORY

Chapter Three

EARLY HISTORICAL TRADITION AND THE FIRST ISLAMIC POLITY

A. The Character of Early Islamic Historiography

IN VIEW of the astonishing events which occurred in the seventy-year period between the foundation of an autonomous Muslim community in 622 and the consolidation of Marwanid power in the 690s, we should expect to find an unusually wide-ranging body of sources. Muslims, we would suppose, must surely have taken great care to record their spectacular achievements, while the highly literate and urbanized societies which they had subjugated could hardly avoid coming to grips with what had happened to them. And indeed the sources relating to this period appear formidable. In addition to a very large number of Muslim Arabic narrative texts, we have a growing corpus of archaeological traces, the Greco-Arabic papyri of Egypt, and fascinating remnants of Byzantine, Syriac, and Armenian chronicle, polemic, and hagiography. A comprehensive survey of the literary sources is now in preparation, under the title *Late Antiquity and Islam: A Critical Guide to the Literary Sources*, ed. by Averil Cameron and Lawrence I. Conrad. Pending the appearance of this work, however, the detailed review of the material pertaining to Iraq in Michael Morony, *Iraq after the Muslim Conquest* (1984), pp. 537–654, demonstrates how much is available for a single region. If few would still proclaim that Islam was born in the full light of history, nevertheless the situation seems a very hopeful one—all the more so if we compare it to our knowledge of contemporaneous events in Byzantium or Latin Europe.

Sadly, it is not so. The true contemporary sources (papyri, archaeology, and Christian writings) are tantalizing indeed, but are either fragmentary or represent very specific or even eccentric perspectives. An adequate and convincing reconstruction of Islam's first century from these materials alone is simply not possible. That leaves us with the Muslim Arabic literary sources. If our goal is to comprehend the way in which Muslims of the late 2nd/8th and 3rd/9th centuries understood the origins of their society, then we are very well off indeed. But if our aim is to find out "what really happened"—i.e., to develop reliably documented answers to modern questions about the earliest decades of Islamic society—then we are in trouble.

The Arabic narrative sources represent a rather late crystallization of a fluid oral tradition. These sources can become an adequate foundation for "scientific" history only when we have learned a great deal more than we presently know about this oral tradition: its origins, the social and cultural institutions by which it was shaped and transmitted, the variations and transformations it underwent in the course of transmission, the circumstances in which it was first committed to writing, the degree of alteration suffered by early written versions before they at last achieved their definitive form in the mid-3rd/9th century, etc. Questions of this kind have been discussed over and over by modern scholars, but so far their conclusions remain more in the realm of speculation than of demonstration. The evidence is such, in fact, that reasonable certainty may be beyond our grasp.

The point may be illustrated by the controversy surrounding F. M. Donner's *The Early Islamic Conquests* (1981), a work notable not only for its clarity and its admirably integrated interpretation, but also for its cautious approach to the sources. Where there are gaps or irreconcilable contradictions, Donner is content to live with ambivalence and uncertainty. Even so, he is confident that we can construct a reliable account of the main events and institutions of the Conquest era. His critics are not convinced—see, for example, the sympathetic but critical view of G. R. Hawting (*BSOAS*, xlvii [1984], 130–133), who sums up Donner's handling of the Arabic sources in the following statement: "When contradictions between different accounts cannot be resolved, broad generalization is resorted to . . . and there is a tendency to accept information which is consistent with the thesis being argued while rejecting or even ignoring that which is inconsistent." In general, Hawting argues, Donner's interpretation is surely plausible, but quite contradictory ones are no less so.

The first seventy years of Islamic history command our attention, therefore, not only because of the enormous intrinsic interest of this period, but also because of the extraordinary methodological problems posed by our principal sources for it. In what sense, then, is it possible to reconstruct the political history of early Islam?

This general question in fact stands for a lengthy series of distinct though interrelated issues, each of which requires separate attention:

1. In what form has the ancient historical tradition—that which claims to recount the events of the first seven decades—come down to us?
2. How accurately and fully does the extant form of this tradition reflect its primitive form? In particular, how stable were concepts of historical process, political and religio-ethical values and attitudes, and narrative structures?
3. Is the ancient historical tradition, as we now have it, in any meaningful sense an authentic reflection of the persons and events of early Islam? To put the issue another way, does criticism of the tradition annihilate it, so to speak, or does it simply refine it of later accretions and distortions?
4. Are there reliable criteria by which we can determine whether these texts are authentic or spurious?

5. Even if this historical tradition can be critically reconstructed in something like its original form, can we presume to use its data (selected and articulated within a 7th-century frame of reference) to respond to questions which reflect distinctively 20th-century concepts and concerns?

1. The Present Form of the Ancient Tradition

The bulk of our historical texts on early Islam are to be found in a body of compilations and digests composed roughly between 850 and 950 A.D. A few earlier works are still extant, to be sure, but these are too scattered and fragmentary to give us any adequate picture of the scope and methods of early Arabic historical writing. For much the same reasons, of course, they cannot support a synthetic account of early Islamic history. (To both these strictures there is one extremely important exception. As it happens, our principal accounts of the life of Muhammad were all composed in their definitive form between 750 and 850—i.e., about a century earlier—by Ibn Isḥāq [d. 150/767], al-Wāqidī [d. 207/823], and Ibn Saʿd [d. 230/845].)

The classical compilations of the 3rd/9th and 4th/10th centuries are not our only resource for early Islamic history, to be sure. They are supplemented in important ways by certain universal chronicles, biographical dictionaries, and encyclopaedias written in later centuries, for these often preserve otherwise unknown citations from early writings. A few examples must suffice. The vast commentary of Ibn Abī al-Ḥadīd (d. 656/1258) on the sayings of the fourth caliph ʿAlī b. Abī Ṭālib, the *Sharḥ nahj al-balāgha*, contains numerous historical texts (from a Shiʿite perspective, of course) in addition to a mass of other philological and theological data. The lengthy biographical dictionaries on Muhammad's Companions compiled by Ibn ʿAbd al-Barr (368–463/978–1070), Ibn al-Athīr (555–630/1160–1233), and Ibn Ḥajar al-ʿAsqalānī (773–852/1372–1449), preserve a great deal of early material that is otherwise lost. The biographical dictionaries of Damascus by Ibn ʿAsākir (d. 571/1176) and Aleppo by Kamāl al-Dīn ibn al-ʿAdīm (d. 660/1262) contain a mass of information on the first Islamic century which has yet to be examined systematically. Finally, we might note a late but important compilation dealing with the early conquests, the *Kitāb al-ghazawāt* by the Andalusian traditionist Ibn Ḥubaysh (d. 584/1188). But on the whole late works of this kind follow very closely the interpretive paradigms and narrative plots established in the compilations of the period 850–950; they are in no sense independent readings of the ancient historical tradition.

Perhaps the best way to get a comprehensive view of the whole body of this tradition is through the ten folio volumes of Leone Caetani, *Annali dell'Islam* (1905–26). Caetani attempted a critical survey, year by year and event by event, of all the historical texts available to him for early Islamic history, from the Hijra down to the assassination of ʿAlī in 40/661. He proceeds by intertwining three levels of presentation: (a) a translation or close paraphrasing (usually but not always reliable) of extensive citations from a remarkable array of sources; (b) a critique of the data contained in these texts; (c) wide-ranging and often daring essays on general problems. His conclusions on many points have naturally been contested, but this detracts neither from the immense value of his labors nor from the intellectual courage which they required. The *Annali* remain the starting point for serious research in this period.

So great was the prestige of the classical compilations, and so compelling were the interpetations that they proposed, that most of the texts written earlier simply ceased to be copied or read in any systematic way, though it is clear that many titles were still available (and occasionally studied) down at least to the 7th/13th century. On the other hand, we might argue that the compilations made between 850 and 950 become classics not only because of their intrinsic merit and comprehensiveness, but also because after the mid-4th/10th century the problems and topics which had heretofore been the center of concern no longer seemed so acutely relevant. Specifically, from 132/750 on the crucial religio-political issue for every historian had been what stance he ought to take in regard to the Abbasids—whether to see them as usurpers either of Umayyad or ʿAlid rights, as legitimate successors to the continuing and unbroken caliphal succession since Abū Bakr, or even as restorers of the purity and integrity of the primitive Community. On one's resolution of this delicate problem rested his whole interpretation of Islamic history during the century and a half before the Abbasid Revolution. With the collapse of Abbasid power and the rise of autonomous regional states in the early 4th/10th century, however, Abbasid legitimacy became increasingly a moot issue. In any case, by that time a historian could be content to adopt one of the several interpretive paradigms of early Islamic history already in circulation.

Some of the works from the period 850–950 are properly digests rather than compilations; the best-known cases would be the *Taʾrīkh* of al-Yaʿqūbī (d. 283/897), *al-Akhbār al-ṭiwāl* of Abū Ḥanīfa al-Dīnawarī (d. 281/894), the *Kitāb al-maʿārif* of Ibn Qutayba (d. 276/889), and the *Murūj al-dhahab wa-maʿādin al-jawhar* of al-Masʿūdī (d. 345/956). These authors attempt to work the voluminous and extremely disparate materials produced by the early historical tradition into a single narrative line, loosely knit but coherent, with the aim of offering a fairly clear and unambiguous interpretation of Islamic history. Even so, these digests remain a useful source for earlier historical writing, since they were composed less by melding older materials into an integrated story than by quoting or paraphrasing (in a very selective manner, to be sure) from a stock of fixed anecdotes and sayings already in circulation.

Without question, however, the crucial historical works of the late 9th and early 10th centuries are the massive compilations of two scholars: Aḥmad b. Yaḥyā al-Balādhurī (d. 279/892) and Abū Jaʿfar Muḥammad b. Jarīr al-Ṭabarī

(d. 310/923). It is these which preserve for us the broadest cross-section of earlier historical writing and which therefore most fully represent the ancient historical tradition. In principle, such compilations aimed to bring together all the reliable and well-attested accounts pertaining to each event and person whom they include. For each event, the compilers would state their sources in the form of an *isnād* (literally, "support," but normally translated as "chain of authorities.") Although these "chains" often claim to go back to contemporaries of the events described, the compilers of the period 850–950 were in fact taking their materials from older collections of historical material which had been written down roughly a century before, in the decades around 800. These, not the alleged original narrators, are their true sources. (The vexing issue of the sources used by the late 2nd/8th and early 3rd/9th century writers will be taken up later on in this chapter.)

In contrast to the digests, the compilations make no effort to construct a connected narrative of events; rather, they consist of a series of discrete anecdotes and reports (Ar., *khabar*, pl. *akhbār*), which vary in length from one line to several pages. These *akhbār* are not explicitly linked to one another in any way; they are simply juxtaposed end to end, so to speak, each being marked off from the others by its own *isnād*. In principle, it was thought proper for a compiler to abridge or paraphrase the *akhbār* found in his sources, and he might even blend a number of them together into a single account so long as he did no violence to their substance. (In the scholarly literature, this latter procedure is often called a "collective tradition.") Normally, a compiler would select several reports for each event or topic to be covered; these reports might then repeat, supplement, overlap, or flatly contradict one another.

These compilations did not claim to include all the materials which the ancient historical tradition had produced. On the contrary, a compiler would select only a small number of those known to him. Unfortunately, the compilers never spell out for us the criteria which guided their choice, except vague ones of "reliability" or "suitability." Nor do they state the principles of sequence and linkage which governed their efforts to give order, coherence, and meaning to the highly disparate materials which they had brought together. Our only hints in regard to such matters are occasional sub-headings identifying the subject-matter of a group of *akhbār*, and the external frameworks—annalistic, biographical, dynastic, etc.—within which the *akhbār* have been fitted. As full a statement on method as we have is the following passage, which concludes al-Ṭabarī's introduction to his *Ta'rīkh al-rusul wa'l-mulūk* (Chronicle of Prophets and Kings):

> Let him who studies this book of ours know that in everything I say about the subjects which I have decided to recount there, I rely only on what I transmit from explicitly identified reports (*akhbār*) and from accounts (*āthār*) which I ascribe by name to their transmitters. I do not achieve understanding through rational proofs nor do I make discoveries by intuition (*fakr al-nufūs*), save to a very limited degree. For

> knowledge about the men of the past and current news about men of the present cannot be obtained by one who has not himself witnessed these men or whose lifetime does not reach back to theirs. [In the latter situation knowledge can be obtained only] by the statements of reporters and transmitters, not by rational deduction or intuitive inference. And if we mention in this book any report about certain men of the past which the reader finds objectionable or the hearer offensive, to such a degree that he finds in it no sound purpose or truth, let him know that this is not our fault, but is rather the responsibility of one of those who has transmitted it to us. We have presented (such reports) only in the form in which they were presented to us. (Leiden, I, 6–7)

The reluctance of men like al-Ṭabarī to speak in their own voice, to state explicitly the sense and significance of the materials which they have so laboriously assembled, has been an acute problem for many an Orientalist. In some cases it has even led to the conclusion that these scholars did not think at all, that they were in fact mere compilers. But most of them, far from being cloistered antiquarians, were experienced men of affairs who were deeply immersed in the political and intellectual controversies of their times. In view of this fact, I would prefer to connect their apparent diffidence not to pious modesty or arid objectivity, but rather to the concept of knowledge in early Islamic culture. In this milieu, the historian's proper task was to convey objective knowledge of those past events which were generally believed to possess legal, political, or religious significance. Such knowledge (*ʿilm*) consisted of accounts of these events which could be traced back to reliable authorities—in the ideal case, eyewitnesses of known veracity, but in any case reputable early scholars who had obtained their information from such persons. The historian's task was decisively *not* to interpret or evaluate the past as such; rather, he was simply to determine which reports about it (*akhbār*) were acceptable and to compile these reports in a convenient order.

There is of course another dimension to this problem. As we have noted, everyone recognized historical events as religiously and politically crucial. If they were not, why record them in the first place? Thus, if a would-be historian spoke about these matters in his own words, he would inevitably be regarded as no serious scholar but as a mere propagandist for one or another faction. For an historian to be accepted as an objective transmitter of reliable facts about these religiously sensitive events, he had to disclaim personal responsibility for the statements in his works. He had to be able to show that these statements were to be ascribed not to himself, but to men whose authority could not be questioned, the revered early masters and the authorized transmitters of their works.

In spite of its crucial cultural significance, the historical writing produced in the late 3rd/9th and early 4th/10th centuries has received little scholarly attention for its own sake. Overwhelmingly, modern researchers have regarded these men not as influential historians with something of their own to say, but merely as repositories of archaic texts. Even the great compilers, al-Balādhurī and al-Ṭabarī, have only recently begun to attract serious attention in their own right. Franz Rosenthal has given us (at last!) a critical and well-documented study of al-Ṭabarī's life and writings in his general introduction to the complete English translation now being edited by Ehsan Yar-Shater (*The History of al-Ṭabarī*, Vol. I, 1989; pp. 5–154). Heretofore one had to make do with M. J. de Goeje's comments—largely textual rather than biographical or cultural—in Vol. XIV (1901) of the great edition which he supervised (*Annales quos scripsit Abu Gaᶜfar at-Tabari*); the article by Rudi Paret in *EI*[1], iv, 578–79; and Sezgin's interesting but concise statements in *GAS*, i, 323–25. For al-Balādhurī we still have very little. In addition to the article by Carl Becker and Franz Rosenthal in *EI*[2], i, 971–72, see the important introduction by S. D. Goitein to Vol. V (1936) of al-Balādhurī, *Kitāb ansāb al-ashrāf*.

Beyond these contributions, one can get at what al-Ṭabarī and his contemporaries were trying to do only through general studies (which are few and far between) on Islamic historiography. There are some typically elliptical comments by H.A.R. Gibb, "Taʾrīkh," *EI*[1], Suppl., 235–37 (reprinted in Gibb, *Studies on the Civilization of Islam*, 116–19); these are perceptive but now require revision. A more recent survey of this type is Claude Cahen, "L'historiographie arabe des origines au viiᵉ s. H.," *Arabica*, xxxiii (1986), 142–149; his statements are perceptive and up-to-date but are inevitably very general. Many pertinent remarks can be found here and there in Franz Rosenthal, *A History of Muslim Historiography* (1958; 2nd ed., 1968), especially in chapters 3 and 5, dealing with the forms of historical writing. The present author has attempted to characterize the underlying interpretive framework of this literature in "Qurʾānic Myth and Narrative Structure in Early Islamic Historiography," in F. M. Clover and R. S. Humphreys, eds., *Tradition and Innovation in Late Antiquity* (1989). The relevant chapter in D. S. Margoliouth, *Lectures on Arabic Historians* (1930), is now badly outdated. The most recent scholarly survey covering this period is Shākir Muṣṭafā, *al-Taʾrīkh al-ᶜarabī wa'l-muʾarrikhūn* (2 vols., in progress, 1978–), I, ch. 6 (202–264); he is concise but well worth attention.

The authors of the digests have been somewhat better dealt with, no doubt because the relative brevity and cohesion of their works makes them easier to manage, as well as causing their personal orientations to be more visible. Al-Yaᶜqūbī wrote one of the most important of these digests, the earliest universal chronicle in Arabic in the sense of a work going from the Creation down to his own time; he has been examined in an unpublished dissertation by William Millward, "A Study of al-Yaᶜqūbī, with Special Reference to His Alleged Shi'ite Bias" (1962); see also Yves Marquet, "Le šīᶜisme au ixᵉ siècle à travers l'histoire de Yaᶜqūbī," *Arabica*, xix (1972), 1–45, 101–138. Al-Masᶜūdī was a prolific writer, but of his many historical works only the *Murūj al-dhahab wa-maᶜādin al-jawhar* (a book meant as much to entertain as to instruct) and the *Kitāb al-tanbīh wa'l-ishrāf* (a supplement to his other writings rather than an independent contribution) still survive. Ironically, he has received more attention than any other historian of the period 850–950, even though he is the least useful among them as a source either for early Islam or for the ancient historical tradition. On the other hand, his curiosity and erudition in regard to pre-Islamic and non-Islamic societies is very striking, and it is this aspect of his work which has most readily attracted modern scholarship. See S. Maqbul Ahmad and A. Rahman, eds., *Al-Masʿūdī Millenary Commemoration Volume* (1960); Tarif Khalidi, *Islamic Historiography; the Histories of Masʿūdī* (1975), and Ahmad Shboul, *Al-Masʿūdī and His World* (1979). Finally, we have an important and influential critical study on Ibn ʿAbd al-Ḥakam (d. 257/871), an Egyptian jurist whose *Futūḥ Miṣr wa-akhbāruhā* is our fullest source for the Arab campaigns in North Africa: Robert Brunschvig, "Ibn ʿAbdalhakam et la conquête de l'Afrique du Nord par les arabes," *AIEO*, vi (1942–47), 108–155; reprinted in *Études sur l'islam classique et l'Afrique du Nord* (1986).

2. The Primitive Form of the Early Historical Tradition

In the authors and books reviewed so far, we have had the advantage of dealing with extant works; whatever problems these present, at least we possess them essentially in the forms in which their authors intended to leave them. But when we ask to what degree these texts reflect the original or primitive form of the ancient historical tradition, we enter into one of the most controversial areas of Islamic studies. The issue is not whether our 3rd/9th–4th/10th century texts have reproduced *verbatim* the sources which they claim to be quoting. Rather, the issue is how far, and in what ways, the concepts of historical process, the religio-political concerns, and the literary structures of the extant texts have diverged from accounts originally composed (whether orally or in writing) during the 1st/7th century.

The answer to this question requires us to construct a precise history of the origins and development of Arabic historiography down to the middle of the 3rd/9th century, and this we are simply unable to do. It is in fact not clear that such a history will ever be possible. For the time being, in any case, we have to restrict ourselves to the identification of key problems and the framing of working hypotheses. To be sure, there has been no lack of effort to deal with this subject. In addition to the general surveys named above—viz., Margoliouth, *Lectures*; Gibb, "Taʾrīkh", 108–116; Cahen, "L'historiographie arabe", 135–142; Shākir Muṣṭafā, *al-Taʾrīkh al-ʿarabī*, Vol. I—several studies merit attention. ʿAbd al-ʿAzīz al-Dūrī, *The Rise of Historical Writing among the Arabs*, trans. L. I. Conrad (1983), which gives a sensible and balanced account from a conservative perspective, is a good place to begin. (Its value is enhanced by Conrad's thorough bibliography of texts and studies.) Dūrī's emphasis on the formation of "schools" of history in the 2nd/8th century has been disputed, and he can also be criticized for taking too simple a view of how religio-political commitments, established forms of narrative, etc., shaped all historical writing in the first two Islamic centuries, but he makes a plausible case for the authenticity and reliability of at least some strands of the early tradition.

Fuat Sezgin's account (*GAS*, I, 235–389) is indispensable, for he provides a comprehensive overview of known authors and works, whether these are preserved in independent manuscripts or only in the citations of later authors. However, his entries for the Umayyad and early Abbasid period must be regarded as conjectural. His "Einführung" (pp. 237–256) is important but controversial—he insists on the early origin and accurate transmission of written history in Islam—and should be read together with his related arguments regarding the hadith in the same volume (pp. 53–83). Sezgin's approach is independently advocated by Nabia Abbott in two meticulously produced volumes: *Studies in Arabic Literary Papyri*: Vol. I, *Historical Texts* (1957); Vol. II, *Qur'anic Commentary and Tradition* (1967). The evidence which she amasses in these volumes is very impressive in itself. Still open to question is whether this evidence means what she believes it to mean, for there is at least a trace of circularity in her arguments. Her conclusions, based on relatively short fragments, should now be reevaluated in the light of work by R. G. Khoury, who has published two long papyri of similar type from the Heidelberg collection: (1) *Wahb b. Munabbih* (1972), which contains legends about King David and a text on the campaigns of the Prophet Muḥammad by this 2nd/8th-century folklorist/historian; (2) *ʿAbd Allāh ibn Lahīʿa (97–174/715–790): juge et grand maître de l'école égyptienne* (1986), a very early collection of hadith.

Some studies which deal with more narrowly focused topics of course have important implications for the evolution of Arabic historiography. Among these, Josef Horovitz, "The Earliest Biographies of the Prophet and their Authors," *IC*, i (1927), 535–559; ii (1928), 22–50, 164–182, 495–526, is a mine of information, though Horovitz is far more willing to accept Muslim tradition on this matter than most Western scholars have been. In contrast, a highly critical approach is taken in E. L. Petersen, *ʿAlī and Muʿāwiya in Early Arabic Tradition: Studies on the Genesis and Growth of Islamic Historical Writing until the End of the Ninth Century* (1964). Here Petersen attempts to reconstruct the overall development of Arabic historiography by analyzing the treatment of a few crucial events—in particular the Siffin arbitration imbroglio—between the composition of the earliest identifiable texts (ca. 725–750) and the final shaping of these narratives in al-Ṭabarī 150 years later. Other scholars have identified significant flaws in Petersen's analysis, which is in any case afflicted by an awkward and sometimes barely intelligible English translation. His general approach to the problem, however, remains in my opinion important and persuasive. See also two related studies by the same scholar:

(a) "ʿAlī and Muʿāwiya: the Rise of the Umayyad Caliphate, 656–661," *Acta Orientalia*, xxiii (1959), 157–196; (b) "Studies on the Historiography of the ʿAlī-Muʿāwiya Conflict," *Acta Orientalia*, xxvii (1963), 83–118. It must be admitted that Dūrī, Sezgin, Abbott, and Petersen yield no consensus; on the contrary, their conclusions are utterly irreconcilable. Even so, they do acquaint us with the range of issues and difficulties which must be confronted in dealing with this literature.

Further progress in establishing the primitive forms of Islamic historiography will require a serious scrutiny of the 2nd/8th-century compilations which were the direct sources for al-Ṭabarī, al-Balādhurī, et al. These have received some attention, to be sure, but not remotely enough. A concise survey is given by Dūrī, "The Iraq School of History in the Ninth Century," in Lewis and Holt, *Historians of the Middle East*, 46–53. One of them, the Kufan Abū Mikhnaf (d. 157/774), has been studied by Ursula Sezgin, *Abū Mikhnaf: ein Beitrag zur Historiographie der umaiyadischen Zeit* (1971)—a detailed monograph which throws much light on the whole period. But other scholars of his period were even more influential contributors to Islamic historical tradition, and they remain neglected. Among them would be the following:

a. Ibn Isḥāq (d. 150/767), best known for his biography of the Prophet (on which see below), but also the author of a history of the Caliphs (*Taʾrīkh al-khulafāʾ*), cited at several points by al-Ṭabarī and extant in one papyrus fragment (Abbott, *Literary Papyri*, I, 80–99).

b. Sayf b. ʿUmar (d. ca. 180/796), who was al-Ṭabarī's principal source for the early Arab conquests and the history of the Caliphate down to the death of ʿAlī.

c. Muḥammad b. ʿUmar al-Wāqidī (d. 207/823), a biographer of the Prophet second in importance only to Ibn Isḥāq, but also the main informant of al-Balādhurī in several chapters and extensively used by al-Ṭabarī for chronological data and variant narratives.

d. Muḥammad ibn Saʿd (230/845), apparently the chief editor and transmitter of al-Wāqidī, and the compiler of the first major biographical dictionary, the *Kitāb al-ṭabaqāt al-kabīr*.

e. ʿAlī b. Muḥammad al-Madāʾinī (d. ca. 225/840), a crucial source especially for the Arab conquests in Iran.

Ibn Isḥāq is certainly the best-studied of these authors, due largely to the fame and influence of his *Sīrat Rasūl Allāh*. This work has received an extremely valuable though not always reliable translation by Alfred Guillaume, *The Life of Muhammad* (1955; reprinted 1967, 1978), on which see the review article by R. B. Serjeant, *BSOAS*, xxi (1958), 1–14. The *Sīra* has also attracted several substantial studies:

a. Johann Fück, *Muḥammad ibn Isḥāq: literarhistorische Untersuchungen* (1925).

b. James Robson, "Ibn Isḥāq's Use of the Isnād," *BJRL*, xxxviii (1955–56), 449–465.

c. W. M. Watt, "The Materials Used by Ibn Isḥāq," in Lewis and Holt, *Historians of the Middle East*, 23–34.

d. ʿAbd al-ʿAzīz al-Dūrī, *Dirāsa fī sīrat al-Nabī wa-muʾallifihā Ibn Isḥāq* (1965).

e. Rudolf Sellheim, "Prophet, Chalif, und Geschichte: die Muḥammad-Biographie des Ibn Isḥāq," *Oriens*, xviii–xix (1967), 33–91.

His work can be placed within the general development of the *sīra* genre through the pertinent chapters (16–18, by J.M.B. Jones, M. J. Kister, and J. T. Monroe) in the *Cambridge History of Arabic Literature: Arabic Literature to the End of the Umayyad Period* (1983).

Sayf ibn ʿUmar suffers from a malign reputation due to the scathing critique devoted to him in Julius Wellhausen's *Prolegomena zur ältesten Geschichte des Islams* (1899). These strictures can perhaps be softened to some degree in light of the conclusions of Albrecht Noth, "Der Charakter der ersten grossen Sammlungen von Nachrichten zur frühen Kalifenzeit," *Islam*, xlvii (1971), 168–199. Neither scholar, unfortunately, addresses squarely the question of Sayf's own method, purpose, narrative structuring, religio-political affiliations, etc. If only because of Sayf's paramount place in al-Ṭabarī's account of early Islam, he certainly merits a far closer examination than he has heretofore received. For the time being, a few attempts to sketch the character of Sayf's work are given in the translators' introductions to the relevant volumes in *The History of al-Ṭabarī* (e.g., Vol. XIII, *The Conquest of Iraq, Southwestern Persia, and Egypt*, trans. by G.H.A. Juynboll [1989]; and Vol. XV, *The Crisis of the Early Caliphate*, trans. R. S. Humphreys [1990]).

For al-Wāqidī and Ibn Saʿd, we have no significant monographic studies, and for al-Wāqidī we must be content with such scraps as we can glean from work on other historians. On the other hand, the biographical genre which Ibn Saʿd established can be explored in two brief essays and a fairly substantive survey:

a. H.A.R. Gibb, "Islamic Biographical Literature," in Lewis and Holt, *Historians of the Middle East*, 54–58.

b. Malak Abiad, "Origine et développement des dictionnaires biographiques arabes," *BEO*, xxxi (1979), 7–15.

c. Ibrahim Hafsi, "Recherches sur le genre 'Ṭabaqāt' dans la litterature arabe," *Arabica*, xxiii (1976), 227–265; xxiv (1977), 1–41, 150–186.

Al-Madāʾinī has begun to receive some serious attention in recent years: see Badrī M. Fahd, *Shaykh al-akhbāriyyūn: Abū'l-Hasan al-Madāʾinī* (1975); U. Sezgin, "al-Madāʾinī," *EI²*, v, 946–48; and Gernot Rotter, "Zur Überlieferung einiger historischer Werke Madāʾinīs in Ṭabarīs Annalen," *Oriens*, xxiii–xxiv (1974), 103–133.

The authors discussed above are all Iraqi or Medinese, and this fact has not gone unnoticed. It is still disputed whether Syria failed to produce much historical writing in the late 8th and early 9th centuries, or whether a once-significant Syrian historiography was (deliberately or otherwise) pushed out of circulation. The latter interpretation is propounded in F. M. Donner's intelligent overview of the matter: "The Problem of Early Arabic Historiography in Syria," in *Proceedings of the Second Symposium on Bilād al-Shām during the Early Islamic Period*, ed. M. A. Bakhīt (3 vols., 1987), Vol. I, 1–27. Donner's conclusions are supported by two recent studies which focus on writers heretofore overlooked or dismissed as later forgeries: (a) Gernot Rotter, "Abū Zurʿa ad-Dimašqī (st. 281/894) und das Problem der frühen arabischen Geschichtsschreibung in Syrien," *Welt des Orients*, vi (1971), 80–104; (b) L. I. Conrad, "Al-Azdī's History of the Arab Conquests in Bilād al-Shām: Some Historiographical Observations," in *Second Symposium on Bilād al-Shām during the Early Islamic Period*, Vol. I, 28–62.

Scholarly discussion on the historiography of the period 750–850 has undoubtedly been contentious, but the bitterest controversy has been aroused by the earliest phase of historical collecting and composition. This is unsurprising, since our evidence for the decades before 750 consists almost entirely of rather dubious citations in later compilations. Deprived of direct evidence, scholars have had to compensate with bold surmises and moral certitude.

The only monograph devoted to the period of origins as a whole is N. A. Faruqi, *Early Muslim Historiography: a Survey of the Early Transmitters of Arab History from the Rise of Islam up to the End of the Umayyad Period* (1979). Many readers will find Faruqi's rather traditional interpretation of his subject unacceptable, all the more as he writes in unidiomatic English and is only poorly acquainted with the Western scholarly literature. On the other hand, he does present a wealth of data gleaned from wide reading in the Arabic texts; the book certainly merits being consulted. In addition, there are a few shorter studies of real substance. Two of these focus on the critical figure of Ibn Shihāb al-Zuhrī (d. 124/742), a Medinese scholar with close ties to the Umayyad court who is usually regarded as the first systematic collector of historical narratives. The authenticity and value of the accounts ascribed to him were challenged by Joseph Schacht, "On Mūsā ibn ʿUqba's *Kitāb al-maghāzī*," *Acta Orientalia*, xxi (1953), 288–300. A serious response to Schacht's attack was made by Dūrī, "Al-Zuhrī: a Study on the Beginnings of History Writing in Islam," *BSOAS*, xix (1957), 1–12. In addition, see J.M.B. Jones, "Ibn Isḥāq and al-Wāqidī: the Dream of ʿĀtika and the Raid to Nakhla in Relation to the Charge of Plagiarism," *BSOAS*, xxii (1959), 41–51, where the author concludes that "the greater part of the *sīra* was already formalized by the second century A.H. [i.e., by 720 A.D.], and . . . later writers shared a common corpus of . . . material, which they arranged according to their own concepts and to which they added their own materials."

Discussions on the origins of Arabic historiography have focused almost exclusively on two issues: (1) whether there really was any properly historical collecting and composition by the turn of the 1st/8th century; (2) whether the accounts ascribed by our extant texts to the scholars of that period are substantially genuine or later fictions. The two issues are of course intimately related, but they are nonetheless distinct conceptually. We might well imagine a situation in which "historical" research was going on by 700 A.D., but where this primitive historiography was forgotten or falsified beyond recognition a half-century later. However, most modern scholars have insisted on linking the two propositions: i.e., *either* there was an authentic primitive historiography which was substantially passed on to later generations, *or* there was no such thing, and the later texts ascribed to this early period are blatant forgeries.

The debate on these issues has been closely connected to the critique of *isnāds*. The question is whether *isnāds* (at least those produced by reputable scholars) represent genuine lines of transmission, or are instead forgeries intended to legitimize statements first circulated at a later period. The problem is extraordinarily complex, and no cut-and-dried rules of *isnād*-criticism can be given; it is enough to say that no *isnād* should be accepted at face value. Medieval Muslim scholars were of course aware of this and ultimately evolved a very elaborate science on the subject. Unfortunately, the procedures of this science were not fully articulated until the 4th/10th century, well after the the major compilations of hadith and historical *akhbār* had been assembled. Even so, *isnāds* and the principles which govern them are only intelligible through the work of Muslim scholars; any modern analysis must reflect a sound knowledge of their critique.

A summary of this is given by James Robson in *EI*²: "al-Djarḥ wa't-Taʿdīl," ii, 462; and "Ḥadīth," iii, 23–28. These can be followed up by the items cited above in Part I, Ch. 2.A (pp. 22, 35): Sezgin, *GAS*, I, 53–83; al-Ḥakīm al-Naisābūrī, *An Introduction to the Science of Tradition*, trans. J. Robson (1953); William Marçais, "Le *Taqrīb* de en-Nawawī," *JA*, ser. ix (1900–01).

Formal statements of methodology are only a first step. The substance of traditional *isnād*-criticism is buried in a series of biographical works which deal specifically with the early transmitters of hadith, with the aim of evaluating their reliability. Among these four have become standard references:

1. Abū ʿAbdallāh al-Bukhārī (d. 256/870), *al-Ta'rīkh al-kabīr* (4 vols., 1361–77/1940–58).
2. Shams al-Dīn al-Dhahabī (d. 748/1348), *Mīzān al-iʿtidāl fī naqd al-rijāl* (3 vols., 1325/1907; new ed. by A. M. al-Bījāwī, 4 vols., 1963).
3. Ibn Ḥajar al-ʿAsqalānī (d. 852/1449), *Tahdhīb al-tahdhīb* (12 vols., 1325–27; new ed. by A. M. al-Bījāwī, 8 vols., 1970–72).
4. Idem, *Lisān al-mīzān* (6 vols., 1329–31/1911–13. An abridgement of al-Dhahabī.).

These works are monuments of devoted scholarship, but they must be used critically; see the careful, sympathetic, and rather disturbing analysis of their contents (in particular the *Tahdhīb* of Ibn Ḥajar) recently presented in Chs. 4 and 5 of G.H.A. Juynboll, *Muslim Tradition* (1983).

A number of very capable modern scholars have defended the general authenticity of *isnāds*. An important early contribution was Josef Horovitz, "Alter und Ursprung des Isnād," *Islam*, viii (1918), 39–47, 299; xi (1921), 264–65, who connected the earliest use of *isnāds* to the turmoil of the second civil war of the 60s/680s when it became an urgent matter to be able to identify the provenance of doctrinally loaded statements concerning Muḥammad and the Companions. (As we shall see below, Horovitz's chronology was sharply challenged by Joseph Schacht and others, but on this point at least he has recently been supported by Juynboll, "The Date of the Great *Fitna*," *Arabica*, xx [1973], 142–59.) More elaborate statements of this position have come along since Horovitz. In addition to several studies already noted (Sezgin, *GAS*, I, 53–83; Abbott, *Studies in Arabic Literary Papyri*, I–II; Robson, "Ibn Isḥāq's Use of the Isnād"; U. Sezgin, *Abū Mikhnaf*), see the following:

a. M. M. Azmi, *Studies in Early Hadith Literature* (1968).
b. Fuat Sezgin, *Buharī'nin kaynakları hakkında araştırmalar* (1956).
c. Jawād ʿAlī, "Mawārid Taʾrīkh al-Ṭabarī," *MMII*, i (1950), 143–231; ii (1951), 135–90; iii (1954), 16–58; viii (1961), 425–436.

The majority of Western scholars have regarded *isnāds* with deep suspicion ever since the work of Julius Wellhausen and Ignaz Goldziher at the turn of the century. Wellhausen's works on early Islamic history (which are still fundamental) were informed by the hypothesis that the old historical tradition preserved for us by the 3rd/9th and 4th/10th century compilations fell into two parts: (1) an authentic primitive tradition, definitively recorded in the late 2nd/8th century, and (2) a parallel version which was deliberately concocted to rebut this. This second, "artificial" tradition was written down at more or less the same time as the first and is in some way based upon it, but it is filled with tendentious distortions and fictitious tales invented for their literary impact. The authentic tradition is found in citations from such scholars as Abū Mikhnaf, al-Wāqidī, and al-Madāʾinī, while the falsified version is typified by Sayf b. ʿUmar. Wellhausen refers to this hypothesis at many points, but his most explicit statement of method seems to be the following:

> By the term "original reporters" I mean the oldest historical writers. These are of course also collectors, in the sense in which every historian is. They have not spun their fabric from their fingertips but have brought it together from sources. . . . They are not compilers of disparate and contradictory traditions, but are rather representatives of a unified historical outlook, to which all the data collected by them corresponds, with certain explicitly stated exceptions. As a rule, then, one need go no further into the motley *isnāds* of separate traditions (*Einzeltraditionen*), but on the

contrary may treat historians like Abū Mikhnaf, Ibn Isḥāq, Abū Maʿshar, al-Wāqidī, etc. as his ultimate authorities. This is what al-Balādhurī and al-Ṭabarī do when they are content to say, "Ibn Isḥāq says," "al-Wāqidī says," without adducing the *isnād* on which these latter rely. It can be asserted, in fact, that for us the value of the *isnād* depends on the value of the historian who deems it reliable. With bad historians one cannot put faith in good *isnāds*, while good historians merit trust if they give no *isnād* at all, simply noting that "I have this from someone whom I believe." All this permits a great simplification of critical analysis. (*Prolegomena*, 4)

The validity of Wellhausen's argument only seemed to be deepened by the work of his contemporary Ignaz Goldziher, who demonstrated that a vast number of hadiths accepted even in the most rigorously critical Muslim collections were outright forgeries from the late 2nd/8th and 3rd/9th centuries—and as a consequence, that the meticulous *isnāds* which supported them were utterly fictitious. (*Muslim Studies*, II, "On the Development of the Hadith.")

Goldziher's findings could not be mindlessly applied to historical texts, to be sure, if only because of the distinction in character between hadith and historical *akhbār*. A hadith is seldom concerned with an event as such, and normally does not even specify time and place; its purpose is rather to communicate some religious doctrine and to give this doctrine Prophetic authority. A historical report, in contrast, may carry some legal or theological implications, but its overt aim is to convey information about some concrete incident. But even with this reservation taken into account, Goldziher's work demanded the attention of historians. In terms of their formal structures, the hadith and the historical *khabar* were very similar indeed; more important, many 2nd/8th and 3rd/9th century scholars had devoted their efforts to both kinds of text equally. Altogether, if hadith *isnāds* were suspect, so then should be the *isnāds* attached to historical reports.

Goldziher's conclusions were pursued further by Joseph Schacht, who proposed two major theses: (1) that *isnāds* going all the way back to the Prophet only began to be widely used around the time of the Abbasid Revolution—i.e., the mid-2nd/8th century; (2) that, ironically, the more elaborate and formally correct an *isnād* appeared to be, the more likely it was to be spurious. In general, he concluded, *no* existing hadith could be reliably ascribed to the Prophet, though some of them might ultimately be rooted in his teaching. And though he devoted only a few pages to historical reports about the early Caliphate, he explicitly asserted that the same strictures should apply to them. Schacht's important and enormously influential arguments are most fully stated in two publications: (a) "A Revaluation of Islamic Traditions," *JRAS* (1949), 143–154; (b) *Origins of Muḥammadan Jurisprudence* (1950), in which see especially Part II, pp. 138–159.

Schacht's conclusions were too well documented to be wished away, and they have left succeeding students of the subject with only three possible strategies. First, we might try to demonstrate that Schacht did not properly understand the processes of hadith transmission in early Islam; this is the approach of Fuat Sezgin, M. M. Azmi, and Nabia Abbott. Second, we might argue that he has taken a sound line of analysis too far. This has been suggested by W. M. Watt (in *Muḥammad at Mecca* [1953], pp. xi–xvi; and "The Materials Used by Ibn Isḥāq"). Far more systematically, G.H.A. Juynboll, *Muslim Tradition: Studies in Chronology, Provenance, and Authorship of Early Hadith* (1983), has tried to do justice both to medieval Islamic views and Schacht's critique. His cautious attitude toward his data and his intricate logic tend to veil his conclusions on certain issues, but this work is surely the most sophisticated and wide-ranging assessment of the evidence we have yet had. Juynboll's tentative counter-revisionism seems to be supported by M. J. Kister's close analysis of a number of particularly troublesome hadiths (collected in *Studies in Jāhiliyya and Early Islam*, 1980). Kister is able to show that several of these hadiths are extremely archaic in both language and content; whether or not they represent the teaching of the Prophet, they clearly reflect the ideas and problems of the first decades of Islam. But Juynboll's findings are explicitly provisional, and Kister deals with only a few odd cases. In the end, we may decide simply that Schacht is right and set out to explore the full implications of his thought.

It is the latter strategy which has recently produced some of the most provocative studies in the history of Western Orientalism. These are associated first of all with the name of John Wansbrough: (a) *Qur'anic Studies: Sources and Methods of Scriptural Interpretation* (1977); (b) *The Sectarian Milieu: Content and Composition of Islamic Salvation History* (1978). A definitive evaluation of Wansbrough's work will not be possible for a long time. It is perhaps tempting to think of him as one of those scholars whose premises and conclusions are drastically wrongheaded, but whose argumentation is brilliant and filled with intriguing perspectives. (To be sure, it is often difficult to say just what his arguments are, for he affects a ferociously opaque style which bristles with unexplained technical terms in many languages, obscure allusions, and Teutonic grammar.) In *Qur'anic Studies* Wansbrough hopes to establish two major points: (1) that Islamic scripture—not merely hadith but the Qur'ān itself—was generated in the course of sectarian controversy over a period of more than two centuries, and then fictitiously projected back onto an invented Arabian point of origin; (2) that Islamic doctrine generally, and even the figure of Muḥammad, were molded on Rabbinic Jewish prototypes. Proceeding from these conclusions, *The Sectarian Milieu* analyzes early Islamic historiography—or rather the interpretive myths underlying this historiography—as a late manifestation of Old Testament "salvation history" (*Heilsgeschichte*).

In *Hagarism, the Making of the Islamic World* (1977), Michael Cook and Patricia Crone have taken an even more radical step than Wansbrough. They regard the whole established version of Islamic history down at least to the time of ʿAbd al-Malik (65–86/685–705) as a later fabrication, and reconstruct the Arab Conquests and the formation of the Caliphate as a movement of peninsular Arabs who had been inspired by Jewish messianism to try to reclaim the Promised Land. In this interpretation, Islam emerged as an autonomous religion and culture only within the process of a long struggle for identity among the disparate peoples yoked together by the Conquests: Jacobite Syrians, Nestorian Aramaeans in Iraq, Copts, Jews, and (finally) Peninsular Arabs. Unsurprisingly, the Crone-Cook interpretation has failed to win general acceptance among Western Orientalists, let alone Muslim scholars. However, their approach does squarely confront the disparities between early Arabic tradition on the Conquest period and the accounts given by Eastern Christian and Jewish sources. The rhetoric of these authors may be an obstacle for many readers, for their argument is conveyed through a dizzying and unrelenting array of allusions, metaphors, and analogies. More substantively, their use (or abuse) of the Greek and Syriac sources has been sharply criticized. In the end, perhaps we ought to use *Hagarism* more as a "what-if" exercise than as a research monograph, but it should not be ignored.

The problems in early Arabic historiography are addressed more explicitly by Patricia Crone in two later monographs: (1) *Slaves on Horses: the Evolution of the Islamic Polity* (1980); and (2) *Meccan Trade and the Rise of Islam* (1987). In the former work she utterly dismisses the whole Arabic tradition relating to the primitive Caliphate (i.e., down to the 60s/680s) except as a corpus of prosopographical data. The narratives are useless fictions; only names survive as hard grains of historical fact. In *Meccan Trade* she stresses the internal contradictions which fill this material, and suggests that many allegedly historical reports are no more than fanciful elaborations on difficult Qur'anic passages. Crone's critique awaits close analysis; in the meantime, it will show how treacherous the use of this material can be.

Clearly, then, an extended debate has led to no agreement on two major issues: when serious historical study among Muslims commenced, and whether the extant accounts substantially reflect the statements of the early reporters to whom they are attributed. A third and perhaps even more crucial issue has so far only begun to attract attention: viz., the problem of how historical narratives might have been altered—in language, intention, structure, and conceptual framework—between the time they were originally formulated (hypothetically, ca. 700) and the point (ca. 850–900) when they took their definitive form.

The cultural meaning and value of any event inevitably alters with the passage of time. In turn, changes in meaning and value almost inevitably entail changes in the way an event is recounted. Thus we might argue that an event perceived by the participants (e.g., Arab warriors settled in Iraq during the 20s/640s) as a question of tribal honor or fiscal rights would be reinterpreted as a religious issue by the men of late Umayyad times. Such a reinterpretation would require a complete recasting of narratives about the event; an original emphasis on a tribe's heroic deeds, for example, might be subordinated to themes of piety and devotion to Islam. But to track down the interpretive development of the ancient historical tradition is a very elusive task—perhaps an impossible one in view of our inability to establish a reliable corpus of primitive texts.

So far, only E. L. Petersen, *ʿAlī and Muʿāwiya,* has made a serious attempt at this, and quite apart from a number of factual errors, his efforts are compromised by the extremely narrow body of texts which he has used. Two important studies by Albrecht Noth at least approach this issue, in that they focus on the formal elements in Arabic historiography: (a) "Iṣfahān-Nihāvand. Eine quellenkritische Studie zur frühislamischen Historiographie," *ZDMG*, cxviii (1968), 274–296; (b) *Quellenkritische Studien zu Themen, Formen, und Tendenzen frühislamischen Geschichtsüberlieferung.* Teil I: *Themen und Formen* (1973). Noth's thesis is that the crucial constitutive element of early Arabic historiography is the *topos*—i.e., a fixed element, ranging in scale from a simple motif to a complex plot, which is found in a number of narrative settings which ostensibly recount different events. A *topos* often looks like a simple factual statement, but it is in fact a symbol; it does not represent an event per se, but rather points to the inner meaning of that event. Though Noth's analysis is precise and astute, however, it is generally achronic in character; his comments on the two-centuries-long evolution of the literary patterns which he has identified are scattered and rather vague.

The problem of narrative change in early Arabic historiography can be successfully addressed only when we understand the process of transmission. Presumably, most of our accounts concerning the first six or seven decades of Islam originated as oral statements, and were only committed to writing at some later point. But as we have seen, scholars do not agree as to the time when such oral accounts began to be systematically collected and written down. Nor is it likely that once a given *khabar* was committed to writing, it would remain fixed in that form forever after. And even after written compilations had become commonplace (probably no later than the mid-2nd/8th century), oral transmission clearly still had a vital role; a scholar could best ensure the dissemination of his collection of *akhbār* by dictating them to his associates and disciples. By the early 3rd/9th century, Muslim scholars had begun to evolve some fairly effective controls to ensure the authenticity and accuracy of orally transmitted materials, but such controls could hardly be applied to the texts produced in earlier generations when these techniques were either unknown or at best far less regular. In brief, the way in which the ancient historical tradition was recorded and transmitted left room for manifold sins of omission and commission.

It is no easy thing for a modern scholar to come to terms with such modes of transmission; they are too remote from our own habits and experience. An excellent practical introduction to them is available in Jan Vansina, *Oral Tra-*

dition: a Study in Historical Methodology, trans. H. M. Wright (1965). Vansina deals chiefly with contemporary Central Africa, but any Islamist should see at once the usefulness of his approach. A more theoretical and very wide-ranging reconsideration of this subject is provided in the same author's *Oral Tradition as History* (1985). From the perspective of comparative literature, much can be learned from the classic study of Yugoslav folk-epic by Albert Lord, *The Singer of Tales* (1960), whose principles have recently been applied to ancient Arabic poetry by Michael Zwettler, *The Oral Tradition of Classical Arabic Poetry* (1978). Finally, Régis Blachère, *Histoire de la littérature arabe* (3 vols., 1952–66), is very alert to the problems of a semi-oral tradition—see especially Vol. I, 85–186. For the period in which the study of hadith and historical *akhbār* became highly formalized (the mid-3rd/9th century at latest), it can usefully be compared with the methods of textual study used in a closely related cultural setting; see B. Gerhardsson, *Memory and Manuscript: Oral Transmission and Written Transmission in Rabbinic Judaism and Early Christianity*, trans. E. J. Sharpe (1961).

3. An Authentic Kernel?

So far we have been discussing the relationships among texts, hypothetical early ones and extant late ones. But implicitly, we have also been asking whether our texts really do reflect the persons and events of primitive Islam. To put it another way, when we have finished the process of source-criticism, what is left; what do we actually know about the things which they purport to describe?

This is an issue which seems to invite extreme positions—a good indication of the complexity and elusiveness of these texts. In fact, no one is wholly agnostic. Even Crone, who completely rejects the narrative and chronological structures of the Arabic historical tradition, believes that it can be made to yield a reliable corpus of personal and tribal names. When this data is collated and analyzed, some of the underlying structural realities—though *not* the sequence of events—of early Islamic history will emerge. In comparison to Crone, Robert Brunschvig appears almost optimistic:

> [Ibn ʿAbd al-Ḥakam's narratives on North Africa] can only be fully explained in light of religio-legal problems, which were no doubt often not the result of a given historical fact, but rather the *raison d'être* or point of departure for this or that narrative.... Of all these facts, in the final analysis only a few remain which are certain or even merely probable—some outlines, a summary sketch of the sequence of major events, some proper names, a very small number of established dates. It is enough to inform us about the rather slow process and the difficulties of the Conquest in eastern Barbary (for lands further west things remain very obscure), but we cannot pretend to any certainty as to the details. ("Ibn ʿAbdalhakam et la conquête de l'Afrique du Nord," 152, 155)

I think it is reasonable to take Brunschvig's position as the minimum, unless we want to give up altogether the effort to write the history of early Islam. As to the most optimistic position available to a critical scholar, it may be represented by Watt:

> In general [the traditional historical material regarding Muḥammad's career] is to be accepted; only where there is internal contradiction is it to be rejected; where "tendential" shaping is suspected it is as far as possible to be corrected. Perhaps the coherence of the resulting account of Muḥammad's career will be accepted as an additional argument for the soundness of this procedure. . . . The critique of Islamic traditions by European scholars . . . has been based mainly on the legal traditions found in the standard collections by al-Bukhārī, Muslim, and others, that is, on the section of the traditional historical material where distortion is most to be expected. It is thus not surprising if sceptical views about the traditions have resulted. If, however, one considers the undisputed or purely historical section of the traditional historical material, it is apparent that there is a solid core of fact. (*Muḥammad at Medina*, 336–38)

In short, Watt believes that the narrative structure given by the extant texts is fundamentally sound, and constitutes an accurate description of events and processes as contemporaries perceived them. The legal, political, and theological conflicts of later times have of course caused some distortion and reshaping, but no wholesale fabrication. Since such anachronistic elements can normally be spotted, it is possible to identify the core of fact even in texts which have been so tainted.

There is ultimately no reconciling the positions represented by Brunschvig and Watt, since they proceed from radically different understandings of how early historical tradition was generated and transmitted. However, the terms of the debate might be clarified by two further observations. First, Petersen has shown (in *ʿAlī and Muʿāwiya*) that many of the disparities among the various accounts of the same event have come about not because of conflicting "eyewitness" reports, but because the texts were generated in a kind of dialogue with one another. If account A took a pro-Umayyad stance, then opponents of Umayyad claims had to circulate a contrasting account B which would both contradict crucial elements in A and support their own position. In other words, the historical tradition, once launched, was autonomous; it could evolve quite independently of the events which it claimed to describe. As to which reports are the original ones and which the rejoinders, there is often no sure way to know.

The second observation is suggested by F. M. Donner's *The Early Islamic Conquests* (1981). Donner argues that the great conquests of the 630s and 640s were specifically Islamic, in that they were rooted in the proto-state institutions and the dynamic ideology created by the new revelation. Now an attentive reading of the ancient historical tradition shows that the actors' intentions and motivations are indeed almost wholly expressed in terms of Islam. Moreover, the issues debated among the various protagonists in these accounts are often precisely those generated by the political-theological controversies of the late Umayyad and early Abbasid periods. There is surely no reason to doubt that Muḥammad's close associates, who had risked so much to follow him, did try to shape their behavior and values according to the imperatives of the new religion. On the other hand, it is far from clear that this religion was at first thought to require a wholesale jettisoning of old ways; we might well argue that the Qur'ān and Muḥammad were demanding simply a reform (within a new theological context, to be sure) of traditional custom. But however that may be, ought we to imagine that the mass of new Muslims—reluctant converts from Quraysh and the rebellious tribes of the Ridda wars—had more than an inkling of what the new revelation was or how it ought to affect their lives? Should we not assume that they continued to direct their conduct in large part according to the values and attitudes of the Jāhiliyya?

4. A Criterion of Authenticity

If this hypothesis is correct, then we are faced with a serious dilemma. The ancient historical tradition describes the events and personalities of the mid-1st/7th century, but it does so in terms of an interpretive framework and rhetoric shaped by the religio-political conflicts of the late 2nd/8th century. Lacking independent evidence for the development of values, attitudes, and concepts over the intervening 125 years, how can we decide whether or not this 8th-century framework is valid for the earlier period? So long as we restrict our consideration to the early historical tradition per se, we can seldom get beyond circular arguments. That is, if we begin by asserting that the earliest Muslims could not have thought in a certain way, we will then reject any text which shows them thinking in that manner. But in fact we have no basis whatever for such assertions *except* the very texts which we are trying to evaluate.

Very occasionally, however, it may be possible to establish the authenticity of a crucial text, and this one text will then provide a firm (albeit very limited) criterion for the assessment of other, still doubtful texts. A very important example would be the agreement between ʿAlī and Muʿāwiya at Ṣiffīn to negotiate an end to their dispute; this agreement has been meticulously reconstructed by Martin Hinds, "The Ṣiffīn Arbitration Agreement," *JSS*, xvii (1972), 93–129, and his work appears to give us our one solid point of repair in analyzing the first civil war. His conclusions concerning this text seem to concur with those of R. B. Serjeant. In a general survey of allegedly archaic documents preserved in the historical tradition, Serjeant rejects the claims of several items, but he also argues that some do appear to meet both linguistic and substantive criteria for authenticity: "Early Arabic Prose," *Cambridge History of Arabic Literature*, Ch. 3, especially p. 128ff.

More broadly, F. M. Donner attempts to assess the historical tradition by going outside it, in "The Formation of the Islamic State," *JAOS*, cvi (1986),

283–296. Drawing on well-attested documentary evidence (coins, inscriptions, papyri) from the first Islamic century to address a series of questions about the earliest political and administrative institutions of Islam, he suggests that the answers to these questions do conform to the general picture provided by the traditional literary sources.

Unfortunately, documents in the strict sense are rare, and few historical texts can be rigorously authenticated. We might then ask whether non-historical writing suggests any criteria for dating historical *akhbār*. Early theological discourse would seem an ideal choice, since so many political and social conflicts had a religious dimension. Unfortunately, only a few theological writings can be attributed to the early 2nd/8th century, and the authenticity even of these is hotly debated; see Josef van Ess, *Zwischen Ḥadīṯ und Theologie* (1975), and *Anfänge muslimischen Theologie* (1977); and the sharp challenge to his relatively optimistic conclusions by Michael Cook, *Early Muslim Dogma: a Source-Critical Study* (1981).

On balance, our best control on the historical tradition may be early Islamic poetry. One of the main functions of poetry in the Jāhiliyya and early Islam was the vaunting of one's own group and the vilification of others. That is, it is political verse, often composed for a specific occasion, and addressing (sometimes directly and sometimes allusively) the events and persons of the day. Insofar as this verse may be authentic, it would provide an excellent check on the attitudes, values, and concepts found in historical narratives.

The poetry of early Islam has come down to us in two forms: (1) in separate collections (*dīwāns*) of each poet's verse; (2) in citations, sometimes very extensive, in literary anthologies and historical compilations. The function of verse citations in the historical texts has never been properly studied, but I believe that they serve much the same purpose as the speeches and letters which are periodically introduced—viz., to allow the historian to convey an explicit interpretation or evaluation of persons and events without having to speak for himself. Poetry, in short, is editorial comment, safely attributed to others. Among the *dīwāns*, the most important one from the pre-Marwanid era is that of the Prophet's "laureate," Ḥassān ibn Thābit, which is available in a splendid critical edition by Walīd N. ʿArafāt (2 vols., 1971).

Here as in every category of early Islamic literature, authenticity is a critical issue. Blachère, *Histoire de la littérature arabe*, I, 156–179, discusses the general problem perceptively and gives some sensible guidelines for evaluating particular cases. See also two studies by ʿArafāt: (a) "Early Critics of the Authenticity of the Poetry of the *Sīra*," *BSOAS*, xxi (1958), 453–463; (b) "An Aspect of the Forger's Art in Early Islamic Poetry," *BSOAS*, xxviii (1965), 477–482.

Altogether, then, we do have a few tools (not terribly precise ones, to be sure) for testing our historical texts. Moreover, from the middle of the 2nd/8th century on, we possess reliable testimony on the broader currents of cultural change in Islam. We can at least guess—though we do not know directly—how change on this level may have affected the form of the historical narratives that have come down to us. What still escapes us, however, is a reliable way of deciding which statements in these reports constitute usable fact. It is certainly possible—by comparing early versions with late ones, by dissecting *isnāds*, etc.—to show that much in them is mere falsification, accretion, or distortion. But what about the residue: does this represent an "authentic core," or is it in turn only the tendentious reshaping of a now irrecoverable primitive narrative? Perhaps we should admit that in this matter we are guided more by intuition than by scientific knowledge, and that a universal consensus is not to be hoped for.

5. Traditional Texts and Contemporary Concepts

Suppose, however, that an agreed-on body of fact could be established. Even in this case, many questions of central importance in modern political studies could not be adequately answered. The problem is that we are not dealing with raw documents but with a consciously shaped literary tradition, and this tradition has constructed its body of historical "fact" according to its own aims and criteria, not ours. We might like to know about social stratification, urban demography, and the like, but the early Muslim historians were concerned with other things—political legitimacy, the nature of right government, whether the redemptive promise of Muḥammad's mission had been fulfilled or betrayed by the course of events. The names, actions, statements, and dates which would constitute the facts of Islamic history were determined within this framework, and we are compelled to make do with these.

This does not prevent us from asking our own questions and using the data at our disposal to respond to them as well as we can. At the very least, we can define the limits within which an acceptable answer must fall. Moreover, in some cases we can make progress simply by restating the Muslim historians' questions in our own terms. For example, we would not debate whether ʿUthmān's failings merited his deposition and death, but instead would ask from which segments of the Community his opponents were drawn, and which aspects of his policies had antagonized them. By making our questions congruent with those of the early Muslim historians in this way, we can make maximum use of the material which they have bequeathed us.

B. Two Cases from the Early History of Islam

Our discussion so far has been filled with qualifications and tentative hypotheses. The best way to lend it an air of reality is to look closely at two concrete cases from the formative years of the Islamic polity. The first will focus on that rare beast, a document of almost unchallenged authenticity; the other will deal with the body of obviously very tendentious narratives that grew up around the death of the third Caliph. Between these two cases, we should obtain a clear sense of what can and cannot be extracted from the ancient historical tradition.

1. The Constitution of Medina

Immediately after his account of the *hijra*, Ibn Isḥāq makes the following statement: "The Messenger of God wrote a document between the Emigrants and the *Anṣār*, and in it he made a treaty and covenant with the Jews, establishing them in their religion and possessions, and assigning to them rights and duties." Ibn Isḥāq then proceeds, with no *isnād* or other indication of provenance whatever, to reproduce a text of several pages. (*Sīrat Rasūl Allāh*, ed. Wüstenfeld, 341–44; trans. Guillaume, 231–33.) As we shall see, this text is a very remarkable one both in content and language. Even more remarkable, no doubt, is that both Western and Muslim scholars agree unanimously that the piece is authentic, a point originally established by the formidable Wellhausen. He bases his assessment on the following points: (1) a forgery would reflect the outlook of a later period—e.g., the Community would not include non-Muslims; the tribe of Quraysh (from which all the Caliphs stemmed) would not be so severely assailed as the enemy of God; much more would be made of Muḥammad's stature as God's Apostle; etc.; (2) linguistically, the grammar and vocabulary are very archaic; (3) the text is full of unexplained allusions which could only have been intelligible to contemporaries; (4) the text seems to reflect ancient tribal law far more than developed Islamic practice. (Wellhausen, "Muḥammads Gemeindeordnung von Medina" [1889], *Skizzen und Vorarbeiten*, iv [1889], 80.)

Such a refreshing unanimity is not maintained when it comes asking what the document is and what it means, however. On this text, after all, hinges our understanding of the last ten years of the Prophet's career, and indeed of the origins of the Islamic state. In regard to these matters almost everyone has some axe to grind. Thus it is disputed whether it is a single document or a collation of several, at what point it (or its component parts) was drawn up, whether it is a unilateral edict or a negotiated settlement, who the principal parties to it were. It is not even clear how it should be translated, so obscure or ambivalent are many of its key terms. Finally, because the rest of the tradition regarding Muḥammad's life (including the Qur'ān itself) is so bitterly contested, we do not have an agreed-upon documentary context within which the Constitution might be interpreted.

Given such a level of disagreement, we cannot deal here with every aspect of the Constitution; rather, we will focus on the ways in which recent scholarship has handled two major problems. The first study to define clearly the issues raised by this document was Julius Wellhausen, "Muḥammads Gemeindeordnung von Medina," already cited. His conclusions were essentially taken over and placed in a broader context by (a) Leone Caetani, *Annali dell'Islam*, I, 391–408, and (b) A. J. Wensinck, *Mohammed en de Joden te Medina* (1928), 73–98 (translated together with Wellhausen's contribution by Wolfgang Behn as *Muḥammad and the Jews of Medina* [1975]). Study of the Constitution was given new impetus by the translation and discussion in W. M. Watt, *Muḥammad at Medina* (1956), 221–260. R. B. Serjeant devoted many years to the elucidation of this text, drawing in particular on his knowledge of tribal custom in South Arabia; see (a) "The 'Constitution of Medina'," *Islamic Quarterly*, viii (1964), 3–16; (b) "The *Sunna Jāmiʿah*, Pacts with the Yathrib Jews, and the *Taḥrīm* of Yathrib: Analysis and Translation of the Documents Comprised in the So-called 'Constitution of Medina'," *BSOAS*, 41 (1978), 1–42. Finally, Moshe Gil, "The Constitution of Medina: a Reconsideration," *Israel Oriental Studies*, iv (1974), 44–66, has stressed Muslim-Jewish relations as the crucial issue addressed by the Constitution. (Translations of the Constitution are given in most of these studies; a line-by-line comparison of those in Wensinck-Behn, Watt, and Serjeant is most instructive.)

The fundamental problem for students of the Constitution is whether it is in fact one document or several; on the resolution of this apparently technical matter rests one's whole interpretation of its social and political significance. Wellhausen and Caetani regarded it as a unity, and argued that it belonged to the first year or so of Muḥammad's residence in Medina, before the battle of Badr in 2/624. Wellhausen bases this judgment on two considerations. First, Muḥammad is very diffident about his own status in the Constitution, making no claim whatever that it is in any sense divinely revealed or authorized. Second, both its tone and its concrete provisions are consistent throughout with the situation in Medina at this time; in particular, the Jews are still fully accepted as members of the Community but are regarded with some distrust.

Watt contests this view, however. He points to variations between first, second, and third-person forms of address; to repetitions of important clauses at scattered points in the text; to the omission of the names of the three major Jewish clans of Medina, though many minor ones are included. These considerations lead him to reconstruct the development of the Constitution in the following way. Roughly the first half would have been drawn up before Badr; these clauses may even represent the terms under which Muḥammad had been invited to Medina. Later on, a second block of articles was added, governing relations between the Muslims and the Jewish clans. Finally, other clauses were added or dropped at various times to fit changing conditions, so that the Constitution as we have it is a composite of the whole Medina period. However, Watt does not feel able to assign any precise chronology to this development, stating that we should not "base an argument solely on the supposed date of any article of the Constitution." (*Muḥammad at Medina*, 228)

Serjeant carries Watt's conclusions much further: (1) the Constitution is composed of eight discrete documents, arranged generally in their order of composition; (2) each of these documents can be quite precisely dated and connected with a known set of circumstances. Serjeant's criterion for separating the documents is a formal one; he posits a juncture wherever there is a sentence which seems to function as a terminal formula (e.g., "probity protects against treachery."). Once these divisions are made, he finds that each section is far more coherent and internally consistent than had previously seemed to be the case. ("Constitution of Medina," 8–9) Thus, he argues, documents A and B were pacts of alliance negotiated by Muḥammad immediately after his arrival in Medina; more than that, they represent the *sunna jāmiʿa* invoked in the Ṣiffīn arbitration agreement between ʿAlī and Muʿāwiya—the documents which (alongside the Qurʾān) were to govern the negotiations between the two adversaries. Documents C and D, also drawn up before Badr, define Muslim-Jewish relations within the Community of Medina. Document E reaffirms the status of the Jews in the face of serious tensions between them and Muḥammad following Badr. Document F, a very late piece, proclaims Medina to be a sacred enclave (*ḥaram*). Document G returns to Muslim-Jewish relations, this time representing the fatal alliance between the Muslims and the Banū Qurayẓa just before the siege of Medina in 5/627. Document H, finally, is a codicil to F and again concerns the sacred status of Medina.

Moshe Gil, in contrast, asserts the unity of the Constitution, though his reasons for this judgment are not really clear. ("Reconsideration," 47–48) He believes that it represents a specific moment in the Prophet's career, about five months after his arrival in Medina, and that it defines a long-term strategy vis-a-vis both the pagan Meccans and the Jews of Medina.

At this point some notes on method are in order. For all these authors, the Qurʾān and the ancient historical tradition are essential for the correct interpretation of the Constitution. Serjeant, however, also draws heavily on his intimate knowledge of tribal life in 20th-century South Arabia. (It is the knowledge of a colonial officer rather than an academic anthropologist, but none the less imposing for that.) He constantly stresses the close resemblance both in language and content between the Constitution of Medina and the legal documents produced in modern South Arabia, especially those concerned with sacred enclaves. In general, he is a strong advocate of the notion that there is an unbroken continuity in the major values and institutions of Bedouin life from the Jāhiliyya down to modern times. As to Muḥammad himself, "the Prophet was no innovator . . . he accepted, with comparatively minor modifications, the ethical code and social framework of his time. . . ." (Serjeant, "Constitution of Medina," 8; cf. "Sunnah Jāmiʿah," 1–2.) Altogether, then, we are entitled to interpret Muḥammad's actions and words, as reported by the early historical tradition, in the light of the observed behavior of holy men in modern South Arabia. That behavior has been explored by Serjeant in a number of publications; see especially: (a) *The Sayyids of Ḥaḍramaut* (1957); (b) "Ḥaram and Ḥawṭah, the Sacred Enclave in Arabia," in *Mélanges Taha Husain*, ed. A. R. Badawi (1962).

That Muḥammad saw himself as a reformer, and in a sense as a restorer, of the established ethical norms of his environment, is now accepted by many scholars. This is indeed Watt's main theme. Even so, Serjeant's approach is daring and controversial. It has certainly enabled him to give a far more detailed and precise reading of the Constitution of Medina than any of his predecessors. On the other hand, the validity of his reading depends on two assumptions: (1) the applicability of contemporary field data to the events of fourteen centuries ago; (2) the authenticity of the early historical tradition, from which he takes so many details and anecdotes essential to his case. The first assumption is undoubtedly useful, but can easily lead to unwarranted dogmatism. As to the second, we will each have to draw our own conclusions.

In the introductory comments to this section, we noted that much of the difficulty in interpreting the Constitution could be attributed to its archaic vocabulary. The second problem which we will examine emerges from one of these lexical puzzles—viz., the precise meaning of the term *umma*. Again, the solution which we adopt to this issue molds our whole understanding of the kind of social body which Muḥammad meant to establish. The word occurs in the opening clauses of the Constitution, and clearly represents a key concept within it:

1. This is a writing (*kitāb*) from Muḥammad the Prophet . . . between the Believers (*al-muʾminūn*) and the Muslims of Quraysh and Yathrib, and those who follow them, join with them, and strive alongside them;
2. They are a single Community (*umma wāḥida*) apart from other people;
3. Any Jews who follow us have support and parity; they are not to be wronged nor is mutual support to be given against them;
4. The Jews of Banū ʿAwf are a Community (*umma*) along with the Believers (*al-muʾminūn*); the Jews have their religion (*dīn*) and the Muslims have their religion. [This applies both to] their clients and themselves, save for him who commits any wrong and acts treacherously. (That person) destroys only himself and the people of his household. (Clause 4 is repeated for the Jews of eight other clans named in succession.)

What precisely does Muḥammad mean by "*umma*" here? Clearly it cannot be the religiously defined "nation of Islam" as understood in later centuries, because it includes the Jews of Medina. On the other hand, the inhabitants of the Yathrib oasis are not all included on an equal footing. Faced with such a quandary, we naturally turn to the Qurʾān, where the word is widely used in the late Meccan and early Medinan passages (on which see R. Paret, "Umma," EI^1, iv, 1015–16; or *SEI*, 603–4). But the Qurʾān does not really solve the problem either. Thus, Watt argues that an *umma* is a theocratic community, instituted by God to supplant the traditional kinship-based tribes. God creates such theocratic communities through a revelation to one of His prophets, and within them solidarity and cohesion are based on a shared acceptance of this revelation and obedience to the divinely chosen prophet. On the other hand, Watt is forced to concede that "when *ummah* is first used in the Qur'ān it is hardly to be distinguished from *qaum*" (i.e., a kinship-based tribe); only slowly does it acquire its distinctively religious connotations. In the Constitution, he notes that the *umma* includes Jews as well as Muslims, and "this suggests that the *ummah* is no longer a purely religious community." Finally, he sees that the Constitution's *umma* is not a body of individuals but a confederacy of already existing clans. (Watt, *Muḥammad at Medina*, 238–241, 247)

Wellhausen's discussion ("Gemeindeordnung," 74–75) is not terribly different from Watt's, though he stresses the military dimension of the *umma*; it is the Community of God organized for defense (*Schutzgemeinschaft Allahs*). Likewise, he points out that while the Constitution includes the Jews and pagans of Medina in the *umma*, they are clients and subordinate members.

Serjeant proposes (as we would expect) a far more secular interpretation; an *umma* is simply a political confederation between a number of autonomous tribes. Following his usual method, he finds a parallel for this term in a semantically related one, *lummiyya wāḥida*, which is used in modern South Arabia for such confederations. ("Constitution of Medina," 12) At first glance, he seems to withdraw a bit in his second study, where he translates *umma* as "theocratic confederation." But he intends a very restricted sense for theocracy—simply that God is in some sense the guarantor of the pact, and that the confederation has been entered into under the aegis of some "priestly" or holy person. He find examples of such theocratic confederations all over ancient and modern Arabia, so that the *umma* of Muḥammad hardly seems exceptional. Only in the course of time (how much time Serjeant does not say) did the new *umma* become the distinctive Islamic community of faith. ("Sunnah Jāmiʿah," 4–5)

Gil is the simplest case. He knows all the relevant Qur'anic passages, but for him *umma* is a neutral term—"a group" as opposed to individuals. ("Reconsideration," 49–50)

Semantic hairsplitting abounds in these discussions, no doubt, but serious issues are at stake. Scholars are trying first of all to get at Muḥammad's own conception of the new entity which he had founded in Medina, and secondly to determine how broadly his conception was shared by the tribesmen of 7th-century West Arabia. These problems are important in themselves, obviously, but their connection with the fate of the Jews in Medina intensifies our fascination with them. The tragic outcome of the conflict between Muḥammad and the old Jewish clans of the oasis is well known; in view of this, we very much want to know what his original intentions toward them were. Plainly this is a bitter issue, especially in the light of our 20th-century history, and modern scholars find it extremely hard to examine the evidence disinterestedly.

Most of the Muslim commentators, including Ibn Isḥāq and al-Wāqidī, present the Constitution as a treaty with the Jews of Medina. But in the document itself, the Jews seem to occupy a clearly subordinate place; that is, the confederation (*umma*) appears to be primarily one between the Meccan emigrants and the various Arab clans (heretofore pagan) of Medina. Moreover, the three largest Jewish clans (Banū Qaynuqāᶜ, Banū Naḍīr, Banū Qurayẓa) are not mentioned by name in the Constitution, even though these were the groups with whom Muḥammad came into conflict. To establish the place of the Jews in the primitive *umma*, then, requires much reading between the lines.

There is a degree of consensus. All modern scholars agree, for example, that by the time of Muḥammad's arrival in Medina the Jewish clans had become subordinate allies of the leading pagan Arab clans in the oasis. Because of this, the Jews were in no position to enter the new *umma* on their own, but instead were brought in as clients of the Arab clans to which they were allied. But whatever their social status, the Jewish clans clearly were accepted as members of the *umma* and had the rights and obligations entailed by such membership.

At this point the consensus breaks down. Wellhausen, Watt, and Serjeant all take Clause 4 to mean that the Jews could retain their old religion and law. Gil however sharply disagrees. Clause 3, he says, refers only to Jews who convert to Islam: "it can by no means be considered a promise of safety to Jews who wish to keep their faith." ("Reconsideration," 63.) The statement about religion in Clause 4 appears to contradict Gil's assertion, but he reads *dayn* (debt) instead of *dīn* (religion, law), and translates: "The Muslims are responsible for the *debt* both of themselves and their clients." For Gil, this reading of the passage undercuts any argument that Muḥammad's original intention was to reach some accommodation with the Jews of Medina. On the contrary:

> Through his alliance with the Arab tribes of Medina the Prophet gained enough strength to achieve a gradual anti-Jewish policy, despite the reluctance of his Medinese allies. . . . In fact, this inter-tribal law [i.e., the Constitution] had in view the expulsion of the Jews even at the moment of its writing. . . .
>
> The document, therefore, was not a covenant with the Jews. On the contrary, it was a formal statement of intent to disengage the Arab clans of Medina from the Jewish neighbours they had been with up to that time. ("Reconsideration," 64–65.)

It is interesting to note that Wellhausen and Wensinck, who also view the Constitution as a unitary document, concur to some extent with Gil's conclusion. Wellhausen finds that it betrays "a certain mistrust of the Jews." ("Gemeindeordnung", 80.) Wensinck goes considerably further: Muḥammad drafted the Constitution merely to neutralize the politically influential Jewish clans; he was stalling for time until he could find an opportunity to subdue them. (*Mohammed en de Joden te Medina*, 97–98)

In contrast, the thesis of Watt and Serjeant that the Constitution is a composite document leads them to a different conclusion. For Watt, always irenic in disposition, the Constitution per se displays no particular hostility toward the

Jews, though their special religious status of course had to be recognized. The conflict with the Jews is reflected chiefly in a negative fact—the absence of a clause referring to any of their three major clans. Watt's hypothesis is that clauses were added and deleted according to need, and so this silence is exactly what we should expect in the definitive (post 5/627) form of the document.

Serjeant holds that the extant version of the Constitution contains *all* the provisions made during Muḥammad's Medinan years. The text's silence in regard to the three major Jewish clans is irrelevant, since he believes (as do Wellhausen and Gil) that the Jews are identified here not by their own clan names but by those of their Arab allies. Although the original agreements (which include Clauses 3 and 4) show no animus towards the Jews and no change in their status from pre-Islamic times, that is not true of the sections appended later on. Particularly noteworthy is the language of Document E (dating from six months after the battle of Badr, 2/624) and Document G (the treaty between Muḥammad and the Banū Qurayẓa, just before the siege of Medina in 5/627). These two documents convey no explicit threats, but for one who is aware of the historical contexts in which they were drawn up they reflect almost explosive tensions. ("Sunnah Jāmiʿah," 32–34, 36–38)

The Constitution of Medina is undeniably the key to the final decade of Muḥammad's career, and like many master keys it is very hard to use. Even with its limitations and difficulties, however, it allows us to pose quite precise questions, and to define the terms in which those questions must be answered.

2. *The Reign of ʿUthmān ibn ʿAffān*

Our discussion of the historical texts dealing with the reign of ʿUthmān will focus not on the social and political "realities" which they purport to describe, but on the intentions and concerns of the historians who composed them. In taking this approach, we are asking a question for which the historical tradition gives us direct, extensive, and unimpeachable evidence—viz., how was ʿUthmān's reign understood and evaluated by educated Muslims of the late 3rd/9th and early 4th/10th centuries. Inquiries of this kind are by now fairly common in the early Islamic field. On the other hand, they have usually dealt not with the major historical compilations per se, but rather with particular *akhbār* included within them. This method is of course valid and necessary, but it should be obvious that the separate *akhbār* have been transmitted to us only because they were selected to become part of some larger scheme of historical description and interpretation. It is then this broad framework which ought to be the primary focus of our attention.

In order to determine the covert structure and intention of a compilation made up of disjunct, highly disparate reports, we need to devise some approach by which these separate elements can be read as a coherent text. Perhaps the easiest and most direct one is simply to try to identify the set of questions which a given compiler was trying to address. Since (as we noted in the first section of this chapter) we can expect to find very few explicit statements of method and purpose, we must discover these questions mainly through a scrutiny of the compiler's selection and arrangement of *akhbār*; we would ask why he chose to include this set of texts, why he omitted others which were available to him, why he fitted them together in one way rather than another. Our solutions will necessarily be hypothetical, and there is always the danger of over-interpreting. But even so, an inquiry of this kind can permit us to see dimensions of these works that would otherwise remain entirely hidden.

To demonstrate how this approach might be applied, we will examine the account of ʿUthmān's Caliphate given by Aḥmad b. Yaḥyā al-Balādhurī (d. 279/892) in his vast biographical-historical collection, the *Kitāb ansāb al-ashrāf* (ed. S. D. Goitein, v, 1–105). Along with the parallel section in al-Ṭabarī (ed. M. J. de Goeje, I, 2776–3065), al-Balādhurī's text is our principal source for this crucial moment in Islamic history. It is clear from his *isnāds* that he had studied with the great biographer of the previous generation, Muḥammad b. Saʿd (d. 230/845), and through him had a close acquaintance with the tradition of al-Wāqidī (d. 207/823); the latter figure is in fact al-Balādhurī's chief authority for the reign of ʿUthmān. In addition, he cites quite extensively the contrasting accounts of Abū Mikhnaf (d. 157/774), al-Madāʾinī (d. 225/840), and even Ibn Shihāb al-Zuhrī (d. 124/742). Finally, al-Balādhurī quotes (with meticulous *isnāds*) a good deal of hadith material—i.e., statements by the Prophet and widely revered early Muslims which do not recount events per se, but instead pass judgment on the religious merit of various protagonists in the drama.

Al-Balādhurī gives us some dates, but not enough to establish an adequate chronology of ʿUthmān's reign. His whole presentation in fact is achronic, for he has arranged his chapters according to topic, with no regard for their sequence in time. There are eighteen chapters, which seem to fall naturally into four groups:

I. ʿUthmān's genealogy, his moral and personal characteristics, and his standing in the eyes of the Prophet and the Companions, especially his rival and successor ʿAlī b. Abī Ṭālib.

II. ʿUthmān's election as Caliph.

III. ʿUthmān's conduct in office, and the protests and dissension which this aroused.

IV. The rebellion against ʿUthmān and his murder.

The second of these sections displays very clearly the main features and problems of al-Balādhurī's account, and so we will focus our analysis on it. The section begins with ʿUmar's nomination of six senior Companions (including ʿUthmān and ʿAlī) to elect a successor to him; it then covers the election procedures stipulated by ʿUmar, the way in which the choice of ʿUthmān actually came about, and finally the response by various sectors of the Medina Community to this decision. It is composed of thirty separate *akhbār*; of these eighteen rest on the authority of al-Wāqidī, while six come from Abū Mikhnaf and two from al-Madā'inī. The longest single *khabar* runs about a page, but everything else is much shorter, in some cases only a line or two.

This group of sources might in itself suggest a particular religious and political bias in al-Balādhurī's presentation. Abū Mikhnaf was a scholar of Kufa, which had always been a stronghold of pro-ʿAlid sentiment. As for al-Wāqidī, he was born in Medina and spent the first half of his life there before moving to Baghdad. In Medina he was closely connected with Ibn Isḥāq, whose pro-ʿAlīd inclinations are fairly clear, and al-Wāqidī himself was regarded with some suspicion by later Sunni scholars both for his scholarly practices and for his supposed Shiʿite sympathies. Altogether, then, we ought to expect an account of the election distinctly hostile to ʿUthmān.

Al-Balādhurī begins with three *akhbār*, the first from al-Wāqidī and the other two from his "miscellaneous" sources. In the first *khabar*, ʿUmar institutes an electoral committee to name his successor, hoping thereby to avoid the charge of "mere happenstance" which some persons had leveled at the choice of Abū Bakr to succeed Muḥammad. In the event of a tie vote, states ʿUmar, ʿAbd al-Raḥmān ibn ʿAwf (one of the electoral committee's six members) is to make the decision. In the second *khabar*, ʿUmar is preaching the Friday sermon shortly before he is attacked; he refuses to name an heir-apparent (as Abū Bakr had named him), and instead commands the people to obey the decision of the six electors. In the third *khabar*, ʿUmar is lying on his deathbed; with all six electors present, he charges ʿAlī and ʿUthmān to fear God if elected, and warns ʿUthmān against burdening the people with his kinsmen. Likewise, he spells out the things which favor the election of each man—in ʿAlī's case, his kinship with the Prophet, his marriage to the Prophet's daughter Fāṭima, and his religious knowledge (*al-fiqh wa'l-ʿilm*); in the case of ʿUthmān, his great age and his marriage to another of the Prophet's daughters.

These three reports seem perfectly unconnected with one another, and all are related without any narrative context, a knowledge of which is simply taken for granted by al-Balādhurī. They are crucial to his design, however, for taken together they implicitly identify the main issues which he will be addressing in the rest of the section. These issues are as follows:

1. The intensely controversial role of ʿAbd al-Raḥmān ibn ʿAwf, whom Shiʿites came to regard as a man who had knowingly foisted an inferior candidate on the Community.

2. Whether Muslims were obligated to accept the decision of the electoral committee.

3. The rivalry between ʿUthmān and ʿAlī, which will be a key motif in al-Balādhurī's presentation of ʿUthmān's entire reign.

4. The relative qualifications of ʿUthmān and ʿAlī for the Caliphate.

5. ʿUthmān's nepotism, which led him to appoint allegedly corrupt and tyrannical officials, and ultimately brought about an uncontrollable rebellion against him.

These five issues are dealt with quite explicitly, but they point to a set of covert problems in al-Balādhurī's text which are addressed only between the lines. These problems were undeniably crucial ones in the minds of early Muslims, for they shaped much of the religio-political debate throughout Islam's first three centuries. They can be stated in the following form:

1. Did the electoral committee named by ʿUmar really possess the right and authority to choose the head of the Muslim Community?

2. Did the electors carry out their role in a lawful and godly manner, or were they instead governed by faction and selfish ambition?

3. Was ʿUthmān in fact the best available candidate, and was he so acknowledged by all the senior Companions?

4. In the end, was the election of ʿUthmān legally and religiously binding on the entire Community, both at that moment and for all later generations?

Al-Balādhurī uses the remaining twenty-seven *akhbār* in his account of the election to explore the issues which he has stated or implied in the opening three. He never gives us a complete and connected narrative of this event, although we can come close to this by combining four *akhbār* from Abū Mikhnaf which occur at scattered points in the last half of the section. Abū Mikhnaf's version seems to acknowledge the electoral committee's decision as binding, for he has ʿUmar demanding on pain of death that all Muslims accept it. However, he is critical of the manner in which the decision was reached; he stresses the kinship ties between ʿUthmān and the "chief elector" Ibn ʿAwf, the latter's trickery in getting ʿAlī excluded, and the general role of faction and personal ambition in the committee's deliberations. Abū Mikhnaf does not directly challenge ʿUthmān's worthiness or personal integrity, but the electoral process comes across as badly tainted.

On the other hand, the bite of Abū Mikhnaf's account is tempered by the other materials which al-Balādhurī cites. In a sense he uses Abū Mikhnaf's version to set up a list of charges against the validity of ʿUthmān's election, and then draws on other reports to demonstrate that these charges can be refuted, or at least mitigated. For example, was ʿUthmān the best available candidate? Undoubtedly ʿAlī was a very strong contender, but he too had significant flaws. Al-Balādhurī recounts an evaluation by ʿUmar of his possible successors, and all of them are found wanting in some crucial respect. Moreover, in two separate *akhbār* ʿUmar warns both ʿAlī and ʿUthmān not to burden the people with their kinsmen. Finally, one of the most learned and revered Companions, ʿAbdallāh ibn Masʿūd, directly proclaims ʿUthmān to be the best available man—an evaluation which is all the more significant because Ibn Masʿūd is normally portrayed as a severe critic of ʿUthmān's regime. In the final analysis, ʿUthmān emerges as at least the equal of any other candidate, even ʿAlī, and hence a plausible if not flawless choice as Caliph. In much the same manner, al-Balādhurī demonstrates the other points at issue: that ʿAbd al-Raḥmān ibn ʿAwf was legitimately empowered to name the new Caliph; and that allegiance was sworn to ʿUthmān by all the Companions, thus making his election binding on all later generations.

Two or three points in al-Balādhurī's presentation require notice. First of all, there is the crucial role which he assigns to ʿUmar: it is he who establishes the electoral committee and makes its decisions binding, he gives ʿAbd al-Raḥmān ibn ʿAwf the final voice, he publicly evaluates all the potential candidates. However, ʿUmar's commands and judgments would be authoritative only for a Sunni audience, and al-Balādhurī's stress on these entitle us to assume that this is the audience he meant to address. He wanted to show, to anyone who might feel uneasy about the matter, that ʿUthmān's right to the Caliphate was unimpeachable. On the other hand, he in no way denigrates ʿAlī, who is portrayed throughout in the most sympathetic manner. His purpose is simply to demonstrate that ʿAlī was not indisputably superior to ʿUthmān, and that he did recognize the latter's election. All this is in line with the Sunni tendency in the 3rd/9th century to assert the equal religious standing and authority of all the Companions (*taswiyat al-ṣaḥāba*)—a doctrine bitterly contested of course by Shiʿite sympathizers. Thus our initial hypothesis that al-Balādhurī's sources (al-Wāqidī, Abū Mikhnaf) might lead him towards a pro-ʿAlid interpretation of ʿUthmān's reign falls to the ground.

One can subject every section in al-Balādhurī's life of ʿUthmān to this sort of analysis and come up with similar conclusions. At bottom, he is pursuing a fundamental question generated by the religio-political conflict of the preceding centuries: did ʿUthmān's Caliphate represent a break in Islamic government, a betrayal of the new covenant brought by Muḥammad, or did this new dispensation remain intact in at least its essential points? On the answer to this issue depended a Muslim's whole conception of the nature of religious and political authority in Islam and his evaluation of the socio-political system in which he lived. Al-Balādhurī is thus wrestling with no trivial problem. On the other hand, his presentation does not constitute a truly historical analysis—i.e., an effort to describe and explain a process of change. Rather, he is presenting a kind of legal-political dossier, a compilation of evidence for and against ʿUthmān on a series of widely current charges.

Al-Balādhurī's was of course not the only approach adopted by the historians of his age. For example, the concise account given by al-Yaʿqūbī (d. 283/897) in his *Taʾrīkh* (ed. M. T. Houtsma, ii, 186–206) provides us with our earliest full statement of the "Shiʿite paradigm" of early Islamic history. Naturally we would expect to find here both a profound veneration of ʿAlī and an outright condemnation of ʿUthmān and all his works. But this kind of partisan display is not what makes al-Yaʿqūbī worth reading.

Far more significant is his conception of the causal links between the Community and the conduct of its ruler. In the typical Sunni view which had emerged by the end of the 3rd/9th century, the Community and the Caliph are in principle mutually autonomous. Whatever the misdeeds or errors of the ruler, they need not affect the religious and moral integrity of the Community as a whole. Rather, the Community's integrity is preserved by its adherence to the doctrine and example of the pious early Muslims. As the famous hadith proclaims, "My Community will never agree on an error."

For al-Yaʿqūbī, however, the primitive Community was itself the source of the corruption in ʿUthmān's odious regime. That is, the Community did not become corrupt because of ʿUthmān's actions. Rather, he was only elected in the first place because the senior Companions decided to reject the Prophet's own chosen successor, ʿAlī, in favor of a man whose character flaws were well-known to all. It is as if the Community, once deprived of the Prophet's personal guidance, at once rejected his heritage and reverted to the mean struggle of personal ambition. Under ʿUthmān, the Community's leaders went so far as to reinstate the kinship-based social order of the Jāhiliyya, and when this was done tyranny and civil strife were inevitable. From this fatal degeneration only a tiny "saving remnant," consisting of ʿAlī and a few devoted followers, was immune. In short, al-Yaʿqūbī is less concerned to condemn ʿUthmān or praise ʿAlī than to ask how the new God-given order brought by Muḥammad could have collapsed so quickly. In contrast to al-Balādhurī, then, he is trying to present and interpret an historical process, albeit within the transcendental framework of the working-out of God's providence.

If space permitted, we might extend our analysis to other historians. This would do much to show the range of concerns and methods displayed by these scholars, and to bring out the varied cultural meanings which might adhere even to a single topic. But we have said enough to suggest what can be found in this literature. More important, we have uncovered some of the problems which the early historical tradition is likely to present for modern efforts to achieve a "scientific" reconstruction of the first century of Islam.

Chapter Four

MODERN HISTORIANS AND THE ABBASID REVOLUTION

THE ART OF INTERPRETATION

THE ABBASIDS claimed that their seizure of power in the years 129–132/747–750 was no mere change of regime, however dramatic, but rather a decisive turning point in Islamic history. And so it has been portrayed ever since, by Western as well as Muslim scholars. For this reason, it has engendered a substantial scholarly literature—one of the very few topics in Islamic historical studies to do so. Hence we have the opportunity to confront several layers of interpretation and reinterpretation, of polemic and attempted synthesis. We can see the emergence of a scholarly tradition over a period of nearly a century, and reflect on the degree to which discourse on the subject has been channeled by the concerns and methods of its pioneers. Altogether, we are in a far better position here than for most topics to see how well historians of Islam have understood and dealt with the problems and opportunities of their field.

It might be simplest to examine the literature on the Abbasid Revolution through a historical survey of its development, beginning with the seminal works of Van Vloten and Wellhausen and coming down to recent studies by Farouk Omar, M. A. Shaban, Jacob Lassner, and Moshe Sharon. However, a chronologically organized survey is likely to take for granted the questions and approaches actually found in the literature, to assume that these really are the most appropriate ways of dealing with a given topic. But it is precisely this assumption that we must question if we want to discover how fully the possibilities of the subject have been understood and explored.

From this perspective, it seems better to define a broad analytic framework for the Abbasid Revolution, one which is independent of existing studies on the subject and yet commensurate with them. Such an analytic framework would take the form of an integrated set of questions, and these in turn could be compared to the problems addressed in the literature. In this way, we can develop a consistent standard against which to measure various accounts of the Revolution. Ideally, we might frame a questionnaire capable of yielding a definitive and comprehensive account of the Revolution *if* every item in it were adequately answered. In practice, of course, this is impossible, if only because historians are always coming up with new questions and devising novel ways to answer old ones. Hence there can never be a wholly objective and permanently valid standard of evaluation. Even so, we can surely devise a set of questions which both comprehends all the significant issues which scholars have so far raised in connection with the Abbasid Revolution and suggests some new lines of inquiry. If a definitive evaluation is beyond our grasp, this approach will at least give us some sense of the field as a whole, while also allowing us to assess the scope and quality of the individual studies which make it up.

A. Developing an Analytic Framework

The first question to ask is a conceptual one: in what sense was the Abbasid seizure of power a "revolution"? This is of course a word much debased in current usage, where it is commonly applied to new detergents and changes in teen-age apparel. Properly speaking, however, it ought to denote the transformation of an established structure, the supplanting of one order of things by another. In regard to the Abbasid takeover, then, we would ask what aspects of political life, social structure, and culture underwent decisive changes as a result of this event. And if there were such changes, to what extent did this revolution conform to the intentions of those who had brought it about? Put more simply, what changes did the new regime intend to institute, and which ones actually occurred?

Such questions may well tempt us into a bottomless pit. But even a modest appraisal of what is demanded by them will compel us to go well beyond the limits of the Abbasid uprising and consolidation of power—i.e., an account restricted to events in Iraq and Khurasan during the decade 745–755. Rather, we will have to examine a sufficiently long period of time to establish "trends" in the development of political institutions, social systems, and ideology; the issue will then be to decide whether the trends of late Umayyad times were interrupted and redirected subsequent to the Abbasid takeover, or whether they instead continued in much the same direction as before. This sort of decision is of course more a matter of interpretive judgment than objective fact, but if a scholar specifies his criteria of continuity and change with sufficient rigor, his judgment ought to be meaningful and useful.

If we move from the problem of revolutionary change to the revolutionary event itself, the questions before us are hardly less vexing. We can begin with the proposition that the Abbasids did not take power by a simple coup d'état. On the contrary, they recruited a very substantial army from among the alienated elements of Umayyad society and used this army to bring down the regime through an arduous and complicated series of campaigns. But this apparently straightforward statement raises many crucial issues. First of all, which groups were the Abbasids able to attract to their cause, and what discontents among these groups were they able to exploit in order to do this? Second (the reverse side of the first question), what program did the Abbasids devise in order to attract recruits to their cause? Third, how did the Abbasids organize their following into an effective military and political movement, one capable of wearing down and eventually breaking up a formidable and long-established opponent? Fourth, the Abbasid movement was only one of many revolutionary movements in the mid-2nd/8th century; what links and parallels did it have with other such movements in this period, and how was it able to dominate its rivals? Each of these is in fact many questions; we will explore them one by one.

1. The assumption underlying almost all scholarship on the Abbasid Revolution is that men felt discontent with Umayyad rule not as individuals but as members of alienated or oppressed groups. When we ask what groups the Abbasids were able to attract to their cause, then, we must begin by defining the different ways in which people ascribed a social identity to themselves in the first half of the 2nd/8th century. Scholars have looked primarily to three modes of classification: (a) race or ethnicity—i.e., groupings defined by common language, culture, socio-political organization, and (to a far lesser degree) genetic stock; (b) among Arab Muslims, tribal affiliation—an elusive but strongly felt form of social identity; (c) regional loyalty or interest (in the present case, Syrian vs. Iraqi vs. Khurasani). In connection with the Abbasid Revolution, two widely used criteria of social identity have been rather neglected. First, little has been made of the cleavage between Muslim and non-Muslim, though this has seemed crucial in regard to other topics in Islamic history. Second, until very recently economic class—one's place in the system of production and distribution—has either been ignored altogether or treated simply as a function of some other mode of social identity.

If there is a degree of consensus as to the typology of social identity, however, scholars are passionately at odds as to which of these types is decisive. In this light, our evaluation of any account of the Abbasid Revolution might well begin by asking why the author assigns priority to one form of identity rather than another. Partly this is a matter of determining what evidence he has cited and how he has used it. But on a more general level, we need to determine whether his general model of the period's social and political structure is coherent and convincing. To mention only one point, we might ask whether it is sensible to think that people acted only as members of a single type of social group. Should we not expect to find multiple and even conflicting loyalties within the same person, as is the case with ourselves; and would this fact not account for much of the apparent instability, fickleness, and treachery within the Abbasid movement?

When we move from questions of social structure to the nature of the discontents which caused various groups (however defined) to feel alienated from or oppressed by Umayyad rule, we penetrate into a very tangled thicket. We can make our starting point the issue of political legitimacy. When Hishām ascended the caliphal throne in 105/724, the Umayyads could rely on a broad, though hardly universal, consensus among politically relevant groups—in particular, the Arab-Muslim warrior elite—that they were the family best able to ensure the integrity and security of the Community. By 127/745, very few groups were willing to concede them this status. On this level, then, the study of the Abbasid Revolution is in large measure a study of how the Umayyads lost their right to govern.

This way of putting the problem suggests several questions. We might ask how different social groups were linked to the regime, and what expectations they had of it. Likewise, to what extent did the competition for status, power, and wealth among different groups translate itself into resentment against a regime which could not simultaneously meet everyone's demands? From another perspective, we would ask which groups were favored by the regime, and which ones it tried to use in order to assert its control over the others. Finally, are the visible discontents of these various groups best understood as ideological, economic, or political in character? That is, were they connected primarily to questions of legitimate leadership and right social order, of material well-being or deprivation, or of power and influence within the existing order of things? These three dimensions are by no means mutually exclusive; on the contrary, any one of them almost necessarily involves the others. The issue here, however, is which dimension was perceived to be primary, the one in terms of which the others had to be expressed and legitimized.

It is essential to recall that not every discontented group joined the Abbasids. Although almost every province of the Umayyad Empire was wracked by rebellion and violence from the mid-730s on, the Abbasids initially depended entirely on forces raised in Khurasan alone. Nor at the beginning did they obtain support from every group there; they were only one faction among many for almost a year after the Abbasid *daʿwa* was publicly proclaimed, and before that event they were hardly visible in the general ferment in the province. What was it about Khurasan that particularly lent itself to their appeal, and how were they ultimately able to bring under their aegis dissident groups which had originally been quite independent of them?

2. The program devised by the Abbasids to mobilize on their own behalf all these discontents has long been a puzzle to students of the Revolution. Ultimately, their program seems to boil down to a few pious slogans. Though witnesses of the Iranian Revolution have every reason to be aware of the power of pious slogans, it remains difficult to connect Abbasid propaganda with the specific social and political tensions of Khurasan. This problem can only be resolved when we recognize words as symbols whose concrete meaning is defined by the contexts within which they are used. A slogan which is a mere pious commonplace for one group may thus be tremendously moving, even inflammatory, for another. For those who feel deeply wronged by current real-

ities, the simple demand for justice and equity may resound as a telling critique of the established order.

We must then go behind the slogans of Abbasid propaganda and seek for the body of religious, political, and social values which they were intended to mobilize. In other words, we must establish not only the Abbasid program as such, but also the way (or the many ways) in which it was understood by those who responded to it.

This task would surely be difficult enough if the Abbasids had been trying to reach only one group, both because of our fragmentary knowledge of the social structure of Khurasan in the mid-2nd/8th century and because of the vast cultural distance between ourselves and the people of that epoch. But insofar as Abbasid agents were trying to mobilize the widest possible array of alienated groups, the problem becomes far more intractable. In this case we have to keep many possibilities in mind. Perhaps certain statements by Abbasid agents were meant only for one group, and then we must identify their target before we can grasp their true significance. On the other hand, many statements may have been crafted for a mixed audience; in this case, we run the risk of overspecifying, of assigning too concrete a meaning to words which were designedly vague and ambiguous. Accounts of the Abbasid Revolution must be judged in part by their alertness to issues of language, to the complex relationships between speaker and audience.

3. The organization of the Abbasid movement was for a long time an almost insoluble problem. The texts dealing with the subject were too few and tendentious for any well-founded analysis to emerge. Happily, the discovery and publication of new sources has greatly improved the situation in the last two decades. Though many issues still cannot be resolved with certainty, they can at least be meaningfully addressed.

The major obstacle to an analysis of Abbasid organization is that the movement was for thirty years an underground conspiracy, a period during which every effort was made to hide or misrepresent its true character. Then for the three years of open rebellion (129–132/747–750), the movement's conspiratorial apparatus remained essentially intact—but still clandestine—even as a vast army was being recruited and organized. In short, the historian must sort out a dual structure during this crowded and confused period. Finally, in the early 750s, we see the often violent dismantling of the old revolutionary apparatus and the creation of a state machinery which differed sharply in function, structure, and personnel from the previous system. Any adequate analysis of Abbasid organization must start with the knowledge that one is pursuing an ever-changing reality through a maze of fun-house mirrors.

It is a common fallacy to suppose that organizations are adequately explained if one has constructed for them a flow chart or a formal hierarchy. Such taxonomies are a useful exercise, but they are best a beginning. The formal structure of an organization only has explanatory power insofar as it can be related to the actual politics of decision-making and implementation within it. A given organizational structure is not necessarily chosen because it is the most efficient way of reaching a defined goal or because it represents the actual distribution of power and influence among its members. On the contrary, it may be chosen largely for symbolic or "traditional" reasons, or even in order to mask its real character and purpose so as to confuse the opposition.

A potentially useful though easily abused way of getting at the realities of a clandestine revolutionary organization like that of the Abbasids is to search for analogies from better known movements. Analogies can of course tell us nothing about the specific characteristics of the groups being studied, but they can suggest what questions might usefully be applied to them. For the Abbasid Revolution, an obvious modern parallel is the Bolshevik seizure of power in 1917. All the particulars as to ideology, program, internal structure, recruitment, socio-political milieu, etc., will be different, and yet many of the questions we ask about the Bolsheviks would be equally significant in regard to the Abbasids. How, for example, can a small, close-knit revolutionary party mobilize a multitude of disparate, ill-focused frustrations and desires in society at large? How does a clandestine group go about persuading a mass of people that it represents their needs and is the most efficacious instrument for realizing them? What means—rewards, surveillance, coercion, etc.—can a revolutionary group's "central committee" use to ensure that its agents are carrying out its policies? Within the revolutionary group itself, who has the right to participate in the definition of policy, and where is the final locus of authority? How are the group's agents recruited and trained, and what are their social background characteristics? How and under what circumstances does a revolutionary party move from clandestine to public action? Once such a party seizes power, how does it transform itself into a government?

Comparative study, especially when it involves something like the Russian Revolution, obviously has the grave disadvantage of confronting a scholar with an unmanageably vast new literature. But since the point of such an effort is not to achieve a valid original interpretation of the rise of the Bolsheviks, but rather to generate a set of questions which may throw light on the Abbasid *daʿwa*, one's reading can be selective. Perhaps the most productive approach in this case would be to study the statements of the Bolsheviks themselves, Lenin and Trotsky above all. In addition, comparative studies of modern revolutionary movements are not lacking. The sociologically inclined might favor the recent and very difficult book of Theda Skocpol, *States and Social Revolutions* (1979). An older comparative analysis, less sophisticated but highly influential, is Crane Brinton, *The Anatomy of Revolution* (1938; rev. ed., 1952).

4. The Abbasid *daʿwa* can be explained in terms of the social groups which it mobilized, of its ideology and program, and of its organizational structure. However, a full account also requires that we know how the Abbasids defined

themselves in terms of the available political and ideological alternatives of the mid-2nd/8th century.

This is hardly an unstudied problem; the links and parallels between the Abbasids and their revolutionary rivals have attracted scholarly concern since the pioneering monographs of Van Vloten in the 1890s. Two basic points are not in dispute. First, the Abbasids asserted that their cause was not merely political but religious—a fact supported by the very name they gave to their enterprise: "*daʿwa*," a "mission" or "summons to the truth." Second, the Abbasid *daʿwa* had its roots in the Shiʿite realm of ideas and values, and remained an integral part of this realm down to the moment of its final success. These two statements are obviously very general, but they are not trivial. On the one hand, they show that the Abbasids claimed to be more than a frustrated faction which would exercise power in much the same manner as the present ruling clique; on the contrary, their purpose was to realize the divinely revealed imperatives of a just political order. At the same time, their Shiʿite affiliations linked them to those who believed that such a divinely revealed order could only be instituted by a suitable member of the Prophet's own family.

Given the character of our sources, however, to go beyond these initial statements is very difficult indeed. In the early 2nd/8th century, Shiʿism was a broad religious orientation rather than an organized sect. In such a situation, what strategies can we devise in order to define the belief-systems of this shifting and overlapping array of Shiʿite sectarian formations and to locate the Abbasid movement within the spectrum of Shiʿite thinking and activity? At times the Abbasids seemed aligned with extremist groups (*ghulāt*), at others they were the very image of sober respectability. Are we then dealing with real shifts of doctrine and ideology, with cynical tactical maneuvers, or with both? In general, should we regard the Abbasids as an integral part of the Shiʿite milieu or as parasites who fattened on it?

The preceding discussion should make it clear how challenging it is to construct an account of the Abbasid Revolution which will do justice to all the dimensions of this vast, sprawling event. Indeed, the goal of a single comprehensive interpretation may be only a chimaera. Perhaps the next generation of scholarship would be better off to explore broad but carefully defined problems within the topic as a whole. Examples of such problems could be multiplied indefinitely. Early Shiʿite political ideology is an obvious choice; though it has been widely discussed already, there still seems to be much that is vague and ill-understood. Among less studied areas, a very promising one would be regional studies analyzing the socio-political crises which subverted Umayyad rule during its last two decades—in Khurasan first of all, but equally in Iraq, Syria, and even North Africa. For as things are, we know fairly well who rebelled, but not (in any concrete sense at least) why. Through carefully focused investigations of this kind, we might gain not only a more precise grasp of each dimension of the Revolution in itself, but also a more vivid sense of how every aspect of the subject reflects all the others.

B. An Outline of the Sources

Because no description of any event can be any better than the sources from which it is derived, we turn at this point to a concise review of the sort of evidence available to us for the Abbasid Revolution. An initial orientation can be gotten from the survey in Farouk Omar (Fārūq ʿUmar), *The Abbasid Caliphate, 132/750–170/786* (1969), pp. 12–55; and the same author's *Ṭabīʿat al-daʿwa al-ʿabbāsiyya* (1970), pp. 19–72. To this account, Moshe Sharon, *Black Banners from the East* (1983)—a partial translation and adaptation of the author's 1970 Ph.D. dissertation for the Hebrew University of Jerusalem ("Aliyat ha-Abbasim la-shilton")—adds important statements in his detailed footnotes and a terse "Historiographic Note" (pp. 231–37).

Our sources consist almost entirely of literary texts—a fact whose implications will be discussed below. These can be grouped into five classes: (1) chronicles (general, local, and "monographic"), including a few items in Syriac and Persian as well as Arabic; (2) biographical dictionaries, compiled according to widely varying criteria; (3) heresiography (properly, the study of *firaq*, "sects"), a genre which began to emerge only in the 4th/10th century; (4) political treatises and polemics; (5) poetry and belles-lettres; (6) messianic texts, in the form of hadith, *malāḥim* (apocalyptic predictions), and perhaps a few Jewish and Christian sermons and tracts.

In general, the first group has provided not only the bulk of our "facts," but also the narrative structure which defines them and gives them meaning and shape. As is so often the case, the fundamental text has been the vast chronicle of al-Ṭabarī. (The section on the Abbasid Revolution is now available in an English version by John A. Williams, *The History of al-Ṭabarī: The Abbasid Revolution, A.D. 743–750/A.H. 126–132* [1985], vol. 27 in the projected complete translation.) It is true that the last two decades have seen such a flood of new or previously unused texts that we can almost speak of a source revolution. Even so, it is the materials supplied by al-Ṭabarī which have established our program of inquiry, the basic set of questions to be investigated. Traditionally, al-Ṭabarī has been supplemented by al-Balādhurī's *Futūḥ al-buldān* (ed. de Goeje, 1866; trans. by P. K. Hitti and F. Murgotten as *The Origins of the Islamic State*, 2 vols., 1916–23), which contains valuable data on the situation of the Arabs in Khurasan and Transoxiana, and by a group of "minor chronicles": al-Dīnawarī, *al-Akhbār al-ṭiwāl*; al-Yaʿqūbī, *al-Taʾrīkh*; al-Masʿūdī, *Murūj al-dhahab*; and the anonymous *al-ʿUyūn wa'l-ḥadāʾiq fī akhbār al-ḥaqāʾiq* (ed. de Goeje, under the title *Fragmenta Historicorum Arabicorum*, 1869).

In recent years, several new works have attracted much attention. ʿAbd al-ʿAzīz al-Dūrī has published Vol. III of al-Balādhurī's *Ansāb al-ashrāf* (1978), which covers the Abbasid family down through the caliph Abū Jaʿfar al-Manṣūr (136–158/754–775). Though al-Balādhurī uses substantially the same sources as al-Ṭabarī, his independent perspective contributes many valuable points. The *Kitāb al-futūḥ* of Ibn Aʿtham al-Kūfī (8 vols., 1968–75) was composed by a contemporary of al-Ṭabarī, and its length and detail make it appear a highly promising source. In fact it does add new data on the Arab tribes in Khurasan, but continued study has also suggested that it contains much legendary material and must be used with great caution. The recently discovered and edited *Taʾrīkh* and *Ṭabaqāt* of Khalīfa b. Khayyāṭ al-ʿUṣfurī (a Basran traditionist, d. 241/855) are very terse, and their interest lies largely in their early date. The *Taʾrīkh* seems in fact to have been the first general annalistic work to be composed in Arabic. On the other hand, the *Taʾrīkh al-Mawṣil* of Yazīd b. Muḥammad al-Azdī (d. 334/945) is extremely important; although al-Azdī draws on the same historical tradition used by al-Ṭabarī and al-Balādhurī, he cites much otherwise unknown material on the crucial province of the Jazira, thereby doing much both to clarify the crisis of Umayyad power in the 740s and the obstacles faced by the new Abbasid regime. Finally, attention should be paid to two late biographical dictionaries from Syria, the *Taʾrīkh madīnat Dimashq* of Ibn ʿAsākir (d. 571/1176) and the *Bughyat al-ṭalab fī taʾrīkh Ḥalab* of Kamāl al-Dīn ibn al-ʿAdīm (d. 660/1262). Both these works contain a mass of material on the first two Islamic centuries; however, until very recently they have been available only in manuscript (in Damascus and Istanbul) and so remain largely unexploited.

By far the most important new work, however, is an anonymous chronicle discovered in Baghdad in 1955 and published by ʿAbd al-ʿAzīz al-Dūrī and A. J. al-Muṭṭalibī under the title *Akhbār al-dawla al-ʿabbāsiyya* (1971). This work was first discussed by Dūrī in "Ḍaw' jadīd ʿalā al-daʿwa al-ʿabbāsiyya," *Majallat Kulliyyat al-Ādāb wa'l-ʿUlūm* (Baghdad, 1957), 64–82. Recently some of Dūrī's and Sharon's hypotheses concerning its date and authorship have been revised (quite persuasively) by Elton Daniel, "The Anonymous 'History of the Abbasid Family' and its Place in Islamic Historiography," *IJMES*, xiv (1982), 419–434. The text is a sort of quasi-official history of the Abbasid Revolution, probably composed in the late 3rd/9th century. It greatly clarifies many heretofore irresolvable problems—the apparently abrupt shifts in Abbasid ideology, the organization of the movement in its clandestine phase before 129/747, the internal politics behind the revolt proclaimed by Abū Muslim. At least some of the *Akhbār*'s sources had previously been closely held secrets of the Abbasid court, but the compiler clearly intended his work for the public domain. An anonymous Leiden manuscript (*Dhikr Banī al-ʿAbbās wa-sabab ẓuhūrihim*), perhaps composed in the mid-4th/10th century, contains many of the same reports along with some additional material; and yet another anonymous chronicle, this one written in the 5th/11th century, contains an abridged version of the *Akhbār*: *Taʾrīkh al-khulafāʾ*, ed. P. A. Gryaznevich (1967).

A few local histories, for the most part surviving only in late Persian abridgments, contain passages throwing light on the social milieu in which the Revolution occurred. In particular, see Narshakhī, *The History of Bukhara* (trans. R. N. Frye, 1954); and Ḥasan al-Qummī, *Taʾrīkh-i Qumm* (ed., Jalāl al-Dīn Tihrānī, 1353/1934). In Narshakhī especially it is not always easy to sort factual data from folklore, but his regional perspective is very valuable.

The other classes of texts are ancillary to the chronicles and biographical dictionaries, but they are not to be overlooked. The heresiographers, for example, include some of the most astute and sophisticated scholars produced by medieval Islam. Their surveys of the Islamic sects of course have many flaws from our point of view: e.g., they are not concerned with the socio-political milieu in which the various sects arose; many of the groups which they describe are fictional—religious orientations rather than organized sects; doctrinal development within the sects is ignored; etc. Even so, they do provide an overview of the religious beliefs circulating in 2nd/8th-century Iraq and Iran which we can obtain nowhere else. However suspect their account of particular sects, there is little reason to doubt the presence of the ideas which they describe or the capacity of the Abbasid propagandists to exploit these ideas for their own benefit.

Among these works the most important for our purposes are the following:

a. Abū al-Ḥasan ʿAlī al-Ashʿarī (d. 324/935), *Maqālāt al-Islāmiyyīn wa-ikhtilāf al-muṣallīn*, ed. Helmut Ritter (1931).

b. Ibn Ḥazm (d. 456/1064), *Kitāb al-fiṣal fī al-milal wa'l-ahwāʾ wa'l-niḥal* (5 vols., 1317–1321/1899–1903). Partial translation and commentary by Israel Friedlaender, "The Heterodoxies of the Shiites," *JAOS*, xxviii (1907), 1–80; xxix (1908), 1–183. Spanish translation by M. Asin Palacios, *Abenházam de Cordoba y su historia crítica de las ideas religiosas* (1927–32).

c. ʿAbd al-Qāhir al-Baghdādī (d. 429/1037), *al-Farq bayn al-firaq*, ed. M. ʿAbd al-Ḥamīd (1964). Translated as *Moslem Schisms and Sects* by Kate Seelye (Vol. I, 1920) and A. B. Halkin (Vol. II, 1935); Halkin's section is much the more reliable. See also the study of this work by Henri Laoust, "La classification des sectes dans le *Farq* d'al-Baghdādī," *REI*, xxix (1961), 19–59.

d. Ḥasan b. Mūsā al-Nawbakhtī (d. ca. 310/923), *Firaq al-shīʿa*, ed. Helmut Ritter (1931). Trans. A. J. Mashkur, "Les sectes shiʿites," *Revue de l'histoire des religions*, cxliii (1958), 68–78; cxliv (1958), 67–95; cxlv (1959), 63–78.

e. Muḥammad b. ʿAbd al-Karīm al-Shahrastānī (d. 548/1153), *Kitāb al-milal wa'l-niḥal* (ed. William Cureton, 2 vols., 1842; ed. Muḥammad F. Badrān, 1951). Trans. Theodor Haarbrücker as *Religionsparteien und Philosophenschulen* (1850–

51). English translation of Part I by A. K. Kazi and J. G. Flynn, as *Muslim Sects and Divisions* (1984)—fluent, but with a very thin annotation. Though relatively late, Shahrastānī's is doubtless the finest achievement of this genre.

Obviously we would benefit enormously if we had direct access to the political arguments and polemics of the Revolutionary period (ca. 735–760), instead of having to reconstruct these from materials composed more than a half-century later. What does survive are two essays by the Iranian *mawlā* Ibn al-Muqaffaᶜ (d. 142/759): the *Kitāb al-ādāb al-kabīr*—an important but rather general mirror for princes—and a remarkable private memorandum, the *Risāla fī al-ṣaḥāba*, written either for the caliph al-Manṣūr (136–158/754–775) or one of his uncles. The *Risāla* is clearly intended to address a concrete historical situation, but it does so in an enigmatic and elusive manner which resists any definitive exegesis. There is now a reliable edition and translation, with an important introduction, by Charles Pellat, *Ibn al-Muqaffaᶜ, "conseilleur" du calife* (1976). See also F. Gabrieli, "L'opera di Ibn al-Muqaffaᶜ," *RSO*, xiii (1931), 231–35; and S. D. Goitein, "A Turning Point in the History of the Muslim State," *IC*, xxii (1949), 120–135—reprinted in Goitein, *Studies in Islamic History and Institutions* (1966), 149–167. (Goitein's discussion is fundamental, a "turning point" in its own right.)

During the middle decades of the 3rd/9th century, ᶜAmr b. Baḥr al-Jāḥiẓ—acting more or less at the behest of the Abbasid court—produced a series of brilliant politico-religious treatises. A tantalizing sample of these, together with an excellent bibliography, can be found in Charles Pellat, *The Life and Works of Jāḥiẓ* (1969); see especially pp. 56–86. Though late, these writings contain many passages suggesting that the social and ideological issues raised by the Revolution were still alive. Unfortunately very little of his work has been studied from this perspective; an important exception is Jacob Lassner, *The Shaping of Abbasid Rule* (1980), Ch. 5, "The Regiments of the Imperial Army: Notes on al-Jāḥiẓ's Epistle to al-Fatḥ b. Khāqān." (This treatise was published by G. van Vloten, *Tria Opuscula* [1903], 1–56, and A. M. Hārūn, *Rasāʾil al-Jāḥiẓ* [2 vols., 1964], I, 1–86; trans. J. Harley-Walker, *JRAS* [1915], 631–697.)

Information of all sorts is supplied by poetry and belles-lettres. The verse composed in late Umayyad and early Abbasid times may well be our most direct source for the propaganda and polemics of the Revolutionary era; Sezgin, *GAS*, II (1975) provides the data for a systematic approach to this material. Rather little seems to have been done with poetry; Wellhausen could occasionally put a piece of verse to good use, but he has had few successors.

Among prose works, the most extensively consulted have been the major anthologies compiled in the late 3rd/9th and 4th/10th centuries:

a. Ibn ᶜAbd Rabbihi (d. 328/940), *al-ᶜIqd al-farīd*, ed. Aḥmad Amīn et al. (8 vols., 1947–53).

b. Muḥammad b. Yazīd al-Mubarrad (d. 284/898), *al-Kāmil* (ed. William Wright, 2 vols., 1864–92).

c. Abū al-Faraj al-Iṣfahānī (d. 356/967), *Kitāb al-aghānī* (Bulaq ed., 20 vols., 1284–85/1867–69; vol. 21, ed. R. Brünnow, 1888; Cairo ed., 24 vols., 1929–in progress). The Cairo edition is far superior to the old Bulaq version but retains its pagination in the margins, thus allowing readers to use the excellent indices prepared by Ignazio Guidi (1895–1900).

A work just beginning to reveal its value for the Abbasid Revolution is the *Sharḥ nahj al-balāgha* of Ibn Abī al-Ḥadīd (see above, p. 71). To some degree these anthologies simply provide alternative versions of *akhbār* known to us from the chronicles, but they also contain significant texts which have otherwise disappeared. A note of caution: the anthologists selected texts because of their eloquence and grammatical interest, not their historical veracity, and since these items occur in a non-historical context, it is even more difficult than usual to decide what they "really" mean and how to use them.

As we shall see shortly, tribal conflicts (or at least conflicts so labeled) played a critical role in bringing about a revolutionary situation. The extensive genealogical literature produced during the 3rd/9th century can be of real value in disentangling the protagonists in these struggles. Beyond allowing us to determine which tribe or clan stood on which side of a given conflict, accurate genealogical data may yield vital clues as to the material interests and ideological issues at stake. The most famous compilation of this kind is the *Jamharat al-nasab* of Hishām b. Muḥammad al-Kalbī (d. 206/821)—a work most conveniently used through the detailed analysis of Werner Caskel, *Ǧamharat an-Nasab. Das genealogische Werk des Hišām ibn Muḥammad al-Kalbī* (2 vols., 1966). Vol. I contains a study of the text and its author, along with 334 genealogical tables (prepared by Gert Strenziok) abstracted from Ibn al-Kalbī's prose; the bulk of Vol. II is an index of every personal name in these tables, with capsule biographical data and detailed references to the sources for each entry. A more traditional but very convenient reference tool is ʿUmar Riḍā Kaḥḥāla, *Muʿjam qabāʾil al-ʿArab al-qadīma wa'l-ḥadītha* (5 vols., 1368–1395/1949–1975). As the name suggests, this is an alphabetically arranged dictionary of tribes and tribal sections; each entry contains concise genealogical data and references to a considerable array of Arabic sources.

At this point a few general comments seem in order. Our sources for the Abbasid Revolution are plainly as partisan and tendentious as any body of texts could be. We have to take it for granted that every statement reflects a hidden agenda, that it is as much a commentary on current events as on the Revolution per se. Moreover, since almost all accounts of these events took their present form and context about a century after the Revolution, we must be aware of at least three levels of meaning in them: (1) their data, authentic or otherwise, about the event being described; (2) the intention or program of an account's original authors; (3) the secondary intention of the final compiler.

Because Arabic historical writing was already well-launched at the time of the Abbasid Revolution, we should not expect the primitive narratives concerning this event to be so heavily reshaped as those which describe the Conquests and the Early Caliphate may have been. Even so, every effort must be made to locate parallel versions of each *khabar* and to account for even slight differences among them. This is no mere philological exercise; rather, it is a matter of discovering the religio-political dialogue in which the narrator of a given account was engaged. Of course a story may be intensely partisan in tone and intention and still be factually accurate, but if we fail to grasp the various messages which this story carried for contemporary readers, then we will miss important dimensions of the event which it recounts. Such a close reading of the texts is seldom encountered in the literature on the Abbasid Revolution, but some idea of the possibilities can be gained from two recent monographs. Tilman Nagel, in *Untersuchungen zur Entstehung des abbasidischen Kalifates* (1972), was the first to try to reconstruct the purpose and original milieu of the historical narratives dealing with the Abbasid movement. On the methodological level, Nagel's performance remains astute and perceptive, though his conclusions now require rethinking in light of the *Akhbār al-dawla al-ʿabbāsiyya*, which was not available to him. Jacob Lassner's *Islamic Revolution and Historical Memory* (1986) revisits this material and comes away with even more agnostic conclusions. He argues that our historical record is essentially the residue of a complex Abbasid propaganda campaign that began during the movement's clandestine phase, and then was subjected to a constant retouching as the new regime had to speak to changing audiences and defend itself against shifting challenges to its legitimacy. The *akhbār* produced by this campaign are not simply invented; they are based on real people and real events, but these things are so transformed by the processes of polemic and debate that analysis can no longer recover the reality imbedded within the texts. Lassner has been accused of being over-subtle, and the charge is not without merit—he is a very frustrating scholar to read. But nowhere else can one gain so exact a sense of how these texts were produced and used and transmuted into new forms.

C. Analyses and Interpretations

The basic questionnaire which has guided the study of the Abbasid Revolution for almost the last century was first proposed in two works by the Dutch Orientalist Gerlof van Vloten: (1) *De Opkomst der Abbasiden in Chorasan* (1890); (2) "Recherches sur la domination arabe, le chiitisme, et les croyances messianiques sous le Khalifat des Omayades" (1894). Like many youthful works, these assert their conclusions with far more force and confidence than the evidence really warrants, and of course by now van Vloten's documentation is hopelessly obsolete. Nevertheless, both still merit study, both because of the clarity with which the author states his theses, and because these theses have remained tremendously influential even for authors who have exerted every effort to discard them. Moreover, if van Vloten did not put the puzzle together in a way which seems satisfactory to us now, he did discover the pieces which were needed to solve it.

In *Der Opkomst der Abbasiden*, van Vloten focuses on three aspects of the Revolution: (1) the alleged designation by ᶜAlī's grandson Abū Hāshim of his cousin Muḥammad b. ᶜAlī (a grandson of the Prophet's uncle al-ᶜAbbās) to succeed him as chief of the Hāshimiyya sect; (2) the reorganization of the sect under Muḥammad b. ᶜAlī and its underground agitation in Khurasan over a period of three decades; (3) the uprising in that province led by Abū Muslim, which finally brought down the Umayyads. In "Recherches sur la domination arabe," the author focuses on the social and ideological context within which the Revolution took place. The Abbasid triumph, he says, is to be explained by three things: "(1) the inveterate hatred of a subject population for its foreign oppressors; (2) Shiᶜism—i.e., the cult of the descendants of the family of the Prophet; (3) the expectation of a liberator or messiah." ("Recherches," 2)

Van Vloten's account is more nuanced than is often supposed. For example, he does not posit a crude racial interpretation of the revolt in Khurasan, but a socio-political one: it was less a question of Persians against Arabs than of oppressed subjects (mostly Iranian) against the ruling class (mostly Arab). Likewise, although he stresses the movement's use of messianic themes and symbols and links these to a specifically "non-Arab" extremist Shiᶜism, he recognizes that the Abbasids also had to appeal to the moderate and sober Shiᶜism of Khurasan, which looked to the House of the Prophet not for a Savior but simply for a just ruler. As with many scholars, van Vloten's real interpretation is to be located in the texture of his argument rather than in a few sweeping and enthusiastic generalizations.

If van Vloten was the pioneer in this subject, the imam is without doubt Julius Wellhausen. *Das arabische Reich und sein Sturz* (1902; trans. M. G. Weir as *The Arab Kingdom and Its Fall*, 1927) remains even after ninety years one of the sovereign achievements of Western Orientalism. Wellhausen was the first to grasp the whole socio-political milieu within which the Abbasid Revolution occurred, and he reconstructed this milieu with a richness of detail never since attained. Here we find many topics slighted by van Vloten: the bloody internecine strife within the Umayyad dynasty after the death of Hishām (125/743) and the devastating political effects of this feud throughout the Empire; the whole array of Kharijite as well as Shiᶜite revolts which broke out in Iraq and Mesopotamia during the 740s; the complex politics of the Arab armies in Khurasan in the 730s and 740s; the acute discontents not only of the

Iranian peasants in that province but also of the half-assimilated Arab tribesmen who had settled there.

It is true that Wellhausen still sees the Abbasid Revolution as fundamentally an Iranian uprising at the beginning, but he is far less categorical than his predecessor. As he presents it, the *daʿwa* in Khurasan was largely headed by Arabs (mainly drawn from clans which had settled in Marv in the late 1st/7th century). When Abū Muslim (himself a *mawlā*) proclaimed the rebellion in 129/747, "the majority of his adherents consisted of Iranian peasants and of the Mawālī of the villages of Marw, but there were Arabs among them also, who mostly occupied leading positions." (*Arab Kingdom*, 532.) He stresses that many groups, not merely Iranian converts, had reason to feel disgusted with Umayyad rule by the late 740s. Religion was the glue that held this motley coalition together—not some extravagant heresy, but a sober, catholic orientation which sought just government and the political equality of all Muslims.

So imposing was Wellhausen's achievement that almost nothing else was done on the subject for the next forty years. (This is a regrettably common pattern in Islamic studies; major syntheses are too often taken not as a challenge but as established doctrine.) Only in the 1940s do we begin to find a new generation of scholars willing to re-examine the issues he had raised. However, the sporadic essays of that decade (by Dennett, Moscati, Lewis, and Frye) have developed since 1960 into what passes in the Islamic field for a flood of publications. As proposed in the opening section of this chapter, these can be evaluated most effectively by seeing what they contribute to the solution of a series of general problems:

1. Was the Abbasid Revolution really a revolution?
2. What groups were the Abbasids able to recruit to their cause?
3. What was the ideology of the Abbasid *daʿwa*?
4. What were the links between the Abbasid *daʿwa* and the other religio-political movements of the period?
5. How were the Abbasids able to organize their adherents into an effective political movement and military force?
6. How can we explain the Umayyad failure to suppress this movement?

Van Vloten and Wellhausen had no doubt that the Abbasids did usher in a revolution: "The Abbasids called their government the 'dawla'— i.e., the new era. The revolution effected at this time was indeed prodigious." (*Arab Kingdom*, 556.) But a recent student of these events is not so sure. "The Abbasids came," he says, "the millenium did not." (Lassner, *Shaping of Abbasid Rule*, 112.) Any meaningful decision on this issue requires a solid knowledge of both late Umayyad and early Abbasid politics and society. The former we have to some degree; the latter, until very recently, has been almost a blank.

For Khurasan and Transoxiana under the Umayyads, Wellhausen's work has been brought up to date in M. A. Shaban, *The Abbasid Revolution* (1970), which is really a study of the Arab tribes in Khurasan from the first campaigns there in the 650s down to the Abbasid revolt. Shaban's account is generally clearer and more tightly argued than Wellhausen's, but his interpretation differs from his predecessor's far less than he believes. Moreover, some of his more daring assertions seem very weakly supported by the sources. The same reservations apply, but to an even higher degree, to his general survey, *Islamic History, a New Interpretation: I, A.D. 600–750* (1971). Wellhausen and Shaban should be compared with an early but still valuable work by H.A.R. Gibb, *The Arab Conquests in Central Asia* (1923); and the classic synthesis of W. Barthold, *Turkestan down to the Mongol Invasion* (orig. Russian ed., 1902; 3rd rev. English ed., 1968), which contains a few dense but telling pages (180–197) on 2nd/8th–century Khurasan and the Revolution. On Syria and Mesopotamia under the later Umayyads, see below, pp. 126–127.

As to the consequences of the Abbasid seizure of power, these have only begun to be studied. Wellhausen's comments on this subject are hasty and represent not his own research but the received Orientalist doctrine of his day. A concise initial orientation to the new dynasty and its policies can be obtained in several places:

a. B. Lewis, "Abbasids," *EI*², I, 15–23.

b. H.A.R. Gibb, "Government and Islam under the Early Abbasids," in *L'Elaboration de l'Islam* (1961), 115–127.

c. Dominique Sourdel, "The Abbasid Caliphate," *Cambridge History of Islam*, (1970), I, 104–139.

d. Roy Mottahedeh, "The Abbasid Caliphate in Iran," *Cambridge History of Iran*, IV (1975), 57–89.

In view of the dynasty's spectacular beginnings, book-length surveys are surprisingly scarce. An intelligent account focusing on questions of power and administration can be found in Hugh Kennedy, *The Early Abbasid Caliphate: a Political History* (1981), which goes down to the reign of al-Maʾmūn (198–218/813–833). A much fuller account of the first three decades of Abbasid rule is given in Farouk Omar, *The Abbasid Caliphate, 132/750–170/786*; the Arabic version, *al-ʿAbbāsiyyūn al-awāʾil* (2 vols., 1970–73), has some additional materials and is much more attractively produced. Full-scale histories of the whole Abbasid period down to 656/1258 exist only in Arabic. Shākir Muṣṭafā, *Dawlat Banī al-ʿAbbās* (2 vols., 1973) is a comprehensive political-administrative history which tries also to cover the "international relations" of the period. The old survey by ʿAbd al-ʿAzīz al-Dūrī, *al-ʿAṣr al-ʿabbāsī al-awwal* (1945), still gives an essentially sound narrative of political events. (A word of warning: M. A. Shaban, *Islamic History, a New Interpretation: II, A.D. 750–1050* (1976) is full of dogmatic but ill-documented assertions; it is more useful as a challenge to complacency than as an interpretation in its own right.)

Even when we turn from general surveys to monographic studies, the literature remains rather thin; the whole issue of the extent to which the observable changes in society, politics, and culture in the later 2nd/8th century can be attributed to the Abbasid Revolution remains very much in dispute. To begin with, there is no comprehensive study of the seminal reign of Abū Jaʿfar al-Manṣūr (136–158/754–775), who undertook the task of transmuting the Abbasid revolutionary apparatus into a state. Moshe Sharon is said to have such a study in preparation, and meantime the essays collected in Lassner, *The Shaping of Abbasid Rule*, illuminate many difficult issues. The political ideas ascribed to al-Mansur are presented in Albert Dietrich, "Das politische Testament des zweiten abbasidischen Kalifen al-Manṣūr," *Islam*, xxx (1952), 133–165. Al-Mahdī (158–169/775–785) has received somewhat more attention; see two works by Sabatino Moscati: (a) "Studi storici sul califfato di al-Mahdī," *Orientalia*, xiv (1945), 300–354; (b) "Nuovi studi storici sul califfato di al-Mahdī," *Orientalia*, xv (1946), 155–179. Finally, the official ideology of the new regime is outlined in a widely cited paper by Bernard Lewis, "The Regnal Titles of the First Abbasid Caliphs," *Dr. Zakir Husayn Presentation Volume* (1968), 13–22.

The issue at stake in all this is the degree to which the early Abbasid caliphs changed the rules of politics, how far they altered the criteria for regular, effective participation in the decision-making process. Or, since both the Umayyads and the Abbasids were autocratic regimes, we can put the issue more concretely: whom did the early Abbasid caliphs choose as their servants, what powers did they give them, and to what extent did these things differ from Umayyad practice?

Administrative history can be an excellent way of approaching such problems. The best starting point is Dominique Sourdel, *Le vizirat abbaside* (2 vols., 1959–60), who demonstrates quite conclusively that the early decades of Abbasid rule saw much less "Persianization" and "bureaucratization" than was once supposed. The royal household, albeit much swollen, continued to be the chief engine of government as it had been under the Umayyads. We shall need many further studies, however, before we understand in any precise way how the early Abbasids recruited and organized their household.

Relations between the central government and the provinces are central to any understanding of what was "new" in the Abbasid regime. This question has only begun to be studied, though there are useful statements in some of the works cited above. For Ifriqiya (modern Tunisia) one can consult the initial chapters in Mohammed Talbi, *L'Émirat aghlabide, 184–296/800–909*, (1966). Egypt, Syria, and the Jazira in the late 2nd/8th century have been almost entirely neglected, but Iran is better served—not surprisingly in view of Khurasan's crucial role in the Revolution. On a general level, Barthold's *Turkestan down to the Mongol Invasion* (pp. 197–207) will always repay close study; and Bertold Spuler, *Iran in frühislamischer Zeit* (1952), has gathered together, though not really analyzed, a vast amount of material. Abbasid government in Iran down to the 830s was constantly troubled by religiously inspired revolts. These have been covered in G. H. Sadighi, *Les mouvements religieux iraniens du iie et iiie siècle de l'Hégire* (1938), which remains very useful though badly dated by its nationalistic perspective. Many standard notions about religio-political ferment in early Abbasid Khurasan have been challenged in Elton Daniel, *The Political and Social History of Khurasan under Abbasid Rule, 747–820* (1979), who rejects both "Iranian nationalism" and "heresy" as concepts possessing any explanatory power. Rather, the revolts of the late 2nd/8th century "typically represented the efforts of peasant communities to resist subjugation by the new 'Muslim,' Arabo-Iranian, urban elite in Khurasan" (p. 126). One might have qualms about two aspects of Daniel's intelligent and well-documented study: (1) his use of a rather vague concept of feudalism to analyze Khurasani society; (2) his tendency to look for consensus in his sources rather than to subject them to a rigorous criticism.

These works all deal primarily with politics, administration, and ideology. Concerning the impact of the Abbasid Revolution on the less visible but probably more durable (or intractable) facts of social structure and economic life, only a few lines of inquiry have been proposed. See Claude Cahen, "Fiscalité, propriété, antagonismes sociaux en Haute-Mésopotamie au temps des premiers Abbasides, d'après Denys de Tell-Mahré," *Arabica*, i (1954), 136–152; and Oleg Grabar, "Umayyad 'Palace' and Abbasid 'Revolution'," *SI*, xviii (1963), 5–18.

The second major question on our agenda—viz., what groups did the Abbasids try to recruit to their cause—brings us back to the late Umayyad period. Van Vloten, as we have seen, argued for an economic cleavage (conqueror vs. conquered) which coincided with and was reinforced by an ethnic division (Arab vs. Iranian). Wellhausen tended to accept this, but he also saw the Abbasids exploiting a purely political conflict among the Arabs of Khurasan which pitted the tribal confederation of Muḍar (aligned with the Umayyad regime) against a Yemen-Rabīʿa coalition (which felt itself unjustly subordinated to the former). Wellhausen in fact lays great stress on such tribal conflicts, but he seems at a loss to account for them in any rational way; for him they are atavistic vestiges of the Jāhiliyya.

Because Wellhausen's analysis is complex and not always clearly articulated, he has been the principal target of revisionists. Here we may distinguish two strands: one insists that the Abbasid *daʿwa* was aimed almost exclusively at dissident Arab factions, while the other argues that it was a mass movement of all the groups in Khurasan, however defined, which felt themselves aggrieved by the Umayyad regime and the native Iranian aristocracy which worked in league with it. The latter is the thesis of Elton Daniel (*Khurasan under Abbasid Rule*). He argues that efforts to identify the ethnic identity of the Revolution's leaders are doomed to failure in view of the character of our sources. In addition, he is impressed by evidence of widespread revolt throughout Khurasan and by the continuing turbulence of the province even after the Abbasids had seized power. Daniel's interpretation may reflect in part a reluctance to commit himself, but it also shows a laudable desire not to force his unruly evidence into an over-simple interpretive schema. Likewise, his lonely effort to define a "class basis" for the Revolution merits further examination.

The "Arabist" interpretation of the Revolution seems to have first been adumbrated in two articles by Richard Frye: (a) "The Role of Abū Muslim in the Abbasid Revolt," *MW*, xxxvii (1947), 28–38; (b) "The Abbasid Conspiracy and Modern Revolutionary Theory," *Indo-Iranica*, v (1952–53), 9–14. But this approach was only fully elaborated in Farouk Omar, *The Abbasid Caliphate, 132/750—170/786* (1969), and *Ṭabīʿat al-daʿwa al-ʿabbāsiyya* (1970). Almost simultaneously it was presented in a somewhat different context by M. A. Shaban, *The Abbasid Revolution* (1970) and *Islamic History, I* (1971). For both scholars, the *daʿwa* in Khurasan was organized and led by Arabs, and from the first was aimed chiefly at the Arabs there, both long-time settlers and active troops. Iranian *mawālī* were of course not excluded, but they simply followed the lead of their Arab patrons, and for this very reason many *mawālī* supported the pro-Umayyad factions among the Arabs. To this basic framework Shaban adds two elements: (1) the Arab factions in Khurasan were not, despite their names, atavistic tribal groupings, but rather rational political parties with conflicting programs; (2) though the Abbasid movement was essentially "Arab," it strove to realize a catholic and assimilationist program, the legal and political equality of all Believers within the universal Community of Islam. Both Omar and Shaban seem to use their evidence rather selectively, and Shaban's assertive dogmatism is not so well-founded as he imagines. Even so, they do underline aspects of the Abbasid Revolution which had been slighted (though not ignored) in earlier accounts.

An interpretation which builds on Wellhausen and Omar, but reshapes their conclusions into the clearest synthesis to date, is Moshe Sharon, *Black Banners from the East* (1983). His argument runs essentially as follows. During the long clandestine phase, Abbasid propagandists aimed at the broadest possible recruitment: villagers and townsmen, Arabs and Iranian *mawālī*, Muḍar and Yemeni tribesmen, settlers and active-duty soldiers. However, when Abū Muslim proclaimed open rebellion in 129/747, he had to mobilize massive support among the regular Arab armies in Khurasan, since only these soldiers could possibly hold their own against Umayyad forces. This he achieved by appealing to the disaffected leaders of the Yemen tribal confederation. As a result the Abbasid revolutionary army was overwhelmingly Arab in command and membership. However, the new army was organized on a non-tribal basis, and this organizational structure would ultimately have genuinely revolutionary consequences for military administration and recruitment in the Abbasid state. On the other hand, these consequences made themselves felt only in the decades following the establishment of the new regime. Sharon is persuasive and his reconstruction of Abbasid recruitment strategies has been widely accepted; for precisely this reason, the reader needs to take account of two severe and exceptionally intelligent reviews: by Patricia Crone, in *BSOAS*, l (1987), 134–136; and by Elton Daniel, in *IJMES*, xxi (1989), 578–583.

However disaffected one or another group in Khurasan may have been, it was not self-evident either that the Umayyads should be overthrown or that the obscure Abbasid claimants should replace them. Clearly there had to be an ideology and program capable of persuading the dissidents to join the Abbasid cause. On this matter the scholarly literature seems initially to present a broad consensus, but a closer reading shows much vagueness and uncertainty. The problem has been complicated by two things. First, Abbasid propagandists were extremely discreet and evasive in their public statements, so that until very recently (with the discovery of the *Akhbār al-dawla al-ʿabbāsiyya*) it was impossible to be sure what the official line really was. Second, the Abbasid movement grew up within a broader Shiʿite milieu, some elements of which were clearly doctrinal extremists (*ghulāt*), and the Abbasids in fact claimed to be the direct spiritual heirs of one of these extremist groups, the Hāshimiyya.

Van Vloten and Wellhausen established the links of the Abbasid *daʿwa* with Shiʿism. Likewise, both scholars (but especially the latter) noted that the actual content of the Abbasid message seems to have been far more sober than one might suppose in view of the movement's Hāshimiyya ancestry. But was this sobriety in reality deliberate vagueness—the exploiting of powerful symbolic formulas which would give no offense to theological moderates who wanted only to be rid of the Umayyads, but at the same time would allow free rein to the imagination of extremists? Another possibility, hinted at by some scholars but still not fully explored, is that Abbasid propaganda was indeed "extremist" down to the embarrassing affair of their agent Khidāsh in 118/736 and only took a turn towards moderation after the revival of active propaganda in Khurasan in the early 740s.

The most intense controversy in this regard has swirled around the figure of that consummate man of mystery, Abū Muslim. In his influential *EI*[1] article (i, 101–2), Barthold judged him to have preached a syncretic religion, blending elements of ancient Iranian beliefs with Islam. R. N. Frye, "The Role of Abū Muslim" (cited above, p. 122) rejected this, though without fully stating his reasons. It was left to Sabatino Moscati, "Studi su Abū Muslim, II: Propaganda e politica religiosa di Abū Muslim," *Acc. Lincei, Rend. Morali*, ser. viii, vol. 4 (1949), 474–495, to show that there was no real basis for Barthold's portrayal.

Abū Muslim continued to be a powerful presence after the Abbasid seizure of power, and even after his own death. His political dealings with the Abbasid court are examined in several studies:

a. S. Moscati, "Studi su Abū Muslim, I; Abū Muslim e gli Abbasidi"; III, "La fine di Abū Muslim." *Acc. Lincei, Rend. Mor.*, ser. viii, vol. 4 (1949), 323–335; ser. viii, vol. 5 (1950), 89–105.

b. J. Lassner, *The Shaping of Abbasid Rule*, 59–68.

c. E. Daniel, *Khurasan under Abbasid Rule*, 100–124.

After his death in 137/755, Abū Muslim became an almost mythical figure in Khurasan and Transoxiana, and as such the inspiration for a long series of revolts there; see Irène Mélikoff, *Abū Muslim, le porte-hache de Khorassan* (1962).

The general problem of the connection between the Abbasid *daʿwa* and early 2nd/8th-century Shiʿism was carefully explored in Claude Cahen, "Points de vue sur la 'Révolution abbaside'," *Revue Historique* (1963), 295–338. Cahen's thesis is that the Abbasid *daʿwa* was an authentic Shiʿite movement as that term was understood down through the 130s/750s, and their propaganda represented a kind of minimum consensus of Shiʿite views. In this period, he argues, Shiʿism was only an orientation, not an organized sect. As such, it demanded three things: (1) rule by an appropriate member of the House of the Prophet (*ahl al-bayt*)—still a vague concept which could include the descendants of al-ʿAbbās as well as ʿAlī; (2) government in accordance with the Qur'ān and Sunna; (3) vengeance for the martyrs of the House of the Prophet. Cahen's thesis was refined by Tilman Nagel, *Entstehung des abbasidischen Kalifates* (cited above, p. 116), who gives a precise and sophisticated discussion of the origins and changing levels of meaning of the various slogans used by Abbasid propagandists.

Cahen's approach has held up well overall, but the work of Lassner and Sharon has modified it in significant ways. Their conclusions are conveniently summarized in Lassner, "The ʿAbbāsid *Dawla*: An Essay on the Concept of Revolution in Early Islam," in Clover and Humphreys, *Tradition and Innovation*, 247–270. The convoluted trail of Abbasid ideology and propaganda is explored in much greater detail, and with more tentative results, in the same author's *Islamic Revolution and Historical Memory*. Finally, in *Black Banners from the East*, Sharon examines these issues in their political context. Lassner and Sharon make two main points: (1) the Abbasid program—correctly outlined by Cahen—was not at all vague in nature, but a messianic call for a restoration of the original Community in Medina; (2) the Abbasids exploited pro-Alid feelings, carefully concealing their own identity and ambitions until the actual proclamation of Abū al-ʿAbbās as caliph in 132/749. They began to appeal to a broad concept of the House of the Prophet only a quarter-century after they had seized the caliphate, in a deliberate ideological shift intended to distance them from their beginnings as the chiefs of an extremist sect. Within their innermost circle of followers, at least, they had previously based their claims strictly on the testament of Abū Hāshim.

Abū Hāshim b. Muḥammad b. al-Ḥanafiyya (d. 98/716) was a grandson of ʿAlī b. Abī Ṭālib through a woman from the tribe of Ḥanīfa; he was also the leader of one of the most intriguing proto-Shiʿite groups, the Kaysāniyya-Hāshimiyya. His alleged testament, by which he bequeathed the leadership of his movement to the Abbasids, has been a perpetual focus of scholarly controversy. Sabatino Moscati, "Il testamento di Abū Hāshim," *RSO*, xxvii (1952), 28–46, reviewed all the texts then available and tried to demonstrate its authenticity. Nagel (*Entstehung des abbasidischen Kalifates*) is equally convinced that it is spurious, a device used by the Abbasids to seize control of the previously autonomous revolutionary apparatus in Khurasan. Nagel's argument is important and revealing, but Sharon, using the best documentation so far, seems able to confirm Moscati's conclusions.

Abū Hāshim's sect had its origins not in pure theological speculation but in political violence—sc., the messianic revolt led by Mukhtār b. Abī ʿUbayd in Kufa during the years 66–67/685–687. Mukhtār's movement was short-lived but spectacular; it is hardly surprising that it has so captured the imagination of modern scholarship. And drama aside, it certainly foreshadows many of the central issues of the Abbasid Revolution. The classic analysis of both the political and religious dimensions of this revolt was given by Julius Wellhausen in *Die religiös-politischen Oppositionsparteien im alten Islam* (1901; trans. by R. C. Ostle and S. M. Walzer as *The Religio-Political Factions in Early Islam*, 1975). Wellhausen's monograph is still indispensable, but it should be supplemented by Gernot Rotter, *Die Umayyaden und der zweite Būrgerkrieg (680–692)* (1982), a meticulous survey of this crucial episode in Islamic history Finally, Hichem Djaït throws much light on the urban setting in which Mukhtār's revolt occurred in *Al-Kūfa: Naissance de la ville islamique* (1986)—in spite of its name, no narrowly focused monograph, but rather a wide-ranging, sometimes speculative essay on the nature and origins of early Islamic urbanism.

The broad Shiʿite milieu within which the Abbasids operated can be approached through several studies. The best place to begin is the concise but reliable and wide-ranging survey of Wilferd Madelung, *Religious trends in Early Islamic Iran* (1988). W. M. Watt, *The Formative Period of Islamic Thought* (1973), is still useful, though it shows its age at certain points. Watt's documentation is solid and he poses the crucial problems quite effectively, but he sometimes has a way of side-stepping solutions to them. A very different but equally comprehensive approach can be found in Henri Laoust, *Les schismes dans l'Islam* (1965). A Shiʿite perspective, informed by traditional doctrine but scholarly in tone, is given by S.H.M. Jafri, *The Origins and Early Development of Shīʿa Islam* (1979). The specific question of Shiʿism's development into a coherent sect is dealt with in S. Moscati, "Per una storia dell'antica Šīʿa," *RSO*, xxx (1955), 261–267; and M.G.S. Hodgson, "How Did the Early Shīʿa Become Sectarian?" *JAOS*, lxxv (1955), 1–13. On the

Hāshimiyya—the ancestor of the Abbasid movement—and its origins, see two studies by Wadad al-Qadi: (a) "The Development of the Term '*Ghulāt*' in Muslim Literature with Special Reference to the Kaysāniyya," *Akten, VII Kong. Arabistik* (1974); (b) *al-Kaysāniyya fī al-ta'rīkh wa'l-adab* (1974).

A revolutionary movement cannot succeed merely because of effective propaganda directed at powerful and disaffected groups. Recall that by 129/747 the Umayyads had been facing major crises and rebellions almost throughout their ninety years in power, and they had mastered them all. Nor was the present caliph, Marwān II, in any way inferior to his predecessors in intelligence, energy, or experience. The capacity of the Abbasid rebels to defeat such a formidable opponent in a long series of pitched battles obviously speaks well for their political and military organization. At the same time, we must ask why the Umayyads were unable to act with their usual decisiveness, why their best generals (including Marwān himself) were defeated one after another. In short, we are dealing here not only with a triumphant revolution but with a state in collapse; both sides of the coin are necessary for an adequate account of the Abbasids' success.

On the internal organization of the Abbasid movement, the best-documented account is Sharon's. Farouk Omar has had access to almost the same set of sources and uses them effectively, but in general he seems less adept than Sharon is resolving their many gaps and contradictions. Nor should Nagel's account be overlooked, for he brings out two important issues: (1) at what point did the Abbasids begin to assert effective control over the underground revolutionary movement in Khurasan; (2) did the Khurasani army raised by Abū Muslim owe its astonishing successes to ideological commitment or to solid administration and discipline?

As to the abrupt and unexpected collapse of Umayyad power after 129/747, the standard account is still that of Wellhausen, who links it to the exhausting civil wars in Syria among various Umayyad pretenders in 126/744, and to the constant Shiʿite and Kharijite uprisings in Iraq and Mesopotamia throughout the 740s. This chaos in the Umayyad heartland was reflected in Khurasan, so that no sustained response to the Abbasid uprising could be made until the latter was already solidly organized. Wellhausen's very detailed though often confusing account of the last decades of Umayyad rule can be supplemented and clarified by a number of more specialized studies. Umayyad authority was already under serious challenge in the later years of Hishām (105–125/724–743) and collapsed almost immediately upon his death. His reign is studied in a monograph by Francesco Gabrieli, "Il califfato di Hishām," *Mémoires de la Société Archéologique d'Alexandrie*, vii/2 (1935). On his able but doomed successor Marwān II (127–132/744–750), consult the unpublished Ph.D. dissertation of D. C. Dennett, "Marwān ibn Muḥammad: the Passing of the Umayyad Caliphate" (Harvard, 1939). In his concern for the Umayyad civil war in Syria and the Jazira, Dennett has unfortunately had few successors.

Nagel does have a useful chapter on this issue, which makes use of the newly discovered chronicle of Khalīfa b. Khayyāṭ. Undoubtedly it would be extremely useful to analyze the data given in al-Azdī's *Ta'rīkh al-Mawṣil* (which was not available to Wellhausen or Dennett) to see whether this text might warrant a restudy of the Jazira during the last decade of Umayyad power.

In the end, how adequate an understanding of the Abbasid Revolution can we obtain from the findings of modern scholarship? As regards the Revolution per se—i.e., its ideology and propaganda, its internal organization, its recruitment of dissident individuals and groups, the sequence of events which brought it to power—we probably know as much as we ever shall. Definitive answers to many of these problems have not been given and perhaps cannot be, but at least we know the range of plausible solutions. All this speaks very highly of the persuasiveness and durability of the basic interpretive framework devised by van Vloten and Wellhausen. As to the social milieu within which the Revolution occurred, something has been done, but clearly there is a long way to go. We still have no exact picture of the social, economic, and religious discontents in Khurasan which the Abbasids were able to mobilize. Perhaps a comparative study of other "messianic" outbursts against established authority in medieval Islam would suggest some productive lines of inquiry in this regard. Finally, we return to our initial problem—was the Abbasid seizure of power truly a revolution? An answer to this question cannot be given until we have an integrated interpretation of Islamic society (especially in Iraq and Iran) in the half-century between 725 and 775. Such an interpretation, in turn, must wait upon monographic studies of administration, land tenure, urban development, political recruitment and participation during this period. These will surely be slow in coming, but studies of this kind will provide the most challenging field of investigation during the coming years.

Chapter Five

BAYHAQĪ AND IBN TAGHRĪBIRDĪ

THE ART OF NARRATIVE IN ISLAMIC HISTORICAL WRITING DURING THE MIDDLE PERIODS

> These stories may be far from history, where one usually reads that a certain king sent a certain general to such and such a war, and that on such and such a day they made war or peace, and that this one defeated that one or that one this one, and then proceeded somewhere. But I write what is worthy to be recorded.
>
> (Abū al-Faḍl Bayhaqī, *Taʾrīkh-i Masʿūdī*)

IN AMERICAN and modern European history the study of politics is based on an analysis of the direct traces of political action—the correspondence and diaries of participants, official reports, records of parliamentary debates, etc. These materials are of course shot through with errors, falsehoods, partisanship, and personal rancor. Nevertheless, they are both part and product of the political process, and for that reason they permit us to construct an independent description of it. That is, with such materials we are in a position to select, according to our own criteria, the set of events which seems most significant to us, to link these events together in patterns of sequence and causation, and to propose a wide range of interpretive schemas quite separate from the concerns and values of participants and contemporaries.

For the political history of medieval Islam, however, such an independent description is not possible. Down at least to 1500 (and in many regions much later than that) our knowledge of political affairs must be derived almost exclusively from narrative texts—i.e., from retrospective literary accounts which were composed expressly to describe and interpret events for those who had not witnessed them. These narrative accounts—usually entitled "*taʾrīkh*" (chronicle) or "*akhbār*" (reports)—undoubtedly have many merits, and taken as a whole far surpass the the average standard of the historical writing done in Latin Europe at least until the fifteenth century. Many Muslim historians indicate, at least in a general fashion, the sources for their statements, and the more scrupulous authors take care to give alternative versions of events where these sources diverge. Those who had regular access to official documents give summaries or even verbatim transcripts of many of them. But even granting all this, we must remember that these texts are not neutral repositories of information but consciously shaped literary structures. Their authors have chosen for us the events to be recounted, their sequence and causal connections with one another, and the cultural significance which they bear. All this means that our basic political data, however full and accurate it may be, exists only in and through interpretive schemas which others have constructed to suit their own needs and tastes.

Can we devise any reliable strategies through which the information in these texts can be disengaged from its original matrix and turned to our purposes? Bound as we are to such sources, to what extent can we achieve an independent description of events? Can we in fact escape the role of critic and commentator—a role in which we can indeed elucidate the difficulties and underlying patterns of our texts, but are ultimately confined within the boundaries which they have established?

A comparative study of two dynastic chronicles, one composed in Afghanistan in the 5th/11th century, the other in Egypt in the 9th/15th, can suggest ways of addressing such issues. These texts can only be superficially intelligible, however, unless they are read in the broad context of Middle Period historiography—i.e., that written between the collapse of caliphal power in 334/945 and the rise of the Ottoman and Safavid states around 900/1500. An overview of this literature is thus the first step in our analysis.

A. The Character of Islamic Historical Writing in the Middle Periods

The historiography of the Middle Periods of course stems directly from that of the 3rd/9th and early 4th/10th centuries. Far from continuing established forms and subject matter, however, it strikes out in a number of new directions.

First of all, the new historiography is written in two languages (Arabic and Persian) instead of one only. Many genres of history are found in both languages, but we should not think of the difference between the two as merely linguistic. To a great extent each language enshrines a specific cultural tradition almost from the beginning. Persian historians draw far more heavily than their Arabic-writing counterparts on the themes of neo-Sassanian culture, not only for rhetorical ornament or exemplary tales, but to form the underlying conceptual paradigms and narrative patterns of their accounts. Likewise, the better Persian writers seem more interested in contriving a fully integrated narrative than do their Arabic counterparts, at least on the surface level. That is, rather than presenting a series of discrete events, they portray (to follow Aristotle's language) a single action, a unified story leading up to a clear dramatic resolution. We might attribute this dramatic coherence to an effort by Persian historians to apply the plot-lines and characterizations which they found in the epic poetry of Firdawsī (d. 411/1020) and his successors to the events and persons which filled their own writings, but at present such statements can only be speculation.

The Persian and Arabic traditions also differ in their approach to chronology. The Arabic historians in general try to be as precise as possible, giving the day of the week as well as the year and day of the month. Their concern for chronological exactitude is also exhibited in their wide use of an annalistic framework. Persian historians, in contrast, are often infuriatingly vague even about the year, let alone smaller units of time. In the post-Mongol period (7th/13th century and later), they sometimes use a Türkmen framework which reflects the alternation between summer and winter pasture (*yaylaq-qıshlaq*), and sometimes allude to the Chinese "animal" calendar—but to relate either of these to the Hijri calendar is a frustrating chore. Again, the contrasting approaches to chronology of the two traditions might be linked to their disparate narrative styles—the integrated story versus the sequence of discrete events.

The "new" historiography (both Arabic and Persian) also involves a redirection of subject matter. In general, historians from the mid-4th/10th century on were no longer concerned to collect new materials for the first two and a half centuries of Islamic history—down roughly to the reign of the caliph al-Mutawakkil (232–247/847–861). As noted above (p. 72), the crucial issue confronting historians of the 3rd/9th century had been the legitimacy of Abbasid rule, and more broadly, the validity of the religious and political evolution of the whole Islamic community. On one level, their work might be read as an interpretation of early Islamic history within the framework of a Qur'anic myth of Covenant, Betrayal, and Redemption. But after the political catastrophes of the reign of al-Muqtadir (295–320/908–932) and his successors, these perspectives could no longer seem terribly compelling. Henceforth, history would become chiefly a source of political prudence and moral admonition—"philosophy teaching by example." And though specifically Islamic values—those based on Qur'ān, hadith, and *sharī'a*—would continue to have a major role in historical writing, many of the most distinctive themes of Middle Period historiography (e.g., impersonal fate, the glorification of the king as God's earthly viceroy) were rooted in the ideologies of Sassanian Iran. For the most part, historians after the mid-4th/10th century are content to cover early Islam simply through abridgments or resumes of al-Ṭabarī, though a few do make an effort to draw on other sources as well. (Ibn al-Athīr, for example, uses al-Balādhurī's *Ansāb al-ashrāf* and al-Azdī's *Ta'rīkh al-Mawṣil*; his relationship to al-Ṭabarī is discussed in Carl Brockelmann, *Das Verhältnis von Ibn-el-Aṯīrs Kāmil fit-ta'rīḫ zu Ṭabarīs Aḫbār errusul wal mulūk* [1890].)

The altered concerns of Muslim historians naturally led them to focus on recent and contemporary events rather than the remote past. Typically, an author would draw on one or a few already existing chronicles for his account of events down to the most recent decades; these would sometimes be cited almost verbatim, but more often in highly condensed form. Once a writer reached his own lifetime, he would then complete his sources by writing a "continuation" (*dhayl*) based on a knowledge of events gained through direct participation, oral information gathered from friends, current official reports, etc. In a sense, the *dhayl* became the real focus of the historian's efforts. (To be sure, even contemporary events might be largely copied from someone else's chronicle, with or without acknowledgement; never assume without checking that a "first-person" account is what it purports to be.) Historians who composed large-scale works might in fact draw on many earlier authorities, but for the most part they cite their sources one at a time, rather than trying to synthesize them into a unified presentation. There are of course a few notable exceptions: e.g., Ibn al-Athīr's universal chronicle, *al-Kāmil fī al-taʾrīkh*, or the dynastic history by Ibn Wāṣil (d. 697/1298), *Mufarrij al-kurūb fī akhbār Banī Ayyūb*. For the modern historian, of course, such synthetic works can be extremely treacherous to use precisely because the provenance of their data is masked by their method of blending their sources. Our needs are often better served by the crude methods of hack chroniclers.

A third major difference between early Islamic and Middle Period historiography lies in the development of new genres. Historians down to the early 4th/10th century had tended to produce either "monographs"—i.e., collections of *akhbār* dealing with a single event or topic—or comprehensive treatments of Islamic history. Historians in the Middle Periods retained the "universal chronicle," but they developed a number of new genres as well. Two of these achieved an especially wide popularity, the dynastic chronicle and the local history.

The subject matter of the former is more or less self-explanatory, though these works vary enormously in terms of size, internal organization, rhetoric (from simple, almost colloquial, to exceedingly florid), political perspective (some are sycophantic, others covertly critical, still others openly hostile to the regimes they describe), and scope (some cover dynasties from beginning to end, others are biographies of a single exemplary ruler). Works of this kind were commonly composed by bureaucrats. Some of these were very highly placed (like ʿImād al-Dīn al-Kātib al-Iṣfahānī [d. 597/1201] and Ibn ʿAbd al-Ẓāhir [d. 692/1292], privy secretaries to Saladin and Baybars respectively), while others, such as Miskawayh and Abū al-Faḍl Bayhaqī, were men of relatively modest rank. Not surprisingly, perhaps, the writers in the latter category tend to give more critical and independent accounts of the dynasties which they served. For them, the theme of political wisdom was more significant than royal glorification. Some of the most notable dynastic chroniclers, however, were trained as men of religion and regarded themselves primarily as *ʿulamāʾ*, though they normally had close if unofficial ties to the palace; among these, Ibn al-Athīr, Ibn Wāṣil, and al-Maqrīzī are especially prominent, but there are many others.

The second genre, local history, is in fact two. Some local histories are chronicles of events which happened in and around a particular locality. These events often stretch far back into the dim pre-Islamic past, but the emphasis tends to be on the most recent decades. Works of this kind are usually written in simple, rather conversational prose, though rhetorical flourishes crop up here and there. While broad generalizations are inevitably misleading, these works seem to have been produced particularly in cities and regions with a strong tradition of political autonomy, places that the big empires found it difficult to digest. In Arabic, an early example (and also a very fine piece of political history) would be the *Dhayl ta'rīkh Dimashq* of Ibn al-Qalānisī (d. 555/1160), available in partial translations by H.A.R. Gibb (*The Damascus Chronicle of the Crusades*, 1932—very reliable, but omitting passages which describe only the "internal affairs" of Damascus) and Roger LeTourneau (*Damas de 1075 à 1154*, 1952). In Persian, the anonymous *Ta'rīkh-i Sīstān* (ed. Malik al-Shuʿarā' Bahār, 1314/1935; trans. Milton Gold, *The Tarīkh-e Sīstān*, 1976) covers the history of this remote and intractable region from the Arab conquest down to the Seljukid invasions of the mid-5th/11th century, with a strong focus on the long period of local autonomy represented by the Saffarid dynasty (253–393/867–1003). It was composed sometime before 455/1063 by an ardent Sistani patriot—which is to say that it is almost exactly contemporaneous with the court chronicle of Bayhaqī which will be studied later in the chapter.

The other framework used for local history was the biographical dictionary. These would normally focus on the noted men of religion (with perhaps a smattering of amirs and sultans) who had resided in a given city; in some cases they were prefaced with a substantial topographical description of the place. This genre of historical writing did not reflect a tradition of local political autonomy as such, but it was rooted in local patriotism, the desire of the urban notables to show that their native cities were major centers of Islamic piety and learning. Such dictionaries are, so to speak, an expression of civic pride—a means as potent as gardens and mosques for displaying the merit and prestige of a city before the world. The model for this genre was the immense *Ta'rīkh Baghdād* of al-Khaṭīb al-Baghdādī (d. 463/1071), containing some 7800 entries. But many others are equally imposing—or were so in their original form. One historian used his materials to compose a major work in both types of local history, though in this regard he is very much the exception: Kamāl al-Dīn b. al-ʿAdīm (d. 660/1262), *Bughyat al-ṭalab fī ta'rīkh Ḥalab* (an unpublished biographical dictionary, only about a quarter of which is extant, in 10 thick Istanbul mss.), and a concise local chronicle, the *Zubdat al-ḥalab fī ta'rīkh Ḥalab* (ed. Sāmī al-Dahhān, 3 vols., 1951–68).

Although an understanding of the methods, concepts, and forms used by the historians of the Middle Periods is obviously essential to our capacity to "deconstruct" their accounts of the past, we still have very few studies which address such questions. Only two surveys can be recommended with any enthusiasm. Sections II and III of Claude Cahen, "L'historiographie arabe: des origines au VII[e] S. H.," *Arabica*, xxxiii (1986), 150–198, combine its author's unmatched knowledge of the texts with a deep understanding of the political milieux in which they were produced. As the title implies, however, he only alludes to Persian historiography, nor does he take the story beyond the mid-7th/13th century. There is still much of value in the terse and allusive sketch by H.A.R. Gibb, "Ta'rīkh," *EI*[1], Suppl., 233–245 (repr. Gibb, *Studies on the Civilization of Islam*, 108–137), especially the second and third sections. In spite of his vast erudition, Gibb inevitably makes a number of errors. More important, his assessments of Persian historiography are oddly prejudiced and yield little insight. It may be useful to compare the approaches of Cahen and Gibb with my own essay on "Historiography (Islamic)," in *DMA*, vol. VI, 249–255.

Franz Rosenthal, *A History of Muslim Historiography* (1952; 2nd rev. ed., 1968) is important but has a rather misleading title. Rosenthal does not chronicle the development of historical writing in Islam, but rather attempts to analyze the role of historical thought in medieval Islamic culture, and to create a typology of the formal organization, rhetoric, and subject matter used by Muslim historians. He emphasizes topics rather than individual historians, and the Arabic rather than the Persian tradition. Like Gibb's article, Rosenthal's analysis yields full value only when one comes to it after having read a great many historical texts on his own. Likewise, it displays some signs of its author's generation, for some of Rosenthal's general assessments of traditional Islamic scholarship now seem rather narrow and ungenerous.

As things are, a general knowledge of the historical writing of the Middle Periods is best obtained by working through the relevant sections of *GAL* and Storey. The former should be supplemented by Vol. II of Shākir Muṣṭafā, *al-Taʾrīkh al-ʿarabī wa'l-muʾarrikhūn* (1978). This exercise is doubtless tiresome, but it is unavoidable. There is no other way to get acquainted with the range of genres and subject matter pursued by Muslim historians, or to acquire a working repertory of authors and works.

A good synthetic study of this literature will not be possible until we have a foundation of monographs dealing with the methods, concepts, and literary structures used by particular authors and historiographic "schools." Only a few such historians have benefited from such studies, however, and these are of very uneven quality.

Miskawayh (d. 421/1030—also called Miskawayhī and Ibn Miskawayh), was not only the most important chronicler of the Buyid era (334–448/945–1055), but also the first major *extant* historian in Islam to have focused his attention on recent and contemporary events. He has attracted attention for his philosophical and ethical writing as well. The later (and more valuable) portions of his great universal chronicle, *Tajārib al-umam*, have been edited with a sound English translation by H. F. Amedroz and D. S. Margoliouth, *The*

Eclipse of the Abbasid Caliphate (Arabic text, vols. 1–3; trans., vols. 4–6; preface and indices, vol. 7; 1920–21). Among modern studies on him, see first of all Mohammed Arkoun, *Contribution à l'étude de l'humanisme arabe au ive/xe siècle: Miskawayh, philosophe et historien* (1970). A monograph by M. S. Khan, *Studies in Miskawayh's Contemporary History* (1980), deals largely with philological problems (models, predecessors and sources), but also has useful statements on Miskawayh's method and conception of his subject. Finally, the admirable monograph of Roy Mottahedeh, *Loyalty and Leadership in an Early Islamic Society* (1980), presents an analysis of the vocabulary of social interaction in Iraq and western Iran during the 4th/10th–11th century. As such, it can also be read as an explication of the ethical and political code which shaped the historical writings of Miskawayh and other historians of his period. Finally, a detailed survey of the cultural and intellectual milieu within which Miskawayh lived and worked is given in Joel L. Kraemer, *Humanism in the Renaissance of Islam* (1986).

The most perceptive and exact of medieval Persian historians may well have been a younger contemporary of Miskawayh, the chancery clerk Abū al-Faḍl Bayhaqī (385–470/995–1077), whose work we shall examine more closely below. Only a fragment of his massive chronicle of the Ghaznavid dynasty is extant—viz., the volume which covers the fatal reign of Sultan Masʿūd (421–433/1030–1041)—but in his terse, allusive prose, he displays a profound understanding of the political life of his era. There is a good recent edition of the *Taʾrīkh-i Masʿūdī* (ed. A. A. Fayyāḍ as *Tārīkh-i Bayhaqī*, 1350/1971), but regrettably no complete translation. He has been studied in a monograph by Marilyn R. Waldman, *Toward a Theory of Historical Narrative: a Case Study in Perso-Islamicate Historiography* (1980), though she sometimes seems more concerned with questions of theory than with the actual interpretation of the text. She has appended a substantial body of translated passages to her work, but these should be used with care.

Although we now have many solid philological studies of the rich historiography of Egypt and Syria during the Ayyubid-Mamluk period, some of which will be reviewed below, only a few scholars have looked at the structural and cultural dimensions of this literature. An early example is H.A.R. Gibb, "*Al-Barq al-Shāmī*: the History of Saladin by the Kātib ʿImād al-Dīn al-Iṣfahanī," *WZKM*, lii (1953), 93–115 (repr. in Gibb, *Saladin: Studies in Islamic History* [1972], 76–103). A number of concise but suggestive papers have been collected in D. O. Morgan, *Medieval Historical Writing in the Christian and Islamic Worlds* (1982): by P. M. Holt on the biographies of Sultan Baybars; Michael Brett on the Banū Hilāl invasion of Tunisia in Fatimid historiography; D. S. Richards on Ibn al-Athīr; and Morgan himself on Persian accounts of the Mongol invasions. On a larger scale, Ulrich Haarmann's published dissertation, *Quellenstudien zur frühen Mamlukenzeit* (1970), gives a perceptive comparative analysis of al-Jazarī (658–739/1260–1338) and Ibn al-Dawādārī (682–736/1283–1336). Haarmann has been especially concerned with the popular and folkloric elements in Mamluk historical writing; see in particular "Auflösung und Bewahrung der klassischen Formen arabischer Geschichtsschreibung in der Zeit der Mamluken," *ZDMG*, cxxi (1971), 46–60.

Ideally, we ought to have book-length analyses of the interplay between a historian's life and career, the cultural currents in which he was immersed, and the development of his thought and writing. For the periods dealt with in this book, only Ibn Khaldūn (732–808/1332–1406) has been treated along these lines, and he is obviously a very exceptional figure. Moreover, the overwhelming bulk of the literature on him focuses not on his universal chronicle (the *Kitāb al-ʿibar*) per se, but on his *Muqaddima*, a work absolutely unique in Arabic literature. Muhsin Mahdi, *Ibn Khaldun's Philosophy of History* (1957), formulated the terms of contemporary debate on Ibn Khaldūn. Although his study has been challenged on many points, it remains a classic account. More recently, the critique and interpretation by Aziz al-Azmeh has attracted much attention; see (1) *Ibn Khaldūn in Modern Scholarship: a Study in Orientalism* (1981) and (2) *Ibn Khaldūn: an Essay in Reinterpretation* (1982). The former contains a thorough bibliography of some 850 items. See also the bibliography prepared by W. J. Fischel as an appendix to Franz Rosenthal's translation of the *Muqaddima* (3 vols., 1958; 2nd rev. ed., 1968; iii, 483–521). Though no other historian possesses Ibn Khaldūn's conceptual originality, several major figures merit extended intellectual biographies—Ibn al-Jawzī (d. 597/1200), Ibn al-Athīr (d. 630/1233), ʿAṭā-Malik Juvaynī (d. 681/1283), Taqī al-Dīn al-Maqrīzī (d. 845/1441), to name only a few of the most obvious subjects. Ottoman historiography is more fortunate; one of its great masters has now received an excellent study of this kind in Cornell Fleischer, *Bureaucrat and Intellectual in the Ottoman Empire: a Biographical Study of the Historian Mustafa Ali, 1541–1600* (1986).

Questions of concept, method, and structure are essential to understanding how a historian has constructed his account of events, and hence to our efforts to achieve an independent interpretation of those events. Equally important, however, and in a sense logically prior, is the technical matter of determining the provenance of his data. We need not discuss the general problems and procedures of *Quellenkritik* here, since these are dealt with adequately in many places; the meticulous treatment of the subject in Bernheim's *Lehrbuch der historischen Methode*, pp. 411–447, for example, still stands up very well. Not many good source-critical studies have been produced for Middle Period historiography, however; for a long time, Orientalists preferred to use late compilations because they were clear and comprehensive; it was supposed that such texts must be "reliable" simply because they were digests of true contemporary sources. As to efforts to locate or reconstruct these sources, and to determine precisely how they had been used, there was very little.

The scholar most responsible for changing these attitudes has undoubtedly been Claude Cahen. Among his many historiographic articles and reviews, two demonstrate his approach and method with particular clarity:

(a) "Quelques chroniques anciennes relatives aux derniers Fatimides," *BIFAO*, xxxvii (1937), 1–27; (b) "The Historiography of the Seljukid Period," in Lewis and Holt, *Historians of the Middle East* (1962), 59–78. In addition, see the items cited above, p. 133.

In general, the most systematic source analysis during the past two decades has been done on Mamluk historiography—a sensible choice, since historians were thick on the ground, and the bulk of their work has been preserved (though not published). The first full-length monograph was D. P. Little, *An Introduction to Mamluk Historiography* (1970), a meticulous disentangling of the web of narrative sources for the first two decades of the reign of the sultan al-Nāṣir Muḥammad (693–740/1293–1241). Early Mamluk historical writing has received ongoing attention from the Orientalisches Seminar at the University of Freiburg, and a number of Ph.D. dissertations produced by its students have been published in the series *Islamkundliche Studien*. In addition to Haarmann's work cited above, see the following:

a. Barbara Schäfer, *Beiträge zur mamlukischen Historiographie nach dem Tode al-Malik an-Nāṣirs* (1971).

b. Samira Kortantamer, *Ägypten und Syrien zwischen 1317 und 1341 in der Chronik des Mufaḍḍal b. Abī-'l-Faḍā'il* (1973).

c. Shah Morad Elham, *Kitbuġā und Lāǧīn. Studien zur Mamluken-Geschichte nach Baibars al-Manṣūrī und an-Nuwairī* (1977).

Obviously an enormous amount of work remains to be done in this field. It is still difficult even to agree on a list of the most important works of Middle Period historiography—i.e., those which were most influential and widely cited by other writers of the time. As to how history was written, we are just beginning to understand this problem either on the philological or the conceptual level. We can only make educated guesses regarding the techniques which these writers used to collect their materials and weave them into cohesive works of history. Paradoxically, we can do better with the "deeper" level of their concepts, values, and structural patterns, because for these matters we have the direct evidence of the texts themselves. But even here little work has been done, and what we have is of very uneven quality.

B. Two Perspectives on Royal Autocracy: Bayhaqī and Ibn Taghrībirdī

General issues of this kind are best explored through the study of specific texts. In order to maintain both a broad view and a reasonably well focused line of argument, we will discuss two historians who share a certain type of subject matter, but are widely separated by time, space, language, and the formal organization of their materials. Moreover, we will restrict our attention to conceptual rather than philological problems.

Abū al-Faḍl Bayhaqī's *Ta'rīkh-i Mas'ūdī* was composed around 1060 and is one of the most important monuments of early New Persian prose. Bayhaqī himself was a prominent and well-connected bureaucrat in the Ghaznavid kingdom of Afghanistan, Khurasan, and Northwest India. He stemmed from a landholding family in Khurasan, and in this way he represents a very common Middle Islamic type—viz., a member of the indigenous Iranian social elite who has entered the service of foreign (in this case Turkish) masters. It is obvious from his writings that he was deeply imbued with the neo-Sassanian values and culture which had established themselves (or at least re-emerged into the full light of day) in eastern Iran during the 4th/10th century, and which had found definitive expression only a generation earlier in Firdawsī's *Shāh-nāmeh*.

The second writer, Abu al-Maḥāsin ibn Taghrībirdī (874/1470), was likewise a fairly typical figure within the political system which he described, the Mamluk Sultanate of Egypt and Syria. His father was ethnically a Rūmī (i.e., a Christian—either Greek or Armenian—from Anatolia). At the same time, he belonged to the Turkish-speaking military elite, and was in fact one of the most powerful figures in the Mamluk state at the turn of the 9th/15th century. Ibn Taghrībirdī was also well-connected with the great *'ulamā'*, for his older sister was successively the wife of the Ḥanafī and Shāfi'ī chief qadis in Cairo. In accordance with Mamluk custom concerning the sons of *mamlūks*, Ibn Taghrībirdī was effectively barred from high office in the army or government. Even so, he still had regular access to the court and was socially accepted among the ruling military caste. Ibn Taghrībirdī's situation was thus the mirror image of Bayhaqī's—viz., he was a slightly declassé member of the "Turkish" political-military elite who had at least partly assimilated himself to the indigenous urban notables and their culture. Again in contrast to Bayhaqī, his historical writing—a vast biographical dictionary, a history of Egypt since the coming of Islam, and a contemporary chronicle—did not represent something innovative, but rather belonged to the mature phase of an Arabic literary tradition dating back at least four centuries.

The passages to be examined here both deal with high politics, the struggle for power within the ruling elite: Bayhaqī recounts the downfall of the powerful vizier Ḥasanak in 422/1031, while Ibn Taghrībirdī narrates the rise to power of the sultan al-Mu'ayyad Shaykh (815–824/1412–1421). But even within this shared framework their presentations present many contrasts in method, structure, and values. Among these differences we will focus our discussion on two.

First, how does each writer analyze the political process? Is the struggle one between individuals or groups? Insofar as groups are involved, what is the nature of them? Who is entitled to participate in the political game? What are the rules (tacit or explicit) by which this game is played? What are the causes of success or failure?

Second, how do the two historians evaluate the events which they recount? These texts should be read not merely as descriptions and analyses of political life, but also as attempts to apply the concerns of Islamic political discourse to actual events and persons. On that level, Bayhaqī and Ibn Taghrībirdī are asking about the religious and ethical significance of the struggle for power, and about the standards of moral judgment which can appropriately be applied to those engaged in it. Ultimately, they must confront the issue of the nature of just government, and decide whether such government is actually possible given the realities and necessities of politics.

The religio-ethical level of questioning is in fact more visible in these texts than the political, and so it makes good sense to begin our discussion there. Moreover, for Bayhaqī and Ibn Taghrībirdī—as for Plato and Aristotle—political analysis begins with ethical concern and is unintelligible outside that context.

Ibn Taghrībirdī sums up in these words the character and conduct of his protagonist:

> He was a great, respected, brave, intrepid, intelligent and discerning Sultan. . . .
>
> Al-Muʾayyad was lofty of ambition, undertaking many campaigns and journeys, expert in planning, astute in government, administering affairs in person, with complete knowledge, adroitness, sagacity, and good judgment in all his affairs, acting with great severity toward his amirs and mamluks, but gentle with his intimate friends and boon companions; . . .
>
> With all this he preserved the prescriptions of royalty and in all his affairs and movements acted in accordance with the dispositions of the rulers before him. He had become Sultan when the conditions of the sultanate were disordered because of the innovations of al-Malik al-Nāṣir Faraj [801–815/1399–1412] in the matter of official positions and the increase in the number of intimate attendants, until it exceeded a thousand individuals. Al-Muʾayyad continued dealing with them until he made their number eighty as it had been in the days of his master al-Malik al-Ẓāhir Barqūq [d. 801/1399]. . . . [In the same way he drastically reduced the ranks of the other court officers.] All this he did out of regard to precedent. . . .
>
> He educated his *mamlūks* exceedingly well, and promoted them only after a long time; therefore none of them after his death was obscure, as far as I know. He was partial to the Turkish race and advanced them, so that most of his amirs were Turks. . . .
>
> . . . Someone said to him, "Men say of you that you have put to death about eighty of the chief amirs." He said, "I did not kill anyone unless he had deserved before to be killed; and it is the Sultan's right to kill whomever he chooses to kill." His words were regarded as shameful by the Turks who did not understand their meaning, those whose intelligence falls short of grasping implications.
>
> His pious deeds were many; he was the creator of benefactions which are known by his name and he built many buildings, the greatest of which is the Muʾayyad Mosque, than which none more ornamental has been built in Islam since the Umayyad Mosque in Damascus. . . . (*History of Egypt*, iii, 87–89)

The criteria by which a ruler should be judged are clearly etched in this passage. His fundamental moral obligations are to his subjects (and ultimately, of course, to God); the common people must be treated with justice and restraint, while true religion and its exponents must be upheld and generously supported. But justice toward the subjects is rooted in the good order of the state. Such order, in turn, requires two things: stability and fear. First, a ruler must maintain the institutions bequeathed him by his great predecessors. Innovation is expensive in the first place, but more important, it undermines the structure of expectations and loyalties through which men know their roles and can fulfill them properly. Second, the ruler must be willing to use the utmost severity, indeed outright brutality, against other members of the political elite, for only through fear can they be restrained from rebellion against him and tyranny toward the subjects. In this context, a ruler's behavior toward his subordinates is morally irrelevant so long as it is effective. These themes have an old history in Islamic thought, and are perhaps most unambiguously expressed in the *Siyāsat-nāmeh* of the Seljukid vizier Niẓām al-Mulk (d. 485/1092).

Another set of themes in Ibn Taghrībirdī's account emerges in his account of al-Muʾayyad Shaykh's seizure of power—to the modern reader and at least some Mamluk observers a tale of unrelieved treachery and violence (*History of Egypt*, iii, 1–28). It begins with a revolt of Shaykh and another senior amir, Nawrūz, against the reigning sultan al-Nāṣir Faraj, who was the son of their own master al-Ẓāhir Barqūq. While Faraj was penned up in Damascus by the forces of the two rebel amirs, they pressured the current caliph—usually barely even a figurehead in the Mamluk state—into accepting the sultanate, in spite of his evident reluctance, and swore elaborate and binding oaths to support him loyally. Ultimately Faraj was compelled to surrender. In return for acceding to his deposition, he was given written pledges of security for his own person. But no sooner was he in the rebels' hands than they arraigned him before a council of amirs and ʿ*ulamāʾ*, by whom he was at once condemned to death and executed.

Shaykh made a show at least of opposing this decision, and his reasoning—or Ibn Taghrībirdī's account of it—provides an intriguing insight into the bases of political loyalty in the Mamluk state:

> Shaykh's purpose in arguing for [al-Nāṣir Faraj's] life was that through him he might arouse fear in Nawrūz if a disagreement arose between the two; also he stood by his oath, fearing the evil consequences of violating oaths and promises; and furthermore he was moved by what he owed to al-Nāṣir's father for past favors. He said: "He" (meaning al-Nāṣir Faraj) "conquered us but spared us more than once, although we were his own *mamlūks*; then how shall we, gaining a victory over him but once, put him to death? Reports of that will be spread abroad among the sovereigns of all regions and it will be condemned as a most abominable act on our part." (*History of Egypt*, iii, 7-8)

In a milieu which often seemed to be a war of every man against every man, only a few bonds had real force. Oaths—voluntary compacts between individuals—were doubtless significant, but they were easily violated. Far more binding was the tie which bound a *mamlūk* to his master. To this latter a *mamlūk* owed everything he had in this world; if he rebelled against his master he was literally an outlaw, a man who could command the trust and respect of no one. From this perspective, Shaykh and Nawrūz owed loyalty to Faraj not because he was the sultan, but because he was the son of their master Barqūq and had thereby inherited his father's rights in their regard. Respect for his person was a matter of piety. By appealing to this bond, however hypocritically, Shaykh put himself on unassailable moral grounds in the oncoming struggle for supremacy with Nawrūz.

Upon the murder of Faraj, Shaykh moved quickly. He tricked Nawrūz into accepting the governorship of Syria, while he himself returned to Egypt with the sultan-caliph al-Mustaᶜīn. Once in Cairo, Shaykh set about isolating al-Mustaᶜīn from all potential sources of support; within a few months he was able to have him deposed and imprisoned, and to take the sultanate for himself under the title of al-Malik al-Muʾayyad. It was now Nawrūz's turn. In the second year of his reign, al-Muʾayyad felt strong enough to attack and besieged him in the Damascus citadel. As with the unfortunate Faraj, solemn oaths of personal security were sworn, and once Nawrūz was in hand, they were just as blatantly violated. His head was taken to Cairo and suspended on the Zuwayla Gate; "the bands sounded the good news and Cairo was decorated for the event."

How could Ibn Taghrībirdī take so benign a view of a man who behaved no better than a gangster? Partly, no doubt, because al-Muʾayyad's ally and enemy Nawrūz had forfeited all claim to fidelity by his conduct toward al-Nāṣir Faraj. But on a deeper level, Ibn Taghrībirdī's positive judgment of al-Muʾayyad is connected with the political discourse of the Mamluk period, in particular the ideas of Badr al-Din ibn Jamāᶜa (d. 733/1333) and Ibn Taymiyya (d. 728/1328). They argue—if we may conflate the views of two bitter opponents—that it is religiously and morally irrelevant how a ruler has come to power; in fact we may assume that he has done so not by election or hereditary right but by violence and fraud. Judgment must be reserved for his conduct once he is in office; only at that point is it meaningful to insist on adherence to the *sharīᶜa* and justice toward the subjects. Whether or not Ibn Taghrībirdī's thought was consciously shaped by this doctrine, his political attitudes unmistakably conform to it.

Paradoxically, Ibn Taghrībirdī's frank acceptance of the imperatives of political power allows him to reach a relatively hopeful conclusion. The commandments of Islamic morality simply do not apply to the internal workings of the political elite. Here effectiveness and rationality are the sole criteria. *Sharīᶜa*-based norms certainly are relevant in judging a ruler's conduct toward his subjects, but even in this context a nit-picking observance of them may sometimes be superseded by his fundamental duty to uphold the state. For Ibn Taghrībirdī, then, religiously acceptable and morally sound government is an attainable goal, albeit one difficult to achieve, within the circumstances of his age.

The moral evaluation of politics developed by Bayhaqī, in contrast, is dark and tragic, one in which normal religious and ethical standards seem only a bitter irony. The story which Bayhaqī recounts is that of the trial and execution for heresy of the powerful Ghaznavid vizier Ḥasanak, who was put to death in 422/1031. Ḥasanak was brought to his fate through a three-cornered conflict between himself, his subordinate and rival Bū Sahl Zawzanī, and the new sultan, Masʿūd b. Maḥmūd. The dramatic situation, then, seems structurally quite similar to that presented by Ibn Taghrībirdī. But whereas Ibn Taghrībirdī presents a carefully dated chronological sequence of discrete events, Bayhaqī builds his story by citing a series of reports from men who had been involved in the affair. He is not much concerned with a clear step-by-step sequence of incidents; on the contrary, his reports overlap or are nested within one another, and often allude to crucial actions which are never explicitly spelled out. Confusing as it is, however, this procedure has real advantages, for it permits Bayhaqī to introduce a range of perspectives, levels of judgment, and shifts of tone which are quite absent from the direct, square statements of Ibn Taghrībirdī.

As with Ibn Taghrībirdī, we begin with the sultan, who is the focal point of all political concern. What judgment should be levied against Masʿūd for having put to death a devoted servant of his father and one of the most capable men in his empire? In this regard Bayhaqī follows the newly emerging Perso-Islamic tradition: Masʿūd had the right to do whatever he wished with his servants, and Ḥasanak had in fact merited punishment by his own arrogance:

> Servants and bondsmen should restrain their tongues in speaking with their lords, for jackals cannot dispute with lions.
>
> . . . [Ḥasanak once said to another official] "Tell your master Masʿūd that I do everything in accordance with my master Maḥmūd's orders. Should he one day become sultan, Masʿūd must execute me." Thus when Masʿūd ascended the throne, Ḥasanak mounted the scaffold. What did Bū Sahl or anyone else have to do with this? Ḥasanak suffered for his own temerity and impropriety. A king must never tolerate three things: defamation of the ruler, divulgence of secrets, and outrage against women.

The basic principle in Bayhaqī's political thought is thus much the same as Ibn Taghrībirdī's. An autocratic political system could maintain itself only insofar as the ruler was able to instill awe and terror in the hearts of his courtiers and officials. Autocracy was based on submission and deference, and without fear, deference would soon evaporate.

Bayhaqī, however, sees in this proposition a corollary which we do not find in his Egyptian counterpart—viz., that an official must not openly oppose the ruler even when he considers him guilty of a grave injustice. One of the officials involved in the case of Ḥasanak was a certain Khwāje Aḥmad, whose profoundest desire was clearly to be left out of the whole affair. However, when it became apparent from Sultan Masʿūd's persistent inquiries into Ḥasanak's orthodoxy that he was seeking some plausible grounds for the latter's death, Khwāje Aḥmad spoke as follows:

> Tell His Majesty that since Almighty God spared me when I was in Kalanjar Castle and my life was in danger, I have solemnly vowed never to say anything about the shedding of any man's blood, justly or unjustly. . . . The lord sultan is the sovereign; let him order that which should be ordered, for even if Ḥasanak is proved a heretic, I shall say nothing about shedding his blood lest he suspect that I might have some design in his predicament. This I say frankly so that nothing might be said to him concerning me, for I abhor bloodshed. Even though this is so, I shall certainly not withhold counsel from the sultan—for that would be tantamount to treason—whether or not to shed his blood or that of anyone else, for bloodshed is not a game.

This is designedly a very slippery passage to interpret. Presumably Khwāje Aḥmad meant to indicate that the charges against Ḥasanak were obviously trumped up, and he wished to say nothing that could be used as evidence against him. At the same time, he knew that he was utterly powerless to oppose the sultan. In these circumstances he contented himself with a general expression of deference to the royal authority. As to the specific matter in question, his silence could (if the sultan wished) be taken to imply consent, and thus be construed as the positive counsel which had been demanded.

In fact Khwāje Aḥmad could not escape a deeper involvement, for he was put in charge of the proceedings at which Ḥasanak was made to transfer all his possessions to Sultan Masʿūd. In the face of this humiliating task, the only way in which Khwāje Aḥmad could signal his true feelings was to show some tact and courtesy to the condemned man, and we see him insisting on the most meticulous etiquette throughout the whole business. Khwāje Aḥmad, compelled to participate in injustice, was entangled in a system from which he could no more escape than could Ḥasanak. For him as for all officials of an autocratic regime, morality and humanity were reduced to a farce; only dignity of bearing could allow a man to preserve at least a shred of his self-respect. Unlike Ibn Taghrībirdī, then, Bayhaqī does not assess the internal politics of the elite merely in terms of effectiveness and rationality. There is a relevant moral dimension to politics, but the tragic reality is that this moral dimension cannot be fulfilled. (Implicit in all this is a very important issue, of course: why did the Ghaznavid political elite accept with no apparent protest a system rooted in fear and humiliation? But that is a question to be examined a bit further on.)

Moral evaluation is clearly an integral part of the description and interpretation of events in both historians. Indeed, their narratives are built around events which have been included in large part on the basis of specifically moral criteria. The moral judgments governing these narratives are not inductively established by the facts and events recounted; on the contrary, they are extrinsic and conceptually prior to them. Thus if we mean to use the factual data in Bayhaqī and Ibn Taghrībirdī for our own political analyses, it makes sense to begin by identifying the moral framework within which this data was selected and shaped.

History is then a morally significant tale, but it is not only that. For both men, it is also a fund of practical *exempla* which can guide the conduct of future rulers and officials. Bayhaqī in particular stresses the role of an individual's character in political success or failure; Ḥasanak's downfall is founded in his own arrogance, the venomous envy of Bū Sahl Zawzanī, and the wounded vanity of Sultan Masʿūd—failings which are sharply contrasted with the far-sighted prudence of Bū Naṣr Mishkān and the integrity of Khwāje Aḥmad. But perhaps Bayhaqī and Ibn Taghrībirdī meant their histories to be even more than repositories of useful but isolated examples of political wisdom or foolishness. They may also have regarded them as general guides to the underlying laws of politics. We cannot expect a high degree of explicit generalization in Islamic historical writing, but our two authors may well have thought that an intelligent reader would know how to draw the appropriate conclusions from their narratives.

Bayhaqī uses a number of devices to draw attention to critical passages in his narrative—exemplary tales (*ḥikāyāt*) from the Sassanian tradition, a sprinkling of wise saws and proverbs at appropriate points, or passing references to the stock embodiments of wisdom, piety, or tyranny (e.g., Nūshīrvān, ʿUmar, Pharaoh, and Haman). These are signals to the alert reader to reread and ponder the passage before him. Such devices are of course part of the stock-in-trade of New Persian historiography, the usual way of lending dignity and significance to the vicissitudes of political life. But Bayhaqī meant his account to be more than a series of banal parables. Rather, his rhetorical devices are clues; read properly, they show how to decode his narratives and penetrate the inner workings of the Ghaznavid political system. Moreover, Bayhaqī clearly assumed that what was true for this polity would hold true for any autocratic state constructed within a framework of Perso-Islamic conceptions and values—i.e., for any state which he could imagine.

The fundamental characteristic of such states, as Bayhaqī presents the matter, is that they are extremely fragile. They are built on nothing more solid than the willingness of every member of the political elite to display absolute submission to the monarch. Such deference could bring immense material rewards, and it is obvious from Bayhaqī's account that these were a powerful incentive for a man to enter royal service. But deference is rooted equally strongly in fear—the pervasive anxiety that one's life and property might be lost at any moment to the king's displeasure. This fear stems not only from the risk that one might directly offend the ruler, but even more from the knowledge that his peers and subordinates are constantly intriguing against him. The only defense against such intrigue is the hope that the ruler will be a strict and disinterested mediator of disputes among his servants. In the case of Ḥasanak, obviously, this hope fails: Ḥasanak had recklessly offended Masʿūd, and now the sultan was all too willing to accede to the wiles of Bū Sahl Zawzanī.

What is striking even here, however, is the sultan's punctilious concern for form and due process. We see a complex charade: caliphal envoys from Baghdad presenting complaints to Masʿūd about Ḥasanak's supposed conduct on the Pilgrimage, the sultan reluctantly submitting to caliphal commands to rid his kingdom of heretics, and demanding formal charges and proofs of guilt, a solemn assembly in which Ḥasanak legally transfers all his property to the sultan, etc. What is all this about? Bayhaqī's answer is only implicit, but it is unmistakable. In order for the state to maintain itself, there must appear to be law even when there is no law. Without a careful observance of this fiction, chaos would ensue.

The reason is that the monarch must stand above the internecine struggles of his servants. For if he is perceived to be involved in them, then he is in a real sense only one more intriguer, the sanctity of his role as supreme arbiter is lost, and he can no longer act as the sole focus of loyalty and cohesion within the political system. Bayhaqī is a realist; he knows that no king really fulfills the criteria demanded by his role: complete disinterestness, aloofness, and repression of personal whim. But the maintenance of form in a kind of theatrical performance permits the illusion to be sustained, and this illusion—so long as reality does not too grossly violate the ideal—lends at least a degree of credibility to the system.

Bayhaqī's interpretation of politics is coherent, powerful, and dramatic. On the other hand, these very qualities imply that his materials will have been selected and shaped according to a program of inquiry very different from any we might have. For example, if we think of politics as the way in which a society organizes itself to dispose of its common resources, then we would want to know about such things as the social background characteristics of the Ghaznavid bureaucrats, recruitment and training patterns for new officials, channels of access between subjects and the court, etc. We might ask whether the bureaucrats accepted the risks of high office because they saw no other way to defend the interests of the Khurasanian landholding class from which so many seem to have come. Information regarding such matters can be gleaned from Bayhaqī, but he surely was not thinking about politics in this way. Even within his own ethical-didactic framework, he does not tell us everything we might want to know. In particular, the sultan's role in the Ḥasanak affair, which must have been far more active than Bayhaqī allows, is left quite obscure. We cannot even reconstruct in any detail the sequence of legal procedures which were used to convict Ḥasanak. Bayhaqī narrates only those critical moments in the whole event which bring out his chosen themes.

Ibn Taghrībirdī's political analysis is conveyed by means quite different from those used by Bayhaqī. In the historiographic tradition to which he belonged, the use of moralizing *ḥikāyāt* and proverbs was generally avoided, except for an occasional verse from the Qur'ān; thus in his writing we do not find flags marking the significant passages. Likewise, his strict adherence to a chronologically ordered presentation gave him less flexibility than Bayhaqī in the selection and arrangement of his materials. Finally, his tone is normally extremely dry and impersonal, a sharp contrast to the melancholy irony of his Iranian counterpart. But Ibn Taghrībirdī compensates for his lack of art with directness. He offers many passages where he explicitly analyzes the institutions or general issues exemplified by this or that event. Even where he does not intervene directly in this manner, he calls attention to crucial events by the detail with which he reports them. In the end, he is able to convey a general analysis of the Mamluk political system which is precise, persuasive, and comprehensive.

In the Mamluk polity, the sultan is not—in contrast to Bayhaqī's monarch—a figure above and apart from the struggle for power. Rather, he is frankly recognized as a member of the military elite, a man constantly engaged in a deadly struggle with the other members of this elite (who are essentially his peers, not his servants) to take power and maintain himself against them. Even ideally, he cannot be an impartial and dispassionate arbiter of conflict; rather, he must be the most skillful conspirator and faction-builder of all.

The only thing which prevents the struggle for power from degenerating into total chaos is the institution of the *mamlūk* household. Almost every member of the military elite had been at one time a military slave (*mamlūk*), and thus had belonged to one or another of the many *mamlūk* regiments which made up the standing army. At the same time, each was now a senior officer in his own right, and thus had at least begun the process of forming a *mamlūk* regiment of his own. A contender for the sultanate would try to assemble a whole string of alliances with other officers to achieve his goals, but in the nature of things these were fragile, *ad hoc* coalitions which would fall apart as soon as they had achieved the immediate goals of their members. A man could find relatively reliable, long-term support only in two places: among his comrades in the regiment where he had once served, or in his personal regiment. The latter was in principle far better, since it was made up of his own *mamlūks*, but most of the men in it were likely to be young and politically inexperienced until their master had been in power for many years. As to the former, it might contain as many potential rivals as supporters. The trick was somehow to be recognized by one's old regiment as the most effective advocate of its interests, the man best able to realize the various ambitions of its individual members. If a would-be sultan could gain the support of his old regimental comrades and simultaneously create a regiment of his own, then his chances of seizing and holding onto the sultanate were fairly good. Even then, of course, to stay in power required a discriminating use of terror and violence against dissidents and potential rivals.

Ibn Taghrībirdī's fullest and most explicit statement on this process is found in his comments regarding the rise of new factions during al-Muʾayyad Shaykh's final illness—always a crucial moment in Mamluk political life:

> In the meantime the amirs and the army had divided into factions; one faction consisted of the principal Muʾayyadīs [i.e., the *mamlūks* purchased and trained by al-Muʾayyad Shaykh], their head being the amir Ṭaṭar, who had inveigled them by his artful words and great cunning, to the effect that he would assist their master's son, would administer their government as one of them, all authority being theirs while he would comply with whatever they wished. Furthermore, he made them fear the revolt and open rebellion of Qujqār al-Qardamī because of his ambition to rule. . . . At the same time Ṭaṭar also secretly had the support of a large number of his barrack mates, the Ẓāhirīs.
>
> A second faction consisted of the principal amirs and sultan's *mamlūks* of Tatar race, and those who had been *mamlūks* of earlier amirs. Their chief was Qujqār al-Qardamī; he was conceited at the same time that he was simple-minded, as those of Tatar race customarily are, exceedingly ignorant and devoted to pleasure night and day.
>
> Another faction, different from the other two, belonged to neither the one nor the other; they were the Ẓāhirīs, *mamlūks* of Barqūq, whose chief was the amir Tanbak Miyiq; they inwardly favored their companion Ṭaṭar, but they feared the results of Ṭaṭar's unfitness for their support since there were on his heels amirs such as Alṭūnbughā al-Qirmishī and the amirs who were with him and for whom there was great respect in men's minds; . . . And to all of this was added the multiplicity of the Muʾayyadī *mamlūks* and their bravery, so that even if Ṭaṭar were a match for all the amirs he would not be able to seize the rule from these Muʾayyadīs. For this reason many of his fellows refused to join him at the outset of the matter. (*History of Egypt*, iii, 85–86)

Due to Ibn Taghrībirdī's impersonal manner and his apparently rigid and mechanical framework, it is easy to miss the criteria which really govern his choice and structuring of events. But if we approach the text with an independent set of questions, it is clear soon enough that such criteria are at work. For example, Ibn Taghrībirdī (like most Egyptian chroniclers of the 9th/15th century) supplies quite a bit of data on prices, mortality due to epidemics, etc. But if we try to use this data to construct a clear and coherent picture of economic trends in the Egypt of his time, we cannot do so. On closer inspection, this data either falls into the traditional category of *ʿajāʾib* ("marvelous occurrences,"), or it is meant to illustrate the impact of intra-elite conflicts on everyday life. In the end, the struggle for power within the military elite is Ibn Taghrībirdī's central concern, and he interprets this struggle in terms of the institutions, values, and rules of behavior peculiar to that group. If we wish to write a different kind of political history, we must make do with whatever allusions and fragments of data he may give us.

A few general observations will serve for a conclusion. Bayhaqī and Ibn Taghrībirdī, like many of their colleagues in the Middle Periods, give us persuasive and well-integrated accounts of political life; it is very tempting simply to follow their lead, reproducing what they have to say with a few corrections and critical notes. But if we want to construct an independent interpretation, we must approach them in a highly conscious manner. First, we need to decide precisely what we want to know, quite apart from what our sources have chosen to tell us; when we read these texts, we need to bring with us a questionnaire of our own making. We cannot of course learn things concerning which they are utterly silent, but at least we will have an independent perspective on the information they do contain. Second, we need to understand the conceptual and literary structures within which this information is imbedded. On a certain level, their data can never really be disengaged from these structures; in a sense it exists only in the context given it by these historians. On the other hand, to know the concepts, values, and purposes which have governed the selection and shaping of a body of facts means that we can use them in ways which their authors did not imagine. To some degree, at least, we can guess what they have left out and imagine the original contexts of the data which they do supply. Complete independence from our sources is obviously not possible, but at least we can attain a certain ironic distance from them—and irony is after all the soul of history.

Chapter Six

IDEOLOGY AND PROPAGANDA

RELIGION AND STATE IN THE EARLY SELJUKID PERIOD

IN ANY socio-political system the question of legitimacy is fundamental, for such a system can hope to survive only if its distribution of wealth, status, and power seems generally right to those groups (or at least the politically articulate ones) which constitute it. In a stable society—i.e., one at peace within itself and not seriously threatened by any outside force—the concepts which legitimize the existing order may not be expressed in the form of abstract propositions. On the contrary, such concepts will typically be imbedded in the ceremonials, visual symbols, and myths through which that society asserts its identity and internal cohesion. But whenever the established order is felt to be threatened, either by internal dissent or external force, then the spokesmen for this order must begin to explain why things are as they are. On the other side, dissenters must try to say what is wrong and how they intend to alter existing institutions so as to create or restore a right order of things.

Such attempts to define in abstract general statements what the socio-political system is and what it ought to be constitute ideology. The means by which ideology is communicated (public ceremonial, architecture, inscriptions, pamphlets, sermons, etc.) are then propaganda. More formally, we can define ideology as a critique of a given socio-political system which both describes that system and calls upon its members to sustain, alter, or overthrow it. Ideology, in short, is both an analysis and a call to action.

Ideologies are utopian; each claims that the achieving of its program will establish the best social order of which man is capable, an order whose rightness and legitimacy will be self-evident to everyone. The utopian goal is often portrayed as the re-establishment of a once existing but now lost Golden Age, but it may also represent a realization of dreams and aspirations only adumbrated in the past. Some ideologies are millenarian, aiming to bring about the end of history. Others are contingent; they can be fully realized only for a moment, under a specific and essentially unpredictable set of circumstances—e.g., the reign of a perfectly just monarch like Khusraw Anūshīrvān. Others, finally, are cyclical; their goals are achieved periodically as one stage in a recurrent process—e.g., the era of Muḥammad and the other major prophets in early Ismāʿīlī thought. As a general rule, ideologies of the millenarian or cyclical type demand radical change in the established order, while those of the contingent type most often buttress conservative claims.

Ideologies are almost invariably integrated with some comprehensive interpretation of the nature of the cosmos. That is, they are linked to systems of thought which variously assert that visible phenomena are produced by purely material forces, by a dualistic struggle between good and evil principles, by the intervention of an active personal deity or deities, or by the lawful but impersonal governance of providence. The claims of ideology thus tend to be absolute, because they are rooted in absolute truth. Extremism in ideology is no mere accident, a matter of carrying a sensible idea too far.

Ideology has a distinctive rhetoric, one which is simultaneously rational and emotive. Because ideology tries to incite people to action, it is seldom presented simply as a logical sequence of abstract propositions. To be sure, ideology contains such general propositions, but they are almost always framed in forceful, value-laden language. In particular, ideology appeals to deep-rooted cultural symbols to convey its message. These symbols, in turn, become a kind of shorthand for the ideology as a whole. It is possible to spell out in detail the ideas which lie behind them, but ordinarily symbols are grasped intuitively by both speaker and audience. Hence the tendency of ideology to be reduced to the chanting of slogans. In Islamic discourse, for example, one commonly calls for adherence to the *sharīʿa*, following the path of the pious ancestors (the *salaf*), and government according to the Qur'ān and Sunna. Taken in themselves these are very vague notions indeed. Which interpretation of the *sharīʿa*, we want to ask, which ancestors, what passages in the Qur'ān? But in an appropriate social and political milieu, such slogans will express not only vague longings and eternal ideals but a specific program, or at least the outlines of such a program.

No adequate bibliography on the concept of ideology can be given here. In addition to the classic if rather turgid analysis of Karl Mannheim, *Ideology and Utopia* (trans. Louis Wirth and Edward Shils, 1936), several studies of Clifford Geertz are very stimulating. See especially "Ideology as a Cultural System" in *The Interpretation of Cultures* (1973), pp. 193–233. Finally, a wide-ranging discussion is given by Edward Shils and Harry M. Johnson, "Ideology," in *International Encyclopaedia of the Social Sciences*, vii (1968), 66–85.

Ideology is a salient feature of Islamic history right from the outset. The Qurʾān itself proclaims an ideology, a program of social and political action aimed at the creation of a godly society, and Muḥammad's career was in large part devoted to carrying out this divinely authorized program of action. After Muḥammad, most of the Community's internal crises generated a host of conflicting ideologies. We have already noted this in regard to the Abbasid Revolution, but it is equally the case for the early Kharijite and Shiʿite rebellions, the Carmathian and Fatimid revolts of the late 3rd/9–10th century, the Almoravid and Almohad movements in the Maghrib, the Safavid uprising, and many others. Even regimes like the Buyids, originally founded on nothing more than brute force, soon enough tried to construct some ideology which would make them acceptable to the politically articulate among their subjects. Invaders from outside the Dār al-Islām, once they began to accommodate themselves to the values and attitudes of their Muslim subjects, likewise developed ideologies which would justify in specifically Islamic terms both their rule and the socio-political order which they fostered.

We should note at the outset that Islamic ideologies are not all of a piece. Some hoped only to replicate the outlook of the Qur'ān and the historical experience of the primitive Community—to recover and re-establish that Community in all its purity. But alongside such "revivalist" ideologies (perhaps best exemplified by the Almohads and, in early modern times, the Wahhābiyya), we find others which derived their values, logic, and vocabulary not only from purely Islamic sources (Qur'ān and Sunna), but from many other traditions as well—the Greek philosophy of Late Antiquity, the political and ethical writings of Sassanian Iran, a whole array of regional folk cultures in the steppes and mountains (among which the Turkic traditions of Central Asia came to be the most influential). Thus Fatimid ideology (among the elite at least) was based on a neo-Platonic interpretation of the Islamic concept of the Imamate; the Buyids claimed to be restorers of the glories of Iranian kingship; the Jalayirids of post-Mongol Iraq tried to create a marriage of Chingiz-Khanid and *sharīʿa* norms. The possible combinations were almost limitless, and for this reason any student of Islamic ideology must constantly be aware of the vast array of cultural traditions available to medieval Muslims—traditions among which several were likely to seem equally valid and compelling to any one person or group.

Propaganda in medieval Islam naturally mirrored the complexity of ideology. There were of course no mass media in our sense, but both governments and their opponents had effective ways of getting their message across to all the politically relevant groups in society. (By politically relevant, I mean all groups, however defined, which could expect as a matter of right or custom to have some direct part in the formulation and execution of state policy, or which could organize enough force to make the authorities take them into account. The social groups which fulfilled these criteria were of many types: *mamlūk* regiments, nomadic tribes, Sufi confraternities, urban notables and *ʿulamā'*, etc.) No one means of communication could be effective among all the groups which it was desirable to reach, and so propaganda had to be targeted. Moreover, in a largely illiterate society governed less by abstract principles than by tradition and primordial loyalties, we should expect visual symbols and ceremonial to be no less important than words.

What then were the chief instruments of propaganda, both verbal and visual? Among verbal instruments, the distinction between written and oral is not entirely clear-cut, for the majority of texts were meant to be recited and discussed aloud. We must be attentive not only to the words themselves but even more to the setting in which they would be read. Thus the *khuṭba* (the formal sermon at the Friday prayer) was declaimed before a congregation of worshippers—in principle all the adult males of a town or quarter. Poetry would be recited among gatherings of friends (*majlis*) in private homes or elsewhere. Hadith and legal or theological texts might also be studied in a private *majlis*, but were equally likely to be presented to a circle of students in a mosque or madrasa. Some genres of history at least were handled in the same manner. Informal preaching took place in a mosque or in any other place where a crowd could be gathered. Essays and treatises were often composed for recitation before a specific audience, whose members would be known to the writer as he worked. The interplay of oral and written materials in a traditional, semi-literate society such as medieval Islam, needs much more study than it has received; some useful thoughts on the matter, together with further references, are brought together in Michael Zwettler, *The Oral Tradition of Classical Arabic Poetry* (1978).

Monumental inscriptions, placed over the portals or along the facades of public buildings, were of course different; they were not meant to be read aloud nor aimed at a select audience. On the contrary, they could be read by any marginally literate passerby. The audience for these inscriptions was doubtless far larger than we might suppose. Most Muslim boys in the towns, even if not literate in our sense of the word, had learned to recite the Qur'ān and could write it down from dictation; in this way they were familiar with the alphabet and many key words. Since inscriptions usually had a rudimentary grammar and lexicon—they consisted largely of names, epithets, and slogans—they would be readily intelligible to anyone who could make out the letters. A foundation inscription (i.e., an inscription identifying the character of the monument on which it was placed, the date of construction, and the name of those who had caused it to be built) could therefore be a very efficacious instrument of propaganda. (For a general discussion on Islamic inscriptions, see above, pp. 53–59.)

Only a few genres of medieval Islamic writing (panegyric poetry, mirrors for princes and political polemics) openly identify themselves as propaganda—i.e., as a medium for the conveying and reinforcing of ideology. The ideological dimension in a text, the hidden agenda which has shaped the author's choice and treatment of his subject, must usually be sought between the lines. Moreover, a text's true ideology may differ from or even contradict its apparent content and purpose. It is easy to take this rule too far; we may begin to see goblins wherever we look, distorting the true intention and cultural significance of a work in an obsessive search for its ideological underpinnings. Still, the double risk of naivete and hypercriticism should only heighten alertness and sensitivity.

Visual propaganda raises problems of its own. In pre-modern times very few societies bothered to spell out in abstract terms the "meaning" of their rituals, ceremonies, architecture, painting and plastic arts, etc.—nor could they have done so if pressed. Yet precisely these things were the most immediate and effective symbols of identity, solidarity, and legitimacy within traditional society. In our times, of course, no one can so much as paint a picture without writing a manifesto which explains the social significance of his art. In medieval Islamic society we face an intermediate situation. Ideology was, as we have noted, a significant element in political life and hence received careful verbal expression. Likewise, Islamic art and architecture often seems to "fit" the ideologies of the era which produced it, but Muslim authors almost never discuss the ideological dimensions of this art and architecture. It is only through the actual uses of these things that we can approach their role as propaganda. (As it happens, much the same problem arises in late Roman and early medieval European art; see E. B. Smith, *Architectural Symbolism of Imperial Rome and the Middle Ages* [1956], pp. 3, 10–12, et passim. For more general considerations, see Geertz, "Ethos, World View, and the Analysis of Sacred Symbols," in *The Interpretation of Cultures*, 126–141.)

As to ritual and ceremonial in Islam, we know much about formal worship, but this was essentially unchanging, at least after the earliest decades, and thus it could convey ideological significance only when it was explicitly connected to the always changing context of current political issues and conflicts. Of court ceremonial we have some knowledge, and it was of course ideological by its very nature, but it represents the political ideas and values only of the political elite. Regrettably we know very little of the rites and ceremonies of the *futuwwa* and *aḥdāth* organizations, which presumably represent a more popular orientation.

Modern scholars have been slow to investigate the ideological elements in the art and architecture of medieval Islam, but there are some useful essays in this direction. To date, Oleg Grabar has developed the most comprehensive and provocative body of ideas; these have been brought together in *The Formation of Islamic Art* (1973; rev. ed., 1987). In a narrower field of inquiry, the political symbolism of the mosque in Umayyad times is explored in Jean Sauvaget, *La mosquée omeyyade de Médine* (1947), a study whose conclusions are sometimes dubious but whose argument is unfailingly brilliant and illuminating. A similar effort has been made by the present author in "The Expressive Intent of the Mamluk Architecture of Cairo: a Preliminary Essay," *SI*, xxxv (1972), 69–119. On the other hand, the pitfalls of this sort of analysis are demonstrated by Jonathan Bloom's critique of my interpretation of one monument in "The Mosque of Baybars al-Bunduqdārī in Cairo," *AI*, xviii (1982), 45–78 (see esp. pp. 51–52).

In Western culture, painting has been one of the most widely used and effective means of communicating socio-political values. The same is less true of the Islamic world, however, not because Islam did not have painting but because painting was (especially in later centuries) chiefly an art of the book, and hence private rather than public in character. Illustrated books could not be mass-produced, of course, and it is almost certain that they were produced not for general sale but at the behest of a particular patron. Unless we know the patron, or at least the broad group to which he belonged (prince, wealthy merchant, etc.), we are in no position to interpret the ideological significance of the images. Down to the 5th/11th century, mural painting and figural sculpture seem to have been fairly common elements in palace decoration, but these were made for the pleasure of the ruler and his intimate courtiers. Again, they represent a private art. Other figural media—ceramics, metalwork, and painted glass—were widely circulated, but the iconography of most of these pieces is too simple and stylized to have conveyed more than the most general ideological concepts. The exceptions to this rule are again luxury pieces which were fabricated for specific princes and high officials. On these issues, a number of useful ideas together with an important (though now outdated) bibliography will be found in Oleg Grabar, "The Visual Arts," in *Cambridge History of Iran*, v (1968), 641–657.

Royal ceremonial in Islam is at last beginning to receive serious attention, though the field remains spotty; likewise, most accounts are descriptive rather than interpretive in approach. An excellent overview is given by D. and J. Sourdel in chapter 7, "Le palais et l'entourage souverain," of their *La civilisation de l'Islam classique* (1968). Particular points are covered in various articles in *EI*²: " ʿAnaza," " ʿAṣāʾ," "Balāt," "Burda," "Ḳaḍīb," "Khilʿa." Many interesting citations, focusing particularly on the 4th/10th century, are gathered in Chapter IX of Adam Mez, *Die Renaissance des Islam* (1922).

Sources and studies relating to particular dynasties are widely scattered. The Umayyads are most conveniently treated in Oleg Grabar, "Notes sur les ceremonies umayyades," in Miriam Rosen-Ayalon, ed., *Studies in Memory of Gaston Wiet* (1977), 51–60. On the Abbasids, see Dominique Sourdel, "Questions de cérémonial ʿabbāside," *REI*, xxviii (1960), 121–148. Two fundamental Abbasid texts are available in translation:

1. Hilāl al-Ṣābiʾ, *Rusūm dār al-khilāfa*, ed. Mikhāʾīl ʿAwād (1964); trans. Elie Salem as *The Rules and Regulations of the Abbasid Court* (1977).
2. pseudo-Jāḥiẓ, *Kitāb al-tāj*, ed. Aḥmad Zakī (1914); trans. Charles Pellat as *Livre de la couronne* (1954); on the authorship of this treatise see G. Schoeler, "Verfasser und Titel des dem Ǧāḥiẓ zugeschriebenen sog. *Kitāb al-Tāǧ*," *ZDMG*, cxxx (1980), 217–225.

The Fatimids have been discussed by Marius Canard, "Le cérémonial fatimide et le cérémonial byzantin: essai de comparaison," *Byzantion*, xxi (1951), 355–420; and in ongoing work by Paula Sanders. Pending the publication of her dissertation (1984), see "From Court Ceremony to Urban Language: Ceremonial in Fatimid Cairo and Fusṭāṭ," in *Essays in Honor of Bernard Lewis* (1989), 311–321. Buyid ceremonial has not been presented in any general way, but a particularly important incident is analyzed in Heribert Busse, "The Revival of

Persian Kingship under the Buyids," in D. S. Richards, ed., *Islamic Civilization, 950–1150* (1973), pp. 47–69; their bitter rivals in eastern Iran, who had a particularly important role in evolving a distinctive Perso-Islamic conception of government, have been treated in C. E. Bosworth, *The Ghaznavids: their Empire in Afghanistan and Eastern Iran* (1963)—see in particular pp. 129-141. Oddly enough, the Seljukids have been neglected from this point of view, in spite of their enormous influence as an exemplary dynasty in the Middle Periods. The Mamluks of Egypt and Syria have attracted some attention, though much remains to be done; a general description of their ceremonial (quite innocent of analysis) can be found in M. Gaudefroy-Demombynes, *La Syrie à l'époque des Mamelouks, d'après les auteurs arabes* (1923); there are also important points in P. M. Holt, "The Position and Power of the Mamluk Sultan," *BSOAS*, xxxviii (1975), 237–249.

In dealing with ceremonial and the visual arts, as with texts, it is a fallacy to suppose that once we have identified some ideological aspect in an object, we have thereby discovered its true meaning. Most images, objects, and rites carry significance on many levels simultaneously. To study their ideological dimensions is not to unmask their "real" nature or purpose, but simply to put them in a specifically political context.

Ideology and propaganda were undoubtedly pervasive elements in the political life of medieval Islam, but for just this reason they are also elusive ones. At this point, it will be useful to turn to a specific time and place, and to ask how ideology functioned there both as a body of ideas and as a reflection of a specific socio-political milieu. From this perspective, the early Seljukid period seems to offer a particularly challenging set of problems.

During the six decades from their first incursions into Khurasan in the 1030s down to the death of Malikshāh in 485/1092, the Seljukids presided over a major ideological effort to restate the principles of Iranian kingship in Islamic terms. The resulting ideology, which we might call "Perso-Islamic autocracy," did not even in its own time have the field to itself. On the contrary, the 5th/11th century was also the age which produced the classic definitions of caliphal authority, and it is apparent that these definitions (which have in some respects remained normative down to the present day) were formulated at least partly to resist and undercut the emerging Perso-Islamic synthesis. Even so, Seljukid political concepts remained extremely influential throughout the Nile-to-Oxus region down to the end of the 9th/15th century.

Since ideology is not an autonomous body of ideas, but rather a response to a specific socio-political situation, we need to begin by defining that situation in Iran and Iraq during the 5th/11th century. The following questions, reflecting the process by which the struggle for power generates ideology, represent one approach to the task:

1. What political formations (i.e., states, dynasties, tribal confederations, military juntas) were involved in the struggle for autonomy and/or paramountcy?

2. What were the politically relevant groups within these formations?

3. How did these groups define their political identity, their social role, and their concrete interests?

4. What were the specific conflicts and tensions which compelled these groups to articulate an ideological response?

There is no full-length, comprehensive study on the politics of 5th/11th-century Iran and Iraq, certainly none which explicitly addresses this set of questions. However, in *Continuity and Change in Medieval Persia* (1988), A.K.S. Lambton gives a detailed survey of the administrative and fiscal institutions of Iran between the 5th/11th and 8th/14th centuries. Though these institutions were always subject to evolution and innovation, they were assuredly far more stable than the regimes which utilized them. They constitute, so to speak, the rules of the game, the enduring framework within which the struggle for power and paramountcy was played out. To the complex and confusing dynastic history of the period, Lambton is an indispensable guide.

Dynastic history has acquired an unenviable reputation among modern historians, but however arid and antiquated it may seem, it is unavoidable. No serious analysis of ideology is possible without a solid knowledge of the four major political formations of this period: the Caliphate, the Buyids of Iraq and western Iran, the Ghaznavids of Khurasan and Afghanistan, and the Seljukids themselves. Beyond articles in *EI²* (among which Claude Cahen's on the Buyids is especially important) and the relevant chapters in the *Cambridge History of Iran*, vols. IV and V, see the following studies:

a. On the Buyid confederation, see Heribert Busse, *Chalif und Grosskönig: die Buyiden in Iraq (945–1055)* (1969), which is now the standard account, and Mafizullah Kabir, *The Buwayhid Dynasty of Baghdad* (1964). Both these works focus on the Iraq branch of the family, though at various times Shiraz and Rayy were more significant political centers within the confederation. R. P. Mottahedeh, *Leadership and Loyalty in an Early Islamic Society* (see above, p. 134), is fundamental for an understanding of the rules and values which shaped political behavior in the Buyid environment.

b. As regards the Ghaznavids, there is a sound narrative account of the most famous of them, with an emphasis on his spectacular campaigns in India: Muḥammad Nazim, *The Life and Times of Sultan Mahmud of Ghazna* (1931). Far more analytic in character is the admirable study of C. E. Bosworth, *The Ghaznavids: their Empire in Afghanistan and Eastern Iran* (1963). Bosworth has an important chapter on the cities and their ambivalent relations with the central government, as well as a careful examination of the beginnings of the Seljukid empire. Finally, W. Barthold's classic *Turkestan down to the Mongol Invasion* (orig. ed., 1900; 3rd ed., 1968; see esp. pp. 254–333) must be consulted for both the Ghaznavids and Seljukids—as indeed for every dynasty in eastern Iran and Transoxiana—for he anticipates many of the most productive lines of inquiry developed by Cahen, Bosworth, et al. over the last few decades. It is tedious reading but richly repays the time spent.

c. For the early Seljukids, the literature is badly scattered. There is no full-length narrative in a Western language even of war and politics. This need is partly met—but only partly—by Gary Leiser's translation of the long article on the dynasty in *IA*: *A History of the Seljuks: İbrahim Kafesoğlu's Interpretation and the Resulting Controversy* (1988). A.K.S. Lambton has analyzed Seljukid politics and administration in a long series of books and articles; she gives a concise but not always well-focused synthesis of her views in "The Internal Structure of the Saljuq Empire," in *Cambridge History of Iran*, v (1968), 203–282. Claude Cahen has also contributed many essential studies; his ideas are most conveniently summed up in "The Turkish Invasion: The Selchükids," in K. M. Setton, ed., *A History of the Crusades*, i (1955; repr. 1969), 135–176. Much of the best work on the Seljukids is in Turkish; the following are good places to begin:

a. İbrahim Kafesoğlu, *Sultan Melikşah devrinde Büyük Selçuklu İmparatorluğu* (1953).

b. M. A. Köymen, *Büyük Selcuklu İmparatorluğu Tarihi, I: Kuruluş Devri* (1979).

c. Osman Turan, *Selçuklular Tarihi ve Türk-İslam Medeniyeti* (1965).

d. The 5th/11th-century Caliphate has traditionally been neglected as a ghost institution of no practical significance. However, this interpretation has been sharply and effectively challenged by George Makdisi, *Ibn ʿAqīl et la résurgence de l'Islam traditionaliste au xiᵉ siècle* (1963), esp. pp. 69–164. Makdisi demonstrates that the caliphs were able to carve out for themselves at least a local role in Baghdad by playing off rival amirs and would-be sultans against one another, and by mobilizing certain segments of the Baghdad populace (in particular the Ḥanbalīs) in their support.

Some of these studies, especially those of Bosworth and Makdisi, not only outline the inter-dynastic struggle for hegemony, but also examine the competition for power and influence within each political system. However, the rules which governed this competition are not easily inferred from either the factual data or the interpretive statements contained in these works. Political conflict often comes across as no more than a struggle among ambitious and unprincipled individuals. At other points, the players in the game do form themselves into groups, but these groups are defined by varying and often rapidly shifting criteria—ethnic (e.g., Turk vs. Tajik); confessional (e.g., Ḥanafī vs. Shāfiʿī or Ḥanbalī vs. Shīʿī); tribal affiliation; place of residence (e.g., one urban neighborhood vs. another); or even voluntary association (e.g., *futuwwa* clubs or youth gangs).

In the face of such confusion, a modern historian is tempted to say that all these groups must really reflect some hidden factor, such as opposing economic interests. It somehow seems mere mystification to claim that Ḥanbalīs attacked Muʿtazilīs in Baghdad because of differing doctrines concerning the relationship of God's speech to God Himself. Likewise, ethnic conflicts can be seen as an irrational displacement of the competition for scarce resources. But to brush aside the names which groups give themselves or the motives which they claim for their actions is a serious mistake. In so doing we overlook the forms of identity, solidarity, and social value in terms of which political action was actually expressed and carried out. After all, it is precisely a person's understanding of his place in the social and political system which underlies his attempts to formulate an ideology. In short, in order for us to understand what an ideology meant to its adherents, we must recognize the terms in which they analyzed their own society, defined the goals of political action, and tried to form themselves into politically effective groups.

Serious efforts to present the social history of the early Seljukid period, and hence to know what groups counted in the politics of that age, are still sparse and provisional. The majority of titles, as we shall see, deal with urban society and politics, and there is some reason for this. The peasantry, who constituted the great majority of the population in most areas, were almost never "politically relevant" (as we have defined the term) save on the most local level. Even those men whose political power derived from their landholdings resided in the cities. The pastoral tribes are obviously another matter altogether, but they have usually been dealt as marauders or soldiers, not as social groups in their own right.

An overview of these problems is provided by Claude Cahen, "Tribes, Cities, and Social Organization," in *Cambridge History of Iran*, iv (1975), pp. 305–328. D. S. Richards, ed., *Islamic Civilization, 950–1150* (1973), contains papers on several relevant topics. On the pastoral tribes and their impact on the region's social structure and economic life, for example, see the careful and sympathetic treatments by Cahen, "Nomades et sédentaires dans le monde musulman du milieu du Moyen Age," and Lambton, "Aspects of Saljuq-Ghuzz Settlement in Persia," both in Richards, 93–102, 105–125. (The former is reprinted in Cahen, *Peuples musulmans dans l'histoire* [1977], 423-437.) The broad ethnic group to which the Seljukids belonged has been surveyed in the synthesis of Faruk Sümer, *Oğuzlar (Türkmenler): tarihleri, boy teşkilatı, destanları* (1972). On the groups which constituted urban society, the pioneering study (still very important) was Cahen, "Mouvements populaires et autonomisme urbain dans l'Asie musulmane du Moyen Age," *Arabica*, v (1958), 225–250; vi (1959), 25–56, 233–265. The red herring of urban guilds was disposed of by Cahen, "Y a-t-il eu des corporations professionelles dans le monde musulman classique," and by S. M. Stern, "The Constitution of the Islamic City," both in A. H. Hourani and S. M. Stern, eds., *The Islamic City* (1970), pp. 25–64. Finally, a useful heuristic model for urban socio-political organization during this period has been proposed by Ira M. Lapidus, "Muslim

Cities and Islamic Societies," in Lapidus, ed., *Middle Eastern Cities* (1969), pp. 47–79.

On the basis of this literature, we can construct something like the following picture of the struggle for hegemony in Iraq and Iran. Four principal powers were involved, each one representing a very distinct type of political formation. The Caliphate, because of its immense prestige, was effectively immune from extirpation by its competitors; on the other hand, its real military power was so slight that it could manage at best a degree of local influence in Baghdad and the Sawad by playing on rivalries within and between the Buyid and Seljukid rulers. The only reliable long-term support available to the caliphs was the Sunni segment of the Baghdad populace.

As to the Buyids, their regime had begun as an outright military dictatorship, based simply on the mercenary troops whom they had led to power: the Daylami mountaineers from whom they had sprung and who provided their elite infantry, and their Turkish *mamlūk* cavalry. In addition, as Twelver Shiʿites they could garner some popular support from their co-religionists in Baghdad and certain other towns such as Qumm.

Like the Buyids, the Ghaznavids were a military dynasty, whose authority rested in the first instance on their formidable professional army. But there were crucial differences as well. First, their center of power was in Eastern Iran and Afghanistan, so that for them the caliphs were not rivals, but rather a potential source of legitimacy. Second, caliphal backing was all the easier to obtain since the Ghaznavids were militant Sunnis. This fact also enabled them to draw support from the influential Sunni religious notables of Khurasan. Third, the Ghaznavids were Turks—their first sultans had in fact been *mamlūks*—and thus they represented what was already the paramount military group of the day. Their Turkishness did not necessarily make them any more "alien" to the regions they ruled than the Buyids, however, for the founders of the Ghaznavid polity had been servants of the Samanids, a native Iranian dynasty, and they regarded themselves as legitimate heirs of this kingdom and its traditions.

From mid-century on the Seljukids became the dominant political force in the region. The Seljukid sultans had originally been simply the war-leaders of a coalition of Türkmen bands drawn from the Oğuz tribes living east of the Aral Sea, and they always retained, willy-nilly, their status as chiefs and patrons of their Türkmen followers. In addition, however, the Seljukids had to rule an urban and agrarian society, and this task required the support of certain elements of the indigenous population. The regime relied in particular on three groups which were functionally distinct but had a partially overlapping membership: the Iraqi-Iranian bureaucracy, the urban notables, and the Sunni religious elite. As rulers of an urban-agrarian society, the Seljukids needed a regular military force which was more reliable and less predatory than the Türkmen, and could indeed be turned against these latter if need be. This force they found—as did everyone else in that age—in a Turkish *mamlūk* guard, a group which would soon supply most of the senior military officers (including provincial governors) in the state. As regards the Caliphate, the Seljukid princes portrayed themselves as its loyal servant and guardian, but in fact they had to wrestle with it as a persistent and troublesome rival, especially in Iraq.

The preceding sketch clearly implies which groups possessed political relevance in the conflicts of the Seljukid era. First, there were two groups at court: the indigenous (Arab and Iranian) civil bureaucracy, and the professional standing army. Second, the Türkmen tribes, who represented both a distinct socio-economic element in the region and an autonomous, sometimes dissident military force. Third, the indigenous urban elites: merchants, landholders, and high-ranking *ʿulamāʾ*. Fourth, the urban populace in a few large centers like Baghdad or Nishapur; these were sometimes organized through the *madhāhib* (legal-theological schools), sometimes in the form of youth gangs or neighborhood militia. At times these broad groups would act as solid classes, each with clear objectives and interests at stake. More often, however, each such group was internally fragmented into a host of competing factions, and these factions would align and realign themselves with one another in a giddy series of shifting coalitions. Thus we see an amir from the standing army recruiting followers among the Türkmen and Kurdish tribes. Likewise, the Sunni *ʿulamāʾ* of Baghdad who were partisans of al-Ashʿarī's theology would seek the support of the Seljukid court against their traditionalist colleagues, while these in turn looked for caliphal backing.

Having developed some sense of the complex and fluid political environment of this period, we can now turn to the ideologies which emerged within it. It is no surprise that there were many of these, but we do not know them all equally well. The nature of our sources ensures that we are best informed about the "official" ideologies, which articulated the conflicting claims to legitimacy of the various dynasties. As to ideologies of protest, we find many traces of these in our sources, but few fully stated formulations.

There is no general survey of ideology as such in the Seljukid period; that is, we have no broad study devoted not only to the political ideas of that age, but also to rhetoric, symbolism, and propaganda. Indeed, we have only one serious study of this kind for any portion of the Middle Periods, the admirable monograph of Emmanuel Sivan, *L'Islam et la Croisade: idéologie et propagande dans les réactions musulmanes aux Croisades* (1968). Sivan's book falls outside the chronological limits of this chapter, but its focus on a cluster of Seljukid successor states makes it highly relevant. The problem confronting these states (a Christian occupation of Muslim territories) was unique, but their ideological response to it was framed in terms developed under the Seljukids. More than that, Sivan's precision, his broad documentation, and his alertness to the ways in which slight verbal changes can signal major shifts in policy, all combine to make his study a model for work in this area.

As things are, we must be content to start with analyses of political thought, which has been fairly well studied, proceeding from there to the other aspects of ideology so far as the literature will permit. The best overall survey now is probably A.K.S. Lambton, *State and Government in Medieval Islam* (1981), who wisely focuses on the *sharīʿa* tradition, akin to our constitutional law. Her account can be compared with the classic study of Louis Gardet, *La cité musulmane: vie sociale et politique* (orig. ed., 1954; rev. ed., 1961; see esp. pp. 147–188), which presents a comprehensive analysis of Sunni values and concepts within an explicitly Thomist perspective. These studies can be supplemented by E.I.J. Rosenthal, *Political Thought in Medieval Islam* (1958), which is thin and derivative on the *sharīʿa* jurists but has useful things to say about the philosophers properly speaking, like al-Fārābī and Ibn Sīnā.

The *sharīʿa* tradition naturally centered on the institution of the caliphate. The classic statement of its religious necessity and political pre-eminence is no doubt the famous treatise by Abū al-Ḥasan al-Māwardī, *al-Aḥkām al-sulṭāniyya* (edited by R. Enger, 1853, as *Constitutiones Politicae*; and in Cairo, 1928). Al-Māwardī was the Shāfiʿī qadi of Baghdad and a confidant of the caliph al-Qādir (381–422/991–1031), at whose behest he composed the work, probably ca. 420/1030. It has received a skillful translation by Émile Fagnan, *Les statuts gouvernementaux, ou règles de droit public et administratif* (1915). However, al-Māwardi's was not the only work of this genre in its time; the Ḥanbalī qadi of Baghdad, Abū Yaʿlā b. al-Farrāʾ (d. 458/1066) composed a book with the identical title (ed. Cairo, 1357/1938), also apparently at the caliph's request. Clearly these writings represent not disinterested theorizing, but a concerted campaign by the Abbasids to reassert their political authority.

Abū Yaʿlā's treatise, though published a half-century ago, has yet to be seriously studied. Al-Māwardī, in contrast, has attracted considerable attention. The pioneering studies were by H.A.R. Gibb: (a) "Al-Māwardī's Theory of the Khilāfah," *IC*, xi (1937), 291–302; (b) "Some Considerations on the Sunni Theory of the Caliphate," *Archives d'histoire du droit oriental*, iii (1939), 401–410; (c) "Constitutional Law," in M. Khadduri and H. Liebesny, eds., *Law in the Middle East* (1947), 1–29. (The first two items are reprinted in Gibb, *Studies on the Civilization of Islam*, 141–165.) The most thorough analysis is that of Henri Laoust, "La pensée et l'action politiques d'al-Māwardī (364–450/974–1058)," *REI*, xxxvi (1968), 11–92, who examines both his theory of government and the political context in which it was written.

George Makdisi's *Ibn ʿAqīl* (see above, p. 156) broadens the context in which formal treatises like al-Māwardī's must be interpreted through its astute analysis of the ideological significance of religious creeds, which are ostensibly theological rather than political statements. His discussion (pp. 299–310) can be compared with that of his mentor, the indispensable Laoust, in the latter's introduction to *La profession de foi d'Ibn Baṭṭa* (1958)—a work by a 4th/10th century Iraqi jurist who wrote during the height of the Buyid tyranny.

At the end of the 5th/11th century, Abū Ḥāmid al-Ghazālī (450–505/1058–1111) restated the theory of caliphal political supremacy, albeit with some rather explicit concessions to the current realities of Seljukid military domination. He presents his fullest discussion of this issue in the *Kitāb faḍā'iḥ al-Bāṭiniyya wa-faḍā'il al-Mustaẓhiriyya*, published and studied by Ignaz Goldziher in *Die Streitschrift des Ġazālī gegen die Bāṭiniyya-Sekte* (1916). A more concise statement is given in *al-Iqtiṣād fī al-iʿtiqād* (ed. Cairo, 1327/1909), analyzed by Leonard Binder in "Al-Ghazālī's Theory of Islamic Government," *Muslim World*, xlv (1955), 229–241. A comprehensive study of his political thought (within which the caliphate is only one element) can be found in Henri Laoust, *La politique de Ġazālī* (1970). Most recently Carole Hillenbrand has published a careful, somewhat revisionist overview of the Ghazalian political corpus: "Islamic Orthodoxy or Realpolitik? Al-Ghazālī's Views on Government," *Iran*, xxvi (1988), 81–94.

The fundamental political reality facing the Caliphate, of course, was that it had to act within the constraints imposed on it by a number of military dictatorships, some happily quite distant but others embarrassingly close-by. The studies cited above recognize his problem, to be sure, but in addition there are others specifically devoted to it:

a. W. Barthold, "Kalif i Sultan," *Mir Islama*, i (1912), 202–226, 345–400; analyzed in C. H. Becker, "Barthold's Studien über Kalif und Sultan," *Islam*, vi (1916), 350–412; partial translation by N. S. Doniach in *Islamic Quarterly*, vii (1963), 117–135.

b. A. H. Siddiqi, "Caliphate and Kingship in Medieval Persia," *IC*, ix (1935), 560–579; x (1936), 97–126, 260–279, 390–408; xi (1937), 37–59. (Essentially a survey of political events from Tahirid to late Seljukid times.)

c. Émile Tyan, *Institutions du droit public musulman, II: sultanat et califat* (1957). (A valuable study, but note the highly critical review of Claude Cahen in *Arabica*, v [1958], 70–76.)

Among these dictatorships, the Buyids of course posed the most acute problem, since they controlled Baghdad and lower Iraq, and were in addition Shiʿites who did not recognize the Abbasids as rightful heads of the Community. On the other hand, the Buyids exploited their Shiʿism only on the local level, as we have already noted (see above, p. 158). Not only did they reject Fatimid claims to the imamate, they never tried to act as vicegerents for the Hidden Imam, the spiritual if absent head of their own Twelver sect. When the Buyids began to feel the need for some source of legitimacy beyond the sword, they hoped to find it in the traditions of ancient Iranian kingship. This effort at cultural revival is linked especially to the formidable ʿAḍud al-Dawla Fanā-Khusraw (338–372/949–983). In addition to Busse's "The Revival of Persian Kingship under the Buyids" (see above, pp. 153–154), see the two following articles:

a. W. Madelung, "The Assumption of the Title Shāhānshāh by the Buyids and 'The Reign of Daylam (*Dawlat al-Daylam*)'," *JNES*, xxviii (1969), 84–108, 168–183.

b. Lutz Richter-Bernburg, "Amīr-Malik-Shāhānshāh: ʿAḍud ad-Daula's Titulature Re-examined," *Iran*, xviii (1980), 83–102.

Our knowledge of Buyid royal ideology is largely based on the titles which they claimed. Certainly we possess no formal treatises by men like al-Jāḥiẓ, al-Ghazālī, al-Māwardī, Niẓām al-Mulk, et. al., which spell out the Buyid understanding of Iranian kingship. Our most useful source is probably Buyid coinage; in addition we can glean some data from the chronicles and state correspondence (the latter preserved not in its original form of course but in *inshā*ʾ-collections). All the necessary references are in J. C. Bürgel, *Die Hofkorrespondenz ʿAḍud ad-Daulas und ihr Verhältnis zu anderen historischen Quellen der frühen Buyiden* (1965).

The Buyid revival of Iranian kingship was a tentative thing, largely restricted to royal ceremonial and titulature. In the following generation, however, the ideals and criteria of rulership on this model would receive a definitive statement in Firdawsī's vast *Shāh-nāmeh*, composed largely at the Samanid court in Bukhara but ultimately presented to Sultan Maḥmūd of Ghazna (see also above, p. 137). Henceforth neo-Sassanian values and attitudes would imbue every piece of political writing in Iran, every inscription and coin, every ceremony, down through the medieval period. For this reason, it is useful to be aware of the literature on pre-Islamic kingship in Iran. The standard survey is Arthur Christensen, *L'Iran sous les Sassanides* (1936; 2nd rev. ed., 1944); see especially chapter 8, dealing with the monarch who most fully exemplified Iranian ideals, Khusraw Anūshīrvān. There is a wealth of material here, but it must be used with extreme caution because much of our data on the Sassanians comes from sources written in Islamic times, and Christensen's critical sense sometimes fails him. The subject has also been studied by Geo Widengren, "The Sacral Kingship of Iran," in *The Sacral Kingship* (1959), 242–258. The article by R. N. Frye, "The Charisma of Kingship in Ancient Iran," *Iranica Antiqua*, iv (1964), 36–54, has many interesting points but does not live up to its title. Sassanian art developed a powerful iconography of kingship. The striking silver vessels produced for the court have now been superbly catalogued and studied in Prudence Harper, *Silver Vessels of the Sassanian Period. Volume One: Royal Imagery* (1981), which has excellent plates and a thorough bibliography dealing with all aspects of Sassanian art. The imposing rock reliefs commemorating enthronements and major victories are surveyed (not very perceptively, unfortunately) in Roman Ghirshman, *Iran: Parthes et Sassanides* (1962), trans. S. Gilbert and J. Emmons as *Iran: Parthians and Sassanians* (1962). Monumental in scale, these were of course extremely impressive pieces of dynastic propaganda.

The transmission of the Sassanian royal tradition to Islam is a major subject in itself, and we can give only a few references here. C. E. Bosworth has contributed a brief essay, "The Heritage of Rulership in Early Islamic Iran and the Search for Dynastic Connections with the Past," *Iran*, xi (1973), 51–62. As regards architecture and imagery, there are many valuable suggestions in Oleg Grabar, *The Formation of Islamic Art*; see especially pp. 141–178. On the literary side, many themes came into circulation through the famous Shuʿūbiyya controversy in the late 2nd/8th and 3rd/9th centuries, involving the proponents of Iranian culture on one side and the defenders of Arab pre-eminence on the other. Ignaz Goldziher brought together the main facts in his *Muhammedanische Studien*, I, pp. 147-216 (*Muslim Studies*, I, 137–198). H.A.R. Gibb provided a socio-political rather than cultural interpretation for this conflict in a famous article, "The Social Significance of the Shuʿūbiyya," in *Studia Orientalia Ioanni Pedersen Dicata* (1953), 105–114; repr. in *Studies on the Civilization of Islam*, 62–73. See also R. P. Mottahedeh, "The Shuʿūbiyah Controversy and the Social History of Early Islamic Iran," *IJMES*, vii (1976), 161–182. The relevant texts are innumerable; the first chapter of the famous anthology of Ibn Qutayba (d. 276/889) will demonstrate how acceptable Sassanian political concepts had become even in conservative Islamic circles: "Kitāb al-sulṭān," in *ʿUyūn al-akhbār* (4 vols., 1343–49/1924–30), i, 1–106; trans. Josef Horovitz as "The Book of Government," *IC*, iv (1930), 171–198, 331–362, 487–530; v (1931), 1–27.

Though Turkish by race, the Ghaznavids tried as hard as the Buyids, and more successfully, to link themselves to Iranian royal tradition. In contrast to their rivals, however, they attempted also to create a synthesis between the Iranian and the specifically Islamic bases of their regime; the Ghaznavids are in fact the true founders of the model of government which we have referred to in this book as Perso-Islamic autocracy. Using this model, they portrayed themselves as warriors striving to expand the realm of Islam, as defenders of Sunnism and suppressors of heresy, and as loyal allies and agents of the Abbasid caliphs. In this way they simultaneously proclaimed the values of royal absolutism and the Iranian concept of justice. As with the Buyids, the titles used by the Ghaznavid sultans are very revealing; see C. E. Bosworth, "The Titulature of the Early Ghaznavids," *Oriens*, xv (1962), 210–233. In regard to their art and architecture, there is a good brief survey (already somewhat dated) by J. Sourdel-Thomine in *EI²*, ii, 1053–55. The best statement of their ideology is probably Bayhaqī's *Taʾrīkh-i Masʿūdī*, on which see the analysis in the preceding chapter. In addition, the famous *Siyāsat-nāmeh* of Niẓām al-Mulk, though written for the Seljukid sultan Malikshāh (465–485/1072–1092) closely mirrors the values and ideas of the Ghaznavid monarchy, in whose service Niẓām al-Mulk had begun his career. The best edition and translation is that by Hubert Darke, *The Book of Government or Rules for Kings* (Persian text, 1960; rev. ed. 1968, using an important new manuscript; English version, 1960; rev. ed., 1978).

The various strands of ideology produced by the Caliphate, the Buyids, and the Ghaznavids were all inherited by the Seljukids, who became, as we noted earlier in this chapter, the exemplary Islamic state in the later Middle Periods. In spite of their immense influence and prestige, however, we still have no general examination of Seljukid ideology. The closest approach to this will be found in several studies by A.K.S. Lambton on medieval Iranian concepts of kingship, which have been brought together in *Theory and Practice in Medieval Persian Government* (1980). Among these, two in particular have been widely cited: (a) "Quis Custodiet Custodes: Some Reflections on the Persian Theory of Government", *SI*, v (1956), 125–148; vi (1956), 125–146; (b) "Justice in the Medieval Persian Theory of Kingship," *SI*, xvii (1962), 91–119. These articles are full of interesting ideas; on the other hand, they deal only with particular aspects of the overall subject, and in addition they try to cover all the major dynasties of Islamic Iran, not just the Seljukids.

Lambton's work is based on texts written explicitly to spell out the criteria of right government. Among the several important works of this type produced under the Seljukids, we have already noted the *Siyāsat-nāmeh* of Niẓām al-Mulk. In addition, see the *Naṣīḥat al-Mulūk* attributed to al-Ghazālī, a treatise which reads almost as if it had been composed in direct response to Niẓām al-Mulk. In this work the author (whether al-Ghazālī or someone else) pays no attention to the Caliphate and its claims; he is writing specifically for a Seljukid governor in eastern Iran. Hillenbrand ("Islamic Orthodoxy or Realpolitik?" Cited above, p. 161) regards the piece as spurious. In any case, the *Naṣīḥat* has a complex textual history and is most easily consulted in the translation by F.R.C. Bagley, *Ghazali's Book of Counsel for Kings* (1964). Finally, there is the elegant *Qābūs-nāmeh* of the prince Kay Kā'ūs b. Iskandar (fl. 475/1082), ed. and trans. Reuben Levy as *A Mirror for Princes* (1951).

These three works share a common concept of the status and role of the monarch, which they present in both a neo-Sassanian and an Islamic framework, but in their tone and ethos they differ markedly from one another. Niẓām al-Mulk regards the sultan's task with grim realism; for him, the sultan can achieve justice and tranquillity only by imposing his will on his subordinates, and this can be done only through unremitting vigilance and the constant threat of coercion. By justice, he means a right social order, a divinely established and fixed relationship among stable classes. Because this just social order is ordained by God, it follows that the sultan must do all in his power to uphold true religion among his subjects and to quash heresy. On the other hand, Niẓām al-Mulk seems to regard justice as something which is both rationally knowable and advocated by all decent religions, not Islam alone. From this perspective, the relationship between government and religion is a functional one: the ruler upholds the *established* religion because that religion legitimizes and reinforces the *established* social order, not because of that religion's abstract truth-value.

In the *Naṣīḥat al-mulūk*, the author is concerned first of all with the character and motivation of the ruler; he implicitly argues that if the ruler's own thought and conduct have been rightly shaped, then his policies will be sound and his regime will flourish. For him, however, the truth-value of religion is primary; every aspect of the ruler's behavior must flow from a personal commitment to this truth. (Cf. Lambton's analysis in "The Theory of Kingship in the *Naṣīḥat al-Mulūk* of Ghazālī," *Islamic Quarterly*, i [1954], 47–55.)

The *Qābūs-nāmeh* is certainly the most attractive and humane of these texts, though from a theoretical point of view it is the least important. It consists of worldly (but not cynical) advice from a petty dynast to his son on how to make his way in a dangerous world, and how to conduct himself at all times as befits a prince.

All three of these treatises were meant primarily for the rulers themselves; all are private memoranda as much as public documents. In order to reach other groups, Seljukid ideology had to be expressed through different genres. A good deal of Seljukid historiography (a form of writing which would most directly concern the bureaucrats) was quite overtly ideological in character. This literature has not been adequately studied, but Claude Cahen has contributed two important articles: (a) "Le Malik-nāmeh et l'histoire des origines seljukides," *Oriens*, ii (1949), 31–65; (b) "Historiography of the Seljuqid Period," in Lewis and Holt, eds., *Historians of the Middle East*, 59–78.

Among the *ʿulamāʾ* and their followers, the dynasty's role as "defender of the faith" could be symbolized by its patronage of religious institutions. The mosques and *madrasa*s of Seljukid times unfortunately survive only in bits and pieces, and what we have has been badly neglected by modern scholars. For a brief overview of what is known, see Oleg Grabar, "The Visual Arts," in the *Cambridge History of Iran*, v, 626–641. Likewise, Seljukid epigraphy has never been the object of a synthetic study, though its value for the development of ideology is self-evident. An indication of what might be learned can be found in two studies by Nikita Elisséeff on a Seljukid successor prince in 6th/12th century Syria, Nūr al-Dīn Maḥmūd b. Zangī: (a) "La titulature de Nūr ad-Dīn d'après ses inscriptions," *BEO*, xiv (1952–54), 155–196; (b) "Les monuments de Nūr ad-Dīn," *BEO*, xiii (1949–51), 5–43. Elisséeff's interpretation adheres closely to the framework established by Max van Berchem in *CIA*; the latter's remarks on the Seljukids remain perceptive but are terribly scattered.

So far we have spoken as if the Seljukids regarded themselves simply as Perso-Islamic autocrats and as protectors of Sunni Islam and the Caliphate. But they were also Türkmen chiefs, at least in the beginning, and it is necessary to ask what impact this fact had on their political thinking. Even the realistic Niẓām al-Mulk alludes to this facet of their identity only in passing, when he advises Malikshāh not to neglect or offend the Türkmen who had brought the dynasty to power. In regard to Türkmen political concepts and values, however, he says not a word. Nevertheless, it clear that the Turkic peoples of Inner Asia had deep-rooted traditions of their own, some of which at least they carried with them as they penetrated beyond the Oxus in the early 5th/11th century.

A particularly important example of these is the notion that territorial sovereignty was the property not of an individual but of a whole family. That is, the leading member of the paramount family within a polity was obliged to share his authority by assigning portions of his territories as autonomous appanages to other members of his house. This kind of political structure can be given various names; among those in current use are "collective sovereignty," "family confederation" and "appanage state." The institution was first identified by Barthold (*Turkestan down to the Mongol Invasion*, 268), but his insight was not followed up until Claude Cahen called attention to this pattern of behavior in his articles on the Ayyubids and the Buyids in *EI*[2]. The institution has been most systematically examined in two recent monographs: (a) R. S. Humphreys, *From Saladin to the Mongols: the Ayyubids of Damascus, 1193–1260* (1977); and (b) John E. Woods, *The Aqquyunlu: Clan, Confederation, Empire* (1976). There can be no question that the code of collective sovereignty strongly shaped Seljukid political behavior, but it seems to have been mostly an unspoken affair—a body of ideas and values which affected their dealings with one another and with their Türkmen followers, but which never formed part of their public claims to authority over Muslim lands and peoples.

The Seljukids took great pride in being Turkish—a point evident in an early 5th/11th century essay, the *Tafḍīl al-Atrāk* of Ibn Ḥassūl (Arabic text and Turkish translation by S. Yaltkaya, study by ʿAbbās al-ʿAzzāwī, *Belleten*, iv [1940], 235–266). On the other hand, the Seljukids never sponsored a literature in Turkish, though the model for this was provided by the Qara-Khanids of Transoxiana in the mid 5th/11th century. Under their patronage a Turkish mirror for princes was composed which in fact slightly antedates any extant Persian text of this kind, the *Kutadgu Bilig* of Yusuf Khass Hajib, translated by Robert Dankoff as *The Wisdom of Royal Glory* (1983). Even more impressive was the great *Dīwān Lughāt al-Turk* of Maḥmūd al-Kāshgharī (on which see above, p. 15). But in general, we begin to see an officially sponsored Turkish literature only in the second half of the 9th/15th century.

It has been argued that from an early time the Seljukids regarded themselves as a people with a divine mandate to rule the world, though I find the thesis a doubtful one. This theme has been most fully (if somewhat chauvinistically) explored by Osman Turan, *Türk Cihan Hâkimiyeti Mefkûresi Tarihi* (2 vols., 1969); the same author gives a concise statement of it in "The Idea of World Domination among the Medieval Turks," *SI*, iv (1955), 77–90. One aspect of Turkish traditions of rulership has been explored in J. P. Roux, "L'origine celeste de la souveraineté dans les inscriptions paléo-turques de Mongolie et de Siberie," in *The Sacral Kingship*, 231–241. For the Seljukids' use of an old Turkish symbol of royal power, the bow and arrow, see Claude Cahen, "La tuġrā seljukide," *JA*, ccxxxiv (1943–45), 167–172.

We should not exaggerate the salience of Turkish concepts and symbols in the public image which the Seljukids tried to project. Doubtless these were important for the way in which they understood themselves, but they could hardly have done much to legitimize Seljukid rule among their Iranian, Arab, and Kurdish subjects. To be sure, such ideas were clearly very important among the Il-Khans and their Turco-Mongol successors such as the Jalayirids, Qara-Quyunlu, and Timurids. But the Mongols began their domination in Iran and Mesopotamia as pagans, men imbued with the traditions of Inner Asia and quite oblivious of Perso-Islamic ideas. For the Seljukids, in contrast, specifically Islamic and neo-Sassanian criteria seem to have controlled their public political statements, and hence the image of kingship and social order to which they aspired.

If we go back to the general comparative framework for ideology and propaganda which we developed at the beginning of this chapter, we can now try to locate the Seljukids within it. First of all, they entered the Islamic world at a moment of profound political and cultural turmoil there. In such circumstances they (or more accurately, their indigenous spokesmen) could not avoid defining their role and purposes—i.e., formulating an ideology which justified their domination over established Muslim populations. They were barbarians, but barbarians who wished to preserve, so far as possible, the established urban-agrarian social order in Iran and the Fertile Crescent. This stance compelled them to align themselves with the indigenous classes who were committed to that order—the landholding bureaucracy and the urban notables (*ʿulamāʾ* and merchants). For this reason, the Seljukid ideology would necessarily be one which tried to justify and defend things as they were. This conservative perspective was reinforced by the decision of the interlopers to link themselves with the Abbasid Caliphate.

Tension and conflict were built into the Seljukid order of things, and their apologists hoped to resolve these by framing conceptual pairs which would assert the inner harmony between apparently opposing elements—hence their stress on the complementary role of key ethnic groups (Turk and Tajik) and political institutions (caliphate and sultanate). In the same way, they presented the Seljukid regime as one which could satisfy all the criteria of ideal rulership which had arisen in early Islam, Sassanian Iran, and Turkic Central Asia, however contradictory these might seem on the surface.

Because the established order was under attack from various quarters, most visibly the Ismaʿili wing of Shiʿism, Seljukid conservatism was inevitably militant and even strident in tone. Their propaganda was the propaganda of men who are free to speak in public and who control vast resources. Their supporters could teach in the mosques and *madrasas*, put major literary works into circulation, and endow magnificent religious institutions. Was all this effective? It could not of course save the Seljukid empire as such from its own structural weaknesses. But the ideology thus evolved did address squarely the political needs of military dynasties trying to rule within an established framework of Islamic values and attitudes. Moreover, it was able to make later generations look back on the early Seljukids as a moment of restored glory for Islam, a moment which they should struggle, however vainly, to recapture for themselves.

Chapter Seven

THE FISCAL ADMINISTRATION OF THE MAMLUK EMPIRE

ADMINISTRATIVE history is without doubt the dullest genre in the field, and yet it is essential to almost everything else we want to do. Administration, we should remember, is simply the body of practices and institutions through which a political elite tries to extract and distribute, in a fairly regular and predictable manner, the "surplus resources" produced by the society which it governs. To analyze an administrative system, then, is to understand the character of a society's political elite, to perceive the dividing line between "public" and "private" goods, to define the purposes for which public resources are expended, and to reconstruct many of the linkages between the elite and the mass of citizens or subjects. Precisely because administration is in some sense the engine which runs the whole political system, it must not be treated in isolation as a self-contained piece of machinery whose only function is to operate elegantly and with a minimum of friction. Of all fields, administrative history is the one where tunnel history is the most appealing approach, and where it is most strenuously to be avoided. For administration tells us more than anything else can of the purposes for which government was instituted in a given time and place, of who was expected to benefit and who would pay the costs.

In contrast to the Germanic peoples in Latin Europe, the Arabs destroyed the old empires of the Middle East, but not the administrative structures which they had created. On the contrary, the new Arab elite made a concerted and largely successful effort to maintain them, albeit with certain reforms and changes of emphasis. Throughout the medieval period, even in moments of grave governmental weakness, at least a skeleton of centrally controlled administration always remained, and into such skeletons a vigorous ruler could breathe new life almost at a moment's notice. The tradition is unbroken: dynasties come and go, but always there is some dynasty—and always there is the tax-collector, with his proven techniques, to see to its financial needs.

Among the states of the medieval Islamic world, the one whose administrative institutions and practices we know best is certainly the Mamluk Empire of Egypt and Syria. For Mamluk administration we have a range and quantity of source material which is unmatched in any other Islamic state except the Ottoman Empire. Here if anywhere we can achieve a description which is not only formally correct but well integrated with other dimensions of political, social, and economic history. In some sense, then, the Mamluk Empire (and Egypt in particular) can act as a paradigm for medieval Islamic administration. Obviously Mamluk data cannot be applied in a mechanical way to other regions and political entities. But because this data is so rich, we can use it to generate guidelines suggesting how separate practices and bureaux might fit together, how at least the outlines of a system can be discerned through disjointed scraps of information, and what values, goals, and skills were typically possessed by the bureaucrats of medieval Islam. Moreover, since the Mamluk administration was heir to so many Middle Eastern traditions (most directly, Fatimid and Seljukid), a careful and astute scholar can deconstruct its institutions so as to throw light on the administrative systems of its ancestors and cousins.

Many major gaps remain, but the Mamluk Empire has been relatively well served, both in quantity and quality, as regards the publication of administrative texts and documents. In spite of a number of important achievements, however, the same is not true of interpretive studies—whether of processes and procedures, of the personnel of the bureaux, or of the "interface" between the bureaucracy and other social groups and institutions (e.g., the amirs, the ports and markets, the peasantry). In view of this situation, perhaps the most sensible way to proceed is to begin by reviewing our documentation, and then to ask what possibilities are opened up by it. By focusing on the sources actually available, we may be able to generate questions which would not have occurred to us *a priori*, as well as to avoid problems which are in the end insoluble.

An intelligent review of the sources is given by Hassanein Rabie, *The Financial System of Egypt, A.H. 564–741/A.D. 1169–1341* (1972), pp. 1–25. We do not need to repeat what he has said; rather, we will concentrate our attention on a few exemplary publications of sources, which suggest what can be done, and on the major gaps which desperately need to be filled.

Administrative history ought to begin with official documents—decrees, tax registers, cadastral surveys, etc. But those pertaining to fiscal matters in the Mamluk Empire are all gone now, at least in their original form, and so we have to devise various indirect ways of getting at them and their contents.

One such device is to examine the extant official documents from the non-fiscal agencies of the Mamluk state. Of these the most important collection by far is the archive of petitions and decrees of protection held at St. Catherine's Monastery on Mt. Sinai. It is important because of its range and completeness, with state documents reaching from Fatimid to Ottoman times, but also because elements of it have been published in an utterly exemplary manner. An overall survey of the archive's contents has been provided by A. S. Atiya, *The Arabic Manuscripts of Mount Sinai* (1955). But for our purposes the most important work has been that done by Samuel M. Stern:

a. *Fatimid Decrees: Original Documents from the Fatimid Chancery* (1964).

b. "Three Petitions of the Fatimid Period," *Oriens*, xv (1962), 172–209. (These in fact are Geniza pieces, but the article belongs to this series in other respects.)

c. "Petitions from the Ayyubid Period," *BSOAS*, xxvii (1964), 1–32.

d. "Two Ayyubid Decrees from Sinai," in S. M. Stern, ed., *Documents from Islamic Chanceries* (1965), 9–38, 207–216.

e. "Petitions from the Mamluk Period," *BSOAS*, xxix (1966), 233–276. (In part a review article on Ernst, *Sultansurkunden*, on which see below.)

Obviously most of these publications refer to the pre-Mamluk period, but Stern demonstrates a striking degree of continuity in script, format, and procedure from beginning to end, such that all of these studies are equally important for the student of Mamluk diplomatics.

Stern's principal concern throughout is to reconstruct the exact procedure by which these documents were initiated, drafted, and officially promulgated. This he does by a meticulous comparison of their features with the description of procedure given by al-Qalqashandī's *Ṣubḥ al-aʿshā*. But he brings in as many Islamic documents from other periods and regions as possible, as well as comparative materials from the chancery practice of medieval Spain and Italy. As narrowly focused as his work appears to be, in short, it is placed within a very broad context and thereby throws light on a whole array of issues besides those he is explicitly addressing.

The documents collected by Stern can be supplemented with a number of others. Most directly relevant is Hans Ernst, *Die mamlukischen Sultansurkunden des Sinai-Klosters* (1960), which contains transcriptions and translations of seventy decrees issued directly by the Mamluk sultans. There are no facsimiles, however, and his historical-diplomatic annotations, though useful, are not up to the level of Stern's. An archive similar in character to St. Catherine's, though smaller, is that of the Franciscan Custodia Terrae Sanctae in Jerusalem. Twenty-six decrees and deeds from this collection have been published with fascimiles by N. Risciani, *Documenti e firmani* (1931). (On this study and a catalog by E. Castellani, see Stern, "Mamluk Petitions," pp. 234–235 and n. 7.)

None of these documents directly address the needs of a student of fiscal administration, obviously—even where they allude to taxes and dues, they do not use a technical vocabulary and contain no numbers. As to procedures, they were not issued through the fiscal bureaux, but by the *dīwān al-inshā*ʾ (Office of Correspondence) and the *kātib al-sirr* (Confidential Secretary). Even so, a detailed knowledge of chancery procedures may suggest ways of interpreting the hints and allusions we find in our textual sources. More than that, these documents do show how the Mamluk government dealt with one class of its subjects on a routine official level.

The most intriguing body of documents otherwise are those registered by Muḥammad Amīn, *Catalogue des documents d'archives du Caire, de 239/853 à 922/1516* (1981) (in Arabic). These consist of *waqf* endowment deeds, contracts of sale and conveyance, and the like. These are private rather than state documents, to be sure, drawn up by notaries (*shuhūd*) rather than government clerks (*kuttāb*). In this sense they pertain to the kinds of issues discussed below in Chapter Seven. On the other hand, because so many of them were drafted for sultans and senior officials, they can help us understand those economic relations between rulers and subjects which were non-fiscal in nature, and how the state intervened in matters which were in theory religious. Decrees were sometimes recorded in inscriptions, which were typically placed on the walls of congregational mosques. These are not in their original form, obviously, but even so they retain their official character. A list of those in Syria (with terse French summaries but no Arabic texts) is given by Gaston Wiet, "Répertoire des décrets mamlouks de Syrie," *Mélanges René Dussaud* (1939), ii, 521–537. Sixty-two such inscriptions have been published, with valuable though now outdated commentary, by Jean Sauvaget, "Décrets mamelouks de Syrie" *BEO*, ii (1932), 1–52; iii (1933), 1–29; xii (1947–48), 5–60. Sauvaget's decrees contain a wealth of data especially on the *mukūs* (market taxes and fees of dubious legality), which they unceasingly claim to be abolishing. We have here a lengthy repertory of names for these taxes, details as to their administration, and valuable allusions to the contexts in which they were imposed. Since these urban taxes are so inadequately discussed in our textual sources, and since Syria is so much less well known than Egypt, Sauvaget's material is all the more valuable.

For the later Circassian period at least (from 872/1468 on), we have a very valuable and unexpected resource in the materials collected and summarized by the Ottomans in the 1520s, who of course had to inform themselves on the economic situation and administrative institutions of the vast territories which they had seized in 921–22/1516–17. Only the first steps have been taken to analyze this trove of fiscal data and procedure, but the following items will give an example of what is already available:

a. Robert Mantran and Jean Sauvaget, *Règlements fiscaux ottomans: les provinces syriennes* (1951). (A translation of chapters from Ö. L. Barkan, *XVve XVIıncı asırlarda Osmanlı İmparatorluğunda zirâi ekonominin hukuki ve mali esasları*. Vol. I, *Kanunlar* (1943).

b. Stanford J. Shaw, *The Financial and Administrative Organization and Development of Ottoman Egypt, 1517–1798* (1962). (A pioneer work, written when archive-based administrative studies on the Ottoman Empire were in their infancy, but still a valuable fund of data.)

c. Amnon Cohen and Bernard Lewis, *Population and Revenue in the Towns of Palestine in the Sixteenth Century* (1978).

Obviously Ottoman documents must be used cautiously; they reshape the data of the Mamluk administration to fit Ottoman terminology and classification, and Mamluk institutions and procedures were surely treated in the same way. Even so, the Ottomans seem to have taken a conservative course in the old Mamluk dominions, and we have enough Mamluk materials to serve as a check. Altogether, it is clearly irresponsible not to make the fullest possible use of the Ottoman records.

More immediately rewarding than any of the above resources, however, is the truly remarkable series of administrative digests and encyclopedias produced by Ayyubid and Mamluk authors. These contain detailed (if often confusing and obscure) discussions of procedure in every branch of the administration, surveys of the administrative geography of Egypt and Syria, digests of tax statistics and *iqṭāʿ* assignments, scores of transcripts of official documents of every kind, etc. Though other dynasties produced an occasional volume of this sort, there is nothing—even from the Ottoman Empire—which remotely approaches the Mamluk tradition in this field. Where the information contained in these texts can be tested against original documents (as in Stern's studies) it has proved to be remarkably accurate and precise. In light of all this, it will be useful to review each of the major items, proceeding in chronological order. We begin with a group of Ayyubid texts, because it was Saladin and his associates who established the peculiar marriage of Fatimid and Seljukid institutions so characteristic of Egypt in the later Middle Ages.

1. ʿAlī b. ʿUthmān al-Makhzūmī. *Kitāb al-minhāj fī ʿilm kharāj Miṣr*. Partial edition by Claude Cahen and Yūsuf Rāghib (1986). Originally composed 565/1169-70, revised ca. 581/1185.) This work, held in the British Museum, but lacking a title page and many substantial sections, was first identified by Claude Cahen around 1960. ("Un traité financier inédit d'époque fatimide-ayyubide," *JESHO*, v [1962], 139–159.) To it he has devoted a number of special studies, now gathered together in a volume called *Makhzumiyyat: Études sur l'histoire économique et financière de l'Égypte médiévale* (1977), which constitutes an indispensable commentary to the published text. As Cahen points out more than once, al-Makhzūmī's is a very frustrating work to use, but it contains invaluable materials on military administration, import and export dues (with model tax statements, selective tariff rates, etc. Cahen has supplied provisional French translations of all the published sections of the text in the articles collected in *Makhzumiyyat*, but further efforts in this direction may well yield additional clarifications.

2. Ibn Mammātī, *Kitāb qawānīn al-dawāwīn*, ed. A. S. Atiya (1943). A work similar in date (Ibn Mammātī died in 606/1209) and character to al-Makhzūmī's, though more complete and better organized. It is especially valuable for the procedures used to assess and allocate agricultural taxes. On the other hand, its numerical data is very limited, and it glosses over many problems concerning the structure of the bureaucracy. According to Richard S. Cooper, the most recent student of Ibn Mammātī, Atiya's edition contains many significant errors. Cooper has prepared an English translation ("Ibn Mammātī's Rules for the Ministries," Ph.D. thesis, Univ. of California-Berkeley, 1973), and has published two concise but exact studies: "Land Classification Terminology and the Assessment of the Kharāj Tax in Medieval Egypt,"

JESHO, xvii (1974), 91–102 (includes a translation of Ibn Mammātī, ch. 4); "The Assessment and Collection of Kharāj Tax in Medieval Egypt," *JAOS*, xcvi (1976), 365–382.

3. ʿUthmān b. Ibrāhīm al-Nābulsī: (a) *Ta'rīkh al-Fayyūm*, ed. B. Moritz as *Description du Fayyoum* (1899); (b) *Kitāb lumaʿ al-qawānīn al-muḍiyya fī dawāwīn al-Diyār al-Miṣriyya*, ed. C. Becker and C. Cahen, *BEO*, xvi (1958–60), 119–134; selected passages translated by C. Cahen, "Quelques aspects de l'administration égyptienne médiévale vus par un de ses fonctionnnaires," *BFLUS*, xxvi (1948), 97–118. Al-Nābulsī wrote during the reign of al-Ṣāliḥ Ayyūb (637–647/1240–1248). The *Ta'rīkh al-Fayyūm* is a detailed fiscal description of the Fayyūm district; it has been studied and its rich fund of numerical data broken down into tabular form by Cahen, "Le régime des impots dans le Fayyūm ayyubide," *Arabica*, iii (1956), 8–30; reprinted in *Makhzumiyyat*. It is as close as we will ever get to an official tax register for Mamluk Egypt. The *Kitāb lumaʿ al-qawānīn* is more a personal memo, in which al-Nābulsī points out administrative corruption and malfeasance and specifies necessary reforms. Whatever its biases and distortions, it gives a vivid picture of the Egyptian fiscal administration at work.

4. ʿIzz al-Dīn ibn Shaddād, *al-Aʿlāq al-khaṭīra fī dhikr umarā' al-Shām wa'l-Jazīra*. The various sections of this work have been published separately, as follows: (a) Aleppo: ed. D. Sourdel (1953). (b) Damascus: ed. Sāmī al-Dahhān (1956). (c) Jordan, Lebanon, Palestine: ed. Sāmī al-Dahhān (1963); (d) North Syria excluding Aleppo: ed. Anne-Marie Eddé, *BEO*, xxxii–xxxiii (1981–82), 265–402; annotated translation by A.-M. Eddé-Terrasse, as *Description de la Syrie du Nord* (1984). (e) Jazira: ed. Yāsīn ʿAbbāra (2 vols., 1977–78). Parts of the Jazira volume have been translated by Claude Cahen, "La Jazira au milieu du xiiie siècle d'après ʿIzz ad-Dīn ibn Chaddâd," *REI*, viii (1934), 109–128. Ibn Shaddād (d. 684/1285—*not* the well-known biographer of Saladin) composed this historical-geographical survey of Syria and the Jazira for Sultan Baybars in the 1270s. The volumes are of varying usefulness, but those on Aleppo and the Jazira contain some valuable summaries of late Ayyubid tax revenues and troop contingents. Since we are generally so much less well informed on Syrian administration than Egyptian, this work, in spite of its spottiness, has much to offer.

5. Aḥmad b. ʿAbd al-Wahhāb al-Nuwayrī (d. 732/1332), *Nihāyat al-arab fī funūn al-adab*. Of the 30 original volumes, nos. 1–25 have been published, the rest remain in manuscript. The latter half of the work is a "universal chronicle" of Islamic history, useful chiefly for Fatimid times and the reign of al-Nāṣir Muḥammad (693–741/1294–1340). The earlier section belongs to the old *adab al-kātib* ("art of the clerk") genre; it describes the skills a government clerk must have, with an outline of the fiscal bureaux in Vol. VIII.

6. Aḥmad b. Faḍlallāh al-ʿUmarī (d. 749/1349): (a) *Masālik al-abṣār fī mamālik al-amṣār* (partially published; the best set of manuscripts is in Is-

tanbul, Ayasofya 3415–3439); (b) *al-Taʿrīf bi'l-muṣṭalaḥ al-sharīf* (1894). The latter work is a sort of vade-mecum, a useful companion to a clerk who needed to know the correct formulas of address for state correspondence, or the localities within a given administrative district. The section on the administrative divisions and postal communications in Egypt and Syria has been translated by Richard Hartmann, "Politische Geographie des Mamlukenreichs: Kapitel 5 und 6 des Staatshandbuchs Ibn Fadlallah al-Omari's," *ZDMG*, lxx (1916), 1–40, 477–511; lxxi (1917), 429–430. As for the *Masālik al-abṣār*, one of the most impressive works produced in the Mamluk period, the sections on the Il-Khanid Empire and North Africa have been published and studied, by Klaus Lech (1968) and M. Gaudefroy-Demombynes (1927) respectively. But until recently the detailed chapters on Egypt and Syria have been both unpublished and unstudied, though they were available in a perfectly accessible Paris manuscript (BN Schefer 5867). Presumably the recent edition by A. F. Sayyid, *L'Égypte, la Syrie, le Ḥiğāz et le Yemen* (1985), will encourage greater scholarly attention.

7. Abū al-ʿAbbās Aḥmad al-Qalqashandī (d. 821/1418) *Ṣubḥ al-aʿshā fī ṣināʿat al-inshāʾ* (14 vols., 1913–1920). A general index was published in 1972 by M. Q. al-Baqlī; and the same scholar has now supplied a glossary of technical terms (*al-Taʿrīf bi-muṣṭalaḥāt Ṣubḥ al-aʿshā*, 1984.) Walther Björkman provides a detailed synopsis in *Beiträge zur Geschichte der Staatskanzlei im islamischen Ägypten* (1928). This is without doubt the most valuable single source we have for the entire administrative history of Islamic Egypt, a *summa* of almost every skill and form of knowledge needed by a government clerk in the Mamluk state. Five volumes are filled with accurate and dated transcripts of examples of official correspondence drawn largely from the archives. But for our purposes the precise descriptions of chancery procedure and of the structures of the central and provincial governments are even more valuable. A translation of the chapters on Syria, with excellent notes and a useful though outdated introduction, is given by Maurice Gaudefroy-Demombynes, *La Syrie à l'époque des Mamelouks* (1923). Al-Qalqashandī's account of the financial administration has been analyzed in B. Michel, "L'organisation financière de l'Égypte sous les sultans mamelouks d'après Qalqachandi," *BIE*, vii (1925), 127–147. The *Ṣubḥ al-aʿshā* does have shortcomings, obviously: (a) it contains very little financial data; (b) more important, it gives a normative, somewhat idealized and static account which minimizes change and glosses over the realities of actual political-bureaucratic behavior.

8. Taqī al-Dīn Aḥmad al-Maqrīzī (d. 845/1442), *Kitāb al-mawāʿiẓ wa'l-iʿtibar fī dhikr al-khiṭaṭ wa'l-āthār* (more commonly, the *Khiṭaṭ*). The "standard" Bulaq edition (2 vols., 1270/1853–54) is not only ill-printed and full of errors, but has no index. What amounts to an index of personal names was provided by Gaston Wiet in his analytic resume of an early biographical com-

pendium by Ibn Taghrībirdī, *Les biographies du Manhal Safi*, in *MIE*, xix (1932). The pressing need for a complete index is at last being met by Aḥmad A-M. Harīdī, *Index des Ḫiṭaṭ: Index analytique des ouvrages d'Ibn Duqmāq et de Maqrīzī sur le Caire* (3 vols., in progress, 1983–); this work will include not only personal and group names, but also dates, sources cited by al-Maqrīzī, technical terms, etc. Wiet also began, but never finished, a true critical edition in *MIFAO*, xxx, xxxiii, xlvi, xlix, liii (5 vols., 1911–27). A French translation, also incomplete, was undertaken by Urbain Bouriant and Paul Casanova, "Description historique et topographique de l'Égypte," *MMAF*, xvii (1900); *MIFAO*, iii–iv (1906–20). Finally, a brief but invaluable section has been superbly presented in Andre Raymond and G. Wiet, *Les marchés du Caire: traduction annotée du texte de Maqrizi* (1979). The *Khiṭaṭ* is essentially an historical geography of Islamic Egypt; under the name of each locality, al-Maqrīzī presents the topographic and historical data which he had been able to assemble in his vast reading. Among this data is a precious (though scattered and uneven) fund of fiscal and administrative material gleaned from sources now lost. The specifically historical character of the *Khiṭaṭ* makes it an essential supplement to the static descriptive geography of al-Qalqashandī, especially for the scholar who is concerned with the concrete effects of the administrative system on Egyptian society. (Works of roughly similar character and value pertaining to Syria are surveyed below, Chapter Ten.)

9. Yaḥyā b. Shākir, called Ibn al-Jīʿān (d. 885/1480), *al-Tuḥfa al-saniyya bi-asmāʾ al-bilād al-Miṣriyya*. Ed. B. Moritz (1898; repr. 1974). An administrative geography of Egypt based on the famous cadastral survey of al-Nāṣir Muḥammed in 715/1315, the *rawk al-Nāṣirī*, which remained the foundation of Egyptian fiscal administration until the fall of the Mamluk Empire. Ibn al-Jīʿān was an accountant (*mustawfī*) and his is an accountant's book. For each locality he cites data for each of two years, ca. 1375 and ca. 1475 as follows: the land area under cultivation, the nominal fiscal yield of the district (its *ʿibra*) and the names of the *iqṭāʿ*-holders. We thus have a cross-section of the army land-registers at two critical points in Mamluk history—one while the settlement of al-Nāṣir Muḥammad was still relatively intact, the other after a century of demographic, economic, and political crisis. We can thus plot many of the administrative and fiscal changes suffered by Egypt during that period, though of course we cannot with this data alone reconstruct the *process* by which these things happened. Ibn al-Jīʿān's data, combined with the similar though less complete material of Ibn Duqmaq (dating from ca. 1395) has been abstracted and presented in clear tabular form, with cross-references to other sources, by Heinz Halm, *Ägypten nach den mamlukischen Lehensregistern* (2 vols., 1979–82). Little use has as yet been made of Halm's work, but it is potentially a very powerful research tool, and should become the constant companion of anyone working on the institutions of Mamluk Egypt.

These texts, together with numerous others not cited here, contain a good deal of numerical data on tax revenues. This material has been collected and abstracted by Prince Omar Toussoun, *Mémoire sur les finances d'Égypte depuis les Pharaons jusqu'à nos jours*, in *MIE*, vi (1924)—pretentiously titled perhaps, but a useful and convenient if not terribly sophisticated contribution.

All the sources so far discussed are specifically administrative in nature; they were produced by bureaucrats as part of their work or for the edification of generations of bureaucrats yet to come. In order to make the most effective use of them, however, they must be read together with the vast array of narrative sources—chronicles and biographical dictionaries—left to us by Mamluk authors. There is no room to review them here, for the number of titles runs into the scores if not hundreds, and new works are constantly being brought to light. It will suffice to point to the encyclopedic comprehensiveness of these writers and to their broad range of interests. Moreover, the Mamluk historians belonged to many disparate elements in society—the military elite, *ʿulamāʾ* both petty and great, the bureaucracy, even some non-Muslims (all of them Copts in this period)—so that we have in their writings many contrasting perspectives on politics and society. All this puts us in an unusually good position to examine the broader sociopolitical significance of technical administrative institutions and procedures. By this point, it goes without saying that many of the most remarkable narrative sources remain unpublished, or are available only in incomplete or inferior editions.

How, then, is this immense trove of material to be exploited? It is tempting to undertake a systematic examination of the subject as a whole—to try to pin down in one volume the essential institutions and procedures which characterized the Mamluk fiscal machinery throughout its long existence. This is a temptation (admittedly not alluring to everyone) to which a number of scholars have succumbed, and it has led to some undeniably useful and important work. In English two such studies merit special attention. William Popper, *Egypt and Syria under the Circassian Sultans, 1382–1468 A.D.: Systematic Notes to Ibn Taghribirdi's Chronicles of Egypt* (2 vols., 1955–57) is very much what its title implies, a compendium whose purpose is to supply the background information necessary to read the author's translation of Ibn Taghrībirdī intelligently. It is less a synthetic account of the Mamluk state than a critical digest of various chapters from al-Qalqashandī. But Popper's intelligence and erudition make it an invaluable resource in many ways: its systematic and meticulous survey of offices and ranks, its materials on weights, measures, currency and prices, etc. Altogether it is probably the most sensible place to begin.

Hassanein Rabie, *The Financial System of Egypt* (mentioned above) is a work of radically different character. For the period which it covers (down to 741/1341) it has an exhaustive documentation, and Rabie's detail and exactitude are remarkable. Its organization makes this a difficult book to use for anyone who wants a synthetic description, however. It is arranged topically rather than historically, and it pays little attention to the broad societal and political context in which taxes, bureaux, and officials functioned. It is perhaps best regarded as a critical repertory of data, to which we must bring our own set of questions if we hope to use it effectively.

French scholarship has less to offer in this area—surprisingly, in view of the distinguished literature on administration and institutions in this language in many other fields. Besides the article of Michel cited above, see the long introduction (100 pp.) to Gaudefroy-Demombynes, *La Syrie à l'époque des Mamelouks.* Seriously outdated in many respects, this account remains distinguished by its clarity and coherence, and has much to offer on ceremonial, the order of precedence among state offices, and other specific topics. In German, Björkman's *Staatskanzlei im islamischen Ägypten* is useful but superficial. In Arabic, there is a substantial and well-documented work which has not been as widely used as it would seem to merit: Ibrāhīm ʿAlī Ṭarkhān, *al-Nuẓum al-iqṭāʿiyya fī al-Sharq al-Awsaṭ fī al-ʿUṣūr al-Wusṭā* (1968). In spite of its title, it focuses on Mamluk Egypt, and tries to deal with the *iqṭāʿ* in a very comprehensive way—not only fiscal and administrative questions, but also the political and social significance of the institution. But Ṭarkhān's work is afflicted by the same problem as all these general works—viz., it is ahistorical in conception. Change is recognized to some degree, but it is not the organizing principle of the presentation. As a result, the variations and contradictions in our information seem merely arbitrary and unpredictable rather than part of an intelligible process. Such rigid and schematic approaches mean that we cannot even ask how and why the visible changes (in tax rates, organization and procedures, etc.) took place. Were they connected to long-term economic processes, to purposeful revamping of the fiscal system, to factional feuds, to simple manipulation for personal profit? Unless we alter the framework of our investigations, we have no way to know.

The necessary focus, coherence, and developmental perspective might be achieved if we could direct our attention to a crucial office or institution, one whose evolution would accurately mirror that of the whole political-administrative system. Here we would be thinking of something like Dominique Sourdel, *Le vizirat abbaside de 749 à 936* (2 vols., 1959–60), which follows meticulously the development not only of the vizierate itself but of the administrative apparatus attached to it. Sourdel refuses to range very far afield from his stated subject, but his account reveals much about patterns of political conflict in the Abbasid state. In the Mamluk system, however, there was nothing equivalent to the Abbasid vizierate; the sultan relied on a constantly shifting array of military officers and senior bureaucrats to run things, and hence no one office has much to tell us about the long-term evolution of the administrative system.

An alternative approach would be to situate Mamluk administration within an explicitly developmental framework—one which seeks to clarify and explain Mamluk tax assessment, collection, and allocation procedures by determining how they fit into the evolution of Egypt's fiscal institutions from the

Arab Conquest down to Ottoman times. Such an approach seems all the more promising in that the extreme ends of this process have been quite thoroughly studied. The Ottoman period is scrutinized in Stanford J. Shaw, *The Financial and Administrative Organization and Development of Ottoman Egypt, 1517–1798* (1962). Shaw's monograph is extremely detailed, but it should be recalled that this is one of the pioneer investigations of Ottoman tax registers, and that it represents an early stage of the author's career. Another look at the Ottoman materials would surely not be out of place.

For the early Islamic period, the *locus classicus* is C. H. Becker, "Steuerverhältnisse im ersten Jahrhundert," in his *Beiträge zur Geschichte Ägyptens unter dem Islam* (2 vols., 1902–3), pp. 81–112. (The main themes of this piece are developed and further documented in Becker's other publications. See especially *Papyri Schott-Reinhardt* [1906], and two papers in Vol. I of his *Islamstudien* [2 vols., 1924–32]: "Die Entstehung von ʿUšr- und Ḫarāǧland in Ägypten," pp. 218–233; "Historische Studien über das Londoner Aphroditowerk," pp. 248–262.) Becker's masterful work shaped all further research on the subject for the next four decades, until D. C. Dennett offered a brilliant rebuttal in Chapter Five of his *Conversion and the Poll Tax in Early Islam* (1950). Dennett's revisionism held sway in turn for many years, but recently there has been a swing back towards Becker in Kosei Morimoto, *The Fiscal Administration of Egypt in the Early Islamic Period* (1981). Morimoto's contribution is especially important in the present context because he carries the story down to the end of the Abbasid period, with some reference to the crucial Fatimid developments. The debate among these scholars has taught us much, but it is hard to think that we can expect a final word on the first three Islamic centuries any time in the near future.

The Fatimid and Ayyubid regimes mark a crucial shift in Egypt's fiscal institutions, from a centrally controlled apparatus for the collection and distribution of tax revenues to a partially decentralized system in which soldiers collected their incomes directly from lands and villages assigned to them. In short, the Abbasid system is exchanged for a modified Seljukid one. To understand this process it is essential to have a solid knowledge of Seljukid administrative institutions as they developed in their Iranian homeland; this task has been considerably eased by A.K.S. Lambton, *Continuity and Change in Medieval Persia: Aspects of Administrative, Economic and Social History, 11th–14th Century* (1988). The Ayyubid synthesis of Fatimid and Seljukid practices is analyzed in Cahen's indispensable (albeit sometimes maddening) *Makhzumiyyat.* Michael Brett, "The Way of the Peasant," *BSOAS*, xlvii (1984), 44–56, clarifies some of the issues raised by Cahen.

To see Mamluk fiscal institutions in the context of a millenium-long evolution should do much to clarify administrative structures and points of detail. However, the relationship between fiscal administration and the political system as a whole can only be determined insofar as we understand the character of the Mamluk polity. The Mamluk Empire was a military oligarchy, and its central institution was necessarily the army. From another perspective, the army was the principal beneficiary of the system, and it supervised, manipulated, and interfered in the collection and disbursement of the revenues which supported it. Yet the army was not the bureaucracy, whose internal organization and procedures existed in a quite distinct world of their own. What a knowledge of the army allows us to grasp is how expenditures were allocated and distributed within the political system (or at least the most crucial element of it). In short, it allows us to make a vital connection between technical administrative problems and the issues of general history.

At the interface between the army and the bureaucracy, the most sensitive and revealing point of contact was certainly the *iqṭāʿ*, the system of revocable revenue assignments (usually but not exclusively on agricultural land) to individual officers and soldiers through which they received the bulk of their pay. The *iqṭāʿ* was an administrative device, controlled by the bureaucracy on behalf of the sultan; at the same time, it had been created as and always remained a response to the financial needs of military regimes. Hence we can approach it from either a military-political or fiscal-administrative perspective.

It had already had a long history by the time the Mamluks took it up, of course; it appeared under the first Buyid amir of Iraq in the mid-10th century, and quickly became an essential element in the fiscal-military structure of the majority of states in Western Iran and Mesopotamia. The Seljukid Empire generalized it throughout the Fertile Crescent and the whole of Iran, while the Ayyubids brought it to the Nile Valley. In spite of the immense importance of the *iqṭāʿ*, however, there is still only one reliable account of its origins and development: Claude Cahen, "L'évolution de l'iqṭāʿ du ixᵉ au xiiiᵉ siècle," *AESC*, viii (1953), 25–52; to be supplemented by the same author's "Iḳṭāʿ," *EI*², iii, 1088–1091. In light of the central role of the Buyids and the Seljukids in the development and spread of this institution, one should consult C. E. Bosworth, "Military Organization under the Buyids of Persia and Iraq," *Oriens*, xviii–xix (1967), 143–167; Tsugitaka Sato, "The Iqṭāʿ System of Iraq under the Buwayhids," *Orient* (Tokyo), xviii (1982), 83–105 (worth struggling through in spite of the author's extremely unidiomatic English); and A.K.S. Lambton, *Landlord and Peasant in Persia* (1953), and "Reflexions on the Iqṭāʿ," in G. Makdisi, ed., *Arabic and Islamic Studies in Honor of H.A.R. Gibb* (1965), 358–376. For Zangid and Ayyubid Syria, see the materials in N. Elisséeff, *Nūr ad-Dīn* (3 vols., 1967), III, 726–729, and R. S. Humphreys, *From Saladin to the Mongols* (1977), 371–375 et passim. On early Mamluk Syria, there are astute and well-documented observations in Robert Irwin, "Iqṭāʿ and the End of the Crusader States," in P. M. Holt, ed., *The Eastern Mediterranean Lands in the Period of the Crusades* (1977), 62–77.

The far richer data which we have for Mamluk Egypt has so far not been exploited at its full value. Again, a historical perspective, which takes change as the central fact to be explained and which links institutions to a broad context of financial imperatives, political interests, and policy goals, is essential, and such a perspective we do not as yet have. The valuable general studies of Rabie and Ṭarkhān give, as we have noted, a rather static presentation, in which the *iqṭāʿ* system seems to consist mostly of exceptions and special cases. A more historical approach is attempted in several studies by A. N. Poliak, but these are now obsolete, and are full of misleading notions and unsupported assertions. They are still interesting but must be used skeptically: *Feudalism in Egypt, Syria, Palestine, and the Lebanon (1250–1900)* (1939); "La féodalité islamique," *REI*, x (1936), 247–265; "Some Notes on the Feudal System of the Mamluks," *JRAS* (1937), 97–107; "The Ayyubid Feudalism," *JRAS* (1939), 428–432. (I have been unable to see E. E. al-ʿArīnī, *al-Iqṭāʿ al-ḥarbī fī zaman salāṭīn al-Mamālīk* [1956]; the title is promising, at least.)

On the other hand, we do now have some good analyses of the single most important event in the development of the Mamluk *iqṭāʿ*—the great cadastral survey and systematic reallocation of *iqṭāʿ* lands by al-Nāṣir Muḥammad in 715/1315, an act which created the framework for military administration down to the fall of the Empire. See Tsugitaka Sato, "The Evolution of the Iqṭāʿ System under the Mamluks—an Analysis of al-Rawk al-Ḥusāmī and al-Rawk al-Nāṣiri," *Memoirs of the Research Department of the Toyo Bunko*, no. 37 (Tokyo, 1979), 99–131. This study should be compared to the discussion in Heinz Halm, *Ägypten nach den mamlukischen Lehensregistern*, i, 8–34, which is especially useful in regard to the pre-Mamluk cadastral surveys. Sato's article seems at last to give us the necessary point of repair from which we can follow out the changes in the Mamluk *iqṭāʿ* system over the next two centuries, all the more as his conclusions can be combined with Halm's painstaking digest of the data supplied by Ibn Duqmāq and Ibn al-Jīʿān. There are vast gaps in our information obviously, but a systematic combing of the chronicles might well yield reliable indications if not ironclad conclusions. It is simply a matter of much time and more patience.

Such an historical account of the *iqṭāʿ*, and of the administrative bureaux connected with it (the *dīwān al-jaysh* in particular), will require an exact knowledge of the changing structure of the Mamluk army. Though there is still a very great deal to be done in this regard, the essential foundation has been laid in a lengthy series of studies by David Ayalon. Most of these have recently been grouped together in two volumes: (a) *Studies on the Mamluks of Egypt (1250–1517)* (1977); (b) *The Mamluk Military Society* (1979). His major conclusions are summed up in "Mamlūk," *EI²*, vi, 314–321. Although almost everything from Ayalon's pen is worth studying, the contributions most pertinent to our concerns in ths chapter are the following: "Studies on the Structure of the Mamluk Army," *BSOAS*, xv (1953), 203–238, 448–476; xvi (1954), 57–90; "The System of Payment in Mamluk Military Society," *JESHO*, I (1958), 37–65, 257–296.

These two studies go far toward explaining the intricate array of ranks and offices and the disparate corps making up the Mamluk army to which the *iqṭāʿ*-system had to be keyed. He has relatively little to say about the administrative machinery which supported the army, but does much to make this machinery seem intelligible and purposeful. Certain gaps and problems in his approach require notice, however. First of all, the sources available to Ayalon when he published this work date overwhelmingly from the Circassian period (9th/15th century), and he tends to be quite vague and general in dealing with the late 13th and 14th centuries, which represented the apogee of Mamluk economic and military power. In the 1950s this flaw was almost unavoidable, but a new body of texts from the earlier period simply demands that this part of his work be redone. Second, Ayalon focuses strongly on the army of Egypt and all but ignores the very differently constituted forces of Syria, which in fact did much of the Empire's fighting against its foreign enemies, and which administratively were no less significant than the Egyptian army. Finally, there is a problem of organization—Ayalon is certainly not oblivious to problems of change in the Mamluk army, and indeed refers to these constantly, but the topical structure of his discussion means that the processes of change which he discerns do not emerge clearly. On another level, he often seems to talk about change as a moral issue—a matter of greed, indiscipline, declining standards, etc.—and does not systematically examine the demographic, economic, and social milieu within which it was occurring. It is true that several of his later studies do look at these issues of milieu, but the tone of moral censure is not muted.

Few scholars besides Ayalon have seriously examined the Mamluk military system. Attempts at a different perspective can be found a few places, however: (a) the classic article of H.A.R. Gibb, "The Armies of Saladin," *Cahiers de l'histoire égyptienne*, ser. iii, no. 4 (1951), 304–320; repr. in *Studies on the Civilization of Islam*, 74–88, which focuses on a specific moment in the development of Syro-Egyptian military institutions; (b) R. S. Humphreys, "The Emergence of the Mamluk Army," *SI*, xlv (1977), 67–99; xlvi (1977), 147–182, which tries to describe the transition from late Ayyubid to early Mamluk institutions (ca. 1220–1280); (c) Ulrich Haarmann, "The Sons of Mamluks as Fief-holders in Late Medieval Egypt," in Tarif Khalidi, ed., *Land Tenure and Social Transformation in the Middle East* (1984), pp. 141–168, which deals especially with the late 8th/14th century—a crucial but heretofore almost unstudied period. Gibb's article can be supplemented (though it is not much altered) by the relevant chapters in the comprehensive synthesis of Ramazan Şeşen, *Salâhaddîn devrinde Eyyûbiler Devleti* (1983).

An institution-centered approach to administrative history allows for a high degree of consistency and continuity in one's discussion, and it can also demonstrate in very concrete terms the linkages between the fiscal bureaucracy and other key institutions of the state. But such an approach is necessarily impersonal, focusing on rules, procedures, and policies. Popular imprecations to the contrary, however, bureaucrats are not faceless and bloodless. They have families, and so long as they are in office they represent the values and interests of their families. To a large degree, the administrative system works in the way they want it to work. There is in short much to be said for neglecting institutions and procedures in favor of personalities.

The basic fund of information about bureaucrats is to be found in the biographical dictionaries which the Mamluk period produced in such profusion. These do not give an exhaustive repertory of names, however: the majority of functionaries were far too obscure to merit inclusion in such works, which focused on persons noted for their religious learning or political power. Likewise, in Egypt a great many bureaucrats, especially in the final bureaux, were Copts or recent converts to Islam, and would be excluded as such by Muslim authors. One must be grateful for the occasional dictionary like the *Tālī wafayāt al-aʿyān*, written in the early 14th century by a man who was both a Copt and a middle-level bureaucrat (Ibn al-Ṣuqāʿī, d. 726/1325), and who included a rather large number of his own kind. In the chronicles, however, bureaucrats are surprisingly visible, and a careful search of these texts can yield a great deal.

At this point only the barest beginnings of a prosopographical approach to Mamluk administration can be found in the literature. Half a century ago, Gaston Wiet provided a very useful survey of the holders of the influential post of *kātib al-sirr* (confidential secretary) in the 9th/15th century, with capsule sketches of the careers of each man based on the texts then available: "Les secrétaires de la chancellerie (*kuttāb al-sirr*) en Égypte sous les Mamlouks circassiens (784–922/1382–1517)," *Mélanges René Basset* (1923), i, 271–314. Wiet attempts no general conclusions, however, and his study is simply a starting point. A similarly conceived work is Aḥmad ʿAbd al-Rāziq, "Le vizirat et les vizirs d'Égypte au temps des Mamluks," *AI*, xvi (1980), 183–239. ʿAbd al-Rāziq's survey is better documented than Wiet's, but the biographical data is pared down radically, to the subject's dates of birth, death, and service in the vizierate. Though useful as it stands, it is more an index to the sources than a developed study.

The one scholar so far to attempt a synthetic study of the men of the bureaucracy is Carl F. Petry, *The Civilian Elite of Cairo in the Later Middle Ages* (1981). Petry's study is based on the computer analysis of a mass of data aggregated from two 15th-century biographical dictionaries, and the possibilities and problems posed by this method will be discussed in the next chapter. Here it is more useful to note those aspects of his discussion which pertain to the bureaucrats. First of all, he is not very interested in them as men of the state, but rather as members of the native, Arabic-speaking society of Syria and Egypt who had somehow risen to positions of some influence and visibility in a Mamluk-controlled political system. They are treated as but one element in a native, non-military social elite which was really dominated by men of religion. Second, he is interested in only a few aspects of their lives—viz., their geographic origins (whether Cairene, Upper Egyptian, North Syrian, etc.); their residence patterns in Cairo; and their career patterns—i.e, the degree of mobility between one profession and another enjoyed by members of this civilian elite. Questions about family background, education, sources of income, political roles, are often alluded to but are not systematically explored. In short, he creates for us a solid (though far from comprehensive) framework within which we can place the careers of the men of the civil administration, but the dynamics of bureaucratic life—the ways in which men chose career lines, tried to fend off rivals and claw their way to the top, influence policy-making by the sultan and the senior amirs, reinforce their personal ties to other members of the military and civilian elites, assert prestige and leadership within the indigenous society from which they had emerged—all these things can be perceived only dimly. Nor do we gain any sense of the precise role of the bureaucracy in the endemic political and economic crises of the 9th/15th century. One scholar cannot do everything, of course, at least not in one book, and Petry's solid achievement shows how very far we have to go before we can begin to understand in depth the manifold political and social roles of the bureaucrats of the Mamluk Empire.

In spite of the admirable work produced along the lines explored above, very few scholars have tried to integrate administrative problems into a comprehensive view of Mamluk history, at least in an explicit and systematic way. And yet precisely this (as we argued at the outset of the chapter) should be the goal of administrative history. In this light, the achievements of two major studies are all the more distinctive:

1. Ahmad Darrag, *L'Égypte sous le règne de Barsbāy, 825–841/1422–1438* (1961).
2. Jean-Claude Garcin, *Un centre musulman de la Haute-Égypte médiévale: Qūṣ* (1976).

Darrag has adopted a framework which is commonplace in most fields of history, but is seldom used in medieval Islamic studies: the political history of a particular reign. His approach is saved from conventionality by his interpretation: he sees Barsbāy's policy as a response—often ingenious but desperate and destructive as well—to the long-term economic crisis in which Egypt was mired. His efforts to assert the paramountcy of the Mamluk state in the Eastern Mediterranean and to preserve the prerogatives of the military elite both had to be carried out within a context of economic depression. One-third of the book is explicitly devoted to the economic situation and Barsbāy's administrative responses to it.

Darrag certainly conveys a wealth of information—in particular, he makes good use of the fiscal inscriptions published by Wiet and Sauvaget—but in the end his account seems adequate neither from the economic nor from the administrative point of view. On the administrative side, he focuses on the themes of corruption, malfeasance, and extortion without really exploring the development of the administrative machinery as such. He piles up anecdotes and figures—very revealing in themselves—without showing precisely where they fit into the administrative system or what kind of process they add up to. As to the economic situation, his description again tends to be anecdotal. He recognizes that the numbers he cites are often contradictory and doubtful, but he does not present them in a systematic form nor does he evaluate them rigorously. Finally, and most critically, he has no model of the Syro-Egyptian economic system to guide his discussion; he can show us that this economy was in serious trouble in the early 9th/15th century, but he cannot demonstrate how its many problems were related to one another. Obviously an elaborate econometric model of the contemporary sort is out of the question; on the other hand, an outline in verbal form of the main sectors of the economy and their linkages to one another is possible and very much needed. Darrag was of course a pioneer (in the peculiar context of Islamic studies) in the effort to integrate political and economic history, and should not be berated for conceptual shortcomings of the kind suggested here. But his successors may need to do some careful reading in the economics of developing countries (admittedly a terribly vexed field, and especially thickly strewn with ideological mines). Even more to the point, they need to read widely on economic structures and trends in Mediterranean Europe between the 7th/13th and 9th/15th centuries. In this period the economies of these lands were affected by many of the same forces (most obviously the Black Death) as Egypt and Syria, and were closely linked to them through a highly developed commercial network. Mediterranean Europe is thus a mirror (however distorted) of economic life in the Mamluk Empire.

Garcin's *Qūṣ* is a different sort of book altogether; it attempts to develop a comprehensive history of a small region, in which political, economic, social, and cultural dimensions are not only represented but fully integrated with one another. The region chosen is interesting: a rather under-developed province, geographically remote from the main centers of economic and political power in Egypt but not isolated from them. It would be extremely misleading to claim that Qūṣ and its district represent the "real Egypt," but clearly they represent an aspect of the Empire that one can never grasp from a Cairene perspective. Even for its innumerable poor, after all, Cairo was a place which consumed the surpluses produced elsewhere, a sort of colonial metropolis into which the production of all Egypt and Syria flowed, and on the most favorable terms of trade. Qūṣ, in contrast, was only a point of administration and exchange, a place through which rural revenues and the Red Sea trade passed on their way to the capital. The experience of Qūṣ, however distinctive, certainly resembled far more than Cairo's that of the vast majority of the Empire's population.

Garcin devotes a lengthy chapter to an analysis of the various roles played by Qūṣ within the structure of the early Mamluk state—e.g., control over the Bedouin, security of the trade and pilgrimage routes between the Nile and the Red Sea—and in this context he sifts through the data given by Ibn al-Jīʿān in order to explore the allocation of *iqṭāʿ*s in Upper Egypt ca. 1375. Although Garcin presents a meticulous account of the amirial grants, he is particularly interested in how the sultan exploited the "crown estates" of the district. He suggests a bias toward commercial livestock grazing, and examines the administrative offices and their personnel (largely Christian). Altogether, the precision and historical concreteness of Garcin's discussion are a most refreshing change from the usual mechanical survey of such topics. But his approach reveals its true merit when he comes to examine the dismal events of the 9th/15th century. Because his initial description is both placed in a broad political-economic context and securely anchored in a specific time and place, he is able to reconstruct an intelligible account (which is not necessarily to say a correct or definitive one) of administrative trends during the century following 1375. For once, we see how the degradation in administrative institutions and procedures is rooted in demographic decline, the economic crises of the early 1400s, etc. We are no longer compelled to attribute unpleasant changes to such permanent (and hence explanatorily useless) elements of human nature as greed, ambition, and malice.

Garcin, in brief, seems to me to have achieved more fully than anyone else the integration of specifically administrative problems into a broad historical framework. Here if anywhere the pitfalls of tunnel history and the mechanistic view of administration are avoided. Obviously his approach cannot be replicated for other provinces in any simple-minded way, not only because our sources for them vary so widely, but also because Qūṣ' frontier location gave it such a distinctive social, cultural, and political profile. But the spirit which informs this work certainly can be transferred, and regions like the Fayyūm, the Delta, or the Syrian provinces would profit immensely from studies carried out from such a perspective. Certainly no other strategy seems likely to yield so much insight into what the Mamluk state was and how it worked.

Chapter Eight

A CULTURAL ELITE

THE ROLE AND STATUS OF THE ʿULAMĀʾ *IN ISLAMIC SOCIETY*

Ulamalogy is a noble science—at least we have to think so, because it is almost all the Islamic social history we will ever have. . . .
(Roy P. Mottahedeh, in *JAOS*, xcv [1975], 495)

WHO AND WHAT are the *ʿulamāʾ*? It is easier to say what they are not, for they are neither a socio-economic class, nor a clearly defined status group, nor a hereditary caste, nor a legal estate, nor a profession. They appear in our texts as semi-literate village imams and erudite qadis, as rabble-rousers and privy counselors to kings, as spiritual directors and cynical politicians. Some are scions of wealthy and influential families, others are impoverished immigrants from remote villages. Some are landowners, some are salaried professors or bureaucrats, some are merchants or humble artisans. The great majority are men, but there are a number of notable women in their ranks as well. In short, they seem to cut across almost every possible classification of groups within Islamic society, playing a multiplicity of political, social, and cultural roles. But in spite of this ambiguity, they are plainly a crucial element in Islamic society—the one group which in fact makes it "Islamic" rather than something else—and wherever we turn we encounter them.

Perhaps the *ʿulamāʾ* seem so complex and elusive simply because we know so much about them, at least relative to other groups in medieval Islamic society. Such a degree of knowledge should not be surprising, to be sure, for they wrote the bulk of the prose texts which have come down to us, and they naturally tended to talk about themselves and their own concerns. But more specifically, they evolved a scientific-literary genre which focuses strongly (though far from exclusively) on men of religious learning and prestige. This is the biographical dictionary. The mere mass of these works would make them an essential tool for the study of the *ʿulamāʾ*, but equally to the point is that they yield an astonishingly complete and exact self-image of this group. We can know these people in their own terms far more directly and comprehensively than we can any other element in Islamic society.

For two reasons, then—their omnipresence, and the caliber of our data—the *ʿulamāʾ* demand special attention by the social historian. It would be extremely misleading to say that we can generalize from the *ʿulamāʾ* to the rest of society, but we can use a precise, critical knowledge of their behavior to throw light into nooks and crannies of the social system that would otherwise remain obscure. By seeing how they dealt with one another and with non-*ʿulamāʾ*, we should be able to develop a sense of the patterns of social action which were available to medieval Muslims generally.

Since our principal source is the biographical dictionary, we will begin our investigation with a discussion of its characteristics. Biographical dictionaries, in their hundreds or thousands, come in every conceivable size and format, and useful generalizations are difficult to make. However, there is a clear and perceptive introduction to the subject in H.A.R. Gibb, "Islamic Biographical Literature," in Lewis and Holt, *Historians of the Middle East*, 54–58. (Gibb's persistent anti-Iranian bias is evident even here, however.) A more detailed survey is that of Ibrahim Hafsi, "Recherches sur le genre 'Ṭabaqāt' dans la littérature arabe," *Arabica*, xxiii (1976), 228–265; xxiv (1977), 1–41, 150–186. Hafsi gives a good overview of the forms of organization and the types of subject matter to be found in such works, but his study is not a comprehensive examination of the biographical dictionary. Rather, he is specifically concerned with the meaning and usage of the term "*ṭabaqāt*" ("classes"—lit., "layers," "strata"), and he refers only to texts which include this word in their titles. Finally, we now have a very useful reference tool in Paul Auchterlonie, *Arabic Biographical Dictionaries: A Summary Guide and Bibliography* (1987), a selective but judicious overview of this immense body of texts. Auchterlonie focuses on the needs of librarians and researchers, however, and provides little on the development or the literary structures of this genre.

The biographical dictionary appears very early in the development of Islamic historical writing. Our first three extant works (all of them available in printed editions) were compiled in the middle years of the 3rd/9th century: the *Kitāb al-ṭabaqāt al-kabīr* of Ibn Saʿd (d. 230/845), the disciple and "secretary" (*kātib*) of al-Wāqidī; the *Kitāb al-ṭabaqāt* of Khalīfa b. Khayyāṭ al-ʿUṣfurī (d. 240/854); and the *Ṭabaqāt al-shuʿarāʾ al-jāhiliyya wa'l-islāmiyyīn* of Muḥammad ibn Sallam al-Jumaḥī (d. 231/846). Thereafter the chain of biographical works is almost unbroken, and this fact has important implications for the student of the "learned classes" in Islam: whatever doubts we may have as to the authenticity of our information on the Companions and the Successors, from the late 2nd/8th century on we have solid—indeed often contemporary—biographical data. Mistakes and bias abound, but there is at least little pure invention.

Earlier biographical works tended to focus on religious scholars—hadith-transmitters, *faqīhs*, Qurʾān-reciters, etc.—but with the passage of time the net was spread more broadly. Thus there came to be by the late 4th/10th century specialized dictionaries of poets and other men of letters, Sufis, physicians, even senior bureaucrats. The first great general dictionary, one including men of distinction in all fields, was Ibn Khallikān's well-documented but highly selective (some 850 entries) *Wafayāt al-aʿyān fī anbāʾ abnāʾ al-zamān*, completed in Cairo in 672/1274. It is striking and instructive, however, that the productive classes of society—the farmers, merchants, and artisans—never made it into the dictionaries as such, though a few persons of such background do appear under a more respectable rubric.

The earlier dictionaries attempted to provide comprehensive coverage for those broad classes (hadith specialists or poets, usually) which they included in their purview. But in the 4th/10th century we see a growing tendency to include only subgroups, defined by place of residence, legal or theological sect, etc. Such changes in the criteria for inclusion have important cultural implications, obviously; thus there seems to be a feeling that one's Islam is not defined by his fidelity to Scripture (Qurʾān and hadith) but by the way in which he interprets it, or that a locality can properly be a Muslim's primary (though not ultimate) focus of cultural identity. Only in the 7–8th/13–14th centuries, and then chiefly in the Mamluk dominions, does a universal, encyclopedic impulse reassert itself: on this point Ibn Khallikān perhaps marks the watershed, but the culmination is reached only in the colossal (no hyperbole in this case) *al-Wāfī bi'l-wafayāt* of Muḥammad b. Aybak al-Ṣafadī (d. 764/1363).

Although a single author would sometimes write both chronicles and biographical dictionaries, these are very distinct genres as to sources, methods, and subject matter, and they convey very different kinds of information. This remains true to a considerable degree even when both genres are combined in a single work, as in the *Muntaẓam* of Ibn al-Jawzī (d. 597/1200), the first of a long succession of works which systematically followed the events of a given year or decade with obituaries of the notable persons who had died therein.

Arabic is almost the exclusive language for dictionaries focused on men of religion, wherever and whenever they were compiled, but from the 6th/12th century Persian was widely used for lives of Sufis and poets.

Even more than in other genres, biographical compilers copy from their predecessors and even contemporaries. As a result, several of the lives devoted to a particular individual are likely to be paraphrases or abridgements of a single original text. There are relatively few examples where we have truly independent lines of testimony about a given person, though of course this problem must be resolved separately for each case. This feature of the biographical literature can be very frustrating, obviously, but it also means that a great many texts which are otherwise lost—some of them of great antiquity—can be reconstructed quite reliably. Thus Ibn Ḥajar al-ʿAsqalānī (d. 852/1449) wrote works on the Companions and early traditionalists which preserve many statements from 2nd–3rd/8th–9th century materials still extant in his day. (On this point, however, see the cautionary remarks of G.H.A. Juynboll, *Muslim Tradition: Studies in Chronology, Provenance and Authorship of Early Hadith* [1983], pp. 135–137, 237–241.)

Keeping these points in mind, we can now begin to ask what sort of knowledge about the *ʿulamāʾ* can be gleaned from these works—about, in short, the very men who wrote them. As always, we should begin by trying to understand a text in its own terms, by identifying the questions which its author was trying to answer. We can find a fairly typical biographical entry (Ar., *tarjama*) in the following text from the Andalusian scholar Ibn al-Abbār (595–658/1199–1260), *Kitāb al-takmila li-kitāb al-ṣila* (ed. F. Codera, *BAH*, V, no. 792, p. 246):

> Muḥammad b. ʿAbd al-ʿAzīz b. ʿAlī b. ʿĪsā b. Saʿīd b. Mukhtār al-Ghāfiqi, from the people of Cordoba. His kunya was Abū al-Ḥasan, and he is known as al-Shaqūrī because his family originally came from Shaqūra [modern Segura de la Sierra]. He studied (hadith) with Abū ʿAbdallāh b. al-Aḥmar al-Qurashī; Abū Bakr b. al-ʿArabī; Abū Jaʿfar al-Biṭrūjī; Abū al-Qāsim b. Rāḍī; Abū ʿAbdallāh b. Makkī; Abū Aḥmad b. Rizq; Abū Muḥammad al-Nafazī; Abū Bakr b. Mudīr; ʿAbd al-Raḥīm al-Ḥajjārī [or al-Ḥijāzī]; Abū al-Ṭāhir al-Tamīmī; Abū Isḥāq b. Thibāt; Abū Bakr Yaḥyā b. Mūsā al-Birzālī; Abū Muḥammad ʿAbdallāh b. ʿAlī b. Faraj; and others. Abū al-Walīd b. Khayra, Ibn al-Dabbāgh, and Ḥaydar b. Yaḥyā al-Bajīlī licensed him (to teach their works). He knew by memory the history of Andalus. He was devoted to the study of hadith—he travelled widely in order to hear it, could discriminate among its transmitters, was deeply versed in the channels (through which it had been handed down), and [in short] had a complete mastery of this subject. He was equal to anyone in Arabic philology, and shared the asceticism, merit, and fine reputation of his father and family as regards the acquisition and transmission (of knowledge). He held the qadiship of Shaqūra, the town of his ancestors. His conduct was praiseworthy; he was just in his judgments, firm in regard to the right, and not fretful of (the problems) which he encountered in office. He dictated hadith and people of standing copied it on his authority; he did not study with his father concerning (topics) wherein he was more knowledgeable. He was born in 520 and died on Wednesday, 2 Muḥarram, 579. He was buried in the cemetery of Umm Salama, at the bend of the road facing the tomb of Hārūn b. Sālim. Abū al-ʿAbbās al-Majrīṭī led the funeral prayers for him. Most of (this account) is on the authority of Ibn Ḥawṭ Allāh.

It is rather an austere entry. It gives us only a few facts about al-Ghāfiqī—not even everything we would look for in a modern capsule obituary. In regard to his principal public office (the qadiship of Shaqūra), for example, we are not told when or by whom he was appointed. As much attention is given to his funeral as to any other facet of his life. But this entry is in fact fuller than most of those in Ibn al-Abbār, and the question naturally arises, what are we to do with this kind of biographical data? If it is a question of al-Ghāfiqī as an individual, the answer is plainly very little. But if we are willing to see him as just one member in a collectivity, then we might take a more hopeful view. At least six points can be made to support this contention.

First of all, we have a full genealogy, comprising six generations, together with a tribal *nisba*. If some of his ancestors were also men of learning (as seems likely from other data in the biography), then we might be able by searching Ibn al-Abbār and other Andalusian dictionaries to trace the emergence of a prominent learned family. Genealogies are not easy to use, to be sure, and many times they are quite fictitious once one goes back more than three or four generations, since men of Berber or native Spanish descent would often try to claim a noble Arabian tribal origin for themselves.

Second, we know al-Ghāfiqī's place of residence in his earlier years (Córdoba) and his family's place of origin (Segura). Like many men of ambition and some talent, then, a fairly recent ancestor had abandoned a small provincial town to seek his fortune in a major city. A systematic survey of the dictionaries for such data could tell us much about the major centers of learning in each region, their connections with one another, the cultural hinterlands over which they held sway, the kinds of study pursued in each place, the geographic origins of the *ʿulamāʾ*, etc.

Third, we have a good list of the men with whom al-Ghāfiqī studied. Since many of these are likely to have been scholars of some prominence, it should in principle be possible to trace them in the dictionaries. (The fact that most here are identified only by *kunyā* and *nisba*, while most dictionaries in this period arrange their entries by *ism*, obviously complicates matters.) Insofar as this task could be achieved, the personal network within which al-Ghāfiqī was trained and began his career could be re-established. Depending on one's skill and doggedness, this network could be linked to political factions, religious circles, various kinds of social groupings (clans, classes, etc.). This kind of prosopographic investigation is always slow and painstaking at best, and its results are often exiguous; it is only likely to be useful if one goes in knowing quite precisely what problems he wishes to explore.

Fourth, we are given al-Ghāfiqī's dates of birth and death. Death dates at least are almost always cited in the biographical literature, and this fact allows us to construct a time-series, hence to examine the several dimensions of *ʿulamāʾ* life within a framework of time and change.

Fifth, a valuable insight into cultural and religious life is afforded by the list of subjects which al-Ghāfiqī had studied. This sort of material, repeated with little variation in almost all entries, allows us to construct a profile of intellectual activity. Since such profiles are based on aggregate data, they are rather stiff and lifeless by themselves, but they can provide an objective context for a scholar who is trying, for example, to assess the cultural place and significance of a particular work or writer.

Finally, al-Ghāfiqī's one major public office is mentioned. This type of data is not given in systematic, predictable ways, because it is not always germane to the purposes of the biographical literature. Still, there is enough to give us some valuable indications as to the typical career patterns and sources of income of the *ʿulamāʾ*.

The methodological implications of the above discussion can be summed up in the following way. First of all, the kind of data given in the typical biographical dictionary can almost never support a detailed biographical study of an individual; for a serious investigation of a man's career and personality, a great many other materials must be available. On the other hand, it is precisely the repetitive, formulaic character of their data that permits quantitative and prosopographic approaches to the *ʿulamāʾ*; for no other group in Islamic society can we construct such a systematic and comprehensive profile. Because of their narrow scope, however, biographical dictionaries cannot be used in a vacuum; the aggregate data derived from them can be given life and substance only when it is fleshed out from other sources. (In this context, it should be said that the impersonality of the biographical dictionary, and of its cousin the chronicle obituary, is much less marked in certain works of the Mamluk and post-Mamluk period. Thus al-Sakhāwī [d. 902/1497] in *al-Ḍawʾ al-lāmiʿ fī aʿyān al-qarn al-tāsiʿ*, is direct, vividly detailed, and often virulent in his judgments of personality. ʿAbd al-Raḥmān al-Jabartī [d. 1240/1825] gives remarkably lifelike portraits of the 18th-century figures included in his *ʿAjāʾib al-āthār*—though amirs fare better than *ʿulamāʾ*. But even in these cases we are not dealing with biography in our sense of the term.)

Given the characteristics and possibilities of the biographical literature, what are the strategies through which it can best be exploited? We shall explore this question simply by looking at the different ways in which modern scholars have tried to deal with the *ʿulamāʾ* as social actors. It is tempting, no doubt, to think of some of these approaches as "old-fashioned," others as "revolutionary." But that is a useless game. Our goal is to achieve a comprehensive, or at least many-dimensioned, understanding of the *ʿulamāʾ*. All we need to know is what each available approach has been able to contribute to this goal, and how different approaches can be made to complement and reinforce one another.

We have already noted that biographical studies are not favored by the sources at our disposal. But when two conditions are met, biography has proved to be an approach worth pursuing: (1) when a subject has left a large body of work in which he comments fairly regularly on his own experience; (2) when he is so public a figure that his statements and actions are extensively recorded in contemporary chronicles. For the *ʿulamāʾ* these two conditions occur but rarely. Their writing was for the most part technical scholarship, dry and impersonal in tone. As for writing about one's personal life and inner experience—the very stuff of biography as we know it—that was crude and indiscreet; it was simply not done by people who cared about their dignity. Even a man like al-Jāḥiẓ (half an *ʿālim* at least), with his exceptionally direct and personal manner, tells us almost nothing about his own doings and feelings. Nor were most *ʿulamāʾ*, however well placed, likely to be engaged in the kind of actions that political chroniclers would note. Only those who were notorious rabble-rousers and gadflies could expect much attention from this quarter.

In only a small number of cases, and these very atypical, can we hope to find those connections between social milieu and the development of personality which are the essence of biography. They are not to be dismissed because of their atypicality, however, for they are one of our few avenues of escape from abstract trends and processes, and towards a recognition of how the *'ulamā'* thought and behaved in concrete situations. In addition to its humanistic value, biography can suggest lines of inquiry and working hypotheses even for contexts where this method cannot be applied.

It must be said that none of the biographical studies so far done on the *'ulamā'* is a comprehensive "life and times" in the manner of Robert Blake's *Disraeli*. Rather, they are what we could call intellectual biography—efforts to reconstruct the outer circumstances of a man's life in order to comprehend better the character and development of his thought.

The classic essay of this kind is certainly Henri Laoust, *Essai sur les doctrines sociales et politiques de Taki-d-Din Ahmad B. Taimiya* (1939). Here a meticulous examination of Ibn Taymiyya's thought is prefaced by a biographical-historical essay of about 150 pages. It is rather conventional in form (though skillfully handled), dealing with the origins of Ibn Taymiyya's family, the general political and cultural milieu of the late 13th and early 14th centuries, his "formation intellectuale et morale," and his public career. Laoust firmly directs these pages towards those aspects of Ibn Taymiyya's life which seem to throw a direct light on his thought. He makes no effort to reconstruct his complex personality, nor does he try to identify his place as a social actor—that is, Laoust does not explicitly ask what it meant to be an activist Sunni scholar within the framework of an autocratic-military state. In other words, politics is background here, not a set of values, expectations, and rules of behavior within which an individual actor tries to define and achieve his goals. Laoust's presentation is masterful in its own terms, but it is important to realize that he does not broach all the issues that a contemporary biographer might want to discuss. Two such issues have been followed up in a pair of articles by D. P. Little, "The Historical and Historiographic Significance of the Detention of Ibn Taymiyya," *IJMES*, iv (1973), 311–327; and "Did Ibn Taymiyya Have a Screw Loose?" *SI*, xli (1975), 93–111.

In view both of the very large number of texts available for these years, and of the light which Ibn Taymiyya's career sheds on the religious establishment and its relations with the Mamluk state, a new biographical study—this time socio-political rather than intellectual in intention—seems well worth the effort. The fact that we have an unusual degree of insight into Ibn Taymiyya's personality, since he was never a man to let dignity and tact interfere with his acts and statements, only adds to the possible rewards of the task.

A second figure who has attracted a fair amount of biographical study is Ibn Khaldūn. Obviously the scope and originality of his intellect have been the prime focus of scholarly interest, as can be attested by a glance at the "Selected

Bibliography" which Walter J. Fischel has appended to the translation of the *Muqaddima* by Franz Rosenthal, 2nd rev. ed. (1967), iii, 485–521. On the other hand, most students of Ibn Khaldūn have felt that an exact knowledge of the external facts of his life is critical to a valid interpretation of his thought. Thus Muhsin Mahdi prefaces his classic (though by no means unchallenged) analysis with a substantial biographical essay: *Ibn Khaldun's Philosophy of History* (1957), pp. 17–62. Mahdi interprets his subject's very turbulent public career as a kind of Platonic search for the ideal ruler. The accounts given by Rosenthal (*Muqaddima*, vol. I, xxix–lxvii) and Muḥammad Talbi ("Ibn Khaldūn," *EI*[2], iii, 825–831) are drier and in the latter case more skeptical, but both continue to see Ibn Khaldūn's personal political experience as a fundamental element of his thought.

It is thus all the stranger that we have no adequate full-scale biography of this man, though we are admittedly better provided for in his case than in most others. A worthy but now dated account is that of Muḥammad ʿInān, *Ibn Khaldūn, ḥayātuhu wa-turāthuhu al-fikrī* (1933), published in English as M. A. Enan, *Ibn Khaldūn, His Life and Work* (1941: 2nd ed., 1946). By far the most significant work, however, has been done by W. J. Fischel; see especially *Ibn Khaldūn and Tamerlane: Their Historic Meeting in Damascus, A.D. 1401 (803 A.H.)* (1952), and *Ibn Khaldūn in Egypt (1382–1406)* (1967). Both studies are based closely on Ibn Khaldūn's celebrated autobiography (a very rare genre in Islamic literature), which received its final recension in 1405; of this there is a good edition by Muḥammad Ṭāwīt al-Ṭanjī, *al-Taʿrīf bi-Ibn Khaldūn wa-riḥlatuhu gharban wa-sharqan* (1370/1951). Using a less complete recension, de Slane provided a fluent French version in the introduction to his famous translation of the *Muqaddima: Prolégomènes historiques d'Ibn Khaldoun* (1862).

We will close our discussion on biography with a unique figure who has been dealt with in a unique way; Louis Massignon's *La passion d'al-Hallaj* (1922; 2nd rev. ed., 1975; trans. by Herbert Mason as *The Passion of al-Hallaj*, 4 vols., 1982) is an astonishing tour de force which cannot be—and perhaps should not be—duplicated. Massignon has given us what might be called a spiritual biography, one based on a profound knowledge of the texts, but also, and more decisively, on intuition and empathetic understanding. In terms of hard facts, we have only a skeleton of al-Ḥallāj's career, and much of what we are told about him is saintly hagiography rather than earth-bound history. Massignon was not deterred by such obstacles, because his goal was not to establish a chronology of al-Ḥallāj's actions, but somehow to penetrate to the core of his spiritual personality, and to see it as a vital response to the totality of his milieu. Such a program required no simple background sketch, but an effort to reconstruct the political crises, socio-religious life, and intellectual resources not only of Iraq in the early 4th/10th century, but of all those places where al-Ḥallāj had lived and studied: Fars, Khurasan and Transoxiana, even India.

Massignon's work is extraordinarily evocative, and full of insight on every topic he touches. It is no surprise that he should have inspired an entire generation of French Orientalists, including such major figures as Henri Laoust, Roger Arnaldez, and Louis Gardet. On the other hand, Massignon was also (as one colleague has put it) a prophet who saw so deep and so far that sometimes he perceived things that were not there. Most notoriously, he argued that Ismailism was the ideology of the artisan guilds in Islamic cities—a statement that led generations of scholars astray until Claude Cahen and Samuel Stern demonstrated that Ismailism had no particular connection with artisanal groups, and that in fact there were no guilds at all in early Islamic times. But the problems associated with Massignon's empathy and intuition go further; he was himself a mystic, steeped in the Catholic tradition, and like all mystics he tended to transfer the symbolic forms of one religious system to another. Without this tendency he could perhaps not have grasped al-Ḥallāj and his spiritual world at all; on the other hand, his reconstruction of the Muslim mystic is an intensely personal one, strongly colored by his own religious experience. It is hard to think that we can, through Massignon, perceive al-Ḥallāj as he perceived himself.

If Massignon cannot be a model for most scholars, however, he remains an almost inexhaustible source of ideas and suggestions. The value of his work might be grasped in two ways—through the evaluation of him in Jacques Waardenburg, *L'Islam dans le miroir de l'Occident* (1967), or by setting his book side-by-side with that of others. An extreme case might be Charles Pellat's *Le milieu basrien et la formation de Ǧāḥiẓ* (1953). Pellat's is an austere work which nails down all the objective data available to us on Basra in the late 2nd/8th century, but in which the sense of time and place, the feeling for what was morally and philosophically at stake, is almost completely undeveloped. One has a far surer guide in Pellat than in Massignon, but the journey is infinitely less rewarding.

All three of the figures discussed above were men who set themselves apart, by choice or otherwise, from their fellows; it thus makes fairly good sense, the state of the sources permitting, to try to deal with them as individuals. But the vast majority of *'ulamā'* did not stand out so clearly from the crowd, and indeed had no desire to do so. In their ideal self-image, they embodied the values of the Community and saw their work as a collective enterprise. If we want to deal with them as social actors, then one of our chief goals must be to define the types of collectivities with which they identified themselves and through which they tried to act. Among these collectivities, some were professional in function and recruitment (e.g., the *madhhab* or the *madrasa*), while others (clans, factions, urban settlements) were constitutive elements of society as a whole.

From the point of view of the *'ulamā'*, at least from the 3rd/9th century on, the crucial collectivity was doubtless the "school of law" or *madhhab*—a typical medieval Islamic institution in its amorphousness, elusiveness, and extraordinary durability. It assured continuity and stability both in education and doctrine, and through affiliation with a *madhhab* a scholar became connected with a wide-ranging professional and social network. It was in brief the main instrument through which one found his place in the world of the *ʿulamāʾ*. On the *madhhab* as a societal-professional institution (as opposed to a body of legal doctrine), relatively little work has been done. The most systematic body of research in this field is probably represented by a series of studies by Henri Laoust on the Ḥanbalis, a natural extension of his work on Ibn Taymiyya:

a. "Aḥmad ibn Ḥanbal," *EI²*, i, 280–286.

b. "Le Hanbalisme sous le Califat de Bagdad, 241/855–656/1258," *REI*, xxvii (1959), 67–128.

c. "Le hanbalisme sous les Mamlouks Bahrides, 658–784/1260–1382," *REI*, xxviii (1960), 1–72.

d. *Le précis de droit d'Ibn Qudāma (541/1146–620/1223).* (1950), pp. ix–lvi.

e. *La profession de foi d'Ibn Baṭṭa (m. 387/997)* (1958), pp. vii–cxxxviii.

Besides the great fund of data which Laoust's studies contribute, they bring out several important concepts. First of all, the sense in which Islamic law and theology were a collective enterprise emerges with great clarity. One learns in Laoust's surveys not to look for a few outstanding masterpieces, but to see a continual elaboration and distillation by disciples of the teachings (both oral and written) of their masters. In this process, we should regard extant works merely as momentary crystallizations of a continuously developing tradition. Second, Laoust shows us the very personal nature of the *madhāhib*; they are networks of colleagues, masters, and disciples, united on the ideological level by their proclaimed fidelity to the doctrines of a great *imām*, and knit together socially by a variety of personal ties, including clientship, marriage, and descent. Third, Laoust brings out the constant interplay and tension between the course of politics and the evolution of doctrine.

As in his *Ibn Taimiya*, Laoust pays little heed to social structures and institutions per se, and we get no clear sense of how the Ḥanbalīs fit into the general social and economic life of Baghdad or Damascus. Likewise, his treatment of politics is fairly narrow and selective; it is the politics of the court, not the whole range of social decision-making, that he treats, and this naturally limits the context in which the *ʿulamāʾ* are perceived as politically relevant actors. Finally, Laoust's approach has a limitation connected with his subject rather than his method. The Ḥanbalīs were normally the smallest, the most cohesive, and the most localized of the *madhāhib*. Hence we should be reluctant to use the Ḥanbalīs as a model for the analysis of the other schools, which were far larger, more diffuse, and socially and politically more complex. As a result, we would expect them to be far more liable to internal faction, doctrinal quarrels, class or ethnic or status divisions, etc.

The program implied by Laoust's approach has been most fully worked out in George Makdisi's imposing *Ibn ʿAqīl et la résurgence de l'Islam traditionaliste au xie siècle* (1963). (See also above, pp. 156, 160) Makdisi's work is in fact many studies simultaneously: a detailed review of the biographical literature relative to 5th/11th-century Baghdad; a survey, one by one, of all the major scholars in the city during this period; a narrative account of the Ḥanbalī movement and its sometimes violent clashes with other religio-political groups; finally, an outline of the career of the Ḥanbalī jurist-theologian Ibn ʿAqīl (with particular attention, in the manner of the old *ṭabaqāt*, to his teachers and students). Makdisi does not attempt to develop the personality of his subject; rather, he sees Ibn ʿAqīl as a point of intersection for the religious, political, and intellectual cross-currents of his epoch. His real protagonist in the end is the Ḥanbalī *madhhab* of 5th/11th-century Baghdad; the collectivity, not the individual, is primary.

The world of learning as Makdisi presents it is no serene academy, but a complex religio-political system, full of tension and conflict on many levels. It is however a world made up mostly of elites (religious and political), where the masses are present only as a lump of humanity which the elites can occasionally mobilize or goad into violence for their own purposes. But precisely how the masses are mobilized, why they feel involved in these disputes, the structure of religious institutions at the quarter level, the links between popular groups like *futuwwa* clubs or *ʿayyār* gangs and religious leaders—of all this we get only occasional glimpses. That the leading *ʿulamāʾ* were on several levels a powerful political presence, taken very seriously by men like the caliph al-Qāʾim or the viziers ʿAmīd al-Mulk al-Kundurī and Niẓām al-Mulk, of this there is no doubt. But the mechanisms through which they were able to translate religious leadership into political power are not so clear.

Whatever the limitations of Laoust's approach—even as modified by Makdisi—one would dearly love to see studies of this kind for the other schools. For the Ḥanafīs and Mālikīs we currently have no surveys at all, though at least for the latter there is a rich documentation assembled over many centuries. For the Shāfiʿīs, however, there is now a very useful skeleton history in Heinz Halm, *Die Ausbreitung der šāfiʿitischen Rechtschule von den Anfängen bis zum 8/14 Jahrhundert* (1974). (This is one of the Beiheften to *TAVO*, on which see above, p. 16. The maps numbered 13.VIII.16–18 are specifically devoted to the several *madhāhib*.) Halm has used a wide array of sources, some of them in manuscript, in order to identify as many scholars as possible in each significant center of Shāfiʿī jurisprudence. His work is organized geographically, moving more or less southwestward from Transoxiana and Khurasan. For each major urban center he presents a list of the known qadis whatever their *madhhab*, and in a few cases he is also able to reconstruct family trees for important Shāfiʿī clans. Each individual named is footnoted to an Arabic text. What we have of course is not a history of this *madhhab* but rather a *catalogue raisonnée* of the materials needed for that purpose.

Halm's compilation opens up some very interesting research possibilities. In particular, he makes it relatively easy to undertake a series of regional and comparative studies. We can for example use his outline to discover the degree of scholarly exchange and communication (or conversely, mutual isolation and autonomy) among the major towns of a given region; or to compare the growth of the Shāfiʿī *madhhab* in a number of different regions, distinguished from one another by their economic structures, ethnic makeup, political circumstances, etc. In general, I would argue that regional and comparative essays of this kind are likely to move us farther and faster than either narrowly focused monographs or broad general essays.

The *madhhab*-oriented approach of Laoust, Halm, and Makdisi deals very effectively with the *ʿulamāʾ* as professionals, as scholars bound together by common doctrines and interlocking career patterns. This approach can also be integrated quite readily with ideological currents and the course of politics. It is less easy, however, to connect it to broader problems of social and political structure. A laudable but perhaps premature essay in this direction is Richard Bulliet, *The Patricians of Nishapur* (1972). The heart of Bulliet's monograph is a 150-page survey of the religious notable families—those whom he terms patricians—of Nishapur between the mid-10th and mid-12th centuries. Here career patterns and social backgrounds are traced, family trees constructed, and political roles and connections sketched. The approach he uses is prosopographic—i.e., he attempts to establish as many facts as possible about all those who seem to be connected with the Nishapur patriciate, and then to convert these facts into a collective portrait of this group.

Bulliet's source for this survey consists chiefly of three very terse abridgments of two biographical dictionaries of the religious notables of Nishapur. In a very real sense, then, the set of persons that he will discuss has been preselected for him, and we must ask whether he has found the most productive way to analyze this group. What he has done is to begin by positing a class of patricians, "made up of a limited number of wealthy extended families whose dominance remained relatively stable over a long period of many generations. The prestige and power of these families derived from . . . landholding, trade, or religion." (*Patricians*, p. 20). This definition clearly derives from a scrutiny of the texts, and yet it posits a group not identified as such within them, as he frankly admits: ". . . the concrete reality of the patriciate has not been demonstrated. There is no word, no 'patricians' or 'burgher' or 'citizen' to signal its existence." (p. 85). But if that is the case, is there not a danger that Bulliet's analysis will wind up an exercise in circular logic? We might well be better off—especially in light of the character of the sources—to begin with the language and conceptual categories of the texts themselves. Using this perspective, we would pursue the following questions. What are the characteristics of the group, taken as a whole, contained in the biographical dictionaries of Nishapur? What aspects of their lives and careers are we told about? What audiences and what purposes do these texts address? From this perspective we could move on to matters of social structure and political role in some confidence that our texts were not leading us blindly by the nose. It represents only a subtle change in approach from Bulliet's, but potentially a highly significant one.

Bulliet prefaces his prosopographic survey with an essay on the character and roles of the Nishapur patriciate. The essay is full of interesting ideas, but in the end it leaves more questions than it answers. His goal is to account for the bitter and almost unceasing strife between two factions of patricians, one labeled by the texts as "Ḥanafī," the other as "Shāfiʿī." Rejecting a number of superficially plausible explanations, Bulliet finally proposes that the Ḥanafīs represented a conservative aristocratic party, which "conceived of a social order dominated by law and rationality and crowned by a patrician class which merited its pre-eminence by its monopoly of legal and religious knowledge." (p. 39). The Shāfiʿīs in contrast represented a progressive party, "in the literal sense of supporting those trends which were comparatively new in society" (e.g., mysticism, theological semi-determinism, populism). The problem with all this is a certain vagueness as to what a patriciate is, what it does, how it is linked to other social and political actors. For example, not all *ʿulamāʾ* are patricians, nor vice-versa; and yet religious prestige and learning is the essence of being a patrician—one is a patrician in the full sense only if he has the right to teach the religious sciences (p. 56ff.). In effect, then, patrician and *ʿālim* are functionally identical. Bulliet thus contributes valuable material on the *ʿulamāʾ* of a major urban center, together with a number of interesting hypotheses as to how *madhhab*s might function as political parties. Yet in the end the historical reality of this process is unclear, and his hypotheses remain hypotheses.

In order to move beyond the stage to which Makdisi's Ibn ʿAqīl and Bulliett's Nishapur have brought us, several things are necessary. First, we need a far more exact definition of who the *ʿulamāʾ* are and how they are linked to other groups in society. Second, we want a more detailed knowledge of the religious and educational institutions within which the *ʿulamāʾ* functioned. Finally, we must develop a more comprehensive and coherent view of the social order within which the *ʿulamāʾ* were embedded, and in terms of which their activities had meaning and value.

On the institutional side of things, the most important recent work has been done by George Makdisi, who sums up some two decades of research in *The Rise of Colleges: Institutions of Learning in Islam and the West* (1981). (He gives a concise but thoroughly documented statement of his ideas in "Madrasa," *EI*², v, 1123–1134; consult also Robert Hillenbrand's careful survey of the architectural development of this institution, *ibid.*, 1136–1154.)

Among his earlier work, see especially "Muslim Institutions of Learning in Eleventh-century Baghdad," *BSOAS*, xxiv (1961), 1–56. Makdisi's conception of his topic is very much rooted in that time and place, and even though *The Rise of Colleges* includes much material from Ayyubid-Mamluk Cairo and Damascus, he is not quite so much at home there.

In spite of the title, *The Rise of Colleges* is not really historical in nature; it is less concerned with origins and development than with the complex body of institutions and practices which the *madrasa* represented in its "mature" form. In short, his analysis is static and synchronic rather than dynamic and diachronic. He locates the *madrasa* within a typology of Islamic institutions of learning, and shows how it is legally a product of the law of *waqf.* He relates the curriculum to general concepts of knowledge in medieval Islam. Finally, he examines the "scholastic community"—professors, staff, and students.

Makdisi gives us here a very exact account of how the *ʿulamāʾ* functioned as *ʿulamāʾ*, but it is very much an autonomous, self-contained world that he portrays. The relations of the *ʿulamāʾ* with other elements in society, whether sultans or peasants, are not spelled out. And while we see very clearly the common cultural commitments and activities which made the *ʿulamāʾ* a definable, coherent group, we can only surmise why and in what ways these commitments and activities were significant to other members of society.

Makdisi's account is formalist rather than functionalist—i.e., he bases his discussion on an explication of the formal categories of rank, office, and subject-matter used within the educational system. In a certain sense, in fact, this book might be regarded as a lexicon, an attempt to survey and define the intricate technical vocabulary of Islamic higher education; certainly it is so organized that it can readily be used in this way. Makdisi seeks a hard-edged clarity, without ambiguity or vagueness. This he achieves, but perhaps at the cost of more definiteness than the subject will allow of. He portrays things in terms of a firm, consciously organized system, especially in regard to the curriculum of legal studies. Moreover, he uses a vocabulary which recalls (and clearly is meant to) that used for Western universities—e.g., "fellows," "syllabus," "courses," "graduate" and "undergraduate." This of course is related to his concern in Chapter 4 to show the very close parallels between higher education in Islam and Latin Christendom. This challenging and extremely controversial chapter cannot detain us here, but clearly it represents a major goal of his entire inquiry and has strongly shaped the earlier chapters dealing only with the Islamic world.

A study which in a sense tries to blend the concerns of Laoust, Makdisi, and Bulliet is represented by Louis Pouzet, *Damas au vii^e/xiii^e s. Vie et structures religieuses dans une metropole islamique* (1988). Pouzet's goals are very ambitious indeed—to portray the totality of religious life in Damascus during that century and to integrate it into the era's exceedingly complex political history. Hence he deals with both the membership and the main doctrines of the various *madhāhib* (including the Shīʿa), with the institutions of justice, education, and worship, with mysticism and popular religion, with the place of Christians and Jews in an overwhelmingly Muslim environment, and finally, with the interactions between men of religion and the rulers. Inevitably there are some errors, but item by item Pouzet's presentation is rich and full of interest. As a whole, however, the book lacks clarity and focus; it is too dense, there are too many intersecting themes, for even a well-informed reader to grasp it as a whole. It is invaluable, but must be digested in small pieces.

Since Makdisi and Pouzet deal mostly with the 5th/11th and later centuries, something is needed on the educational system of earlier times. For the time being, we must make do with Munir-ud-Din Ahmed, *Muslim Education and the Scholars' Social Status up to the Fifth Century Muslim Era in the Light of Taʾrīkh Baghdād* (1968). Though Ahmed's book is in many ways superficial, it is well documented, and his clear discussion of technical terms and the organization of education can usefully be compared to Makdisi's. He stresses the extreme informality and individualism of the early centuries. He does make an effort (unlike Makdisi) to integrate scholars in a larger social setting, but his account here is too idealized to have much value. In regard to the educational system, it is still worth perusing A. S. Tritton, *Materials on Muslim Education in the Middle Ages* (1957)—a mere miscellany of information with precious little analysis or even organization, but full of interesting and valuable data.

Perhaps the most successful efforts to date to comprehend the *ʿulamāʾ* as part of a broader socio-political order have been those which do not focus on them, but rather try to reconstruct a whole socio-political system. In so doing they must inevitably grapple with the *ʿulamāʾ* as part of this system. Two works in particular suggest the possibilities of such an approach: Ira M. Lapidus, *Muslim Cities in the Later Middle Ages* (1967; reprinted without notes, 1984), and Jean-Claude Garcin, *Un centre musulman de la Haute-Égypte médiévale: Qūṣ* (1976). Both works are urban studies, but they contrast markedly in approach: Lapidus is sociological and comparative, while Garcin is historical. (On Garcin's study, see also above, pp. 185–186; Lapidus is discussed below, p. 246.)

In his study of urban life in Mamluk Cairo and Syria, Lapidus deals with the *ʿulamāʾ* principally in Chapters 4 and 5. He begins with the problem of social integration and cohesion. Specifically, how was it possible for urban populations to see to such common needs as education, charity, public and the regulation of commerce and public morality, in view of the lack of city-wide organizations (guilds, communes, etc.) and the narrow military and fiscal concerns of the state? He finds the answer in the *ʿulamāʾ*, "a category of persons . . . permeating the whole of society. . . . they played a crucial role in the processes by which social communication was carried on and thus in the integration of the society into a working whole" (p. 108). Because they stemmed from or had marriage connections to all respectable groups in society, they could in a sense represent the whole system simply through their socio-economic networks and background. Moreover, "this basis for a larger community was reinforced by the crystallization of associational life around the *ʿulamāʾ* " (p. 111). This associational life consisted in the study groups which formed around leading scholars. The official *ʿulamāʾ*—qadis, their deputies, notaries—also were the foci of associations, and of course were leading members of their respective *madhhabs*. The groups which coalesced around the *ʿulamāʾ* were voluntary associations, with no legal foundation and no formal organizational structure governing membership, leadership, roles, finance, etc. But precisely for that reason the *ʿulamāʾ*-centered groups cut across and mitigated the divisiveness of *mamlūk* corps, youth gangs, neighborhood factions, clans, etc. "An undifferentiated elite," (p. 114) they were the essential glue of Mamluk urban life.

At the same time, because they had no means of coercion at their disposal and no formal organization, they could only carry out their socio-political roles in uneasy collaboration with the Mamluk state. More than that, they depended heavily on the gifts and endowments supplied by the military elite, who controlled and manipulated the main sources of wealth in society. *ʿUlamāʾ* deference to the regime should not be construed as loyalty in any fundamental sense, but purely as collaboration, intended to secure a degree of law and order and an Islamic way of life. Collaboration took the form of legitimizing the regime in various ways—e.g., the issuance of *fatwā*s (legal opinions), preaching, acceptance of office, etc. The crucial figure in this regard was the qadi: the chief judicial official of the state, overseer of orthodoxy and sound morals in the mosques and *madrasas*, supervisor of endowments and appointments. Many *ʿulamāʾ* entered the bureaucracy as chancery and fiscal officials as well. They were never entirely co-opted; the middle and lower echelons in particular were more closely linked to the urban populace, and some even earned part of their living as retailers or artisans. Moreover, the group as a whole placed a high value on keeping one's distance from the regime and the moral corruption which tainted all its acts.

Lapidus' pages on the *ʿulamāʾ* are an excellent distillation of ideas generated by Orientalist thought over a long period of time, from Snouck Hurgronje to Gibb (his own mentor), restated here in the language of functionalist sociology. The vocabulary chosen by Lapidus is consciously not culture-specific, but general and abstract, and this fact makes his description a very appropriate one for comparative analysis. It can readily be applied to and tested against other historical contexts in medieval Islam. (He has in fact tried—quite successfully—to show its general applicability in "Muslim Cities and Islamic Societies," in Lapidus, ed., *Middle Eastern Cities* [1969], pp. 47–79.)

Lapidus' work clearly adds a significant dimension to our comprehension of the *ʿulamāʾ*; for the first time in the literature surveyed in this chapter, we see them living and working as members of a whole society; we see the several ways in which they are able to define themselves as a coherent element in that society; we discern the kinds of links they form with other groups—not merely the court, but popular groups as well. Nevertheless, there are significant problems in an approach of this kind. First of all, Lapidus has almost nothing to say about the concrete ideas purveyed by the *ʿulamāʾ*; the ideological dimension—a crucial aspect of their social role—is therefore very much attenuated. Between the doctrinal analysis of Laoust and the sociological presentation of Lapidus there is a real gulf, and neither seems inclined to bridge it. A second shortcoming (noted by Lapidus himself in his more recent work) is perhaps related to this one—viz., that we are given very little sense of what Mamluk writers thought about the status and role of the *ʿulamāʾ*, even though their texts are full of evaluations of specific incidents and personalities. Again we return to a basic motif in this book, that historical analysis should begin (though it cannot end) with an effort to reconstitute a society's description of itself. Both these problems doubtless stem from the abstract, general language of Lapidus' approach, in which historical concreteness has been sacrificed for analytic clarity and comparability.

Finally, there is the issue of change: the 250 years of Mamluk history obviously saw profound changes in many spheres of life, and necessarily these must have affected the situation of the *ʿulamāʾ*. But functionalist analysis is very poorly equipped to deal with such problems, and in fact tends to minimize evidence of change in favor of discerning stable institutions. In a functionalist framework, indeed, change often seems arbitrary disruption rather than an intelligible, rational process. None of the above is said to minimize a fine achievement, but simply to show that no one approach, however coherent and persuasive in its own terms, is adequate to the complex reality of the *ʿulamāʾ*.

Jean-Claude Garcin's study of Qūṣ represents an effort to restore a sense of concrete time and place and the dimension of change. He deals not only with the town of Qūṣ proper but its region, and covers the whole period from the beginnings of Islamic rule down to the collapse of the Circassian Mamluks, with some attention even to 18th and 19th-century developments. In such a broad context religious institutions and leaders can be only a single element; yet for Qūṣ' apogee as a regional center under the Ayyubids and early Bahri Mamluks, Garcin regards them as altogether crucial:

> It is then the *madrasa* which creates a process of upward mobility among the people of the Upper Egyptian countryside, even as it normally holds them in a position of inferiority relative to the town-dwellers [of Qūṣ] properly speaking. . . . It is the *madrasa* also—together with the holding of judicial office—which contributes to the creation of a network of new relationships among localities which were otherwise united only in a common subjection by their common financial exploitation; a new social space, that of the province (of Qūṣ), comes into being, defined by the scope of the *madrasas*' influence and by intersecting judicial careers. . . .
>
> A "provincial milieu" is thus born from the *madrasa* education of these semi-rural people. . . . The culture of this provincial milieu is not rich; rather, it remains

> strongly oriented towards the practical application of the semi-technical disciplines taught in the *madrasas*. . . . In Egypt, where the countryside is always so close to the city, and in this remote province, it is this minimum of linguistic, legal, and religious education, rather than a distinct way of life, which characterizes the process of urbanization. . . . (pp. 356–357)

As in Lapidus' analysis, then, it is the *ʿulamāʾ* who are the kernel of social integration, though in this case the society in question is not urban in a narrow sense, but instead is regional in character. Nor is it the presence of *ʿulamāʾ* as such which is vital, but rather the existence of *madrasas*, formally endowed institutions of religio-legal education. It was the presence of such institutions (sixteen altogether) which gave Qūṣ its prestige in the surrounding area. They also connected it to the great world outside, for the leading families of Qūṣ would send some of their members to Cairo, where in some cases they were able to achieve major careers (e.g., al-Nuwayrī and Ibn Daqīq al-ʿĪd). Moreover, the qadi of the province of Qūṣ had the authority to appoint deputy-qadis throughout the province, and this fact gave the small-town and village *faqīh*s educated in Qūṣ some opportunity to use their new skills.

Garcin's documentation for the *ʿulamāʾ* of Qūṣ is extremely limited—essentially a single biographical dictionary of some 600 entries, composed in Cairo in the 740s/1340s by an emigré scholar from Edfou in Upper Egypt, Kamāl al-Dīn Jaʿfar al-Udfuwī: *al-Ṭāliʿ al-saʿīd al-jāmiʿ li-asmāʾ al-fuḍalāʾ wa'l-ruwāt bi-aʿlā al-Saʿīd* (Ed., Cairo, 1914; new ed. by S. M. Ḥasan, 1966). The innumerable chroniclers of Mamluk Egypt noted events in the south only when they threatened the regime, and the great dictionary compilers, like Ibn Ḥajar al-ʿAsqalānī and al-Sakhāwī, included only those Saʿīdis who had made notable careers in Cairo. We thus have a fairly systematic conspectus of the *ʿulamāʾ* of Qūṣ only down to 1348. Moreover, we see them only in their relations with one another, as academics and judicial officials, rather than in other dimensions of their social experience (as landholders, merchants, town notables, etc.).

But if the patterns of academic life are carefully established, and correlated with patterns derived from different evidence (on the Red Sea commerce, fiscal administration, and political developments), then we can integrate them into a comprehensive structure of society in Qūṣ. More than that, we can locate the role of the *ʿulamāʾ* and their institutions within a slow, hardly perceptible process, through which Qūṣ was connected to the cosmopolitan forms of Islamic life and thought known in Cairo. Early Mamluk rule in this province was not merely a matter of administrative control and fiscal exploitation, but also one of social and cultural assimilation. On some level Islamic history must always be a history of provinces and their relations with the center; in this light the perspective brought by Garcin is one that should be followed up wherever possible.

The analyses of both Lapidus and Garcin are almost entirely qualitative; numbers are used sparingly, and only to illustrate propositions advanced within a purely verbal framework. It is natural to wonder whether quantitative analysis might not be the surest means to achieve substantial progress beyond the level of interpretation established by them. At this point it is hard to say. Quantitative data of a sort are certainly available, or at least can be constructed, but the question remains whether such data can be used to deal with problems that could otherwise not be resolved or even effectively posed. The characteristic pitfall in quantitative analysis, after all, is the investing of prodigious ingenuity and effort in order to reinvent the wheel. A historian considering this route might begin by looking at some of the work done in other fields, such as the American colonial period or early modern Europe, to decide whether the game is worth the candle. In addition, there are two general guides for the historian, now old but still useful, as to what can be done and what mathematical techniques are needed:

1. Roderick Floud, *An Introduction to Quantitative Methods for Historians* (1973);
2. C. M. Dollar and R.J.N. Jensen, *Historian's Guide to Statistics: Quantitative Analysis and Historical Research* (1971).

If one is going to get serious about such things, clearly some formal statistical and computer training is in order; for this the best advice is to go visit one's colleagues in the appropriate departments as soon as possible.

An early quantitative essay dealing with the *ʿulamāʾ* is an often-cited article by Hayyim J. Cohen, "The Economic Background and the Secular Occupations of Muslim Jurisprudents and Traditionists in the Classical Period of Islam (until the Middle of the Eleventh Century)," *JESHO*, xiii (1970), 16–61. Cohen's results are interesting and suggestive, but his methodology—both as to questionnaire and analysis—is extremely simple. The piece is best regarded as heuristic rather than demonstrative. All the same, the issue he has dealt with is unquestionably a crucial one—in the age before *madrasa*s, when salaried positions were at last available, how did scholars manage to make a living? What connections did they have to the productive groups in the economic system, and to what extent did they themselves actively participate in the production of wealth? Such questions were not new with Cohen, obviously, but his essay allowed a far more exact sense of what the evidence regarding these issues was. It is unfortunate that no one so far has really tried to carry out more systematic and technically sophisticated investigations in this area. (There is a partial exception to this stricture in an article on 6th/12th-century Damascus, a period representing an early stage in the professionalization of the *ʿulamāʾ*: Joan E. Gilbert, "Institutionalization of Muslim Scholarship and Professionalization of the *ʿulamāʾ* in Medieval Damascus," *SI*, lii (1980), 105–134.)

On a technical level, at least, two recent studies do mark a genuine step forward. In both cases the machinery constructed may be more elaborate than the results would seem to warrant; on the other hand, both studies are explicitly heuristic in intention. They have been undertaken at least partly to explore and develop new research strategies. In this instance, the strategy being explored is the possibility created by the computer of aggregating and analyzing the prosopographic data locked up in the apparently arid formulas of the biographical dictionary. The kinds of questions posed by each scholar are quite different, however, and this may help us to get some sense of the range of issues that a computer can help us address.

Carl F. Petry, *The Civilian Elite of Cairo in the Later Middle Ages* (1981), is by far the most ambitious study we have of the "learned classes" in any one time or place in Islamic history. Petry has constructed a census of some 4600 learned men of the 9th/15th century. The principal criterion for inclusion is known residence in Cairo, and the census is drawn from two major dictionaries: 4000 figures from al-Sakhāwī's *al-Ḍawʾ al-lāmiʿ* (completed in 1491, and containing a total of some 12,000 entries), supplemented by some 600 additional persons from Ibn Taghrībirdī's *al-Manhal al-ṣafī wa'l-mustawfī baʿd al-wāfī*. Petry does not restrict his field of vision to *ʿulamāʾ* in the narrow sense, but includes all those who followed a literate profession. He divides his people into six broad occupational categories, following the widely used classification of William Popper, *Egypt and Syria under the Circassian Sultans* (2 vols., 1955–57): scil., military-executive, bureaucratic, legal (qadis, notaries, *muḥtasib*s), artisan-commercial, scholarly-educational, religious functionaries. This group of men is then analyzed as to their geographic origins, their places of residence and employment in Cairo, and occupational mobility—i.e., the degree to which people held jobs in different categories.

Petry carries out his analysis very carefully, and though there are few surprises, there are many significant nuances. Thus we learn that the greatest sources of manpower for the learned establishment in Cairo were the Delta and Damascus. In terms of prestige, the *madrasa*s of the old Fatimid compound far surpassed even the richly endowed amirial institutions near the Citadel, and scholars of non-Egyptian origin were in fact heavily concentrated in the former zone. A final example: the learned class was not undifferentiated, but formed a tripartite elite. That is, movement between the three principal career patterns (bureaucratic, judicial-scholarly, religious) was possible but certainly not easy or commonplace. Each of these groups was recruited from distinct social groups, and each played a specific and well-recognized role in the Mamluk socio-political order.

Petry's results are far from negligible, and even where they simply confirm what has long been suspected, they do nail down these notions with a solid documentation. On the other hand, there are many possible lines of questioning which he does not explore. For example, he has very little to say about the social background characteristics of his subjects—family occupations, ethnic identity, inheritance of "learned" status, etc. He does not try to establish the sequences of occupations, the *cursus honorum*, pursued by these men; we would naturally wonder what career paths might be followed by ambitious young men on their way up. The 9th/15th century is treated essentially as a single block, with no serious attempt to do a time-series over decade or twenty-year intervals. Again, his statistical treatment is of the simplest: he gives only percentages and (for geographic origins only) a simple coefficient of concentration, nor are there any graphs, which would often be helpful in discerning the significance of his elaborate tables. To a surprising extent he builds his conclusions simply through visual examination of the data. Perhaps Petry's most significant limitation, however, is his caution. He means to integrate his inquiry into the existing literature, and that is without a doubt a laudable goal; certainly it means that his work is a useful test of the hypotheses and conceptual frameworks already advanced by Abū Lughod, Ayalon, Popper, and (above all) Lapidus. But by working within such parameters, he forgoes the opportunity to ask questions of his own, and to explore the many new possibilities and perspectives which computer-based analysis might open up.

In *Le monde des ulemas andalous du ve/xie au viie/xiiie siècle* (1978), Dominique Urvoy does try to use computer-analyzed aggregate data to grapple with questions which could not otherwise be posed. Whereas Petry's is a sociological study, Urvoy's is an essay in intellectual history, focusing on the following set of issues: (1) the identification of the main centers of study in Spain between the fall of the Caliphate (420/1030) and the collapse of Almohad power (630/1233 sqq.); (2) the characteristic fields of study (hadith, *furū' al-fiqh*, grammar, etc.) pursued in each region, with special attention to the differences between them; (3) the links established by migration and travel between these regions; (4) the networks of students through which the leading scholars in each area were connected with one another; (5) the patterns of change in each of the above dimensions, analyzed through twenty-year segments. Oddly and most frustratingly, she uses no maps. Her data is mostly presented through a series of complicated and hard-to-read tables, though for No. 4 (Student Networks) she has generated a series of complex geometric figures to illustrate her results.

Although Urvoy's source base is very limited (on this and other points see the review by Rachel Arié, *Islam*, lx [1983]), and although one may not always accept her conclusions, she does succeed in showing how a quantitative approach can lead to a very productive set of questions even in a field which has always been the sacred preserve of close textual analysis. Her terse presentation is less effective than it might have been, since she takes for granted the context of institutions and individual cases needed to show the cultural significance of her data. In this respect, it is very much a specialist's monograph. More striking is that she applies no formal statistical treatment to the pages of numbers which she has so laboriously compiled. Her tables would come off far better simply by being paired with a few linear curves and bar graphs, but there are none to be found. There are not even any percentages. Having constructed a body of aggregate data, she has simply examined it visually in order to deduce strictly verbal propositions. It could be argued (most of all by a serious statistician) that with the data base available to her, formal mathematical procedures could yield no significant results. But I would respond that since the book's goals are heuristic, the opportunity for statistical testing and manipulation ought to have been taken. On the other hand—with Urvoy as with Petry—there is nothing to prevent a reader from trying this for himself. Indeed, in light of the stupefying effort needed to construct aggregates of the kind presented by these two authors, it would make sense for anyone contemplating a quantitative approach to begin by experimenting with the tables of Petry and Urvoy, to see what else might be extracted from them, and to decide whether the proposed project is likely to be worth the cost in time and money.

As with every other approach discussed in this chapter, quantitative analysis is clearly not the final key to the puzzle of determining who and what the *ʿulamāʾ* were. Its effectiveness depends entirely on the quality of the hypotheses and categories of data to be used. These, at least so far, have been defined by more traditional forms of inquiry. But traditional investigations in turn have tended to focus too much on the *ʿulamāʾ* as a closed group, one whose members interact chiefly with one another. This is a natural enough bias, and certainly one which our principal source, the biographical dictionary, does everything to encourage. It is nevertheless extremely misleading. For the future, we need to deal with the *ʿulamāʾ* as members of a whole socio-cultural system, and our task must be to determine the totality of the social relations and cultural relations into which they entered. It may indeed be that the *ʿulamāʾ* are the only major group in medieval Islamic society which we can ever know directly. But if we get to know them well enough, they can lead us to a sound understanding of the society in which they lived and which they did so much to shape.

Chapter Nine

ISLAMIC LAW AND ISLAMIC SOCIETY

UNTIL very recently historians of Islam have been extremely reluctant to regard law and jurisprudence as a significant source for social and economic life. For anyone familiar with the importance of law in the study of Roman or English history, such behavior must seem simply obtuse. Yet there are reasons for it. First of all, most Western scholars have been more interested in the theoretical jurisprudence of Islam (*uṣūl al-fiqh*) than in the practical application of the principles of law to specific cases (*furūʿ al-fiqh*). Most Orientalists, after all, are not lawyers but students of culture. Thus they have tended to approach Islamic law as a religious orientation and a mode of thought rather than as a body of rights, obligations, and rules of procedure.

It is not merely professional bias which has shaped the traditional Orientalist approach, however, but also the correct perception that *fiqh* is more than jurisprudence, and that the body of rules which it produces—*sharʿ* or *sharīʿa*—is more than a code of law. Its concerns encompass not merely personal status, contracts, criminal acts, etc., but worship and ethics. It makes no distinction between acts which have concrete legal consequences and those which can be judged by God alone. As the founder of Islamic legal studies in the West, Christiaan Snouck Hurgronje, pointed out almost a century ago,

> *Fiqh* is distinguished from modern and Roman law in that it is a doctrine of duties [*une déontologie*] in the broadest sense of the word, and cannot be divided into religion, morality, and law. It deals only with "external" duties—i.e., those which are susceptible to control by a human authority instituted by God. However, these duties are without exception duties toward God, and are based on the unfathomable will of God Himself. All duties which men can perceive being carried out are dealt with—all the duties of man in whatever circumstances and in their connections with anyone whatever. (*Selected Works*, ed. J. Schacht and G. H. Bousquet, 261)

Profound as this insight was, it had the unfortunate consequence of establishing a highly idealized view of *fiqh*—as if it embodied only the vain dreams of aged *ʿulamāʾ* cloistered in their mosques and did not hope to mold the affairs of everyday life.

However, even Snouck Hurgronje himself subscribed to this idealized image only at certain moments. He was after all a superb observer of contemporary Islamic society in Mecca and the Dutch East Indies, and to a large degree his thesis was meant as a protest against the misperceptions found in the bulk of studies on Islamic law and jurisprudence in his time. These studies—predominantly translations or analyses of the digests of positive law used in the *sharīʿa*-courts of India and Southeast Asia—were often written specifically to assist colonial administrators in their dealings with native society. It was in short a pragmatic scholarship, based on the supposition that the *sharīʿa* actually did reflect and govern the attitudes and behavior of Muslims. Much produced by these scholars was culturally naive, conceptually inadequate, and full of errors. But taken as a whole, their work does suggest that *fiqh* and *sharīʿa* were rooted not only in social ideals but also in social reality.

To say that Islamic law is both idealizing and realistic does not get us very far, to be sure; such a statement offers no criteria for deciding which aspects of it reflect the actualities of life, or in what way. An Egyptian scholar's rejoinder to the usual Orientalist view may suggest a better formulation of the problem; the *sharīʿa*, he says, was "an ideal doctrine for a very real society." (Galal El-Nahal, *The Judicial Administration of Ottoman Egypt in the Seventeenth Century* [1979], p. 73.) That is, *fiqh* tries to establish a body of rules of behavior which, taken together, define a specifically Islamic way of life—one which assures Muslims that they are obeying God and His Prophet, but which also deals concretely and effectively with the everyday needs of social life. Within this framework, obedience to God's will is doubtless primary, as Snouck Hurgronje thought, while immediate social utility is secondary. However, this hierarchy of values is to a large extent a conceptual rather than a practical matter; it affects the way in which a *faqīh* structures his argument more than his concrete resolution of particular cases. In general, Muslim jurists supposed that God desired the best for man, and therefore social utility could most reliably be attained through obedience to the divine will. In *fiqh* there is thus a constant interplay between the pragmatic demands of social reality, the traditional norms and values of the Community in being, and the transcendant ideals of Scripture. Actual life is always under scrutiny and evaluation from the point of view of apparently fixed ideals, according to a rigorous scholastic method, and yet the way in which this method is used to interpret those ideals depends on the jurist's perception of real needs and interests.

Of course the balance of realism versus idealism varies greatly between schools and even individual scholars. By the end of the 3rd/9th century at latest, a great many texts were clearly composed chiefly as scholastic exercises, as elements within a self-contained literary and scientific tradition rather than as commentaries on society at large. But this must never be taken for granted; at all periods there were multitudes of legal writings meant to address current political, social, and economic problems. The fact that these latter are formally identical to purely academic work simply means that historians of Islamic law have to be exceptionally alert to the concrete issues of the periods which they study.

Robert Brunschvig is without doubt the scholar who has most closely sought out the elements of realism in classical *fiqh*. His method has been to gauge the provisions of selected legal texts against the socio-economic structures and patterns of behavior which are suggested by independent evidence. Among his many studies on Islamic jurisprudence, see in particular the following:

a. "Considérations sociologiques sur le droit musulman ancien," *SI*, iii (1955), 61–73.

b. "Urbanisme médiéval et droit musulman," *REI* (1947), 127–155.

c. "Métiers vils dans l'Islam," *SI*, xvi (1962), 41–60.

d. "Conceptions monétaires chez les juristes musulmans (viiie–xiiie siècles)," *Arabica*, xiv (1967), 113–143.

e. "Propriétaire et locataire d'immeuble en droit musulman médiéval (jusqu'à vers l'an 1200)," *SI*, lii (1980), 5–40. (The first four of these are reprinted in Brunschvig, *Études d'islamologie*, ed. A. M. Turki, 2 vols., 1976. The latter can be found in his *Études sur l'Islam classique et l'Afrique du Nord*, 1986.)

Less concrete than Brunschvig's studies but still suggestive are the comments of Claude Cahen, "Considerations sur l'utilisation des ouvrages de droit musulman par l'historien," in *Atti del III Congresso di studi arabi e islamici* (1967); reprinted in Cahen, *Les peuples musulmans dans l'histoire*, 81–89.

The elusive balance between "realism" and "idealism" must be established for each text and each case. However, it is governed to some degree by the characteristic attitudes and approaches of the different schools of law which grew up in early Islamic times. (The word "school" translates *madhhab*, pl. *madhāhib*; it represents not a formal organization but a shared method and doctrine—a school of thought, so to speak.) Among the four main schools of Sunni Islam, the Ḥanafī and Mālikī *madhhab*s display the most realistic orientation, in that both of them drew the substance of their legal rulings from the established social traditions of the regions in which they grew up in the late 8th and early 9th centuries. The Ḥanafīs, centered in Kufa and then Baghdad, reflect the complex, fluid society of lower Iraq, with its mixed agrarian and mercantile economy, its ethnic variety, and its cosmopolitan culture. In addition, the Ḥanafīs' proximity to the caliphal court induced in them a certain deference to political and administrative imperatives. The Mālikīs in contrast were formed by the pietism and the patriarchal, still quasi-tribal traditions of Medina, as reshaped by the Prophet and the early caliphs. The Shāfiʿīs, in line with the rigorous temperament of their founder, seem primarily concerned to evolve a fully rationalized, internally consistent body of doctrine derived from the strict application of analogical reasoning to Qur'ān and Sunna. Finally, the Ḥanbalīs (originally a populist movement which arose in Baghdad in opposition to the Abbasid court) were the most moralistic, with the goal of recapturing the whole tone of life in the primitive Community of Medina.

Scholars (both Western and Muslim) have normally regarded the period from the mid-2nd/8th to the late 3rd/9th century as the most creative phase of Islamic jurisprudence, in the sense that during those years *faqīhs* were freest to define the principles of their inquiry and to determine main rules which ought to govern Muslim life. In view of the immense authority ascribed to the "founding fathers" and established tradition in all pre-modern societies, it is no wonder that later generations of jurists felt some pressure to conform both to the methodologies and to the substantive legal opinions laid down in this period. This devotion to tradition and precedent was described in several ways among Muslims: as following the ways of the earliest generations of Muslims (the *salaf*), or as adhering to the doctrine of the authoritative scholars (*imāms*, in the Sunni sense of that term) of the 2nd/8th and 3rd/9th centuries, or as the consensus of the learned (*ijmāʿ*).

By the late 5th/11th century, the idea had begun to spread that the "gate of *ijtihād*" was closed—that is, that future jurists were not entitled to evolve new theories of jurisprudence, or even (in more rigid formulations) to depart from the established rulings of their *madhhab* where these were applicable to the case before them. This was no simple and rapid process, however, nor does it mean that *fiqh* became more and more a purely scholastic enterprise devoid of flexibility and realism. In the first place, many jurists contested the new doctrine for several centuries; it was not universally accepted until the 10th/16th century. Second, *ijtihād* (the application of reason to the solution of legal issues) is a very complex concept which comprises many different levels of inquiry. Even a *faqīh* who felt bound by the teachings of his masters would often encounter situations for which no clear precedents could be found, thus requiring him to exercise at least a limited *ijtihād* in order to resolve the case before him. Moreover, within a given *madhhab* there was often much dissension among the leading authorities as to the correct solution to a given problem, and in this situation a *faqīh* would make his own choice of the most appropriate ruling. (This account of the closing of the gate of *ijtihād* follows a revisionist line of argument recently suggested by several scholars—Fazlur Rahman, George Makdisi, and Bernard Weiss—and elaborated in an article by Wael B. Hallaq, "Was the Gate of Ijtihād Closed?" *IJMES*, xvi [1984], 3–41. The standard introductions to Islamic jurisprudence by Joseph Schacht and N. J. Coulson, cited below, give good statements of the older and still more usual interpretation.)

All this suggests the following approach to the use of *fiqh* as a source for social history. In the 2nd/8th and 3rd/9th centuries, *fiqh* constituted a quite immediate response to social realities, within the broad religio-moral framework established by Qurʾān and Sunna. In later centuries, *fiqh* certainly continued to address current reality, but now it did so in terms of the categories and logic of established legal doctrine. In this context, legal discussion was concerned to fill gaps and resolve contradictions in the existing body of doctrine quite as much as to deal with the real problems of Islamic society. This latter point requires us to look into the methodology of Islamic jurisprudence and to survey the kinds of documents produced by legal inquiry and practice.

The method of *fiqh* can be defined as both *scholastic* and *casuistic*. It is scholastic in that *fiqh* was not primarily the work of legislators, administrators, or judges, but rather of private scholars who saw their task as the discovery and interpretation of God's will for mankind. Thus *sharīʿa* was not defined in the form of royal decrees and court judgments, but through treatises and non-binding opinions by jurisconsults (*fatwā*s). Moreover, much of its subject-matter is hypothetical: "Suppose such-and-such a situation, what should the ruling be?" In principle, the decisions made by qadis in actual litigation were supposed to conform to the solutions already contrived by scholars and summarized in their authoritative textbooks. Court decisions as such established no true precedents; they were simply applications of an independently defined law. On the other hand, *fiqh* is casuistic; it is elaborated through an examination of all the possible (even far-fetched) cases which may occur to a *faqīh* studying a given area of law. Such cases are in fact worked out through the application of a consistent and complex set of legal principles. However, such principles are seldom presented as a body in special chapters or treatises, but occur only within the analysis of specific cases. An approach of this kind has the advantage of being highly concrete, but it also means that the rulings dealing with many crucial topics—e.g., freedom vs. slavery, legal competence, contract—are scattered far and wide.

Fiqh and the *sharīʿa*-court system obviously produced an immense literature. The question is whether this literature constitutes a significant source for social history. But whatever historical value these legal texts may or may not possess, they are hardly transparent. They can only be used by those acquainted with their peculiar technical language (lawyers have changed little over the centuries) and with the institutions through which they were generated.

The best place to begin is certainly Joseph Schacht, *An Introduction to Islamic Law* (1964), although his authority is no longer so unquestioned as it was during his lifetime. His account of the origins and early development of *fiqh* (both legal theory and positive law), though widely accepted among Western scholars, is controversial and open to serious debate at many points. (His complex arguments on this subject are developed in much greater detail in *The Origins of Muhammadan Jurisprudence* [1950].) And in regard to later times, as we have already noted (p. 212), recent research is beginning to suggest that *fiqh* did not become so rigid and fossilized after the 4th/10th century as he believed. On the other hand, Schacht's views cannot be dismissed; they have been enormously influential, they continue to provoke many new lines of inquiry, and they are supported by great erudition and critical thinking. On a practical level, Schacht's *Introduction* provides a concise glossary of technical terms as well as a meticulously organized bibliography which includes almost everything of value down to 1964.

Schacht's work builds upon foundations laid in the late 19th century. His guiding concepts of the nature and purpose of Islamic jurisprudence are rooted in the work of Christiaan Snouck Hurgronje, whose scholarship can be sampled in *Oeuvres choisies/Selected Works*, ed. G. H. Bousquet and J. Schacht

(1957). On another level, Schacht's approach to the origins of *fiqh* was inspired by Ignaz Goldziher's famous study "On the Development of the Hadith," *Muslim Studies*, ii (1971), originally published in 1890. Goldziher's interpretations of Islamic law and theology reflect both immense erudition and careful thought; they undoubtedly merit their extraordinary influence, and they remain challenging and productive even now. A synopsis of Goldziher's views is given in his *Vorlesungen über den Islam* (1910; rev. ed., 1925); trans. by Ruth and Andras Hamori (with additional bibliography and notes) as *Introduction to Islamic Theology and Law* (1981).

Schacht's treatment can be supplemented by N. J. Coulson, *A History of Islamic Law* (1964), and *Conflicts and Tensions in Islamic Jurisprudence* (1969). Coulson's interpretation does not diverge greatly from Schacht's, though he shows a greater awareness than the latter of the realistic elements in *fiqh*. The collective volume edited by Majid Khadduri and H. J. Liebesny, *Law in the Middle East*, vol. I, *Origin and Development of Muslim Law* (1955), is uneven but has a number of useful chapters on positive law as well as jurisprudence. Until very recently Shiʿite jurisprudence has been grossly neglected in Western-language studies. We still do not possess anything like Schacht or Coulson, but the gap is partly filled by Hossein Modarressi Tabatabaʾi, *An Introduction to Shīʿī Law: A Bibliographical Study* (1984). Part I is a concise but authoritative exposition of the nature and development of Shīʿī *fiqh*, while Part II provides a detailed survey of the major works produced within this tradition. The survey is organized according to legal topic, and includes both published works and those extant only in manuscript.

Such introductory treatments of course cannot give us a real grip on Arabic legal texts, with their elliptical grammar and formidable technical vocabulary. Perhaps the best way to acquire at least the rudiments of Arabic legal usage is to study those digests of positive law which are available in sound annotated translations. A thorough bibliography of such works is given in Schacht, *Introduction*, pp. 261–269. The following are especially useful:

a. Abū Isḥāq al-Shīrāzī (Shāfiʿī, d. 476/1083), *al-Tanbīh*; trans. G. H. Bousquet (4 vols., 1949–52).

b. Muwaffaq al-Dīn ibn Qudāma (Ḥanbalī, d. 620/1223), *al-ʿUmda*; trans. Henri Laoust as *Le précis de droit d'Ibn Qudāma* (1950).

c. Khalīl ibn Isḥāq (Mālikī, d. 767/1365), *al-Mukhtaṣar*; trans. I. Guidi and D. Santillana as *Sommario del diritto malechita* (2 vols., 1919); and G. H. Bousquet as *Abrégé de la loi musulmane selon le rite de l'imam Malek* (4 vols., 1956–62).

While these digests can acquaint us with terminology and the main rules of law, they contribute little towards an understanding of legal method and reasoning. In this regard the studies by Robert Brunschvig collected in Vol. II of his *Études d'islamologie* are particularly helpful. A systematic analysis of the doctrine of one *madhhab* is provided by the classic study of David Santillana,

Istituzioni di diritto musulmano malichita, con riguardo anche al sistemo sciafiita (2 vols., 1926). The studies of Chafik Shehata are likewise of high value. In addition to his *Études de droit musulman* (2 vols., 1971–73), see his analysis of conceptions of contract, with extensive citations from the sources: *Théorie générale de l'obligation en droit musulman hanefite* (1969).

At this point, we can turn to the texts produced by Islamic jurists and ask what light these may throw on the actual workings of Islamic society. Treatises on method (*uṣūl al-fiqh*) can be noted simply in passing. Anyone who hopes to use Islamic jurisprudence as a source for social history must of course be broadly familiar with the *uṣūl* in order to interpret his texts, but such treatises are in themselves quite theoretical. They are not likely sources either for actual behavior or for the norms which were supposed to govern that behavior. (On this point, however, it is worth looking at a moderately revisionist article by Wael Hallaq, "Considerations on the Function and Character of Islamic Legal Theory," *JAOS*, civ [1984], 679–689.) In general, whatever guidance *fiqh* can give us will be found in works of positive law (*furūʿ al-fiqh*). These in turn fall into several categories of varying usefulness.

Most convenient to use, but perhaps least significant from the social historian's point of view, are the manuals or digests which presented outlines of the doctrine of each of the schools. These served both as introductory textbooks for novice *faqīh*s and as a quick reference for harassed or ignorant qadis. While these digests do provide a brief statement of the main rules of conduct (*ḥukm*, pl. *aḥkām*), they have serious drawbacks: they give no variant opinions, no explanations of the reasoning which led to a particular ruling, no discussion of the cases in which this ruling would apply. It is however precisely this kind of information which we need in order to interpret the social significance of the *aḥkām*.

We must therefore examine the great compilations, composed mostly between the late 2rd/8th and the 7th/13th centuries. These works attempt to give the whole teaching, including variant and minority opinions, of all the recognized masters in each *madhhab*. (Naturally enough they emphasize the compiler's personal judgments, but in most cases he would rank as one of the outstanding *faqīh*s of his time.) Here we can expect to find detailed explorations of the possible cases which might occur under each subject heading (e.g., marriage, manumission, partnership contracts). Works of the earliest period sometimes take the form of a dialogue between a master and his disciples; examples would be the vast *Kitāb al-aṣl* of the Ḥanafī scholar Muḥammad al-Shaybānī (d. 189/204) or *al-Mudawwana al-kubrā* by the Mālikī Saḥnūn (d. 240/854). In the 5th/11th and later centuries, these compilations were often presented as commentaries on one of the school's authoritative digests. To this class belong the *Kitāb al-mabsūṭ* of al-Sarakhsī (Ḥanafī, d. 483/1090) and the *Kitāb al-mughnī* of Muwaffaq al-Dīn ibn Qudāma (Ḥanbalī, d. 620/1223). Many of the most important of these compilations are (predictably) still available only in manuscript. One can however get some sense of the older "dialogue" works through Majid Khadduri, *The Islamic Law of Nations: Shaybani's Siyar* (1966), a translation of the chapters on warfare and taxation from the *Kitāb al-aṣl.*

More limited in scope, but of no less value, are treatises on special topics (Ar., *risāla*; pl., *rasāʾil*). Of these the best studied are certainly the books on taxation, the *kitāb al-kharāj* genre. To this group in fact belongs the oldest extant work of positive law, the *Kitāb al-kharāj* of Abū Yūsuf (d. 182/798), who was Abū Ḥanīfa's most brilliant and influential student as well as chief qadi of the Abbasid Empire under Hārūn al-Rashīd. There is an excellent French translation by E. Fagnan, *Livre de l'impôt foncier* (1921); and a usable but less satisfactory English version by A. Ben Shemesh, *Taxation in Islam*, Vol. III (1969). Apart from Abū Yūsuf, see the important treatises of Yaḥyā b. Ādam (d. 203/818) and Qudāma b. Jaʿfar (fl. early 4th/10th cen.), which have been published in facsimile and translated by A. Ben-Shemesh, *Taxation in Islam*, vols. I (1958; rev. ed., 1967) and II (1965).

Such works have been examined many times as a source for the origins and development of administrative practice under the caliphate (on which see below, Chapter Twelve, pp. 302–303). However, a few studies have adopted a specifically legal perspective, in which the reasoning which produced or rationalized rules of law takes precedence over their impact on state finance. This approach can give us an excellent insight into the mix of pragmatic, religio-moral, or purely scholastic motivations in early *fiqh*, especially when it is combined with the more positivist investigations hitherto favored by Western scholars. A systematic review of the fiscal doctrines evolved in *fiqh* can be found in the old but still useful study of Nicholas P. Aghnides, *Mohammedan Theories of Finance* (1916; reprinted 1961). More recently, H. M. Tabatabaʾi, *Kharāj in Islamic Law* (1983), provides a concise but clear legal analysis of the often conflicting concepts of taxation to be found among traditional Muslim jurists, both Sunni and Shiʿite. Few cultivators were freeholders; in this light, Ziaul Haque examines a crucial aspect of tax law in *Landlord and Peasant in Early Islam. A Study of the Legal Doctrine of Muzāraʿa or Sharecropping* (1977). For the doctrinal shifts of a later era, see Baber Johansen, *The Islamic Law of Land Tax and Rent: The Peasants' Loss of Property Rights as Interpreted in the Ḥanafite Legal Literatures of the Mamluk and Ottoman Periods* (1988).

A second group of special treatises consists of works on the crucial institution of the *waqf* (charitable trust). Two early works by Hilāl al-Raʾy (d. 245/859) and Khaṣṣāf (d. 261/874) are of particular interest; they have been studied in a broad historical and sociological context by Claude Cahen, "Reflexions sur le *waqf* ancien," *SI*, xiv (1961), 37–56; reprinted in *Les peuples muṣūlmans dans l'histoire*, 287–306.

A third group, as yet little exploited in spite of its obvious importance for Muslim society, consists of the works on inheritance (*farāʾiḍ*, "compulsory shares in an estate"). These can be approached through a monograph by N. J. Coulson, *Succession in the Muslim Family*, 1971). A number of such works have been translated, most notably by the famous Sir William Jones in connection with his duties in the East India Company; for references, see Schacht, *Introduction to Islamic Law*, p. 264.

A particularly intriguing category is that of treatises on the *ḥiyal*, legal stratagems by which one could sidestep inconvenient provisions in the *sharīʿa* while still adhering to the letter of the law. This genre was first seriously examined by Joseph Schacht. In addition to his editions of several important texts, see the following: (a) "Die arabische *ḥijal*-Literatur. Ein Beitrag zur Erforschung der islamischen Rechtspraxis," *Islam*, xv (1926), 211–232; (b) *Introduction to Islamic Law*, pp. 78–82; (c) "Ḥiyal," *EI²*, iii, 510–13. This type of writing was especially cultivated among the Ḥanafīs and seems characteristic of their realistic (not to say worldly) approach to *fiqh*. The other *madhhabs*, in contrast, regarded *ḥiyal* with suspicion and sometimes outright condemnation, though they were not always above the use of certain stratagems in their own jurisprudence.

Among the Mālikīs, adjustment to social realities took the form of *ʿamal*, a concept which allowed a qadi or *muftī* to take some account of established local custom and necessity in framing his rulings. See J. Berque, " ʿAmal," *EI²*, i, 427–28.

We will simply allude to the manuals of *ḥisba* (market inspection and the censorship of public morals). These treatises are certainly rooted in the legal and moral concerns of *fiqh*, and until late Mamluk times (mid-9th/15th century) it was taken for granted that a *muḥtasib* ought to be at least an adequate *faqīh*. Nevertheless, manuals on the *ḥisba* are far from works of *fiqh*; they are in no sense statements of rules of conduct (*aḥkām*) derived through the *uṣūl*, but practical guides to the enforcement of public morality in specific urban settings. Further comments are given below (pp. 242, 272); for the present, see Cl. Cahen and M. Talbi, "Ḥisba," *EI²*, iii, 485–89; and the major study by Pedro Chalmeta Gendron, *El "señor del zoco" en España* (1973).

As the positive content of *sharīʿa* was increasingly defined by authoritative compilations, commentaries, and digests, the *fatwā* became the most important device for addressing contested issues. The *fatwā* (pl., *fatāwā*) was a juristic opinion on a particular issue of ritual or conduct and was issued by a *faqīh* in response to a petitioner's question. *Fatwā*s are thus quite similar to rabbinic responsa, Roman rescripts, or even Papal decretals. The petitioner might be an ordinary Muslim with a question about some ritual observance, a qadi seeking guidance in a difficult piece of litigation, or a ruler wishing to establish the lawfulness of an act of state. In either case, the *faqīh*'s opinions were presumably authoritative but in principle non-binding, and a petitioner could always seek a plurality of opinions. In earlier centuries, any *faqīh* might serve as a *muftī*, but with the establishment of the *madrasa* system and the professionalization of the *ʿulamāʾ*, beginning in the 5th/11th century, the giving of *fatwā*s became somewhat more regularized. The ruler and his chief qadi would now intervene to prevent unqualified men from acting as *muftīs*. Only under the Ottomans, however, did a rigorous system emerge; here the *muftīs* formed a parallel hierarchy to the qadis, and only "licensed" scholars were entitled to give authoritative opinions to the courts.

From the 6th/12th century, it became common for eminent *faqīhs* (or their disciples) to collect and publish their *fatwās*. Many such collections have been printed (for these see Schacht, *Introduction to Islamic Law*, pp. 261–62), and scores of others are to be found scattered throughout Brockelmann, *GAL*. An excellent introduction to the genre is a compilation by the great Mālikī jurist Aḥmad b. Yaḥyā al-Wansharīsī (d. 914/1508), translated (or sometimes paraphrased) by Émile Amar as "La pierre de touche des fetwas," *Archives Marocaines*, xii–xiii (1908–1909). The potential yield of the *fatwā* literature for social history may seem disappointing at first glance. *Fatwās* are composed in an abstract, impersonal form; the great majority deal with ritual issues rather than law in our sense; and a great many are purely scholastic and theoretical in character. Even at its most routine, however, this type of writing does much to clarify the values and ideals which actually informed daily life in the societies of medieval Islam. On a more concrete level, *fatwās* can reveal the workings of certain crucial institutions (e.g., the *waqf*) or throw light on the dynamics of some types of social conflict, such as inter-confessional strife. Efforts to use them in this way are unfortunately still rare; as an example, see H. R. Idris, "Le mariage en Occident muṣūlman. Analyse de fatwās médiévales extraites du 'Miʿyār' d'al-Wansharīsī," *ROMM*, xii (1972), 45–62; xvii (1974), 71–105; xxv (1978), 119–138.

Anyone intending to deal with contracts (a very broad category indeed) must become familiar with the formularies or collections of model documents called *shurūṭ* (lit., "stipulations"). Again, these were first seriously studied by Joseph Schacht, who published some important examples of the genre. This literature is best approached, however, through Jeanette Wakin, *The Function of Documents in Islamic Law: The Chapters on Sales from Ṭaḥāwī's Kitāb al-Shurūṭ al-Kabīr* (1972). She prefaces her edition of the vast, only partly extant formulary-*cum*-commentary of al-Ṭaḥāwī (d. ca. 321/933) with a valuable analysis of the role of written documents in Islamic judicial practice (which in principle does not recognize them as valid evidence) and the internal structure of contracts. By comparing al-Ṭaḥāwī's model documents with contracts preserved among the papyri, Wakin is able to establish the close parallels between theoretical doctrine and actual usage. Finally, she emphasizes the guiding principle in al-Ṭaḥāwī's presentation: that the notary who draws up a contract must try to foresee every possible challenge to its validity from a qadi of any *madhhab*, even if he follows only a minority opinion within that *madhhab*. This principle not only illustrates al-Ṭaḥāwī's realism, but also demonstrates the practical significance of the differences of opinion among *faqīhs*, which have often been regarded as merely academic quarrels. In addition to Wakin's discussion, based upon early Islamic doctrine and practice, see also the Mamluk-period text published and studied by Gabriela Linda Guellil, *Damaszener Akten des 8./14. Jahrhunderts nach al-Ṭarsūsīs Kitāb al-Iʿlām* (1985); Guellil's analysis of al-Ṭarsūsī's formulary (Part II of her study) is less detailed than Wakin's, but it provides useful points of comparison.

In addition to the literary materials surveyed above, the Islamic legal system of course produced mountains of documents properly speaking. A surprising number of these survive, though they are badly scattered. Naturally enough, most of what remains dates from Ottoman times, and only fragments are available for the periods covered in this book. The extant legal documents can be divided into three broad classes, as follows:

1. *Sharīʿa*-court records: *maḥāḍir* (minutes of court hearings) and *sijillāt* (registers of the qadis' decisions).
2. Deeds of *waqf*, which are variously termed *waqfiyya*, *ḥujjat waqf*, and *kitāb waqf*.
3. Contracts (*ʿaqd*, pl. *ʿuqūd*) on subjects of all kinds—marriage, sale, partnership, etc.

The publication of legal documents is in its infancy, but we do have access to two small but highly important collections, each of which contains a cross-section of documentary types. D. P. Little, *A Catalogue of the Islamic Documents from al-Ḥaram aš-Šarīf in Jerusalem* (1984), gives a terse resume in English of each document in this remarkable 8th/14th-century trove. Obviously this hardly does away with the need to refer to the originals, but it enormously simplifies the identification of materials likely to be relevant to a given topic. From another corner of the Islamic world, Monika Gronke has published (with detailed commentaries) twenty-five judicial and notarial documents from the shrine of Shaykh Ṣafī al-Dīn in Ardabil: *Arabische und persische Privaturkunden des 12. und 13. Jahrhunderts aus Ardabil (Aserbaidschan)* (1982). (See also Part I, Chapter Two, p. 49.)

Sharīʿa-court records have obviously been kept since very early times, and a very long chapter (still unpublished) of al-Ṭaḥāwī's *Kitāb al-shurūṭ* demonstrates that an elaborate body of forms for such documents had already been established by the end of the 3rd/9th century. However, only a few surviving registers predate Ottoman times, and these remain unstudied. A detailed survey of the extant registers of Syria and Jordan is given in Jon E. Mandaville, "The Ottoman Court Records of Syria and Jordan," *JAOS*, lxxxvi (1966), 311–319, which also contains references to the scholarly literature on other regions of the Ottoman Empire. More recently, see A. K. Rafeq, "Les régistres des tribunaux de Damas comme source pour l'histoire de Syrie," *BEO*, xxvi (1973), 219–226. For the judicial archives of Egypt there are useful discussions in André Raymond, "Les documents du Maḥkama comme source pour l'histoire économique et sociale de l'Égypte au xviiie siècle," in J. Berque and D. Chevallier, *Les Arabes par leurs archives, xvie-xxe siècles* (1976), pp. 125–140; and Galal El-Nahal, *The Judicial Administration of Ottoman Egypt in the Seventeenth Century* (1979), pp. 9–11, 77. Unfortunately, there appears to be no survey of a similar kind for Iran.

Very few *sharīʿa*-court registers have as yet been published, even in calendar form. An example of their contents can be found in D. P. Little, "Two Fourteenth-Century Court Records from Jerusalem concerning the Disposition of Slaves by Minors," *Arabica*, xxix (1982), 16–49.

Deeds of *waqf* survive in considerable numbers, though they are terribly scattered. Typically the founder (*wāqif*) would retain one copy of the deed and deposit the other with the chief qadi of his district, who was a sort of controller-general of *awqāf*. Many such deeds are still in mosque repositories or in private hands, but in the former Ottoman territories, at least, most of them have been deposited in the national ministries of *awqāf* established in the late 19th and 20th centuries. Catalogs and surveys are a rarity, but for Egypt we now do have a very important one in Muḥammad Amīn, *Catalogue des documents d'archives du Caire, de 239/853 à 922/1516* (1981); as noted above (pp. 47, 171–172), Amīn includes many types of legal paper here, but the *waqfiyyas* are very numerous.

A few deeds of *waqf* have been published and more appear every year. As an appendix to his catalog, Amīn has provided facsimiles and printed transcriptions (with concise notes) of two of them. A very early deed of *waqf*, dating from 435/1043, has been published by D. Sourdel and J. Sourdel-Thomine, "Biens fonciers constitués *waqf* en Syrie fatimide pour une famille de Šarīfs damascains," *JESHO*, xv (1972), 269–296. For early Ottoman Egypt see an important study by R. Vesély, "Trois certificats delivrés pour les fondations pieuses en Egypte au xvie siècle," *Oriens*, xxi–xxii (1968–69), 248–299.

Related to the deed of *waqf* are a variety of other documents. One type is the summary recording all the properties endowed in favor of a given institution, together with income and expenses. Such summaries have no legal force, but they do contain the concrete data of most interest to the majority of historians. A good example is the text edited by Ahmad Darrag, *L'acte de waqf de Barsbay (Ḥuǧǧat waqf Barsbāy)* (1963). Likewise, summary versions of deeds of *waqf* are often given in the inscriptions on religious and charitable buildings (see above, Part I, Chapter Two, p. 58). Many examples can be found in *RCEA*, though so far as I am aware there are no studies primarily based on inscriptions of this kind. The Ottomans carefully surveyed and recorded in register form the *awqāf* of their dominions, and these often give valuable data on the pre-Ottoman period. Some of these surveys have been published for Anatolia and the Balkans, but the empire's Arab provinces remain neglected. As an example of what the Ottoman documents contain, see Ö. L. Barkan and E. H. Ayverdi, *İstanbul vakıfları tahrir defteri, 953 (1546) tarihli* (1970). On a more modest scale, see Suraiya Faroqhi, "*Vakıf* Administration in Sixteenth Century Konya, the *Zâviye* of Sadreddin-i Konevi," *JESHO*, xvii (1974), 145–172, which draws on tax and *waqf*-registers, the endowment's account books, and *sharīʿa*-court registers.

Finally we turn to contracts. Though a written contract was not per se valid evidence in court, no important transaction was made without one. In theory anyone might draw up a contract, but most persons preferred to go to a recognized notary (*shāhid*, pl. *shuhūd*) for this purpose. Contracts survive in considerable numbers from quite early times, and they are well represented among the papyri and Geniza papers. (See Part I, Chapter Two, pp. 41–42, 46–48.) Vols. I and II of Grohmann's *Arabic Papyri in the Egyptian Museum* are devoted to legal texts. A very old and important group of ten contracts (relating variously to partnership, marriage, and obligations for future delivery of textiles), dating from 250–58/864–872, has been superbly presented in Yūsuf Rāghib, *Marchands d'étoffes du Fayyoum au iiie/ixe siècle, I: les actes des Banū ʿAbd al-Muʾmin* (1982). Almost as old, and even more precious because of their non-Egyptian origin, are the documents published by D. Sourdel and J. Sourdel-Thomine in "Trois actes de vente damascains du début du ive/xe siècle," *JESHO*, viii (1965), 164–185. From the Mamluk period, Amīn's catalog includes many sales and transfers of property, among which he has published two 9th/15th-century examples. The Ḥaram collection from Jerusalem has some sixty contracts, along with nearly a hundred acknowledgments of legal obligation (*iqrār*). A few of these have been studied by D. P. Little in "Six fourteenth-century purchase deeds for slaves from al-Ḥaram aš-Šarīf," *ZDMG*, cxxxi (1981), 297–337. Outside Egypt and Syria-Palestine, such documents are scarce; a happy exception are those (marriage contracts for the most part) published in Wilhelm Hoenerbach, *Spanisch-Islamische Urkunden aus der Zeit der Nasriden und Moriscos* (1965).

The institutional machinery through which *fiqh* was applied has been much less carefully studied than the doctrine itself. We do have one major effort at a synthesis, however: Émile Tyan, *Histoire de l'organisation judiciaire en pays de l'Islam* (orig. ed. 2 vols., 1938–43; 2nd rev. ed., 1960). In spite of his title, Tyan's approach is formal rather than historical. Having traced the origins and development of the office of qadi during the first 150 years of Islam, he thereafter follows a broad institutional approach which pays little attention to issues of change and social milieu. Beyond that, he bases his study on a limited selection of literary texts and makes no use of true documentary evidence. In its own terms, Tyan's is a solid and useful piece of work, but we cannot really understand the significance of judicial institutions in Islamic society until we know precisely how they functioned in specific times and places. Inquiries of this sort are assuredly demanding, since they require the skills of both a legal and a social historian—a rare combination. The best documented studies to date on court procedure concern the Ottoman period, as we would expect, though none of these displays a sophisticated knowledge of classical *fiqh*. We have already mentioned the monograph of Galal El-Nahal on 11th/17th-century Egypt. See also a series of studies by R. C. Jennings: (a) "The Office of Vekil (Wakil) in 17th-Century Ottoman Sharia Courts," *SI*, xlii (1975), 147–169; (b) "Kadi, Court, and Legal Procedure in 17th-Century Ottoman Kayseri," *SI*, xlviii (1978), 133–172; (c) "Limitations of the Judicial Powers of the Kadi in 17th-Century Ottoman Kayseri," *SI*, l (1979), 151–184. For pre-Ottoman times, we have Joseph H. Escovitz, *The Office of Qāḍī al-Quḍāt in Cairo under the Baḥrī Mamluks* (1984), a solid monograph necessarily based on chronicles and biographical dictionaries rather than legal documents, of which very few survive for this period. Escovitz has a chapter on court practice, but essentially he presents a prosopographic study aimed at clarifying the identity and social background of these judges and the political milieu within which they had to operate.

The notarial system, so essential for the drafting of legal documents of all kinds, is described in the excellent monograph of Tyan, *Le notariat et la régime de la preuve par écrit dans la pratique du droit muṣūlman* (1945), which should of course be compared with J. Wakin, *The Function of Documents in Islamic Law*, and G. L. Guellil, *Damaszener Akten des 8./14 Jahrhunderts*.

Apart from modern studies, medieval Muslim authors wrote a number of treatises on the administration of justice. These tend to be prescriptive and idealizing, but they should not be ignored. Most accessible is perhaps Ibn Khaldūn's chapter entitled, "The Functions of the Religious Institution of the Caliphate" (*Muqaddima*, trans. F. Rosenthal, vol. I, 448–465). Abū'l-Ḥasan al-Māwardī included three chapters on judicial institutions in his famous *al-Aḥkām al-sulṭāniyya*; these can be consulted in Fagnan's translation (*Les statuts gouvernementaux* [1915]) or in an English resume and study by H. F. Amedroz: (a) "The Office of Kadi in the Aḥkām Sulṭāniyya of Mawardi," *JRAS* (1910), 761–796; (b) "The Maẓālim Jurisdiction in the Aḥkām Sulṭāniyya of Mawardi," *JRAS* (1911), 635–674; (c) "The Ḥisba Jurisdiction in the Aḥkām Sulṭāniyya of Mawardi," *JRAS* (1916), 77–101, 287–314. Al-Māwardī also composed a treatise on judgeship, *Adab al-qāḍī* (ed. M. H. al-Sirḥān, 1971), a major work which has yet to be studied. Among later works of this type, two are available in Western languages: (1) Guellil's *Damaszener Akten des 8./14. Jahrhunderts* (3. Teil); and (2) the *Kitāb al-wilāyāt* of al-Wansharīsī (d. 914/1518), trans. H. Bruno and M. Gaudefroy-Demombynes as *Le livre de magistratures* (1937). For further references see Schacht, *Introduction*, pp. 230–31, 283.

We return at last to the question with which we opened this chapter: what contributions can we expect *fiqh* to make to the history of Islamic society? Among the many aspects of life which might be examined from this perspective (e.g., family structure, property ownership, social stratification), we shall focus our attention on trade and commerce during early Islamic times, down to ca. 1100. This choice is suggested by several considerations. First, we have a major study which uses *sharīʿa* doctrine as its principal tool for reconstructing the commercial institutions of early Islam. Second, we have a limited but extremely interesting group of external sources against which we can compare the results obtained from *fiqh*. Finally, we have a sufficient number of studies on the history of commerce and commercial institutions in the medieval Mediterranean to provide a broad comparative framework.

A. L. Udovitch, *Partnership and Profit in Medieval Islam* (1970), tries to define the main institutions of commercial investment and business organization in early Islamic times (down to ca. 1100) through a close analysis of the discussions found in the major early compilations of Ḥanafī and Mālikī *fiqh*. He sticks close to his authorities, but does try to go beyond them in several respects: (1) by showing that their diverse and scattered doctrines add up to a coherent and remarkably flexible set of institutions; (2) by underscoring the jurists' concern to shape their doctrine so as to fit the traditional usages and imperatives of merchants without doing violence to the religio-ethical conceptions which underlay *fiqh*; (3) by comparing the results of his textual analysis to the contracts found among the Geniza papers in order to bring out the close parallels between juristic doctrine and actual usage. (In regard to this last point, it is interesting that Udovitch makes limited use of the numerous Islamic papyri published by Grohmann and others. In view of the rapidly growing number of published commercial documents, it might be a productive exercise to reconstruct Islamic doctrines and procedures on commerce directly from the documents, and then to compare such empirical results with the statements of the jurists.)

It might well be possible to push Udovitch's analysis further and to place it in a more general frame of reference, but even as it stands it is sufficient to indicate what kinds of questions *sharīʿa* texts can and cannot answer. Several things emerge very clearly from Udovitch's sources. First of all, they establish the techniques of investment and finance which were available to Muslim merchants (or to *dhimmīs* who wanted the protection of the qadis' courts). Second, they document the different ways in which artisans and merchants organized their enterprises; from this we can reasonably infer the scale and complexity of business organization in Abbasid times. Third, they show the manifold ways in which the conduct of business was intertwined with the legal and judicial system. Finally, we can infer from them the "mental set" of values, expectations, and goals which shaped economic behavior in this period.

Obviously all this adds up to a significant fund of knowledge. Yet there are many aspects of commerce and economic life which we cannot get at through *fiqh*. Let us note two in particular.

1. *Fiqh* is in principle universal, applying equally to every individual without regard to time and place. It tells us almost nothing about such concrete

realities as products of exchange, trade routes, centers of production and distribution, or the economic roles of different groups within the Islamic world. Yet without facts of this kind, the real economic significance of forms of business organization, financial instruments, etc., cannot be determined.

2. *Fiqh* in theory establishes rules of conduct which are valid and binding for all time. Although some jurists take note of established custom and social realities in formulating their rulings, none recognizes change and development as a legitimate element in jurisprudence. It is thus all but impossible to use *fiqh* to trace historical change within the commercial institutions of Islam.

For both reasons, external evidence is essential—legal documents (contracts, *sharīʿa*-court records, etc.) where these exist, non-legal sources otherwise.

Within this latter class, we have a substantial fund of business documents which are not legal in character, such as letters, invoices, letters of credit, etc. In view of their routine, occasional nature, these have been preserved only by chance, and since chance favors things Egyptian, that is where most of them come from. Grohmann places such "economic texts" in Vols. V and VI of *Arabic Papyri in the Egyptian Museum*. See also Albert Dietrich, *Arabische Briefe aus der Papyrussammlung der Hamburger Staats- und Universitäts-Bibliothek* (1955). Business papers from the Cairo Geniza have been widely published; the best and most attractive introduction to them is certainly S. D. Goitein, *Letters of Medieval Jewish Traders* (1973).

As to the literary sources, certain genres in particular yield tantalizing bits of data, though seldom enough to permit a fully satisfactory resolution of any major problem. By far the most useful and widely consulted genre has been geography, especially the remarkable series of 3rd/9th and 4th/10th-century texts in the *BGA*. (See also Part I, Chapter One, pp. 17–18.) These texts are our most reliable and comprehensive source for trade routes, the identification of centers of administration, production, and exchange, the most visible (though not necessarily the most important) products of various localities, and urban topography. A concise overview of the evolution, approach, and contents of geographical writing can be obtained from S. Maqbul Ahmad, "Djughrāfiya," *EI²*, ii, 575–587, as well as from the old but still valuable contributions of J. H. Kramers: (a) "Geography and Commerce," in T. Arnold and A. Guillaume, eds., *The Legacy of Islam* (1931, often reprinted), pp. 79–108; and (b) "La littérature géographique classique des muṣulmans," in Kramers, *Analecta Orientalia* (2 vols., 1954–56), i, 172–204. I. I. Krachkovskii's important monograph, *Arabskaia geograficheskaia literatura*, vol. IV of *Izbrannye sochineniia* (1957), has been ensured a limited readership due to its language; there is however a good Arabic translation by Ṣalāḥ al-Dīn U. Hāshim, *Taʾrīkh al-adab al-jughrāfī al-ʿarabī* (2 vols., 1963–65). Finally, André Miquel has published an impressive series of volumes under the title *La géographie humaine du monde muṣūlman jusqu'au milieu de 11ᵉ siècle* (3 vols., in progress;

1967–1980). The first discusses the evolution and role of geographical writing within Arabic literature; the second examines how Muslim geographers described the lands and cultures which lay outside the boundaries of Islam; the third deals with the treatment of physical geography by Muslim writers. Unfortunately, a volume on the ways in which Muslim geographers approached the cultures and peoples of Islam itself has yet to appear.

The materials supplied by the geographers can be supplemented by scattered statements in the chronicles and biographical dictionaries. Even more useful, however, are the compilations of edifying and entertaining anecdotes which were so popular a literary genre in the 3rd/9th and 4th/10th centuries. These deal not only with the elites of caliphal society—bureaucrats, courtiers, generals, the *ʿulamāʾ*—but also with a surprising number of ordinary folk as well. For our purposes, the most informative writers in this genre are al-Jāḥiẓ (Abū ʿUthmān ʿAmr b. Baḥr, 160–255/776–868) and al-Muḥassin b. ʿAlī al-Tanūkhī (329–384/940–994). A superb example of the narrative skill and social realism of al-Jahiz can be found in his *Kitāb al-bukhalāʾ* (ed. M. T. al-Ḥājirī, 1948), trans. Charles Pellat as *Le livre des avares* (1951). Al-Tanūkhī's was a slenderer talent; he is less a realist than his great predecessor, and more concerned to illustrate the commonplace moral stereotypes of his day (e.g., the just monarch, the humble but upright artisan, the religious charlatan). Nevertheless, his most important work, *Nishwār al-muḥāḍara*, is full of characteristic detail and repays close analysis. Moreover, the fact that he was a qadi lends an extra degree of authenticity and credibility to his many accounts of legal conflicts, however fictionalized these may be. The extant portions have been translated (with a degree of bowdlerization) by D. S. Margoliouth as *The Table-Talk of a Mesopotamian Judge* (Part I, 1922; Parts II and VIII in *IC*, iii–vi [1929–1932]). Obviously the data contained in such collections is extremely unsystematic. The relevant anecdotes illustrate vividly many commercial practices and attitudes; on the other hand, they are not sufficient by themselves to indicate the institutional patterns within which these things occurred. In principle, at least, it would be an interesting exercise to try to fit this anecdotal evidence into the legal framework established by Udovitch, Wakin, Brunschvig, et al.

Two older studies still provide the best examples of the results which can be obtained by a systematic ransacking of geographical, historical, and anecdotal texts:

1. Adam Mez, *Die Renaissance des Islam* (1922; repr. 1968. The English translation by S. Khuda-Bukhsh and D. S. Margoliouth, *The Renaissance of Islam* [1937, repr. 1973, 1975], is not always reliable).
2. R. B. Serjeant, "Materials for a History of Islamic Textiles," *Ars Islamica*, ix–xvi (1942–51); separately reprinted as *Islamic Textiles: Material for a History up to the Mongol Conquest* (1972).

Neither of these works attempts an integrated interpretation; rather, both are compilations—Serjeant's the more critical and thorough—of texts in resume or translation.

Unfortunately the character of our sources seldom permits us to pursue biographical and family studies, which have been so productive for the economic history of later medieval Europe. Even where we do have enough data, it concerns atypical elite figures; to this category belongs H. L. Gottschalk's study of an important family of financiers and officials, *Die Mādarā'ijjūn, ein Beitrag zur Geschichte Ägyptens unter den Islam* (1931). For Jewish merchants (more fully discussed below, Chapter Eleven) we are somewhat better informed because of the Geniza papers. There is some valuable material on them in the Islamic literary sources as well, however; this has been brought together in W. J. Fischel, *Jews in the Economic and Political Life of Mediaeval Islam* (1937, repr. 1968).

In view of the importance and prestige of commerce in Islamic history, we might suppose that there would be a considerable literature of commercial ethics, practical advice for merchants, etc. In fact there is very little; apparently the merchants in medieval Islamic society identified themselves on a cultural plane with the *ʿulamāʾ* and the civil bureaucracy and produced no distinctive literature of their own. In contrast, the *ʿulamāʾ* would occasionally comment in religious and ethical works on the proper role and status of merchants, and two essays make good use of this material:

1. S. D. Goitein, "The Rise of the Middle-Eastern Bourgeoisie in Early Islamic Times," in *Studies in Islamic History and Institutions* (1966), pp. 217–241.
2. A.K.S. Lambton, "The Merchant in Medieval Islam," in W. B. Henning and E. Yarshater, eds., *A Locust's Leg: Studies in Honour of S. H. Taqizade* (1962), 121–130.

We do have one major mercantile text, *Kitāb al-ishāra ilā maḥāsin al-tijāra* ("On the excellence of commerce"), composed by a certain Abū'l-Faḍl al-Dimashqī. He seems to have written in Fatimid Egypt during the 5th/11th century, but otherwise we know nothing about him. His treatise is an attempt to integrate the commercial practice of his day into a general Islamic value-system. To this end he presents a conception of economics derived from the ideas of Late Antiquity, a survey of prestige articles of exchange, hadith citations proclaiming the dignity of commerce, and bits of advice on techniques of trade. The work was studied and partly translated by Helmut Ritter, "Ein arabisches Handbuch der Handelswissenschaft," *Islam*, vii (1917), 1–91. See also the additional comments of Claude Cahen, "À propos et autour d'*Ein arabisches Handbuch der Handelswissenschaft*," *Oriens*, xv (1962), 160–171. Less significant than al-Dimashqī but still worth noting are two brief essays:

1. al-Jāḥiẓ, *Fī madḥ al-tujjār wa-dhamm ʿamal al-sulṭān* ("In praise of merchants and condemnation of government service"); brief excerpts are translated in Charles Pellat, *The Life and Works of Jāḥiẓ*, trans. D. M. Hawke (1969), 272–73.

2. Pseudo-Jāḥiẓ, *al-Tabaṣṣur bi'l-tijāra* ("A clear view of commerce"); trans. Ch. Pellat, *Arabica*, i (1954), 153–165.

Obviously many vital problems concerning the commerce and industry of early medieval Islam are effectively closed to us. We cannot, for example, construct a useful model of the economy of any region, with the possible exception of Egypt for certain periods. We can perhaps identify the main sectors of the economy, but we will have no idea of their relative (let alone absolute) size and importance. A serious economic history, whether neo-classical or Marxist in inspiration, thus seems out of the question. On the other hand, manifold opportunities remain open in regard to the forms of economic life; we can learn in great detail what people made and traded, and how they went about these activities. Within an institutional approach of this kind, *fiqh* ought to be an invaluable resource. We can get full value from it, however, only through a systematic comparison of the statements of *fiqh* with the evidence supplied by documents and literary sources. In regard to documents, important results have already been achieved, though they remain tentative and to some degree mutually contradictory. On the other hand, students of Islamic law and Arabic literature continue to inhabit different realms and hardly communicate with one another. Until this barrier is pierced, we will have only an impoverished and distorted sense of what might be learned about the economic life of medieval Islam.

Chapter Ten

URBAN TOPOGRAPHY AND URBAN SOCIETY

DAMASCUS UNDER THE AYYUBIDS AND MAMLUKS

A. General Perspectives on Urban History in Islam

THE CITY has long been considered the hallmark of Middle Eastern civilization, and though Orientalists of a Romantic stamp have sometimes been obsessed with the notion that Islam belongs to the desert, the cities of Islam—Cordoba, Fez, Cairo, Istanbul, Baghdad, Isfahan, Samarqand—are legendary. It is true that until very recent times only a small minority of Middle Easterners lived in anything which could be called a city; the majority were always peasants, and in certain times and places nomadic pastoralists have outnumbered city-dwellers. But even so, we cannot deny the crucial place of cities in Islamic society and politics. They were the residence of that society's elites (whether cultural, economic, social, or political), the centers of administration, and the nexus of commerce and investment even in rural areas. Urban culture was often remote from the lifeways of the village and steppe, but it always provided the norms in terms of which non-urban cultural patterns were to be evaluated and legitimized.

In spite of all this, the systematic study of urban history is a rather recent development in Islamic studies. The reasons for this lag in scholarly awareness probably lie in two things: first, the focus in Orientalism before World War I on religion and political history; second, the widespread attitude among Western scholars that Islamic cities were mere agglomerations, without the municipal institutions and political self-consciousness that would make them true urban entities like those of Classical Antiquity or medieval Europe.

Although Adam Mez published a paper on the Islamic city as early as 1912 (included as Chapter 22 of *Die Renaissance des Islam* [1922]), far more influential was the article of William Marçais, "L'Islamisme et la vie urbaine," *Comptes-rendus de l'Académie des Inscriptions et Belles-Lettres* (1928), 86–100 (reprinted in the author's *Articles et conferences*, 1961)—a piece which marks the beginning of the great French tradition of Islamic urban studies. The succeeding two decades saw a thin but steady stream of publications (the majority of them by French scholars) on various aspects of the topic. Among these were a number of monographs on specific towns and regions, some of which we shall note in due course. There were also, however, several efforts to follow the lead of W. Marçais in proposing general definitions or characterizations of the Islamic city—attempts to capture the essence of Islamic urbanism, we might say.

Among the most perceptive of these were three pieces by Georges Marçais (the younger brother of William):

1. "L'urbanisme musulman," *Revue africaine* (1939–40), 13–34;, repr. in G. Marçais, *Mélanges d'histoire et d'archéologie de l'Occident musulman* (2 vols., 1957), i, 219–231.
2. "La conception des villes dans l'Islam," *Revue d'Alger*, ii (1945), 517–533.
3. "Considerations sur les ville musulmanes et notamment sur le rôle du mohtasib," *Recueils Société Jean Bodin*, vi (1954), 249–262.

Marçais focuses on the towns of North Africa, naturally enough. In spite of its title, the first of these articles places little emphasis on Islam per se as a determining factor in urban life, stressing instead such concrete matters as security and defense, water, heterogeneous populations, and the organization of marketplaces. In the two later papers, however, Marçais ascribes a central role to religion: "... chaque ville musulmane est une citadelle de la foi ... ce rôle religieux est presque sa raison d'être." ("La conception des villes," p. 524).

Following in this path, Gustave von Grunebaum, in "The Structure of the Muslim Town," (*Islam, Studies in the Nature of a Cultural Tradition* [1955], pp. 141–158), constructs an ideal type in the manner of Max Weber, and tries to show how the characteristics of this urban type are rooted in Islamic culture. Von Grunebaum's essay displays formidable erudition and great logical coherence, but its usefulness is restricted by a static, ahistorical framework in which problems of change and adaptation can hardly be addressed. Likewise, its cultural perspective, in which the Classical city is the measure of all things, no longer seems persuasive.

Since the early 1960s, the field has almost exploded with activity. The once dominant Marçais-von Grunebaum paradigm has been sharply assailed from many directions, though none of its critics has been able to win sole possession of the field for his own mode of analysis. Indeed, the whole subject has become intensely pluralistic, and all we can do is to indicate the most interesting of the many approaches now available. Perhaps the best introduction to urban life in medieval Islam currently is the chapter "La ville et les milieux urbains," in D. and J. Sourdel, *La civilisation de l'Islam classique* (1968), pp. 397–466, which is well documented, concrete, and highly cognizant of social and political change. See also the excellent volume edited by A. H. Hourani and S. M. Stern, *The Islamic City: a Colloquium* (1970); Hourani's introduction ("The Islamic City in the Light of Recent Research", pp. 9–24, brings out most effectively the general issues implicit in the individual contributions.

An early critique of the notion of "the Islamic city" was presented in two papers by Claude Cahen: (a) "L'histoire économique et sociale de l'Orient musulman médiéval," *SI*, iii (1955), 93–115; (b) "Zur Geschichte der städtischen Gesellschaft im islamischen Orient des Mittelalters," *Saeculum*, ix (1958), 59–76. The former is essentially an outline of the kinds of questions which need to be asked and a discussion of the prospects for productive research in this field. In the second paper, Cahen argues that down to the 11th century the cities of Islam largely maintained the patterns of Late Antiquity, that their salient characteristics closely resembled those of early medieval Europe, and that in any case a still nascent Islam could hardly have had much impact at such an early period.

Adopting a specifically sociological perspective, Ira Lapidus has sought to define the complex interactions between the social groups which made up the urban populace. From this point of view, religious ideals and the physical appearance of the city—the principal focus of analysis in Marçais and von Grunebaum—are of very secondary significance. His main ideas are summed up in two articles: (a) "Muslim Cities and Islamic Societies," in Lapidus, ed., *Middle Eastern Cities. A Symposium on Ancient, Islamic, and Contemporary Middle Eastern Urbanism* (1969), pp. 47–79; (b) "The Evolution of Muslim Urban Society," *Comparative Studies in Society and History*, xv (1973), 21–50.

In contrast to Lapidus, Oleg Grabar has emphasized anew the significance of the monuments for our understanding of the character and meaning of urban life in Islam. In so doing, he restores something obscured in the approaches of Cahen and Lapidus—viz., the cultural dimension of urban life, a sense of the values and ideals held by the Muslims who dwelt in these cities. At the same time, Grabar is very alert to questions of change and the particularities of time and place. See (a) "The Architecture of the Middle Eastern City from Past to Present: the Case of the Mosque," in Lapidus, ed., *Middle Eastern Cities*, pp. 26–46; and (b) "Cities and Citizens," in Bernard Lewis, ed., *The World of Islam* (1976), pp. 89–116.

In recent years, urban geographers in Germany have been producing a series of monographs which are both carefully executed and conceptually sophisticated. Much of this work is brought together in an impressive article by Eugen Wirth, "Die orientalische Stadt. Ein Überblick aufgrund jüngerer Forschungen zur materiellen Kultur," *Saeculum*, xxvi (1975), 45–94. Wirth is especially concerned with the spatial organization, land-use patterns, and economic functions exhibited by the cities of the pre-modern Islamic world. He argues that the "Islamic city" is substantially identical in these respects to the towns of the ancient Near East, and indeed shares important features with Greco-Roman, medieval European, and even modern cities. In his view, the only major innovation of Islamic urban life is the bazaar, the central market complex which sets the towns from Morocco to Afghanistan apart from all others. So central is the bazaar to Wirth's interpretation that he has devoted a lengthy study to it: "Zum Problem des Bazars (sūq, çarşı). Versuch einer Begriffsbestimmung und Theorie des traditionellen Wirtschaftszentrum der orientalisch-islamischen Stadt," *Islam*, li (1974), 203–260; lii (1975), 6–46. (For "case studies" on

Aleppo and Isfahan by the same author, see below, pp. 233, 244.) Wirth is not a historian and thus shows little concern for change and development, but his analysis does provide a new and revealing way of interpreting the visible features of the cities of Islam.

The cities of medieval Islam were not recognized as legal entities in any sense, and most scholars have thus assumed that the *sharīʿa* has nothing to say about urban life per se. However, Robert Brunschvig, "Urbanisme médiéval et droit musulman," *REI*, xv (1947), 127–155 (reprinted in Brunschvig, *Études d'islamologie*, ii [1975], pp. 7–35), demonstrated that later Mālikī jurists did address specifically urban issues. After a long hiatus, this theme has recently been picked up again in studies by Baber Johansen; see (a) "Eigentum, Familie, und Obrigkeit im hanafitischen Strafrecht," *Welt des Islams*, N.S. xix (1979), 1–73; (b) "The All-Embracing Town and its Mosques," *ROMM*, xxxii (1981), 139–161.

The contrasting (and sometimes incommensurate) concepts and methods of these scholars are to a large degree rooted in their differing choice of sources. At this juncture, then, we need (1) to develop an overview of the resources available to us for the study of urban history in Islam, and (2) to explore ways of using these resources to maximum effect. We will begin with a few notes on the possibilities offered by the Ottoman period, not merely to induce longing and regret among students of earlier centuries, but also because the Ottoman sources throw much light at least on the 9th/15th century, as well as forming a useful standard of comparison for scholars who must rely on a thinner documentation.

Ottoman archival documents have many shortcomings and are far from easy to use, but even so they transform our knowledge of urban society in the Fertile Crescent and the eastern and southern Mediterranean basin. Bernard Lewis was the first to discuss the significance of these materials for the Arab provinces, in "The Ottoman Archives as a Source for the History of the Arab Lands," *JRAS* (1951), 139–155. Since that time, Ottoman archival collections have been much discussed and occasionally used, but very few have been published or indexed in detail. Lewis himself has published some tax registers on the towns of Palestine, however: (a) "Studies in the Ottoman Archives, I," *BSOAS*, xvi (1954), 469–501; (b) (with Amnon Cohen), *Population and Revenue in the Towns of Palestine in the Sixteenth Century* (1978). The tax code for Ottoman Syria is given in Robert Mantran and Jean Sauvaget, *Règlements fiscaux ottomans: les provinces syriennes* (1951). For lower Iraq, see Mantran, "Règlements fiscaux ottomans: la province de Bassora," *JESHO*, x (1967), 224–277. The vast fund of Ottoman documents in Cairo was first surveyed a half-century ago by Jean Deny, *Sommaire des archives turques du Caire* (1930), but it was not systematically put to use until S. J. Shaw, *The Financial and Administrative Organization and Development of Ottoman Egypt, 1517–1798* (1962)—an important pioneering work in which the presentation of data still dominates attempts at interpretation. An early effort to make sense of the

Ottoman census data, and one which remains the starting point for the study of urban demography in the later Middle Ages, is Ö. L. Barkan, "Essai sur les données statistiques des régistres de recensement dans l'Empire Ottoman aux xve et xvie siècles," *JESHO*, i (1958), 9–36. Finally, we should recall the *shari'a*-court records (discussed above, Chapter Nine, pp. 219–221), which are critically important for the urban historian.

Historians of the Ottoman city benefit also from the writings of European travellers to the Middle East, who by the 16th century were not only numerous but relatively sophisticated. Though religious and cultural antagonisms were still very vivid indeed, Europeans were now sufficiently objective to give descriptions of enduring scientific value. By the early 19th century, some were formidable scholars as well as acute observers—e.g., John Lewis Burckhardt, Edward William Lane, Alfred Freiherr von Kremer—and what they saw in the Muslim world represented a still unbroken (though of course constantly changing) social and cultural tradition. Obviously travellers' accounts must be used critically, but their testimony remains an excellent first-hand source.

Finally, Ottomanists have the advantage of being able to view directly the object of their studies, for the remaining "traditional quarters" in Middle Eastern cities date largely from Ottoman times. Obviously these districts contain important vestiges and layers from earlier periods, but the final elaboration of the traditional urban topography is a product of the Ottoman period. Admittedly this advantage grows less important with each passing year, as the traditional sections are abandoned, razed for new construction, or otherwise mutilated beyond recognition. But such change can be of no comfort to students of earlier periods, for whom the archaeological evidence is disappearing even more rapidly. In view of these facts, it is especially unfortunate that Ottoman neighborhoods and monuments were almost ignored until very recently, perhaps because the Ottoman era was for so long regarded as one of "cultural decline"—whatever that may mean. An important exception to this rule is Cairo, where the topography of the late Ottoman city was meticulously recorded by E. F. Jomard in the vast *Description de l'Égypte: état moderne* (vol. II, part 2, pp. 579–786) produced by the Napoleonic expedition of 1798.

A number of important studies exploiting these sources have appeared in recent years. To take only the Arab provinces of the Empire, a concise but detailed survey of six towns (Algiers, Tunis, Cairo, Damascus, Mosul, and Baghdad) is given in André Raymond, *Les grandes villes arabes à l'époque ottomane* (1985). Far narrower in scope, but important for the insight which they give into the ways in which archival and archaeological research can be combined, are two recent monographs:

1. Jean-Claude David, *Le waqf d'Ipšir Paša à Alep (1063/1653)* (1982).
2. Jean-Paul Pascual, *Damas a la fin du xvie siècle, d'aprés trois actes de waqf ottomanes* (1983).

Beyond doubt the most imposing achievement is Andre Raymond's *Artisans et commercants au Caire au xviii*^e^ *siècle* (2 vols., 1973), a comprehensive study of the economic life of late Ottoman Cairo and of the social and political structures through which it functioned. Obviously scholars who work on less richly documented periods cannot duplicate Raymond's results. However, the book indicates more clearly than any other in the Islamic field the range of questions which urban historians need to confront, and just as important, it demonstrates a most effective approach to the integration of highly disparate topics within a common interpretive framework.

Our resources for non-Ottoman lands, or for the centuries before 1500 are much thinner than those available to Ottomanists. In place of comprehensive archives we have only scattered documents; foreign travellers are few and ill-informed; archaeological traces are often vestigial and hard to interpret, especially for the earlier periods. But though the task is harder it is not impossible; for those who know how to look, much even from the Roman past survives. And if foreign visitors fail us, Muslim authors produced geographical surveys and urban topographies in great profusion. Mamluk Egypt and Syria and late medieval North Africa in particular present major research opportunities. An outstanding example of what can be done by combining textual sources with close observation of the 20th-century city is provided by the study of Roger Le Tourneau, *Fès avant le Protectorat* (1949), though at the time he wrote it the royal archives in Morocco were not yet open to Western researchers. Roughly similar in approach is a volume edited by R. B. Serjeant and Ronald Lewcock, *Ṣanʿāʾ, an Arabian Islamic City* (1983)—superbly (indeed lavishly) produced, though inevitably less focused and cohesive than Le Tourneau's classic, since it is the work of many hands. The monuments and ensembles of two Syrian cities have been meticulously inventoried and analyzed in Michael H. Burgoyne, *Mamluk Jerusalem: An Architectural Study* (1987); and in Heinz Gaube and Eugen Wirth, *Aleppo. Historische und geographische Beiträge zur baulichen Gestaltung, zur sozialen Organisation und zur wirtschaftlichen Dynamik einer vorderasiatischen Fernhandelsmetropole* (1984).

Iran, unfortunately, does not offer quite the same prospects, in part because archival materials are so scattered and fragmentary, at least down to the Qajar period (19th century). It is true that the country was much visited and commented on by European travellers, and until recent years major segments of the traditional urban topography were extant. But this latter resource was just beginning to be exploited effectively by the 1970s, and one can only guess at the destruction wrought since the end of that decade. (What might have been done is suggested by Heinz Gaube and Eugen Wirth, *Der Bazar von Isfahan* [1978], on which see below, p. 244.)

Finally, we should note a pair of recent monographs on the garrison towns (*amṣār*) founded during the early Islamic conquests. These are of interest not only because of the substantive data which they provide on a crucial period, but because their sources are the mirror image of each other. In *Al-Fusṭāṭ: Its Foundation and Early Urban Development* (1987), Wladyslaw Kubiak studies an urban center whose early history is sketchily recorded in the texts, but for which there is a rich archaeological record. In contrast, Hichem Djaït's *al-Kūfa, naissance de la ville islamique* (1986) deals with a town which was the cradle of early Islamic historical tradition, but where actual excavations have been very limited. The two books thus illustrate neatly the differing (and somewhat incommensurate) images of the past created by archaeology on the one hand and textual analysis on the other.

Even at best, the study of urban history in Islam demands a good deal of speculation. Any item of hard data must be squeezed for all it is worth, and broad interpretations are inevitably erected out of bits and pieces that might have been put together quite differently. The whole process is feasible only if we approach our subject with a well-defined set of hypotheses. Inevitably these will be to some degree *a priori* propositions, in the sense that they are derived from the study of other, better-known urban systems and from general social and political theory. But without such hypotheses our evidence will make no sense—indeed, we will not be able to recognize many potentially significant phenomena as evidence at all.

The scholar who best exemplified this approach among Islamists was without doubt Jean Sauvaget (1901–1950). Occasionally he fell victim to its pitfalls, for he sometimes became fascinated with his hypotheses as ends in themselves, but he could also exploit its possibilities with rare sophistication and effectiveness. He was deeply concerned throughout his career with issues of method; while these are touched upon in almost everything he wrote, they are most fully developed in two places: (a) "Comment étudier l'histoire de l'Orient musulman," *Revue Africaine*, xc (1946), 5–23 (repr. in *Mémorial Jean Sauvaget* [2 vols., 1954], i, pp. 167–186); (b) *La mosquée omeyyade de Médine* (1947). Both of these were based on his lectures at the Collège de France, and the latter was explicitly presented as an exercise in method. Between them, these two pieces spell out the logic and underlying attitudes which governed all of Sauvaget's writing, and anyone using his work needs to become familiar with them.

Since we are concerned here with Sauvaget as an urban historian, however, we will focus our attention on his great thesis: *Alep: essai sur le développement d'une grande ville syrienne des origines au milieu du xixe siècle* (2 vols., 1941). Vol. I is the text proper, Vol. II a splendid album of seventy photographs by the author. This work represents the culmination of some thirteen years' residence and research in Syria, in circumstances far more favorable than any enjoyed there by Western scholars before or since. Since Syria was under French Mandate, Sauvaget had *carte blanche* to see what he wanted. Moreover, in spite of considerable damage during the 1925 revolt and the beginnings of modernization (an even more destructive force than war), the traditional topography and organs of urban life in Syria were substantially intact. Many old monuments were in a sad state of decay and neglect, but at least they were still there.

Sauvaget argues that one must begin with the visible evidence, with the actual condition of the city—its buildings (including the humblest and most tumbledown), its street plan, its facilities for collective action and communal life. One must quite literally note every stone and try to determine when and why that stone had been put where it was. In large part, this approach reflected Sauvaget's concern for the physical form of the city; for him, the purpose of urban history was to explain how a city had come to look the way it did. At the same time, he believed that a city's monuments, topography, and settlement patterns were a direct and undistorted reflection of its social history, and these material witnesses to the past had to be scrutinized as closely as any written sources. The texts were obviously essential, not only for names and dates, but also for the political institutions and social values which shaped urban life. But only a scholar who could control and interpret texts through his knowledge of the archaeological evidence could really understand what they had to say. Such a program may seem intuitively obvious, but when Sauvaget wrote archaeologists knew no Arabic and Arabists knew no archaeology. Even today, only a few historians seem to look closely at what they write about.

It is worth noting that though Sauvaget regarded himself as an archaeologist, he never carried out an excavation. On the contrary, he always confined his attention to surface evidence. In a way he had no choice, for he was studying living urban centers, where any sort of large-scale excavation was out of the question. On the other hand, this approach meant that he would inevitably miss a good deal of significant, even crucial evidence, and in using his work we have to keep this in mind.

Sauvaget's method governs the structure of his book. It is organized in twelve chapters, each reviewing one epoch in the city's long history. These epochs are defined in political terms—i.e., each is identified with one of the dynasties or empires which ruled Aleppo for some substantial period of time. In turn, each political epoch is correlated with a specific set of changes in the city's physical topography and social structure. Every chapter is laid out in an identical manner, according to a four-part scheme: (1) a concise essay setting down the broad trends of politics and international relations within a given period; (2) a discussion of the impact of these political trends on urban administration and the internal political life of Aleppo; (3) a presentation of the changes in the city's topography and monuments, with emphasis on the still visible evidence of these changes; (4) an essay which tries to integrate the materials previously presented into a general interpretation of the characteristics and evolution of urban life in Aleppo during the period under study.

Alep is altogether a remarkable achievement, one which fully merits its many accolades. Like any work of such scope, of course, it has certain failings both in content and method. To some degree this is merely a result of scholarly progress. For example, we now know vastly more about pre-Hellenistic history and culture in North Syria than Sauvaget could hope to, and every year adds something of importance. Likewise, we now have access to many more texts from the Islamic period (due largely to the initiatives of Sauvaget and his students, in fact)—and just as important, we are now in a position to do third and fourth readings of texts which he was the first to use. Other problems, however, are matters of approach and cultural attitude; it is easy to miss these, for Sauvaget's argumentation possesses a seductive power and clarity.

First of all, he displays a very rigid concept of the linkages between politics, social institutions, and urban topography. Political and administrative stability are equated with social peace, large-scale public construction, and regular urban planning. (And of course the reverse is also true.) So strong are these linkages that Sauvaget will assert them even in the absence of positive evidence. For example, he attributes the appearance of two characteristic features of the late Ottoman town—the closed or walled quarter (*ḥāra*) and the highly irregular market streets—to the "dark age" of the 4th/10th and 5th/11th centuries. The quarters, he argues, were carved out of the previously open city, while the markets were simply the colonnaded avenues of Roman times transformed. His argument for this dating goes as follows:

> The chronological place which I assign to this phenomenon is, I repeat, purely hypothetical. However, the historical milieu presents all the circumstances we need in order not to think this a rash opinion: the instability of power, annihilating any possibility of control; the weakening of governmental authority, thus leaving more scope for individual initiatives; general administrative corruption, which facilitated illegal actions; a need for security, which induced a manner of grouping shops together which would leave them less exposed; the quickness of popular reactions, which made governmental administration difficult; the frequency of disorders, which caused much damage to the city; the poverty of architectural thinking. (*Alep*, 102–3.)

Reasoning of this kind is undeniably plausible, but it also displays at least a degree of circularity.

More significant, perhaps, is the myth which underlies Sauvaget's presentation. He regards the history of Aleppo as a morally significant process, one which exemplifies the city's ultimate failure to sustain the urban ideal which it had embodied at one moment in its history. For Sauvaget, this urban ideal is crucial, both as the effective starting point of the city's millenia-long history and as the standard of value against which all later developments must be measured. He locates the realization—or rather the definition—of the urban ideal in the long Hellenistic-Roman period (333 B.C. to 286 A.D.). Before this time Aleppo had been a sort of overgrown village, but during Classical Antiquity (which he treats almost as a single moment), "the essential elements [of the city] were already chosen, put into place, and their scale defined: the centuries still to be traversed would hardly do more than work out this initial theme." (*Alep*, p. 53.) As to the urban ideal itself, Sauvaget defines it in the following terms: "urbanism . . . expresses itself not merely in the drawing of a plan, but rather through systematic and coherent administrative regulation, elaborated after due reflection for a defined purpose and then firmly applied." (*Alep*, p. 52.) A true city is thus created by the application of public law to every aspect of its life; in this way a city becomes an "organic unity" and a "moral person."

All the later chapters in the book are devoted, at least in part, to showing how Aleppo bit by bit fell away from this great ideal. The Byzantine period already reflects "a dangerous negligence of the principles of urbanism," (*Alep*, p. 67), and if the city more or less held its own under the early caliphate (down to 836), during the three centuries of anarchy which followed it became no more than "an aggregate of quarters," where "each person was in some sense the enemy of all others," and was governed only by "individual, egoistic, and incoherent initiatives." (*Alep*, pp. 107–8.) Even the Zengid and Ayyubid periods (1128–1260), which brought renewed prosperity and an architectural renaissance, introduced a new element of urban disaggregation by creating opposing classes of Turkish masters and Arab subjects. Nor did the Mamluk hegemony (1260–1516) resolve this fundamental illness. Under them Aleppo indeed became a metropolis (*une grande ville*)—i.e., a composite of relatively autonomous though adjoining and interacting settlements. Worse, its prosperity was but a function of Europe's: "It is the grandeur of Venice which, by ricochet, assures that of Aleppo." (*Alep*, p. 185)

In reading any work of Sauvaget, it is crucial to recognize how profoundly his analysis was shaped by his idealization (which few scholars now would share) of the Hellenistic and Roman city and by his ascription of decisive moral value to this ideal. His approach has the merit of allowing a superbly unified and coherent account of a vast subject, but it inevitably leads to a suppression of contradictory data and to a misunderstanding of those institutions and values in Islamic times which do not conform to Classical ideals. To put this point in another way, Sauvaget demonstrates in many places how deeply medieval Islam was rooted in Classical Antiquity—and he was one of the first who fully comprehended this—but too often he fails to perceive the integrity and authenticity of Islamic life in its own terms.

Whatever the shortcomings of Sauvaget's work, however, it provides a excellent methodological model which should have been far more widely applied. Relatively few cities are amenable to such treatment, to be sure, for Sauvaget's approach requires both a relatively intact "old city" and a substantial body of historical and topographical texts. For many crucially important urban centers such as Baghdad, Kufa, or Nishapur other strategies would have to be devised. Still, it is enough to name Damascus, Jerusalem, Cairo, and Isfahan to suggest what might yet be achieved along these lines.

B. A Case Study: Damascus in the Later Middle Ages

There is little merit in blind imitation of Sauvaget; the point is to use his method to address a different set of questions from those which seemed central to him. In order to explore this possibility we will look at one city during a single (albeit broadly defined) period: Damascus, from the Seljukid occupation in 471/1078 down to the Ottoman conquest in 922/1516. Damascus is an especially good choice for several reasons. (1) We possess the whole array of sources which we can hope to find for any pre-Ottoman town. (2) It has attracted a fair amount of serious scholarly attention. (3) The "old city" is sufficiently small and coherent to enable a scholar to master its monuments and topography.

The textual sources for the history of Damascus are unmatched by any other Muslim city except Cairo. First of all, between the mid-6th/12th and the 20th centuries, Damascene scholars produced a truly remarkable series of historical topographies. The first of these was written by the *faqīh* Ibn ʿAsākir (d. 571/1176) as the introduction to his vast biographical compilation, *Taʾrīkh madīnat Dimashq*. Ibn ʿAsākir collects here numerous traditions—many of them obviously spurious—on his city's claims to religious merit (*faḍāʾil*), with special attention to the splendid Umayyad Mosque. But more important for our purposes is his meticulous cataloging of the city's mosques, places of pilgrimage (*ziyārāt*), churches, palaces, gates, and innumerable canals and public baths. By his time there were already some two dozen *madrasas*, but he does not regard these as a separate category and merely notes them among the mosques. Likewise, he has no chapter on the bazaars and caravanserais of Damascus, presumably because these things bore no religious or political prestige; however, his text does contain many allusions to such structures. Though the *Taʾrīkh* is still only partly published, there is a reliable edition of this segment by Ṣalāḥ al-Dīn al-Munajjid (1954), as well as an invaluable translation by Nikita Elisséeff, *La Description de Damas d'Ibn ʿAsākir* (1959), which has detailed notes and a superb map of the 6th/12th-century city.

Ibn ʿAsākir modeled his compilation on the *Taʾrīkh Baghdād* of al-Khaṭīb al-Baghdādī (on whom see above, p. 132). Useful insights into the purpose and method underlying his topography can be gotten by comparing it with the Khaṭīb's famous introduction, of which there are two translations: (a) Georges Salmon, *L'introduction topographique à l'histoire de Baghdadh* (1904); (b) Jacob Lassner, *The Topography of Baghdad in the Early Middle Ages* (1970).

Ibn ʿAsākir's text in its turn became the basis for almost the entire succeeding topographical tradition in Damascus. A century later, it was incorporated nearly *in toto* in the historical geography of Syria and Mesopotamia written by ʿIzz al-Dīn ibn Shaddād for Sultan Baybars, *al-Aʿlāq al-khaṭīra fī dhikr umarāʾ al-Shām wa'l-Jazīra*. (See also above, p. 174.) To his predecessor's work, however, Ibn Shaddād appended lists of the mosques and baths—many scores of them—which had been erected during the intervening century. In addition, he added material on restorations to the Umayyad Mosque, the history of the Citadel, and a separate chapter on the city's more than eighty *madrasas*, with cursory notes on their founders and professors.

Ibn Shaddād's volume on Damascus provided the skeleton for the admirable compilation of ʿAbd al-Qādir al-Nuʿaymī (d. 927/1521), *Tanbīh al-ṭālib wa-irshād al-dāris fī mā fī Dimashq min al-jawāmiʿ wa'l-madāris*, (published by Jaʿfar al-Ḥassānī under the title of *al-Dāris fī ta'rīkh al-madāris*, 2 vols., 1948–51). To the jejune lists of Ibn Shaddād, al-Nuʿaymī adds a wealth of historical and biographical data drawn from very diverse sources, thus making his work a wonderful compendium of the social and religious history of Damascus over a period of some four centuries. A late 16th-century abridgement by ʿAbd al-Basīṭ al-ʿAlmāwī was translated by Henri Sauvaire (with a mass of notes compiled from unpublished manuscripts and inscriptions) as "Description de Damas," *JA*, ser. ix, nos. 3–7 (1894–96); printed separately in two volumes (1895–96). A desperately needed index was compiled by Émilie Ouéchek, *Index générale de la Description de Damas de Sauvaire* (1954). Sauvaire's work is outdated at many points, but it remains the most convenient and comprehensive starting point for the study of the city's historical topography.

A history along similar lines of the important suburb of Ṣāliḥiyya was compiled by al-Nuʿaymī's contemporary, the noted chronicler Shams al-Dīn ibn Ṭūlūn (d. 953/1546): *al-Qalāʾid al-jawhariyya fī ta'rīkh al-Ṣāliḥiyya* (2 vols., ed. M. A. Duhmān, 1949–56, with an excellent map).

Ibn Shākir al-Kutubī (d. 764/1363) has some independent information. He drew on Ibn ʿAsākir in the introduction to his chronicle *ʿUyūn al-tawārīkh* but does not follow the expanded framework devised by Ibn Shaddād. Sauvaire translated a portion of this work in his "Description de Damas" (*JA*, ser. ix, no. 7 [1896], pp. 369–421), but we still await an up-to-date edition and complete translation.

Yet another kind of topography is represented by the *Kitāb al-ishārāt ilā maʿrifat al-ziyārāt* of the mendicant sufi and government agent ʿAlī al-Harawī (d. 611/1215), ed. J. Sourdel-Thomine (1953) and translated by her as *Guide des lieux de pélerinage* (1957). This work is a sort of religious geography, identifying sacred locales throughout the Near East (including Tunisia and Anatolia) which merit a pious visit. The chapter on Damascus, which is particularly rich in such sites, has been studied by Sourdel-Thomine in "Les anciennes lieux de pélerinage damascains d'après les sources arabes," *BEO*, xiv (1952–54), 65–85.

Finally, the 20th-century scholar Muḥammad Kurd ʿAlī (d. 1953), though acquainted with modern Orientalism, wrote his two principal works in a traditional manner. They bring together a great deal of scattered information and are standard references: (a) *Khiṭaṭ al-Shām* (6 vols., 1343–47/1925–28); (b) *Ghūṭat Dimashq* (1949; rev. ed., 1952), on the villages and monuments of the oasis of Damascus.

The historical topographies form the foundation for any attempt to reconstruct the evolution of Damascus. However, several other kinds of texts have a vital contribution to make as well. There is first of all an important tradition of local chronicle and biography going from the mid-6th/12th century down to the Ottoman conquest, and reaching its apogee sometime around 700/1300. The earliest work of this kind is perhaps also the most impressive: Ibn al-Qalānisī, *Dhayl taʾrīkh Dimashq* (ed. H. Amedroz, 1908), a political chronicle of affairs in Damascus and central Syria from the Fatimid domination (ca. 359/970) down to the occupation of the city by Nūr al-Dīn (549/1154). There are two partial translations. H.A.R. Gibb, *The Damascus Chronicle of the Crusades* (1932) is excellent, but gives only those passages which touch on the wars with the Crusaders, thus omitting a large proportion of Ibn al-Qalānisī's detailed and irreplaceable accounts of the city's internal politics. Roger Le Tourneau, *Damas de 1075 à 1154* (1952) is complete for the portion translated. Ibn al-Qalānisī was extensively cited by later chroniclers (especially Sibṭ ibn al-Jawzī and Ibn al-Athīr), who knew a good thing when they saw it.

He had no true successors, but a second local tradition was begun about a century later by Sibṭ ibn al-Jawzī (d. 654/1256), who had migrated to Damascus from Baghdad in the early 7th/13th century. His *Mirʾāt al-zamān fī taʾrīkh al-aʿyān* was meant to be a universal chronicle, and was modeled on the *Muntaẓam* of his famous grandfather Ibn al-Jawzī (d. 597/1201): for each year the most notable events were recorded, and then concise obituaries were given for the important persons who had died during that year. Down to 1200 or so, Sibṭ in fact does give us a true universal chronicle, and one of great value especially for the 5th/11th century. But after that date he gives up all pretense of covering the Islamic world as a whole and increasingly narrows his focus to the affairs of Damascus. On his adopted city, however, he is a gold mine, and his work became the starting point for a long-lived "school" of Damascene historians: Abū Shāma (d. 665/1268), al-Jazarī (d. 739/1338), al-Birzālī (d. 739/1338), Quṭb al-Dīn al-Yūnīnī (d. 726/1326), al-Dhahabī (748/1347), Ibn Shākir al-Kutubī (d. 764/1363), and Ibn Kathīr (d. 774/1373). Abū Shāma follows Sibṭ very closely, with additional notes, down to the end of his chronicle in 652/1254. The next three—al-Jazarī, al-Birzālī, and al-Yūnīnī—whose writings are closely linked to one another in ways that are still not wholly clear—regarded themselves as Sibṭ's continuators, and al-Yūnīnī in fact prepared the finished (albeit slightly abridged) recension of Sibṭ's rough and incomplete draft. Al-Dhahabī, al-Kutubī, and Ibn Kathīr all composed universal histories (of which the first and third are of high value), but relied quite heavily on Sibṭ ibn al-Jawzī for their account of Ayyubid Damascus and on his continuators for the early Mamluk period. The 9th/15th century saw some attenuation of historical writing in Damascus, but was still able to produce major chronicles by Taqī al-Dīn ibn Qāḍī Shuhba (d. 851/1448) and Shams al-Dīn ibn Ṭūlūn. On the historiographic tradition of Damascus during these centuries we still lack a really adequate account; provisionally, see the following:

a. M.H.M. Ahmad, "Some Notes on Arabic Historiography during the Zengid and Ayyubid Periods (521/1127–648/1250)," in Lewis and Holt, *Historians of the Middle East*, 79–97.

b. Sami Dahan (= Sāmī al-Dahhān), "The Origin and Development of the Local Histories of Syria," in *ibid.*, 108–117.

c. Ulrich Haarmann, *Quellenstudien zur frühen Mamlukenzeit* (1970)—which in fact focuses on al-Jazarī.

Among the numerous biographical dictionaries produced during these centuries, the most important is certainly the titanic *Ta'rīkh madīnat Dimashq* of Ibn ʿAsākir, already mentioned several times in this book. Access to this crucial work is unfortunately no easy thing. A condensed edition (*tahdhīb*) was begun by ʿAbd al-Qādir Badrān and Aḥmad ʿUbayd (7 vols., 1911–32), but it covers only the first third of the alphabet and is unsatisfactory in any case. A complete version was undertaken in the 1950s by the Arab Academy in Damascus, but progress has been uneven; three volumes appeared promptly, and then there was a hiatus of nearly a quarter-century. Several new volumes have been issued since the early 1980s, however, so there may be hope. In addition, there is now a quite useable facsimile edition (really a xerographic copy) of the Damascus manuscript, issued in nineteen volumes by Dār al-Bashīr in Amman. This great work, together with the similar though only partly extant compilation on Aleppo by Kamāl al-Dīn ibn al-ʿAdīm (*Bughyat al-ṭalab fī ta'rīkh Ḥalab*), ought to be the indispensable foundation for research on the social and religious history of Syria from the Arab conquest down to the 7th/13th century. The fact that both works are still only partially available in acceptable printed editions, and that both have been almost entirely neglected by modern scholarship, demonstrates all too clearly the state of research in the Islamic field.

Ibn ʿAsākir had no real successors. However, a new biographical tradition was established in the mid-7th/13th century with the immensely popular and influential dictionary of Ibn Khallikān (d. 681/1282), *Wafayāt al-aʿyān wa-anbā' abnā' al-zamān*. Ibn Khallikān's collection was universal (though very selective) in scope, including some 850 persons from all periods and regions in Islam. However, he resided for most of his adult life in Cairo and Damascus, and his entries for the 6th/12th and 7th/13th centuries clearly favored the men of Egypt and Syria. Moreover, his work was widely cited in the later chronicles mentioned above, and at least two continuations of it were composed by writers living principally in Damascus: (a) Ibn al-Ṣuqāʿī (d. 725/1325), *Tālī wafayāt al-aʿyān*, ed. and trans. Jacqueline Sublet (1974); (b) Ibn Shākir al-Kutubī, *Fawāt al-wafayāt*, ed. M. M. ʿAbd al-Ḥamid (2 vols., 1951–52).

Damascus and its oasis always attracted attention from the geographers. Since their works were designed as compendia of the whole Islamic world, none of them devotes more than a few pages to the city. However, their testimony, terse as it is, can be very enlightening. The most important Arabic texts have been discussed above, pp. 17–18, 224. The most convenient collection of this material in English is G. Le Strange, *Palestine under the Moslems* (1890), pp. 224–273; however, his versions are paraphrases rather than exact translations, and he does little to explicate the passages presented. More satisfying, though it deals with only a single text, is André Miquel's annotated translation of sections (including the chapter on Damascus) of al-Muqaddasī's *Aḥsan al-taqāsīm fī maʿrifat al-aqālīm* (1963)—a very concise but telling portrait of the 4th/10th century city and its people by a man who knew them all too well.

Because Damascus was so much a part of the Islamic heartland, travellers seldom felt impelled to say much about it. One of them, however, makes a very important contribution to our knowledge of the city's monuments and topography in the late 6th/12th century. The description by the Andalusian pilgrim Ibn Jubayr (d. 601/1204) was especially esteemed for its precise and vivid account of the Umayyad Mosque, but it has much else besides. His account of his journeys (usually referred to as the *Riḥla*) was first published by William Wright (1852; revised by M. J. de Goeje, 1907), and has been translated several times. The English version by R.J.C. Broadhurst, *The Travels of Ibn Jubayr* (1952) is usable, but the version by M. Gaudefroy-Demombynes, *Ibn Jobayr, Voyages* (3 vols., 1949–56) is more scholarly and reliable. The famous Ibn Baṭṭūṭa (d. 770/1368) is a disappointment in this case—as in fact he often is—for his account of Damascus is mostly copied from Ibn Jubayr, though he does add some information on the Black Death which raged in the city shortly before his visit.

The Mamluk administrative literature pertaining to Damascus has already been discussed above (Chapter Seven); here it will suffice to mention the texts by al-ʿUmarī and al-Qalqashandī presented in M. Gaudefroy-Demombynes, *La Syrie à l'époque des Mamelouks* (1923). However, special note should be made of a manual of *ḥisba* written in Damascus in the late 6th/12th century by a certain al-Shayzarī, *Nihāyat al-rutba fī ṭalab al-ḥisba*, which gives a remarkably detailed picture of the organization of manufacturing and commerce in the city. The text was edited by Bāz al-ʿArīnī (1365/1946) and translated by Walther Behrnauer, "Mémoire sur les institutions de police chez les Arabes," *JA*, xvi (1860), 347–392; xvii (1861), 5–76.

Finally we turn to the inscriptions of Damascus. These are extremely numerous, and a systematic though very uncritical effort to collect them was made in the late 19th century by William Waddington. This corpus, known as the Recueil Schéfer, contains more than 600 items; although it is full of mistakes, it is the sole basis for many entries in *RCEA* and for Sauvaire's epigraphic notes in the "Description de Damas." On it see the important critique by Gaston Wiet, "Les inscriptions arabes de Damas," *Syria*, iii (1922), 153–166.

A more scientific effort was undertaken before World War I by Moritz Sobernheim and Ernst Herzfeld, as part of Max van Berchem's project for a *Corpus Inscriptionum Arabicarum* (on which see above, Part I, Chapter Two, pp. 56–57). Sobernheim did publish the Citadel inscriptions: "Die Inschriften der Zitadelle von Damaskus," *Islam*, xii (1922), 1–28. His readings now require revision, however, and there are some new discoveries; see Gaston Wiet, "Notes d'épigraphie syro-musulmane: inscriptions de la citadelle de Damas," *Syria*, vii (1926), 46–66; and N. Elisséeff, "À propos d'une inscription d'al-Malik al-Muʿaẓẓam ʿĪsā: contribution à l'étude de son règne: *AAS*, iv–v (1954–55), 3–28. As for Herzfeld, he published only his architectural notes, and then only thirty years later (see below, p. 245).

The inscriptions of Damascus preserve a number of government decrees, and many of these have been collected and published by Jean Sauvaget: (a) *Quatre décrets seldjoukides* (1947); (b) "Décrets mamelouks de Syrie," *BEO*, ii (1932), 1–52; iii (1933), 1–29; xii (1948), 5–60. A convenient list of such texts is given in Gaston Wiet, "Répertoire des décrets mamlouks de Syrie," *Mélanges René Dussaud* (1939), 521–537, to which the last installment of Sauvaget's "Décrets mamelouks" makes important additions and corrections. (See also pp. 58, 172 above.)

The recent work of Heinz Gaube, *Arabische Inschriften aus Syrien* (1978) is a collection of newly recorded items, this time critically edited, but it makes no effort to correct the errors in the Recueil Schéfer. In addition, the critical apparatus and commentary are very slender, and the majority of the entries date from Ottoman times. There may be reason for hope, however, in a re-edition of the inscriptions of Damascus undertaken by D. Sourdel and J. Sourdel-Thomine. To date, see "Dossiers pour un *Corpus* des inscriptions arabes de Damas", *REI*, xlvii (1979), 119–171 (covering the years 444/1052 to 544/1149).

To this remarkably comprehensive if not always easily accessible body of texts, we can add a wealth of archaeological evidence—not only individual monuments such as mosques and colleges, but also street plans, market layouts, and irrigation networks. During the period under discussion, Damascus consisted of the following elements: (1) a walled compound of some 130 hectares; (2) three suburbs immediately adjoining the walled city; (3) a number of nearby agricultural villages in the oasis; (4) the new settlement of Salihiyya about two kms. to the northwest, founded in the mid-6th/12th century by Ḥanbalī refugees from Crusader Palestine. Today, the medieval walls, though extensively damaged, still contain many elements from the later Middle Ages. Likewise, the section of the walled compound which was the core of Muslim life—the northwest quarter lying between the Citadel and the Umayyad Mosque—still contains (sometimes intact, sometimes only in vestiges) a large number of medieval structures, the bulk of them from the 6th/12th and 7th/13th centuries. Finally, the main artery in Ṣāliḥiyya, largely a creation of the Ayyubid period (589–658/1193–1260), is intact to an astonishing degree. Although the markets of the walled city have migrated quite a bit over the centuries, the street plan of the northwest quarter has been remarkably stable.

That a rather precise reconstruction of the streets and marketplaces of the 6th/12th century is possible has been demonstrated by Nikita Elisséeff in two places: (a) the beautiful map of the walled city which accompanies his translation of Ibn ʿAsākir, where he attempts to localize every building, water channel, and street named in the text; (b) "Les corporations de Damas sous Nur al-Dīn; matériaux pour une topographie économique de Damas au xiie siècle," *Arabica*, iii (1956), 61–79. Here too the various trades are localized on a map of the city, and Elisséeff has appended a very useful glossary of technical terms used for the different classes of goods and merchants. It would be even better, of course, to have something like the splendid monograph of Heinz Gaube and Eugen Wirth, *Der Bazar von Isfahan* (1978). This study is divided into three parts: the first reviews the cartographic and textual sources for the study of the bazaar; the second gives an overview of the topic from several perspectives—economic, historical-geographic, and architectural; the third and longest is a detailed catalogue of all the streets and buildings imbedded in the bazaar. Finally, there are thirty-two plates of drawings and photographs, and an impressive set of maps.

Damascus is the creature of its splendid oasis, the Ghūṭa, and two major studies have been devoted to the water-system and its impact on urban life. For the oasis as a whole, see Richard Tresse, "L'irrigation dans la Ghouta de Damas," *REI* (1929), 459–574. On water-management in the city proper, see Michel Écochard and Claude Le Coeur, *Les bains de Damas* (2 vols., 1942–43). Neither study represents a historical perspective, but both were written at a time when traditional techniques were substantially intact.

On the architecture of medieval Damascus, we have numerous provisional surveys and preliminary studies, but these have never led to comprehensive and detailed syntheses of the sort that Creswell devoted to Cairo. In view of the rapid destruction of the city's medieval heritage, it is questionable how long studies of that kind will be possible. The substance of what we know at present is contained in four works. The oldest of these is Karl Wulzinger and Carl Watzinger, *Damaskus, die islamische Stadt* (1924). This ground-breaking study was an effort to present a complete repertory of all the medieval and

Ottoman monuments still extant at that time, together with capsule descriptions, dates, and (where possible) concise historical data. It is a very creditable achievement and still provides an indispensable foundation for modern studies. On the other hand, the authors had only a limited knowledge of Islamic architecture, which was a field of study still in its early infancy, nor did they have access to most of the crucial texts which have since been published. In short, it is only a starting point and must be used with caution.

The identifications and dates given by Wulzinger and Watzinger can often be corrected through an early work of Sauvaget, *Les monuments historiques de Damas* (1932). This is a concise handbook, without references but full of its author's usual insights. It too is by now seriously dated.

Architectural studies in the proper sense had to wait until the eve of World War II. The first to be published were by Jean Sauvaget and Michel Écochard, *Les monuments ayyoubides de Damas* (3 fascicles, 1938–48). This work consists of sixteen concise studies, each devoted to a separate monument from the 6th/12th and 7th/13th centuries. For each building, the authors discuss its history and function, its construction and decor, and the special characteristics or problems connected with it. The only textual evidence is that suuplied by Sauvaire's "Description de Damas," but this is well used. The destruction of some of the collected materials in Paris near the end of World War II and Sauvaget's premature death unfortunately terminated this very important enterprise; like so many projects in Islamic studies it remains a torso.

At about the same time Ernst Herzfeld began to publish the very important (though often idiosyncratically interpreted) architectural notes which he had originally gathered in Damascus three decades earlier for a projected volume in the *CIA*: "Damascus: Studies in Architecture," *Ars Islamica*, ix (1942), 1–53; x (1943), 13–70; xi–xii (1946), 1–71; xiii–xiv (1948), 118–138. For the next four decades, little of substance appeared, in spite of the obvious gaps and shortcomings of the existing literature and in spite of the rapid disappearance of many of the city's historical quarters and monuments.

In this context, two recent dissertations demand notice. The numerous monuments in Syria and the Jazira which were built at the behest of Nūr al-Dīn have been studied from both an architectural and cultural-historical perspective in Yasser al-Tabba, "The Architectural Patronage of Nūr al-Dīn (1146–1174)" (2 vols., New York University, 1982); a separate chapter is devoted to the nine extant monuments in Damascus which date from this period. In addition, the imposing citadel has been meticulously re-examined by Paul A. Chevedden in "The Citadel of Damascus" (2 vols., UCLA, 1986); Chevedden's data are far more precise than any heretofore available, and his conclusions substantially modify those of his predecessors Wulzinger, Watzinger, and Sauvaget.

Whatever the problems in our documentation, then, we undeniably possess an enormous mass of material. What can be made of it? We know what Sauvaget would have done from an early essay, "Esquisse d'une histoire de la ville de Damas," *REI*, viii (1934), 421–480, which remains the best single account of the city's evolution despite its age. It should be supplemented by N. Elisséeff, "Dimashḳ," *EI²*, ii, 277–291—a concise, densely packed survey which sticks close to the interpretive framework developed by Sauvaget. A more general approach is offered by the present author in "Damascus," *DMA*, iv, 80–85.

Sauvaget's prominence and persuasiveness make it tempting simply to follow him, but I think it is essential to find an independent approach, if only to test the limits and possibilities of his approach. The main alternative currently available focuses on the structure of politics in the city—not merely the formal administrative institutions through which the princely courts and the generals imposed their demands on their subjects, but rather the ways in which the urban population was able to organize its own affairs, compel recognition from the court and army, and achieve a degree of effective political participation. This socio-political approach was first developed in an article by E. Ashtor-Strauss, "L'administration urbaine en Syrie médiévale," *RSO*, xxxi (1956), 73–128, who called attention especially to the capacity of the local notables and urban militias of Aleppo and Damascus in the first half of the 6th/12th century to assert themselves against the weak Turkish princes of that period. Ashtor's results were reviewed and placed in a broad comparative perspective, which included militias and youth gangs not only in Syria but in Baghdad and Iran as well, in a truly seminal (though allusive and difficult) study by Claude Cahen, "Mouvements populaires et autonomisme urbain dans l'Asie musulmane du Moyen Age," *Arabica*, v (1958), 225–250; vi (1959), 25–56, 233–265.

A further step was taken in the comprehensive and superbly integrated analysis of urban political structures—specifically, those which evolved in Mamluk Damascus, Aleppo, and Cairo—presented in Ira M. Lapidus, *Muslim Cities in the Later Middle Ages* (1967). Lapidus' interpretation does present certain problems, to be sure. (1) His functionalist approach is ill-suited to dealing with change and development; in his presentation, patterns of political action appear to remain much the same throughout a 250-year period which was riddled with major crises (e.g., the Black Death, the invasion of Timur) as well as constant turmoil within the political elite. (2) His account aims at a high level of generalization; as a result we get little sense of real persons and events, of time and place. (3) Finally, his analytic framework is very much a contemporary one, and hence cannot really convey how his subjects understood or described their own lives (see also above, pp. 201–203).

Among the most urgent tasks confronting the princes of twelfth-century Syria was that of imposing some order on an urban populace which was not only turbulent but fairly cohesive and well-organized. The Fatimid and early Seljukid milieu in which this kind of urban autonomy emerged has been studied in three substantial monographs:

1. Gerhard Hoffmann, *Kommune oder Staatsbürokratie? Zur politischen Rolle der Bevölkerung syrischer Städte vom 10 bis 12 Jahrhundert* (1975); a Marxist-Leninist analysis by an East German scholar.

2. Axel Havemann, *Riʾāsa und Qaḍā. Institutionen als Ausdruck wechselnder Kraftverhältnisse in syrischen Städten vom 10 zum 12 Jahrhundert* (1975).

3. Thierry Bianquis, *Damas et la Syrie sous la domination fatimide (359–468/969–1076)* (2 vols., 1986–89)—an invaluable analysis of this confused and little-known era; Bianquis offers not only a precise and well-focused narrative, but also a perceptive reading of the ways in which his sources construct the past for their own purposes.

None of these works makes any serious use of the evidence afforded by urban topography and architecture, and so it is not surprising that none of them pays much attention to the issues suggested by such evidence. If we want to go beyond political analysis and investigate such topics as population size and density, land use and spatial organization, or the kinds of social differentiation suggested by settlement patterns, we need to look elsewhere for a model.

The question of population size provides one useful way to explore the feasibility of such lines of inquiry. Our textual sources for Ayyubid and Mamluk Damascus give no figures of any kind even for the city's overall population, let alone statements which would permit us to construct a more complex demographic profile of it. Still, we might hope to be able to estimate the total population with reasonable accuracy. Michael Dols attempts just such an exercise in *The Black Death in the Middle Ages* (1977), pp. 194–204. His goal here is to determine the peak populations of Cairo and Damascus ca. 1340, so as to get some sense of the losses inflicted by the Black Death. For both places, he adopts the method of establishing the surface area of the walled city, and then multiplying this figure by an estimated population density. A check on the results is provided by Ottoman census reports from the 10th/16th century, which are fairly reliable though difficult to interpret. Dols' strategy is unfortunately crippled by an utter lack of consensus as to the probable population density of these cities—an issue which he confronts frankly. Estimates range from the very conservative figure of J. C. Russell (150 per hectare) to a high of 400 per hectare proposed by Thorkild Jacobsen. (In *Land behind Baghdad* [1965], pp. 24–25, 122–24, Robert Adams deals sensibly but inconclusively with precisely the same issue.)

In the end, Dols is compelled to settle for a plausible guess. He adopts a population density of 348 persons per hectare, which is the number calculated by L. Torres Balbás for the towns of Muslim Spain on the basis of the average area per urban dwelling (a measurable quantity) and average family size (sheer hypothesis). Dols multiplies this figure by an estimated area of 154 hectares for the walled enclosure of Damascus—an estimate which is in fact too high. He thereby obtains a population of some 53,500 within the walled city, to which he adds another fifty per cent for the adjoining suburbs, for a total of 80,000. If we alter Dols' 154 hectares to the correct figure of 130, we would get a total of 67,750. It is pleasant to discover that this figure accords fairly well with Barkan's reconstruction of the Ottoman census—57,326 in 1530 and 42,779 in 1595. In view of our severely limited data, Dols' procedure is probably as good as any. It does not create certainty, but it does impose rationality and method on our speculations, and suggests at least an order of magnitude.

At this point a note of caution must be sounded. Dols' exercise is a good demonstration of the value of the Ottoman archives even for historians of far earlier periods. On the other hand, they raise as many questions as they resolve. First of all, the numbers supplied by the Ottoman bureaucrats were intended to answer their questions, not ours. Ottoman censuses record households or hearths rather than individuals; to convert these numbers into population figures, we must once again find an appropriate multiplier. Barkan uses the figure of five persons per household, but that is only an educated guess. In a careful review of the 1005/1596–97 tax register, J.-P. Pascual (*Damas à la fin du xvi*^e^ *siècle*, pp. 18–29) suggests that seven would be more realistic. He thus proposes a 1596 population for Damascus plus its suburbs ranging from 44,500 (at five per household) to 57,000 (at seven per household), with a clear preference for the higher number.

As a check on his hypotheses, Pascual also works a figure for inhabitants per hectare. He points out a crucial fact overlooked by Dols—viz., that a substantial part of any urban area represents open or public space. He argues that out of the 230 hectares which made up the "Damascus metropolitan area," the city's residential zones could have totaled no more than 200 hectares. This latter figure is of course the one to which estimates of population density must be applied. With an inhabitated area of 200 hectares, then, the lower population estimate would yield 220 persons per hectare, the higher a more satisfying 285 persons per hectare—in either case, far lower than Dols' estimate. Finally, Pascual shows that two-thirds of the total population of Damascus lived *outside* the walled city.

Obviously Pascual's results cannot be mechanically applied to the Damascus of 1340, but they do throw some doubt on three points in Dols' argument: (1) his decision to posit 348 inhabitants per hectare; (2) his application of this figure to the total urban area; (3) his hypothesis that the suburban population would equal half the walled city's. In short, the apparent harmony between Dols' estimates and the numbers in the Ottoman censuses may be just a happy accident.

By its very limitations, however, Dols' essay in quantitative method suggests another question: is there any way to construct a more elaborate set of numbers, capable of helping us deal with more complex issues in urban history?

We have already noted in Chapter Eight that the information in biographical dictionaries, due to its repetitious, formulaic character, is quite amenable to numerical aggregation. But though this genre of text tells us much about an urban cultural elite (the *ʿulamāʾ*), it yields little about the urban milieu as a whole. However, a much broader corpus of data can be derived from three categories of the sources just reviewed: urban topographies, inscriptions, and the monuments themselves. Taken together, these permit us to construct a remarkably complete and systematic profile of architectural patronage in Damascus between the 6th/12th and 10th/16th centuries. The study of architectural patronage, in turn, can be a revealing way of analyzing the internal structure and mutual relationships of the city's social and political elites during the later Middle Ages.

By identifying the persons who demanded and paid for the buildings and public monuments of Damascus, we learn as well who controlled its resources of land and money. More broadly, the socio-economic groups from whom such patrons of architecture were drawn will almost certainly represent the elite elements of urban society. It is at least plausible to argue that the role and relative importance of each of these groups in architectural patronage must reflect its social and political influence within the community as a whole. From another perspective, if we can determine the kinds of building which an individual patron tended to favor, we should get a good idea of the beliefs, values, and institutions which seemed most important to that patron. If we go a step further, and assume that patrons belonging to the same social group would consistently tend to favor the same kinds of monuments, then the "architectural preferences" of each group should give us a direct insight into that group's conception of its social role. In addition, by comparing the preferences displayed by different groups, we should be able to decide whether they all shared similar social values and aims, or whether each had evolved autonomous and perhaps conflicting value-systems.

It would be helpful if our data gave us an accurate cross-section of architectural activity—if every type of building had an equal chance of survival and was equally likely to be noted in the texts. Unfortunately, though predictably, we face a severe problem of bias. On the material level, a city's poorer buildings are far more subject to decay and neglect than its great public monuments—palaces, major mosques, even caravanserais—and among these, secular monuments suffer a much higher mortality rate than do religious structures. As to our principal written source, the urban topographies, the men who wrote them were without exception men of the Sunni religious establishment in Damascus. As such, they were concerned with the monuments of their city only insofar as they embodied specifically Islamic values and served Islamic purposes. Except for public baths and fortifications (both of which can be connected with Islamic themes—ritual ablutions in the one case and *jihād* in the other), secular architecture receives only sporadic attention. Commercial structures are seldom mentioned unless they were part of the endowment for a mosque or *madrasa*, and private dwellings usually crop up only when they were being converted to some religious function or if they had a special prestige. In general, we are very poorly informed as to those buildings which provided housing, food, and commerce—obviously an extremely serious gap.

The bias of our sources in favor of religiously significant buildings might entail a secondary bias in favor of two groups of patrons, high state officials and the *ʿulamāʾ*. We would predict this for two reasons: first, because these two groups were presumably those most committed to the material support of Islamic institutions; second, because they were the persons whom the topographers could most easily identify and on whom the fullest biographical data was available. On the other hand, it is not certain that the hypothetical tendency of our sources to favor the *ʿulamāʾ* and men of the state really does obscure the social role of any other group. It is at least reasonable to suppose that the dominance of these two classes accurately mirrors the reality. For one thing, all our other texts portray the *ʿulamāʾ* and the high officials as the two poles of socio-political leadership. Moreover, it seems unlikely on *a priori* grounds that any group which took little or no part in providing the physical structures essential to Islamic life could claim a position of social leadership. In general, we are probably justified in thinking that every "elite" group will show up in our data, and that we will be able to perceive important aspects of their social roles and their dealings with one another. On the other hand, we should not expect to see the whole range of their concerns and activity.

What kind of information can we get from our sources? For the monuments per se, at least five categories of data can be recovered. (1) For every building, we know at least the Arabic term for the monumental type to which it belonged. This sounds trivial but is not. It makes a difference whether a place of worship is called *masjid*, *jāmiʿ*, or *mashhad*, whether a sufi convent is known as a *khānqāh* or *zāwiya*. Likewise, we need to know that a building identified as a *madrasa* (college of *sharīʿa* jurisprudence) in its foundation inscription is named as a *masjid* (simple mosque) in a text written a century later. (2) In the great majority of cases, we can also determine the functions served by the building—worship, education, commemoration of a saint, etc. It is important to note that the Arabic term for a building does not always identify its function—for example, *zāwiya* may refer both to a sufi retreat and to a locale for the teaching of *fiqh*. In determining function, archaeological evidence is obviously essential. (3) Most buildings can be located, at least by quarter, even if they are no longer extant. (4) Dates are a sometime thing. Sometimes we can reconstruct in precise detail the whole history of a building; in other cases we can hardly be sure of the century when it was erected. Still, at least approximate dates can be assigned to the majority of monuments, and this fact allows us to construct some revealing albeit provisional time-series charts. (5) We can often determine whether a given monument represents original construction or the conversion of an old edifice to some new use. The typical case in Damascus would be the conversion of an amir's private mansion to a *madrasa* on his death.

In regard to the patrons (i.e., those persons at whose behest and with whose wealth construction was carried out), we can typically obtain the following categories of information: (1) ethnic or racial origin, (2) birthplace or place of origin, (3) ordinary place of residence, (4) personal status (free or slave), (5) gender, (6) date of death, (7) occupational class (ruling family, military, court and bureaucracy, religious establishment, sufis, merchants and artisans, (8) *madhhab*.

Information of this sort is readily tabulated into what looks like a census of monuments and patrons, but how reliable a census is it? To the modern eye, numbers look like the hardest of facts, and once they have been put on paper they take on a life of their own. Under these circumstances, incomplete or unreliable data will lead us off into worse than our present ignorance. In the case of medieval Damascus, our data falls into three distinct categories, each of which must be treated quite separately.

I. We can construct a highly complete and accurate census of certain types of structures and their patrons: educational institutions, congregational mosques, sufi convents, mausolea, shrines, and fortifications. This category of data can validly—and perhaps usefully—be subjected to simple forms of statistical handling.

II. A second category of buildings are noted only haphazardly in our sources: commercial structures, private residences, aqueducts and fountains, etc. Tabulations of this material have no statistical value and must not be blended in with the first category; they are simply a convenient way of organizing our material.

III. Two very common types of monument—the ordinary mosque and the public bath—belong in a category by themselves. From Ibn ʿAsākir on, many authors compiled lists, allegedly exhaustive, of all such structures in the city. However, we seldom have enough information to date these individually or to identify their patrons. The best we can do is to estimate the number of these built in each successive period. However, this at least gives us some idea of overall construction in each period, and also indicates which districts of the city and its suburbs were relatively active or stagnant within that period.

To create aggregate data in this way is an extremely tedious task, worth undertaking only if it allows us to develop new lines of inquiry, or at least to answer old questions in a clearly more adequate manner. A useful way to explore this issue is to examine Elisséeff's assertion that the "renaissance" of Damascus in the first half of the 7th/13th century was due above all to the presence there of a major princely court (*EI*², ii, 284). We need to know two things about this statement: (1) whether it is true at all; (2) the exact nature of the causal sequence which it posits. In order to test it, we will draw on a census (provisional and as yet unpublished) of architecture and patronage in Ayyubid Damascus which I have compiled along the lines laid out above. (A more detailed version of the following discussion is given in my paper "Politics and Architectural Patronage in Ayyubid Damascus," in *Essays in Honor of Bernard Lewis*, 151–174.)

That the Ayyubid period (589–658/1193–1260) saw a very high level of construction activity is not in doubt; our Category I census data clearly shows that the number of religious and educational buildings founded or undergoing major restorations was twice as high during these seven decades as in either of the two equally long periods (Seljukid-Zangid, Early Mamluk) preceding and following. It is also beyond question that the Ayyubid princes of Damascus, several of whom were highly educated men, were active patrons of Arabic letters and the religious sciences. But does this fact mean that they were in any direct way responsible for the architectural renaissance of the period?

Our census data on the career backgrounds of patrons throws some doubt on this hypothesis:

Career Backgrounds of Patrons
(*Category I Data*)

Members of the Ayyubid Clan	24
Non-Ayyubid Princes	2
Amirs and Their Families	38
Religious Establishment (*ʿUlamāʾ*, Qadis)	23
Civil Bureaucracy	9
Sufis	15
Courtiers (Ayyubid Household)	7
Merchants and Artisans	2
TOTAL	120

Clearly it is not the Ayyubid family which supplied the largest number of patrons, but the men and women of the military class. The number of Ayyubid patrons is in fact no greater than those from the religious establishment. Indeed, if we recall that the religious establishment and the civil bureaucracy were recruited from men of the same social background, we can combine the number of patrons from each for a total of 32. (This is not an arbitrary maneuver; contemporary writers customarily lumped the two groups together under the name of *mutaʿammimīn*—"men of the turban.") In any case, the royal patrons make up only 20 percent of the total number.

Other data show the Ayyubid family in a more prominent role, to be sure. For example, out of the 197 separate "acts of construction" in our Category I data, they sponsored 29 percent, the military sponsored 25 percent, and the *mutaʿammimīn* sponsored 20 percent. But if we remove fortifications (which were in effect a royal monopoly), the amirate again becomes the most important group, and the role of the *mutaʿammimīn* is equal to that of the Ayyubids. In sum, we are dealing with a tripartite elite, in which no one of the component groups really dominated the system of architectural patronage.

What then might the Ayyubid role have been in the efflorescence of Damascus? If we suppose that the military class, the religious establishment, and the bureaucracy were composed chiefly of long-established residents of Damascus—i.e., of persons who were financially independent of the Ayyubid court and would have been living in Damascus in any case—then surely the city would have flourished, perhaps not mightily but at least decently, without the Ayyubids. To test this hypothesis, we would have to determine what proportion of these three groups were *originaires* of Damascus, and how many had come there as immigrants. Likewise, we would need to know whether or not their wealth depended on the largesse of the court. Finally, we would want to know how firm were the ties binding them to Damascus.

We begin with the military class, since it represents the largest group of patrons. The general political situation under the Ayyubids would have favored widespread migration, for there were many autonomous and often hostile courts competing with one another for skilled soldiers. In such a situation, the survival of the court of Damascus would depend on its capacity to offer favorable terms of service. An able and ambitious man would remain only so long as his thirst for both power and wealth could be satisfied there. In fact this seems to be the case. We know the birthplace or regional origin of only 13 amirs (out of a total of 38 military patrons), but of these only 2 were natives of Damascus. The other 11 came equally from Egypt, North Syria, and the Jazira. In general, both the numbers and circumstantial evidence suggest that the military class's role in architectural patronage was linked to the presence in Damascus of a wealthy and relatively powerful court.

A rather similar line of argument can be constructed for the *ʿulamāʾ* and the bureaucrats. Out of the 28 whose place of origin can be identified, 10 were born in Damascus, and 18 were immigrants. Of the latter group 7 were from Egypt, the others equally from Iraq, North Syria, the Jazira, and South Syria; in short, Damascus was drawing far outside its immediate hinterland. What was the role of the Ayyubid court in regard to these people? Here we seem to find the fruits of a conscious policy first developed by Nūr al-Dīn (541–569/1146–1174), to establish a solid alliance between the court and the Sunni scholars. This policy was pursued on many levels, but clearly the royal patronage of *madrasa*s was a crucial part of it. Nūr al-Dīn was not content to found *madrasa*s, however; he also sought the most noted *ʿulamāʾ* to staff them, attracting a great many men from the Jazira and from Iran. The Ayyubids continued this policy in the most energetic way; any talented scholar who found his way to Damascus could be sure that a place would be made for him—as a *madrasa* professor, a qadi, a preacher in a congregational mosque. Because so many of the *ʿulamāʾ* were newcomers, however, they were directly dependent on royal favor both for their high status and their capacity to patronize construction of their own. Their position was assuredly not so vulnerable to political change as that of the amirs. On the other hand, if Damascus ceased to be a major political center, it would become increasingly difficult to retain prestigious scholars or to attract new immigrants.

The case of the bureaucracy was rather different. These men were almost always proteges of a particular prince, not local notables who could staff the offices of whoever happened to hold the throne. As it happens, a stable hereditary succession was never established in Ayyubid Damascus, and the repeated coups d'etat of the period ensured a constant influx of new senior bureaucrats. Among the 9 bureaucratic patrons, 8 were just such immigrants.

We can thus sum up our data on immigrant patrons by noting that out of 60 patrons (excluding members of the Ayyubid family) whose places of origin can be determined, only 13 were natives of Damascus—fewer than one-quarter of the total. From another perspective, out of the 197 "acts of construction" in our Category I census data, 58 were sponsored by immigrant patrons, and 57 by members of the Ayyubid family. This constitutes a minimum of three-fifths of the total patronage recorded in Category I—a minimum, because we do not know the place of origin of 57 patrons.

The argument sketched here suggests a far more nuanced evaluation of the role of the Ayyubid court than we had imagined at the outset. It is not enough to say that the Ayyubid princes sponsored a substantial body of construction, but were really no more than the equals of the amirs or the *mutaᶜammimīn*. On the contrary, we can now identify this tiny group of men and women (some two dozen in all) as the hub of the whole mechanism. They were the hub not because they personally did so much, but because they attracted the immigrants who did. In this light, the foundations of the architectural vitality of Ayyubid Damascus seem very frail, because all this activity depended on an intricate and inherently unstable system of politics. The Mongol conquest and Mamluk occupation in 658/1260 did not just obliterate the Ayyubid regime in Syria; they also shattered the fragile social groupings which had brought about the city's growth and development during the previous century.

We should not suppose that a semi-quantitative approach of the kind proposed above can replace the archaeological method of Sauvaget or the close textual analysis of Cahen and his successors. Such an approach cannot always be made to work, and in any event the data which it yields can only be interpreted through a careful reading of archaeological data and traditional historical texts. But it does suggest one way of achieving greater certainty and precision and of generating new lines of questioning. In view of the severe problems inherent in our sources, the development of new approaches of this kind must be a major aim of urban historical studies.

Chapter Eleven

NON-MUSLIM PARTICIPANTS IN ISLAMIC SOCIETY

A. The Role and Status of the *Dhimmī*

ISLAMIC HISTORY is not a history of Muslims alone. From the beginning, the non-Muslim elements of society have been at the very center of life. Without attention to their role, it is hard to imagine a sound history of crafts and commerce, of science and medicine, even of governmental administration. And though we always tend to think of non-Muslims as a minority, we must remember that in many Islamic polities they have been the overwhelming majority—the early Caliphate, for example, or the Ottoman Empire down to the conquests of Selim I. Simply on the level of intrinsic interest, then, the study of the role and status of non-Muslims in Islamic society is fully merited.

Such studies are merited on more general grounds as well, however. On one level, we might say that no society can be adequately understood if we exclude from consideration some significant portion of its members. Recall how impoverished a picture of American society and culture we would have if we omitted (as was once very common, of course) women and racial minorities. But on a deeper level, we might argue that to study a society's subordinate groups gives an insight into the structure and functioning of the whole—and even of the dominant groups themselves—which cannot otherwise be obtained. In doing this, we see a society from the perspective of its weakest members, those who are systematically excluded by law or custom from the enjoyment of all the benefits which that society has to confer. Thereby, we can learn what it meant, as a practical matter, to be a member of a subordinate or excluded group. We can see what kinds of social interaction were actually possible between "insiders" and "outsiders," and to what extent the world-view and ethos of these two groups differed or were held in common. In short, we might argue that a society's cohesion and integration are most sharply revealed through the study of its subordinate groups.

I have gone to some pains in the preceding discussion to avoid the term "minorities," and for this there is a very sound reason. Most societies have reserved full participation in their rights and responsibilities for a relatively small number of persons; it is probably quite rare that those excluded partially or wholly from such participation actually constitute a numerical minority of the total population. Obviously this pattern is by no means extinct. In Islamic societies, as we have already mentioned, the proportion of non-Muslims varied enormously, and it is extremely misleading to refer to them as the "religious (or confessional) minorities." In fact, groups are seldom excluded from full participation in a society simply because they are few in number, and one of the most crucial tasks in studying any society is to determine the criteria governing participation within it.

In any social or political system dominated by Muslims, down at least to the middle of the nineteenth century, the essential criterion for membership was of course religion. This fact is so universally recognized, however, that it has often lured us into thinking that religion was the only significant criterion. Obviously this cannot be true; Islamic polities and societies have varied enormously, and each one has developed criteria of status and participation specific to itself. One or two examples will suffice to make the point. During the early caliphate it was not enough to be a Muslim in order to obtain all the legal and financial benefits of membership in the *umma* or *jamāʿa*; one also had to be a full member of an Arab tribe and to be registered as such in the government *dīwān*. Under the Mamluk Sultanate (1250–1517) society was divided into a number of estates; entry into the wealthiest and most powerful of these, the "men of the sword," required one to be a Muslim in religion, Turkish or Circassian in race, and generally even to have been a *mamlūk* or military slave. In many periods, to be black was a disability though seldom an absolute barrier. It is true, however, that all such criteria of race, culture, and economic class are conditional and variable, while adherence to Islam is effectively universal. In the study of Islamic societies, it is not enough to know whether a person is a Muslim or not, but that is the first thing which we must know.

What was the formal status enjoyed by non-Muslims within the Islamic polity, then, and what was the range of social roles which they were actually able to play? A response to the first question involves a review of legal and institutional history, while the second calls for an examination of the internal life of non-Muslim communities in particular times and places. In the latter case, we do not want to think of the non-Muslim communities as self-contained entities; rather, we need to perceive the web of relationships which bound them to the larger society. Any number of problems might serve to develop this theme, but here we shall restrict ourselves to two: the Jewish community of Egypt between the 11th and 13th centuries as revealed by the Cairo Geniza; and the question of conversion to Islam—the processes by which a small Muslim elite ultimately became the overwhelming majority in almost every region they ruled. Each of these problems is quite well documented, but in very different ways. Each presents a distinct problem of methodology and different possibilities of knowledge about the life of non-Muslim communities under Islam.

A broad if not exhaustive bibliography on the non-Muslim communities, with emphasis on modern times, is given by Erhard Franz, *Minderheiten im*

Vorderen Orient: Auswahlbibliographie (1978). For our purposes, however, it makes sense to begin with some of the general statements on Muslim/non-Muslim relations. There are two articles in *EI*² by Claude Cahen, who takes a relatively optimistic view of the relations between Muslims and non-Muslims: "Dhimma" (ii, 227–231), and "Djizya" (ii, 559–562). The former deals with the "pact of protection" which defined the status and rights of non-Muslims under Islam and which gives them their usual Islamic name, *dhimmī* (sing.) or *ahl al-dhimma* (collective); the latter with their most visible badge of subjection, the head tax or capitation. More recent and generally more guarded assessments of the situation can be found in the following essays:

a. Benjamin Braude and Bernard Lewis, eds., *Christians and Jews in the Ottoman Empire; the Functioning of a Plural Society* (2 vols., 1982); Editors' Introduction, i, 1–36.

b. C. E. Bosworth, "The Concept of Dhimma in Early Islam," *ibid.*, i, 37–51.

c. Bernard Lewis, "L'Islam et les non-musulmans," *AESC*, xxxv (1980), 784–800.

d. A. L. Udovitch, "The Jews and Islam in the High Middle Ages," *Settimane di studio del Centro italiano di studi sull'alto medioevo*, xxvi, 1978 (Spoleto, 1980), 655–711.

e. Rudi Paret, "Toleranz und Intoleranz in Islam," *Saeculum*, xxi (1970), 344–365.

With these general perspectives in mind, one can make good use of two more narrowly conceived studies. A. S. Tritton, *The Caliphs and Their Non-Muslim Subjects: a Critical Study of the Covenant of Umar* (1930; repr. 1970) is a collection of materials—paraphrases from medieval Arabic and Syriac texts—whose purpose is to portray the actual historical relations between Muslims and non-Muslims (for the most part Christians) from the Arab Conquests down to the collapse of the Mamluk Empire (1516–17), and to compare these relations with the ideal set of doctrines and attitudes contained in the so-called Covenant of ʿUmar, composed in its definitive form ca. 1100. Tritton, no believer in overly systematic organization, arranges his materials under very loose topical headings; for this reason the reader might best begin with his concise "Conclusion," p. 229ff.

Antoine Fattal, *Le statut légal des non-musulmans en pays d'Islam* (1958) is precisely what the title implies. After examining the origins (in the time of Muhammad and the first Conquests) of the distinctive juridical and administrative status of non-Muslims under Islamic rule, Fattal analyzes the doctrines proposed by Muslim jurists under several headings—family and personal status, economic rights and constraints, freedom of worship, fiscal obligations, etc. The author is quite exact as to variations in doctrine among the different jurists and *madhāhib*, but he shows little concern for problems of development and change in doctrine after the ninth century (i.e. the age of the first "classic" formulations of *fiqh*). And though he cites a good deal of historical material, this is used simply to illustrate applications of formal doctrine rather than to show how ideal norms were generated by or addressed to specific socio-political contexts. Though both Tritton and Fattal are quite ahistorical in conception, however, they do provide the materials from which one can elicit an historical framework for the study of the development of *sharīʿa* doctrine regarding non-Muslims, on both a formal and a socio-political level. (As we noted in Chapter Nine, historical issues of this kind are only beginning to be addressed in Islamic legal studies.)

Status—a notoriously slippery term—might be defined simply as the way in which one is regarded by the dominant groups in his or her society. From this perspective, our principal source for defining the status of non-Muslims would be found in statements made by members of the Muslim political and cultural elites. Obviously there is no shortage of these, even if we exclude purely theological polemic and disputation. On the other hand, statements which throw light on the status of non-Muslims were seldom embodied in systematic treatises on the subject; quite the contrary, they must largely be gleaned (as Tritton and Fattal try to do) from a vast array of texts which are focused on entirely different issues. Almost every genre of Arabic and Persian literature has some contribution to make to the question of non-Muslim status, and here we will content ourselves with a few of the better known examples. (Fattal has a good, though far from exhaustive, bibliography of Arabic texts, and this can be supplemented for Syriac and Persian from the very terse entries in Tritton.)

We begin of course with the Qur'ān, both for what it says about relations between Muslims and non-Muslims at the very origins of the new religion, and because it defined the norms to which all later practice had to conform. The problem (not only for us but for medieval Muslims as well) is that the Qur'ān seems to speak with many voices on this issue. The berating of the Jews in Sura II, the hostility to the "People of Scripture" in Sura IX (whose famous and controversial verse 29 calls on the Prophet to fight them until they pay tribute "out of hand"—or perhaps "by hand," i.e., directly and in person—and are humbled), must be balanced against many other verses calling for tolerance and restraint. (Many such verses can be found in Suras III and V.) Western scholars have tended to take an evolutionary view of Qur'anic teaching on this issue, arguing that the Qur'ān evinces a growing hostility toward Jews and Christians, and that a stance of grudging and conditional toleration should be understood as its final and definitive doctrine on the matter. To my mind this interpretation is somewhat misleading. The Qur'ān as we know it represents a very complex interweaving of discrete revelations received over a period of some twenty years. On the other hand, the Muslim community has from the outset accepted the whole body of revelation as definitive; verses and suras were not preserved and transcribed because of their "historical" value, but because they were believed to communicate a message vital for human life and salvation. The assumption that if verse A was revealed later than verse B and appears to contradict this latter, then A supersedes B, is a very crude and inadequate way of representing the Muslim understanding and use of the Qur'ān. Both a lenient and rigorist view of non-Muslim communities are equally a part of the Qur'ān, and both enter into the way Muslims have thought about and dealt with these communities. Sometimes one is salient, sometimes the other, but that is linked to changing circumstances and attitudes, which the Qur'ān may legitimize but does not determine.

Inevitably the Qur'ān enters into other writings, most particularly *fiqh*. Almost every treatise on substantive law (*furū*ᶜ *al-fiqh*) contains relevant material, much of it in chapters on the *jizya*—for example Abū Yūsuf, *Kitāb al-Kharāj* (tr. Fagnan), pp. 184–197. However, we will get a better sense of Muslim attitudes, as opposed to formal rules, from certain types of writing: *fatwā*s (legal opinions addressed to specific questions), manuals of *ḥisba*, and the occasional treatise dealing with the status of non-Muslims in Islam. Among *fatwā*s, one of the earliest studied in Europe was that of Ibn al-Naqqāsh (written 759/1357), translated by M. A. Belin as "Fetwa relatif à la condition des zimmis . . . en pays musulmans depuis l'établissement de l'Islam jusqu'au milieu du 8ᵉ siècle de l'hégire," *JA*, 4ᵉ ser., xviii (1851), 417–516; xix (1852), 97–140. The 124 *fatwā*s on this subject in al-Wansharīsī's great compilation are briefly summarized and indexed in H. R. Idris, "Les tributaires en Occident musulman médiéval d'après le Miᶜyār d'al-Wanšarīsī," in *Mélanges d'islamologie dediés à . . . Armand Abel*, vol. I (1974), 172–196. Translations of these can be found in E. Amar's translation in *Archives marocaines*, xii–xiii (1908–09).

Many of these texts are quite late (14th–15th centuries) and represent a period when the status of non-Muslims had sharply degenerated from earlier times; here as elsewhere no one text should be made the basis for sweeping generalizations. Among manuals of *ḥisba*, particularly striking—but not necessarily typical—are the strictures of the Spaniard Ibn ᶜAbdūn, writing in the last years of Almoravid domination (ca. 1100). His *risāla* was published by E. Lévi-Provençal in *JA* (1934), and translated by the same scholar as *Séville musulmane au début du xiiᵉ siècle* (Paris 1941). (Partial English translation by Bernard Lewis, *Islam from the Prophet Muhammed to the Capture of Constantinople* [Harper and Row, 1974], ii, 157–165.) One of the few jurists to have been studied systematically is Ibn Taymiyya (d. 1328). His statements on the *ahl al-dhimma* are discussed in Henri Laoust, *Essai sur les doctrines . . . d'Ibn Taymiyya* (1939), pp. 265–277.

Hadith, a field of study closely related to *fiqh* but distinct from it, is a particularly rich source of Muslim attitudes as these crystallized and were accepted as part of the Prophetic heritage between the 8th and 10th centuries. Consult A. J. Wensinck, *Handbook of Muhammadan Tradition*, especially under the headings "Dhimma (ahl al-)," "Djizya," and "Jews" (commonly occurring as

"Jews and Christians"); and the *Concordance de la Tradition Musulmane*, under "dhimma," "jizya," "ahl al-kitāb," "yahūd," and "naṣārā." But many references to non-Muslims are buried in contexts where they are not likely to be indexed; to find and evaluate these we need to survey the hadith material on our own. A convenient and comprehensive collection for this task is the 14th-century *Mishkāt al-maṣābīḥ*, trans. James Robson (4 vols., 1960–65). On the Jews, see Georges Vajda, "Juifs et musulmans selon le ḥadīṯ," *JA*, ccxxix (1937), 57–127.

There is a rather small genre of polemic directed against non-Muslim officials because of their alleged disloyalty, tyranny, etc. A widely cited example is the quasi-historical tract of an obscure and disgruntled official of early Mamluk times named Ghāzī ibn al-Wāsiṭī (fl. 692/1292), edited and translated by Richard Gottheil as "An Answer to the Dhimmis," *JAOS*, xli (1921), 383–457; in addition to anecdotes drawn from the time of the Prophet and the early Caliphs, it contains a wealth of scurrilous tales about the nefarious doings of *dhimmī* officials in late Fatimid, Ayyubid, and early Mamluk times. Whatever the historical merit of his stories, they do embody the demonology to be found in some circles. More recently, see Moshe Perlmann, "Asnawi's Tract against Christian Officials," *Ignaz Goldziher Memorial Volume*, ed. Samuel Löwinger et al., (2 vols., 1958), ii, 172–208.

An enormous amount of material on Muslim attitudes towards non-Muslims is contained in works of history and belles-lettres. Obviously we cannot survey this here, but a few general comments on method may be in order. First of all, chroniclers' reports on Muslim-*dhimmī* relations are like their reports on prices—they only report moments of crisis and conflict, which in the nature of things tell us very little about the ordinary tenor of life. On the other hand, let us admit that the attitudes and forms of behavior which surface in a time of crisis are very likely to reflect feelings which are normally unspoken and repressed, but are still very much present. The civility of everyday relations may only mask the latent alienation, tension, and hostility felt by each group toward the other. Thus, there is little to indicate that the Christians and Jews of Damascus in the early 13th century suffered any unusual oppression either from the city's Muslim populace or from the normally easy-going Ayyubid regime. But when the Mongols (led by a Nestorian general from the Naiman Turks, and accompanied by forces from Cilician Armenia and Crusader Antioch) entered Damascus in the spring of 1260, the local Christians took every opportunity to humiliate the beaten Muslims. And in their turn, when the Muslims of Damascus learned of the great victory of ʿAyn Jālūt, they launched a savage pogrom against the city's Christians and (to a markedly lesser extent) its Jews. In such incidents, rare as they are in the totality of Islamic history, one detects underlying emotions and attitudes on both sides which could easily explode into violence. A second point would be that the reports and stories of Muslim writers about non-Muslims are not based on knowledge but on ignorance. (The reverse is equally true, of course.) That is, their accounts record perceptions rather than objective facts—a construction of phenomena according to a Muslim standard of value and meaning.

In general, then we should probably conclude that the anecdotes of historians and belles-lettrists are most valuable to us for their tone of voice, for the concepts, logic, values, and self-perception which have shaped them. Only secondarily, and only with great caution, should they be accepted as factual records of events. Another way to put this point might be as follows. A group's status in society is less a direct consequence of events per se than of the way in which these events are interpreted. In this light, it is more important to identify the cultural meaning ascribed to events than to establish what "really happened."

When we pass from questions of status to questions of role, what we want to learn from our sources changes quite drastically. "Status" is to some degree a static category; it tends to assume that society is a structure in which each social group has been assigned its place. "Role," in contrast, is a rather more dynamic category; we talk about roles when we think of society as a process—properly, as a kind of drama in which different groups interact in constantly evolving ways. In thinking of roles, we ask what kinds of actions and events groups were involved in, and how these actions and events created a social process. In this altered perspective, how different groups thought about and evaluated one another is distinctly secondary to what they actually did. We might say that when we talk about the status of a group within a given society, we are concerned primarily with that society's self-perception. When we talk about a group's role, we are looking at that society from the outside; we construct a temporal process, and seek to identify the parts played by its constituent groups within that process. As we turn to our two case-study problems, "role" will replace "status" as the focus of our attention.

B. Autonomy and Dependence in the Jewish Communities of the Cairo Geniza

The vast surge of conquests in the 7th and early 8th centuries brought a host of religious communities under Islamic domination. But of all these, three broad groupings were to prove most significant in the development of Islamic society and culture—the "Zoroastrians" of Iraq and Iran, the Christians of the Eastern Mediterranean lands, and the Jews. From the late 9th century on, however, the Zoroastrians declined abruptly in numbers and cultural vitality. The Christians remained a far more important element in society, down at least to Mongol and post-Crusade times, and they are still a very considerable minority in Egypt and the Fertile Crescent. Even so, it is obvious that the great majority of Christians ultimately turned to Islam; and Antioch and Alexandria, which had been major centers of conflict and creative thought down to the Arab conquest, soon ceased to be so.

The fate of the Jews was rather different. Always the smallest of the religious communities, and before Islam the one most liable to persecution, it was under Islamic rule the most durable and culturally vital. The Jewish communities of the Middle East and North Africa lost some of their number to conversion, and in Mamluk times and in North Africa after 1150 or so they led a rather marginal existence. Even so, on the whole they maintained their integrity and cohesion remarkably well, and many of the greatest names in Jewish life and thought—among them Saadya Gaon, Judah ha-Levi, and Maimonides—flourished in an Islamic milieu. Moreover, for at least one time and place, the Jews are also the most visible of the non-Muslim communities, due largely to a stroke of fortune which has preserved a body of sources unequalled in medieval Islamic studies for its range, coherence, and intimacy. The study of Jewish history in medieval Islam, then, is valuable not only because of the high intrinsic interest of this community, but also because it can yield social history of a depth which we cannot achieve for any other group, even the highly articulate and vastly larger Muslim majority.

The trove which makes such a thing possible was found in the storage room (Geniza) of the synagogue of Old Cairo or Fustat in the 1890s. It is a miscellaneous assortment of papers numbering more than a quarter-million leaves, for the most part deposited there between the 11th and 13th centuries. The vast majority of these materials are literary in character, and they have of course given an enormous impetus to Biblical, Talmudic, and medieval Hebrew studies of every kind. But some 10,000 leaves (in addition to uncounted fragments) are "documents"—e.g., business and personal correspondence, wills, contracts of all kinds, bills of account and shipping manifests, etc. This latter class of material was ignored for some time after its discovery, but with the work of Jacob Mann after World War I, it became apparent that it would permit a far better history of Jewish life in medieval Egypt than could ever have been imagined previously. Mann still relied mostly on Hebrew-language material, but as it came to be realized that the great bulk of the documents were in Arabic (albeit written in Hebrew script), scholars who were trained in Islamic as well as Judaic studies began working with them. This work has issued in literally hundreds of monographs and published documents, and it has attained a first synthesis in the studies of S. D. Goitein, whose work will be reviewed in some detail below. (D. S. Richards has described another, though much smaller, documentary collection for the Karaite community, which is especially useful for late Mamluk and Ottoman times: "Arabic Documents from the Karaite Community in Cairo," *JESHO*, xv [1972], 105–162).

We can get a general familiarity with the Geniza materials, and the history of their discovery and study, through several articles. A beginning would be Norman Golb, "Sixty Years of Geniza Research," *Judaism*, vi (1957), 3–16, though this is of course now obsolete. Good descriptions of the documentary portion of the Geniza can be found in S. D. Goitein, "The Documents of the Cairo Geniza as a Source for Islamic Social History," *Studies in Islamic History and Institutions*, 279–295; and *A Mediterranean Society: the Jewish Communities of the Arab World as Portrayed in the Documents of the Cairo Geniza*, Vol. I (1967), 1–28. Among the 10,000 or so documents of the Geniza there are some 1200 letters; eighty of these have been translated and analyzed by Goitein in *Letters of Medieval Jewish Traders* (1973)—perhaps the most direct and pleasurable way to introduce oneself to these texts. Finally, a systematic survey of what had been done in this field down to 1964 is given by Shaul Shaked, *A Tentative Bibliography of Geniza Documents* (1964).

At this point, it may be useful to digress in order to compare our sources for the history of that far larger "minority," the Eastern Christians, with those for the Jews of Fatimid and Ayyubid times. We are far from badly informed, for Eastern Christian writers down to the late 13th century produced an extensive historical and quasi-historical literature in Arabic, Syriac, and Armenian. Moreover, the great bulk of this literature has been not only edited but translated. (Many, perhaps a majority, of the translations are done in Latin, a language evidently felt to be particularly appropriate for such ecclesiastical works.) For some periods, in particular the age of the Crusades, scholars have found these sources to be of enormous value for general political history; for example, the chronicle of the Jacobite patriarch Michael the Syrian (d. 1199) is one of the outstanding historical works produced within the medieval Islamic world. On the other hand, almost all the extant writing produced by Eastern Christians, of whatever genre, was written by churchmen highly placed in their respective hierarchies. As the literature of an elite, it tends to reflect elite concerns—in this case, problems of ecclesiastical organization, relations between the Churches, relations of the official hierarchy with Muslim rulers, the doings of Muslim rulers and officials insofar as these impinged on the status and privileges of the Churches, etc. Problems of social history are not entirely absent from the Eastern Christian chronicles, but they are very much a subordinate and occasional theme. It is as if the very organizational strength and complexity of the Christian communities ensured that only the concerns and outlook of the hierarchy would be preserved and transmitted.

No doubt because of the bias of our texts—and also because most modern students of Eastern Christianity are also clergymen—the great bulk of the scholarly literature on Eastern Christian communities under Islam is ecclesiastical and doctrinal in orientation. Much of this work is extremely good—we might name in particular the numerous studies of J. M. Fiey among recent writers—but it is in no sense social history. Examples of the very rare essays in this direction would be the article of Claude Cahen, "Fiscalité, propriété, antagonismes sociaux en Haute Mésopotamie au temps des premiers Abbassides, d'après Denys de Tell Mahré," *Arabica*, i (1954), 136–152; and the work of Michael G. Morony, now summed up in his massive *Iraq after the Muslim Conquest* (1984), especially Chapter 12, "Christians," pp. 332–383.

With this excursus, we may return to the unique opportunities and problems offered by the Geniza documents. Every historian of remote periods dreams of nothing more than getting his hands on such papers, written not for posterity or for public display but for the needs of the moment. At the same time, it is precisely such documents which are hardest to interpret. Because they are practical and unself-conscious, they do not bother to explain themselves. The identities of the persons named in them, the social, economic, and political institutions which they reflect and without which they are unintelligible, the meanings of once commonplace colloquial expressions or technical terms, the cultural values and attitudes with which they are imbued—all these things must be teased out bit by bit from statements which take them utterly for granted. For all these reasons, the Geniza documents present a formidable challenge to any scholar. Because of the milieu which produced them, it helps to have been brought up in an observant Jewish home and to have had some training in rabbinics. But even this is only a beginning, for we are not dealing with modern Judaism, however tradition-minded it may be, but with a specific Jewish community having its characteristic patterns of life and thought, and imbedded in a specific, always rapidly changing Muslim milieu. Thus before a would-be student of the Geniza can hope to achieve anything serious with the documents themselves, he must learn what he can about the institutions and traditions within which they were created.

It is logical to begin with an overview of the development of Jewish life and thought under Islam, and of the relations between the two communities. The literature on this subject is staggering, and anyone who tries to master all of it will do nothing else. Fortunately, there is now an excellent bibliographical essay to help one make the necessary choices: Mark R. Cohen, "The Jews under Islam: from the Rise of Islam to Sabbatai Zevi," in *Bibliographical Essays in Medieval Jewish Studies* (New York: Ktav, 1976), 169–229. (Reprinted with a supplement on works published between 1973 to 1980 as *Princeton Near East Paper, No. 32*, Program in Near Eastern Studies, Princeton Univ., 1981). There is also a good bibliography in Norman A. Stillman, *The Jews of Arab Lands: a History and Source Book* (1979). The body of Stillman's book is divided into two parts: a concise but broadly conceived survey of Jewish history in the Muslim lands down to the late nineteenth century; and an anthology of translated texts keyed to the historical survey. Stillman's book is a very good one, though it might be criticized on two points. First, both the historical survey and the translated documents perhaps give more attention to incidents of violence and overt oppression than is really warranted. Second (though this is in a sense to rebuke the author for not writing another book), the other non-Muslim communities, in particular the Christians, are almost entirely invisible. The importance of this is that a naive reader might misconstrue certain actions and institutions in the light of modern European anti-Semitism or the Arab-Israeli conflict, instead of understanding them as part of the general structure of Muslim/non-Muslim relations in the Middle Ages. A third introduction to the subject, popular in tone and purpose but wide-ranging and superbly informed, is S. D. Goitein, *Jews and Arabs: Their Contacts Through the Ages* (1955; revised eds., 1964, 1974). Of particular value for our purposes here are Chapters VI ("The Economic Transformation and Communal Reorganization of the Jewish People in Islamic Times") and VII ("The Cultural Development of the Jewish People inside Arab Islam"). Finally, see a recent work by Bernard Lewis, *The Jews of Islam* (1984), written with its author's customary ease, erudition, and breadth. In all works of such scope there is an unavoidable tendency to overgeneralize, of course. One might also ask whether the familiar categories of tolerance/intolerance and efflorescence/decline are the most useful ones to apply to this subject. They respond to our concerns, but how well do they reveal the concrete realities of Jewish life in an Islamic milieu?

At this point, one may be ready to profit from the massive synthesis of Salo W. Baron, *A Social and Economic History of the Jews* (2nd ed., 18 vols., 1957–1980). The relevant portions of this work are found in Vols. III–VIII, which deal with the High Middle Ages (from 500 to 1200), and Vol. XVII, which covers the later Middle Ages and the era of European Expansion, from 1200 to 1500. Volumes III–V and XVII deal with political and social questions, while Vols. VI–VIII focus on the complex cultural and intellectual achievement of Middle Eastern Jews in the Islamic period. Baron's annotation is lavish and important, and there is an index volume for Vols. I–VIII. On the other hand, Baron is not an Arabist, and this means that his interpretation of the Islamic milieu and of the ways in which Jews functioned within it is necessarily somewhat derivative and second-hand.

Baron's work opens up unlimited vistas (or perhaps a bottomless pit), and so it is well to remember that our purpose is not to master medieval Jewish culture and institutions as an end in itself, but to understand what roles were played by the Geniza community within Fatimid-Ayyubid society. We want to see the Jews not as a self-contained object of study, but as one element within a larger universe of thought and behavior. For this reason, a student of the Geniza documents needs a very extensive familiarity with the Fatimid and Ayyubid socio-political systems—systems which were beyond the control of the Geniza Jews but which created the expectations, opportunities, and constraints which governed their lives.

A thorough survey of the main works on Fatimid and Ayyubid politics and institutions is not possible here; for our purposes we need only the principal studies. There are a number of surveys of the Fatimid Caliphate, though a true political analysis is still lacking. The most detailed are two works in Arabic: Ḥasan Ibrāhīm Ḥasan, *Taʾrīkh al-Dawla al-Fāṭimiyya* (1948); and

Muḥammad Jamāl al-Dīn al-Surūr, *al-Dawla al-Fāṭimiyya fī Miṣr* (1965–66). In English, see Marius Canard, "Fāṭimids," *EI*[2], ii, 850–862, and the same author has contributed the entry on the crucial figure of al-Ḥākim bi-Amr Allāh (386–411/996–1021), *EI*[2], iii, 76–82. See also Abbas Hamdani, *The Fatimids* (1962). Finally, the old survey of F. Wüstenfeld, *Geschichte der Fatimiden-Chalifen nach dem arabischen Quellen* (1881), is still of value, though of course its source-base is obsolete. Valuable interpretive statements were contributed by Grunebaum and Bernard Lewis in *Colloque Internationale sur l'histoire du Caire* (Cairo, 1970).

For the Ayyubids we are somewhat better served. The present author's *From Saladin to the Mongols: the Ayyubids of Damascus, 1193–1260* (1977), attempts to survey the whole period of Ayyubid domination, though it focuses on Syria, about which the Geniza papers have very little to say, rather than Egypt. More concise introductions can be found in the brilliant article of Claude Cahen, "Ayyubids," *EI*[2], i, 796–807, and H.A.R. Gibb, "The Aiyubids," in K. E. Setton, ed., *A History of the Crusades* (1962; repr., 1969), Vol. II, pp. 693–714. As to individual Ayyubid rulers, the most important in the present context are Saladin (564–589/1169–1193) and his nephew al-Kāmil Muḥammad (615–635/1218–1238). On the latter we have a very thorough and exact monograph by H. L. Gottschalk, *al-Malik al-Kamil und seine Zeit* (1958). On Saladin there are a plethora of biographies, though most are of no scholarly interest. Stanley Lane-Poole, *Saladin* (1898), was well-documented for its time, but now seems romantic and old-fashioned. H.A.R. Gibb did several studies of great value, though his apotheosis of Saladin as a selfless warrior for the unity of Islam lies beyond proof or disproof; his work is summed up in *Saladin* (1973). A. S. Ehrenkreutz, *Saladin* (1972), is a vigorous (perhaps overly so at points) riposte to Gibb, and is especially important for the first ten years of Saladin's reign. Most recently, we have M. C. Lyons and David Jackson, *Saladin: the Politics of the Holy War* (1982)—a meticulous and sober study with important new documentation, but narrowly focused.

The works just cited give the framework of events and personalities which the Geniza communities pursued their way, but they have little to say about the administrative and fiscal institutions which were for non-Muslims the most ubiquitous manifestations of a Muslim polity. On these matters in general, see above, Chapter Seven; here we need only recall a few of the most essential titles. The invaluable studies of Claude Cahen on late Fatimid and early Ayyubid fiscal practice have been collected in *Makhzumiyyat: Études sur l'histoire économique et financière de l'Égypte médiévale* (1977). The chancery procedures of the Fatimid government are elucidated in the fundamental study of S. M. Stern, *Fatimid Decrees* (1964)—of particular importance here because most of these decrees were issued as edicts of protection and privilege to a *dhimmī* institution, the Greek Orthodox Monastery of St. Catherine's on Mt. Sinai. Though it deals with a period later than the classical Geniza, there is interesting material in C. E. Bosworth, "Christian and Jewish Religious

Dignitaries in Mamluk Egypt and Syria: Qalqashandī's Information on their Hierarchy, Titulature, and Appointment," *IJMES*, iii (1973), 59–74, 199–216. Hassanein Rabie, *The Financial System of Egypt, A.H. 564–741/A.D. 1169–1341* (1972), is an extremely useful collection of materials, based on a wide knowledge both of sources (including some Geniza papers) and the literature, even though the author's general conclusions are sometimes open to challenge. Finally, a useful general survey of Fatimid institutions is ʿAbd al-Munʿim Mājid, *Nuẓum al-Fāṭimiyyīn wa-rusūmuhum* (2 vols., 1953–56). The extensive material presented by the 9th/15th century encyclopedist al-Qalqashandī on the subject is available in Marius Canard, *Les institutions des Fatimides en Égypte* (1957). (Canard's writings on Fatimid subjects are very extensive and important, though badly scattered; his articles at least are now gathered in three stout *Variorum Reprints* volumes.)

Under the Fatimid and Ayyubid regimes, formal ideology only occasionally affected in any direct way the relations between the Jews of Egypt and the state. On the other hand, the harsh militance of early Mamluk times certainly had a most deleterious impact; we can follow the gradual emergence of this outlook in the brilliant monograph of Emmanuel Sivan, *L'Islam et la Croisade: idéologie et propagande dans les réactions musulmanes aux Croisades* (1968), which touches on all three of the relevant dynasties.

Finally, one should be familiar with a few studies which try to discuss the situation of the "protected communities" specifically within the Fatimid and Ayyubid polities. Some of these are general statements, others focus on a particular incident or personality. Good starting points are C. E. Bosworth, "The Protected Peoples (Christians and Jews) in Medieval Egypt and Syria," *BJRUL*, lxii (1979), 11–36; and Emmanuel Sivan, "Notes sur la situation des chrétiens sous les Ayyubides," *RHR*, clxii (1967), 117–130. Among the Muslim rulers of this long period, who obviously played a crucial role in determining the status and role of their non-Muslim subjects, only two have been studied. Eli Strauss (= Eliyahu Ashtor) has written "Saladin and the Jews," *Hebrew Union College Annual*, xxvii (1956), 305–326. For the Fatimid Caliph al-Ḥākim bi-Amr Allāh, who launched a frightful persecution first of Christians but later also of Jews and even Muslims, one should begin with the article in *EI²* by Marius Canard; on a famous incident in his reign, see the same author's "La destruction de l'Église de la Resurrection par le calife Hakim et l'histoire de la descente du feu sacré," *Byzantion*, xxxv (1955), 16–43. A very few *dhimmī*s took a major role in affairs of state. The most famous of these was in fact a convert to Islam, Yaʿqūb ibn Killis, the wazir of the Caliph al-ʿAzīz (975–996) and one of the principal architects of the Fatimid state in Egypt. On him see Walter J. Fischel, *Jews in the Economic and Political Life of Medieval Islam* (1937; repr. 1968), pp. 45–68; and most recently, Yaacov Lev, "The Fatimid vizier Yaʿqūb b. Killis and the Beginning of the Fatimid Administration in Egypt," *Islam*, 1 (1981), 237–249. Of almost equal interest are the Banū Sahl al-Tustarī, who are also studied in Fischel, *op. cit.*, 68–89. On a Christian vizier of the early 12th century, see Marius Canard, "Un vizir chrétien à l'époque fatimite, l'Arménien Bahram," *AIEO*, xii (1954), 84–113; and "Notes sur les Arméniens à l'époque fatimite," *AIEO*, xiii (1955), 143–157.

All this may seem a very long introduction to the Geniza documents themselves (and of course it is very far from complete). But without this kind of background, one is simply in no position to locate these documents in their political or cultural milieu—and by extension one cannot use them either to reconstruct the inner workings of the community which created them or to identify the place of this community in the general social structure of the age.

In view of the extraordinary demands placed on the researcher by these documents, we are fortunate that the first scholar to attempt a synthesis of them was fully equipped to perceive and exploit their possibilities. S. D. Goitein brought to his task a broad knowledge of Judaica, close acquaintance with a living Oriental Jewish community (that of Yemen, perhaps the most "traditional"—i.e. un-Westernized—Jewish community still to be found in the 1920s and 1930s), and finally solid training and research in Arabic and Islamic studies. All this allowed him to create almost single-handed a reliable foundation for work in the Geniza field. (A guide to Prof. Goitein's voluminous writing, already obsolescent, is Robert Attal, *Bibliography of the Writings of Professor Shelomo Dov Goitein*, 1975). From the early 1950s on, his research appeared in scores of articles, but the bulk of this has been summed up in *A Mediterranean Society: the Jewish Communities of the Arab World as Portrayed in the Documents of the Cairo Geniza*. There are five volumes, as follows: Vol. I, *Economic Foundations* (1967); Vol. II, *The Community* (1971); Vol. III, *The Family* (1978); Vol. IV, *Daily Life* (1982); Vol. V, *The Individual* (1988). The order of publication of this massive series is not necessarily the best order in which to read it. The most satisfactory starting point is probably Vol. II, which describes the internal workings of the Jewish community and its links to the several Islamic regimes which dominated it. Vols. I and IV deal with the crucial business of making a living. Finally, Vols. III and V lead the reader into the more intimate realms of kinship, sexuality, and self-identity.

Goitein's work is one of the most impressive and moving achievements in the history of our field. It is distinguished of course by its enormous erudition, which has resolved—or at least brought into clear focus—a host of technical and lexical problems. But more than that, the reader is struck by the almost conversational ease of Goitein's presentation; he was very much at home not only with the documents themselves but with the people who wrote them. For this reason he was able to give us an extraordinarily rich and detailed account of the world as it was perceived and experienced by these people. In doing this, Goitein necessarily sticks close to his texts, to their language, world-view, and ethos. He quite consciously eschewed any attempt to develop an analysis based on the application of contemporary concepts of society and culture to his materials; anyone who seeks here the overt influence of Max Weber, Talcott Parsons, Claude Lévi-Strauss, or Clifford Geertz will have sought in vain. It is for this reason that I would call *A Mediterranean Society* a first-level synthesis. It is no compilation of raw materials, but a rational and well-ordered presentation of their contents. On the other hand, the discrete bits of data which make up this presentation are still quite visible, and can be used to support far more complex, structured interpretations. One might think of it as a fine mosaic—very much an artistic unity as it stands, but its constituent tesserae can be used to construct quite a different image.

In speaking of Goitein's work as the first true synthesis of the Geniza materials, I of course do not mean to disparage earlier studies of this kind. In particular, the works of Jacob Mann written between the wars still contain much of value, but they are really collected monographs, focused largely on questions of communal organization, and they are obviously based on a far narrower body of texts. In addition, one needs to be a competent Hebraist to get full value from them, since Mann does not transliterate many key terms and phrases, and texts are given in the original rather than in translation. On the whole, one is better off consulting Mann for his treatment of specific problems after having absorbed what Goitein has to say. For our purposes, Mann's most valuable and influential work was *The Jews in Egypt and in Palestine under the Fatimid Caliphs* (2 vols., 1920–22; repr. in one volume, with preface by S. D. Goitein, 1970). There is also much of importance in *Texts and Studies in Jewish History and Literature* (2 vols., 1931–35; reprint with preface by Gerson D. Cohen, 1972). The prefatory essays by Goitein and Cohen in the Ktav reprints are extremely useful and make these editions the ones of choice.

Goitein's work, which focuses on the Jews of Egypt and (to a lesser degree) Tunisia—i.e. on those who left us the Geniza papers—can be used even more effectively if one has read surveys dealing with the important although less well-documented Jewish communities of neighboring lands and periods. Unfortunately for the majority of Islamists, the best of these are in Hebrew. Eliyahu Ashtor has contributed two important studies:

1. *Toledot ha-Yehudim be-Mizrayim ve-Suria tahat Shilton ha-Mamlukim*. 3 vols., 1944–70. (*History of the Jews in Egypt and Syria under Mamluk Rule*. Vol. I, 1250–1382; Vol. II, 1382–1517; Vol. III, texts of 74 Geniza documents cited.) On Vol. III, see a very critical review by Goitein in *Tarbiz*, xli (1971–72), 59–81, with English summary.
2. *Korot ha-Yehudim bi-Sefarad ha-Muslemit*. 2 Vols., Jerusalem: Kiryat Sefer, 1960–66. English translation: *The Jews of Muslim Spain* (1973–79).

On the very important Jewish communities of North Africa, the standard survey (already dated in many respects) is H. Z. Hirschberg, *Toledot ha-Yehudim be-Afrika ha-Zefonit*, (2 vols., 1965); English translation by M. Eichelberg of Vol. I, *A History of the Jews in North Africa: I, From Antiquity to the Sixteenth Century* (1974). (The English translation of Vol. I has been severely criticized by N. A. Stillman, *IJMES*, viii [1977], 405–407.) There is a comprehensive bibliography by Robert Attal, *Les juifs de l'Afrique du Nord: bibliographie*

(1973), containing some 5600 entries in all languages. Studies on the Jews of Iraq are far more scattered and uneven; refer to Cohen, "Jews under Islam," pp. 183–187; the lack of a comprehensive, methodologically sophisticated study in this area is especially regrettable in that the "Babylonian" community was the intellectual and demographic center of Jewish life in late Antiquity and the early Middle Ages. Finally, the Jews of the Ottoman Empire have recently begun to claim attention. This allows us to bring to bear a documentation which is different from the Geniza but equally as powerful. In addition to a few of the pieces in Braude and Lewis, see especially Amnon Cohen, *Jewish Life Under Islam: Jerusalem in the Sixteenth Century* (1984). Altogether, then, the student of the Geniza people is in a fortunate (and in our field extremely rare) position; Goitein's work provides a reliable and solid foundation, while the Jewish communities of adjoining periods and regions are well enough known for Geniza research to be placed in a quite detailed historical, social, and cultural context.

We are now in a position to pursue two questions. (1) What are the areas which Goitein's work has opened up either to specialized investigation or to more elaborate levels of interpretation? (2) What strategies are likely to prove most effective in exploiting this material?

As to the former of these, there is almost no area of life about which we cannot make some reasonable statement. Definitive results are not always possible, but at least we can propose testable hypotheses grounded in a reasonable body of empirical evidence. Only a few topics have so far been explored, to be sure, and these only in a provisional way, generally with more emphasis on the presentation of documents than on synthesis and interpretation. Some of this work focuses on the legal dimension of social organization; thus we have Moshe Gil, *Documents of the Jewish Pious Foundations from the Cairo Geniza* (1976), and Mordechai (Milton) Friedman, *Jewish Marriage in Palestine: a Cairo Geniza Study* (2 vols., 1980–81). Interesting work has also been done on the great merchant families whose heads, prominent both in commerce and in learning, provided vital leadership to the Geniza community in all areas of life:

a. Murad Michael, "The Archive of Nahray ben Nissim, Business Man and Public Figure in Egypt in the Eleventh Century" (In Hebrew). Ph.D. Diss., Hebrew University, Jerusalem, 1963. (Based on 261 documents presented in the text.)

b. Norman A. Stillman, "The Eleventh-century Merchant House of Ibn ʿAwkal (a Geniza Study)," *JESHO*, xvi (1973), 15–88.

On balance, however, perhaps the best-integrated and most finished monograph to follow up the lines of inquiry traced by Goitein is Mark R. Cohen, *Jewish Self-Government in Medieval Egypt: The Origins of the Office of Head of the Jews, ca. 1065–1126* (1980). This is not a comprehensive synthetic statement on the internal organization of the Geniza community or on the whole range of political-administrative links between it and the Fatimid government. The second volume of *A Mediterranean Society* is still the only comprehensive effort of this kind. Rather, Cohen focuses on a single problem: the emergence and institutional consolidation of a government-appointed *raʾīs al-Yahūd*, who within the Jewish community commonly had the honorary title of *nagid*. Cohen discusses the historical situation out of which this office emerged, the social-background characteristics of the Jewish notables who oversaw its creation, the precise powers over communal affairs which the *nagid*s claimed for themselves, and the struggle for power among competing factions. Particularly decisive, in his view, were the following: the collapse of public authority in Egypt and Palestine in the 1060s–70s; the Crusader conquest of Palestine and Lebanon; the irreversible erosion in the traditional authority of the Palestinian Academy and its head (the Gaon) over the Egyptian community as a result of these events; and—an extremely important point—the migration to Egypt of many prominent and learned Jews in the mid-11th century from Tunisia and Palestine, for it was these immigrants who oversaw the creation of the nagidate and hence established the autonomy of the Egyptian community within the Jewish world as a whole.

Cohen's monograph is in many ways a model of what a political study ought to be. First, it is based on a broad yet well-focused notion of politics, which is seen here not merely as a struggle for power among a narrow elite but as the way in which a social group defines its collective goals and organizes itself in order to achieve them. Second, it rests on precise definitions of its key terms. Third, it has a very low ratio of speculation to hard evidence. Finally, and most crucially, it is very attentive to problems of change, and to the ways in which change can be masked by the traditional language of our sources.

In spite of its qualities, Cohen's study is of course not the final word on the political life of the Geniza community. In what follows, we will sketch one alternative approach, and this will also allow us to deal with the second question posed above (p. 270)—viz., what strategies can be used to exploit the Geniza materials?

One might argue that a political system is only meaningful insofar as we understand the social structure which underlies it, and moreover that every society is first and foremost a system of production and distribution. If this postulate is accepted, it would imply that we can usefully search for a class basis of politics in the Geniza community. This kind of inquiry certainly poses serious conceptual problems—e.g., a clear definition of economic class, relationships between class and status in Geniza society, a determination of the exact mechanisms by which one's class position could be translated into a greater or lesser degree of political influence and participation, etc. But even more difficult are problems of method. To take only one point, Geniza writers generally speak in a language of status, not of class. How then can we construct the class system of their community from the casual and highly variable references to persons and groups in their letters, contracts, and depositions? (Goitein has given us a useful essay in this direction [*Mediterranean Society*, vol. I, 75–80], but in his discussion concepts of class and status are mixed together; this confusion simply reflects the language of his sources, to be sure, but it also obstructs analysis.)

One strategy would be to tabulate all the different occupations cited in a given bloc of letters, then trying to attach these to general economic functions in society. The latter step can of course only be performed if one has worked out an economic model of Geniza society, at least in broad outline. To some extent, this is an a priori process, for—except for Ibn Khaldun, and there only in a sketchy, inchoate manner—there are no indigenous economic models to be found. But the manuals of *ḥisba* mentioned in previous chapters (especially the 7th/13th-century Damascene al-Shayzarī and his 8th/14th-century Egyptian adapter Ibn al-Ukhuwwa) can provide significant help—not only a quite exhaustive description of market and artisanal occupations, but also many hints as to how these were integrated into a functioning economic system. (See also pp. 217, 242.) Economic models of the kind we are discussing are very crude, certainly; they are qualitative and intuitive, not econometric. Most of all, they are not cast in bronze; they are heuristic, guides for the organization and assessment of evidence, and as we acquire new data from the Geniza and other texts, we should expect to alter, and even completely recast, the model we are using.

A procedure of this kind could eventually lead to a reasonable understanding of how different occupations were related to one another to form an economic system. And once a framework of economic action has been established, it should be no great matter to deduce from it the class structure which it embodies. But how do we move from the definition of a class structure to determining a "class basis" (if in fact it does exist) for politics in the Geniza community. Here we would proceed from the most exact knowledge possible of Jewish communal offices in this period. We would be concerned less with the formal functions of communal officers than with their actual interactions with one another; that is, we would first want to understand politics as a closed system of relations among those entrusted with the collective needs and goals of the community. From this knowledge, we would try to construct the hierarchy of offices—a hierarchy in which one's position was determined not only by formal function but also by status and effective power both within the community and in relation to the Muslim government. Once we have established a hierarchy of offices, it should not be difficult to correlate each office with the economic class of the individuals who held it. If class was a significant determinant of political power, that fact should show up at this point.

It must be admitted that this kind of analysis can be very misleading; it can lead us to suppose that class is the sole criterion of a person's place in the political system, when in the minds of those involved other (sometimes contradictory) criteria were decisive, such as hereditary right, learning and piety, etc. But a class analysis of the kind just sketched does permit us to integrate in an effective way our knowledge of an economic and a political system—two things which are crucial but often apparently incommensurate aspects of any society. There is another problem as well: the presuppositions of this sort of study are plainly Marxist, and so it is easy to suppose that its results must conform to a Marxist schema. That is not the case, however; the line of questioning outlined here asks whether class is politically salient, but it does not assert that it must be. Obviously we should beware of insisting on class struggle rather than communal solidarity, or of imposing a vocabulary ("feudal," "agrarian" vs. "merchant capital," "petite bourgeoisie," "proletariat," etc.) which obscures rather than elucidates the concrete realities revealed by the data.

We have explored one possibility opened up by Goitein's research, the political life of the Geniza community, because it has been developed in a very good monograph. But other possibilities are perhaps even more exciting, in that they allow us to link Jewish experience with that of the broader Muslim and Mediterranean worlds. Goitein has in fact chosen the title of his *magnum opus* precisely to bring out this point, and has argued for it in "The Unity of the Mediterranean World in the 'Middle' Middle Ages," *Studies in Islamic History and Institutions*, 296–307. The linkage between Jewish and other communities can be made in many areas, but it is most striking and complete in commerce. Perhaps it is not surprising that few scholars, either Islamists or students of medieval Europe, have as yet tried to use the vast fund of material made available in the first volume of *A Mediterranean Society* in a broader synthesis, for the linguistic demands alone of such a task are absolutely staggering. But there is a real need for someone to apply the data of the Geniza papers to the main problems of Mediterranean commerce and economic organization. To a large degree, these issues have been explored by Europeanists, who know Latin, Greek, Italian, etc., but no Arabic, let alone the Judaeo-Arabic of the Geniza documents. Even Claude Cahen, equally at home on all shores of the Mediterranean, has largely left the Geniza aside in his important studies in the area's economic history. The most promising attempts along these lines are perhaps those of A. L. Udovitch; as an example, see "Time, the Sea, and Society: Duration of Commercial Voyages on the Southern Shores of the Mediterranean during the High Middle Ages," *La navagazione mediterranea nell'alto medioevo* (Spoleto, 1978), pp. 503–563. Still, we should hope that more scholars will enter the fray, for while the Geniza documents enrich our knowledge of the Islamic lands in many areas, in the field of economic history they utterly transform it.

C. The Problem of Conversion

I have already pointed out in several places in this chapter that the Muslims were at the outset a small minority—a warrior elite—in most of the lands they ruled. They became a majority not by displacing the indigenous peoples but by converting them. Conversion to Islam was thus a massive process, one with vast if not always easily definable consequences, and yet it remains one of the most poorly examined fields in Islamic studies. All the truly important studies on this subject could probably be listed on a single page. There is no standard work which defines the field and lays out the directions of future research. (In this regard, the collection edited by Nehemiah Levtzion, *Conversion to Islam* (1979) is certainly very useful; but it focuses on modern times, and thus deals mostly with regions which lie outside the old Islamic lands which are our principal concern here.) Rather, we have a few essays—methodological explorations or impressionistic surveys as the case may be—even fewer monographs devoted to a specific population, and various brief discussions imbedded in books devoted chiefly to other subjects.

Under these circumstances, our approach must be very different from the one we followed in discussing the Geniza community. We will begin by investigating the kinds of issues which the student of conversion must confront, indicating also some of the sources and techniques which might throw light on these issues. Finally, we will examine two recent studies on conversion—one a methodological essay, the other detailed inquiry into a particular historical situation.

What was conversion to Islam and what did it entail for the would-be convert? First of all, conversion is a matter of exchanging one set of religious beliefs and rituals for another. Western orientalists, up through World War I at least, tended to have a condescending if not overtly hostile attitude toward Islam, and this frame of mind led them to regard this as somewhat aberrant behavior, a business of exchanging a patently superior creed (i.e., Christianity or Judaism) for one which was both alien and relatively primitive. Moreover, because religious affiliation in Europe and America by the late 19th century was largely an individual and voluntary matter, one's professed beliefs presumably stemmed from conscience and personal commitment. From this perspective, it was (and for most of us still is) difficult to understand how large numbers of people could—often quite casually to all appearances—shed one religion for another unless they were coerced into doing so. A more disinterested and historical view, however, will suggest how misleading these two attitudes can be. We should not suppose that a medieval Christian or Jew, if he were discontented with his received faith, would have any reason to regard Islam as alien and primitive; on the contrary, as the constant stream of interconfessional apologetic and polemic shows, the three scriptural religions shared a core vocabulary, and each was equally able to demonstrate the inanity of the other two. More to the point, however, in medieval times religion was socially determined; that is, one's creed was not a matter of personal choice but of the community in which he lived. As Clifford Geertz in particular has pointed out (*Islam Observed*, p. 107ff.), many adherents of a religion in such circumstances are only superficially committed to it as a set of doctrines. If their social situation changes, they do not find it difficult to exchange one religion for another, for religion is a question of what is socially appropriate as well as of what is transcendentally true. For most converts to Islam, then, we should expect that the change of creed and ritual was the least of their concerns.

What would their real concerns have been? First of all, in almost all premodern societies a religion has been not only a creed but also a law, and as such a way of life. Thus in converting one expected to exchange one way of life for another, a change which would affect dress, rules of marriage and divorce, inheritance, and many other things; much of the texture of everyday life would be altered. Second, to convert was not only to join a new community but in large measure to leave an old one; at least temporarily, then, it might engender a degree of social isolation unless and until one could weave a new web of personal bonds to replace those severed by his decision to convert. (For some of the legal consequences of conversion in marriage and inheritance, see Fattal, *Statut légal des non-musulmans*, pp. 127–143.) Conversion, then, involved not simply, or even mainly, decisions about what one believed, but about how he wanted to live his life; it was in concrete terms one of the gravest choices which anyone could confront.

All these comments suggest that we should try to view the process from four distinct perspectives: (a) that of the individual would-be convert; (b) that of a given social group (village, tribe, urban quarter, etc.) whose members were involved in the conversion process; (c) that of the organized non-Muslim religious community from which converts were being drawn; (d) that of the Muslim community which was receiving them. These perspectives, I believe, are all accounted for in the following set of questions:

1. What was the nature of the Muslim community which the convert would enter? Did it represent a substantial majority of the region's population, was it a small elite controlling the government, did it consist rather of a small number of transient or resident "foreigners" such as merchants or mendicant Sufis, was it an old or a recently established community?
2. What was the attitude of the Muslim community—or rather of its political and religious chiefs—toward conversion?
3. What benefits would conversion predictably offer to non-Muslims? Conversely, why was it worthwhile to face the problems created by leaving one's community?
4. In the time and place under study, did conversion occur principally among isolated individuals or as a fairly broad-based social movement? Should we think of a change of allegiance among individuals or among social groupings?
5. As a corollary of no. 4, what was the pace of conversion in the period under study?

6. What groups within the non-Muslim society being studied seem to have been particularly prone to conversion, and conversely, which resisted most stubbornly?

7. What was the structure and character of the religious community from which conversion occurred: what instruments did it have to oppose conversion, what weaknesses and conflicts within it might have induced its members to want to leave?

All this implies, of course, that conversion was not a process which was broadly the same throughout Islam; on the contrary, conversion is only intelligible within specific historical, social, and cultural contexts, and these contexts must be expected to vary enormously from one time and place to another. The questions we have posed are universal in form; they can be applied with roughly equal validity to any pertinent body of phenomena. But the answers will in no two cases be the same. Indeed, we might argue that the study of conversion to Islam is one of our most effective ways of reconstructing the specific characteristics of each of the constituent societies of medieval Islam.

What kinds of resources do we have for questions of the kind posed here? There is no one body of sources which is uniquely devoted to the problem of conversion, so that in this area we must be prepared to draw on the whole array of literary, documentary, and archaeological evidence left us by medieval Islam. A brief survey of the sorts of data we might expect to derive from each is thus needed.

The Muslim chronicles, the foundation of our knowledge of political history and institutions, have only isolated incidents to report even in regard to Muslim/non-Muslim relations overall, let alone the specific problem of conversion. A broad (though far from exhaustive) selection of what they have to say can be found in Tritton's *The Caliph and His Non-Muslim Subjects*, though of course Tritton is concerned with the legal and social status of non-Muslims under Muslim rule, not conversion per se. An essay which suggests what can be learned from the historical texts is I. M. Lapidus, "The Conversion of Egypt to Islam," *Israel Oriental Studies*, ii (1972), 248–262. Lapidus' study is only a sketch, but it suffices to show that the chronicles can give us both the general political context within which conversion occurred and the government's major policy initiatives in this area. Lapidus' generalizations can be followed up in the concise but lucid monograph of Joseph Cuoq, *Islamisation de la Nubie chrétienne, viie–xvie siècle* (1986). Subtler but perhaps more decisive aspects of the process—e.g., constant undercurrents of social pressure, economic trends, etc.—are of course likely to slip through the coarse net of the chronicles.

A second historical genre, the biographical dictionary, might have more to offer. Richard Bulliet has contrived an ingenious though controversial method of exploiting this resource, which we shall examine below. More traditional methods, however, would involve scrutinizing the entries for accounts of converts or sons of converts. Though the personal data of the biographical dictionaries is usually meager and stereotyped, it should be possible to combine it with contextual information derived from chronicles and other sources. This work, if carried out for enough individuals (of course carefully distinguished by region and period), should allow us to assess the kinds of circumstances and motives which favored conversion, at least for that elite which is registered in the biographical literature.

This last point brings up a very real difficulty: the majority of biographical dictionaries are devoted to those who were distinguished by their erudition in the Islamic religious sciences, and in these we can expect little information on converts, who obviously could not expect to attain much religious prestige. Some dictionaries are based on criteria which do include non-Muslims and converts, however, and these might repay close examination. Thus, Ibn Abī Uṣaybiʿa's (d. 1284) great dictionary of physicians, *ʿUyūn al-anbāʾ fī ṭabaqāt al-aṭibbāʾ*, (2 vols., 1399/1882), is not only wide-ranging and richly detailed, but includes persons without reference to religion. For early Mamluk times, there is the *Tālī wafayāt al-aʿyān* of Ibn al-Ṣuqāʿī (ed. and trans. Jacqueline Sublet, 1974)—an early 8th/14th century continuation of Ibn Khallikān which is distinctly inferior to its model in most respects, but which was written by a Christian bureaucrat who includes many of his co-religionists.

What about the many important historical texts written by Christians—might not they have a special value for this problem? Several of these, written by laymen, in fact have little or nothing to say about the Christian experience per se, but are simply general political chronicles, not different in nature or orientation from those written by Muslims. Examples might be the chronicles of Yaḥyā al-Anṭākī (an extremely important text, however, for Fatimid-Byzantine relations) and two Coptic writers of the early Mamluk period, al-Makīn ibn al-ʿAmīd (d. 672/1274) and al-Mufaḍḍal ibn Abī al-Faḍāʾil (d. 759/1358). On the other hand, as we have mentioned above (p. 263) in another context, there is a rich tradition of ecclesiastical history composed by churchmen, written in Arabic, Syriac, and Armenian. This ecclesiastical tradition often has much to contribute to our knowledge of Muslim political history properly speaking—though it must be admitted that many of its products are astonishing in their ignorance and narrowness. But in any case they do inform us directly and vividly about two crucial topics: the experience of the organized church under Islam (or at least the bishops' and monks' perception of this experience), and the internal workings of the ecclesiastical hierarchy. Without these texts it would be extremely difficult to answer questions such as those raised under no. 7 above.

We cannot here give even a cursory outline of Christian historiography under Islam. For Syriac and Arabic works, the reader can consult the bio-bibliographic surveys of Baumstark and Graf (cited above, Part I, Chapter Two, p. 29), but there seems to be nothing equivalent for the Armenian tradition. However, three comprehensive works will suggest what may be learned.

First, the universal chronicle of Michael the Syrian (d. 1199), ed. with French translation by J. B. Chabot (4 vols., 1899–1914. Vol. IV, Syriac text; Vols. I–III, French translation and appendices)—a remarkable compilation which draws on and in a sense sums up the whole Syriac historiographical tradition, and is written with unusual intelligence. The Armenian tradition, during the critical period of the early Seljukid occupation of Anatolia, can be followed in the work of Matthew of Edessa (d. 1136): *Chronique de Matthieu d'Édesse, 962–1136, avec la continuation de Grégoire le Prêtre jusqu'à 1162*, ed. and trans. Ed. Dulaurier (1858). There is also a modern Turkish translation by Hrant Andreasyan, *Urfalı Mateos Vekayı-namesi*, with notes by Dulaurier and M. H. Yinanç (1962). I am unable to assess its quality, however. Finally, we should mention a collective work compiled over many centuries, the *History of the Patriarchs of Alexandria*, begun in the 4th/10th century by Severus (Sawīrūs) ibn al-Muqaffaʿ and continued down to the mid-7th/13th century by other hands (Vol. I, ed. F. Seybold, 1904; Vols. II–IV, ed. and trans. O.H.E. KHS-Burmester, Y. ʿAbd-al-Masīḥ, A. S. Atiya, 1943–1974).

Historical works, both Muslim and non-Muslim, are clearly a major source for dealing with the sorts of questions we have posed in this section. But other kinds of texts must not be neglected. One of the most revealing, if used critically and perceptively, should be legal texts, already discussed from the point of view of the status of *dhimmīs*. But of course the non-Muslim communities also generated reams of legal prose, and some of this clearly had to address the problem of conversion, if only by implication. The Zoroastrians are not really well studied; for a start, however, see an article of Jean de Menasce, "Problèmes des mazdéens dans l'Iran musulman," *Festschrift für Wilhelm Eilers* (Wiesbaden, 1967), pp. 220–230. A tenth-century Pahlavi lawbook has been published by B. T. Anklesaria, *The Pahlavi Rivayat of Aturnfarnbag and Farnbag-sros* (2 vols., 1969). For studies on the multitude of responsa produced by the Gaonim of Iraq and Palestine down to the eleventh century, and later by Jewish leaders like Maimonides, guidance can be found in Mark Cohen, "The Jews Under Islam." (In Israel there is an ongoing effort to create a broad index of the responsa, for historical as well as strictly legal and religious purposes.) Finally, the Christian churches published the acts of their numerous synods and councils; see J. B. Chabot, ed. and trans., *Synodicon orientale, ou recueil des synodes nestoriens*, in *Notices et extraits des manuscrits de la Bibliothèque Nationale*, (Paris) t. xxxviii (1902). Legal texts, of whatever genre, are of course difficult to interpret historically, since they attempt to state universal rules in general language and to link these rules to ancient, unchanging tradition. In every case, we must try to discern the exact time and place in which a statement of law was issued, and the situation which it was intended to address—a pious truism easier to state than to carry out, but too often neglected by the few scholars who have tried to use these texts.

Original documents—official decrees, court cases, letters, etc.—would obviously be very useful indeed. But as we have had to say so many times in this book, these usually come from Egypt—a very important but by no means typical region of the Muslim world—or from Ottoman times. Within Egypt, the Geniza papers discussed above are of course the main body of documents produced by a non-Muslim community. They throw only a dim and occasional light on the process of conversion to Islam, however, because the Jewish community lost relatively few of its members until well into Mamluk times. It was the Coptic Church which was transformed from the embodiment of the Egyptian nation to an insecure and dwindling minority; but so far as we know, there are only a few papyri in which the Copts speak for themselves. On the other hand, the numerous administrative papyri from Umayyad and early Abbasid times have much to contribute if read correctly; a hint of what might be done is the discussion on Egypt in D. C. Dennett, *Conversion and the Poll-Tax in Early Islam* (1950), p. 82ff. and 114–115.

Finally, there is the evidence of archaeology. Anyone who travels in Syria and Anatolia will see a number of mosques which are clearly converted churches and shrines. Throughout the Central Islamic Lands, there are countless abandoned cultic centers—fire temples, monasteries, etc. All of this in itself suggests the vast religious and cultural change which once occurred in these countries. A very useful way of approaching the problem of conversion, then, would be to try and determine the period and circumstances in which a given non-Muslim place of worship was abandoned or converted to Islamic functions. This determination would rest both on direct archaeological evidence and on any relevant texts which could be discovered. In this regard, the urban topographies reviewed in Chapter Ten would be especially useful, and to these we should add at least two works which look at Christian monuments:

1. Abū Ṣāliḥ (13th cen.), *The Churches and Monasteries of Egypt*, trans. B. Evetts and A. J. Butler (1894–95).
2. al-Shābushtī, *Kitāb al-Diyārāt* (The Book of Monasteries), ed. Girgis ʿAwwāḍ. (1951; repr. 1966).

There are unfortunately very few if any studies of conversion which make serious use of archaeological evidence. One important monograph should be noted, however: J. M. Fiey, *Mossoul chrétienne: essai sur l'histoire, l'archéologie, et l'état actuel des monuments chrétiens de la ville de Mossoul* (1959).

In light of the preceding discussion, it should be possible to assess two of the more systematic and imaginative efforts to deal with the issue of conversion: (a) Richard W. Bulliett, *Conversion to Islam in the Medieval Period: an Essay in Quantitative History* (1979); (b) Speros Vryonis, *The Decline of Medieval Hellenism in Asia Minor and the Process of Islamization from the Eleventh through the Fifteenth Century* (1971).

Prof. Vryonis' book is much the longer and more detailed of the two, and it is also more conventional in its choice and use of sources—though "conventional" hardly means commonplace or uninteresting. In addition to Greek, Persian, and early Ottoman chronicles, he has drawn on Muslim hagiography, travellers both Muslim and Christian, published deeds of waqf, acts of Church synods in Constantinople and other ecclesiastical documents. Where possible, he alludes to (without really examining) archaeological evidence, which so far has been only sparsely published for late Byzantine and early Turkish times. He has thus used most of the categories of evidence reviewed above, and he presents the ecclesiastical material in particular very extensively.

His basic thesis is straightforward though not simple. Down to the Seljukid invasions of the mid-eleventh century, Anatolia was a land deeply permeated by Orthodox Christianity and the Greek language and culture (of course in its Byzantine form); all classes and regions were within the sphere of a specifically Hellenic and Christian way of life. The framework which supported this way of life was first of all the Byzantine government, of course, but also—and perhaps even more important—the Orthodox Church, with its networks of bishoprics in almost every town and its rich monasteries dotting the countryside. Both this way of life and the organizations which sustained it were badly damaged in the wave of Turkish conquests beginning in the 1060s–1070s: the populations in many areas fled or were enslaved or in some instances massacred; the bishops were cut off from their dioceses; churches were ruined and the properties which supported them confiscated; Byzantine administration disappeared, to be replaced by ungoverned troops of Türkmen nomads. In spite of the shock, however, both the Greek populace and the Orthodox Church survived to a considerable degree, and even began to recover somewhat in the late 12th and early 13th centuries, due largely to two processes: the emergence of a strong Seljukid government in Turkish Anatolia which valued order and stability, and the Byzantine consolidation of its political and administrative position in coastal and Western Anatolia. Even in this period of respite there was a constant pressure for assimilation and conversion, but it proceeded in a gradual manner.

A new age of disorders, far worse and more fatal in its effects than the first, opened in the late 13th century with the simultaneous crumbling of Seljukid authority and Byzantine power, due largely to the Mongol conquest of the Seljukids and the consequent uncontrolled influx of new Türkmen groups into Anatolia. Now even the coastal regions and the west were exposed to Türkmen depredations. In the turmoil, Byzantine administration disappeared forever, the Orthodox Church was left utterly impoverished and demoralized, the Greek population was constantly subject to violence and enslavement. Moreover, Muslim culture had now evolved powerful positive institutions which could encourage conversion and assimilation: the dervish orders, the *futuwwa* brotherhoods, networks of charitable and educational institutions with which the Church could no longer compete. When a new era of security and order was established, it was under the aegis of a state that had finally obliterated the Byzantine Empire and put the Orthodox Church in tutelage. There were still many islands of Greek Christians, but the dominant forces were the Islamic faith and Turkish culture.

The general outline of Vryonis' argument is certainly plausible, but there are important flaws and omissions, as Claude Cahen noted in a long critical review (*IJMES*, iv [1973], 112–117). Thus he quite ignores the non-Greek, non-Orthodox populations of Syrian Jacobites and Armenians who were the majority of the indigenous population in eastern Anatolia and upper Mesopotamia. He overlooks the possible effects of the centuries-long Arab-Byzantine wars which had created a broad frontier zone in the Taurus Mountains and central Anatolia. On a methodological level, Vryonis has a tendency to apply evidence from the well-documented late 14th and 15th centuries to the thinly documented 13th and early 14th. One might also ask whether he treats Muslim hagiography with sufficient caution. He tends to look at this literature as containing a kernel of historical truth hidden within veils of legend. I would not deny that some historical data might be tucked away in this literature, but its essence is myth and allegory. What we can get from it on a historical level are things like its attitudes toward non-Muslims, the degree to which crucial Christian practices and beliefs could be accommodated in popular Islam, etc. Finally, we might argue that the picture presented by Vryonis for the 14th century in particular is too bleak: of course churchmen from Constantinople would stress instances of violence and deprivation, but how did the Christian communities in Anatolia view things? They are almost voiceless, so we do not know, but the survival of large Greek populations in Anatolia until World War I should suggest that in many places Greek Orthodox society was able to propagate itself in a Turkish Muslim world.

None of the above implies that Vryonis did not do his homework; it simply suggests the enormous complexity of the problem of conversion, and the range of skills and concepts which a scholar must draw on to deal with it effectively.

The second book to be considered is altogether different in character. Whereas Vryonis hopes to reconstruct in detail a social and cultural process in one period and region, Bulliet intends only to present a heuristic essay, to suggest a method for assessing the rate and degree of conversion to Islam, and to show the results yielded by this method when it is applied in a provisional manner to several disparate and widely separated parts of the medieval Muslim world. In this context, the fact that he has used an extremely incomplete documentation is not a valid criticism, and the promise of the method is more important than the inconclusiveness of his results.

Briefly, Prof. Bulliet's goal is to determine when a Muslim majority was attained in the various regions conquered by the Arabs, and at what rate this majority had come into being. Secondarily, he tries to correlate these findings with the chronology of political events so as to suggest some of the possible causes and consequences of the conversion process per se. His principal source is the biographical dictionary, which is usable precisely because of its repetitious and formulaic presentation. By far his most important and intriguing innovation, however, is his attempt to use formal statistical methods to analyze the data which he extracts from his texts. He argues that conversion takes place along a bell-shaped curve, similar in principle to the curve describing a population's adoption of technological innovations. He hopes to support this notion by showing that the empirically established conversion process for two Iranian cities (Isfahan and Nishapur) in fact approximates a bell-shaped curve very closely. Having established the plausibility of such a curve for a place where the evidence is "good," he hopes then to apply it in situations where the evidence is much less direct.

What kinds of evidence has Bulliet been able to find in the biographical dictionaries? There is almost nothing on converts as such, as we have already noted. Thus one must read between the lines. For Iran, Bulliet believes that naming patterns are the key; when a man converted to Islam, he might take a Muslim name for himself, and he would certainly give a Muslim name to his children, in order to demonstrate their (and his own) adherence to the new faith. If we read through the lineages (*nasab*) attached to each person entered in the dictionary, we find that all the names are specifically Muslim until the last (i.e. the name of the most remote ancestor), which will be Iranian. Presumably this figure is the first convert in the family. By counting back through the generations, then, it should be possible to establish the date of a family's conversion to Islam. Naming patterns are also the key in Arabic-speaking areas—Iraq, Syria, Egypt, Tunisia, Spain—but here (except to a degree in Spain) they are much less obvious. In these countries he charts the popularity of a set of purely Muslim names (Muḥammad, Aḥmad, ʿAlī, Ḥasan, Ḥusayn) as an index of conversion.

Bulliet's method is a daring one; it is built not merely on one or two hypothetical propositions, but on complex syllogisms of such hypotheses, all of which must be valid for the syllogism to hold. Taken one at a time, each of his hypotheses is at least plausible; but one gets uneasy at the thought of an argument resting only on layers of unproved and perhaps unprovable propositions. To establish Bulliet's method as a sound one—or to show it is unworkable—will require two kinds of tests. The first would be to show that Bulliet's results are broadly consonant with the results obtained by more traditional kinds of analysis, such as that attempted by Vryonis. Bulliet attempts a few brief essays in this direction; obviously he is gratified by the result. More important and encouraging, however, is that an historian of medieval Spain has found Bulliet's conversion curve for that country to be persuasive and useful: Thomas F. Glick, *Islamic and Christian Spain in the Early Middle Ages* (1979)—see esp. pp. 33–35. The second kind of test would be to try to construct a conversion curve from a far broader and more exhaustive body of data than any used by Bulliet. For Syria, we might use the huge dictionaries compiled by Ibn ʿAsākir (d. 571/1176) for Damascus, or Kamāl al-Dīn ibn al-ʿAdīm (d. 660/1262) for Aleppo. These dictionaries are far more detailed, and are compiled on the basis of more inclusive criteria, than those cited by Bulliet. In using them, we would at least have some assurance that we had access to most of the relevant cases.

Serious work on conversion is clearly in its infancy. Its future depends both on the emergence of new ways of tackling the problem, and on scholars who have the patience to exploit the techniques already developed. In any case, it is hard to think of any topic which would repay such efforts with higher dividends.

Chapter Twelve

THE VOICELESS CLASSES OF ISLAMIC SOCIETY

THE PEASANTRY AND RURAL LIFE

MEDIEVAL Islamic society was overwhelmingly a society of peasants, and on their unremitting labor was built the whole glittering edifice of that civilization. The peasant's bitter toil earned him little but contempt and exploitation in his own day, however, and while we are ready enough to accord him at least a modicum of respect (if not to romanticize him beyond recognition), we have had very little to say about him. This neglect in part reflects the neglect of our sources, to be sure; illiterate and politically marginal, the peasant could not speak for himself, while the literate citied classes who lived from his labors were too preoccupied with the service of God and the heroics or antics of kings to pay him much heed. In medieval Islamic culture, the peasant seems both voiceless and invisible.

Even so, far more might have been done. Scholars of early medieval Europe (down to ca. 1100) and Byzantium are confronted by a similar conspiracy of silence, and yet for generations they have assiduously exploited the scraps available to them. We thus return to an oft-repeated theme of this book—that Islamic specialists require a far broader historical culture than they usually possess. A serious acquaintance with major studies on rural history produced by medievalists and Byzantinists would have suggested not only interesting areas of inquiry, but also types of sources that might be used and more inventive strategies for exploiting them. In the end, our neglect of the peasant in Islamic studies is a failure of curiosity—and perhaps also a failure (induced by the image of the "timeless East") to suppose that he had any history.

Given this situation, it is sensible to begin by looking at a few of the major synthetic works on the rural history of medieval Europe. We shall concentrate our attention here on France. England, due to the Domesday Book and the early centralization of royal authority, is a case apart from the point of view of sources, while the rural history of Italy and Spain remains little explored. As to Germany and Central Europe, the scholarly literature is mostly unavailable in English.

The scientific study of rural life and agrarian institutions in France goes back to the 18th century, and has been cultivated with considerable vigor since the last quarter of the 19th century. The first great synthesis, however, was Marc Bloch's *Les caractères originaux de l'histoire rurale française* (1931); English trans. by Janet Sondheimer, *French Rural History: an Essay on its*

Basic Characteristics (1966). Bloch's work (originally a series of lectures) still impresses by its vividness, its sense of intellectual excitement, and by the author's love for his subject. Many of his specific conclusions will no longer stand, of course, and the book should not be thought of as a guide to current thinking on the subject. But its real achievements have not been antiquated.

First of all, there is Bloch's method—one begins with the known (in this case the land-tenure rules and farming practices of the 18th century) and works back to the unknown. The present is not to be projected onto the past, but is rather used to generate a set of questions and working hypotheses. These are then applied to whatever documents and artifacts survive from the period under study. Bloch's point is that where contemporary documentation is fragmentary, it cannot be the sole basis for the reconstruction of a social system; it can only be made to speak if one asks how the conditions it alludes to differ from those (usually of a later time) which are much better known. This method of course assumes a high degree of continuity within an ongoing social system, but not stagnation; Bloch is in fact exceptionally alert to evidences of change and innovation. Moreover, as the documentation from remoter periods dries up, he is careful to emphasize the provisional character of his statements.

The second characteristic of Bloch's approach is his search for a valid comparative method. By comparative history, he does not mean a feature-by-feature comparison of two or more periods or locales. Rather, his goal is to establish a common set of questions about agrarian life—questions which can be applied to Poland and Sicily as well as to Normandy and Provence—so that our knowledge of highly disparate places can be brought within a unified framework. Questions of this kind are by no means easy to define, and Bloch only adumbrates such a method without fully achieving it, but his approach remains a compelling one.

Finally, Bloch is a master of integration; he has a vision of the whole which allows him to bring together the most disparate kinds of data. The type of plow is related on the one hand to soil conditions and on the other to forms of land tenure. It is hardly an original notion that every facet of life reflects every other, but Bloch succeeds far better than most in conveying this sense of wholeness.

A book which in some ways can be read as a commentary on Bloch (though it stands on its own merits) is the critical survey of Georges Duby, *L'économie rurale et la vie des campagnes dans l'Occident médiéval* (1962); English trans. by Cynthia Postan, *Rural Economy and Country Life in the Medieval West* (1968). The ambience of the two works is very different indeed—where Bloch is vivid and full of excitement, Duby is dry and reserved; where Bloch boldly generalizes, Duby cautiously enumerates particular cases. But Duby builds on Bloch's achievement with great skill, and far better than his predecessor he indicates what we really do and can know. Duby's overt method is to begin each chapter with a review of the available evidence for a given problem (e.g., the spread of cultivated land in the 12th–13th centuries), then to cite particular cases to illustrate our knowledge of that problem, and finally to propose (with all due reserve) a few tentative generalizations in the form of concrete, testable hypotheses. His covert method is rather different. He has adopted the conclusions of his predecessors (Bloch of course, but Pirenne, Dopsch, and many others as well) as a tacit program for his book. The issues which they have identified as primary form the framework of his discussion. In a sense, he proceeds by accepting their statement of the issues, but critically dissects their hypotheses about them, and where necessary replaces them by revised and more nuanced statements. His method is thus scientific in a strict sense of the term, and provides an excellent model of how to proceed on the basis of very spotty evidence—at least if a field of study has already generated a substantial body of working hypotheses.

The contrasting but complementary approaches of Bloch and Duby can provide a methodological framework for further reading. The most convenient way to approach the voluminous literature is probably through the *Cambridge Economic History of Europe, I: The Agrarian Life of the Middle Ages* (1st ed., 1942; 2nd revised ed., 1966). (This work, like Duby's, has a very substantial bibliographie raisonnée.) Reference-survey works of this kind are not to be read naively as a mine of brute fact, but rather should be studied for the insights into sources, problems, and strategies which they can yield when used critically.

If we move from Latin Europe to the Central Islamic Lands, can we find any works displaying the same conceptual and methodological sophistication as those just reviewed? A study which attempts (with considerable success) to build a bridge between Europe and the Islamic world is Thomas F. Glick, *Irrigation and Society in Medieval Valencia* (1970). Glick divides his investigation into two parts: first, a reconstruction, based on very extensive archival and archaeological data, of the irrigation communities of the Christian Kingdom of Valencia between the 13th and 15th centuries; second, an effort to locate the roots of this irrigation system (both its technological and administrative apparatus) in the much less well attested period of Muslim domination. Glick's study suggests as well as any how we can follow the dictum of Bloch to work from a recent "known" to a remoter "unknown." Glick's research was eased by a number of factors which can not always be obtained in the Islamic field, to be sure—e.g., easy access to the region, and a rich body of archival sources directly concerned with irrigation. But his advantages should not be overestimated. The Arabic texts are very sparse, and the cultural politics of modern Spain have created a thicket of polemics over the last century or so.

Within the Muslim world proper, we now have one work which attempts a comprehensive account of rural life and the peasantry, and through which we can obtain something like Bloch's "known" for the region which it studies. Lucette Valensi, *Fellahs tunisiens: l'économie rurale et la vie des campagnes aux 18e et 19e siècles* (1977); English trans. by Beth Archer, *Tunisian Peasants in the 18th and 19th Centuries* (1985), is striking for its comprehensiveness, its conceptual sophistication, and its documentation. Like Glick, Valensi is fortunate in the period she has chosen. She has a nearly complete series of state fiscal registers for the period that she studies, and can draw on nearby European archives as well (e.g., those of the Marseilles Chamber of Commerce). We shall have occasion elsewhere in this chapter to note how valuable the Ottoman archives can be for late medieval and early modern agrarian history, but she is the first to use them systematically for this purpose. Second, the French occupation of the country in 1881 means that its geography and ethnography were closely surveyed during the decades immediately following the period studied by her. Third, both Arab and foreign visitors have criss-crossed the country for centuries and have given us a very substantial descriptive literature. Finally, she has as background to her study the classic work of Robert Brunschwig, *La Berbérie orientale sous les Hafsides* (2 vols., 1940–47). Such a documentation, both direct and contextual, would be hard to match for earlier periods and for many other regions. On the other hand, it is not there just for the picking; to use it requires enormous labor and intelligence. Valensi's work is deeply informed by the concepts and concerns of contemporary anthropology, and these she uses to achieve a comprehensive interpretation of her subject. Almost every aspect of rural life is linked together in a pattern of historical change—physical environment, the material and symbolic dimensions of life (from grain varieties to wedding ceremonies), and socio-political structures (including both lineage patterns and the state apparatus).

For North Africa, at least, we now have a starting point for historical research into remoter periods, based on the era just before Tunisia's integration into a European-dominated world market and all the changes brought by that process. Surely something of the kind could be done for many other areas—Egypt and Syria-Palestine at least, and perhaps also parts of Iran. Such research would do much to end the dependence of historians of the countryside on the late 19th-20th century (the colonial and modernizing periods) as a model and point of reference for the practices and institutions of medieval times.

Given our current situation, however, what can be done? We might begin by asking what a comprehensive history of rural life would look like. If it is to center on the peasant himself, it must include all the things, from weather to market conditions, which govern his thinking and behavior. At the same time, it must see these elements not as ends in themselves, but as forming the environment within which the peasant shapes his social institutions and his culture. In an ideal world, we might well start with a close description of these latter topics, expanding outward from them to include whatever aspects of the natural and social environment seemed necessary to elucidate our principal themes. In terms of the final presentation of our material, this might well be an appropriate literary strategy to adopt. As a research strategy, however, it will not work at all for medieval times, because (as a general rule) we have so little direct access to peasant life and culture. It is necessary first to define the environment, and then to use our knowledge of this to help us decipher the scattered hints and casual descriptions which we find in our sources.

The peasant's life begins with the soil he works. Geographical determinism has no place in modern historical thought, but it is undeniable that climate and landscape set the parameters, the limits of possibility, in a peasant's life. The story of any peasant community is in large part a story of how it has come to terms with its physical environment.

This implies a second level of inquiry—viz., what technologies have been devised to give peasant communities some advantages beyond the hunter-gatherer, some small measure of predictability and control in a range of extremely demanding physical settings? Technology is a deceptive word; it suggests tools and machines, and obviously it makes a real difference to a farmer whether he has a sickle, a scythe, or a mechanical harvester. But in fact "technology" should be understood to include the whole array of arts by which people adapt themselves to their environment, and try to shape an environment to their own goals. We must think of the choice of crops grown, of techniques of water management, even forms of labor organization. Likewise, we must recognize that no peasant solves such problems of environmental management *ex nihilo*. On the contrary, any peasantry is always heir to long-established traditional solutions to such problems. Here we must be careful: traditions, however firmly rooted, do change, but usually slowly and quietly; innovation occurs, but mostly within an established and apparently even rigid context. Abrupt major changes in agricultural technology are likely to come from external actors—new ethnic groups which have settled alongside or supplanted older ones, or some figure from outside the village (perhaps a ruler or a capitalist) who has decided to invest in a lucrative new crop. Changes of this kind inevitably disrupt the whole fabric of peasant society, and for that reason alone are unlikely to have stemmed from a peasantry which lives too close to the bone to take such risks.

Just as soil and water imply technology, so in its turn technology implies social structure. We have already noted that technology is a social artifact, the creation of a collectivity over a long period of time. In a very real sense, a given technology shapes and maintains a social order; the kinds of tasks that need to be done will tend to maintain a certain division of labor within a group, and hence the class and status differences implied by this division. Conversely, existing class and status differences will shape the ways in which work is divided. Technology and society are each mirrors to the other, and each is unintelligible without its counterpart.

We should not fall into the Marxist fallacy of supposing that technology—the "means of production"—rigidly determines a social order in the manner suggested by the statement, "the hand-mill gives us a society with a feudal lord; the steam-mill gives us a society with an industrial capitalist." (Cited in E. H. Carr, *What is History?* [1961], p. 60.) If nothing else, the enormous differences between societies with a roughly similar technological base should disabuse us of any such mechanistic connections. To comprehend the peasant's world, we need to comprehend the whole set of mutual relations (with family, clan, fellow villagers, and outsiders) within which he acted on a regular, predictable basis. Here an almost endless series of questions arises: what was the basic unit of settlement, how was membership within it defined, how were the available resources (land, water, tools, seed, labor, credit, etc.) allocated to its members, what things determined one's rank and status within the settlement, what ties (besides common residence) linked the members of a settlement, what decisions were made within the settlement and by what processes . . . ?

Peasant societies do not exist within a vacuum, of course; we have several times referred to "outsiders" already. But these external actors are a very real element in peasant society, no less a part of the web of human interaction than one's kinsman or neighbor. We need to know who these external actors are (landlords, tax-collectors, merchants) and in what ways they make their presence felt, through taxes, corvees, rents, the administration of justice, etc. Especially when the outsiders are powerful, as is usually the case, it is tempting to think of peasant society as a passive victim of their machinations. A victim the peasant may be, but he is not passive, and we need to look at how he shapes his society and patterns of action in order to deal with the threats and possibilities presented by external actors.

Finally, we need to move beyond the "objective" realities of physical setting, technology, and social structure, to look for "the symbolic dimensions of social action" (Geertz, *The Interpretation of Cultures*, p. 30), for the ways in which peasants have described and interpreted their own lives. The study of culture, defined in this way, does not involve a different subject matter from what we have so far discussed; we are viewing the same soils, tools, tax systems, etc. as before. But now we want to know what value and meaning were ascribed by the peasants to this body of experience. At this point the voicelessness of the medieval peasant comes back to haunt us, but simply to have asked the question is to begin to think of at least some ways of getting answers.

All the above adds up to an extremely ambitious agenda. To what degree can we hope to carry it out? The response to this will differ according to the aspect of rural life that we examine.

A. The Physical Setting

For this dimension of his subject the historian is remarkably well off. Not only is the landscape there to be observed, but it has also been the subject of a growing number of increasingly sophisticated studies, some concerned with the contemporary situation, others with historical change within the natural environment over the last ten to fifteen millenia. The standard handbook in English has long been W. B. Fisher, *The Middle East: a Physical, Social, and Regional Geography* (orig. ed., 1950; currently in 7th rev. ed., 1978). Perhaps more modern in conception, and very effectively presented, is P. Beaumont, G. H. Blake, and J. M. Wagstaff, *The Middle East: a Geographical Study* (1976); it does not give such even coverage as Fisher, but in turn it is better focused on specific topics and problems, among which agriculture is very well represented. See also W. C. Brice, *Southwest Asia* (1966); and P. Birot and J. Dresch, *La Méditerranée et le Moyen Orient* (2 vols., 1953–56; revised edition of vol. I, on the Western Mediterranean, 1964). The latter is detailed and wide-ranging; however, its geological concepts and information are of course obsolete by now, and it does not include areas east of the Tigris River. From general overviews of this kind, we can move to a number of regional and country surveys. Recent examples would include the following:

a. J. Despois and R. Raynal, *Géographie de l'Afrique du Nord-Ouest* (1967): arranged on a country-by-country basis, and within each, district-by-district.

b. E. Wirth, *Syrien: eine geographische Landeskunde* (1971): primarily an economic geography (and one of outstanding quality), but opening with a substantial survey of the physical geography of Syria.

c. E. Wirth, *Agrargeographie des Irak* (1962).

d. *Cambridge History of Iran, I: The Land of Iran*, ed. by W. B. Fisher (1968): uneven, but by far the most comprehensive survey of this vast and complex area.

e. Xavier de Planhol, *De la plaine pamphylienne aux lacs pisidiens, nomadisme et vie paysanne* (1958): on southwestern Anatolia.

Surveys like those just noted are absolutely indispensable, but they can also be somewhat misleading. Surveys naturally have a contemporary orientation, but in many crucial respects natural environments may have changed significantly even in historic times. A classic example would be the systematic deforestation of Anatolia in Hellenistic and Roman times, a process studied in a well-known article of W. C. Brice, "The Turkish Colonization of Anatolia" (*BJRL*, 1955). In many places once substantial mineral deposits have been depleted, fertile soils salinized. In brief, a physical geography which is adequate for our purposes must be historically conceived; it must try to identify the patterns of change in landscape and climate. And because many (though not all) of these changes are connected with a human presence, such a geography must treat human exploitation and occupation as an integral part of the processes it describes. Most of the geographies surveyed above are quite aware of these issues, to be sure, but their information on environmental change—and in particular the land-man dimension of it—tends to be somewhat secondhand. At times they even seem to resort to the speculations of historians who knew no geography.

We certainly do not have enough historically oriented studies, but some well-documented and challenging material is available. A collective work edited for UNESCO has several useful contributions: L. Dudley Stamp, *A History of Land Use in Arid Regions* (1961). Of particular value are F. K. Hare, "The causation of the arid zone," pp. 25–30, and K. W. Butzer, "Climatic change in arid regions since the Pliocene," pp. 31–56. A collection which focuses almost wholly on long-term natural processes is W. C. Brice, ed., *The Environmental History of the Near and Middle East since the Last Ice Age* (1978). Though of little direct value for the physical environment of the Islamic period, this collection does help establish the rather narrow parameters of climatic change over the last several millenia, and warns historians away from a facile reliance on such factors to explain great historic movements.

B. Technology and the Human Impact

At this point we can no longer sustain the illusion that the natural environment is an autonomous, self-contained system; we need to examine the impact of human settlement and—more narrowly—to ask what kinds of tools and techniques man has devised to shape nature to his own purposes. An introduction (by no means entirely satisfactory) to this problem is R. O. Whyte, "Evolution of land-use in south-western Asia," in Stamp, *History of Land Use in Arid Regions* (1961). On a more detailed level, we can begin at the beginning with the widely cited articles of K. V. Flannery: "The Ecology of Early Food Production in Mesopotamia," *Science*, cxlvii, no. 3663 (1965), 1247–1255; and "The Origins and Ecological Effects of Early Domestication in Iran and the Near East" (in P. J. Ucko and G. W. Dimbleby, *The Domestication and Exploitation of Plants and Animals*, 1969).

Once we reach the historic period, a larger number of studies are available. These, however, tend to focus on two areas, the great flood-plains of the Nile and the lower Tigris-Euphrates. Second, they tend to focus on the ancient periods, before the Islamic conquests and even before Alexander. In this context, the Islamic period is mostly regarded as a kind of appendage to the problems posed by the rise of the first great civilizations in these regions, and vast areas of crucial importance like the Iranian plateau and Syria-Palestine are largely ignored.

By far the most impressive set of studies are those dealing with lower Iraq and southwestern Iran (Khuzistan). One should begin with the extremely influential study of Robert McC. Adams, *Land Behind Baghdad: a History of Settlement on the Diyala Plains* (1965). Adams is concerned with the origins and development (down to the end of the 19th century) of the irrigation network of the alluvial plain between the Tigris and Diyala Rivers, and with the patterns and density of settlement which this network has supported during the 6000 years of its existence. His principal tool for this reconstruction is the surface survey—a technique worked out some fifty years ago by Thorkild Jacobsen but never previously applied so systematically and on such a large scale. A surface survey is simply the collection, identification, and tabulation of ceramic fragments found on the surface of the area being studied; it is based on the assumption that in continuously inhabited zones where the soil is constantly being turned over, the quantity and distribution of surface shards will reflect the relative densities of settlement throughout the whole history of human occupation. (See also a systematic elaboration of this method in C. E. Redman and P. L. Watson, "Systematic, Intensive Surface Collection," *American Antiquity*, xxv [1970], 279–291.)

Adams integrates the data thus collected, first with information on the geomorphology of the area, and then with what is known about its human ecology (including of course techniques of traditional agriculture). Moving from a contemporary-ecological framework to a historical one, he tries to correlate the data of the shards with a sketch (based largely on textual evidence) of the socio-political development of the region. It should be stressed that this is just a sketch, a framework for a rural-agrarian history, but not the history itself. Its logic is very clear, and it is based on a broad and imaginatively used documentation, but Adams' statements are very general indeed, with only some illustrative detail. Even so, it is the most impressive study of the relationship between man and his environment that Middle Eastern studies has produced, and the indispensable starting point for further work.

Adams has extended and refined his work for other districts of Mesopotamia; this has now been synthesized (with some important revisions regarding the Diyala plain) in *Heartland of Cities: Surveys of Ancient Settlement and Land Use on the Central Floodplain of the Euphrates* (1981). In addition to surface surveys, this work uses aerial and LANDSAT photos, and interprets its array of data through some rather sophisticated statistical tools. All of Adams' work is characterized by a constant interplay between history and anthropological-geographical theory on one level, between data and its methodological implications on another. With Valensi, then, it can stand as a model for the kind of work required for the history of the Middle Eastern peasantry and countryside.

An essay which attempts to combine archaeology and contemporary anthropology to analyze the human impact on the Tigris-Euphrates floodplain is McGuire Gibson, "Violation of Fallow and Engineered Disaster in Mesopotamian Civilization," in M. Gibson and T. E. Downing, *Irrigation's Impact on Society* (1974), pp. 7–20. Gibson's thesis is simple and provocative: that a relatively stable agriculture on the Tigris-Euphrates alluvium requires a low-level extensive exploitation of the soil, something which occurs only in a context of weak, decentralized government control, where local communities make most of the decisions regarding investment and production. In contrast, highly centralized states pursue policies of short-term revenue maximization through massive irrigation schemes, intensive exploitation of the soil, etc. Inevitably this leads to a system breakdown and near-catastrophic agricultural regression. Although he is describing a recurrent pattern in the region, he finds his model of social structure and political action in the Iraq of the late 1950s, as analyzed by R. W. Fernea, *Shaykh and Effendi: Changing Patterns of Authority among the El Shabana of Southern Iraq* (1970). The importance of contemporary anthropology, both theory and substantive findings, for the reconstruction of medieval rural society is a theme which will often recur in this chapter.

Though Khuzistan belongs to the Tigris-Euphrates complex both geographically and historically, it has been much less intensively studied than Mesopotamia. Adams however contributed an early article "Agriculture and urban life in early southwest Iran," *Science*, cxxxvi (1961), 109–122. His conclusions have been tested for a rather remote corner of the region by J. A. Neely, "Sassanian and early Islamic water-control and irrigation systems on the Deh Luran Plain, Iran" (Downing and Gibson, *Irrigation's Impact on Society*, [1974], pp. 21–42).

The Jazira and Syria have not benefited from long-range ecological studies of this kind, and only for Egypt do we again find an important one, though it is on a distinctly smaller scale than Adams' work: K. W. Butzer, *Early Hydraulic Civilization in Egypt: a Study in Cultural Ecology* (1976). Butzer's analysis rests not on the surface survey, but on geomorphological evidence combined with the rich literary and archaeological record of ancient Egypt. He focuses on the centuries preceding Alexander's conquest; even so, his conclusions as to irrigation technology, demography, and settlement patterns are of great value for the Islamic historian. He does not give us a full history of these matters—certainly not for the Islamic period—but he does construct an invaluable framework to guide such a history. His argument can be compared with that of G. Hamdan, "Evolution of irrigation agriculture in Egypt" (Stamp, *History of Land-Use in Arid Regions*, 1961), pp. 119–142, whose survey comes down to modern times.

The studies so far reviewed deal with ecological issues—i.e., with the relationship between man and his environment, and in particular with the ways in which human settlement has altered the landscape through attempts to channel massive amounts of water in riverine floodplains. At this point we want to move to technology in a more specific sense, the tools and techniques which people have devised in order to exact a livelihood from the soil. To a very large degree, our knowledge about agricultural technology in medieval Islam is based on extrapolation from modern observation rather than contemporary documentation. For this reason, we must be especially alert to the question of how much agricultural technology has changed over the centuries. Technology is not an indivisible whole; some elements may have seen marked innovations, others have remained much the same since ancient times. It is a natural temptation to assume stability and conservatism, but we should not blandly assert this without evidence to support it. A terse overview of the subject can be gotten from "Filāḥa," *EI*², ii, 899–910 (various authors).

It seems sensible to begin our survey with the crops themselves, for the selection of plants to be cultivated is the basis of any agricultural technology. To a large degree, Muslim peasants everywhere must have continued the grain-centered agriculture of ancient times. But in recent decades a number of studies have been published arguing that a vast array of new crops (and with them new techniques) was introduced to the Middle East in the early Middle Ages, between the 6th and 9th centuries. These were predominantly cash crops (e.g., sugar, cotton, indigo) and fruits, and they spread rapidly throughout the Islamic world, though only slowly and much later did they become widespread in non-Islamic Mediterranean lands, such as Italy, Christian Spain, or southern France. The most systematic attempt to deal with this phenomenon will be found in the writings of A. M. Watson, which are summed up in *Agricultural Innovation in the Early Islamic World* (1983), which contains a very full bibliography and lengthy critical notes. Watson seems rather an enthusiast in places, but his documentation is very wide-ranging and he uses it well. Watson is not the only scholar to have dealt with this issue; among others, see M. Canard, "Le riz dans le Proche Orient aux premiers siècles de l'Islam," *Arabica*, vi (1959), 113–131.

The "green revolution" described by Watson obviously had tremendous social and economic consequences, but for the moment we are only concerned with the tools and techniques needed to exploit this new array of crops. We are surprisingly well off in this regard, though serious chronological and regional gaps remain. First, we have a substantial body of agronomic texts from the medieval Islamic world (chiefly from Iraq and Andalus, but from Mamluk Egypt as well). Second, archaeology has revealed a wealth of information from ancient (but not medieval) times. Finally, we have numerous descriptions of 19th and 20th-century agricultural practice from European observers; many of these are casual, and almost all lack a valid historical perspective, but even so they yield a useful starting point for the interpretation of medieval and ancient data. For some regions, it would be possible to write a solid, well-documented history of agricultural technology from the earliest times down to the present. It is also true that this daunting labor has yet to be undertaken.

For Iran, start with the fine study (based on field observations made in the 1930s, well before the beginning of any serious "modernization" in the Iranian countryside) of Hans E. Wulff, *The Traditional Crafts of Persia* (1966). A.K.S. Lambton also includes a chapter on farming methods in her *Landlord and Peasant in Persia* (1953); her information too is based largely on field observations (from the 1940s), and it too antedates modernization. Finally, there is the concise general survey of H. Bowen-Jones, "Agriculture," in *Cambridge History of Iran*, i (1968), 565–598.

In most of Iran irrigation is the crucial art, and the characteristic device of the underground canal, the *qanāt* or *kārīz*, has attracted a vast literature. In addition to the preceding titles, see (a) D. J. Flower, "Water Use in North-east Iran" (*Cambridge History of Iran*, i [1968], 599–610); (b) Brian Spooner, "Irrigation and society: the Iranian plateau" (Downing and Gibson, *Irrigation's Impact on Society* [1974], 43–58); (c) P. W. English, *City and Village in Iran* (1966), and "The origin and spread of qanāts in the Old World" (*Proceedings, APS*, cxii (1968), 170–181. A regional variant is discussed in J. C. Wilkinson, *Water and Tribal Settlement in South-east Arabia; a Study of the Aflāj of Oman* (1977). The monographs of English and Wilkinson go far beyond technical matters, to deal with the social, economic and legal milieu and significance of irrigation technology.

The tools and farming techniques of ancient and medieval Iran are regrettably much less well served. Except for the very beginnings of settled agriculture on the Plateau (studied most notably by R. J. Braidwood) very little rural-oriented archaeology has been done, and the texts have little to say. There are useful but brief comments in Lambton, "Aspects of Agricultural Organization and Agrarian History in Persia" (*HO*, I/vi/6, 1 [1977]). In regard to medieval times, something can be gleaned from administrative texts (mostly Timurid and Safavid in date) and from the geographers like Ibn Ḥawqal and al-Muqaddasī. On the whole, however, we must reconstruct medieval agricultural technology in Iran by extrapolation from our knowledge of the early 20th century. This expedient is dangerous but unavoidable. Only if we are very certain just what we are looking for can an occasional text be found to confirm or deny a "null hypothesis" of technological stability and conservatism.

Lower Iraq presents a very different picture. Here we have rather little on contemporary agriculture, though the principal exception is a very important piece of work: Eugen Wirth, *Agrargeographie des Irak* (1962). In contrast, we are fairly well-informed on ancient and medieval times. The complex irrigation system of the region has of course drawn most attention. In addition to the studies of Adams and Gibson (above), see the following: Aḥmad Sūsa (LC spelling, Ahmed Sousa), *Irrigation in Iraq* (1945), and *al-Rayy wa'l-ḥaḍāra fī wādī al-Rāfidayn* (1968); E. de Vaumas, "Études irakiennes (2eme serie): le contrôle et l'utilisation des eaux du Tigre et de l'Euphrate," *Revue de géographie alpine*, xlvi (1958), 235–331. These should be compared with an early 11th century fiscal text translated and studied by Claude Cahen, "Le service de l'irrigation en Iraq au début de xie siècle," *BEO*, xii (1949–51), 117–143.

The whole range of agricultural tools and methods are surveyed in a useful study by H. Q. al-Samarraie, *Agriculture in Iraq during the 3rd Century A.H.* (1972). (Unfortunately this book is marred by many misprints, and its numerical data in particular should always be confirmed.) A degree of direct comparison is possible between early Abbasid and Sassanian times through the study of J. Newman, *The Agricultural Life of the Jews in Babylonia between the Years 200 C.E. and 500 C.E.* (1932). Some caution is called for: Newman is dealing with a confessional community whose customs differed in important ways from the Christian and Muslim peasantry described by Samarraie, and his principal source, the Babylonian Talmud, gives a distinctive slant to his data. Finally, some material on ancient agriculture is furnished by A. Salonen, *Agricultura Mesopotamia nach sumerisch-akkadischen Quellen* (1968).

Medieval Iraq has given us a most remarkable text, which sums up the whole agricultural tradition of Mesopotamia from Seleucid times to the tenth century; this is the *Nabataean Agriculture* (*al-Filāḥa al-nabaṭiyya*) attributed to Ibn Waḥshiyya, an obscure and controversial figure supposed to have flourished in the early tenth century. (A summary of the scholarly disputes about Ibn Waḥshiyya can be found in the article on him by T. Fahd in *EI*², iii, 988–990.) But whatever the provenance, authenticity, and authorship of this vast opus, it certainly represents the agronomic lore available in Iraq ca. 900 A.D., and it had a great influence on later Muslim agronomists from Iran to Andalus. Though there are several manuscripts, the work has never been edited or translated in its entirety, no doubt due to doubts as to its authenticity. A detailed survey of its contents is provided by T. Fahd, "Matériaux pour l'histoire de l'agriculture en Iraq: *al-Filāḥa n-Nabaṭiyya*" (*HO*, I/vi/6, 1; [1977]). Among many studies by the same author of Ibn Waḥshiyya, two are particularly pertinent to our concerns: "Conduite d'une exploitation agricole d'après l'Agriculture nabatéenne," *SI*, xxxii (1970), 109–128; and "Le calendrier de travaux agricoles d'après al-Filāḥa n-Nabaṭiyya" (*Mélanges Pareja*, i [1974], 245–272).

Beyond the Nabataean Agriculture and a few botanical works (like the *Kitāb al-Nabāt* of Abū Ḥanīfa al-Dīnawarī, ed. B. Lewin, 1953), much useful data on Iraq as on other places may be gleaned from the geographers. In addition to the standard works in the *BGA*, see Guy Le Strange, "Description of Mesopotamia and Baghdad, written about the year 900 A.D. by Ibn Serapion," *JRAS* (1895), 1–76, 255–315. The geographers' work on Iraq and Iran is conveniently paraphrased in Le Strange, *Lands of the Eastern Caliphate* (1905). The geographers have nothing to say directly about farming tools and techniques, but something can be reconstructed by combining our knowledge of recent times with such hints as the types of crops grown. An emphasis on barley as a district's staple crop, for example, would suggest high soil salinity, limited water supplies, and winter cropping. But if a district is identified as a major rice producer, we would expect to find ample water and good drainage (or newly opened lands). Rice also demands very distinctive techniques, and so we might ask whether we are dealing with a new population of cultivators, or with an old one somehow retrained for a new array of tasks.

Our direct knowledge of medieval Iraq is not matched by Syria-Palestine; here our information is concentrated at the chronological limits—Biblical antiquity on one side, the late 19th and 20th centuries on the other. There is also a regional imbalance, which is very likely to distort the conclusions of those with a taste for broad generalizations. For obvious reasons we know most about Palestine, although the oasis of Damascus and the Orontes valley have also attracted considerable interest. Very much less has been done in regard to North Syria, the Hawran, and the interior steppe. Our written sources for medieval Islamic times are sparse—a few bits of data in the geographers and chroniclers, but no agronomic works and no major administrative texts of the kind we shall find for Egypt. In compensation, there are the Ottoman archives (so far examined in regard to rural life only for Palestine), and some tantalizing fragments from the Crusader states.

For the 20th century a number of good surveys are available. The most recent is that of Eugen Wirth, *Syrien: eine Geographische Landeskunde* (1971), already cited; chapters 3 and 5, dealing with crop distributions, water management, etc., are especially pertinent here. The book does have a strong contemporary focus, however, and since systematic modernization was already well underway when it was written, it must be used with great care for earlier periods. From the 1930s three good regional geographies can be mentioned:

1. Richard Thoumin, *Géographie humaine de la Syrie centrale* (1936).
2. J. Weulersse, *Le pays des Alaouites* (2 vols., 1940).
3. Idem, *L'Oronte: étude de fleuve* (1940).

On farming in particular, valuable guidance will be found in André Latron, *La vie rurale en Syrie et au Liban* (1936), and in the classic survey of Weulersse, *Paysans de Syrie et du Proche Orient* (1946). All of these works are redolent of the conceptions and concerns of the French Mandate, but their substantive information on agricultural methods and land use remains valid. Finally, the complex irrigation system of Damascus and its oasis are analyzed in the previously cited article by R. Tresse, "L'irrigation dans la Ghouta de Damas," *REI*, iii (1929), 461–574.

Palestine in the early 20th century is treated in two old works: (a) Arthur Ruppin, *Syrien als Wirtschaftsgebiet* (1917), who includes also such information as he could obtain on the rest of Syria; (b) the massive compilation of Gustav Dalman, *Arbeit und Sitte in Palästina* (6 vols. 1928–39), in which vols. I and II are most relevant to our concerns.

For the Islamic Middle Ages, we have only brief essays. The only attempt at a general statement is N. Elisséeff, *Nūr al-Dīn* (3 vols., 1967), iii, 875–900. In fact many of his statements are simple extrapolations from those to be found in the French accounts of modern Syria mentioned above, or in a very valuable study by Joshua Prawer first published in 1952, and recently revised and expanded in his *Crusader Institutions* (1980), pp. 169–180, 184–187. Some points can also be gleaned, along with much good critical advice, from an article of Claude Cahen, "Le régime rural syrien au temps de la domination franque," *BFLUS* (1951), 286–310. A recent study with a promising title (though I have been unable to see it), is Fāliḥ Ḥusayn, *al-Ḥayāt al-zirāʿiyya fī Bilād al-Shām fī al-ʿaṣr al-umawī* (1978).

Is there no more to be learned than the meager yield of these three studies? Perhaps a more extended scrutiny of the sources we have would yield worthwhile returns. It is clear that the Ottoman archives can tell us a good deal about crops, rotations, etc., though very little about the daily work of the farmer. This statement is borne out by the detailed maps of agricultural revenues, broken down by crop, which have been constructed by W.-D. Hütteroth and K. Abdulfattah on the basis of the Ottoman census of 1596–97: *Historical Geography of Palestine, Transjordan, and Southern Syria in the Late 16th Century* (1977). The data of the fiscal registers (*defter-i mufassal*) used by them can be extended by examining the regulations of the Ottoman *kanun-namehs*. A convenient introduction to those issued for Syria is R. Mantran and J. Sauvaget, *Règlements fiscaux ottomans: les provinces syriennes* (1951)—on which see above, pp. 172, 231. There is doubtless an enormous amount of information buried in the *sharīʿa*-court records and *awqāf* registers, for anyone prepared to face the frightful task of ferreting it out.

To what extent can we legitimately extend Ottoman-based data to earlier times? It is unlikely that the 15th century would pose any problems. But for earlier centuries, any statement of continuity would have to rest on an explicit (and as yet undemonstrated) thesis of technological conservatism or stagnation. And even if tools remain much the same from Roman to modern times, the choice of crops, rotations, and the organization of labor are still subject to change. What the Ottoman archives give us, for a few topics, is a solid point of reference at the very end of the epoch surveyed in this book. We must be careful about demanding more information from them than they really have to give.

For Mamluk times, there is a limited administrative literature. It was composed mostly by Egyptians (hence at second-hand in regard to Syrian conditions), and has received very little notice from modern scholars. An exception to this latter stricture is a brief passage in al-Nuwayrī, *Nihāyat al-arab* (composed ca. 1320), translated and studied by Cl. Cahen, "Aperçu sur les impôts du sol en Syria au Moyen Age," *JESHO*, xviii (1975), 233–244; and cited also in Prawer, *Crusader Institutions*, 173. Some bits of data (but disappointingly few) might be extracted from Qalqashandī's *Ṣubḥ al-aʿshā*, of which relevant portions are translated by Maurice Gaudefroy-Demombynes, *La Syrie à l'époque des Mameloukes* (1923). The most valuable of these texts would probably be al-ʿUmarī's *Masālik al-abṣār* (composed ca. 1320), but as noted previously this massive work remains almost unstudied for Egypt and Syria. For pre-Crusade times we have only the geographers, whose work is summarized in Guy Le Strange, *Palestine under the Moslems* (1890). (Note that Le Strange treats Aleppo as a northern extension of Palestine.)

The unique water-use system of Egypt has already been noted in connection with the essays of Butzer and Hamdan. In the present technological context, we should add the old study of William Willcocks, the man who more than any other is the founder of the modern system of perennial irrigation in the country: *Egyptian Irrigation* (1st ed. 1889; the 3rd edition, co-authored with J. I. Craig, 1913, is vastly expanded). The actual art of cultivating the soil has received less attention, but even for Islamic times we are moderately well off. A very interesting body of source material, the almanacs or agricultural-fiscal calendars which are imbedded in the administrative texts of al-Makhzūmī, Ibn Mammātī, and al-Maqrīzī, has recently been published and translated by Charles Pellat, *Cinq calendriers égyptiens* (1986). Claude Cahen has contributed two useful studies of the agricultural data in al-Makhzūmī and Ibn Mammātī: (a) "À propos de quelques almanachs et calendriers de l'Égypte médiévale," *JESHO*, v (1962), 151–159; (b) "Al-Makhzūmī and Ibn Mammātī sur l'agriculture égyptienne médiévale," *AI*, xi (1972), 141–151. (Both items are reprinted in *Makhzumiyyat*.) A good concise synthesis of the subject is given by R. S. Cooper, "Agriculture in Egypt, 640–1800" (*HO*, I/vi/6, 1; [1977]). A detailed survey of irrigation techniques and crops, based on medieval Arabic texts, is given by D. Müller-Wodarg, "Die Landwirtschaft Ägyptens in der frühen Abbasidenzeit," *Islam*, xxxi (1954), 174–227; xxxii (1955–57), 14–78, 141–167; xxxiii (1958), 310–321. Finally, for Mamluk times there is a superbly documented piece from Hassanein Rabie, "Some Technical Aspects of Agriculture in Medieval Egypt," in Udovitch, *The Islamic Middle East, 700–1900* (1981), pp. 59–90. This work, laudable as it is, of course only constitutes a beginning of what is possible; the uniquely rich sources for Egypt could support systematic studies along these lines for almost every period.

The traditional-style technology of early modern times, which provides an invaluable point of reference for the interpretation of medieval statements, can be approached through the attractive though somewhat sentimental book of H. H. Ayrout, *Moeurs et coutumes des fellahs* (1938); English trans. (with revisions) by J. A. Williams, *The Egyptian Peasant* (1963). More systematic are the two volumes by G. P. Foaden and F. Fletcher, *Textbook of Egyptian Agriculture* (1908). The statements of this and Ayrout's account have to be used with caution, however; although Foaden and Fletcher antedate any modern-style mechanization and even the broad extension of perennial (as opposed to basin) irrigation, the crops grown at the turn of the century were very different from those of medieval times. Moreover, the land-tenure system was far removed from that of any previous period, and this fact must have affected farming practices in many direct and indirect ways. So it is still worth looking at the pioneer effort at a systematic, scientific description of Egyptian agriculture—M.P.S. Girard, "Mémoire sur l'agriculture, l'industrie, et le commerce de l'Égypte," in the great *Description de l'Égypte* produced by the savants of Napoleon's expedition.

Antiquity, both Pharaonic and Hellenistic-Roman, is represented by a number of substantial works, among which see the following:

a. Fernande Hartmann, *L'agriculture dans l'ancienne Égypte* (1923).
b. M. Schnebel, *Die Landwirtschaft in hellenistischen Ägypten* (1925).
c. Naphtali Lewis, *Life in Egypt under Roman Rule* (1983).

From Egypt we shall pass directly to Spain, a region of unusual interest because of its geographical isolation from the Islamic East, but even more because Islamic Spain saw a synthesis of two distinct agronomic traditions—one the Iraqi tradition of Ibn Waḥshiyya, the other inherited directly from the Roman world. Of all the Islamic lands, Spain produced the richest and most complex science of agriculture.

What the Roman tradition was, both in theory and practice, can conveniently be studied through K. D. White, *Roman Farming* (1970), and the same author's *Agricultural Implements of the Roman World* (1967). White focuses on Italy, but he has some examples from Spain and North Africa as well. White's work should henceforth be the foundation of any serious study on the agricultural history of the Western Mediterranean; his study can be compared with two chapters in the *Cambridge Economic History of Europe*, I (1966): (a) C. E. Stevens, "Agriculture and Rural Life in the Later Roman Empire," and (b) Charles Parain, "The Evolution of Agricultural Technique."

There is nothing quite so concrete and detailed as White's work for Islamic Spain, but the agronomic tradition of that country and its practical applications have been studied in an important monograph by Lucie Bolens: *Les méthodes culturales au Moyen Age d'après les traités d'agronomes andalous: traditions et techniques* (1974); reprinted as *Agronomes andalous du Moyen Age* (1981), with three new technical studies appended. A brief statement of her conclusions can be found in "L'agriculture hispano-arabe au Moyen Age" (*HO*, I/vi/6, 1; [1977]). Some of the agronomic texts which she has analyzed are available in translation. Of these the most important is doubtless Ibn al-ʿAwāmm, *Kitāb al-filāḥa*: Arabic text published by Banqueri (1802); French trans. by J. J. Clément-Mullet (2 vols. in 3; 1864–67). The very influential text of Ibn Baṣṣāl, *Kitāb al-qaṣd wa'l-bayān* (The Book of Proposition and Demonstration) is available in two forms: (a) a medieval Castilian abridgement, ed. J. M. Millas-Vallicrosa, *Andalus*, xiii (1948), 356–430; (b) an Arabic text, based on fragmentary and anonymous manuscripts, published as *Kitāb al-filāḥa* by Millas-Vallicrosa and M. Aziman (1955). The famous Calendar of Cordova, a miscellany of all sorts of data, seems to have some links with the Egyptian tradition in this genre; see Charles Pellat, *Le calendrier de Cordoue* (1961). As to the other textual sources for Spanish-Islamic agriculture, they are valuable but less characteristic; a concise survey of them can be found in the notes to Rachel Arié, "La vie économique de l'Espagne musulmane" (*HO*, I/vi/6, 1; [1977]).

If we combine the statements of the agronomists with the kind of archival and archaeological materials used by Glick (*Irrigation and Society in Medieval Valencia*), we are in a very good position—almost as good as in Egypt, perhaps better than in Iraq—to reconstruct the farming tools and methods of medieval Islamic society. Such a reconstruction would be of particular value in that Spain is ecologically so different from the Nile and the Tigris-Euphrates valleys, so that we can gain some notion of the *range* of technology available to the medieval Muslim farmer.

C. Agriculture and the Social Order

We have already argued that technology reflects a social order: it is not merely the tools themselves but how they are used which shapes an agricultural system. The obvious next step, then, would be to move to a consideration of the village societies, for these constitute the immediate framework for man's accomodation to and exploitation of his environment. But at this point we shall pass over peasant society and culture, because our direct knowledge of this subject is so meager; the medieval texts have almost nothing to say, and no excavations (which would at least tell us something about material culture) have been undertaken for medieval rural sites. We can reconstruct rural societies and cultures with some degree of confidence only if we can establish the total context within which they arose. This context is partly given by the natural environment, partly by the level of technology, but also by the external social, economic, and political forces based in cities and empires. For a peasant, the complex and often cruel machinery of taxes, land tenure, and urban markets were as much a part of his daily reality as the weather, and hardly more controllable. We need, then, to look briefly at the external agencies which affected the peasant's life—at agrarian fiscal administration, land tenure, and urban-based marketing systems. These are obviously major subjects of inquiry in themselves and some have been dealt with in other chapters (see especially Seven and Nine). Here we need only note their effect on rural society.

Lambton's *Landlord and Peasant in Persia* (which should now be supplemented by her *Continuity and Change in Medieval Persia* [1988], especially Chapters Five and Six) focuses on issues of land tenure and agrarian administration. It is a standard reference, valuable not only for Iran but for other areas which passed under the rule of the Seljukids and their successors—Iraq, the Jazira, Anatolia, and Syria. It has vast scope, a wealth of concrete detail based on a good documentation, and sound critical sense. The author's refusal to generalize from the data for a single region or period is likewise laudable. On the other hand, it is a confusing book to read, because Lambton does not really try to integrate her materials. An important interpretation is there beneath the disjointed surface of particular issues and detail, but it will not be located on a first reading. In simplest terms, she argues that the following theses hold true for Iran's agrarian history throughout Islamic times: (1) that Iranian-Islamic high culture (in some contrast to that of ancient times) all but ignores the peasant and his social role, or at best sees him in a utilitarian light as the source of the revenues which support the state and the elite—there is in short a divorce in values, aspirations, and attitudes between the peasant and his masters; (2) the Iranian landlord has typically derived his wealth and power from service to the state, but ironically the state—the central government—was usually too weak to assert effective control over him or to intervene to protect the legal and customary rights of the peasantry even when it desired to do so; (3) until the time of Reza Shah, at least, the Iranian landlord regarded his properties as a source of social status and more or less secure income, but not as an investment which could be rationally managed and developed; hence his capital inputs into his properties were commonly very slight. In contrast to these continuities, of course, she does demonstrate that the institutional forms governing the landlord-peasant relationship have changed constantly, normally in accordance with the characteristics of the central power.

A very important interpretation of one period in medieval Iranian history is provided by I. P. Petrushevsky, "The Socio-Economic History of Iran under the Il-Khans" (*Cambridge History of Iran*, v [1968], 483–537)—essentially an English summary of his fundamental *Zemledelie i agrarnie otnosheniya v Irane XIII–XIV vekov* (1960), available in a good Persian translation by Karīm Kishāvarz, *Kishāvarzī va Munāsabāt-i ʿArżī dar Īrān-i ʿAhd-i Mughul* (2 vols., 1966). Petrushevsky uses a Marxist framework, obviously, but in an analytical rather than a polemical manner; and in the context of this topic it seems a highly effective approach.

The administrative system of Iraq has attracted a great deal of scholarly attention—under the Abbasids it became the model adopted by most states in the eastern Islamic world—but studies focused specifically on land tenure and agrarian administration are few. A recent overview is given in two chapters of al-Samarraie's *Agriculture in Iraq in the 3rd Century A.H.* (1972). Following this, one can plunge into the thicket through several studies of Claude Cahen—provisional, difficult to follow, but always in close touch with reality: (a) "Le service de l'irrigation en Iraq au début du xie siècle," *BEO*, xii (1949–51), 117–143; (b) "Quelques problèmes économiques et fiscaux de l'Iraq buyide d'après un traité de mathématique," *AIEO*, (1952), 326–363; (c) "Fiscalité, propriété, antagonismes sociaux en Haute-Mésopotamie au temps des premiers Abbasides d'après Denys de Tell-Mahré," *Arabica*, i (1954), 136–152; (d) "L'évolution de l'iqṭāʿ du ixe au xiiie siècle," *AESC*, viii (1953), 25–52. (The last three items are reprinted in *Peuples musulmans dans l'histoire médiévale*.) Much data will also be found in A. A. al-Dūrī, *Taʾrīkh al-ʿIrāq al-iqtiṣādī fī'l-qarn al-rābiʿ al-hijrī* (1948). On the early Islamic period, see two contributions in Udovitch, *The Islamic Middle East, 700–1900*: (a) M. G. Morony, "Landholding in Seventh-Century Iraq: Late Sassanian and Early Islamic Patterns," pp. 135–176; (b) I. M. Lapidus, "Arab Settlement and Economic Development of Iraq and Iran in the Age of the Umayyad and Early Abbasid Caliphs," pp. 177–208.

The classic legal texts on the *kharāj* (by Abū Yūsuf, Yaḥyā b. Ādam, and Qudāma b. Jaʿfar) have much to offer the historian of land tenure and rural administration in Iraq. (See above, Chapter Nine, p. 216.) The older scholarly literature on these subjects has been reviewed and criticized in three works:

1. Frede Løkkegaard, *Islamic Taxation in the Classic Period, with Special Reference to Circumstances in Iraq* (1950). Cf. the review by Cahen, *Arabica*, i (1954), 346–353.
2. D. C. Dennett, *Conversion and the Poll-Tax in Early Islam* (1950). (Dennett also contains a long chapter on Egypt, and interesting though rather sketchy chapters on Syria and Khurasan.)
3. H. M. Tabatabaʾi, *Kharāj in Islamic Law* (1983). (A survey and legal critique of the doctrines contained in the texts rather than an effort to establish an objective historical reality.)

The fiscal administration and land-tenure systems of medieval Syria, almost entirely neglected in the literature, can be passed over here. One study on late Ottoman times, based on the *sharīʿa*-court records, should be noted as an example of the sort of data which might also be found for the end of the Mamluk period: A. K. Rafeq, "Economic Relations between Damascus and the Dependent Countryside, 1743–1771" (Udovitch, *The Islamic Middle East*, 653–686). Egyptian administration, at least for Ayyubid and Mamluk times, we have already examined in Chapter Seven; it will suffice here to recall K. Morimoto, *The Fiscal Administration of Egypt in the Early Islamic Period* (1981), and the review article by Michael Brett, "The Way of the Peasant," *BSOAS*, xlvii (1984), 44–56. As regards the marketing systems in operation there, however, some titles should be noted. S. D. Goitein, *A Mediterranean Society, I: Economic Foundations* (1967) is full of invaluable data from the Fatimid period on prices, how goods were bought and sold, etc.; it is descriptive rather than analytic in conception, however, and no ready-made model of the Fatimid marketplace will be found here. Eliyahu Ashtor in contrast tried to construct an economic interpretation of the vast funds of data on prices and wages which he collected over some thirty years, though his interpretations have failed to convince many experienced historians of the medieval Mediterranean world. He provides a general synthesis of his position in *A Social and Economic History of the Near East in the Middle Ages* (1976). But however controversial his economic models, his data deserves serious if critical scrutiny. Among his many works, it will suffice to mention *Histoire des prix et des salaires dans l'Orient médiéval* (1969); and a recent article, "Quelques problèmes que soulève l'histoire des prix dans l'Orient médiéval"—a work which deals largely with 9th/15th century Egypt, in Myriam Rosen-Ayalon, ed., *Studies in Honor of Gaston Wiet* (1977), 203–234. A critique of this piece is given by Boaz Shoshan, "Money Supply and Grain Prices in Fifteenth-Century Egypt," *Economic History Review*, ser. 2, xxxvi (1983), 47–67. An important effort to analyze the ways in which the Mamluk military elite dominated the grain market is given by I. M. Lapidus, "The grain economy of Mamluk Egypt," *JESHO*, xii (1969), 1–15.

North Africa has been rather neglected, but see the well-documented paper of Mohamed Talbi, "Law and Economy in Ifriqiya (Tunisia) in the Third Islamic Century. Agriculture and the Role of Slaves in the Country's Economy," in Udovitch, *The Islamic Middle East*, pp. 209–250.

For Spain, in addition to the article of Rachel Arié already cited in *HO*, we might add the concise chapters on economic life in her thesis on *L'Espagne musulmane au temps des Nasrides, 1232–1492* (1973). Far richer, but dealing only with the tenth century, is Vol. III, *Le siècle du califat de Cordoue*, of E. Lévi-Provençal's classic *Histoire de l'Espagne musulmane* (3 vols., 1944–53), which contains lengthy chapters on agriculture, economic life, and administration. For the two centuries between Lévi-Provençal and Arié, there are useful raw materials to be quarried from C. E. Dubler, "Über das Wirtschaftsleben auf der Iberischen Halbinsel vom XI zum XIII Jahrhundert" (*Romanica Helvetica*, 1943).

If all this material allows us to establish reasonably well the external forces, constraints, and structures within which the peasant tried to shape his life, can we at last hope to find out what that life actually was? For the mid-20th century, the answer is yes; there are far too few peasant studies of the Middle East, but we have enough to suggest what might still be done. The problem with these studies is their lack of historical depth; almost all our "scientific" observations and interpretations go no further back than World War I at best—that is, to a period when the agrarian life of the region had already been profoundly transformed by its role in a global market system, by new forms of land tenure, by state bureaucracies which could penetrate rural life far more deeply than any of their predecessors. The technological and institutional, if not natural, environment of the peasant had already changed almost beyond recognition, and it would therefore be exceedingly risky to assert that his village-level society and culture had remained stable and untroubled.

There have been a few attempts to reconstruct the peasant society of late Ottoman times, of course. In addition to Valensi's *Fellahs Tunisiens* (1977), we can cite a pioneering study by ʿAbd al-Raḥīm ʿAbd al-Raḥīm, *al-Rīf al-Miṣrī fi'l-qarn al-thāmin ʿashar* (1974). Studies of this kind, partly based on contemporary observation, but able to confirm and correct it through Ottoman documents, can serve as a kind of intermediary check-point for those concerned with more remote periods. They can first of all indicate the steps needed to rid modern studies of their anachronisms; second, they provide a body of facts and statements securely anchored in the pre-colonial, pre-Industrial Revolution era. Except for Valensi (and on a less ambitious level ʿAbd al-Raḥīm), however, we do not yet have such a body of studies; to provide them ought to be a major task of the next generation of scholars.

What do studies on contemporary rural life have to tell us? They can at least suggest the questions we need to be asking, and can alert us to the fragmentary hints of the medieval texts. We cannot survey all these studies, which are in any case becoming more and more numerous; we will thus restrict our comments to three, which have complementary merits and points of view:

1. P. W. English, *City and Village in Iran: Settlement and Economy in the Kirman Basin* (1966).
2. Jacques Weulersse, *Paysans de Syrie et du Proche Orient* (1946).
3. R. T. Antoun, *Arab Village: a Social Structural Study of a Trans-Jordanian Peasant Community* (1972).

English has written an economic geography; he asks how the different regional and social units of the Kirman basin are linked together into a functioning economic whole. His theme is urban domination—i.e., the establishment by the city of Kirman (or rather its elite residents) of a pervasive network of control over the whole network of economic activities in the region. This control can partly be identified with ownership of the means of production (land, sheep, carpet looms), but even more with the control of markets for small town and village products. Ultimately, the city's domination rests on the fact that cultivation in the Kirman basin is impossible without irrigation, and only urban-based elites have had the time and capital to construct the vast system of *qanāt*s. Why are the elites urban rather than rural? In part, at least, because of the traditional role of the city as a center of governmental administration and coercion, and most of the Kirman elite got their start at least as servants—not always faithful ones—of the state.

How well does the peasant himself emerge in English's analysis? As an economic actor, very clearly indeed; his complex role in the system of production and distribution is carefully delineated, and the class structure of the region comes out in high relief. But village society in itself, the patterns of behavior by which villagers relate to one another to create a system of social relations, remains rather vague and sketchy. Nor do we have a clear idea of village politics—the range of decisions made within the village community and the mechanisms by which such decisions are reached.

Such gaps in English's presentation are not flaws so much as a matter of emphasis. But from another perspective we can perceive a shortcoming, for English seems to have a limited sense of historical process. He regards the Basin's economic system as age-old: "the social and economic structure of modern Iran is . . . fundamentally similar to the feudal structures of Parthian and Sassanian Iran" (p. 88). On the other hand, his own language about the control of capital by urban elites, about the influence of international markets on Kirmani rug-weaving, etc., would imply that the term "feudal" is misplaced. One scholar has argued that Kirman's socio-economic structure in fact reflects its growing integration into a world capitalist system since the 17th century. Perhaps even this Wallersteinian formulation is too simplistic, but it is enough to suggest that we cannot simply project English's conclusions into the past, though the clarity and persuasiveness of his analysis makes it very tempting to do so. We can however use his questions: what role does the village have within a given economic system; what functions of economic life are pursued within the village; what kinds of economic decisions can villagers really make; etc.?

Weulersse's *Paysans de Syrie*, in contrast to the regional economic perspective of English, represents a holistic approach to the Syrian village. As a total performance, it is perhaps the most satisfying book yet written about modern peasant society in the Middle East; it deals with all four of the domains governing the peasant's life (environment, technology, external actors, village society and culture), it is exact and richly detailed, and it is vividly and eloquently written. Altogether it fully merits its place in a series (*Le Paysan et la Terre*) founded by Marc Bloch.

Even so there are grave flaws. One is the author's tendency to generalize from two distinctive regions in Syria—the Ghuta of Damascus, and the Orontes Valley and Jabal Anṣāriyya where he did his own dissertation research. More important is a lack of a genuine historical sense (a very common failing among geographers and anthropologists). The situation described by Weulersse grew out of a very specific conjuncture of circumstances linked to the Ottoman Land Reform Law of 1858. Of this political-economic process he seems only dimly aware. In one place he locates the roots of the agrarian situation in a combination of geographical determinism and immemorial tradition (e.g., p. 53 ff.); at another, his explanation is characterological—the fundamental hostility of Arabism (with its nomad-centered culture) and Islam (an urban faith of warriors and merchants) to agrarian life (p. 68 ff.). He asserts a vast and unbridgeable gulf between city and countryside, two distinct populations with almost nothing in common. We even detect allusions to the immemorial conflict of Orient and Occident. On one level, clearly, Weulersse's text must be read as an apologia (certainly a heartfelt one) for the French Mandate in Syria. What we can take from Weulersse is his sense of the whole, his capacity to identify and describe the elements that make up a way of life, and his awareness of the ways in which these elements interact with one another.

A subject to which Weulersse gives only slight attention, however, is the internal social relations of the Syrian village. Here is where the text of Antoun, thinner and less evocative in many ways, has its contribution to make. He brings into sharp focus the complex bonds of descent, marriage, and property which link households and clans to one another. More than that, he shows us the constant interplay between social values and norms on one side, and the goals, ambitions, and conflicts of individuals on the other. No more than anyone else do peasants conform passively to the ideal roles and expectations established by their societies; on the contrary, without abandoning these values, they try to manipulate them to their own advantage. Antoun's statements of fact certainly cannot be applied in any mechanical way even to other villages in Syria and Jordan. But he does give a sense of how a village works—how resources are distributed, what decisions are made, and by whom. To absorb the lessons of this kind of study is to forswear glib language about "families" and "tribes."

A caveat is in order here. *Vox anthropologi vox Dei non est*. Even an experienced and astute anthropologist may be badly misled about what he observes, and his statements are as subject to testing, confirmation, and reinterpretation as those of any source. To see this point, it is only necessary to read the brilliant and influential article of Emrys Peters, "Aspects of Rank and Status among Muslims in a Lebanese Village," in J. Pitt-Rivers, ed., *Mediterranean Countrymen* (1963); repr. in Louise Sweet, ed., *Peoples and Cultures of the Middle East* (2 vols., 1970), i, 76–123, and then to see the author's retraction of his own views a decade later in "Shifts in Power in a Lebanese Village," in R. Antoun and I. Harik, eds., *Rural Politics and Social Change in the Middle East* (1972), pp. 165–197.

All three of the studies we have discussed have some cultural dimension; all of them, that is, have something to say about the ways in which villagers understand and talk about themselves and their place in the world. But good studies focused on the culture of the village, of the kind done most notably by Clifford Geertz for Java and Bali, are still a rarity. We do have some collections of folklore for certain areas, like H. A. Winkler, *Ägyptische Volkskunde* (1936); Winifred Blackman, *The Fellahin of Upper Egypt* (1927); and Hasan el-Shamy, *Egyptian Folktales* (1980). But too often this material is abstracted from the social context which gave it birth; and when it is not (as in Blackman's case) it still conveys some of the condescension of urban or foreign elites. Moreover, we cannot attribute any of this material to earlier centuries without caution, though it is obvious that much of it is of great antiquity. And even where we can track down an exact parallel to some modern practice in a demotic papyrus or medieval manuscript, how do we know that it meant the same thing then as it does now?

We do have a most interesting text from 17th-century Egypt on peasant behavior and norms, the *Hazz al-quḥūf li-qaṣīd Abī Shadūf* of al-Shirbini. The text excoriates the poverty and grossness of village life, and modern Egyptian critics have tended to see in it an attack on the oppression and degradation created by the late Ottoman feudal order. A scholarly evaluation from this perspective is A. R. ʿAbd al-Raheim, "Hazz al-Quḥūf: a New Source for the Study of the Fellahin of Egypt in the XVIIth and XVIIIth Centuries," *JESHO*, xviii (1975), 245–270. This view has been rejected by Gabriel Baer, however, who argues ("Shirbīnī's Hazz al-Quḥūf and its Significance," in *Fellah and Townsman in the Middle East*, [1982], 3–47) that it is an attack on the peasants themselves, by a small-town *ʿālim* anxious to put some distance between himself and a religiously and morally suspect peasantry. In either case, it is an Egyptian view of rural life, and as close as we are ever likely to get to that segment of Islamic society.

Is it then possible to write a valid history of peasant society and culture in the medieval Islamic world? A pessimistic (or realistic) assessment of what we have said above would say that it is not; at best we can hope to create a plausible imaginative reconstruction. Even this is more than we now have, however, and if hypothetical statements are identified for what they are, they do no harm. Indeed, they give us a body of propositions which can be tested against new evidence as it emerges. But whatever evidence there may be, it will be used effectively only by a scholar who is both historian and anthropologist; it is achieving that combination of perspectives and disciplines which is the real challenge.

ABBREVIATIONS

(For starred items [*], full entries and page references to the text are given in the Bibliography. For archaeological periodicals and serials, see also p. 67.)

AAS	*Annales archéologiques de Syrie* (Direction Générale des Antiquités et des Musées, Damascus. Vol. I, 1951–to date. Since Vol. XVI, 1966, published as *Annales archéologiques arabes syriennes*).
AESC	*Annales: Économies, Sociétés, Civilisations* (Paris. Vol. I, 1946–to date).
AI	*Annales islamologiques* (Institut Francais d'Archeologie Orientale, Cairo. Continues *Mélanges islamologiques*, 3 vols., 1954–57).
AIEO	*Annales de l'Institut d'Études Orientales* (University of Algiers, Faculté des Lettres et Sciences Humaines. Vol. I, 1934–Vol. XX, 1962).
AMI	*Archäologische Mitteilungen aus Iran* (Deutsches Archäologisches Institut, Abteilung Teheran. Vol. I, 1929. New Series, Vol. I, 1968–to date).
BAH	*Bibliotheca Arabico-Hispana*. Ed. F. Codera y Zaidín and J. Ribera y Tarrago. 10 Vols. Madrid: (various publishers), 1882–95. (Biographical dictionaries by Ibn Bashkuwāl, al-Ḍabbī, Ibn al-Abbār, Ibn al-Faraḍī, Abū Bakr b. Khayr).
BEO	*Bulletin d'études orientales* (Institut Français d'Études Arabes, Damascus. Vol. I, 1931–to date).
BFLUS	*Bulletin de la Faculté de Lettres de l'Université de Strasbourg* (Vol. I, 1922–Vol. XLVIII, 1970).
*BGA	*Bibliotheca Geographorum Arabicorum.*
BIE	*Bulletin de l'Institut d'Égypte* (Cairo. Vol. I, 1919–to date. Supersedes *Bulletin de l'Institut Égyptien*).
BIFAO	*Bulletin de l'Institut Français d'Archéologie Orientale* (Cairo. Vol. I, 1901–to date).
BJRL	*Bulletin of the John Rylands Library* (Manchester. Vol. I, 1903–to date).
BSOAS	*Bulletin of the School of Oriental and African Studies* (University of London. Vol. I, 1917/20–to date).
*CIA	Berchem, Max van. *Matériaux pour un Corpus Inscriptionum Arabicarum.*
CSCO	*Corpus Scriptorum Christianorum Orientalium.* Ed. J.B. Chabot, I. Guidi, et al. In six sections: Scriptores Aethiopici; Scriptores Arabici; Scriptores Armeniaci; Scriptores Coptici; Scriptores Iberici; Scriptores Syri (Various publishers, 1908–to date).
*DMA	*Dictionary of the Middle Ages.*
*EI^1	*Encyclopaedia of Islam*, original edition.
*EI^2	*Encyclopaedia of Islam*, new edition.
*GAL	Brockelmann, Carl. *Geschichte der arabischen Litteratur.*
*GAS	Sezgin, Fuat. *Geschichte des arabischen Schrifttums.*
*HO	Spuler, Bertold. *Handbuch der Orientalistik.*
*IA	*İslam Ansiklopedisi.*
IJMES	*International Journal of Middle East Studies* (Middle East Studies Association of North America, New York. Vol. I, 1970–to date).

JA	*Journal Asiatique* (Société Asiatique, Paris. Series I, no. 1, 1822–to date).
JAOS	*Journal of the American Oriental Society* (New Haven, Conn. Vol. I, 1843/49–to date).
JESHO	*Journal of the Economic and Social History of the Orient* (Leiden. Vol. I, 1957–to date).
JNES	*Journal of Near Eastern Studies* (Oriental Institute, University of Chicago. Vol. I, 1942–to date. Supersedes *The American Journal of Semitic Languages and Literatures*).
JRAS	*Journal of the Royal Asiatic Society of Great Britain and Ireland* (London. Vol. I, 1834–to date. Vols. not numbered since 1890).
JSS	*Journal of Semitic Studies* (Manchester. Vol. I, 1956–to date).
MIE	*Mémoires présentés à l'Institut d'Égypte* (Cairo. Vol. I, 1919–to date).
MIFAO	*Mémoires publiés par les membres de l'Institut Français d'Archéologie Orientale* (Cairo. Vol. I, 1902–to date).
MMAF	*Mémoires de la Mission Archéologique Française au Caire* (Vol. I, 1884–Vol. XXXI, 1934).
MMII	*Majallat al-Majmᶜa al-ᶜIlmī al-ᶜIrāqī* (Baghdad. Vol. I, 1369/1950–to date).
MW	*Muslim World* (Hartford Seminary Foundation, Hartford, Conn. Vol. I, 1911–to date. Published as *The Moslem World*, 1911–1947).
OLZ	*Orientalistische Literaturzeitung* (Berlin. Vol. I, 1898–to date).
**RCEA*	*Répertoire chronologique d'épigraphie arabe.*
REI	*Revue des études islamiques* (Paris. Vol. I, 1927–to date. Supersedes *Revue du monde musulman. See also* Bibliography: *Abstracta Islamica*).
RHR	*Revue de l'histoire des religions. Annales du Musée Guimet* (Paris. Vol. I, 1880–to date).
ROMM	*Revue de l'Occident musulman et de la Mediterranée* (Aix-en-Provence. Vol. I, 1966–to date).
RSO	*Revista degli studi orientali* (Rome. Vol. I, 1907–to date).
**SEI*	*Shorter Encyclopaedia of Islam.*
SI	*Studia Islamica* (Paris. Vol. I, 1953–to date).
**TA*	*Türkologischer Anzeiger.*
**TAVO*	*Tübinger Atlas des Vorderen Orients.*
**VOHD*	*Verzeichnis der orientalischen Handschriften in Deutschland.*
**WKAS*	*Wörterbuch der Klassischen Arabischen Sprache.*
WKZM	*Wiener Zeitschrift fur die Kunde des Morgenlandes* (Institut der Orientalistik der Universität Wien. Vol. I, 1887–to date. *See also* Bibliography: *Türkologischer Anzeiger*).
ZDMG	*Zeitschrift der Deutschen Morgenländischen Gesellschaft* (Leipzig; since 1945, Wiesbaden. Vol. I, 1858–to date).

BIBLIOGRAPHIC INDEX

In general, entries are made by author. Where more than one item is cited for an author, two rules apply: (1) books and monographs precede articles and chapters in collective volumes; (2) within each of these two categories, works are cited in order of publication. Jointly authored or edited works are listed under the name of the principal author, following all other entries for that author. Anonymous works, encyclopaedias, and text editions combining the writings of several authors are entered by title. Following each entry, on a separate line, the page numbers of places in the text where that item is mentioned are given within diamond brackets: ‹ ›. A few entries do not have such page references: collective volumes from which individual contributions only are discussed, or very recent publications which could not be worked into the text. Certain reference works are cited continually throughout the text (e.g., the *Encyclopaedia of Islam, Handbuch der Orientalistik*); for these items page references are made only to places where they are discussed as a whole. Finally, with few exceptions, authors (both medieval and modern) listed in the Bibliography are not listed in the Index.

Abbott, Nabia. *The Kurrah Papyri from Aphrodito in the Oriental Institute*. Chicago: University of Chicago Press, 1938.
‹P. 42›

———. *Studies in Arabic Literary Papyri, I: Historical Texts*. Oriental Institute Publications, lxxv. Chicago: University of Chicago Press, 1957.
‹Pp. 77, 78, 82, 84›

———. *Studies in Arabic Literary Papyri, II: Qurʾanic Commentary and Tradition*. Oriental Institute Publications, lxxvi. Chicago: University of Chicago Press, 1967.
‹Pp. 77, 78, 82, 84›

———. "Arabic Papyri of the Reign of Ğaʿfar al-Mutawakkil ʿalā-llāh." *ZDMG*, xcii (1938), 88–135.
‹P. 47›

ʿAbd al-Bāqī, Muḥammad Fuʾād, ed. *al-Muʿjam al-mufahras li-alfāẓ al-Qurʾan al-Karīm*. Cairo, 1364/1945.
‹Pp. 21, 56›

ʿAbd al-Raheim, ʿAbd al-Raheim A. (= ʿAbd al-Raḥīm) "Hazz al-Quḥūf: a new source for the study of the fellahin of Egypt in the XVIIth and XVIIIth centuries." *JESHO*, xviii (1975), 245–270.
‹P. 308›

ʿAbd al-Raḥīm, ʿAbd al-Raḥīm. *al-Rīf al-Miṣrī fī al-qarn al-thāmin ʿashar*. Cairo: Maṭbaʿat Jāmiʿat ʿAyn al-Shams, 1974.
‹P. 304›

ʿAbd al-Rāziq, Aḥmad. "Le vizirat et les vizirs d'Égypte au temps des Mamluks." *AI*, xvi (1980), 183–239.
‹P. 183›

Abiad, Malak, "Origine et développement des dictionnaires biographiques arabes." *BEO*, xxxi (1979), 7–15.
‹P. 79›

Abstracta Iranica. Supplément à Studia Iranica. Leiden: E. J. Brill, for the Institut Français d'Iranologie à Téhéran. Vol. I, 1978–to date.
‹P. 9›

Abstracta Islamica. Extrait de la *Revue des études islamiques.* Paris: P. Geuthner. Vol. I, 1927–present.
‹P. 9›

Abū Ṣāliḥ. *The Churches and Monasteries of Egypt.* Trans. by A. J. Butler and B. Evetts. Oxford: Clarendon Press, 1894–95.
‹P. 279›

Abū Yaʿlā al-Farrāʾ. *al-Aḥkām al-sulṭāniyya.* Ed. by M. H. Al-Fiqqī. Cairo: Muṣṭafā al-Bābī al-Ḥalabī, 1357/1938.
‹P. 160›

Abū Yūsuf. *Kitāb al-kharāj.* Trans. by Edmond Fagnan as *Livre de l'impôt foncier.* Paris: P. Geuthner, 1921.
‹Pp. 216, 259, 303›

Ackerman, Phyllis. *See under* Pope, Arthur U.

Adamec, Ludwig W., ed. *Historical and Political Gazetteer of Afghanistan.* 6 vols. Graz: Akademische Druckerei, 1972–85.
‹P. 19›

———. *Historical Gazetteer of Iran.* 3 vols., in progress. Graz: Akademische Druckerei, 1976–88.
‹P. 19›

Adams, Robert McC. *Land behind Baghdad: A History of Settlement on the Diyala Plains.* Chicago and London: University of Chicago Press, 1965.
‹Pp. 247, 291, 295›

———. *Heartland of Cities: Surveys of Ancient Settlement and Land Use on the Central Floodplain of the Euphrates.* Chicago & London: University of Chicago Press, 1981.
‹Pp. 292, 295›

———. "Agriculture and Urban Life in Early Southwestern Iran." *Science,* cxxxvi (1961), 109–122.
‹Pp. 293, 295›

Afrika Kartenwerk. Ed. by J. H. Schultze. Berlin and Stuttgart: Deutsche Forschungsgemeinschaft, 1976–in progress.
‹P. 17›

Afshar, Iraj. *Bibliographie des catalogues des manuscrits persans.* Publications de l'Université de Tehran, no. 485. Tehran, 1337/1958.
‹P. 39›

Aghnides, Nicholas P. *Mohammedan Theories of Finance.* Columbia University Studies in History, Economics and Public Law, 70. New York: Columbia University Press, 1916; repr. Lahore 1961.
‹P. 216›

Ahlwardt, Wilhelm. *Verzeichnis der arabischen Handschriften der Königlichen Bibliothek zu Berlin.* 10 vols. Berlin: L. Schade, 1887–1899.
‹P. 37›

Ahmad, M. Hilmy M. "Some Notes on Arabic Historiography during the Zengid and

Ayyubid Periods (521–648/1127–1250)." In Lewis and Holt, *Historians of the Middle East*, 79–97.
‹P. 241›

Ahmad, S. Maqbul. "Djughrāfiya." *EI*^{2}, ii, 575–587.
‹P. 224›

Ahmad, S. Maqbul, and A. Rahman, eds. *Al-Masʿūdī Millenary Commemoration Volume*. Aligarh, 1960.
‹P. 76›

Ahmed, Munir-ud-Din. *Muslim Education and the Scholars' Social Status up to the Fifth Century Muslim Era in the Light of Taʾrīkh Baghdād*. Zurich: Verlag Der Islam, 1968.
‹P. 201›

Akhbār al-dawla al-ʿabbāsiyya. (Anon.) Ed. by A. A. al-Dūrī and A. J. al-Muṭṭalibī. Beirut: Dar al-Taliʿa, 1971. *See also* Gryaznevich, P. A.
‹Pp. 112–113, 116, 123›

Alarcón y Santón, M. A., and R. G. de Linares. *Los documentos arabes diplomaticos del archivo de la Corona de Aragon*. Madrid-Granada, 1940.
‹P. 46›

Album, Stephen, ed. *Marsden's Numismata Orientalia Illustrata*. New York: Attic Books, 1977.
‹P. 50›

Alderson, Anthony Dolphin. *The Structure of the Ottoman Dynasty*. Oxford: Clarendon Press, 1956.
‹P. 20›

ʿAlī, Jawād. "Mawārid Taʾrīkh al-Ṭabarī." *Majallat al-Majmaʿ al-ʿIlmī al-ʿIrāqī*, i (1950), 143–231; ii (1951), 135–190; iii (1954), 16–58; viii (1961), 425–436.
‹P. 82›

Allan, J., and Dominique Sourdel. "Khātam." *EI*^{2}, iv, 1102–1105.
‹P. 44›

Alparslan, Ali. "Khaṭṭ." *EI*^{2}, iv, 1122–1126.
‹P. 33›

Amar, Emile. "La pierre de touche des fetwas." *Archives Marocaines*, xii (1908), xiii (1909).
‹Pp. 218, 259›

Amari, Michele. *I diplomi arabi del R. Archivio Fiorentino*. Florence, 1863.
‹P. 46›

Amedroz, H. F. "The Office of Kadi in the Aḥkām Sulṭāniyya of Mawardi." *JRAS* (1910), 761–796.
‹P. 222›

———. "The Maẓālim Jurisdiction in the Aḥkām Sulṭāniyya of Mawardi." *JRAS* (1911), 635–674.
‹P. 222›

———. "The Ḥisba Jurisdiction in the Aḥkām Sulṭāniyya of Mawardi." *JRAS*, (1916), 77–101, 287–314.
‹P. 222›

al-ʿĀmilī. *See* al-Ḥurr al-ʿĀmilī.

Amin, Muhammad M. *Catalogue des documents d'archives du Caire, de 239/853 à 922/1516, suivi de l'édition critique de neuf documents*. Cairo: Institut Français d'Archéologie Orientale, 1981.
‹Pp. 47, 171, 220, 221›

Anderson, Margaret. *Arabic Materials in English Translation: a Bibliography of Works from the Pre-Islamic Period to 1977*. Boston: G. K. Hall, 1980.
‹P. 11›

Anklesaria, B. T. *The Pahlavi Rivayat of Aturnfarnbag and Farnbagsros*. 2 vols. Bombay: Industrial Press, 1969.
‹P. 278›

Antoun, Richard A. *Arab Village: a Social Structural Study of a Transjordanian Peasant Community*. Bloomington: Indiana University Press, 1972.
‹Pp. 305, 306–307›

Antoun, Richard, and Iliya Harik, eds. *Rural Politics and Social Change in the Middle East*. Bloomington and London: Indiana University Press, 1972. *See* Peters, Emrys.

Arafat, Walid N. "Early Critics of the Authenticity of the Poetry of the Sira." *BSOAS*, xxi (1958), 453–463.
‹P. 90›

———. "An Aspect of the Forger's Art in Early Islamic Poetry." *BSOAS*, xxviii (1965), 477–482.
‹P. 90›

———. *See also* Ḥassān b. Thābit.

Arberry, A. J., ed. *Specimens of Arabic and Persian Palaeography*. London: India Office, 1939.
‹P. 33›

———. *The Chester Beatty Library: A Handlist of the Arabic Manuscripts*. 6 vols. Dublin: E. Walker, 1955–66.
‹P. 33›

———. *The Chester Beatty Library. A Catalogue of the Persian Manuscripts and Miniatures*. 3 vols. Dublin: Hodges, Figgis, 1959–62.
‹P. 33›

Arié, Rachel. *L'Espagne musulmane au temps des Nasrides, 1232–1492*. Paris: E. de Boccard, 1973.
‹P. 304›

———. "La vie économique de l'Espagne musulmane." *HO*, I/vi/6, pt. 1 (1977), 239–254.
‹Pp. 300, 304›

———. Review of D. Urvoy, *Le monde des ulemas andalous*. *Islam*, lx (1983), 324–325.
‹P. 207›

al-ʿArīnī, E. E. *al-Iqṭāʿ al-ḥarbī fī zaman ṣalāṭīn al-mamālīk*. Cairo, 1956.
‹P. 181›

Arkoun, Mohammed. *Contribution à l'étude de l'humanisme arabe au ivᵉ/xᵉ siècle: Miskawayh, philosophe et historien*. Paris: J. Vrin, 1970.
‹P. 134›

Arnold, T., and A. Guillaume, eds. *The Legacy of Islam*. Oxford: Clarendon Press, 1931. *See* Kramers, J. H.

al-Ashʿarī, Abū al-Ḥasan. *Maqālāt al-islāmiyyīn wa-ikhtilāf al-muṣallīn*. Ed. by Hellmut Ritter. 3 vols. Istanbul: Deutsche Morgenländische Gesellschaft, 1929–33.
‹P. 113›

Ashtor, Eliyahu. *Toledot ha-Yehudim be-Mizrayim ve-Suria tahat Shilton ha-Mamlukim*. 3 vols. Jerusalem: Mossad Harav Kook, 1944–70. *See also* Goitein, S. D.
‹P. 269›

———. *Korot ha-Yehudim bi-Sefarad ha-Muslemit*. 2 vols. Jerusalem: Kiryat Sefer, 1960–66. Trans. by Aaron and Jenny M. Klein as *The Jews of Muslim Spain*. 2 vols. Philadelphia: Jewish Publication Society of America, 1973–79.
‹P. 269›

———. *Histoire des prix et des salaires dans l'Orient médiéval*. Paris: S.E.V.P.E.N., 1969.
‹Pp. 303–304›

———. *A Social and Economic History of the Near East in the Middle Ages*. London: William Collins & Sons, 1976.
‹P. 303›

———. "Quelques problemes que soulève l'histoire des prix dans l'Orient médiéval." In M. Rosen-Ayalon, ed., *Studies in Memory of Gaston Wiet*, 203–234.
‹P. 304›

———. *See also* Ashtor-Strauss, E.; Strauss, Eli.

Ashtor-Strauss, E. "L'administration urbaine en Syrie médiévale," *RSO*, xxxi (1956), 73–128.
‹P. 246›

Asin Palacios, Miguel. *Abenházam de Cordoba y su historia crítica de las ideas religiosas*. Madrid: Tipografia de la "Revista de archivos," 1927–32.
‹P. 113›

al-ʿAsqalānī, Ibn Ḥajar. *Lisān al-Mīzān*. 6 vols. in 3. Hyderabad, Deccan: Dāʾirat al-Maʿārif al-Niẓāmiyya, 1329–31/1911–13.
‹Pp. 71, 81, 189, 204›

———. *Tahdhīb al-tahdhīb*. 12 vols. Hyderabad, Deccan: Dāʾirat al-Maʿārif al-Niẓāmiyya 1325–27/1907–10. New edition by ʿAlī Muḥammad al-Bijāwī. 8 vols. Cairo: Dār Nahḍat Miṣr li'l-Ṭabʿ waʾl-Naskh, 1970–72.
‹Pp. 71, 81, 82, 189, 204›

Atıl, Esin. *Renaissance of Islam: Art of the Mamluks*. Washington, D.C.: Smithsonian Institution, 1981.
‹P. 62›

Atiya, A. S. *The Arabic Manuscripts of Mt. Sinai*. Baltimore: Johns Hopkins University Press, 1955.
‹Pp. 47, 170›

Attal, Robert. *Les juifs d'Afrique du Nord: bibliographie*. Jerusalem: Ben-Zvi Institute, 1973.
‹Pp. 269–270›

———. *Bibliography of the Writings of Professor Shelomo Dov Goitein*. Jerusalem: Hebrew University Press, 1975.
‹P. 268›

Auchterlonie, Paul. *Arabic Biographical Dictionaries: A Summary Guide and Bibliog-*

raphy. Durham: Middle East Libraries Committee, 1987.
‹Pp. 29, 188›

ʿAwwād, Kūrkīs. *Fahāris al-makhṭūṭāt al-ʿarabiyya fī al-ʿālam. Catalogues of the Arabic Manuscripts in the World.* 2 vols. Kuwait: Institute of Arabic Manuscripts; Arab League Educational, Cultural, and Scientific Organization, 1405/1984.
‹P. 39›

Ayalon, David. *Studies on the Mamluks of Egypt (1250–1517)*. London: Variorum Reprints, 1977.
‹Pp. 181, 207›

———. *The Mamluk Military Society*. London: Variorum Reprints, 1979.
‹Pp. 181, 207›

———. "Studies on the Structure of the Mamluk Army." *BSOAS*, xv (1953), 203–238, 448–476; xvi (1954), 57–90.
‹P. 181›

———. "The System of Payment in Mamluk Military Society." *JESHO*, i (1958), 37–65, 257–296.
‹P. 181›

———. "Mamlūk." *EI*[2], vi, 314–321.
‹P. 181›

Ayoub, Mahmoud M. *The Qurʾān and Its Interpreters*. Vol. I. Albany: State University of New York Press, 1984.
‹P. 22›

Ayrout, Henry Habib. *Moeurs et coutumes des fellahs*. Paris: Payot, 1938. Revised and trans. by J. A. Williams as *The Egyptian Peasant*. Boston: Beacon Press, 1963.
‹P. 299›

al-Azdī, Yazīd b. Muḥammad. *Taʾrīkh al-Mawṣil*. Ed. by ʿAlī Ḥabība. Cairo, al-Majlis al-Aʿlā li'l-Shuʾūn al-Islāmiyya, 1967.
‹Pp. 112, 127, 130›

al-Azmeh, Aziz. *Ibn Khaldun in Modern Scholarship: A Study in Orientalism*. London: Third World Center for Research and Publishing, 1981.
‹P. 135›

———. *Ibn Khaldun, an Essay in Reinterpretation*. London: Frank Cass, 1982.
‹P. 135›

Azmi, Mohammad M. (LC listing: al-Aʿẓamī, M. M.). *Studies in Early Hadith Literature*. Beirut: al-Maktab al-Islami, 1968.
‹P. 82, 84›

Babinger, Franz. *Die Geschichtsschreiber der Osmanen und ihre Werke*. Leipzig: O. Harrassowitz, 1927.
‹P. 31›

Baer, Eva. *Metalwork in Medieval Islamic Art*. Albany: State University of New York Press, 1983.
‹P. 62›

Baer, Gabriel. *Fellah and Townsman in the Middle East: Studies in Social History*. London: Frank Cass, 1982.
(a) "Shirbīnī's Hazz al-Quḥūf and its Significance," 3–47.
(b) "Fellah Rebellion in Egypt and the Fertile Crescent," 253–323.

(c) "Village and City in Egypt and Syria, 1500–1914," 49–100. Also in Udovitch, *The Islamic Middle East, 700–1900*, 595–652.

‹P. 308›

Bağdatlı İsmail Paşa. *Īḍāḥ al-maknūn fī al-dhayl ʿalā kashf al-ẓunūn*. Ed. by M. Şerefettin Yaltkaya and Kilisli Rifʿat Bilge. 2 vols. in 1. Istanbul: Milli Eğitim Basımevi, 1945–47.

‹P. 29›

al-Baghdādī, ʿAbd al-Qāhir. *al-Farq bayn al-firaq wa-bayān al-firqa al-nājiya*.

(a) Ed. by M. Badr. Cairo: Matbaʿat al-Maʿarif, 1910.

(b) Ed. by M. ʿAbd al-Ḥamīd. Cairo: Muhammad ʿAli Ṣabīḥ, n.d. [1964?]

(c) Translated as *Moslem Schisms and Sects*. Vol. I, by Kate Seelye (New York: Columbia University Press, 1920); Vol. II, by A. B. Halkin (Tel Aviv: Palestine Publishing Co., 1935).

‹P. 113›

Bakhīt, M. A., ed. *Proceedings of the Second Symposium on the History of Bilād al-Shām during the Early Islamic Period up to 40 A.H./640 A.D.* 3 vols. Amman: University of Jordan, 1987.

al-Balādhurī, Aḥmad ibn Yaḥyā. *Ansāb al-ashrāf*.

Vol. I. Ed. by M. Hamidullah. Cairo: Dār al-Maʿārif, 1959.

Vol. II. Ed. by M. al-Maḥmūdī. Beirut: Dār al-Taʿāruf li'l-Maṭbūʿāt, 1974.

Vol. III. Ed. by A. A. al-Dūrī. Wiesbaden: F. Steiner, 1978.

Vol. IVA. Ed. by Max Schloessinger and M. J. Kister. Jerusalem: Magnes Press, 1971. = Vol. IV, pt. 1, ed. by Iḥsān ʿAbbās. Wiesbaden: F. Steiner, 1979.

Vol. IVB. Ed. by Max Schloessinger. Jerusalem: Hebrew University Press, 1938.

Vol. V. Ed. by S. D. Goitein. Jerusalem: Hebrew University Press, 1936.

Anonyme arabische Chronik, Band XI. Ed. by W. Ahlwardt. Greifswald, 1883.

‹Pp. 72, 75, 78, 83, 99–103, 112, 130›

al-Balādhurī, Aḥmad b. Yaḥyā. *Futūḥ al-buldān*.

(a) Ed. by M. J. de Goeje. Leiden: E. J. Brill, 1866.

(b) Trans. by Philip Hitti and Francis Murgotten as *The Origins of the Islamic State*. 2 vols. Columbia University Studies in History, Economics, and Public Law. Vol. LXVIII, nos. 163, 163a. New York: Columbia University Press, 1916–24.

‹P. 111›

Ball, Warwick, and Jean-Claude Gardin. *Archaeological Gazetteer of Afghanistan*. 2 vols. Paris: Éditions Recherche sur les Civilisations, 1982.

‹P. 64›

Balog, Paul. *The Coinage of the Mamluk Sultans of Egypt and Syria*. New York: American Numismatic Society, 1964.

‹P. 51›

———. *The Coinage of the Ayyubids*. London: Royal Numismatic Society, 1980.

‹P. 51›

al-Baqlī, Muḥammad Qandīl. *al-Taʿrīf bi-muṣṭalaḥāt Ṣubḥ al-Aʿshā*. Cairo: al-Hayʾa al-Miṣriyya al-ʿĀmma li'l-Kitāb, 1984.

‹P. 175›

Barkan, Ömer Lutfi. *XV ve XVIıncı asirlarda Osmanlı Imparatorluğunda zirai ekonom-*

inin hukuki ve mali esasları. Vol. I: *Kanunlar*. Istanbul, 1943. *See also* Mantran, Robert and Sauvaget, Jean.
‹P. 172›

———. "Quelques observations sur l'organisation économique et sociale des villes ottomanes des XVe et XVIIe siècles." *Recueils de la Société Jean Bodin: La Ville*. Brussels, 1955, 289–311.
‹Cf. pp. 231–233›

———. "Essai sur les données statistiques des registres de recensement dans l'Empire Ottoman aux XVe et XVIe siècles." *JESHO*, i (1958), 9–36.
‹P. 232›

Barkan, Ömer Lutfi, and E. H. Ayverdi. *Istanbul vakıfları tahrir defteri, 953 (1546) tarihli*. Istanbul: Baha Matbaasi, 1970.
‹P. 220›

Baron, Salo W. *A Social and Economic History of the Jews*. 2nd ed., 18 vols. New York: Columbia University Press; and Philadelphia: Jewish Publication Society of America, 1957–85.
‹P. 265›

Barthold, W. (= Bartol'd, V. V.)

Bartol'd, V. V. *Turkestan down to the Mongol Invasion*. 1st Russian ed., St. Petersburg, 1900. 1st English ed.: E.J.W. Gibb Memorial, N.S. 5. London: Luzac, 1928. 3d rev. ed., London: Luzac, 1967.
‹Pp. 119, 120, 155, 166›

———. *Istoriko-geograficheskii obzor Irana*. St. Petersburg, 1903. Repr. in Bartol'd, *Sochineniia* (9 vols., Moscow, 1963–76), vii, 29–225. Trans. by Svat Soucek as *An Historical Geography of Iran*. Princeton, NJ: Princeton University Press, 1984.
‹P. 18›

———. "Kalif i sultan." *Mir Islama*, i (1912), 202–226, 345–400. Partial trans. by N. S. Doniach, *Islamic Quarterly*, vii (1963), 117–135. *See also* Becker, Carl.
‹P. 161›

———. "Abū Muslim." EI^{1}, i, 101–2.
‹P. 123›

al-Bāshā, Ḥasan. *al-Alqāb al-islāmiyya fī al-taʾrīkh wa'l-wathāʾiq wa'l-āthār*. Cairo: Maktabat al-Nahḍa al-Miṣriyya, 1957. Reprinted Cairo: Dār al-Nahḍa al-ʿArabiyya, 1978.
‹P. 51›

Bates, Michael L. "Islamic Numismatics." *MESA Bull.*, xii, 2 (May 1978), 1–16; xii, 3 (Dec. 1978), 2–18; xiii, 1 (July, 1979), 3–21; xiii, 2 (Dec. 1979), 1–9.
‹P. 50›

———. "History, Geography, and Numismatics in the First Century of Islamic Coinage." *Revue Suisse de Numismatique*, lxv (1986), 231–263.

Baumstark, Anton. *Geschichte der syrischen Literatur, mit Ausschluss der christlich-palästinensischen Texte*. Bonn: A. Marcus and Weber, 1922; repr. Berlin: W. de Gruyter, 1968.
‹Pp. 29, 277›

Bayhaqī, Abū al-Faẓl Muḥammad b. Ḥusayn. *Taʾrīkh-i Bayhaqī*. Ed. by A. A. Fayyāḍ. Mashhad: University of Mashhad Press, 1350/1971.
‹Pp. xiv, 128, 129, 131, 134, 137–138, 141–145, 147, 163›

Beaumont, Peter; Blake, Gerald H.; and Wagstaff, J. Malcolm. *The Middle East: A*

Geographical Study. London and New York: John Wiley & Sons, 1976.
‹P. 290›

Becker, Carl H. *Beiträge zur Geschichte Ägyptens unter dem Islam*. 2 vols. Strasbourg: Karl Trübner, 1902–3.
‹P. 179›

———. *Papyri Schott-Reinhardt*. Veröffentlichungen aus der Heidelberger Papyrus-Sammlung, III. Heidelberg: Carl Winter, 1906.
‹P. 179›

———. *Islamstudien. Vom Werden und Wesen der islamischen Welt*. 2 vols. Leipzig: Quelle & Meyer, 1924–32.
‹P. 179›

———. "Barthold's Studien über Kalif und Sultan." *Islam*, vi (1916), 350–412. *See also* Bartol'd, V. V.
‹P. 161›

Becker, Carl, and Franz Rosenthal. "al-Balādhurī." *EI²*, i, 971–72.
‹P. 75›

Behn, Wolfgang H. *Islamic Book Review Index*. Berlin: Adiyok (since 1988, Millersport, PA). Vol. I, 1982.
‹P. 7›

———. *Index Islamicus, 1665–1905*. Millersport, PA: Adiyok, 1989.
‹P. 7›

Behrnauer, Walter. "Mémoire sur les institutions de police chez les Arabes, les Persans, et les Turcs." *JA*, series 5: no. xv (1860), 461–508; xvi (1860), 114–190, 347–392; xvii (1861), 5–76.
‹P. 242›

Belin, M. A. "Fetwa relatif à la condition des zimmis, et particulièrement des chrétiens, en pays musulmans depuis l'établissement de l'Islam jusqu'au milieu du 8e siècle de l'hégire." *JA*, series 4: no. xviii (1851), 417–516; xix (1852), 97–140.
‹P. 259›

Ben-Shemesh, A. *Taxation in Islam*. Vols. I–III. Leiden: E. J. Brill, 1958–1969. 2d rev. ed. of Vol. I, 1967.
‹Pp. 216, 303›

Berchem, Max van. *Matériaux pour un Corpus Inscriptionum Arabicarum*.
Ie partie: Égypte
Le Caire. Max van Berchem. *MMAF*, xix (1894–1903).
Le Caire (suite). Gaston Wiet. *MIFAO*, lii (1930).
IIe partie: Syrie
Syrie du Nord: ʿAkkār, Ḥiṣn al-Akrād, Tripoli. Moritz Sobernheim. *MIFAO*, xxv (1909).
Syrie du Sud: Jérusalem. Max van Berchem. 3 vols. *MIFAO*, xliii–xlv (1920–27).
Syrie du Nord: Inscriptions et monuments d'Alep. Ernst Herzfeld. 2 vols. in 3. *MIFAO*, lxxvi–lxxviii (1954–56).
IIIe partie: Asie mineure
Siwas, Diwrigi. Max van Berchem and Halil Edhem. *MIFAO*, xxix (1917).
IVe partie: Arabie
La Mekke: Ḥaram et Kaʿba. H. M. al-Hawary and Gaston Wiet. *MIFAO*, cix (1985).
‹Pp. 56–57, 165, 243, 245›

———. *Opera Minora*. 2 vols. Geneva: Slatkine, 1978.
‹P. 57›

Berghe, L. Vanden. *Archéologie de l'Iran ancien*. Leiden: E. J. Brill, 1959.
‹P. 64›

———. *Bibliographie analytique de l'archéologie de l'Iran ancien*. Leiden: E. J. Brill, 1979.
‹P. 64›

Berlin, Königliche Bibliothek. *See* Ahlwardt, W. and Pertsch, W.

Bernheim, Ernst. *Lehrbuch der historischen Methode und der Geschichtsphilosophie*. 5th–6th rev. edition. Leipzig: Duncker & Humblot, 1908.
‹Pp. 25, 34, 135›

Berque, J., and D. Chevallier. *Les Arabes par leurs archives, XVIe–XXe siècles*. Paris: Centre national de la recherche scientifique, 1976.
‹P. 220›

Berque, Jacques. "ʿAmal." *EI*[2], i, 427–428.
‹P. 217›

Bianquis, Thierry. *Damas et la Syrie sous la domination fatimide (359–468/969–1076). Essai d'interpretation de chroniques arabes médiévales*. 2 vols. Damascus: Institut Français de Damas, 1986–89.
‹P. 247›

Biberstein-Kazimirski, Albert de. *Dictionnaire arabe-francais*. 4 vols. Paris: Maisonneuve, 1860.
‹P. 13›

Bibliotheca Geographorum Arabicorum. Ed. by M. J. de Goeje. 8 vols. Leiden: E. J. Brill, 1879–1939.
Vol. I. Abū Isḥāq al-Fārisī al-Iṣṭakhrī. *Viae regnorum*.
Vol. II. Ibn Ḥawqal. *Opus geographicum*. Ed. by J. H. Kramers.
Vol. III. al-Muqaddasī. *Descriptio imperii moslemici*.
Vol. IV. *Indices, glossarium et addenda et emendanda ad partibus I–III*.
Vol. V. Ibn al-Faqīh al-Hamadhānī. *Compendium libri Kitāb al-Boldān*.
Vol. VI. Ibn Khordādhbeh. *Kitāb al-Masālik wa'l-Mamālik (Liber viarum et regnorum)*.
Vol. VII. Ibn Rusta. *Kitāb al-Aʿlāḳ al-Nafīsa VII*. al-Yaʿqūbī. *Kitāb al-Boldān*.
Vol. VIII. al-Masʿūdī. *Kitāb at-Tanbīh wa'l-Ischrāf*.
See also Ibn Ḥawqal, Ibn Rusta, al-Masʿūdī, al-Muqaddasī, al-Yaʿqūbī.
‹Pp. 14, 18, 224, 296›

Binder, Leonard, ed. *The Study of the Middle East: Research and Scholarship in the Humanities and Social Sciences*. New York: John Wiley and Sons, 1976. *See also* Grabar, Oleg.
‹Pp. 11, 60›

Binder, Leonard. "Al-Ghazālī's Theory of Islamic Government." *Muslim World*, xlv (1955), 229–241.
‹P. 161›

Birnbaum, Eleazar. "Turkish Manuscripts: Cataloguing since 1960 and Manuscripts Still Uncatalogued." *JAOS*, ciii (1983)–civ (1984).
Pt. 1: review of M. Götz and H. Sohrweide, Türkische Handschriften (3 vols., 1968–79). *JAOS*, ciii (1983), 413–420.

Pt. 2: Yugoslavia, Bulgaria, Romania. *JAOS*, ciii (1983), 515–532.
Pt. 3: U.S.S.R., Iran, Afghanistan, Arab Lands (except Palestine), Israel and Palestine, India and Pakistan, China. *JAOS*, ciii (1983), 691–708.
Pt. 4: Hungary, Czechoslovakia, Poland, Great Britain, Ireland, The Netherlands, Belgium, France, Germany, Switzerland, Austria, Italy, Finland, United States, Canada. *JAOS*, civ (1984), 303–314.
Pt. 5: Turkey and Cyprus. *JAOS*, civ (1984), 465–504.
‹Pp. 30–31, 39›

Birot, Pierre, and Jean Dresch. *La Méditerranée et le Moyen Orient*. 2 vols. Paris: Presses Universitaires de France, 1953–56. 2d rev. ed. (Vol. I only), 1964.
‹P. 290›

Björkman, Walther. *Beiträge zur Geschichte der Staatskanzlei im islamischen Ägypten*. Hamburg: Friederichsen de Gruyter, 1928.
‹Pp. 45, 175, 178›

Björkman, W., et al. "Diplomatic." *EI*², ii, 301–316.
‹P. 43›

Blachère, Régis. *Le Coran: traduction selon un essai de reclassement des sourates*. 3 vols. Paris: G. P. Maisonneuve, 1947–1951.
‹P. 22›

———. *Histoire de la littérature arabe*. 3 vols. Paris: Adrien Maisonneuve, 1952–66.
‹Pp. 87, 90›

Blachère, Régis, ed. *Dictionnaire arabe-francais-anglais*. 4 vols., in progress. Paris: Maisonneuve et Larose, 1964–.
‹P. 13›

Blackman, Winifred. *The Fellahin of Upper Egypt: Their Religious, Social, and Industrial Life Today, with Special Reference to Survivals from Ancient Times*. London: George G. Harrap, 1927.
‹P. 307›

Blair, Sheila. *A Corpus of Early Arabic Inscriptions from Iran and Transoxiana (to A.H. 500)*. Leiden: E. J. Brill; projected date of publication, 1991.
‹Pp. 57, 58›

Bloch, Marc. *Les caractères originaux de l'histoire rurale francaise*. Oslo: Institut pour l'Etude Comparative des Civilisations, 1931. Trans. by Janet Sondheimer as *French Rural History: an Essay on its Basic Characteristics*. Berkeley and Los Angeles: University of California Press, 1966.
‹Pp. 284–285, 286›

Bloom, Jonathan. "The Mosque of Baybars al-Bunduqdārī in Cairo." *AI*, xviii (1982), 45–78.
‹P. 152›

Bolens, Lucie. *Les méthodes culturales au Moyen Âge d'après les traités d'agronomie andalous: traditions et techniques*. Geneva: Editions Médecine et Hygiene, 1974. 2d ed., published as *Agronomes andalous du Moyen Age*. Geneva and Paris: Droz, 1981.
‹P. 300›

———. "L'agriculture hispano-arabe au Moyen-Âge." *HO*, I/vi/6, pt. 1 (1977), 255–275.
‹P. 300›

Bombaci, Alessio. *The Kufic Inscription in Persian Verses in the Court of the Royal*

Palace of Masʿud III at Ghazni. Istituto Italiano per il Medio ed Estremo Oriente, Centro Studi e Scavi Archeologici in Asia. Reports and Memoirs, 5. Rome, 1966.
‹P. 55›

Bosworth, C. E. *The Ghaznavids: Their Empire in Afghanistan and Eastern Iran*. Edinburgh: Edinburgh University Press, 1963.
‹Pp. 154, 155, 156›

———. *The Islamic Dynasties: a Chronological and Genealogical Handbook*. Edinburgh: Edinburgh University Press, 1967.
‹P. 20›

———. "The Titulature of the Early Ghaznavids." *Oriens*, xv (1962), 210–233.
‹P. 163›

———. "Military Organization under the Buyids of Persia and Iraq." *Oriens*, xviii–xix (1967), 143–167.
‹P. 180›

———. "Abū ʿAbdallāh al-Khwārizmī on the Technical Terms of the Secretary's Art." *JESHO*, xii (1969), 113–164.
‹P. 44›

———. "Christian and Jewish Religious Dignitaries in Mamluk Egypt and Syria: Qalqashandī's Information on Their Hierarchy, Titulature, and Appointment." *IJMES*, iii (1973), 59–74, 199–216.
‹Pp. 266–267›

———. "The Heritage of Rulership in Early Islamic Iran and the Search for Dynastic Connections with the Past." *Iran*, xi (1973), 51–62.
‹P. 163›

———. "The Protected Peoples (Christians and Jews) in Medieval Egypt and Syria." *BJRUL*, lxii (1979), 11–36.
‹P. 267›

———. "The Concept of Dhimma in Early Islam." In Braude and Lewis, *Christians and Jews in the Ottoman Empire*, i, 37–51.
‹P. 257›

Bosworth, C. E., et al., eds. *The Islamic World from Classical to Modern Times: Essays in Honor of Bernard Lewis*. Princeton, NJ: Darwin Press, 1989. *See also* Humphreys, R. S.; Sanders, Paula.

Bowen-Jones, H. "Agriculture." In *Cambridge History of Iran*, i, 565–598.
‹P. 295›

Boyce, Mary. *A History of Zoroastrianism*. Vol. I: *The Early Period*. *HO*, I/viii/1 (1975).
‹P. 6›

Braude, Benjamin, and Bernard Lewis, eds. *Christians and Jews in the Ottoman Empire: The Functioning of a Plural Society*. 2 vols. London and New York: Holmes and Meier, 1982. *See also* Bosworth, C. E.
‹Pp. 257, 270›

Bregel, Yuri. *Persidskaia literatura: bio-bibliograficheskii obzor*. 3 vols. Moscow: Central Department of Oriental Literature, 1972.
‹Pp. 30, 39›

Brett, Michael. "The Way of the Peasant." *BSOAS*, xlvii (1984), 44–56.
‹Pp. 179, 303›

Brice, William C. *South-west Asia*. London: University of London Press, 1966.

‹P. 290›

———. "The Turkish Colonization of Anatolia." *BJRL*, xxxviii (1955), 18–44.
‹P. 290›

Brice, William C., ed. *The Environmental History of the Near and Middle East since the Last Ice Age*. London and New York: Academic Press, 1978.
‹P. 291›

———. *An Historical Atlas of Islam*. Leiden: E. J. Brill, 1981.
‹P. 16›

Brinton, Crane. *The Anatomy of Revolution*. New York: Norton, 1938. Rev. ed., New York: Prentice-Hall, 1952. 2d rev. ed., New York: Vintage, 1965.
‹P. 109›

British Library. *Third Supplementary Catalogue of Arabic Printed Books in the British Library, 1958–1969*. 4 vols. London: British Museum Publications, 1977.
‹P. 24›

British Museum. Department of Oriental Printed Books and Manuscripts.
(a) *Catalogue of Arabic Printed Books in the British Museum*. 3 vols. London: British Museum, 1894–1901.
(b) *Supplementary Catalogue*. London: British Museum, 1926.
(c) *Second Supplementary Catalogue*. London: British Museum, 1959.
‹P. 24›

———. Department of Oriental Printed Books and Manuscripts. *A Catalogue of the Persian Printed Books in the British Museum*. London: British Museum, 1922.
‹P. 24›

Brockelmann, Carl. *Das Verhältnis von Ibn-el-Aṯīrs Kāmil fit-taʾrīẖ zu Tabaris Aḫbār errusul wal mulūk*. Strasbourg: K. J. Trubner, 1890.
‹P. 130›

———. *Geschichte der arabischen Litteratur*. Original edition: 2 vols., Weimar: E. Felber, 1898–1902. 3 supplement vols., Leiden: E. J. Brill, 1937–42. Rev. edition of Vols. I–II, Leiden: E. J. Brill, 1943–49.
‹Pp. 26–27, 28, 29, 31, 39, 133, 218›

Brunschvig, Robert. *La Berbérie Orientale sous les Hafsides*. 2 vols. Paris: Adrien Maisonneuve, 1940–47.
‹P. 287›

———. *Études d'islamologie*. 2 vols. Paris: G. P. Maisonneuve et Larose, 1976.
‹Pp. 211, 214›

———. *Études sur l'Islam classique et l'Afrique du Nord*. Ed. by A.-M. Turki. London: Variorum, 1986.
‹Pp. 76, 87, 211›

———. "Ibn ʿAbdalḥakam et la conquête de l'Afrique du Nord par les arabes." *AIEO*, i (1942–47), 108–155. Reprinted in Brunschvig, *Études sur l'Islam classique*.
‹Pp. 76, 87›

———. "Urbanisme médiéval et droit musulman." *REI*, xv (1947), 127–155. Reprinted in Brunschvig, *Études d'islamologie*, ii, 7–35.
‹Pp. 211, 231›

———. "Considérations sociologiques sur le droit musulman ancien." *SI*, iii (1955), 61–73. Reprinted in Brunschvig, *Études d'islamologie*, ii, 119–132.
‹P. 211›

———. "Métiers vils dans l'Islam." *SI*, xvi (1967), 41–60. Reprinted in Brunschvig,

Études d'islamologie, i, 145–164.
‹P. 211›
———. "Conceptions monétaires chez les juristes musulmans, viiie-xiiie siècles." *Arabica*, xiv (1967), 113–143. Reprinted in Brunschvig, *Études d'islamologie*, ii, 271–301.
‹P. 211›
———. "Propriétaire et locataire d'immeuble en droit musulman médiéval (jusqu'a vers l'an 1200)," *SI*, lii (1980), 5–40. Reprinted in Brunschvig, *Études sur l'Islam classique*.
‹P. 211›
al-Bukhārī, Abū ʿAbdallāh. *al-Ṣaḥīḥ*. Trans. by O. Houdas and Wm. Marçais as *Les traditions islamiques*. 4 vols. Paris: E. Leroux, 1903–14.
‹P. 22›
———. *al-Taʾrīkh al-kabīr*. 4 vols. Hyderabad, Deccan: Dāʾirat al-Maʿārif al-ʿUthmāniyya: 1361–77/1940–58.
‹P. 81›
Bulliet, R. W. *The Patricians of Nishapur*. Cambridge, MA: Harvard University Press, 1972.
‹Pp. 198–199›
———. Conversion to Islam in the Medieval Period: *An Essay in Quantitative History*. Cambridge, MA: Harvard University Press, 1979.
‹Pp. 279, 281–282›
Bürgel, J. C. *Die Hofkorrespondenz ʿAḍud ad-Daulas und ihr Verhältnis zu anderen historischen Quellen der frühen Buyiden*. Wiesbaden: O. Harrassowitz, 1965.
‹P. 162›
Burgoyne, Michael Hamilton. *Mamluk Jerusalem: An Architectural Study*. London: World of Islam Festival Trust, from the British School of Archaeology in Jerusalem, 1987.
‹P. 233›
Busse, Heribert. *Untersuchungen zum islamischen Kanzleiwesen, an hand Türkmenischer und Safawidischer Urkunden*. Abhandlungen des Deutschen Archaeologischen Institut, Kairo: Islamische Reihe, I. Cairo, 1959.
‹Pp. 43, 45›
———. *Chalif und Grosskonig: Die Buyiden im Iraq (945–1055)*. Beirut: Orient-Institut der Deutschen Morgenländischen Gesellschaft, 1969.
‹P. 155›
———. "Persische Diplomatik in Überblick: Ergebnisse und Probleme." *Islam*, xxxvii (1961), 202–245.
‹P. 45›
———. "Iran under the Buyids." In *Cambridge History of Iran*, iv, 250–304.
———. "The Revival of Persian Kingship under the Buyids." In Richards, *Islamic Civilization, 950–1150*, 47–69.
‹Pp. 153–154, 161›
———. "Farmān." *EI*², ii, 803–804.
‹P. 44›
Butzer, Karl W. "Climatic change in arid regions since the Pliocene." In Stamp, *History*

of Land-Use in Arid Regions, 31–56.
‹P. 291›

———. *Early Hydraulic Civilization in Egypt: A Study in Cultural Ecology*. Chicago and London: University of Chicago Press, 1976.
‹Pp. 293, 299›

Caetani, Leone. *Annali dell'Islam*. 10 vols. Milan: U. Hoepli, 1905–1926.
‹Pp. 71, 72, 93›

———. *Chronographia Islamica*. Paris: P. Geuthner, 1912.

Caʿfer Efendi. *Risāle-i Miʿmāriyye. An Early Seventeenth-Century Ottoman Treatise on Architecture*. Facsimile ed. and trans. by Howard Crane. Leiden: E. J. Brill, 1987
‹P. 63›

Cahen, Claude. *Pre-Ottoman Turkey*. Trans. by J. Jones-Williams. London: Sidgwick and Jackson, 1968.
‹P. 48›

———. *Les peuples musulmans dans l'histoire médiévale*. Damascus: Institut Français de Damas, 1977.
‹Pp. 36, 121, 124, 136, 157, 165, 180, 211, 216, 226, 229, 263, 301›

———. *Makhzūmiyyāt: Études sur l'histoire économique et financière de l'Égypte médiévale*. Leiden: E. J. Brill, 1977. *See also* al-Makhzūmī.
‹Pp. 173, 174, 179, 266, 299›

———. *Introduction à l'histoire du monde musulman médiéval: viie–xve—siècle*. Paris: Jean Maisonneuve, 1982. *See also* Sauvaget, Jean.
‹P. 8›

———. "La Jazira au milieu du xiiie siècle d'après ʿIzz ad-Dīn ibn Chaddād," *REI*, viii (1934), 109–128.
‹P. 174›

———. "Les chroniques arabes concernant la Syrie, l'Égypte, et la Mésopotamie de la conquête arabe à la conquête ottomane dans les bibliothèques d'Istanbul." *REI*, x (1936), 333–362.
‹P. 38›

———. "Quelques chroniques anciennes relatives aux derniers Fatimides." *BIFAO*, xxxvii (1937), 1–27.
‹P. 136›

———. "La tuğrā seljukide." *JA*, ccxxxiv (1943–45), 167–172.
‹P. 167›

———. "Le Malik-nameh et l'histoire des origines seljukides." *Oriens*, ii (1949), 31–65.
‹P. 165›

———. "Le service de l'irrigation en Iraq au début du xie siècle." *BEO*, xii (1949–51), 117–143.
‹Pp. 295, 302›

———. "Notes sur l'histoire des Croisades et de l'Orient latin, II: Le régime rural syrien au temps de la domination franque." *BFLUS* (1951), 286–310.
‹P. 297–298›

———. "Quelques problèmes économiques et fiscaux de l'Iraq buyide d'après un traité de mathématique." *AIEO*, x (1952), 326–363.
‹P. 301›

———. "L'évolution de l'iqṭāʿ du IXe au XIIIe siècle: contribution à une histoire comparée des sociétés médiévales." *AESC*, viii (1953), 25–52. Reprinted in Cahen, *Peuples musulmans*, 231–270.
‹Pp. 180, 301›

———. "Fiscalité, propriété, antagonismes sociaux en Haute-Mésopotamie au temps des premiers Abbassides, d'après Denys de Tell Mahré." *Arabica*, i (1954), 136–152. Reprinted in Cahen, *Peuples musulmans*, 405–422.
‹Pp. 121, 263, 301›

———. Review of F. Løkkegaard, *Islamic Taxation in the Classic Period. Arabica*, i (1954), 346–353.
‹P. 303›

———. "The Turkish Invasion: The Selchükids." In Setton, *History of the Crusades*, i, 135–176.
‹P. 156›

———. "La chronique des Ayyoubides d'al-Makīn ibn al-ʿAmīd." *BEO*, xv (1955–57), 109–184.
‹P. 277›

———. "L'histoire économique et sociale de l'Orient musulman médiéval." *SI*, iii (1955), 93–115. Reprinted in Cahen, *Peuples musulmans*, 209–230.
‹P. 229›

———. "Le régime des impôts dans le Fayyum ayyubide." *Arabica*, iii (1956), 8–30. Reprinted in Cahen, *Makhzumiyyat*.
‹P. 174›

———. "Ayyūbids." *EI^2*, i, 796–807.
‹Pp. 166, 266›

———. "Buwayhids or Būyids." *EI^2*, i, 1350–1357.
‹Pp. 155, 166›

———. "Djizya." *EI^2*, ii, 559–562.
‹P. 257›

———. "Dhimma." *EI^2*, ii, 227–231.
‹P. 257›

———. Review of Sibṭ ibn al-Jawzī, *Mirʾāt al-zamān fī taʾrīkh al-aʿyān. Arabica*, iv (1957), 191–194.
‹P. 36›

———. "Zur Geschichte der städtischen Gesellschaft im islamischen Orient des Mittelalters." *Saeculum*, ix (1958), 59–76.
‹Pp. 229–230›

———. "Mouvements populaires et autonomisme urbain dans l'Asie musulmane du Moyen Âge." *Arabica*, v (1958), 225–250; vi (1959), 25–56, 233–265.
‹Pp. 157, 246›

———. Review of Émile Tyan, *Sultanat et califat. Arabica*, v (1958), 70–76.
‹P. 161›

———. "Reflexions sur le *waqf* ancien." *SI*, xiv (1961), 37–56. Reprinted in Cahen, *Peuples musulmans*, 287–306.
‹P. 216›

———. "The Historiography of the Seljukid Period." In Lewis and Holt, *Historians of the Middle East*, 59–78. Reprinted in Cahen, *Peuples musulmans*, 37–64.
‹Pp. 136, 165›

———. "A propos et autour d'*Ein arabisches Handbuch der Handelswissenschaft.*" *Oriens*, xv (1962), 160–171. Reprinted in Cahen, *Peuples musulmans*, 91–104.
‹P. 226›

———. "Editing Arabic Chronicles: A Few Suggestions." *Islamic Studies* (1962), 1–25. Reprinted in Cahen, *Peuples musulmans*, 11–36.
‹P. 36›

———. "Un traité financier inédit d'époque fatimide-ayyubide." (Appendix: "A propos de quelques almanachs et calendriers de l'Égypte médiévale"). *JESHO*, v (1962), 139–159. Reprinted in *Makhzumiyyat*.
‹Pp. 173, 299›

———. "Points de vue sur la 'Révolution abbaside.' " *Revue Historique* (1963), 295–338. Reprinted in Cahen, *Peuples musulmans*, 105–160.
‹P. 124›

———. "Considérations sur l'utilisation des ouvrages de droit musulman par l'historien." *Atti del III Congresso di Studi Arabi e Islamici* (Naples, 1967). Reprinted in Cahen, *Peuples musulmans*, 81–89.
‹P. 211›

———. "Y a-t-il eu des corporations professionelles dans le monde musulman classique?" In Hourani and Stern, *The Islamic City*, 51–63. Reprinted in Cahen, *Peuples musulmans*,
‹P. 157›

———. "Al-Makhzūmī et Ibn Mammātī sur l'agriculture égyptienne médiévale." *AI*, xi (1972), 141–151.
‹P. 299›

———. "Nomades et sédentaires dans le monde musulman du milieu du Moyen Âge." In Richards, *Islamic Civilization*, 950–1150, 93–102. Reprinted in Cahen, *Peuples musulmans*, 423–437.
‹P. 157›

———. Review of Vryonis, *Decline of Medieval Hellenism*. *IJMES*, iv (1973), 112–117.
‹P. 281›

———. "Tribes, Cities, and Social Organization." In *Cambridge History of Iran*, iv, 305–328.
‹P. 157›

———. "Aperçu sur les impôts du sol en Syrie au Moyen Âge." *JESHO*, xviii (1975), 233–244. [Translation of text of Nuwayri, *Nihāyat al-arab*, viii, 255 ff.]
‹P. 298›

———. "Iḳṭāʿ." *EI*², iii, 1088–1091.
‹P. 180›

———. "L'historiographie arabe: des origines au viiᵉ s. H." *Arabica*, xxxiii (1986), 133–198. [To be published in *Cambridge History of Arabic Literature*, vol. II, part 2.]
‹Pp. 75, 76, 133›

Cahen, Claude, and M. Talbi. "Ḥisba." *EI*², iii, 485–489.
‹P. 217›

Cairo: *al-Nadwa al-duwaliyya li-taʾrīkh al-Qā*hira, Mars-Abril 1969/Colloque internationale sur l'histoire du Caire, Mars-Avril 1969. Cairo: Dār al-Kutub, 1970. *See also* Lewis, Bernard; Grunebaum, Gustave E. von.

Cambridge Economic History of Europe. Vol. I: *The Agrarian Life of the Middle Ages* (2nd ed.). Ed. by M. M. Postan. Cambridge: Cambridge University Press, 1966. *See also* Parain, Charles; Stevens, C. E.
‹Pp. 286, 300›

Cambridge History of Arabic Literature: Arabic Literature to the End of the Umayyad Period. Ed. by A.F.L. Beeston, T. M. Johnstone, R. B. Serjeant, and G. R. Smith. Cambridge and New York: Cambridge University Press, 1983. *See also* Serjeant, R. B.
‹P. 79›

Cambridge History of Arabic Literature: ʿAbbāsid Belles-Lettres. Ed. by Julia Ashtiany, T. M. Johnstone, R. B. Serjeant, and G. R. Smith. Cambridge and New York: Cambridge University Press, 1990.

Cambridge History of Iran. Cambridge: Cambridge University Press, 1968–in progress.
Vol. I. *The Land of Iran*. Ed. by W. B. Fisher (1968).
Vol. II. *The Median and Achaemenian Period*. Ed. by I. Gershevitch (1985).
Vol. III. *The Seleucid, Parthian, and Sasanian Periods*. Ed. by E. Yarshater (1983).
Vol. IV. *From the Arab Invasion to the Saljuqs*. Ed. by R. N. Frye (1975).
Vol. V. *The Saljuq and Mongol Periods*. Ed. by J. A. Boyle (1968).
Vol. VI. *The Timurid and Safavid Periods*. Ed. by P. Jackson and L. Lockhart (1986).
Vol. VII. *From Nadir Shah to the Islamic Republic*. Ed. by P. Avery, G.R.G. Hambly, and C. Melville (1990).
See also Bowen-Jones, H.; Cahen, Claude; Flower, D. J.; Grabar, Oleg; Lambton, A.K.S.; Mottahedeh, R. P.
‹P. 155›

Cambridge History of Islam. Ed. by P. M. Holt, A.K.S. Lambton, and Bernard Lewis. 2 vols. Cambridge: Cambridge University Press, 1970.

Cameron, Averil, and Lawrence I. Conrad, eds. *Late Antiquity and Early Islam: A Critical Guide to the Sources*. [To be published under the auspices of the British Academy.]
‹P. 69›

Canard, Marius. *Les institutions des Fatimides en Égypte; texte arabe extrait du tome III du Kitāb ṣubḥ al-aʿshā fī ṣināʿat al-inshā*. Algiers: Maison des livres, 1957.
‹P. 267›

———. *Byzance et les musulmans du Proche Orient*. Collected Studies, 18. London: Variorum Reprints, 1973.
‹P. 267›

———. *Miscellanea Orientalia*. Collected Studies, 19. London: Variorum Reprints, 1973.
‹P. 267›

———. *L'expression arabo-islamique et ses repercussions*. Collected Studies, 31. London: Variorum Reprints, 1974.
‹P. 267›

———. "Le cérémonial fatimide et le cérémonial byzantin; essai de comparaison." *Byzantion*, xxi (1951), 355–420.
‹P. 153›

———. "Un vizir chrétien à l'époque fatimite, l'Arménien Bahram." *AIEO*, xii (1954), 84–113.
‹P. 268›

———. "La destruction de l'Église de la Resurrection par le calife Hakim et l'histoire de la descente du feu sacré." *Byzantion*, xxxv (1955), 16–43.
‹P. 267›

———. "Notes sur les Arméniens à l'époque fatimite." *AIEO*, xiii (1955), 143–157.
‹P. 268›

———. "Le riz dans le Proche Orient aux premiers siècles de l'Islam." *Arabica*, vi (1959), 113–131.
‹P. 294›

———. "Fāṭimids." *EI^2*, ii, 850–862.
‹P. 266›

———. "al-Ḥākim bi-Amr Allāh." *EI^2*, iii, 76–82.
‹Pp. 266, 267›

Carr, E. H. *What is History?* London: Macmillan; New York: St. Martin's Press, 1961.
‹P. 289›

Caskel, Werner. *Ǧamharat an-Nasab. Das genealogische Werk des Hišam ibn Muḥammad al-Kalbī.* 2 vols. Leiden: E. J. Brill, 1966.
‹P. 115›

Castellani, Eutimio. *Catalogo dei Firmani ed altri documenti legali emanati in lingue araba e turca concernenti i Santuari le proprieta i diritti della Custodia di Terra Santa conservati nell' Archivio della stessa Custodia in Gerusalemme*. Jerusalem: Franciscan Press, 1922.
‹Pp. 48, 171›

Chabot, J. B., ed. and trans. *Synodicon orientale, ou recueil des synodes nestoriens*. In *Notices et extraits des manuscrits de la Bibliothèque Nationale*, xxxviii (Paris, 1902).
‹P. 278›

Chalmeta Gendron, Pedro. *El señor del zoco en España: edades media y moderna. Contribución al estudio de la historia del mercado*. Madrid: Instituto Hispano-Arabe de Cultura, 1973.
‹P. 217›

Chehata, Chafik. *See* Shehata, Shafik.

Chester Beatty Library, Dublin. *See* Arberry, A. J.

Chevedden, Paul E. "The Citadel of Damascus." 2 vols. Ph.D. dissertation, University of California at Los Angeles, 1986.
‹P. 245›

Christensen, Arthur. *L'Iran sous les Sassanides.* Copenhagen: Levin and Munksgaard, 1936. 2d rev. ed., 1944.
‹P. 162›

Clauson, Sir Gerard. *An Etymological Dictionary of Pre-Thirteenth Century Turkish.* Oxford: Clarendon Press, 1972.
‹P. 15›

Clover, F. M., and R. S. Humphreys, eds. *Tradition and Innovation in Late Antiquity.* Madison and London: University of Wisconsin Press, 1989. *See also* Humphreys, R. S.; Lassner, J.

Codrington, Oliver. *A Manual of Musalman Numismatics*. London: Royal Asiatic Society, 1904.
‹P. 51›

Cohen, Amnon. *Jewish Life under Islam: Jerusalem in the Sixteenth Century*. Cambridge, MA: Harvard University Press, 1984.
‹P. 270›

Cohen, Amnon, and Bernard Lewis. *Population and Revenue in the Towns of Palestine in the Sixteenth Century*. Princeton, NJ: Princeton University Press, 1978.
‹P. 172›

Cohen, Hayyim J. "The Economic Background and the Secular Occupations of Muslim Jurisprudents and Traditionists in the Classical Period of Islam (until the Middle of the Eleventh Century)." *JESHO*, xiii (1970), 16–61.
‹P. 205›

Cohen, Mark R. *Jewish Self-Government in Medieval Egypt: The Origins of the Office of Head of the Jews, ca. 1065–1126*. Princeton, NJ: Princeton University Press, 1980.
‹Pp. 270–271›

———. "The Jews under Islam: from the Rise of Islam to Sabbatai Zevi." In *Bibliographical Essays in Medieval Jewish Studies* (New York: Ktav, 1976), 169–229. Reprinted, with supplement on works published 1973–80, as *Princeton Near East Paper*, no. 32 (Program in Near Eastern Studies, Princeton University, 1981).
‹Pp. 264, 270, 278›

Conrad, Lawrence I. "Abraha and Muhammad: Some Observations apropos of Chronology and Literary *Topoi* in the Early Arabic Historical Tradition." *BSOAS*, 1 (1987), 225–240.
‹Cf. p. 86›

———. "Al-Azdī's History of the Arab Conquests in Bilād al-Shām: Some Historiographical Observations." In *Proceedings of the Second Symposium on the History of Bilād al-Shām* , Vol. I, 28–62.
‹P. 80›

———. *See also* Cameron, Averil; al-Dūrī, ʿAbd al-ʿAzīz.

Cook, Michael. *Early Muslim Dogma: a Source Critical Study*. Cambridge and New York: Cambridge University Press, 1981.
‹P. 90›

Cook, Michael, and Patricia Crone. *Hagarism, the Making of the Islamic World*. Cambridge: Cambridge University Press, 1977.
‹Pp. 84–85›

Cooper, Richard S. "Ibn Mammātī's Rules for the Ministries." Ph.D. dissertation, University of California-Berkeley, 1973.
‹P. 173›

———. "Land Classification Terminology and the Assessment of the Kharāj Tax in Medieval Egypt." *JESHO*, xvii (1974), 91–102.
‹Pp. 173–174›

———. "The Assessment and Collection of Kharāj Tax in Medieval Egypt." *JAOS*, xcvi (1976), 365–382.
‹P. 174›

———. "Agriculture in Egypt, 640–1800." *HO*, I/vi/6, pt. 1 (1977), 188–204.
‹P. 299›

Cornu, Georgette. *Atlas du monde arabo-islamique à l'époque classique (ixe–xe siècles)*. Leiden: E. J. Brill, 1985.
‹P. 17›

Corpus Inscriptionium Iranicarum. Ed. by an international committee (President: S. H. Taqizade. Chairman: Harold Bailey). 22 Vols., in progress. London: P. Lund, Humphries, 1973–continuing.
Vol. II: *Khurasan.* Ed. by William Hanaway (1977).
Vol. VI: *Mazandaran.* Ed. by A.D.H. Bivar and E. Yarshater (1978).
‹P. 58›

Coulson, Noel J. *A History of Islamic Law.* Edinburgh: Edinburgh University Press, 1964.
‹P. 214›

———. *Conflicts and Tensions in Islamic Jurisprudence.* Chicago: University of Chicago Press, 1969.
‹P. 214›

———. *Succession in the Muslim Family.* Cambridge: Cambridge University Press, 1971.
‹P. 217›

Creswell, K.A.C. *Early Muslim Architecture.* 2 vols. Oxford: Clarendon Press, 1938–40; 2d rev. ed. of Vol. I, 1969.
‹P. 61›

———. *The Muslim Architecture of Egypt.* 2 vols. Oxford: Clarendon Press, 1952–59.
‹P. 61›

———. *A Bibliography of the Architecture, Arts, and Crafts of Islam.* Cairo: American University of Cairo Press, 1961.
‹P. 63›

———. *A Bibliography of the Architecture, Arts, and Crafts of Islam. Supplement, Jan. 1960 to Jan. 1972.* Cairo: American University of Cairo Press, 1973. *See also* Pearson, J. D.; Scanlon, G.
‹P. 63›

Crone, Patricia. *Slaves on Horses: the Evolution of the Islamic Polity.* London and New York: Cambridge University Press, 1980.
‹P. 85›

———. *Meccan Trade and the Rise of Islam.* Princeton, NJ: Princeton University Press, 1987.
‹P. 85›

———. Review of Sharon, *Black Banners from the East*, in *BSOAS*, l (1987), 134–136. *See also* Cook, Michael.
‹P. 123›

Cuoq, Joseph. *Islamisation de la Nubie chrétienne, viie–xvie siècle.* Paris: P. Geuthner, 1986.
‹P. 276›

Cusa, Salvatore. *I diplomi greci ed arabi di Sicilia.* 2 vols. Palermo, 1868–82.
‹P. 46›

Dahan, Sami (= al-Dahhān, Sāmī). "The Origin and Development of the Local Histories of Syria." In Lewis and Holt, *Historians of the Middle East*, 108–117.
‹P. 241›

Dalman, Gustav. *Arbeit und Sitte in Palästina.* 6 vols. Gütersloh: Deutsche Palästina-Institut, 1928–1939. Reprinted in 7 vols., Hildesheim: Georg Olms, 1974.
‹P. 297›

Daniel, Elton. *The Political and Social History of Khurasan under Abbasid Rule, 747–820.* Minneapolis and Chicago: Bibliotheca Islamica, 1979.
‹Pp. 121, 124›

———. "The Anonymous History of the Abbasid Family and its Place in Islamic Historiography." *IJMES*, xiv (1982), 419–434.
‹P. 112›

———. Review of Sharon, *Black Banners from the East*, in *IJMES*, xxi (1989), 578–583.
‹P. 123›

Darrag, Ahmad. *L'Égypte sous le règne de Barsbāy, 825–841/1422–1438.* Damascus: Institut Français de Damas, 1961.
‹Pp. 184–185›

———. *L'acte de waqf de Barsbāy (Ḥuǧǧat waqf Barsbāy).* Cairo: Institut Français d'Archeologie Orientale, 1963.
‹P. 220›

David, Jean-Claude. *Le waqf d'Ipšīr Pāšā à Alep (1063/1653). Étude d'urbanisme historique.* Damascus: Institut Français de Damas, 1982.
‹P. 232›

Dennett, Daniel C. *Conversion and the Poll Tax in Early Islam.* Cambridge, MA: Harvard University Press, 1950.
‹Pp. 44, 179, 279, 303›

———. "Marwān ibn Muḥammad: The Passing of the Umayyad Caliphate." Ph. D. dissertation, Harvard University, 1939.
‹P. 126›

Dentzer, J. M., Ph. Gautheir, and T. Hackens, eds. *Numismatique antique: problèmes et méthodes. Annales de l'Est, publiées par l'Université de Nancy II.* Mémoire 44. Études d'archéologie classique, IV. Nancy-Louvain: Peeters, 1975.
‹P. 50›

Deny, Jean. *Sommaire des archives turques du Caire.* Cairo: Institut Français d'Archéologie Orientale, pour la Société Royale de Géographie d'Egypte, 1930.
‹P. 231›

———. "Tughrā." *EI*[1], iv, 822–826.
‹P. 44›

Description de l'Égypte, ou, Recueil des observations et des recherches qui ont été faites en Égypte pendant l'expédition de l'armée française, publié par les ordres de Sa Majesté l'Empéreur Napoléon le Grand.
(a) Original edition—19 vols. Paris: Imprimerie Imperiale, 1809–28.
Antiquités: *Descriptions*, 2 vols.; *Mémoires*, 2 vols.; *Planches*, 5 vols.
État Moderne: *Mémoires*, 2 vols. in 3; *Planches*, 2 vols.
Histoire Naturelle: *Mémoires*, 2 vols.; *Planches*, 2 vols. in 3.
Carte Topographique
(b) 2d edition—text, 24 vols. in 26; plates, 12 vols. Paris: C.L.F. Panckoucke, 1821–29.

Despois, J. "Development of land use in northern Africa (with references to Spain)." In Stamp, *History of Land-Use in Arid Regions*, 219–238.
‹Cf. pp. 291, 293›

Despois, Jean, and René Raynal. *Géographie de l'Afrique du Nord-Ouest.* Paris: Payot, 1967.
‹P. 290›

al-Dhahabī, Shams al-Dīn. *Mīzān al-iʿtidāl fī naqd al-rijāl.*
(a) 3 vols. Cairo: Maṭbaʿat al-Saʿāda, 1325/1907.
(b) Ed. by A. M. al-Bijāwī. 4 vols. Cairo: ʿĪsā al-Bābī al-Ḥalabī, 1963–64.
‹P. 81›

Dictionary of the Middle Ages. Ed. by Joseph R. Strayer. 13 vols., New York: Charles Scribner & Sons, 1982–89.
‹P. 6›

Dietrich, Albert. *Arabische Briefe aus der Papyrussammlung der Hamburger Staats- und Universitäts-Bibliothek.* Hamburg: J. J. Augustin, 1955.
‹P. 224›

———. "Das politische Testament des zweiten abbasidischen Kalifen al-Mansur," *Islam*, xxx (1952), 133–165.
‹P. 120›

al-Dimashqī, Abū al-Faḍl. *Kitāb al-ishāra ilā maḥāsin al-tijāra. See also* Cahen, Claude; Ritter, Helmut.
‹P. 226›

al-Dīnawarī, Abū Ḥanīfa. *al-Akhbār al-ṭiwāl.* Ed. by V. Guirgass. Leiden: E. J. Brill, 1888.
‹Pp. 72, 111›

———. *Kitāb al-nabāt.* Ed. by Bernhard Lewin as *The Book of Plants.* Uppsala: Lundequistska Bokhandeln, 1953.
‹P. 296›

Dissertation Abstracts: abstracts of dissertations and monographs in microfilm. V.1–continuing. Ann Arbor: University Microfilms, 1938–present.
‹P. 10›

Dix ans de recherche universitaire française sur le monde arabe et islamique de 1968–9 à 1979. Paris: Editions Recherche sur les Civilisations, for the Association Française des Arabisants, 1982.
‹P. 10›

Djaït, Hichem. *Al-Kūfa, naissance de la ville islamique.* Paris: G.-P. Maisonneuve et Larose, 1986.
‹Pp. 125, 234›

Doerfer, Gerhard. *Türkische und Mongolische Elemente im Neupersischen.* 4 vols. Wiesbaden: Franz Steiner, 1963–75.
‹P. 14›

Dollar, C. M., and R.J.N. Jensen. *Historian's Guide to Statistics: Quantitative Analysis and Historical Research.* New York: Holt, Rinehart, and Winston, 1971.
‹P. 205›

Dols, Michael. *The Black Death in the Middle East.* Princeton, NJ: Princeton University Press, 1977.
‹Pp. 247–248›

Donner, Fred M. *The Early Islamic Conquests.* Princeton, NJ: Princeton University Press, 1981. *See also* Hawting, G. R.
‹Pp. 70, 88–89›

———. "The Formation of the Early Islamic State." *JAOS*, cvi (1986), 283–296.
‹Pp. 89–90›

———. "The Problem of Early Arabic Historiography in Syria." In *Proceedings of the Second Symposium on the History of Bilād al-Shām*, Vol. I, 1–27.
‹P. 80›

Downing, Theodore E., and McGuire Gibson, eds. *Irrigation's Impact on Society.* Anthropological Papers of the University of Arizona, no. 25. Tucson: University of Arizona Press, 1974. *See also* Gibson, McGuire; Neely, James A.; Spooner, Brian.

Dozy, R.P.A. *Supplément aux dictionnaires arabes.* 2 vols. Leiden: E. J. Brill, 1881; repr. 1927, 1960.
‹Pp. 13–14›

Dubler, César E. "Über das Wirtschaftsleben auf der Iberischen Halbinsel vom XI zum XIII Jahrhundert." *Romanica Helvetica* (Geneva), xxii (1943).
‹P. 304›

Duby, Georges. *L'économie rurale et la vie des campagnes dans l'Occident médiéval.* Paris: Aubier, 1962. Trans. by Cynthia Postan as *Rural Economy and Country Life in the Medieval West.* London: Edward Arnold, 1968; Columbia, SC: University of South Carolina Press, 1968.
‹Pp. 285–286›

Duri, A. A. (= al-Dūrī, ʿAbd al-ʿAzīz). "Al-Zuhrī: a Study on the Beginnings of History Writing in Islam." *BSOAS*, xix (1957), 1–12.
‹P. 80›

———. "The Iraq School of History in the Ninth Century—a Sketch." In Lewis and Holt, *Historians of the Middle East*, 46–53.
‹P. 78›

Duri, A. A., et al. "Dīwān." EI^2, ii, 323–337.
‹P. 44›

al-Dūrī, ʿAbd al-ʿAzīz. *al-ʿAṣr al-ʿabbāsī al-awwal.* Baghdad: Maṭbaʿat al-tafwīḍ al-ahliyya, 1945.
‹P. 119›

———. *Taʾrīkh al-ʿIrāq al-iqtiṣādī fī al-qarn al-rābiʿ al-hijrī.* Baghdad: Maṭbaʿat al-Maʿārif, 1948.
‹P. 301›

———. *Baḥth fī nashʾat ʿilm al-taʾrīkh ʿinda al-ʿArab.* Beirut: Catholic Press, 1960. Trans. by Lawrence Conrad as *The Rise of Historical Writing among the Arabs.* Princeton, NJ: Princeton University Press, 1983.
‹Pp. 76–77, 78›

———. *Dirāsa fī sīrat al-Nabī wa-muʾallifihā Ibn Isḥāq.* Baghdad, 1965.
‹P. 79›

———. "Ḍawʾ jadīd ʿalā al-daʿwa al-ʿabbāsiyya." *Majallat Kulliyat al-Ādāb wa'l-ʿUlūm* (Baghdad, 1957), 64–82.
‹P. 112›

Dussaud, Rene. *Topographie historique de la Syrie antique et médiévale.* Paris: P. Geuthner, 1927.
‹P. 18›

Écochard, Michel, and Claude Le Coeur. *Les bains de Damas.* 2 vols. Beirut: Institut Français de Damas, 1942–43.
‹P. 244›

Ehrenkreutz, A. S. *Saladin.* Albany, NY: State University of New York Press, 1972.
‹P. 266›

———. "Studies in the Monetary History of the Near East in the Middle Ages: the Standard of Fineness of Some Types of Dinars." *JESHO*, ii (1959), 128–161.
‹P. 53›

———. "Numismato-statistical Reflections on the Annual Gold Coinage Production of the Tulunid Mint in Egypt." *JESHO*, xx (1977), 267–281.
‹P. 53›

———. "Money." *HO*, I/vi/6, pt. 1 (1977), 84–97.
‹P. 53›

Eickelman, Dale F. *The Middle East: An Anthropological Approach.* Englewood Cliffs, NJ: Prentice-Hall, 1981. 2d rev. ed., 1989.
‹P. 11›

Elham, Shah Morad. *Kitbuġā und Lāǧīn. Studien zur Mamluken-Geschichte nach Baibars al-Manṣūrī und an-Nuwairī.* Freiburg im Breisgau: K. Schwarz, 1977.
‹P. 136›

Elisseéff, Nikita. *Nūr ad-Din, un grand prince musulman de Syrie au temps des Croisades (511–569 A.H./1118–1174).* 3 vols. Damascus: Institut Français de Damas, 1967.
‹Pp. 180, 297›

———. "Les monuments de Nūr ad-Dīn," *BEO*, xiii (1949–51), 5–43.
‹P. 165›

———. "A propos d'une inscription d'al-Malik al-Muᶜaẓẓam ᶜĪsā: contribution à l'étude de son règne." *AAS*, iv–v (1954–55), 3–28.
‹P. 243›

———. "Les corporations de Damas sous Nūr al-Dīn. Matériaux pour une topographie économique de Damas au xiie siècle." *Arabica*, iii (1956), 61–79.
‹P. 244›

———. "La titulature de Nūr ad-Dīn d'après ses inscriptions." *BEO*, xiv (1952–54), 155–196.
‹P. 165›

———. "Dimashḳ." *EI*^{2}, ii, 277–291. *See also* Ibn ᶜAsākir.
‹Pp. 246, 251›

Elwell-Sutton, L. P., ed. *Bibliographical Guide to Iran: the Middle East Library Committee Guide.* Sussex: Harvester Press, 1983. Totowa, NY: Barnes & Noble Books, 1983.
‹P. 9›

Encyclopaedia Iranica. Ed. by Ehsan Yarshater. London and Boston: Routledge & Kegan Paul, 1982–in progress.
‹P. 5›

Encyclopaedia of Islam: A Dictionary of the Geography, Ethnography and Biography of the Muhammadan Peoples. 4 vols. and Supplement. Leiden: E. J. Brill, 1913–1938.
‹Pp. 4, 5›

Encyclopaedia of Islam, New Edition. Leiden: E. J. Brill, 1954–in progress.
‹Pp. 4, 5, 18›

English, Paul W. *City and Village in Iran: Settlement and Economy in the Kirman Basin.* Madison and London: University of Wisconsin Press, 1966.
‹Pp. 295, 305–306›

———. "The Origin and Spread of Qanats in the Old World." *Proceedings of the American Philosophical Society*, cxii (1968), 170–181.
‹P. 295›

Ernst, Hans, ed. *Die Mamlukischen Sultansurkunden des Sinai-Klosters.* Wiesbaden: O. Harrassowitz, 1960.
‹Pp. 47, 171›

Escovitz, Joseph H. *The Office of Qāḍī al-Quḍāt in Cairo under the Bahri Mamluks*. Islamkundliche Untersuchungen, B. 100. Berlin: K. Schwarz, 1984.
‹P. 221›

Ess, Josef van. *Zwischen Ḥadīṯ und Theologie*. Berlin and New York: W. de Gruyter, 1975.
‹P. 90›

———. *Anfänge muslimischer Theologie: zwei antiqadaritische Traktate aus dem ersten Jahrhundert der Hiğra*. Beirut: Orient-Institut der Deutschen Morgenländischen Gesellschaft, 1977.
‹P. 90›

Ettinghausen, Richard. *Arab Painting*. Lausanne: Albert Skira, 1962.
‹P. 61–62›

Fagnan, Edmond. *Additions aux dictionnaires arabes*. Algiers: J. Carbonel, 1923.
‹P. 14›

Fahd, Badrī Muḥammad. *Shaykh al-Akhbāriyyīn: Abū al-Ḥasan al-Madāʾinī*. Najaf: Maṭbaʿat al-Qaḍāʾ, 1975.
‹P. 79›

Fahd, Toufic. "Conduite d'une exploitation agricole d'après l'Agriculture nabatéenne." *SI*, xxxii (1970), 109–128.
‹P. 296›

———. "Le calendrier des travaux agricoles d'après al-Filāḥa n-nabaṭiyya." In J. M. Barral, ed., *Orientalia Hispanica, sive studia F. M. Pareja octogenario dicata* (2 vols. Leiden: E. J. Brill, 1974). Vol I, 245–272.
‹P. 296›

———. "Matériaux pour l'histoire de l'agriculture en Irak: al-filāḥa n-nabaṭiyya." *HO*, I/vi/6, pt. 1 (1977), 276–378.
‹P. 296›

———. "Ibn Waḥshiyya." *EI*^{2}, iii, 988–990.
‹P. 296›

Faroqhi, Suraiya. "Vakıf Administration in Sixteenth Century Konya: the Zaviye of Sadreddin-i Konevi," *JESHO*, xvii (1974), 145–172.
‹P. 221›

Faruqi, Nisar Ahmed. *Early Muslim Historiography: a Study of Early Transmitters of Arab History from the Rise of Islam up to the End of the Umayyad Period*. Delhi: Idarah-i Adabiyat-i Deli, 1979.
‹P. 80›

Fattal, Antoine. *Le statut légal des non-musulmans en pays d'Islam*. Beirut: Imprimerie Catholique, 1958.
‹Pp. 257, 275›

Fekete, Lajos. *Die Siyaqat-Schrift in der türkischen Finanzverwaltung*. Budapest: Akademiai Kiado, 1955.
‹P. 43›

———. *Einführung in die persische Paläographie: 101 persische Dokumente*. Ed. by G. Hazai. Budapest: Akademiai Kiado, 1977.
‹Pp. 42, 43›

Fernea, Robert W. *Shaykh and Effendi: Changing Patterns of Authority among the El Shabana of Southern Iraq*. Cambridge, MA: Harvard University Press, 1970.
‹P. 293›

Fiey, J. M. *Mossoul chrétienne: essai sur l'histoire, l'archéologie, et l'état actuel des monuments chrétiens de la ville de Mossoul*. Beirut: Catholic Press, 1959.
‹Pp. 263, 279›

"Filāḥa." *EI*², ii, 899–910.
‹P. 294›

Fischel, Walter J. *Jews in the Economic and Political Life of Medieval Islam*. London: Royal Asiatic Society, 1937; repr. 1968.
‹Pp. 226, 267›

———. *Ibn Khaldun and Tamerlane: Their Historic Meeting in Damascus, A.D. 1401 (803 A.H.)*. Berkeley and Los Angeles: University of California Press, 1952.
‹P. 194›

———. *Ibn Khaldun in Egypt (1382–1406)*. Berkeley and Los Angeles: University of California Press, 1967.
‹P. 194›

———. "Selected Bibliography." In Ibn Khaldun, *The Muqaddima: An Introduction to History*, trans. by Franz Rosenthal (2d rev. ed. 3 vols. Princeton, NJ: Princeton University Press, 1967). Vol. III, 485–521.
‹Pp. 193–194›

Fisher, W. B. *The Middle East: A Physical, Social and Regional Geography*. 1st ed., London: Methuen, 1950. 7th ed. (rev. and reset), London: Methuen, 1978.
‹P. 290›

Flannery, Kent V. "The Ecology of Early Food Production in Mesopotamia." *Science*, cxlvii, no. 3663 (12 March 1965), 1247–1255.
‹P. 291›

———. "The Origins and Ecological Effects of Early Domestication in Iran and the Near East." In P. J. Ucko and G. W. Dimbleby, *The Domestication and Exploitation of Plants and Animals*. Chicago: Aldine, 1969.
‹P. 291›

Fleischer, Cornell. *Bureaucrat and Intellectual in the Ottoman Empire: A Biographical Study of the Historian Mustafa Ali, 1541–1600*. Princeton, NJ: Princeton University Press, 1986.
‹P. 135›

Floud, Roderick. *An Introduction to Quantitative Methods for Historians*. Princeton, NJ: Princeton University Press, 1973.
‹P. 205›

Flower, D. J. "Water Use in North-east Iran." In *Cambridge History of Iran*, i, 599–610.
‹P. 295›

Flügel, Gustav Leberecht. *Corani Textus Arabicus*. Leipzig: E. Bredtii, 1834; 2nd ed., 1881.
‹P. 21›

———. *Concordantiae Corani Arabicae*. Leipzig: E. Bredtii, 1842; reprinted 1875, 1898.
‹P. 21›

Foaden, G. P., and F. Fletcher, eds. *Textbook of Egyptian Agriculture*. 2 vols. Cairo: National Printing Dept., for the Egyptian Ministry of Education, 1908–1910.
‹P. 299›

Fragner, Bert G. *Repertorium persischer Herrscherurkunden: publizierte Originalurkunden (bis 1848)*. Freiburg im Breisgau: K. Schwarz, 1980.
‹P. 49›

———. "Das Ardabiler Heiligtum in den Urkunden." *WZKM*, lxvii (1975), 169–215.
‹P. 49›

Franz, Erhard. *Minderheiten im Vorderen Orient: Auswahlbibliographie*. Dokumentationsdienst moderner Orient, Reihe A, Bibliographie 10. Hamburg: Deutsches Orient-Institut, 1978.
‹Pp. 256–257›

Freeman-Grenville, G.S.P. *The Muslim and Christian Calendars*. London: Oxford University Press, 1963.
‹P. 19›

Freytag, G.W.F. *Lexicon arabico-latinum*. 4 vols. Halle: C. A. Schwetschke, 1830–1837.
‹P. 13›

Friedman, Mordechai A. *Jewish Marriage in Palestine: a Cairo Geniza Study*. Vol. I: *The Ketubba Traditions of Eretz Israel*. Vol. II: *The Ketubba Texts*. New York and Tel Aviv: Jewish Theological Seminary of America, 1980–81.
‹P. 270›

Frye, Richard N. "The Role of Abu Muslim in the Abbasid Revolt." *MW*, xxxvii (1947), 28–38.
‹Pp. 122, 123›

———. "The Abbasid Conspiracy and Modern Revolutionary Theory." *Indo-Iranica*, v (1952–53), 9–14.
‹P. 122›

———. "The Charisma of Kingship in Ancient Iran," *Iranica Antiqua*, iv (1964), 36–54.
‹P. 162›

Fück, Johann. *Muḥammad Ibn Isḥāq: Literarhistorische Untersuchungen*. Frankfurt am Main, 1925.
‹P. 78›

Gabrieli, Francesco. "L'opera di Ibn al-Muqaffaʿ." *RSO*, xiii (1931), 231–235.
‹P. 114›

———. "Il califfato di Hisham." *Mémoires de la Société Archéologique d'Alexandrie*, vii/2 (1935).
‹P. 126›

Gabrieli, Giuseppe. *Manuale di bibliografia musulmana*. Rome: Tipografia dell' unione editrice, 1916.
‹P. 9›

Garcin, Jean-Claude. *Un centre musulman de la Haute-Égypte médiévale: Qūṣ*. Cairo: Institut Français d'Archéologie Orientale, 1976.
‹Pp. 184, 185–186, 201, 203–205›

Garcin, J.-C., B. Maury, J. Revault, and M. Zakariya. *Palais et maisons du Caire: I -Époque mamelouke (xiiiᵉ–xviᵉ siècles)*. Paris: Centre National de la Recherche Scientifique, 1982.
‹P. 61›

Gardet, Louis. *La cité musulmane: vie sociale et politique*. Paris: J. Vrin, 1954; 2d ed., 1961.
‹P. 160›

Gätje, Helmut. *The Qurʾān and its Exegesis*. Trans. by A. T. Welch. London: Routledge and Kegan Paul, 1976.
‹P. 21›

Gaube, Heinz. *Arabische Inschriften aus Syrien*. Beirut: Orient-Institut der Deutschen Morgenländischen Gesellschaft, 1978.
‹P. 243›

Gaube, Heinz, and Eugen Wirth. *Der Bazar von Isfahan. TAVO*, Beihefte, Reihe B, No. 22. Wiesbaden: L. Reichert, 1978. See also *TAVO*, map A IX, 9.4 (Wiesbaden, 1977).
‹P. 233, 244›

———. *Aleppo. Historische und geographische Beiträge zur baulichen Gestaltung, zur sozialen Organisation und zur wirtschaftlichen Dynamik einer vorderasiatischen Fernhandelsmetropole*. TAVO, Beihefte, Reihe B, No. 58. Wiesbaden: L. Reichert, 1984.
‹P. 233›

Gaudefroy-Demombynes, Maurice. *La Syrie à l'époque des Mamelouks*. Paris: P. Geuthner, 1923 (= al-Qalqashandī, *Ṣubḥ al-Aʿshā*, vol. 4).
‹Pp. 154, 175, 178, 242, 298›

Geertz, Clifford. *Islam Observed: Religious Development in Morocco and Indonesia*. Chicago: University of Chicago Press, 1971.
‹P. 274›

———. *The Interpretation of Cultures*. New York: Basic Books, 1973.
(a) "Thick Description: Toward an Interpretive Theory of Culture," 3–30.
(b) "Ethos, World View, and the Analysis of Sacred Symbols," 126–141.
(c) "Ideology as a Cultural System," 193–233.
‹Pp. 149, 152, 289›

Geiger, Wilhelm. See *Grundriss der iranischen Philologie*.

Gerhardsson, B. *Memory and Manuscript: Oral Transmission and Written Transmission in Rabbinic Judaism and Early Christianity*. Trans. by E. J. Sharpe. Acta Seminarii Neotestamentice Uppsaliensis, 22. Uppsala, 1961.
‹P. 87›

al-Ghazālī, Abū Ḥāmid. *al-Iqtiṣād fī al-iʿtiqād*. Ed. by Muṣṭafā al-Qabbānī al-Dimashqī. Cairo: al-Maṭbaʿa al-Adabiyya, 1320/1902.
‹P. 161›

———. *Nasṣīḥat al-Mulūk*. Trans. by F.R.C. Bagley as *Ghazali's Book of Counsel for Kings*. London and New York: Oxford University Press, 1964.
‹Pp. 164, 165›

———. *Kitāb faḍāʾiḥ al-Bāṭiniyya. See also* Goldziher, Ignaz.

Ghirshman, Roman. *Iran: Parthes et Sassanides*. Paris: Gallimard, 1962. Trans. by Stuart Gilbert and James Emmons as *Iran: Parthians and Sassanians*. London: Thames and Hudson, 1962.
‹P. 162›

Gibb, H.A.R. *The Arab Conquests in Central Asia*. London: Royal Asiatic Society, 1923.
‹P. 119›

———. *The Damascus Chronicle of the Crusades. See also* Ibn al-Qalānisī.

———. *Studies on the Civilization of Islam*. Ed. by S. J. Shaw and W. R. Polk. Boston: Beacon Press, 1962.
‹Pp. 75, 76, 133, 160, 163, 182›

———. *Saladin: Studies in Islamic History*. Ed. by Yusuf Ibish. Beirut: Arab Institute for Publishing and Research, 1972.
‹Pp. 134, 182›

———. *Saladin.* Oxford: Oxford University Press, 1973.
‹P. 266›

———. "Al-Mawardi's Theory of the Khilafah." *Islamic Culture*, xi (1937), 291–302. Reprinted in Gibb, *Studies on the Civilization of Islam*, 151–165.
‹P. 160›

———. "Ta'rīkh." *EI*[1], Suppl., 233–245. Reprinted in Gibb, *Studies on the Civilization of Islam*, 108–137.
‹Pp. 75, 76, 133›

———. "Some Considerations on the Sunni Theory of the Caliphate." *Archives d'histoire du droit oriental*, iii (1939), 401–410. Reprinted in Gibb, *Studies on the Civilization of Islam*, 141–150.
‹P. 160›

———. "Constitutional Organization." In Khadduri and Liebesny, *Law in the Middle East*, I, 3–27.
‹P. 160›

———. "The Armies of Saladin." *Cahiers de l'histoire égyptienne*, ser. iii, fasc. 4 (1951), 304–320. Reprinted in Gibb, *Studies on the Civilization of Islam*, 74–88; and Gibb, *Saladin: Studies* (Ibish), 138–157.
‹P. 182›

———. "The Social Significance of the Shuʿūbiyya." In *Studia Orientalia Ioanni Pedersen Dicata* (Copenhagen: Munksgaard, 1953), 105–114. Reprinted in Gibb, *Studies on the Civilization of Islam*, 62–73.
‹P. 163›

———. "Al-Barq al-Shāmi: the History of Saladin by the Kātib ʿImād al-Dīn al-Iṣfahānī." *WZKM*, lii (1953), 93–115. Reprinted in Gibb, *Saladin: Studies* (Ibish), 76–103.
‹P. 134›

———. "Government and Islam under the Early Abbasids: the Political Collapse of Islam." In *Colloque de Strasbourg, 1959: L'élaboration de l'Islam* (Paris: Presses Universitaires de France, 1961), pp. 115–127.
‹P. 119›

———. "The Aiyūbids." In Setton, *History of the Crusades*, ii, 693–714.
‹P. 166›

———. "Islamic Biographical Literature." In Lewis and Holt, *Historians of the Middle East*, 54–58.
‹Pp. 79, 188›

Gibson, McGuire. "Violation of Fallow and Engineered Disaster in Mesopotamian Civilization." In Downing and Gibson, *Irrigation's Impact on Society*, 7–20.
‹Pp. 292, 295›

Gil, Moshe. *Documents of the Jewish Pious Foundations from the Cairo Geniza.* Leiden: E. J. Brill, 1976.
‹P. 270›

———. "The Constitution of Medina: A Reconsideration." *Israel Oriental Studies*, iv (1974), 44–66.
‹Pp. 93, 94, 96, 97›

Gilbert, Joan E. "Institutionalization of Muslim Scholarship and Professionalization of the ʿUlamā' in Medieval Damascus." *SI*, lii (1980), 105–134.
‹P. 205›

Girard, M.P.S. "Mémoire sur l'agriculture, l'industrie, et le commerce de l'Égypte." *Description de l'Égypte. État Moderne, Mémoires*: Vol. II (1812), 491–714. *État Moderne, Planches*: Vol. II (1817), nos. I–XXX.
‹P. 299›

Glick, Thomas F. *Irrigation and Society in Medieval Valencia*. Cambridge, MA: Harvard University Press, 1970.
‹Pp. 286, 301›

———. *Islamic and Christian Spain in the Early Middle Ages*. Princeton, NJ: Princeton University Press, 1979.
‹P. 282›

Goeje, M. J. de, ed. *Fragmenta Historicorum Arabicorum*. From the anonymous *al-ʿUyūn wa'l-ḥadāʾiq fī akhbār al-ḥaqāʾiq*. Leiden: E. J. Brill, 1869.
‹P. 111›

Goeje, M. J. de. See also *Bibliotheca Geographorum Arabicorum*; al-Ṭabarī.

Goitein, S. D. *Jews and Arabs: Their Contacts through the Ages*. New York: Schocken, 1955; rev. eds., 1964, 1974.
‹P. 265›

———. *Studies in Islamic History and Institutions*. Leiden: E. J. Brill, 1966.
‹Pp. 114, 226, 263, 273›

———. *A Mediterranean Society: The Jewish Communities of the Arab World as Portrayed in the Documents of the Cairo Geniza*. 5 vols., Berkeley and Los Angeles: University of California Press, 1967–88.
‹Pp. 47, 263, 268, 269, 270, 271, 272, 273, 303›

———. *Letters of Medieval Jewish Traders*. Princeton, NJ: Princeton University Press, 1973.
‹Pp. 224, 263›

———. "A Turning-Point in the History of the Muslim State." *Islamic Culture*, xxii (1949), 120–135. Repr. in Goitein, *Studies in Islamic History and Institutions*, 149–167.
‹P. 114›

———. "The Rise of the Middle-Eastern Bourgeoisie in Early Islamic Times." *Journal of World History*, iii (1957), 583–604. Reprinted in Goitein, *Studies in Islamic History and Institutions*, 217–241.
‹P. 226›

———. "The Documents of the Cairo Geniza as a Source for Islamic Social History." In Goitein, *Studies in Islamic History and Institutions*, 279–295.
‹P. 263›

———. "The Unity of the Mediterranean World in the 'Middle' Middle Ages." In Goitein, *Studies in Islamic History and Institutions*, 296–307.
‹P. 273›

———. Review of Vol. III of E. Ashtor, *Toledot ha-Yehudim . . . tahat Shilton ha-Mamlukim. Tarbiz*, xli (1971–72), 59–81, with English summary.
‹P. 269›

Golb, Norman. "Sixty Years of Geniza Research." *Judaism*, vi (1957), 3–16.
‹P. 262›

Goldziher, Ignaz. *Vorlesungen uber den Islam*. Heidelberg: C. Winter, 1910; rev. ed., 1925. Trans. by Felix Arin as *Le dogme et la loi de l'Islam*. Paris: P. Geuthner, 1920. Trans. by Ruth and Andras Hamori as *Introduction to Islamic Theology and Law*.

Princeton, NJ: Princeton University Press, 1981.
‹P. 214›

———. *Streitschrift des Ġazālī gegen die Batinijja-Sekte*. Leiden: E. J. Brill, 1916.
‹P. 161›

———. *Muhammedanische Studien*. 2 vols. Halle: Max Niemeyer, 1889–90. Trans. by S. M. Stern and C. R. Barber as *Muslim Studies*. 2 vols. London: Allen and Unwin, 1967–71.
‹Pp. 36, 82–83, 163, 214›

Gottheil, Richard. "An Answer to the Dhimmis." *JAOS*, xli (1921), 383–457.
‹P. 260›

Gottschalk, H. L. *Die Mādarā'ijjun, ein Beitrag zur Geschichte Ägyptens unter den Islam*. Berlin and Leipzig: W. de Gruyter, 1931.
‹P. 226›

———. *Al-Malik al-Kamil von Egypten und seine Zeit*. Wiesbaden: O. Harrassowitz, 1958.
‹P. 266›

Grabar, Oleg. *The Coinage of the Tulunids*. Numismatic Notes and Monographs, 139. New York: American Numismatic Society, 1957.
‹P. 53›

———. *Sasanian Silver*. Ann Arbor: University of Michigan Museum of Art, 1967.

———. *The Formation of Islamic Art*. New Haven and London: Yale University Press, 1973. 2d rev. ed., 1987.
‹Pp. 55, 60, 152, 163›

———. *The Alhambra*. Cambridge, MA: Harvard University Press, 1978.
‹P. 55›

———. "Umayyad 'Palace' and Abbasid 'Revolution.'" *SI*, xviii (1963), 5–18.
‹P. 121›

———. "The Visual Arts." In *Cambridge History of Iran*, v, 626–658.
‹Pp. 153, 165›

———. "The Architecture of the Middle Eastern City from Past to Present: the Case of the Mosque." In Lapidus, *Middle Eastern Cities*, 26–46.
‹P. 230›

———. "Cities and Citizens." In Lewis, *The World of Islam*, 89–116.
‹P. 230›

———. "Islamic Art and Archaeology." In Leonard Binder, *The Study of the Middle East*, 229–264.
‹P. 60›

———. "Notes sur les cérémonies umayyades." In Miriam Rosen-Ayalon, *Studies in Memory of Gaston Wiet*, 51–60.
‹P. 153›

———. "Between Connoisseurship and Technology: A Review." *Muqarnas*, v (1988), 1–8.
‹P. 62›

Graf, Georg. *Geschichte der christlichen arabischen Literatur*. 5 vols. Vatican City: Biblioteca Apostolica Vaticana, 1944–53.
‹Pp. 29, 277›

Grierson, Philip. *Numismatics*. London: Oxford University Press, 1975.
‹P. 49›

Grimwood-Jones, Diana, Derek Hopwood, and J. D. Pearson, eds. *Arab Islamic Bibliography*. Sussex, England: Harvester Press, 1977.
‹Pp. 8, 9›

Grohmann, Adolf. *Arabic Papyri in the Egyptian Museum*. 6 vols. Cairo: Egyptian Library Press, 1934–62.
‹Pp. 42, 221, 223, 224›

———. *From the World of Arabic Papyri*. Cairo: al-Maaref Press, 1952.
‹P. 42›

———. *Einführung und Chrestomathie zur arabischen Papyruskunde*. Monografie Archivu Orientalniho, XIII. Prague: Czechoslovak Oriental Institute, 1955.
‹Pp. 42, 44, 46›

———. *Arabische Papyruskunde*. *HO*, Ergbd. II, 1966.
‹Pp. 6, 46›

———. *Arabische Chronologie*. *HO*, Ergbd. II, 1966.
‹Pp. 6, 20›

———. *Arabische Paläographie*. 2 vols. Osterreichische Akademie der Wissenschaften, Phil.-Hist. Klasse, Denkschriften, 94. Vienna, 1967–71.
‹Pp. 33, 41, 54›

———. "The Origin and Early Development of Floriated Kufic." *Ars Orientalis*, ii (1957), 183–215.
‹P. 54›

———. "Kāghad." *EI*^{2}, iv, 419–420.
‹P. 41›

———. "Ḳirṭās." *EI*^{2}, v, 173–174.
‹P. 41›

Gronke, Monika. *Arabische und persische Privaturkunden des 12. und 13. Jahrhunderts aus Ardabil (Aserbeidschan)*. Islamkundliche Untersuchungen, B. 72. Berlin: K. Schwarz, 1982.
‹Pp. 49, 219›

Grumel, V. *La chronologie*. Vol. I of *Traité d'études byzantins*. Ed. by P. Lemerle. Paris: Presses Universitaires de France, 1958.
‹P. 20›

Grundriss der arabischen Philologie. 2 vols. Wiesbaden: L. Reichert, 1982–87. Vol. I: *Sprachwissenschaft*, ed. by Wolfdietrich Fischer (1982). Vol. II: *Literaturwissenschaft*, ed. by Helmut Gätje (1987).
‹P. 12›

Grundriss der iranischen Philologie. Ed. by Wilhelm Geiger and Ernst Kuhn. 2 vols. Strasbourg: Karl J. Trübner, 1896–1904. Vol. I: *Sprachgeschichte*; Vol. II: *Literatur, Geschichte, und Kultur.*
‹P. 12›

Grunebaum, Gustave E. von. "The Structure of the Muslim Town." In Grunebaum, *Islam: Studies in the Nature of a Cultural Tradition.* Menasha, WI: American Anthropological Association, 1955. Issued as *The American Anthropologist*, N.S. 57, no. 2, part 2 (April 1955).
‹P. 229›

———. "The Nature of the Fatimid Achievement." In *Colloque Internationale sur l'histoire du Caire*, 199–215.
‹P. 266›

Gryaznevich, P. A., ed. *Arabskii anonim XI veka*. Moscow: Akademiia Nauk SSSR, 1960. See also *Akhbār al-dawla al-ʿabbāsiyya*.

‹P. 113›

Guellil, Gabriela Linda. *Damaszener Akten des 8./14. Jahrhunderts nach at-Tarsusis Kitāb al-Iʿlām. Eine Studie zum arabischen Justizwesen*. Bamberg: aku, 1985.

‹Pp. 219, 222›

Guillaume, Alfred. *See* Ibn Isḥāq, Muḥammad.

Haarmann, Ulrich. *Quellenstudien zur frühen Mamlukenzeit*. Islamkundliche Untersuchungen, B. 1. Freiburg im Breisgau: K. Schwarz, 1970.

‹Pp. 134, 241›

———. "Auflösung und Bewahrung der Klassischen Formen arabischer Geschichtsschreibung in der Zeit der Mamluken," *ZDMG*, cxxi (1971), 46–60.

‹P. 135›

———. "The Sons of Mamluks as Fief-holders in Late Medieval Egypt." In Khalidi, *Land Tenure and Social Transformation in the Middle East*, 141–168.

‹P. 182›

Hafsi, Ibrahim. "Recherches sur le genre 'Ṭabaqāt' dans la littérature arabe." *Arabica*, xxiii (1976), 227–265; xxiv (1977), 1–41, 150–186.

‹Pp. 79, 188›

Ḥajjī Khalīfa (= Kâtib Çelebi). *Kashf al-ẓunūn ʿan asāmī al-kutub wa'l-funūn*.

(a) Ed. and trans. by Gustav Flügel as *Lexicon Bibliographicum et Encyclopaedicum*. 7 vols. Leipzig and London: Oriental Translation Fund of Great Britain and Ireland, 1835–58.

(b) Ed. by Şerefettin Yaltkaya and Kilisli Rifat Bilge. 2 vols. Istanbul: Maarif Matbaası, 1941–43.

‹P. 28›

al-Ḥakīm al-Naisabūrī. *An Introduction to the Science of Tradition*. Trans. by J. Robson. Oriental Translation Fund, 39. London: Royal Asiatic Society, 1953.

‹Pp. 35, 81›

Hallaq, Wael B., "Was the Gate of Ijtihad Closed?" *IJMES*, xvi (1984), 3–41.

‹P. 212›

Hallaq, Wael. "Considerations on the Function and Character of Islamic Legal Theory." *JAOS*, civ (1984), 679–689.

‹P. 215›

Halm, Heinz. *Die Ausbreitung der šāfiʿitischen Rechtschule von den Anfängen bis zum 8/14 Jahrhundert*. *TAVO*, Beihefte, Reihe B, No. 4. Wiesbaden: Ludwig Reichert, 1974.

‹Pp. 197–198›

———. *Ägypten nach den mamlukischen Lehensregistern*. 2 vols. *TAVO*, Beihefte, Reihe B, No. 38/1–2. Wiesbaden: Ludwig Reichert, 1979–82.

‹Pp. 176, 181›

Hamdan, G. "Evolution of irrigation agriculture in Egypt." In Stamp, *History of Land-Use in Arid Regions*, 119–142.

‹Pp. 293, 299›

Hamdani, Abbas. *The Fatimids*. Karachi: Pakistan Publishing House, 1962.

‹P. 266›

Hamdani, Husayn F. "Some Unknown Ismaʿili Authors and their Works." *JRAS* (1933), 359–378.

‹P. 31›

Handbuch der Orientalistik. Ed. by Bertold Spuler. Leiden: E. J. Brill, 1952–in progress.
‹Pp. 5, 6, 12›

Handwörterbuch des Islam. See *Shorter Encyclopaedia of Islam*.

Haque, Ziaul. *Landlord and Peasant in Early Islam. A Study of the Legal Doctrine of Muzāraʿa or Sharecropping*. Islamabad: Islamic Research Institute, 1977.
‹P. 216›

al-Harawi, ʿAlī. *Kitāb al-ishārāt ilā maʿrifat al-ziyārāt*. Ed. by J. Sourdel-Thomine. Damascus: Institut Français de Damas, 1953. Trans. by J. Sourdel-Thomine as *Guide des lieux de pèlerinage*. Damascus: Institut Français de Damas, 1957.
‹P. 239›

Hare, F. K. "The causation of the arid zone." In Stamp, *History of Land-Use in Arid Regions*, 25–30.
‹P. 291›

Harper, Prudence. *Silver Vessels of the Sassanian Period*. Volume One: *Royal Imagery*. New York: Metropolitan Museum of Art, 1981.
‹P. 162›

Hartmann, Fernande. *L'agriculture dans l'ancienne Égypte*. Paris: Librairie-Imprimerie Réunis, 1923.
‹P. 300›

Hartmann, Richard. "Politische Geographie des Mamlukenreichs: Kapitel 5 und 6 des Staatshandbuchs Ibn Faḍlallāh al-Omari's," *ZDMG*, lxx (1961), 1–40, 477–511.
‹P. 175›

Harvard University. *Catalogue of Arabic, Persian, and Ottoman Turkish Books*. 5 vols. Cambridge, MA: Harvard University Press, 1968.
‹P. 24›

———. *Catalog of the Arabic Collection*. Ed. by Fawzi Abdulrazak. 6 vols. Boston: G. K. Hall, 1983.
‹P. 24›

Ḥasan, Ḥasan Ibrāhīm. *Taʾrīkh al-Dawla al-Fāṭimiyya*. Cairo: Maktabat al-Nahḍa al-Miṣriyya, 1948.
‹P. 265›

Ḥassān b. Thābit. *Dīwān*. Ed. by Walid N. Arafat. 2 vols. E.J.W. Gibb Memorial, N.S. 25. London: Luzac, 1971. Reprinted, Beirut: Dar Sader, 1974.
‹P. 90›

al-Hassan, Ahmad Y., and Donald R. Hill. *Islamic Technology: An Illustrated History*. Cambridge: Cambridge University Press; Paris: UNESCO, 1986.
‹P. 63›

Havemann, Axel. *Riʾāsa und Qaḍāʾ. Institutionen als Ausdruck wechselnder Kraftverhältnisse in syrischen Städten vom 10 zum 12 Jahrhundert*. Freiburg im Breisgau: K. Schwarz, 1975.
‹P. 247›

Hawting, G. R. Review of F. M. Donner, *The Early Islamic Conquests*. In *BSOAS*, xlvii (1984), 130–133.
‹P. 70›

Haywood, John A. *Arabic Lexicography. Its History and Its Place in the General History of Lexicography*. Leiden: E. J. Brill, 1960; 2d rev. ed., 1965.
‹P. 13›

Hazard, H. W. *Atlas of Islamic History*. Princeton, NJ: Princeton University Press, 1951.
‹P. 17›

Hennequin, Gilles. *Catalogue des monnaies musulmans de la Bibliothèque Nationale*. Vol. V: *Asie pré-mongole, les Salǧūqs et leurs successeurs*. Paris: Bibliothèque Nationale, 1985.
‹P. 50›

———. "Problèmes théoriques et pratiques de la monnaie antique et médiévale." *AI*, x (1972), 1–51.
‹P. 53›

———. "Nouveaux aperçus sur l'histoire monétaire de l'Égypte à la fin du Moyen-Âge." *AI*, xiii (1977), 179–215.
‹P. 53›

Henning, W. B., and E. Yarshater, eds. *A Locust's Leg: Studies in Honour of S. H. Taqizadeh*. London: Lund, Humphries, 1962.

Hermann, Gottfried. "Urkunden-Funde in Azarbayǧān." *AMI*, N.F. iv (1971), 249–262.
‹P. 49›

Herzfeld, Ernst. "Damascus: Studies in Architecture." *Ars Islamica*, ix (1942), 1–53; x (1943), 13–70; xi–xii (1946), 1–71; xiii–xiv (1948), 118–138.
‹Pp. 243, 245›

Hillenbrand, Carole. "Islamic Orthodoxy or Realpolitik? Al-Ghazali's Views on Government." *Iran*, xxvi (1988), 81–94.
‹P. 161, 164›

Hillenbrand, Robert. "Madrasa. III: Architecture." EI^2, v, 1136–1154.
‹P. 199›

Hinds, Martin. "The Siffin Arbitration Agreement." *JSS*, xvii (1972), 93–129. *See also* Crone, Patricia.
‹P. 89›

Hinz, Walther. *Islamische Masse und Gewichte, umgerechnet ins metrische system*. *HO*, Ergbd. I, 1955; 2d rev. ed., 1970.
‹Pp. 6, 52›

———. "Das Rechnungswesen orientalischer Reichsfinanzamter in Mittelalter." *Islam*, xxix (1950), 1–29; 113–141.
‹P. 45›

Hirschberg, H. Z. *Toledot ha-Yehudim be-Afrika ha-Zefonit*. 2 vols. Jerusalem: Mossad Bialik, 1965. Vol. I: *A History of the Jews in North Africa, I: From Antiquity to the Sixteenth Century*. Trans. by M. Eichelberg. Leiden: E. J. Brill, 1974.
‹P. 269›

Hodgson, M.G.S. *The Venture of Islam: Conscience and History in a World Civilization*. 3 vols. Chicago and London: University of Chicago Press, 1974.

———. "How Did the Early Shīʿa Become Sectarian?" *JAOS*, lxxv (1955), 1–13.
‹P. 125›

Hoenerbach, Wilhelm. *Spanisch-Islamische Urkunden aus der Zeit der Nasriden und Moriscos*. Berkeley: University of California Press, 1965.
‹Pp. 46, 221›

Hoffmann, Gerhard. *Kommune oder Staatsbürokratie? Zur politischen Rolle der*

Bevölkerung syrischer Städte vom 10 bis 12 Jahrhundert. Berlin, DDR: Akademie Verlag, 1975.
‹P. 247›

Hofman, H. F. *Turkish Literature: a Bio-Bibliographical Survey.* Section III: *Moslim Central Asian Turkish Literature.* Part I: *Authors.* 6 vols. Utrecht: Library of the University of Utrecht, 1969.
‹P. 31›

Holt, P. M. "The Position and Power of the Mamluk Sultan," *BSOAS*, xxxviii (1975), 237–249.
‹P. 154›

Hopkins, Simon. *Studies in the Grammar of Early Arabic, Based upon Papyri Datable to before A.H. 300/A.D. 912.* London Oriental Series, vol. 37. Oxford: Oxford University Press, 1984.
‹P. 42›

Horovitz, Josef. "Alter und Ursprung des Isnad." *Islam*, viii (1918), 39–47, 299; xi (1921), 264–265.
‹P. 82›

———. "The Earliest Biographies of the Prophet and Their Authors." *Islamic Culture*, i (1927), 535–559; ii (1928), 22–50, 164–182, 495–526.
‹P. 77›

Horst, Heribert. *Die Staatsverwaltung der Grosselǧuqen und Ĥorazmšahs (1038–1231).* Wiesbaden: F. Steiner, 1964.
‹P. 45›

Hourani, A. H., and S. M. Stern, eds. *The Islamic City: a Colloquium.* Oxford: Bruno Cassirer, 1970. *See also* Cahen, Claude; Stern, S. M.
‹P. 229›

Ḥudūd al-ʿālam. (Anon.) Translation and commentary by V. Minorsky, *The Regions of the World, a Persian Geography 372 A.H.–982 A.D.* E.J.W. Gibb Memorial, N.S. 11. London: Luzac, 1937.
‹P. 18›

Huisman, A.J.W. *Les manuscrits arabes dans le monde: une bibliographie des catalogues.* Leiden: E. J. Brill, 1967.
‹P. 39›

Humphreys, R. S. *From Saladin to the Mongols: The Ayyubids of Damascus, 1193–1260.* Albany, NY: State University of New York Press, 1977.
‹Pp. 166, 180, 266›

———. "The Expressive Intent of the Mamluk Architecture of Cairo: a Preliminary Essay," *SI*, xxxv (1972), 69–119.
‹P. 152›

———. "The Emergence of the Mamluk Army." *SI*, xlv (1977), 67–99; xlvi (1977), 147–182.
‹P. 182›

———. "Damascus." *DMA*, iv, 80–85.
‹P. 246›

———. "Historiography, Islamic." *DMA*, vi, 249–255.
‹P. 133›

———. "Politics and Architectural Patronage in Ayyubid Damascus." In Bosworth et

al., *Essays in Honor of Bernard Lewis*, 151–174.
‹P. 251›

———. "Qurʾanic Myth and Narrative Structure in Early Islamic Historiography." In Clover and Humphreys, *Tradition and Innovation in Late Antiquity*, 271–290.
‹P. 75›

Hurgronje, Christiaan Snouck. *Oeuvres choisies/Selected Works*. Ed. by G. H. Bousquet and J. Schacht. Leiden: E. J. Brill, 1957.
‹Pp. 209, 213–214›

al-Ḥurr al-ʿĀmilī, Muḥammad b. Ḥasan. *Wasāʾil al-Shīʿa ilā taḥṣīl masāʾil al-sharīʿa*. Ed. by A. R. al-Rabbānī, M. al-Rāzī, and A. H. al-Shaʿrānī. 20 vols. Tehran: Maktaba Islāmiyya, 1376–89/1956–69.
‹P. 23›

Ḥusayn, Fāliḥ. *al-Ḥayāt al-zirāʿiyya fī Bilād al-Shām fī al-ʿaṣr al-umawī*. Amman, 1978.
‹P. 298›

Hütteroth, Wolf-Dieter, and Kamal Abdulfattah. *Historical Geography of Palestine, Transjordan, and Southern Syria in the Late 16th Century*. Erlanger Geographischen Arbeiten, Sonderband 5. Erlangen: Frankischen Geographischen Gesellschaft, 1977.
‹P. 298›

Ibn ʿAbd al-Barr, Yūsuf b. ʿAbdallāh. *al-Istīʿāb fī maʿrifat al-aṣḥāb*.
(a) Printed in margins of Ibn Ḥajar al-ʿAsqalānī, *al-Iṣāba fī tamyīz al-Ṣaḥāba*. 4 vols. Cairo: Maktabat al-Saʿāda, 1328/1910.
(b) Ed. by A. M. al-Bijāwī. 4 vols. Cairo: Maktabat Nahḍat Miṣr, 1960 (?).
‹P. 71›

Ibn ʿAbd al-Ḥakam, Abū al-Qāsim ʿAbd al-Raḥmān. *Futūh Miṣr wa-akhbāruhu*. Ed. by C. C. Torrey as *The History of the Conquest of Egypt, North Africa, and Spain*. New Haven: Yale University Press, 1922.
‹Pp. 76, 87›

Ibn ʿAbd Rabbih, Aḥmad b. Muḥammad. *al-ʿIqd al-Farīd*.
(a) 3 vols. Būlāq: al-Maṭbaʿa al-ʿĀmira, 1293/1876.
(b) Ed. by Aḥmad Amīn et al. 8 vols. Cairo: Lajnat al-Taʾlīf wa'l-Tarjama wa'l-Nashr, 1359–72/1940–53.
‹P. 114›

Ibn ʿAbdūn. *Risāla fī al-qaḍāʾ wa'l-ḥisba*.
(a) Ed. by E. Lévi-Provençal, *JA*, ccxxiv (1934), 177–299.
(b) Re-ed. by E. Lévi-Provençal, in *Documents arabes inédits sur la vie sociale et économique en Occident musulman au Moyen-Âge: trois traités hispaniques de hisba*. Cairo: Institut Français d'Archéologie Orientale, 1955.
(c) Trans. by E. Lévi-Provençal as *Séville musulmane au début du xiiᵉ siècle: le traité d'Ibn ʿAbdūn sur la vie urbaine et les corps de métiers*. Paris: G. P. Maisonneuve, 1947.
‹P. 259›

Ibn Abī al-Dunyā. *Kitāb makārim al-akhlāq*. Ed. by James Bellamy. Wiesbaden: F. Steiner, 1973.
‹P. 34›

Ibn Abī al-Ḥadīd. *Sharḥ nahj al-balāgha*. Ed. by Muḥammad A. F. Ibrāhīm. 20 vols. Cairo: ʿĪsā al-Bābī al-Ḥalabī, 1959–64.
‹Pp. 71, 115›

Ibn Abī Uṣaybiʿa. *ʿUyūn al-anbāʾ fī ṭabaqāt al-aṭibbāʾ*. 2 vols. Cairo, 1399/1882.
‹P. 277›

Ibn al-Abbār. *Kitāb al-takmila li-kitāb al-ṣila*. Ed. by F. Codera. *BAH*, v (1887).
‹Pp. 190–191›

Ibn al-ʿAdīm, Kamāl al-Dīn ʿUmar. *Bughyat al-ṭalab fī taʾrīkh Ḥalab*.
(a) Partial edition by Ali Sevim. Ankara: Türk Tarih Kurumu, 1976. [Biographies pertaining to the Seljukids.]
(b) MSS: Ayasofya 3036 (Istanbul, Süleymaniye); Feyzullah Efendi 1404 (Istanbul, Süleymaniye); Ahmet III 2925 (8 vols. Istanbul, Topkapı Saray). [The Paris, British Library, and Mosul volumes are all copies of the Istanbul set.]
‹Pp. 71, 112, 132, 241, 283›

———. *Zubdat al-ḥalab fī taʾrīkh Ḥalab*. Ed. by Sāmī al-Dahhān. 3 vols. Damascus: Institut Français de Damas, 1951–68.
‹P. 132›

Ibn al-Athīr, ʿIzz al-Dīn ʿAlī. *al-Kāmil fī al-taʾrīkh*. Ed. by C. J. Tornberg. 14 vols. Leiden: E. J. Brill, 1851–76. Reprinted (with corrections and new pagination) in 13 vols., Beirut: Dar Sader and Dar Beirut, 1965–67.
‹Pp. 35, 130, 131›

———. *Usd al-ghāba fī maʿrifat al-Ṣaḥāba*. 5 vols. Cairo: al-Maṭbaʿa al-Wahbiyya, 1280/1863.
‹P. 71›

Ibn al-ʿAwwām. *Kitāb al-filāḥa*. Arabic text ed. by Banqueri. 2 vols. Madrid, 1802. French trans. by J.-J. Clément-Mullet. 2 vols. in 3, with glossary. Paris, 1864–67.
‹P. 300›

Ibn al-Jawzī, Abū al-Faraj. *al-Muntaẓam fī taʾrīkh al-mulūk wa'l-umam*. 6 vols. [=Vols. V–X, yrs. 257–574/870–1179]. Hyderabad, Deccan: Dairat el-Maaref Osmania, 1938–40.
‹Pp. 189, 240›

Ibn al-Jīʿān, Yaḥyā b. Shākir. *al-Tuḥfa al-saniyya bi-asmāʾ al-Bilād al-Miṣriyya*. Ed. by B. Moritz. Publications de la Bibliothèque Khédiviale, 10. Cairo, 1898. Reprinted 1974.
‹Pp. 176, 186›

Ibn al-Muqaffaʿ, ʿAbd Allāh (d. 760). *Kitāb al-adab al-kabīr*. Ed. by Muḥammad Kurd ʿAlī in *Rasāʾil al-bulaghāʾ* (Cairo, 1331/1913).
‹P. 114›

———. *Risāla fī al-ṣaḥāba*. Ed. by Muḥammad Kurd ʿAlī in *Rasāʾil al-bulaghāʾ* (Cairo, 1331/1913), pp. 120–131. Trans. by Charles Pellat as *Ibn al-Muqaffaʿ, "conseilleur" du calife*. Paris: G. P. Maisonneuve et Larose, 1976.
‹P. 114›

Ibn al-Qalānisī. *Dhayl taʾrīkh Dimashq*.
(a) Ed. by H. F. Amedroz. Leiden: E. J. Brill, 1908.
(b) Trans. by H.A.R. Gibb as *The Damascus Chronicle of the Crusades*. London: Luzac, 1932.
(c) Trans. by Roger Le Tourneau as *Damas de 1075 à 1154*. Damascus: Institut Français de Damas, 1952.
‹Pp. 132, 240›

Ibn al-Ṣuqāʿī. *Tālī wafayāt al-aʿyān*. Ed. and trans. by Jacqueline Sublet. Damascus: Institut Français de Damas, 1974.
‹Pp. 183, 242, 277›

Ibn al-Ukhuwwa. *Maʿālim al-qurba fī aḥkām al-ḥisba*. Ed. with summary translation by Reuben Levy. E.J.W. Gibb Memorial, N.S. 12. London: Luzac, 1937.
‹P. 272›

Ibn ʿAqīl. *Kitāb al-funūn*. Ed. by George Makdisi. Recherches de l'Institut de Lettres Orientales de Beyrouth, serie I: Pensée arabe et musulmane, tt. 44–45. Beirut: Dar al-Machreq, 1970–71.
‹P. 34›

Ibn ʿAsākir. *Taʾrīkh madīnat Dimashq*.
(a) Abridged edition (incomplete) by ʿAbd al-Qādir Badrān and Aḥmad ʿUbayd. 7 vols. Damascus, 1911–32.
(b) Complete edition in progress. Various editors. Damascus: Majmaʿ al-Lugha al-ʿArabiyya, 1951–in progress.
(c) Xerographic edition of Ẓāhiriyya MS, Damascus. Amman: Dar al-Bashīr li'l-Nashr wa'l-Tawzīʿ, n.d.
‹Pp. 71, 112, 238, 241, 283›

———. *Taʾrīkh madīnat Dimashq*. Vol. I, pt. 2. Ed. by S. D. al-Munajjid. Damascus: Majmaʿ al-Lugha al-ʿArabiyya, 1954. Trans. by Nikita Elisséeff as *La description de Damas d'Ibn ʿAsākir*. Damascus: Institut Français de Damas, 1959.
‹Pp. 71, 112, 238, 241, 244›

Ibn Aʿtham al-Kūfī. *Kitāb al-futūḥ*. 8 vols. Hyderabad, Deccan: Da'irat al-Maaref Osmania, 1968–1975.
‹P. 112›

Ibn Bābawayh. *See* al-Ṣadūq.

Ibn Baṣṣāl. *Kitāb al-qaṣd wa'l-bayān (The Book of Proposition and Demonstration)*. Medieval Castilian compendium: ed. by J. M. Millas-Vallicrosa, *Andalus*, xiii (1948), 356–430. Arabic text: ed. and trans. into Spanish by J. M. Millas Vallicrosa and M. Aziman as *Kitāb al-filāḥa*. Tetouan, 1955.
‹P. 300›

Ibn Baṭṭa. *al-Ibāna*. Trans. by Henri Laoust as *La profession de foi d'Ibn Baṭṭa (m. 387/997)*. Damascus: Institut Français de Damas, 1958.
‹Pp. 160, 196, 198›

Ibn Ḥajar. *See* al-ʿAsqalānī, Ibn Ḥajar.

Ibn Ḥassūl. *Tafḍīl al-Atrāk*. Study and translation by ʿAbbās ʿAzzāwī and Şerefettin Yaltkaya, "Ibni Hassul'ün Türkler hakkīnda bir eseri." *Belleten*, iv (1940), 235–266.
‹P. 166›

Ibn Ḥawqal. *Kitāb ṣūrat al-arḍ*. Ed. by J. H. Kramers. *BGA*, ii (1938–39). Trans. by J. H. Kramers and G. Wiet as *Configuration de la terre*. 2 vols. Paris: G. P. Maisonneuve et Larose, 1964.
‹P. 18›

Ibn Ḥazm, ʿAlī b. Aḥmad. *Kitāb al-fiṣal fī al-milal wa'l-ahwāʾ wa'l-niḥal*. Cairo, 1903. Partial translation by Israel Friedlaender, "The Heterodoxies of the Shiites according to Ibn Hazm." *JAOS*, xxviii (1907), 1–80; xxix (1908), 1–183.
‹P. 113›

Ibn Hishām, ʿAbd al-Malik. *See* Ibn Isḥāq, Muḥammad.

Ibn Ḥubaysh, ʿAbd al-Raḥmān b. Muḥammad. *Kitāb al-ghazawāt*. Ed. by A. Ghunaym. Cairo, 1983.
‹P. 71›

Ibn Isḥāq, Muḥammad. *Sīrat rasūl Allāh* (recension of ʿAbd al-Malik ibn Hishām).

(a) Ed. by F. Wüstenfeld. 2 vols. Gottingen, Dieterichsche Universitäts-Buchhandlung, 1858–60.

(b) Ed. by M. al-Ṣaqqā, I. al-Abyārī, and H. H. Shalabī. 2 vols. Cairo, 1355/1937. Reprinted, 1955.

(c) Trans. by Alfred Guillaume as *The Life of Muhammad*. London: Oxford University Press, 1955. Reprinted, Karachi: Oxford University Press, 1967.

‹Pp. 71, 78, 92›

———. *Taʾrīkh al-khulafāʾ*. *See also* Abbott, Nabia.

‹P. 78›

Ibn Jamāʿa, Badr al-Dīn. *Taḥrīr al-aḥkām fī tadbīr millat al-Islām*. Ed. and trans. by H. Kofler as "Handbuch des islamischen Staats und Verwaltungsrechtes von Badr al-Dīn Ibn Ǧamāʿah," *Islamica*, vi (1934), 349–414; vii (1935), 1–64; Schlussheft (1938), 18–129.

‹P. 140›

Ibn Jubayr. *al-Riḥla*.

(a) Ed. by William Wright. Leiden: E. J. Brill, 1852. 2d ed., rev. by M. J. de Goeje, 1907.

(b) Trans. by C. Schiaparelli as *Viaggio in Ispagna, Sicilia, Siria* ... Rome: Casa editrice italiana, 1906.

(c) Trans. by R. J. Broadhurst as *The Travels of Ibn Jubayr*. London: Jonathan Cape, 1952.

(d) Trans. by M. Gaudefroy-Demombynes as *Voyages*. Documents Relatifs à l'Histoire des Croisades, tt. 4–6. Académie des Inscriptions et Belles-lettres. Paris: P. Geuthner, 1949–56.

‹P. 242›

Ibn Khaldūn. *al-Taʿrif bi-Ibn Khaldūn wa-riḥlatuhu gharban wa-sharqan*. Ed. by Muḥammad Ṭāwīt al-Ṭanjī. Cairo, 1370/1951. Trans. by M. de Slane in *Prolégomènes historiques d'Ibn Khaldoun*. Notices et Extraits des Manuscrits de la Bibliothèque Impériale, t. xix (1862), pp. vi–lxxxiii.

‹P. 194›

Ibn Khaldūn, ʿAbd al-Raḥmān. *Kitāb al-ʿibar*.

(a) Ed. by Naṣr al-Ḥūrīnī. 7 vols. Bulaq, 1284/1867.

(b) Partial edition and translation by W. MacGuckin de Slane, as *Histoire des Berbères et des dynasties musulmanes de l'Afrique Septentrionale*. Arabic text: 2 vols. Algiers:Imprimerie du gouvernement, 1847–51. Translation: 4 vols. Algiers: Imprimerie du gouvernement, 1852–56. Translation reprinted, Paris: P. Geuthner, 1925–56.

‹P. 135›

———. *al-Muqaddima*.

(a) Ed. by E. Quatremère as *Prolégomènes d'Ebn-Khaldoun*. 3 vols. Notices et Extraits des Manuscrits de la Bibliothèque Impériale, tt. xvi–xviii. Paris, 1858.

(b) Trans. by MacGuckin de Slane as *Prolégomènes historiques d'Ibn Khaldoun*. Notices et Extraits des Manuscrits de la Bibliothèque Impériale, tt. xix–xxi. Paris: Imprimerie Impériale, 1862–68.

(c) Trans. by Franz Rosenthal as *The Muqaddima, an Introduction to History*. 3 vols. New York: Bollingen Foundation, 1958. 2d rev. ed., Princeton, NJ: Princeton University Press, for the Bollingen Foundation, 1967.

‹Pp. 34, 45, 135, 193–194, 222, 272›

Ibn Khallikān, Shams al-Dīn. *Wafayāt al-aʿyān wa-anbāʾ abnāʾ al-zamān.*

(a) Ed. by F. Wüstenfeld. 4 vols. Göttingen: R. Deuerlich, 1835–50.

(b) Ed. by M.-D. ʿAbd al-Ḥamīd. 6 vols. Cairo: Dār al-Nahḍa al-ʿArabiyya, 1948.

(c) Ed. by Iḥsān ʿAbbās. 8 vols. Beirut: Dār al-Thaqāfa, 1972.

(d) Trans. by MacGuckin de Slane as *Ibn Khallikan's Biographical Dictionary.* 4 vols. Paris: Oriental Translation Fund of Great Britain and Ireland, 1842–71. (Based on Wüstenfeld edition.)

‹Pp. 188–189, 241›

Ibn Mammātī, al-Asʿad b. al-Khāṭir. *Kitāb qawānīn al-dawāwīn.* Ed. by A. S. Atiya. Cairo, 1943. English translation by R. S. Cooper. "Ibn Mammātī's Rules for the Ministries: Translation with Commentary of the *Qawāwīn al-Dawāwīn.*" Ph.D. dissertation, University of California, Berkeley, 1973.

‹P. 173›

Ibn Qudāma, Muwaffaq al-Dīn. *al-Mughni ʿalā mukhtaṣar Abī al-Qāsim ʿUmar al-Khiraqī.*

(a) Ed. by Rashīd Riḍā. 12 vols. Cairo: Dār al-Manār, 1341–48/ 1922–30.

(b) Ed. by T. M. al-Zaynī. 10 vols. Cairo, 1968–70.

‹P. 215›

———. *al-ʿUmda.* Trans. by Henri Laoust as *Le précis de droit d'Ibn Qudāma (541–620/1146–1223).* Beirut: Institut Français de Damas, 1950.

‹Pp. 196, 198, 214›

Ibn Qutayba, ʿAbd Allāh b. Muslim. *Kitāb al-maʿārif.*

(a) Ed. by F. Wüstenfeld as *Ibn Coteiba's Handbuch der Geschichte.* Göttingen: Vandenhoeck und Ruprecht, 1850.

(b) Ed. by Tharwat ʿUkkāsha. Cairo: Wizārat al-Thaqāfa wa'l-Irshād al-Qawmī, 1960.

‹P. 72›

———. *ʿUyūn al-akhbār.* 4 vols. Cairo: Dār al-Kutub al-Miṣriyya, 1925–1930. Translation of Book I by Josef Horovitz, "The Book of Government." *Islamic Culture,* iv (1930), 171–198, 331–362, 487–530; v (1931), 1–27.

‹P. 163›

———. *Kitāb taʾwīl mukhtalif al-ḥadīth.* Trans. by Gérard Lecomte as *Le traité des divergences du hadith d'Ibn Qutayba.* Damascus: Institut Français de Damas, 1962.

Ibn Rusta. *Kitāb al-aʿlāq al-nafīsa.* Ed. by M. J. de Goeje. *BGA,* vii (1892). Trans. by Gaston Wiet as *Les atours précieux.* Cairo: Société de Géographie d'Égypte, 1955.

‹P. 18›

Ibn Saʿd. *Kitāb al-ṭabaqāt al-kabīr.* Ed. by Eduard Sachau et al. 9 vols. Leiden: E. J. Brill, 1904–1940.

‹Pp. 71, 78, 99, 188›

Ibn Shaddād, ʿIzz al-Dīn. *al-Aʿlāq al-khaṭīra fī dhikr umarāʾ al-Shām wa'l-Jazīra.*

(a) *Taʾrīkh Ḥalab,* ed. D. Sourdel. Beirut: Institut Français de Damas, 1953.

(b) *Taʾrīkh Dimashq,* ed. Sāmī al-Dahhān. Damascus: Institut Français de Damas, 1956.

(c) *Taʾrīkh Lubnān wa'l-Urdunn wa-Filāsṭīn,* ed. Sāmī al-Dahhān. Damascus: Institut Français de Damas, 1963.

(d) *Taʾrīkh al-Jazīra,* ed. Yaḥyā ʿAbbāra. 2 vols. Damascus: Wizārat al-Thaqāfa wa'l-Irshād al-Qawmī, 1977–78.

(e) "Description de la Syrie du Nord," ed. Anne-Marie Eddé. *BEO*, xxxii–xxxiii (1980–81), 265–402. French translation under same title by Anne-Marie Eddé-Terrasse. Damascus: Institut Français de Damas, 1984.
‹Pp. 35, 174, 239›

Ibn Taghrībirdī, Abū al-Maḥāsin. *al-Manhal al-ṣafī wa'l-mustawfī baʿd al-wāfī*. Ed. by Muḥammad M. Amīn. 3 vols. Cairo: al-Hayʾa al-Miṣriyya al-ʿĀmma li'l-Kitāb, 1984–85. *See also* Wiet, Gaston.
‹P. 206›

Ibn Taghrībirdī, Abū al-Maḥāsin Yūsuf. *al-Nujūm al-zāhira fī mulūk Miṣr wa'l-Qāhira*.
(a) 16 Vols. Cairo: Dār al-Kutub al-Miṣriyya, 1929–72.
(b) Partial edition by William Popper. University of California Publications in Semitic Philology, ii, iii, v–vii. Berkeley: University of California Press, 1909–36.
(c) Trans. by William Popper as *History of Egypt, 1382–1469 A.D.* University of California Publications in Semitic Philology, xii–xiv, xvii–xix, xxii–xxiv. Berkeley: University of California Press, 1954–1963.
‹Pp. xiv, 137–143, 145–147›

Ibn Taymiyya, Taqī al-Dīn Aḥmad. *al-Siyāsa al-sharʿiyya fī iṣlāḥ al-rāʿī wa'l-raʿiyya*.
(a) Ed. by S. al-Nashshār and A. Z. ʿAṭiyya. Cairo: Dār al-Kitāb al-ʿArabī, 1951.
(b) Trans. by Henri Laoust as *Le traité de droit public d'Ibn Taimiya*. Beirut: Institut Français de Damas, 1948.
(c) Trans. by Omar A. Farrukh as *Ibn Taimiyya on Public and Private Law in Islam*. Beirut: Khayats, 1966.
‹P. 140›

Ibn Ṭūlūn, Shams al-Din. *al-Qalāʾid al-jawhariyya fī taʾrīkh al-Ṣāliḥiyya*. 2 vols. Edited by M. A. Duhmān. Damascus: 1368–75/1949–56.
‹P. 239›

Ibn Waḥshiyya. *al-Filāḥa al-nabaṭiyya*. *See* Fahd, Toufic; Bolens, Lucie.

Ibn Wāṣil, Jamāl al-Dīn Muḥammad. *Mufarrij al-kurūb fī akhbār Banī Ayyūb*. Vols. I–III, ed. by Jamāl al-Dīn al-Shayyāl. Cairo: Wizārat al-Thaqāfa wa'l-Irshād al-Qawmī, 1953–60. Vols. IV–V, ed. by S.A.F. ʿĀshūr and H. M. Rabīʿ. Cairo: Wizārat al-Thaqāfa, 1972–77.
‹P. 131›

Idris, H. R. "Le mariage en Occident musulman. Analyse de fatwas médiévales extraites du Miʿyār d'al-Wansharīsī." *ROMM*, xii (1972), 45–62; xvii (1974), 71–105; xxv (1978), 119–138.
‹P. 218›

———. "Les tributaires en Occident musulman médiéval d'après le 'Miʿyār' d'al-Wanšarīsī." In P. Salmon, ed., *Mélanges d'islamologie: volume dédié à la mémoire de Armand Abel* (Leiden: E. J. Brill, 1974), 172–196.
‹P. 259›

al-Idrīsī, Abū ʿAbdallāh Muḥammad. *Nuzhat al-mushtāq fī ikhtirāq al-āfāq*.
(a) Ed. by E. Cerulli et al. as *Opus Geographicum*. Leiden: E. J. Brill, for the Istituto Universitario Orientale di Napoli and the Istituto Italiano per il Medio ed Estremo Oriente, 1970–84.
(b) Trans. by P. A. Jaubert as *Géographie d'Edrisi*. 2 vols. Paris: Imprimerie Royale, 1836–40.

(c) Partial translation by M. J. de Goeje and R.P.A. Dozy, *Description de l'Afrique et de l'Espagne par Edrisi.* Leiden: E. J. Brill, 1866; reprinted, 1968.
(d) Partial translation by S. Maqbul Ahmad, *India and the Neighboring Territories.* Leiden: E. J. Brill, 1960.
‹P. 18›

ʿInān, Muḥammad. *Ibn Khaldūn, ḥayātuhu wa-turāthuhu al-fikrī.* Cairo, 1933. English version: M. A. Enan, *Ibn Khaldun, His Life and Work.* Lahore, 1941; 2d ed. 1946.
‹P. 194›

Index Islamicus. See Behn, Wolfgang H.; Pearson, J. D.

International Encyclopaedia of the Social Sciences. 18 vols. New York: Macmillan, 1968–79.

Irwin, Robert. "Iqṭāʿ and the End of the Crusader States." In P. M. Holt, ed., *The Eastern Mediterranean Lands in the Period of the Crusades* (Warminster, England: Aris and Phillips, 1977), 62–77.
‹P. 180›

al-Iṣfahānī, Abū al-Faraj. *Kitāb al-Aghānī.*
(a) 20 vols. Bulaq, 1284–85/1867–69.
(b) Vol. 21. Ed. by R. Brünnow. Leiden: E. J. Brill, 1888.
(c) 24 vols. Cairo: Dār al-Kutub al-Miṣriyya, al-Qism al-Adabī, 1929–in progress.
‹P. 115›

İslam Ansiklopedisi. Islam âlemi coğrafya, etnografya ve biyografya lugatı. Istanbul: Maarif Matbaası, 1940–in progress.
‹P. 5›

Ivanow, W. (= Ivanov, V. A.) *A guide to Ismaili literature.* London: Royal Asiatic Society, 1933; 2d rev. ed., *Ismaili Literature, a Bibliographical Survey.* Tehran: Tehran University Press, 1963.
‹P. 31›

al-Jabartī, ʿAbd al-Raḥmān. *ʿAjāʾib al-āthār fī al-tarājim wa'l-akhbār.*
(a) Ed. Muh. Qāsim. 4 vols. Bulaq, 1297/1880.
(b) Trans. by Chefik Mansour bey, Abdulaziz Kalil bey, Gabriel Nicolas Kalil bey and Iskender Ammoun effendi as *Merveilles biographiques et historiques.* 9 vols. Cairo: Imprimerie Nationale, 1888–96.
‹P. 192›

Jacobsen, Thorkild. *Salinity and Irrigation Agriculture in Antiquity: Diyala Basin Archaeological Report on Essential Results, 1957–58.* Bibliotheca Mesopotamica, 14. Malibu, CA: Undena, 1982.
‹Cf. pp. 247, 291–293›

Jafri, S.H.M. *The Origins and Early Development of Shiʿa Islam.* London and New York: Longman, 1979.
‹P. 125›

al-Jāḥiẓ, ʿAmr b. Baḥr. *Kitāb al-tāj.* Ed. Aḥmad Zakī. Cairo: Imprimerie Nationale, 1914; Trans. by Charles Pellat as *Livre de la couronne.* Paris: Société les Belles Lettres, 1954.
‹P. 153›

———. *Kitāb al-bukhalāʾ.* Edited by M. T. al-Ḥājirī. Cairo: Dār al-Kātib al-Miṣrī, 1948; Trans. by Charles Pellat as *Le livre des avares de Ǧāḥiẓ.* Paris: G. P. Maisonneuve, 1951.
‹P. 225›

———. "Risāla ilā Fatḥ b. Khāqān fī manāqib al-Turk wa-ʿāmmat jund al-khilāfa."
(a) Ed. by G. van Vloten. *Tria Opuscula.* Leiden: E. J. Brill, 1903. Pp. 1–56.
(b) Ed. by A. M. Hārūn. *Rasāʾil al-Jāḥiẓ.* 2 vols. Cairo: Maktabat al-Khanjī, 1964–65. Pp. 1–86.
(c) Trans. by C. T. Harley-Walker. "Jahiz of Basra to al-Fath ibn Khaqan on the 'Exploits of the Turks and the Army of the Caliphate in General.'" *JRAS* (1915), 631–697.
‹P. 114›

———. *Fī madḥ al-tujjār wa-dhamm ʿamal al-sulṭān.*
(a) In *Majmūʿat rasāʾil li'l-Jāḥiẓ: iḥdā ʿashrata risāla.* Cairo, 1324/1906. Pp. 155–160.
(b) Excerpts translated in Pellat, *Life and Works of Jahiz,* 272–273.
‹P. 227›

——— (attributed). *al-Tabaṣṣur bi'l-tijāra. See* Pellat, Charles.

Jennings, R. C. "The Office of Vekil (Wakil) in 17th-century Ottoman Sharia Courts." *SI,* xlii (1975), 147–169.
‹P. 222›

———. "Kadi, Court, and Legal Procedure in 17th-Century Ottoman Kayseri." *SI,* xlviii (1978), 133–172.
‹P. 222›

———. "Limitations of the Judicial Powers of the Kadi in 17th-Century Ottoman Kayseri." *SI,* l (1979), 151–184.
‹P. 222›

Johansen, Baber. *The Islamic Law on Land Tax and Rent: The Peasants' Loss of Property Rights as Interpreted in the Hanafite Legal Literature of the Mamluk and Ottoman Periods.* New York: Croom Helm; Routledge, Chapman & Hall, 1988.
‹P. 216›

———. "Eigentum, Familie, und Obrigkeit im hanafitischen Strafrecht." *Welt des Islams,* n.s. xix (1979), 1–73.
‹P. 231›

———. "The All-Embracing Town and Its Mosques." *ROMM,* xxxii (1981), 139–161.
‹P. 230›

Jomard, Edmé-François. "Description abrégée de la Ville et de la Citadelle du Kaire." *Description de l'Égypte. État Moderne, Mémoires:* Vol. II, Part ii (1822), 579–786. *État Moderne, Planches.* Vol. I (1809), nos. 15–73.
‹P. 232›

Jones, J.M.B. "Ibn Isḥāq and al-Wāqidī: The Dream of ʿĀtika and the Raid to Nakhla in Relation to the Charge of Plagiarism." *BSOAS,* xxii (1959), 41–51.
‹P. 80›

———. "The Maghāzī Literature." *Cambridge History of Arabic Literature,* i, 344–351.
‹P. 79›

al-Jumaḥī, Muḥammad b. Sallam. *Ṭabaqāt al-shuʿarāʾ al-jāhiliyya wa'l-islāmiyyin.* Ed. by Joseph Hell. Leiden: E. J. Brill, 1916.
‹P. 188›

Juynboll, G.H.A. *Muslim Tradition: Studies in Chronology, Provenance and Authorship of Early Hadith.* Cambridge: Cambridge University Press, 1983.
‹Pp. 82, 84, 189›

———. "The Date of the Great Fitna." *Arabica*, xx (1973), 142–159.
‹P. 82›

Kabir, Mafizullah. *The Buwayhid Dynasty of Baghdad*. Calcutta: Iran Society, 1964.
‹P. 155›

Kafesoğlu, İbrahim. *Sultan Melikşah devrinde Büyük Selçuklu İmparatorluğu*. Istanbul: O. Yalin Matbaasi, 1953.
‹P. 156›

———. *See also* Leiser, Gary.

Kaḥḥālah, ʿUmar Riḍā. Muʿjam al-muʾallifīn. 15 vols. Damascus: Maṭbaʿat al-Taraqqī, 1957–61.
‹P. 28›

———. *Muʿjam qabāʾil al-ʿArab al-qadīma wa'l-ḥadītha*. 5 vols. Vols. I–III, Damascus: al-Maṭbaʿa al-Hāshimiyya, 1368/1949. Vols. IV–V, *al-Mustadrak*, Damascus: Maṭbaʿat al-Ḥijāz, 1395/1975.
‹P. 115›

Kai-Kāʾus b. Iskandar. *Qābūs-nāmeh*. Ed. by R. Levy. E.J.W. Gibb Memorial, N.S. 18. London: Luzac, 1951. Trans. by R. Levy as *A Mirror for Princes*. London: Cresset Press, 1951.
‹Pp. 164, 165›

al-Kalbī, Hishām b. Muḥammad. *See* Caskel, Werner.

Kamāl al-Dīn b. al-ʿAdīm. *See* Ibn al-ʿAdīm.

Karatay, F. E. Topkapı Sarayı Müzesi, Kütüphane.
(a) *Arapça yazmalar Kataloğu*. 4 vols., 1962–69.
(b) *Farsça yazmalar Kataloğu*. 1 vol., 1961.
(c) *Türkçe yazmalar Kataloğu*. 2 vols., 1962.
‹P. 38›

al-Kāshgharī, Maḥmūd b. al-Ḥusayn. *Dīwān Lughāt al-Turk*.
(a) Arabic text ed. by Kilisli Muallim Rifat Bilge. 3 vols. Istanbul: 1333–35/1915–17.
(b) Ed. with modern Turkish translation by Besim Atalay. 6 vols. [Vols. 1–3: trans.; Vol. 4: Turkish index; Vol. 5: Arabic facsimile text; Vol. 6: Arabic index.] Ankara: Türk Dil Kurumu, 1939–1957.
(c) Ed. and trans. by Robert Dankoff and James Kelly as *Compendium of the Turkish Dialects*. 2 vols. Sources of Oriental Languages and Literatures, no. 7. General Editors, Şinasi Tekin and Gönül Alpay Tekin. Duxbury, MA: 1982–84.
‹Pp. 15, 166›

Kay Kāʾūs b. Iskandar. *See* Kai-Kāʾūs.

Keçik, Mehmet Şefik. *Briefe und Urkunden aus der Kanzlei Uzun-Hasans: ein Beitrag zur Geschichte Ost-Anatoliens im 15. Jahrhundert*. Freiburg im Breisgau: K. Schwarz, 1975.
‹P. 48›

Kennedy, Hugh. *The Early Abbasid Caliphate: A Political History*. London: Croom Helm, 1981.
‹P. 119›

Khadduri, Majid. *See also* al-Shaybānī.

Khadduri, Majid, and H. J. Liebesny, eds. *Law in the Middle East. Vol. I: Origin and Development of Muslim Law*. Washington, D.C.: Middle East Institute, 1955. *See also* Gibb, H.A.R.
‹P. 214›

Khalidi, Tarif. *Islamic Historiography: the Histories of Masʿūdī*. Albany, NY: State University of New York Press, 1975.
‹P. 76›

Khalidi, Tarif, ed. *Land Tenure and Social Transformation in the Middle East*. Beirut: American University of Beirut, 1984. *See* Haarmann, Ulrich.

Khalīfa b. Khayyāṭ al-ʿUṣfurī. *al-Taʾrīkh*. Ed. by Akram Ḍiyāʾ al-ʿUmarī. 2 vols. Najaf: Maṭbaʿat al-Adab, 1967.
‹P. 112›

———. *Kitāb al-Ṭabaqāt*.
(a) Ed. by Suhayl Zakkār. Damascus: Wizārat al-Thaqāfa wa'l-Siyāḥa wa'l-Irshād al-Qawmī, 1966.
(b) Ed. by A. D. al-ʿUmarī. Baghdad: Maṭbaʿat al-ʿĀnī, 1967.
‹Pp. 112, 188›

Khalīl b. Isḥāq. *al-Mukhtaṣar*.
(a) Trans. by I. Guidi and D. Santillana as *Sommario del diritto malechita*. 2 vols. Milan: U. Hoepli, 1919.
(b) Trans. by G. H. Bousquet as *Abrégé de la loi musulmane selon le rite de l'imam Malek*. 4 vols. Algiers: Editions en-Nahdha algérienne, 1956–62.
‹P. 214›

Khan, Muhammad Sabir. *Studies in Miskawayh's Contemporary History (340–369) A.H.* Ann Arbor, Mich.: University Microfilms International, 1980.
‹P. 134›

al-Khaṭīb al-Baghdādī. *Taʾrīkh Baghdād aw Madīnat al-Salām*. 14 vols. Cairo: Maktabat al-Khanjī, 1931.
‹Pp. 132, 238›

———. *Taʾrikh Baghdād* (Topographical Introduction).
(a) Arabic text: Vol. I of 1931 Cairo edition.
(b) Trans. by G. Salmon as *L'Introduction topographique à l'histoire de Bagdadh d'Abou Bakr Ahmad ibn Thabit al-Khatib al-Bagdadhi*. Paris: Bouillon, 1904.
(c) Trans. by Jacob Lassner as *The Topography of Baghdad in the Early Middle Ages: Text and Studies*. Detroit: Wayne State University Press, 1970.
‹Pp. 132, 238›

Khoury, Raif Georges. *Wahb b. Munabbih*. Teil 1: *Der Heidelberger Papyrus PSR Heid Arab 23; Leben und Werk des Dichters*. Teil 2: *Faksimiletafeln*. Wiesbaden: O. Harrassowitz, 1972.
‹P. 77›

———. *ʿAbd Allāh ibn Lahīʿa (97–174/715–790): juge et grand maître de l'école égyptienne. Avec edition critique de l'unique rouleau de papyrus arabe conservé à Heidelberg*. Wiesbaden: O. Harrassowitz, 1986.
‹P. 77›

al-Khwārizmī, Abū ʿAbd Allāh. *Mafātīḥ al-ʿulūm*. Ed. by G. Van Vloten. Leiden: E. J. Brill, 1895; reprinted 1968.
‹P. 44›

Kister, M. J. *Studies in Jahiliyya and Early Islam*. London: Variorum, 1980.
‹P. 84›

———. "The Sirah Literature." *Cambridge History of Arabic Literature*, i, 352–367.
‹P. 79›

Koprulu, M. F. "Çağatay Edebiyatı." *IA*, iii, 270–323.
‹P. 31›

Kornrumpf, Hans-Jürgen. *Osmanische Bibliographie, mit besonderer Berücksichtigung der Türkei in Europa.* HO, Ergbd. VIII (1973).
‹Pp. 6, 9›

Kortantamer, Samira. *Ägypten und Syrien zwischen 1317 und 1341 in der Chronik des Mufaḍḍal b. Abī'l-Faḍā'il.* Islamkundliche Untersuchungen, 23. Freiburg im Breisgau: K. Schwarz, 1973.
‹Pp. 136, 277›

Köymen, M. A. *Büyük Selçuklu Imparatorluğu Tarihi, I: Kuruluş Devri.* Ankara: Selçuklu Tarih ve Medeniyeti Enstitüsü, 1979.
‹P. 156›

Krachkovskii, I. I. *Arabskaia geograficheskaia literatura.* In *Izbrannye sochineniia* (6 vols. Moscow: Akademiia Nauk SSSR, 1955–1960), Vol. IV. Trans. by S.D.U. Hāshim as *Ta'rīkh al-adab al-jughrāfī al-ʿarabī.* 2 vols. Cairo: Lajnat al-Ta'līf wa'l-Tarjama wa'l-Nashr, 1963–65.
‹P. 224›

Kraemer, Joel L. *Humanism in the Renaissance of Islam. The Cultural Revival during the Buyid Age.* Leiden: E. J. Brill, 1986.
‹P. 134›

Kramers, J. H. "Geography and Commerce." In T. Arnold and A. Guillaume, eds., *The Legacy of Islam* (Oxford: Clarendon Press, 1931. Often reprinted.), 79–108.
‹P. 224›

———. "La littérature géographique classique des musulmans." In Kramers, *Analecta Orientalia: Posthumous Writings and Selected Works* (2 vols. Leiden: E. J. Brill, 1954–56), i, 172–204.
‹P. 224›

Kubiak, Wladyslaw B. *Al-Fustat: Its Foundation and Early Urban Development.* Cairo: American University of Cairo Press, 1987.
‹P. 234›

al-Kulaynī, Abū Jaʿfar Muḥammad. *al-Kāfī.* Ed. by A. A. al-Ghaffārī. 8 vols. Tehran: Maktabat al-Ṣadūq, 1377–81/1957–61.
‹P. 23›

Kurd ʿAlī, Muḥammad. *Khiṭaṭ al-Shām.* 6 vols. Damascus, 1343–47/1925–28.
‹P. 240›

———. *Ghūṭat Dimashq.* Damascus: Arab Academy of Damascus, 1949. Rev. ed. 1371/1952.
‹P. 240›

al-Kutubī, Ibn Shākir. *Fawāt al-wafayāt.* Ed. by M. M. ʿAbd al-Ḥamīd. 2 vols. Cairo: Maktabat al-Nahḍa al-Miṣriyya, 1951–52.
‹P. 242›

———. *ʿUyūn al-tawārīkh. See* Sauvaire, Henri.
‹P. 239›

Lambton, A.K.S. *Landlord and Peasant in Persia: A Study of Land Tenure and Land Revenue Administration.* London: Oxford University Press for The Royal Institute of International Affairs, 1953. 2d ed., 1969.
‹Pp. 180, 294, 301›

———. *Theory and Practice in Medieval Persian Government*. Collected Studies, 122. London: Variorum Reprints, 1980.
‹P. 164›

———. *State and Government in Medieval Islam. An Introduction to the Study of Islamic Political Theory: The Jurists*. London: Oxford University Press, 1981.
‹P. 160›

———. *Continuity and Change in Medieval Persia: Aspects of Administrative, Economic, and Social History, 11th–14th Century*. Albany, NY: State University of New York Press, 1988.
‹Pp. 155, 179, 301›

———. "The Theory of Kingship in the Nasihat al-Muluk of Ghazali," *Islamic Quarterly*, i (1954), 47–55.
‹P. 165›

———. "Quis Custodiet Custodes: Some Reflections on the Persian Theory of Government." *SI*, v (1956), 125–148; vi (1956), 125–146.
‹P. 164›

———. "The Merchant in Medieval Islam." In Henning and Yarshater, *A Locust's Leg* (1962), 121–130.
‹P. 226›

———. "Justice in the Medieval Persian Theory of Kingship." *SI*, xvii (1962), 91–119.
‹P. 164›

———. "Reflexions on the Iqṭāʿ." In G. Makdisi, ed., *Arabic and Islamic Studies in Honor of H.A.R. Gibb*. Cambridge, MA: Harvard University Press, 1965, pp. 358–376.
‹P. 180›

———. "The Internal Structure of the Saljuq Empire." *Cambridge History of Iran*, v, 203–282.
‹P. 156›

———. "Aspects of Saljuq-Ghuzz Settlement in Persia." In Richards, *Islamic Civilization, 950–1150*, 105–125.
‹P. 157›

———. "Aspects of Agricultural Organization and Agrarian History in Persia." *HO* I/vi/6, pt. 1 (1977), 160–187.
‹P. 295›

Lane, Arthur. *Early Islamic Pottery*. London: Faber and Faber, 1947.
‹P. 62›

———. *Later Islamic Pottery*. London: Faber and Faber, 1957.
‹P. 62›

Lane, E. W. *An Arabic-English Lexicon*. 8 vols. London and Edinburgh: Williams and Norgate, 1863–93.
‹P. 13›

Lane-Poole, Stanley. *Catalogue of Oriental Coins in the British Museum*. 10 vols. London: British Museum, 1875–90.
‹P. 50›

———. *The Mohammedan Dynasties*. London: A. Constable, 1894. Reprinted, Beirut: Khayats, 1965.
‹Pp. 20–21›

———. *Saladin and the Fall of the Kingdom of Jerusalem*. London: G. P. Putnam, 1898. (Often reprinted)
‹P. 266›

Langlois, Ch. V., and Ch. Seignobos. *Introduction aux études historiques*. Paris: Hachette, 1898. Trans. by G. G. Berry as *Introduction to the Study of History*. London: Duckworth & Co., 1898.
‹P. 34›

Laoust, Henri. *Essai sur les doctrines sociales et politiques de Taki-d-Din Ahmad b. Taimiya*. Cairo: Institut Français d'Archéologie Orientale, 1939.
‹Pp. 193, 196, 259›

———. *Les schismes dans l'Islam*. Paris: Payot, 1965.
‹P. 125›

———. *La politique de Ġazālī*. Paris: P. Geuthner, 1970.
‹P. 161›

———. "Aḥmad b. Ḥanbal." *EI*², i, 280–286.
‹P. 196›

———. "Le hanbalisme sous le Califat de Bagdad, 241–656/855–1258." *REI*, xxvii (1959), 67–128.
‹P. 196›

———. "Le hanbalisme sous les Mamlouks Bahrides (658–784/1260–1382)." *REI*, xxviii (1960), 1–72.
‹P. 196›

———. "La classification des sectes dans le *Farq* d'al-Baghdādī." *REI*, xxix (1961), 19–59.
‹P. 113›

———. "La pensée et l'action politiques d'al-Māwardī (364–450/974–1058)." *REI*, xxxvi (1968), 11–92.
‹P. 160›

———. *See also* Ibn Baṭṭa, Ibn Qudāma.

Lapidus, Ira M. *Muslim Cities in the Later Middle Ages*. Cambridge, MA: Harvard University Press, 1967. Reprinted without notes: Cambridge University Press, 1984.
‹Pp. 201–203, 207, 246›

Lapidus, Ira M., ed. *Middle Eastern Cities: A Symposium on Ancient, Medieval, and Modern Middle Eastern Urbanism*. Berkeley and Los Angeles: University of California Press, 1969. *See also* Grabar, Oleg.
‹Pp. 202, 207›

Lapidus, Ira M. "Muslim Cities and Islamic Societies." In Lapidus, *Middle Eastern Cities*, 47–79.
‹Pp. 157–158, 202, 207, 230›

———. "The Grain Economy of Mamluk Egypt." *JESHO*, xii (1969), 1–15.
‹P. 304›

———. "The Conversion of Egypt to Islam." *Israel Oriental Studies*, ii (1972), 248–262.
‹P. 276›

———. "The Evolution of Muslim Urban Society." *Comparative Studies in Society and History*, xv (1973), 21–50.
‹Pp. 207, 230›

———. "Arab Settlement and Economic Development of Iraq and Iran in the Age of the Umayyad and Early Abbasid Caliphs." In Udovitch, *The Islamic Middle East, 700–1900*, 177–208.
‹P. 303›

Lassner, Jacob. *The Shaping of Abbasid Rule*. Princeton, NJ: Princeton University Press, 1980.
‹Pp. 112, 114, 120, 124›

———. *Islamic Revolution and Historical Memory: Abbasid Apologetics and the Art of Historical Writing*. New Haven: American Oriental Society, 1986.
‹Pp. 116, 124›

———. "The Abbasid *Dawla*: An Essay on the Concept of Revolution in Early Islam." In Clover and Humphreys, *Tradition and Innovation*, 247–270.
‹P. 124›

———. *See also* al-Khaṭīb al-Baghdādī.

Latron, André. *La vie rurale en Syrie et au Liban: étude d'économie rurale*. Beirut: Institut Français de Damas, 1936.
‹P. 297›

Lavoix, Henri. *Catalogue des monnaies musulmanes de la Bibliothèque Nationale*. 3 vols. Paris: Imprimerie Nationale, 1887–91. *See also* Hennequin, Gilles
‹P. 50›

Le Strange, Guy. *Palestine under the Moslems*. London: Palestine Exploration Fund, 1890. Reprinted, Beirut: Khayats, 1965.
‹Pp. 18, 241, 298›

———. *The Lands of the Eastern Caliphate*. Cambridge: Cambridge University Press, 1905.
‹Pp. 18, 296›

———. "Description of Mesopotamia and Baghdad, written about the year 900 A.D. by Ibn Serapion." *JRAS* (1895), 1–76, 255–315.
‹P. 296›

Le Tourneau, Roger. *Fès avant le Protectorat: étude économique et sociale d'une ville de l'occident musulman*. Publications de l'Institut des Hautes Études Marocaines, t. 45. Casablanca: SMLE, 1949.
‹P. 233›

Leiser, Gary, ed. and trans. *A History of the Seljuks: Ibrahim Kafesoğglu's Interpretation and the Resulting Controversy*. Carbondale, IL: Southern Illinois University Press, 1988.
‹P. 156›

Lev, Yaacov. "The Fatimid vizier Yaᶜqūb b. Killis and the Beginning of the Fatimid Administration in Egypt." *Islam*, lviii (1981), 237–249.
‹P. 267›

Levi-Provençal, Évariste. *Inscriptions arabes de l'Espagne*. Leiden: E. J. Brill, 1931.
‹P. 57›

———. *Histoire de l'Espagne musulmane*. 3 vols. Paris: G. P. Maisonneuve, 1944–53.
‹P. 304›

———. *See also* Ibn ᶜAbdūn.

Levtzion, Nehemiah, ed. *Conversion to Islam*. New York: Holmes and Meier, 1979.
‹P. 274›

Lewis, Bernard, ed. and trans. *Islam, from the Prophet Muhammed to the Capture of Constantinople*. 2 vols. New York: Harper and Row, 1974.
‹P. 259›

Lewis, Bernard, ed. *The World of Islam: Faith, People, Culture*. London: Thames and Hudson, 1976. *See* Grabar, Oleg.

Lewis, Bernard. *The Jews of Islam*. Princeton, NJ: Princeton University Press, 1984.
‹P. 265›

———. "The Ottoman Archives as a Source for the History of the Arab Lands." *JRAS* (1951), 139–155.
‹P. 231›

———. "Studies in the Ottoman Archives, I." *BSOAS*, xvi (1954), 469–501.
‹P. 231›

———. "ʿAbbāsids." EI^2, i, 15–23.
‹P. 119›

———. "Daftar." EI^2, ii, 77–81.
‹P. 44›

———. "The Regnal Titles of the First Abbasid Caliphs." In *Dr. Zakir Husain Presentation Volume* (New Delhi: Dr. Zakir Husain Presentation Volume Committee, 1968), 13–22.
‹P. 120›

———. "An Interpretation of Fatimid History." In *Colloque internationale sur l'histoire du Caire*, 287–295.
‹P. 266›

———. "L'Islam et les non-musulmans." *AESC*, xxxv (1980), 784–800.
‹P. 257›

Lewis, Bernard, and Amnon Cohen. *Population and Revenue in the Towns of Palestine in the Sixteenth Century*. Princeton, NJ: Princeton University Press, 1978.
‹P. 231›

Lewis, Bernard, and P. M. Holt, eds. *Historians of the Middle East*. Oxford: Oxford University Press, 1962. *See* Dahan, Sami; Gibb, H.A.R.; Watt, W. M.

Lewis, Naphtali. *Life in Egypt under Roman Rule*. Oxford: Clarendon Press, 1983.
‹P. 300›

Library of Congress. See *Near East National Union List*.

Little, Donald P. *An Introduction to Mamluk Historiography*. Freiburger Islamstudien, Bd. 2. Wiesbaden: F. Steiner, 1970.
‹P. 136›

———. *A Catalogue of the Islamic Documents from al-Ḥaram aš-Šarīf in Jerusalem*. Beirut: Orient-Institut der Deutschen Morgenländischen Gesellschaft, 1984. *See also* Richards, D. S.
‹Pp. 48, 219›

———. "The Historical and Historiographic Significance of the Detention of Ibn Taymiyya." *IJMES*, iv (1973), 311–327.
‹P. 193›

———. "Did Ibn Taymiyya Have a Screw Loose?" *SI*, xli (1975), 93–111.
‹P. 193›

———. "The Significance of the Ḥaram Documents for the Study of Medieval Islamic History." *Islam*, lvii (1980), 189–219.
‹P. 48›

———. "Six fourteenth-century purchase deeds for slaves from al-Ḥaram aš-Šarīf." *ZDMG*, cxxxi (1981), 297–337.
‹P. 221›

———. "Two Fourteenth-century Court Records from Jerusalem concerning the Disposition of Slaves by Minors." *Arabica*, xxix (1982), 16–49.
‹P. 220›

Løkkegaard, Frede. *Islamic Taxation in the Classic Period, with Special Reference to Circumstances in Iraq*. Copenhagen: Branner & Korch, 1950.
‹P. 303›

Lord, Albert. *The Singer of Tales*. Cambridge, MA: Harvard University Press, 1960.
‹P. 87›

Lyons, M. C., and David Jackson. *Saladin: the Politics of the Holy War*. London: Cambridge University Press, 1982.
‹P. 266›

Maas, Paul. *Textkritik*. 4th ed. Leipzig: B.G. Teubner, 1960. Trans. by Barbara Flower as *Textual Criticism*. Oxford: Clarendon Press, 1958.
‹P. 34›

Madelung, Wilferd. *Religious Trends in Early Islamic Iran*. Albany, NY: State University of New York Press, 1988.
‹P. 125›

———. "The Assumption of the Title Shāhanshāh by the Buyids and 'The Reign of Daylam (Dawlat al-Daylam).'" *JNES*, xxviii (1969), 84–108, 168–183.
‹P. 162›

Mahdi, Muhsin. *Ibn Khaldun's Philosophy of History: A Study in the Philosophic Foundation of the Science of Culture*. London: G. Allen and Unwin, 1957. Reprinted, Chicago: University of Chicago Press, 1964, 1971.
‹Pp. 135, 194›

Mājid, ʿAbd al-Munʿim. *Nuẓum al-Fāṭimiyyīn wa-rusūmuhum*. 2 vols. Cairo, 1953–56.
‹P. 267›

Makdisi, George. *Ibn ʿAqīl et la resurgence de l'Islam traditionaliste au xiᵉ siècle*. Damascus: Institut Français de Damas, 1963.
‹Pp. 156, 160, 197, 198›

———. *The Rise of Colleges: Institutions of Learning in Islam and the West*. Edinburgh: Edinburgh University Press, 1981.
‹Pp. 35, 199–200›

———. "Muslim Institutions of Learning in Eleventh-century Baghdad." *BSOAS*, xxiv (1961), 1–56.
‹P. 200›

———. *See also* Ibn ʿAqīl.

Makdisi, George, and Johannes Petersen. "Madrasa, I: The Institution in the Arabic, Persian, and Turkish Lands." *EI²*, v, 1123–34.
‹P. 199›

al-Makhzūmī, ʿAlī b. ʿUthmān. *Kitāb al-minhāj fī ʿilm kharāj Miṣr*. Partial edition by Claude Cahen and Yūsuf Rāghib. Cairo: Institut Français d'Archéologie Orientale, 1986. *See also* Cahen, *Makhzūmiyyāt*.
‹P. 173›

al-Makīn b. al-ʿAmīd. *See* Cahen, "Chronique des Ayyoubides."

Mandaville, Jon E. "The Ottoman Court Records of Syria and Jordan." *JAOS*, lxxxvi (1966), 311–319.
‹P. 219›

Mann, Jacob. *The Jews in Egypt and in Palestine under the Fatimid Caliphs.* 2 vols. London: Oxford University Press, 1920–22. Reprinted in 1 vol., with preface by S. D. Goitein. New York: Ktav, 1970.
‹P. 269›

———. *Texts and Studies in Jewish History and Literature.* 2 vols. Cincinnati: Hebrew Union College, 1931; Philadelphia: Jewish Publication Society of America, 1935. Reprinted with preface by Gerson D. Cohen. New York: Ktav, 1972.
‹P. 269›

Mannheim, Karl. *Ideology and Utopia.* Trans. by Louis Wirth and Edward Shils. New York: Harcourt, Brace & Co., 1936.
‹P. 149›

Mantran, Robert. "Règlements fiscaux ottomans: la province de Bassora." *JESHO*, x (1967), 224–277.
‹P. 231›

Mantran, Robert, and Jean Sauvaget. *Règlements fiscaux ottomans: les provinces syriennes.* Beirut: Institut Français de Damas, 1951.
‹Pp. 172, 231, 298›

Manuscripts of the Middle East. Ed. by Jan Just Witkam. Vol. I (1986)–to date. Leiden: Ter Lugt Press.
‹P. 39›

al-Maqrīzī, Taqī al-Dīn Aḥmad. *Kitāb al-sulūk li-maʿrifat duwal al-mulūk.* 4 vols. Ed. M. M. Ziyāda et al. Cairo: Lajnat al-taʾlīf wa'l-tarjama wa'l-nashr, 1934–1975. *See* Quatremère, *Histoire des sultans Mamlouks.*

———. *Kitāb al-mawāʿiẓ wa'l-iʿtibār fī dhikr al-khiṭaṭ wa'l-āthār.*
(a) 2 vols. Bulaq, 1270/1853–54. (Editio princeps, often reprinted.)
(b) Ed. by Gaston Wiet (incomplete): *MIFAO*, xxx, xxxiii, xlvi, xlix, liii (1911–27).
(c) Trans. by E. Bouriant and Paul Casanova (incomplete): *MMAF*, xvii (1900); *MIFAO*, iii–iv (1906–1920).
(d) Partial translation by A. Raymond and G. Wiet, as *Les marchés du Caire: traduction annotée du texte de Maqrīzī.* Cairo: Institut Français d'Archéologie Orientale, 1979.
(e) *Index des Khitat. Index analytique des ouvrages d'Ibn Duqmāq et de Maqrīzī sur le Caire.* Ed. by Aḥmad A.-M. Harīdī. 3 vols. Cairo: Institut Français d'Archéologie Orientale, 1983–in progress.
‹Pp. 175–176›

Marçais, Georges. *L'architecture musulmane d'Occident: Tunisie, Algérie, Maroc, Espagne et Sicile.* Paris: Arts et métiers graphiques, 1955.
‹P. 61›

———. "L'urbanisme musulman." *Revue Africaine* (1939–40), 13–34. Reprinted in G. Marçais, *Mélanges d'histoire et d'archéologie de l'Occident musulman* (2 vols. Algiers: Gouvernement général de l'Algérie, 1957), i, 219–231.
‹P. 229›

———. "La conception des villes dans l'Islam." *Revue d'Alger*, ii (1945), 517–533.
‹P. 229›

———. "Considérations sur les villes musulmanes et notamment sur le rôle du mohtasib." *Recueils de la Société Jean Bodin*, vi (1954), 249–262.
‹P. 229›

———. *See also* Saladin, Henri.

Marçais, William. "L'Islamisme et la vie urbaine." *Comptes-rendus de l'Académie des Inscriptions et Belles-Lettres* (1928), 86–100. Reprinted in William Marçais, *Articles et conferences* (Paris: A. Maisonneuve, 1961).
‹P. 228›

———. "Le Taqrīb de en-Nawawī" *JA*, ser. 9: no. xvi (1900), 315–346; no. xvii (1901), 101–149, 193–232, 524–540; no. xviii (1901), 61–146.
‹Pp. 35, 81›

Margoliouth, David S. *Lectures on Arabic Historians*. Calcutta: University of Calcutta, 1930.
‹Pp. 75, 81›

Margoliouth, David S. *See also* al-Tanūkhī, al-Muḥassin b. ʿAlī.

Marquet, Yves. "Le šiʿisme au ixe siècle à travers l'histoire de Yaʿqūbī." *Arabica*, xix (1972), 1–45, 101–138.
‹P. 75›

Martin, Thomas J. *North American Collections of Islamic Manuscripts*. Boston: G. K. Hall, 1977.
‹P. 35›

Mashkur, A. J. "Les sectes shiʿites." *RHR*, cxliii (1958), 68–78; cxliv (1958), 67–95; cxlv (1959), 63–78.
‹P. 113›

Massignon, Louis. *La passion d'al-Ḥallāj, martyr mystique de l'Islam*. 2 vols. Paris: P. Geuthner, 1922. 2d rev. ed., 4 vols. Paris: Gallimard, 1975. Trans. by Herbert Mason as *The Passion of al-Hallaj: Mystic and Martyr of Islam*. 4 vols. Princeton, NJ: Princeton University Press, 1982.
‹P. 194›

———. "Esquisse d'une bibliographie Qarmate." In T. W. Arnold and R. A. Nicholson, eds., *Oriental Studies Presented to Edward G. Browne* (Cambridge: Cambridge University Press, 1922), 329–338.
‹P. 31›

al-Masʿūdī, ʿAlī b. al-Ḥusayn. *Kitāb al-Tanbīh wa'l-Ishrāf*. Ed. by M. J. de Goeje. *BGA*, viii (1894). Trans. by B. Carra da Vaux as *Livre de l'avertissement et de la révision*. Paris: Imprimerie Nationale, 1896.
‹P. 76›

———. *Murūj al-dhahab wa-maʿādin al-jawhar*.
(a) Ed. and trans. by C. Barbier de Meynard and Pavet de Courteille as *Les prairies d'or*. 9 vols. Paris: Imprimerie Impériale and Imprimerie Nationale, for the Société Asiatique, 1861–77.
(b) Revised edition and translation by Charles Pellat, under same title. Arabic text: 7 vols. Beirut: al-Jāmiʿa al-Lubnāniyya, 1965–79. Translation: 5 vols. Paris: Société Asiatique, 1965–74.
(c) Ed. by Y. A. Dāghir. 4 vols. Beirut: Dār al-Andalus, 1956–66.
‹Pp. 72, 75, 111›

———. *See also* Khalidi, Tarif; Shboul, A. M.

Matthew of Edessa. *Chronicle.*
(a) Ed. and trans. by Ed. Dulaurier as *Chronique de Matthieu d'Édesse, 962–1136, avec la continuation de Gregoire le Prêtre jusqu'en 1162*. Paris: A. Durand, 1858.
(b) Trans. by Hrant Andreasyan as *Urfalı Mateos Vekayı-Namesi (962–1136) ve Papaz Grigor'un Zeyli (1136–1162)*. Ankara: Türk Tarih Kurumu, 1962.
‹P. 278›

al-Māwardī, Abū al-Ḥasan ʿAlī. *al-Aḥkām al-sulṭāniyya.*
(a) Ed. by M. Enger as *Maverdii Constitutiones Politicae*. Bonn: A. Marcus, 1853.
(b) Trans. by E. Fagnan as *Les statuts gouvernementaux: ou, Règles de droit public et administratif.* Algiers: A. Jourdan, 1915.
See also Amedroz, H. F.
‹Pp. 160, 222›

———. *Adab al-qāḍī*. Ed. by M. H. al-Sirḥān. Baghdad: Riʾāsat Dīwān al-Awqāf, 1971–72.
‹P. 222›

Mayer, Leo A. *Bibliography of Moslem Numismatics, India Excepted.* Oriental Translation Fund Publications, Vol. XXXV. London: Royal Asiatic Society, 1954.
‹P. 52›

Māzandarānī, ʿAbd Allāh b. Muḥammad. *Die Resāla-ye Falakiyya des Abdollah ibn Mohammad ibn Kiya al-Mazandarani.* Ed. by W. Hinz. Wiesbaden: F. Steiner, 1952.
‹P. 45›

McChesney, R. D. "A Guide to Orientalist Research in Soviet Central Asia." *MESA Bull.*, xii, 1 (1978), 13–25.
‹P. 39›

Meiseles, Gustav. *Reference Literature to Arabic Studies: A Bibliographical Guide.* Tel Aviv: University Publishing Projects, 1978.
‹P. 8›

Mélikoff, Irène. *Abū Muslim, le "Porte-hache" de Khorassan.* Paris: A. Maisonneuve, 1962.
‹P. 124›

Ménasce, Jean de. "Problèmes des mazdéens dans l'Iran musulman." In *Festschrift für Wilhelm Eilers* (Wiesbaden: O. Harrassowitz, 1967), 220–230.
‹P. 278›

Mez, Adam. *Die Renaissance des Islams.* Heidelberg: C. Winter, 1922. Trans. by S. Khuda-Bukhsh and D. S. Margoliouth as *The Renaissance of Islam.* London: Luzac, 1937; reprinted Beirut: United Publishers, 1973; New York: AMS Press, 1975.
‹Pp. 153, 225, 228›

Michael the Syrian. *La chronique de Michel le Syrien.* Ed. and trans. by Jean Chabot. 4 vols. Paris: Académie des Inscriptions et Belles-Lettres, 1899–1914. Reprinted, Brussels: Culture et Civilisation, 1963.
‹Pp. 29, 263, 278›

Michael, Murad. "The Archive of Nahray ben Nissim, Businessman and Public Figure in Egypt in the Eleventh Century." Ph.D. dissertation, Hebrew University, Jerusalem, 1963 (in Hebrew).
‹P. 270›

Michel, Bernard. "L'organisation financière de l'Égypte sous les sultans mamelouks d'après Qalqachandi." *BIE*, vii (1925), 127–147.
‹P. 175›

Michell, George, ed. *Architecture of the Islamic World: Its History and Social Meaning*. New York: Morrow, 1978.
‹P. 60›

Migeon, Gaston. *See* Saladin, Henri.

Miles, George C. *The Numismatic History of Rayy*. Numismatic Studies, Vol. II. New York: American Numismatic Society, 1938.
‹P. 53›

———. "Numismatics." *Cambridge History of Iran*, iv, 364–377.
‹P. 53›

Millward, William G. "A Study of al-Yaʿqūbī with special reference to his alleged Shīʿa Bias." Ph.D. dissertation, Princeton University, 1962.
‹P.75›

Minorsky, Vladimir F., ed. and trans. *Tadhkirat al-Mulūk, a Manual of Safavid Administration (circa 1137/1725)*. E.J.W. Gibb Memorial, N.S. 16. London: Luzac, 1943.
‹P. 45›

———. See also *Ḥudūd al-ʿālam.*

Miquel, André. *La géographie humaine du monde musulman jusqu'au milieu de 11e siècle*. 3 vols. Paris and the Hague: Mouton, 1967–1980.
‹Pp. 224–225›

Miskawayh, Aḥmad b. Muḥammad. *Tajārib al-umam wa-taʿāqib al-himam*. Ed. and trans. by H. F. Amedroz and D. S. Margoliouth for the years 295–369 A.H. as *The Eclipse of the Abbasid Caliphate*. 6 vols. London: Oxford University Press, 1920–21.
‹Pp. 131, 133–134›

Monroe, James T. "The Poetry of the Sīrah Literature." *Cambridge History of Arabic Literature*, i, 368–373.
‹P. 79›

Moravcsik, Gyula. *Byzantino-turcica*. 2d. ed. 2 vols. Berlin: Deutsche Akademie der Wissenschaften, 1958.
‹P. 30›

Morgan, David O., ed. *Medieval Historical Writing in the Christian and Islamic Worlds*. London: School of Oriental and African Studies, University of London, 1982.
‹P. 134›

Morimoto, Kosei. *The Fiscal Administration of Egypt in the Early Islamic Period*. Trans. by Michael Robbins. Kyoto: Dohosha, 1981.
‹Pp. 44, 179, 303›

Moritz, Bernhard. *Arabic Palaeography: A Collection of Arabic Texts from the First Century of the Hidjra till the Year 1000*. Publications of the Khedivial Library; 16. Cairo and Leipzig: Hiersemann, 1905.
‹P. 33›

Morony, Michael G. *Iraq after the Muslim Conquest*. Princeton, NJ: Princeton University Press, 1984.
‹Pp. 44, 69, 264›

———. "Landholding in Seventh-Century Iraq: Late Sasanian and Early Islamic Patterns." In Udovitch, *The Islamic Middle East, 700–1900*, 135–176.
‹P. 303›

Moscati, Sabatino. "Studi su Abu Muslim." *Rendiconti della Reale Accademia dei Lincei.* Series 8, vol. IV (1949–50), 323–335, 474–495; vol. V (1950–51), 89–105.
‹Pp. 123, 124›

———. "Il testamento di Abū Hāshim." *RSO*, xxvii (1952), 28–46.
‹P. 125›

———. "Per una storia dell'antica Šīʿa." *RSO*, xxx (1955), 251–267.
‹P. 125›

———. "Studi storici sul califfato di al-Mahdi." *Orientalia*, xiv (1945), 300–354.
‹P. 120›

———. "Nuovi studi storici sul califfato di al-Mahdi." *Orientalia*, xv (1946), 155–179.
‹P. 120›

Mottahedeh, Roy P. *Loyalty and Leadership in an Early Islamic Society*. Princeton, NJ: Princeton University Press, 1980.
‹Pp. 134, 155›

———. "The Abbasid Caliphate in Iran." *Cambridge History of Iran*, iv, 57–89.
‹P. 119›

———. Review of R. Bulliet, *The Patricians of Nishapur*. *JAOS*, xcv (1975), 491–495.
‹P. 187›

———. "The Shuʿūbiyah Controversy and the Social History of Early Islamic Iran." *IJMES*, vii (1976), 161–182.
‹P. 163›

Muʿādh, Khālid. *See* Ory, Solange.

al-Mubarrad, Muḥammad b. Yazīd. *al-Kāmil.*
(a) Ed. by William Wright. 2 vols. in 1. Leipzig: F. A. Brockhaus, 1864–92.
(b) Ed. by M.A.F. Ibrāhīm and al-Sayyid Shaḥāṭa. 4 vols. Cairo: Maktabat Nahḍat Miṣr, 1956.
‹P. 115›

al-Mufaḍḍal ibn Abī'al-Faḍā'il. *See* Kortantamer, Samira.

Müller-Wodarg, D. "Die Landwirtschaft Ägyptens in der frühen Abbasidenzeit." *Islam*, xxxi (1954), 174–227; xxxii (1955–57), 14–78, 141–167; xxxiii (1958), 310–321.
‹P. 299›

al-Munajjid, Ṣalāḥ al-Dīn, ed. *al-Kitāb al-ʿarabī al-makhṭūṭ ilā al-qarn al-ʿāshir al-hijrī.* Juz' I: *al-Namādhij.* Cairo: Arab League, Institute of Arabic Manuscripts, 1960.
‹P. 33›

Munẓavi, Aḥmad. *Fihrist-i nuskhahā-i khaṭṭī-i fārsī.* 6 vols. Tehran: Mu'assasah-i Farhangī-i Mintaqah'i, 1969–in progress.
‹P. 38›

al-Muqaddasī. *Aḥsan al-taqāsīm fī maʿrifat al-aqālīm*. Ed. by M. J. de Goeje. *BGA*, iii (1906). Partial translation by André Miquel, *La meilleure répartition pour la connaissance des provinces*. Damascus: Institut Français de Damas, 1963.
‹P. 242›

Muṣṭafā, Shākir. *Dawlat Banī al-ʿAbbās*. 2 vols. Kuwait: Wakālat al-Maṭbūʿāt, 1973.
‹P. 119›

———. *al-Ta'rīkh al-ʿarabī wa'l-mu'arrikhūn: dirāsa fī taṭawwur ʿilm al-ta'rīkh wa-maʿrifat rijālihi fī al-Islām.* 2 vols. Beirut: Dār al-ʿIlm li'l-Malāyīn, 1978–in progress.
‹Pp. 75, 76, 133›

al-Nābulsī, ʿUthmān b. Ibrāhīm. *Ta'rīkhkh al-Fayyūm wa-bilādihi*. Ed. by B. Moritz as *Description du Faiyoum au VIIe siècle de l'Hégire*. Cairo: Publications de la Bibliothèque Khédiviale, no. 11, 1899.
‹P. 174›

———. *Kitāb lumaʿ al-qawānīn al-muḍiyya fī dawāwīn al-Diyār al-Miṣriyya*. Ed. by Carl Becker and Claude Cahen. *BEO*, xvi (1958–60), 119–134. Partial translation by Cl. Cahen, "Quelques aspects de l'administration égyptienne médiévale vus par un de ses fonctionnaires." *BFLUS*, xxvi (1948), 97–118.
‹P. 174›

Nagel, Tilman. *Untersuchungen zur Entstehung des abbasidischen Kalifates*. Bonner Orientalische Studien, N.S. 22. Bonn: Selbstverlag des Orientalischen Seminars der Universität, 1972.
‹Pp. 116, 124, 125›

El-Nahal, Galal. *The Judicial Administration of Ottoman Egypt in the Seventeenth Century*. Minneapolis and Chicago: Bibliotheca Islamica, 1979.
‹Pp. 210, 220, 222›

Narshakhī, Muḥammad b. Jaʿfar. *The History of Bukhara*. Trans. by Richard Frye. Cambridge, MA: Mediaeval Academy of America, 1954.
‹P. 113›

Nashriya-i Kitābkhāna-i Markazī-i Dānishgāh-i Tihrān dar barrā-i Nuskhahā-i Khaṭṭī. University of Tehran. Vol. I (1340/1961). (Journal: from vol. IV, the principal title is *Nuskhahā-i Khaṭṭī*.)
‹P. 39›

al-Nawbakhtī, al-Ḥasan b. Mūsā. *Kitāb firaq al-Shīʿa*. Ed. by Helmut Ritter as *Die Sekten der Schiʿa*. Istanbul: Deutsche Morgenländische Gesellschaft, 1931.
‹P. 113›

Nazim, Muhammad. *The Life and Times of Sultan Mahmud of Ghazna*. Cambridge: Cambridge University Press, 1931.
‹P. 155›

Near East National Union List, The. Ed. by Dorothy Stehle. Vol. I: *A*. Washington, D.C.: Library of Congress, 1988.
‹P. 23›

Neely, James A. "Sassanian and early Islamic water-control and irrigation systems on the Deh Luran Plain, Iran." In Downing and Gibson, *Irrigation's Impact on Society*, 21–42.
‹P. 293›

New York Public Library, Reference Department. *Dictionary Catalog of the Oriental Collection*. 16 vols. Boston: G. K. Hall, 1960.
‹P. 24›

New York Public Library, the Research Libraries. *Dictionary Catalog of the Oriental Collection*. First Supplement. 8 vols. Boston: G. K. Hall, 1976.
‹P. 24›

Newman, Julius. *The Agricultural Life of the Jews in Babylonia, between the Years 200 C.E. and 500 C.E.* London: Oxford University Press, 1932.
‹P. 296›

Niẓām al-Mulk, al-Ḥasan b. ʿAlī. *Siyāsat-nāmeh yā siyar al-mulūk*.
(a) Ed. by Hubert Darke. Tehran: Bungāh-i Tarjama va-Nashr-i Kitāb, 1340/1962. Revised edition, on the basis of a newly discovered Nakhchivan manuscript, 1976.

(b) Trans. by Hubert Darke as *The Book of Government, or Rules for Kings*. London: Routledge and Kegan Paul, 1960. Revised trans. 1978.
‹Pp. 139, 163–164, 197›

Nöldeke, Theodor. "Die iranische National-Epos." In Geiger and Kuhn, *Grundriss der iranischen Philologie*, ii, 130–211. Printed separately, Berlin and Leipzig: Vereinigung Wissenschaftlicher Verleger, 1920. Trans. by L. Bogdanov. Bombay: K. R. Cama Oriental Institute, 1930.
‹P. 12›

Northrup, Linda S., and Amal Abul-Hajj. "A Collection of Medieval Arabic Documents in the Islamic Museum at the Ḥaram al-Šarīf." *Arabica*, xxv (1978), 282–291.
‹P. 48›

Noth, Albrecht. *Quellenkritische Studien zu Themen, Formen, und Tendenzen frühislamischen Geschichtsüberlieferung*. Teil I: *Themen und Formen*. Bonner Orientalistische Studien, N.S. 25. Bonn: Selbstverlag des Orientalischen Seminars der Universität Bonn, 1973.
‹P. 86›

———. "Isfahan-Nihawand, eine quellenkritische Studie zur frühislamischen Historiographie." *ZDMG*, cxviii (1968), 274–296.
‹P. 86›

———. "Der Charakter der ersten grossen Sammlungen von Nachrichten zur frühen Kalifenzeit." *Islam*, xlvii (1971), 168–199.
‹P. 79›

al-Nuʿaymī, ʿAbd al-Qādir. *al-Dāris fī taʾrīkh al-madāris*. [Original Title: *Tanbīh al-ṭālib wa-irshād al-dāris fī mā fī Dimashq min al-jawāmiʿ wa'l-madāris*.] Ed. by Jaʿfar al-Ḥassānī. 2 vols. Damascus: Arab Academy of Damascus, 1948–51.
‹P. 239›

al-Nuwayrī, Aḥmad b. ʿAbd al-Wahhāb. *Nihāyat al-arab fī funūn al-adab*. 25 vols., in progress. Cairo: Dār al-Kutub al-Miṣriyya, 1923–continuing.
‹Pp. 174, 298›

Omar, Farouk (= ʿUmar, Fārūq). *The Abbasid Caliphate, 132/750–170/786*. Baghdad: National Printing and Publishing Co., 1969.
‹Pp. 111, 119, 122›

ʿUmar, Fārūq. *al-ʿAbbasīyyūn al-awāʾil*. 2 vols., Beirut: Dār al-Irshād, 1970–73.
‹P. 119›

———. *Ṭabīʿat al-daʿwa al-ʿabbāsiyya*. Beirut: Dār al-Irshād, 1970.
‹Pp. 111, 122›

Ory, Solange, ed. *Archives Max van Berchem, I: Catalogue de la photothèque*. Geneva: Fondation Max van Berchem, 1975.
‹P. 57›

Ory, Solange, and Khālid Muʿādh. *Inscriptions arabes de Damas: les stèles funéraires*. Vol. I: *Cimetière d'al-Bāb al-Ṣaghīr*. Damascus: Institut Français de Damas, 1977.
‹P. 55›

Ouéchek, Émilie. *Index générale de la "Description de Damas" de Sauvaire*. Damascus: Institut Français de Damas, 1954.
‹P. 239›

Parain, Charles. "The Evolution of Agricultural Technique." *Cambridge Economic History of Europe*, i (2d ed., 1966), 125–179.
‹P. 300›

Paret, Rudi. *Der Koran: Kommentar und Konkordanz*. Stuttgart: W. Kohlhammer, 1971.
‹P. 21›

———. "Al-Ṭabarī," *EI*^{1}, 578–579.

———. "Umma," *EI*^{1}, iv, 1015–16; and *SEI*, 603–4.
‹P. 95›

———. "Toleranz und Intoleranz in Islam." *Saeculum*, xxi (1970), 344–365.
‹P. 257›

Pascual, Jean-Paul. *Damas à la fin du xvi*^{e} *siècle, d'après trois actes de waqf ottomans*. Tome I. Damascus: Institut Français de Damas, 1983.
‹Pp. 232, 248›

Pearson, J. D., et. al. *Index Islamicus, 1906–1955. A Catalogue of Articles on Islamic Subjects in Periodicals and Other Collective Publications*. Cambridge: W. Heffer and Sons, 1958. Supplements: i, 1956–1960 (Cambridge: Heffer, 1962); ii, 1961–1965 (Cambridge: Heffer, 1967); iii, 1966–1970 (London: Mansell, 1972); iv, 1971–1975 (London: Mansell, 1977); v, 1976–1980 (in 2 parts. London: Mansell, 1982).
‹Pp. 7, 8, 9, 39, 63›

———. *Quarterly Index Islamicus*. London: Mansell, 1977–continuing.
‹P. 7›

Pearson, J. D. *Oriental Manuscripts in Europe and North America: A Survey*. Bibliotheca Asiatica, 7. Zug, Switzerland: Inter-Documentation, 1971.
‹P. 39›

Pearson, J. D., ed. *A Bibliography of Pre-Islamic Persia*. Persian Studies Series, no. 2. London: Mansell, 1975.
‹P. 10›

Pearson, J. D., and George Ṣcanlon, eds. *A Bibliography of the Architecture, Arts and Crafts of Islam*. Supplement II, January 1972–January 1980. Cairo: American University in Cairo Press, 1984. *See also* Creswell, K.A.C.
‹P. 63›

Pedersen, Johannes. *Den arabiske Bog*. Copenhagen, 1946. Trans. by Geoffrey French as *The Arabic Book*. Ed. by Robert Hillenbrand. Princeton, NJ: Princeton University Press, 1984.
‹P. 32›

———. *See also* Makdisi, George.

Pellat, Charles. *Le milieu basrien et la formation de Ǧaḥiẓ*. Paris: A. Maisonneuve, 1953.
‹P. 195›

———. *The Life and Works of Jahiz*. Trans. by D. M. Hawke. London: Routledge and Kegan Paul, 1969.
‹Pp. 114, 227›

———. *Le calendrier de Cordoue*. Leiden: E. J. Brill, 1961.
‹P. 300›

———, ed. and trans. *Cinq calendriers égyptiens*. Textes arabes et études islamiques, t. xxvi. Cairo and Paris: Institut Français d'Archéologie Orientale, 1986.
‹P. 299›

———. "Ǧāḥiẓiana, I. Le Kitāb al-tabaṣṣur bi-l-tiǧāra attribué à Ǧāḥiẓ." *Arabica*, i (1954), 153–165.
‹P. 227›

———. *See also* Ibn al-Muqaffaʿ.

Perlmann, Moshe. "Asnawi's Tract against Christian Officials." In D. S. Löwinger and J. Somogyi, eds., *Ignace Goldziher Memorial Volume* (2 vols. Vol. I: Budapest, 1948. Vol. II: Jerusalem, 1958), ii, 172–208.
‹P. 260›

Pertsch, Wilhelm. *Verzeichnis der persischen Handschriften der Königlichen Bibliothek zu Berlin*. Berlin: A. Ascher & Co., 1888.
‹P. 37›

———. *Verzeichnis der türkischen Handschriften der Königlichen Bibliothek zu Berlin*. Berlin: A. Ascher & Co., 1889.
‹P. 37›

Peters, Emrys. "Aspects of Rank and Status among Muslims in a Lebanese Village." In Pitt-Rivers, *Mediterranean Countrymen*, 159–200. Reprinted in Sweet, *Peoples and Cultures of the Middle East*, (1970), ii, 76–123.
‹P. 307›

———. "Shifts in Power in a Lebanese Village." In R. Antoun and I. Harik, *Rural Politics and Social Change in the Middle East*, 165–197.
‹P. 307›

Petersen, Erling L. *ʿAlī and Muʿāwiya in Early Arabic Tradition: Studies on the Genesis and Growth of Islamic Historical Writing until the End of the Ninth Century*. Copenhagen: Munksgaard, 1964.
‹Pp. 77, 86, 88›

———. "ʿAlī and Muʿāwiya: The Rise of the Umayyad Caliphate 656–661." *Acta Orientalia*, xxiii (1959), 157–196.
‹Pp. 77–78›

———. "Studies on the Historiography of the ʿAli-Muʿāwiya Conflict." *Acta Orientalia*, xxvii (1963), 83–118.
‹P. 78›

Petrushevsky, I. P. *Zemledelie i agrarnie otnosheniya v Irane XIII–XIV vekov*. Leningrad: Izd-vo Akademii nauk SSSR, 1960. Trans. into Persian by Karīm Kishāvarz as *Kishāvarzī va Munasābat-i ʿArżī dar Īrān-i ʿAhd-i Mughul*. 2 vols. Tehran, 1344/1966.
‹P. 302›

———. "The Socio-Economic History of Iran under the Il-Khans." In *Cambridge History of Iran*, v, 483–537.
‹P. 301›

Petry, Carl F. *The Civilian Elite of Cairo in the Later Middle Ages*. Princeton, NJ: Princeton University Press, 1981.
‹Pp. 183, 206–207›

Pfannmüller, Gustav. *Handbuch der Islam-Literatur*. Berlin and Leipzig: W. de Gruyter, 1923.
‹P. 8›

Philologiae Turcicae Fundamenta. Ed. by Jean Deny et al. 3 vols.–in progress. Wiesbaden: F. Steiner, 1959–continuing.
‹P. 12›

Philon, Helene. *Early Islamic Ceramics: Ninth to Late Twelfth Centuries*. London: Islamic Art Publications, 1980.
‹P. 62›

Pitt-Rivers, Julian, ed. *Mediterranean Countrymen: Essays in the Social Anthropology of the Mediterranean*. Paris and The Hague: Mouton, 1963.
‹P. 307›

Planhol, Xavier de. *De la plaine pamphylienne aux lacs pisidiens: nomadisme et vie paysanne*. Paris: A. Maisonneuve, 1958.
‹P. 290›

Poliak, A. N. *Feudalism in Egypt, Syria, Palestine, and the Lebanon (1250–1900)*. London: Royal Asiatic Society, 1939.
‹P. 181›

———. "La féodalite islamique." *REI*, x (1936), 247–265.
‹P. 181›

———. "Some Notes on the Feudal System of the Mamluks." *JRAS* (1937), 97–107.
‹P. 181›

———. "The Ayyubid Feudalism." *JRAS* (1939), 428–432.
‹P. 181›

Poonawala, Ismail K. *Biobibliography of Ismāʿīlī Literature*. Malibu, CA: Undena, 1977. *See also* Tajdin, Nagib.
‹P. 31›

Pope, A. U., and Phyllis Ackerman. *A Survey of Persian Art*. 6 vols. London and New York: Oxford University Press, 1938–39; Index vol. by Th. Besterman. London and New York: Oxford University Press, 1958; reprinted in 14 vols., Tokyo: Meiji-Shobo, 1964–67.
‹P. 61›

Popper, William. *Egypt and Syria under the Circassian Sultans; 1382–1468 A.D.: Systematic Notes to Ibn Taghribirdi's Chronicles of Egypt*. 2 vols. University of California Publications in Semitic Philology, xv–xvi. Berkeley: University of California Press, 1955–57.
‹Pp. 177, 206, 207›

———. *See also* Ibn Taghrībirdī.

Pouzet, Louis. *Damas au viie/xiiie s. Vie et structures religieuses dans une métropole islamique*. Recherches de la Faculté des Lettres et des Sciences Humaines de l'Université St-Joseph, Beyrouth. Nouv. Ser. A: Langue arabe et pensée islamique, t. 15. Beirut: Dar al-Machreq, 1988.
‹Pp. 200–201›

Prawer, Joshua. *Crusader Institutions*. Oxford: Clarendon Press, 1980.
‹Pp. 297, 298›

al-Qāḍī, Wadād. *al-Kaysāniyya fī al-taʾrīkh wa'l-adab*. Beirut: Dār al-Thaqāfa, 1974.
‹P. 126›

———. "The Development of the Term 'Ghulāt' in Muslim Literature with Special Reference to the Kaysaniyya." *Akten des VII. Kongresses fur Arabistik und Islamwissenschaft, Göttingen, 1974*. Published as *Abhandlungen der Akademie der Wissenschaften in Göttingen, Phil-Hist. Klasse*. Folge 3, Nr. 98 (Göttingen, 1976). Pp. 295–319.
‹P. 126›

Qā'immaqāmī, Jahāngīr. *Muqaddimah-i bar shinakht-i asnādi-i tārīkhī*. Anjuman-i Āsār-i Millī, Silsilah-i Intishārāt, 84. Tehran, 1350/1971.
‹P. 45›

al-Qalqashandī, Aḥmad b. ʿAbdallāh. *Ṣubḥ al-aʿshā fī ṣināʿat al-inshāʾ*. 14 vols. Cairo: Dār al-Kutub al-Khidiwiyya, 1913–20; reprinted, Cairo: Wizārat al-Thaqāfa wa'l-Irshād al-Qawmī, 1963.
‹Pp. 45, 51, 171, 175, 298›

———. *See also* al-Baqlī, M. Q.; Björkman, W.; Canard, Marius; Gaudefroy-Demombynes, M.

Quatremère, Étienne. *Histoire des sultans Mamlouks de l'Égypte*. (Partial translation of al-Maqrīzī, *Kitāb al-sulūk li-maʿrifat duwāl al-mulūk*). 2 vols. in 4 parts. Paris: Oriental Translation Fund of Great Britain and Ireland, 1845.
‹P. 14›

Qudāma b. Jaʿfar. *See* Ben-Shemesh, A.

al-Qummī, Ḥasan b. Muḥammad. *Taʾrīkhkh-i Qumm*. Ed. by Jalāl al-Dīn Tihrānī. Tehran, 1353/1934.
‹P. 113›

Rabie, Hassanein. *The Financial System of Egypt, A.H. 564–741/A.D. 1169–1341*. London: Oxford University Press, 1972.
‹Pp. 45, 46, 170, 177, 181, 267›

———. "Some Technical Aspects of Agriculture in Medieval Egypt." In Udovitch, *The Islamic Middle East, 700–1900*, 59–90.
‹Pp. 181, 299›

Radloff, Wilhelm (= Radlov, Vasilii Vasil'evich). *Versuch eines Wörterbuches der Türk-Dialecte*. 4 vols. St. Petersburg: Imperial Academy of Sciences, 1893–1911. Reprinted with a foreword by O. Pritsak. The Hague: Mouton, 1960.
‹P. 15›

Rafeq, Abdul Karim. "Les régistres des tribunaux de Damas comme source pour l'histoire de la Syrie." *BEO*, xxvi (1973), 219–226.
‹P. 219›

———. "Economic Relations between Damascus and the Dependent Countryside, 1743–1771." In Udovitch, *The Islamic Middle East, 700–1900*, 653–686.
‹P. 303›

Rāghib, Yūsuf. *Marchands d'étoffes du Fayyoum au iiiᵉ/ixᵉ siècle d'après leurs archives (actes et lettres). I, Les actes des Banū ʿAbd al-Muʾmin*. Cairo: Institut Français d'Archéologie Orientale, 1982.
‹Pp. 42, 221›

Raymond, André. *Artisans et commerçants au Caire au xviiiᵉ siècle*. 2 vols. Damascus: Institut Français de Damas, 1973–74.
‹P. 233›

———. *The Great Arab Cities in the 16th–18th centuries: An Introduction*. New York: New York University Press, 1984.
‹P. 232›

———. *Les grandes villes arabes à l'époque ottomane*. Paris: Sindbad, 1985.
‹P. 232›

———. "Les documents du Mahkama comme source pour l'histoire économique et sociale de l'Égypte an xviiiᵉ siècle." In Berque and Chevallier, *Les Arabes par leurs archives*, 125–140.
‹P. 219›

Redman, Charles L. "Archaeology in a Medieval City of Islam." *MESA Bull.*, xiv, 2

(Dec. 1980), 1–22.
‹P. 60›

Redman, Charles L., and Patty Jo Watson. "Systematic, Intensive Surface Collection." *American Antiquity*, xxxv (1970), 279–291.
‹P. 292›

Répertoire chronologique d'épigraphie arabe. Founded by Étienne Combe, Jean Sauvaget, and Gaston Wiet. 17 vols., in progress. Cairo: Institut Français d'Archéologie Orientale, 1931–continuing.
‹Pp. 58–59, 243›

Rescher, Oskar. *Sachindex zu Bokhari nach der Ausgabe Krehl-Juynboll und der Übersetzung von Houdas-Marçais*. Stuttgart: privately lithographed edition of 60 copies, 1923.
‹P. 22›

Revault, J., B. Maury, and M. Zakariya. *Palais et maisons du Caire du xive au xviiie siècle*. 4 vols. Cairo: Institut Français d'Archéologie Orientale, 1975–83. *See also* Garcin, J.-C.
‹P. 61›

Reychman, J., and A. Zajączkowski. *Introduction to Ottoman-Turkish Diplomatics*. Trans. by A. S. Ehrenkreutz. The Hague: Mouton, 1968.
‹P. 43›

Reynolds, L. D., and N. G. Wilson. *Scribes and Scholars: A Guide to the Transmission of Greek and Latin Literature*. London: Oxford University Press, 1968. 2d revised ed., 1974.
‹P. 34›

Richards, D. S., ed. *Islamic Civilization, 950–1150*. Oxford: Bruno Cassirer, 1973. *See* Cahen, Claude; Lambton, A.K.S.
‹Pp. 154, 157›

Richards, D. S. "Arabic Documents from the Karaite Community in Cairo." *JESHO*, xv (1972), 105–162.
‹P. 262›

———. Review of D. P. Little, *A Catalogue of the Islamic Documents from al-Ḥaram aš-Šarīf in Jerusalem*. In *BSOAS*, 1 (1987), 362–364.
‹P. 48›

Richter-Bernburg, Lutz. "Amīr-Malik-Shāhanshāh: ʿAḍud ad-Daula's Titulature Reexamined." *Iran*, xviii (1980), 83–102.
‹P. 162›

Rieu, Charles. *Supplement to the Catalogue of the Arabic Manuscripts in the British Museum*. London: Longman & Co., 1894.
‹P. 31›

Risciani, N. *Documenti e firmani*. Jerusalem: Custodia Terrae Sanctae, 1931.
‹Pp. 48, 171›

Ritter, Helmut. "Ein arabisches Handbuch der Handelswissenschaft," *Islam*, vii (1917), 1–91.
‹P. 226›

Robson, James. "Ibn Isḥāq's Use of the Isnād." *BJRL*, xxxviii (1955–56), 449–465.
‹Pp. 79, 82›

———. "al-Djarḥ wa'l-Taʿdīl." *EI*^{2}, ii, 462.
‹P. 81›

———. "Ḥadīth." *EI*^{2}, iii, 23–28.
‹P. 81›

———. *See also* al-Tibrīzī, Walī al-Dīn.

Roemer, H. R. "Arabische Herrscherurkunden aus Ägypten." *OLZ*, lxi (1966), 325–347.
‹P. 47›

———. "Inshāʾ." *EI*^{2}, iii, 1241–1244.
‹P. 41›

Roolvink, R. et al. *Historical Atlas of the Muslim Peoples*. Amsterdam: Djambatan, n.d. [1957].
‹P. 17›

Rosen-Ayalon, Myriam, ed. *Studies in Memory of Gaston Wiet*. Jerusalem: Institute of Asian and African Studies, Hebrew University, 1977. *See* Ashtor, Eliyahu; Grabar, Oleg.

Rosenthal, E.I.J. *Political Thought in Medieval Islam*. Cambridge: Cambridge University Press, 1958.
‹P. 160›

Rosenthal, Franz. *The Technique and Approach of Muslim Scholarship*. Analecta Orientalia, 24. Rome: Pontificium Institutum Biblicum, 1947.
‹P. 32›

———. *A History of Muslim Historiography*. Leiden: E. J. Brill, 1952; 2d rev. ed., 1968.
‹Pp. 75, 133›

Rotter, Gernot. *Die Umayyaden und der zweite Bürgerkrieg*. Abhandlungen fur die Kunde des Morgenländes, B. XLV, no. 3. Wiesbaden: F. Steiner for the Deutsche Morgenländische Gesellschaft, 1982.
‹P. 125›

———. "Abū Zurʿa ad-Dimašqī (st. 281/894) und das Problem der frühen arabischen Geschichtsschreibung in Syrien." *Welt des Orients*, vi (1971), 80–104.
‹P. 80›

———. "Zur Überlieferung einiger historischer Werke Madāʾinīs in Tabaris Annalen." *Oriens*, xxiii–xxiv (1974), 103–133.
‹P. 79›

Roux, J. P. "L'origine céleste de la souveraineté dans les inscriptions paléo-turques de Mongolie et de Siberie." In *The Sacral Kingship*, 231–241.
‹Pp. 166–167›

Ruppin, Arthur. *Syrien als Wirtschaftsgebiet*. Berlin: Kolonial-Wirtschaftliches Komitee, Deutschen Kolonialgesellschaft, 1917. 2d rev. ed.; Berlin: B. Harz, 1920.
‹P. 297›

Russell, J. C. *Late Ancient and Medieval Population*. Transactions of the American Philosophical Society, xlviii, pt. 3. Philadelphia, 1958.
‹P. 247›

al-Ṣābī, Hilāl. *Rusūm dār al-khilāfa*. Edited by Mikhāʾīl ʿAwad. Baghdad: Maṭbaʿat al-ʿĀnī, 1964. Trans. by Elie A. Salem as *The Rules and Regulations of the ʿAbbasid Court*. Beirut: American University of Beirut, 1977.
‹P. 153›

Sacral Kingship, The. Contributions to the Central Theme of the VIIIth International Congress for the History of Religions, Rome, April 1955. Supplement to *Numen: International Review for the History of Religions*. Leiden: E. J. Brill, 1959. *See* Roux, J. P.; Widengren, Geo.

Sadighi, Gholam Hussein. *Les mouvements religieux iraniens au iie et au iiie siècle de l'Hégire*. Paris: Les Presses Modernes, 1938.
‹P. 121›

al-Ṣadūq, Muḥammad b. ʿAlī b. Bābawayh al-Qummī. *Man la yaḥḍuruhu al-faqīh*. Ed. by H. M. Kharsān. 4 vols. Najaf: Dār al-Kutub al-Islāmiyya, 1957–59.
‹P. 23›

al-Ṣafadi, Khalīl b. Aybak. *al-Wāfī bi'l-wafayāt*. Ed. by Helmut Ritter, Sven Dedering, et al. 22 vols. Istanbul: Deutsche Morgenländische Gesellschaft, 1931–in progress. (Since 1962, Wiesbaden: F. Steiner, for the DMG.)
‹P. 189›

Saḥnūn b. Saʿīd al-Tanūkhī. *al-Mudawwana al-kubrā*. 4 vols. Cairo: al-Maṭbaʿa al-Khayriyya, 1324/1906.
‹P. 215›

al-Sakhāwī, Shams al-Dīn Muḥammad. *al-Ḍawʾ al-lāmiʿ fī aʿyān al-qarn al-tāsiʿ*. 12 vols. Cairo: Maktabat al-Qudsī, 1353–55/1934–36.
‹Pp. 192, 204, 206›

Saladin, Henri, and Gaston Migeon. *Manuel d'art musulman*.
(a) 1st ed., in 2 vols. Vol. I: *L'architecture*. Vol. II: *Arts plastiques et industriels*. Paris: Auguste Picard, 1907.
(b) 2d rev. ed., in 4 vols. Marçais, Georges. *L'architecture: Tunisie, Algérie, Maroc, Espagne, Sicile*, 2 vols. Migeon, G. *Arts plastiques et industriels*, 2 vols. Paris: Auguste Picard, 1926–27.
‹Pp. 60–61›

Saliba, Maurice. *Arabic and Islamic Studies: Doctoral Dissertations and Graduate Theses in English, French, and German (1881–1981)*. Saliba: Antelias, Lebanon, 1983.
‹P. 10›

Salonen, A. "Agricultura Mesopotamia nach sumerisch-akkadischen Quellen." *Annales Academiae Scientiarum Fennicae*, ser. B, 149 (1968).
‹P. 296›

el-Samarraie, Husam Qawam. *Agriculture in Iraq during the 3rd Century A.H.* Beirut: Librairie du Liban, 1972.
‹Pp. 295, 301›

Sanders, Paula. "The Court Ceremonial of the Fatimid Caliphate in Egypt." Ph.D. dissertation, Princeton University, 1984.
‹P. 153›

———. "From Court Ceremony to Urban Language: Ceremonial in Fatimid Cairo and Fustat." In *Essays in Honor of Bernard Lewis*, 311–321.
‹P. 153›

Santillana, David de. *Istituzioni di diritto musulmano malichita, con riguardo anche al sistema sciafiita*. 2 vols. Rome: Istituto per l'Oriente, 1925–38.
‹Pp. 214–215›

al-Sarakhsī, Muḥammad b. Aḥmad. *Kitāb al-mabsūṭ*. 30 vols. in 15. Cairo, 1324–31/1906–13.
‹P. 215›

Sato, Tsugitaka. "The Evolution of the Iqṭāʿ System under the Mamluks—an Analysis of al-Rawk al-Ḥusāmī and al-Rawk al-Nāṣirī." *Memoirs of the Research Department of the Toyo Bunko*, no. 37 (Tokyo, 1979), 99–131.
‹P. 181›

———. "The Iqṭāʿ System of Iraq under the Buwayhids." *Orient* (Tokyo), xviii (1982), 83–105.
‹P. 180›

Sauvaget, Jean. *Les monuments historiques de Damas*. Beirut: Catholic Press, 1932.
‹P. 245›

———. *Alep: essai sur le développement d'une grande ville syrienne des origines au milieu du xixe siècle*. 2 vols. (Vol. I, text; Vol. II, plates). Paris: P. Geuthner, 1941.
‹Pp. 234–238›

———. *Introduction à l'histoire de l'Orient musulman: Éléments de bibliographie*. Paris: Adrien-Maisonneuve, 1943. Revised ed. by Claude Cahen, 1961; English adaptation, *Introduction to the History of the Muslim East*. Berkeley and Los Angeles: University of California Press, 1965. *See also* Cahen, Claude.
‹P. 8›

———. *La mosquée omeyyade de Médine: Étude sur les origines architecturales de la mosquée et de la basilique*. Paris: Vanoest, for the Institut Français de Damas, 1947.
‹Pp. 152, 234›

———. *Quatre décrets seldjoukides*. Beirut: Institut Français de Damas, 1947.
‹Pp. 58, 243›

———, Michel Écochard, and J. Sourdel-Thomine. *Les monuments ayyoubides de Damas*. 4 fascicles. Paris: E. de Boccard for the Institut Français de Damas, 1938–50.
‹P. 245›

———. "Décrets mamelouks de Syrie." *BEO*, ii (1932), 1–52; iii (1933), 1–29; xii (1947–48), 5–60.
‹Pp. 58, 172, 243›

———. "Esquisse d'une histoire de la ville de Damas." *REI*, viii (1934), 421–480.
‹Pp. 245–246›

———. "Comment étudier l'histoire du monde arabe." *Revue Africaine*, xc, nos. 406–409 (1946), 5–23. Reprinted in *Mémorial Jean Sauvaget* (2 vols., Damascus: Institut Français de Damas, 1954), i, 165–186.
‹P. 234›

Sauvaire, Henri. "Matériaux pour servir à l'histoire de la numismatique et de la métrologie musulmanes." *JA*, series 7: no. xiv (1879), 455–533; xv (1880), 228–277, 421–478; xviii (1881), 499–516; xix (1882), 23–77, 97–163, 281–327; series 8: no. iii (1884), 368–445; iv (1884), 207–321; v (1885), 498–506; vii (1886), 124–177, 394–468; viii (1886), 113–192, 479–536; x (1887), 200–259.
‹P. 52›

———. "Description de Damas." *JA*, series 9: no. iii (1894), 251–318, 385–501; iv (1894), 242–331, 460–503; v (1895), 269–315, 377–411; vi (1895), 221–313, 409–484; vii (1896), 185–285, 369–459. Printed separately in 2 vols., Paris: Imprimerie Nationale, 1895–96. *See also* Ouéchek, Émilie.
‹Pp. 239, 243, 245›

Schacht, Joseph. *The Origins of Muhammadan Jurisprudence*. Oxford: Clarendon Press, 1950.
‹Pp. 83–84, 213›

———. *An Introduction to Islamic Law*. Oxford: Clarendon Press, 1964.
‹Pp. 11, 212, 213, 217, 218, 222›

———. "Die arabische ḥijal-Literatur. Ein Beitrag zur Erforschung der islamischen Rechtspraxis." *Islam*, xv (1926), 211–232.
‹P. 217›

———. "A Revaluation of Islamic Traditions." *JRAS* (1949), 143–154.
‹Pp. 83–84›

———. "On Mūsā ibn ʿUqba's Kitāb al-Maghāzī." *Acta Orientalia*, xxi (1950–53), 288–300.
‹P. 80›

———. "Ḥiyal." *EI*^{2}, ii, 510–513.
‹P. 217›

Schäfer, Barbara. *Beiträge zur mamlukischen Historiographie nach dem Tode al-Malik an-Nāṣirs*. Freiburg im Breisgau: K. Schwarz, 1971.
‹P. 136›

Schimmel, Annemarie. *Islamic Calligraphy*. Leiden: E. J. Brill, 1970.
‹P. 33›

Schnebel, Michael. *Die Landwirtschaft im hellenistischen Ägypten*. Münchener Beiträge zur Papyrusforschung und Antiken Rechtsgeschichte, vii: pp. 1–379. Munich: Beck, 1925.
‹P. 300›

Schoeler, G. "Verfasser und Titel des dem Ǧāḥiẓ zugeschriebenen sog. *Kitāb al-Tāǧ*." *ZDMG*, cxxx (1980), 217–225.
‹P. 153›

School of Oriental and African Studies, University of London. *Library Catalogue*. 28 vols. Boston: G. K. Hall, 1963. First Supplement: 16 vols., 1968. Second Supplement: 16 vols., 1973. Third Supplement: 19 vols., 1979.
‹P. 24›

Schwartzberg, Joseph E., ed. *A Historical Atlas of South Asia*. Chicago: University of Chicago Press, 1978.
‹P. 17›

Schwarz, Klaus. *Der Vordere Orient in den Hochschulschriften Deutschlands, Österreichs, und der Schweiz. Eine Bibliographie von Dissertationen und Habilitationsschriften (1885–1978)*. Freiburg im Breisgau: K. Schwarz, 1980.
‹P. 10›

Schwarz, Paul. *Iran im Mittelalter nach den arabischen Geographen*. 9 vols. Leipzig, Zwickau, Stuttgart, Berlin: O. Harrassowitz, 1896–1936.
‹P. 18›

Selim, George Dimitri. *American Doctoral Dissertations on the Arab World, 1883–1974*. 2d ed. Washington, D.C.: Library of Congress, 1976.
‹P. 10›

———. *American Doctoral Dissertations on the Arab World, Supplement, 1975–1981*. Washington, D.C.: Library of Congress, 1983.
‹P. 10›

———. *American Doctoral Dissertations on the Arab World. Supplement, August 1981–December 1987*. Washington, D.C.: Library of Congress, 1989.
‹P. 10›

Sellheim, Rudolf. "Prophet, Chalif, und Geschichte: Die Muḥammed-Biographie des

Ibn Isḥāq." *Oriens*, xviii–xix (1967), 33–91.
‹P. 79›

———. "Ḳirṭās." *EI*^{2}, v, 173–174.
‹P. 41›

———, Dominique Sourdel, et al. "Kātib." *EI*^{2}, iv, 754–760.
‹P. 44›

Serjeant, R. B. *The Saiyids of Hadramawt: An Inaugural Lecture*. London: SOAS, University of London, 1957.
‹P. 94›

———. "Material for a History of Islamic Textiles." *Ars Islamica*, ix (1942), 54–92; x (1943), 71–104; xi (1946), 98–135; xiii–xiv (1948), 75–117; xv–xvi (1951), 29–85. Reprinted in 1 vol. as *Islamic Textiles: Material for a History up to the Mongol Conquest*. Beirut: Librairie du Liban, 1972.
‹P. 225›

———. Review of Alfred Guillaume, *The Life of Muhammad*. In *BSOAS*, xxi (1958), 1–14.
‹P. 78›

———. "Ḥaram and Ḥawṭah, the Sacred Enclave in Arabia." In A. R. Badawi, ed., *Melanges Taha Husain* (Cairo, 1962), 41–58.
‹P. 94›

———. "The 'Constitution of Medina'." *Islamic Quarterly*, viii (1964), 3–16.
‹Pp. 93, 94, 95, 96, 97›

———. "The Sunnah Jāmiʿah, Pacts with the Yathrib Jews, and the Taḥrīm of Yathrib. Analysis and Translation of the Documents Comprised in the so-called 'Constitution of Medina'." *BSOAS*, xli (1978), 1–42.
‹Pp. 93, 94, 95, 96, 97, 98›

———. "Early Arabic Prose." *Cambridge History of Arabic Literature*, i, 114–153.
‹P. 89›

———., and Ronald Lewcock, eds. *Ṣanʿāʾ, an Arabian Islamic City*. London: World of Islam Festival Trust, 1983.
‹P. 233›

Şeşen, Ramazan. *Salahaddin devrinde Eyyubiler Devleti (Hicri 569–589/Miladi 1174–1193)*. Istanbul: Edebiyat Fakültesi Basimevi, 1983.
‹P. 182›

Setton, K. M., ed. *A History of the Crusades*. 6 vols. Vols. I–II: Philadelphia: University of Pennsylvania Press, 1955–62. Rev. ed., Madison: University of Wisconsin Press, 1969. Vols. III–VI, Madison: University of Wisconsin Press, 1975–89. *See* Cahen, Claude; Gibb, H.A.R.

Severus (Sawīrūs) b. al-Muqaffaʿ. *History of the Patriarchs of Alexandria*.
(1) F. Seybold, ed. *Kitāb siyar al-abāʾ al-baṭārika*. In *CSCO (Scriptores Arabici)*, ser. III, t. ix (Paris, 1904–10).
(2) B. Evetts, ed. and trans. In *Patrologia Orientalis*, i, 2 (1904): St. Mark to Theonas (A.D. 300); i, 4 (1907): Peter I to Benjamin; v, 1 (1910): Agathon to Michael I (A.D.766); x, 5 (1915): Mennas to Joseph (A.D. 849).
(3) Publications de la Société d'Archéologie Copte (Cairo), Textes et Documents. *History of the Patriarchs of the Egyptian Church, known as the History of the Holy Church.*

(a) Vol. II, pt. 1: Khael II to Shenouti I (A.D. 849–880). Ed. and trans. by Y. ʿAbd al-Masīḥ and O.H.E. KHS-Burmester. Textes et Documents, t.iii (1943).
(b) Vol. II, pt. 2: Khael III to Shenouti II (880–1046). Ed. and trans. by A. S. Atiya, Y. ʿAbd al-Masīḥ, O.H.E. KHS-Burmester. Textes et Docs., t. iv (1948).
(c) Vol. II, pt. 3: Christodoulos to Michael (1046–1102). Ed. and trans. by Atiya, ʿAbd al-Masīḥ, Burmester. Textes et Docs., t. v (1959).
(d) Vol. III, pt. 1: Ed. and trans. by Antoine Khater and O.H.E. KHS-Burmester. Textes et Docs., t. xi (1968).
(e) Vol. III, pts. 2–3: Ed. and trans. by Khater and Burmester. Textes et Docs., t. xii–xiii (1970). [Vol. III covers A.D. 1102–1216]
(f) Vol. IV, pts. 1–2. Ed. and trans. by Khater and Burmester. Textes et Docs., t. xiv–xv (1974). [Vol. IV covers A.D. 1216–1243]
‹Pp. 29, 278›

Sezgin, Fuat. *Buhari'nin Kaynakları hakkında Araştırmalar.* Istanbul: Ibrahim Horoz, 1956.
‹Pp. 82, 84›

———. *Geschichte des arabischen Schrifttums.* 9 vols. Leiden: E.J. Brill, 1967–in progress.
‹Pp. 22, 27–28, 29, 30, 35, 36, 39, 75, 77, 78, 81, 114›

———, ed. *Beiträge zur Erschliessung der arabischen Handschriften in Istanbul und Anatolien.* 4 vols. Frankfurt am Main: Institut für Geschichte der Arabisch-Islamischen Wissenschaften a. d. Johann Wolfgang Goethe-Universität, 1986.
‹P. 37›

———, ed. *Beiträge zur Erschliessung der arabischen Handschriften in deutschen Bibliotheken.* Frankfurt am Main: Institut für Geschichte der Arabisch-Islamischen Wissenschaftern a. d. Johann Wolfgang Goethe-Universität, 1987.
‹P. 37›

Sezgin, Ursula. *Abū Miḫnaf: ein Beitrag zur Historiographie der umaiyadischen Zeit.* Leiden: E. J. Brill, 1971.
‹Pp. 82, 88›

———. "al-Madāʾinī." *EI²*, v, 946–48.
‹P. 79›

Shaban, M. A. *The ʿAbbāsid Revolution.* Cambridge: Cambridge University Press, 1970.
‹Pp. 118–119, 122›

———. *Islamic History. A New Interpretation.* 2 vols. Vol. I: A.D. 600–750; Vol. II: A.D. 750–1055. Cambridge: Cambridge University Press, 1971–76.
‹Pp. 119, 122›

al-Shābushtī, ʿAlī b. Muḥammad. *Kitāb al-Diyārāt.* Ed. by Girgis ʿAwwāḍ. Baghdad: Maṭbaʿat al-Maʿārif, 1951; repr. 1966.
‹P. 279›

al-Shahrastānī, Muḥammad b. ʿAbd al-Karīm. *Kitāb al-milal wa'l-niḥal.*
(a) Ed. by William Cureton as *Book of Religious and Philosophical Sects.* 2 vols. London: Society for the Publication of Oriental Texts, 1842–46.
(b) Printed with Ibn Ḥazm, *Kitāb al-fiṣal fī al-milal* (q.v.). 5 vols. Cairo, 1317–21/1899–1903.
(c) Ed. by Muḥammad Fatḥ Allāh Badrān. Cairo, 1951.

(d) Trans. by Theodor Haarbrücker as *Religionsparteien und Philosophenschulen*. Halle: C. A. Schwetschke, 1850–51.
(e) Trans. of Part I by A. K. Kazi and J. G. Flynn, as *Muslim Sects and Divisions*. London: Kegan Paul, 1984.
‹Pp. 112–113›

Shaked, Shaul. *A Tentative Bibliography of Geniza Documents*. Paris and The Hague: Mouton, 1964.
‹Pp. 47, 263›

el-Shamy, Hasan. *Egyptian Folktales*. Chicago: University of Chicago Press, 1980.
‹P. 307›

Sharon, Moshe. *Black Banners from the East: The Establishment of the ʿAbbāsid State—Incubation of a Revolt*. Jerusalem: Magnes Press, and Leiden: E. J. Brill, 1983. *See also* Crone, P.; Daniel, Elton.
‹Pp. 111, 122–123, 124›

———. "Un nouveau corpus des inscriptions arabes de Palestine." *REI*, xlii, no. 1 (1974), 185–191.
‹P. 58›

Shaw, Stanford J. *The Financial and Administrative Organization and Development of Ottoman Egypt, 1517–1798*. Princeton, NJ: Princeton University Press, 1962.
‹Pp. 172, 179, 231›

al-Shaybānī, Muḥammad b. al-Ḥasan. *Kitāb aṣl*. Ed. by Shafīq Shaḥāṭa. Cairo: Maṭbaʿat Jāmiʿat al-Qāhira, 1954. (Only 1 fascicle issued.)
‹P. 215›

———. *Kitāb al-siyar*. Trans. by M. Khadduri as *The Islamic Law of Nations: Shaybānī's Siyar*. Baltimore: Johns Hopkins University Press, 1966.
‹P. 216›

al-Shayzarī. *Nihāyat al-rutba fī ṭalab al-ḥisba*. Ed. by Bāz al-ʿArīnī. Cairo, 1946. *See also* Behrnauer, W.
‹Pp. 242, 272›

Shboul, Ahmad M. H. *Al-Masʿudi and His World: A Muslim Humanist and His Interest in non-Muslims*. London: Ithaca Press, 1979.
‹P. 76›

Shehata, Shafik. *Théorie générale de l'obligation en droit musulman hanéfite*. Paris: Sirey, 1969.
‹P. 215›

———. *Études de droit musulman*. 2 vols. Paris: Presses Universitaires de France, 1971–73.
‹P. 215›

Shils, Edward, and Harry M. Johnson. "Ideology." In *International Encyclopaedia of the Social Sciences*, vii (1968), 66–85.
‹P. 149›

al-Shīrāzī, Abū Isḥāq. *Kitāb al-Tanbīh*. Trans. by G. H. Bousquet. 4 vols. Algiers: La Maison des Livres, 1949–52.
‹P. 214›

Shorter Encyclopaedia of Islam. Ed. by H.A.R. Gibb and J. H. Kramers. Leiden: E. J. Brill, 1953. German version: *Handwörterbuch des Islam*. Ed. by A. J. Wensinck and J. H. Kramers. Leiden: E. J. Brill, 1941.
‹P. 4›

Shoshan, Boaz. "Money Supply and Grain Prices in Fifteenth-Century Egypt." *Economic History Review*, ser. 2, xxxvi (1983), 47–67.
‹P. 304›

Sibṭ b. al-Jawzī, Yūsuf b. Qizughlī. *Mir'āt al-zamān fī ta'rīkh al-a'yān.*
(a) Partial edition by Ali Sevim. Ankara: Türk Tarih Kurumu, 1968. [Events connected with the Seljukids, 448–480 A.H.]
(b) Facsimile edition of Part 8 by J. R. Jewett. Chicago: University of Chicago Press, 1907. [Events of 495–654 A.H.]
(c) Printed edition of the Jewett text. 1 vol. in 2. Hyderabad, Deccan: Da'irat al-Maaref Osmania, 1951–52.
‹Pp. 36, 240›

Siddiqi, A. H. "Caliphate and Kingship in Medieval Persia." *Islamic Culture*, ix (1935), 560–579; x (1936), 97–126, 260–279, 390–408; xi (1937), 37–59.
‹P. 161›

Sinor, Denis. *Introduction à l'étude de l'Eurasie centrale*. Wiesbaden: O. Harrassowitz, 1963.
‹P. 10›

Sivan, Emmanuel. *L'Islam et la Croisade: idéologie et propagande dans les réactions musulmanes aux Croisades*. Paris: A. Maisonneuve, 1968.
‹Pp. 159, 267›

———. "Notes sur la situation des chrétiens à l'époque ayyubide." *RHR*, clxxii (1967), 117–130.
‹P. 267›

Skocpol, Theda. *States and Social Revolutions: A Comparative Analysis of France, Russia and China.* Cambridge and New York: Cambridge University Press, 1979.
‹P. 109›

Sluglett, Peter. *Theses on Islam, the Middle East, and North-West Africa 1880–1978, Accepted by Universities in the United Kingdom and Ireland.* London: Mansell, 1983.
‹P. 10›

Smith, E. Baldwin. *Architectural Symbolism of Imperial Rome and the Middle Ages*. Princeton, NJ: Princeton University Press, 1956.
‹P. 152›

Sobernheim, Moritz. "Die Inschriften der Zitadelle von Damaskus." *Islam*, xii (1922), 1–28.
‹P. 243›

Sourdel, Dominique. *Le vizirat abbaside de 749 à 936 (132 à 324 de l'Hégire)*. 2 vols. Damascus: Institut Français de Damas, 1959–60.
‹Pp. 44, 120, 178›

———. "Questions de cérémonial ʿabbaside." *REI*, xxviii (1960), 121–148.
‹P. 153›

———. "The Abbasid Caliphate." In *Cambridge History of Islam*, i, 104–139.
‹P. 119›

Sourdel, Dominique, and Janine Sourdel. *La civilisation de l'Islam classique*. Paris: Arthaud, 1968.
‹Pp. 60, 153, 229›

Sourdel, D., and J. Sourdel-Thomine. "Nouveaux documents sur l'histoire religieuse et sociale de Damas au Moyen Âge." *REI*, xxxii (1964), 1–25.
‹Pp. 47–48›

———. "A propos des documents de la grande mosquée de Damas conservés à Istanbul. Résultats de la seconde enquête." *REI*, xxxiii (1965), 73–85.
‹P. 48›

———. "Trois actes de vente damascains du début du ive/xe siècle," *JESHO*, viii (1965), 164–185.
‹Pp. 48, 220, 221›

———. "Biens fonciers constitués waqf en Syrie fatimide pour une famille de Šarīfs damascains." *JESHO*, xv (1972), 269–296.
‹P. 220›

———. "Dossiers pour un Corpus des inscriptions arabes de Damas." *REI*, xlvii (1979), 119–171.
‹Pp. 58, 243›

Sourdel-Thomine, Janine. "Les anciennes lieux de pélerinage damascains d'après les sources arabes." *BEO*, xiv (1952–54), 65–85.
‹Pp. 239–240›

———. "Khaṭṭ." *EI*^{2}, iv, 1113–1122.
‹P. 32›

Sourdel-Thomine, Janine., et al. "Kitābāt." *EI*^{2}, v, 210–233.

Sourdel-Thomine, Janine, and Bertold Spuler, eds. *Die Kunst des Islam*. Berlin: Propylaen Verlag, 1973. (Vol. IV in *Propylaen Kunstgeschichte*.)
‹P. 61›

Sousa, Ahmed. *See* Sūsa, Aḥmad.

Soustiel, Jean. *Le céramique islamique. Le guide du connaisseur*. Fribourg, Switzerland: Office du Livre, 1985.
‹P. 62›

Spooner, Brian. "Irrigation and society: The Iranian plateau." In Downing and Gibson, *Irrigation's Impact on Society*, 43–58.
‹P. 295›

Spuler, Bertold. *Iran in frühislamischer Zeit*. Wiesbaden: F. Steiner, 1952.
‹P. 120›

Stamp, Dudley, ed. *A History of Land Use in Arid Regions*. Paris: UNESCO, 1961. *See also* Butzer, Karl; Despois, Jean; Hamdan, G.; Hare, F. K.; Whyte, R. O.
‹P. 291›

Stern, Samuel M. *Fatimid Decrees: Original Documents from the Fatimid Chancery*. London: Faber and Faber, 1964.
‹Pp. 42, 43, 45, 47, 170, 266›

———. "Three Petitions of the Fatimid Period." *Oriens*, xv (1962), 172–209.
‹P. 170›

———. "Petitions from the Ayyubid Period." *BSOAS*, xxvii (1964), 1–32.
‹P. 171›

———. "Two Ayyubid Decrees from Sinai." In S. M. Stern, ed., *Documents from Islamic Chanceries* (Oxford: Bruno Cassirer, 1965), 9–38, 207–216.
‹P. 171›

———. "Petitions from the Mamluk Period." *BSOAS*, xxix (1966), 233–276.
‹P. 171›

———. "The Constitution of the Islamic City." In Hourani and Stern, *The Islamic City*, 25–50.
‹P. 157›

Stevens, C. E. "Agriculture and Rural Life in the Later Roman Empire." In *Cambridge Economic History of Europe* (2d ed.), i, 92–124.
‹P. 300›

Stevenson, W. B. *The Crusaders in the East*. Cambridge: Cambridge University Press, 1907.
‹P. 19›

Stillman, Norman A. *The Jews of Arab Lands: A History and Source Book*. Philadelphia: Jewish Publication Society of America, 1979.
‹P. 264›

———. "The Eleventh-Century Merchant House of Ibn ʿAwkal (a Geniza Study)." *JESHO*, xvi (1973), 15–88.
‹P. 270›

———. "Recent North African Studies in Israel: A Review Article." *IJMES*, viii (1977), 405–407.
‹P. 269›

Stojanow, Valery. *Die Entstehung und Entwicklung der osmanisch-türkischen Paläographie und Diplomatik*. Berlin: K. Schwarz, 1983.
‹P. 43›

Storey, Charles Ambrose. *Persian Literature: a Bio-Bibliographic Survey*. 3 vols., in progress. London: Luzac, 1927–84. *See also* Bregel, Yuri.
‹Pp. 30, 39, 133›

Strauss, Eli (= Ashtor, Eliyahu). "Saladin and the Jews." *Hebrew Union College Annual*, xxvii (1956), 305–326.
‹P. 267›

Sümer, Faruk. *Oğuzlar (Türkmenler): tarihleri, boy teşkilatı, destanları*. Ankara: Ankara Üniversitesi Basımevi, 1972.
‹P. 157›

al-Surūr, Muḥammad Jamāl al-Dīn. *al-Dawla al-Fāṭimiyya fī Miṣr*. Cairo: Dār al-Fikr al-ʿArabī, 1965–66.
‹P. 266›

Sūsa, Aḥmad (= Sousa, Ahmed). *Irrigation in Iraq, its History and Development*. [Jerusalem?]: New Publishers Iraq, 1945.
‹P. 295›

———. *Taṭawwur al-rayy fī al-ʿIrāq*. Baghdad: Maṭbaʿat al-Maʿārif, 1946.
‹Cf. p. 295›

———. *Rayy Samarrāʾ fī ʿahd al-khilāfa al-ʿabbāsiyya*. Baghdad: Maṭbaʿat al-Maʿārif, 1948.
‹Cf. p. 295›

———. *Al-Rayy wa'l-ḥaḍāra fī wādī al-Rāfidayn*. Baghdad: Maṭbaʿat al-Adīb al-Baghdādiyya, 1968.
‹P. 295›

Sweet, Louise E., ed. *Peoples and Cultures of the Middle East*. 2 vols. Garden City, NY: Natural History Press, for the American Museum of Natural History, 1970. *See also* Peters, Emrys.

al-Ṭabarī, Abū Jaʿfar Muḥammad b. Jarīr. *Jāmiʿ al-bayān ʿan taʾwīl al-Qurʾān*. Abridged trans. by John Cooper, as *The Commentary on the Qurʾān*. Vol. I. Oxford: Oxford University Press, 1987–in progress.
‹Pp. 21–22›

———. *Ta'rīkh al-rusul wa'l-mulūk.*
(a) Ed. by M. J. de Goeje et al. 15 vols. Leiden: E. J. Brill, 1879–1901.
(b) Ed. by M.A.F. Ibrāhīm. 10 vols. Cairo: Dār al-Maʿārif, 1960–69.
(c) English trans., *The History of al-Tabari.* Various translators; general editor, Ehsan Yarshater. 38 vols. projected. Albany, NY: State University of New York Press, 1985–in progress.
‹Pp. 14, 35, 72–75, 78, 79, 83, 99, 111›

Tabataba'i, Hossein Modarressi. *Kharaj in Islamic Law.* London: Anchor Press, 1983.
‹Pp. 216, 303›

———. *An Introduction to Shiʿi Law: A Bibliographical Study.* London: Ithaca Press, 1984.
‹P. 214›

al-Tabba, Yasser Ahmad. "The Architectural Patronage of Nur al-Din (1146–1174)." 2 vols. Ph.D. dissertation, New York University, 1982.
‹P. 245›

Tadhkirat al-mulūk. See Minorsky, Vladimir.

al-Ṭaḥāwī. *See* Wakin, Jeanette.

Tahir, Bursali Mehmet. *Osmanlı Muellifleri.*
(a) Ottoman script: 3 vols. Istanbul: Matbaʿa ʿAmire, 1333–42/1914–24.
(b) Modern script: 3 vols. Istanbul: Meral Yayınevi, 1971–75.
‹P. 37›

Tajdin, Nagib. *A Bibliography of Ismailism.* Delmar, NY: Caravan Books, 1985.

Talbi, Mohamed. *L'Émirat aghlabide, 184–296/800–909.* Paris: A. Maisonneuve, 1966.
‹P. 120›

———. "Law and Economy in Ifriqiya (Tunisia) in the Third Islamic Century: Agriculture and the Role of Slaves in the Country's Economy." In Udovitch, *The Islamic Middle East, 700–1900*, 209–250.
‹P. 304›

———. "Ibn Khaldūn." *EI²*, iii, 825–831.
‹P. 194›

al-Tanūkhī, al-Muḥassin b. ʿAlī. *Nishwār al-muḥāḍara.* Trans. by D. S. Margoliouth as *The Table-Talk of a Mesopotamian Judge.*
(a) Part I: Oriental Translation Fund, n.s. 28. London: Royal Asiatic Society, 1922.
(b) Parts II and VIII, in *Islamic Culture*, iii (1929), 487–522; iv (1930), 1–28, 223–238, 363–388, 531–557; v (1931), 169–193, 352–371, 559–581; vi (1932), 47–66, 184–205, 370–396. Separately reprinted by *Islamic Culture* (n.d.)
‹P. 227›

Taqizadeh, H. "Various Eras and Calendars Used in the Countries of Islam." *BSOAS*, ix (1937–39), 903–922; x (1940–42), 107–132.
‹P. 20›

Ta'rīkh-i Sīstān. (Anon.) Ed. by Malik al-Shuʿarā' Bahār. Tehran, 1314/1935. Trans. by Milton Gold as *The Tarīkh-e Sīstān.* Rome: Istituto Italiano per il Medio ed Estremo Oriente, 1976.
‹P. 132›

Ṭarkhān, Ibrāhīm ʿAlī. *al-Nuẓum al-iqṭāʿiyya fī al-Sharq al-Awsaṭ fī al-ʿuṣūr al-wusṭā.* Cairo: Dār al-Kātib al-ʿArabī li'l-Ṭibāʿa wa'l-Nashr, 1968.
‹Pp. 178, 181›

Thoumin, Richard. *Géographie humaine de la Syrie centrale*. Tours: Arrault, 1936.
‹P. 297›

al-Tibrīzī, Walī al-Dīn. *Mishkāt al-Maṣābīḥ*. Trans. by James Robson. 4 vols. Lahore: Sh. Mohammad Ashraf, 1960–65.
‹Pp. 22, 260›

Toussoun, Prince Omar. *Mémoire sur les finances d'Égypte dépuis les Pharaons jusqu'à nos jours*. *MIE*, vi (1924).
‹P. 177›

Tresse, Richard. "L'irrigation dans la Ghouta de Damas." *REI*, iii (1929), 459–574.
‹Pp. 244, 297›

Tritton, A. S. *Materials on Muslim Education in the Middle Ages*. London: Luzac, 1957.
‹P. 201›

———. *The Caliphs and Their Non-Muslim Subjects: A Critical Study of the Covenant of Umar*. London: Oxford University Press, 1930; repr. London: Frank Cass, 1970.
‹Pp. 257, 276›

Trotsky, Leon. *History of the Russian Revolution*. Trans. by Max Eastman. New York: Simon and Schuster, 1952.
‹Cf. p. 109›

Tübinger Atlas des Vorderen Orients. Wiesbaden: L. Reichert, 1977–in progress.
‹Pp. 16, 17›

Turan, Osman. *Selçuklular Tarihi ve Türk-İslam Medeniyeti*. Ankara: Türk Kulturunu Araştırma Enstitüsü, 1965. 2d ed., Istanbul: İstanbul Matbaası, 1969.
‹P. 156›

———. *Türk Cihan Hâkimiyeti Mefkûresi Tarihi*. 2 vols. Istanbul: Turan Neşriyat Yurdu, 1969.
‹P. 166›

———. *Selçuklular zamanında Türkiye*. Istanbul: Turan Neşriyat Yurdu, 1971.

———. "The Ideal of World Domination among the Medieval Turks." *SI*, iv (1955), 77–90.
‹P. 166›

Türkiye Yazmaları Toplu Kataloğu/The Union Catalogue of Manuscripts in Turkey. 11 vols., in progress. Ankara: Türkiye Cumhuriyeti Kultur ve Turizm Bakanlığı; Kütüphaneler Genel Müdürlüğü. Various presses, 1979–continuing.
‹P. 38›

Türkologischer Anzeiger. Vienna: Institut fur Orientalistik der Universität Wien. Annual: Vol. I, 1975–to date.
‹P. 9›

al-Ṭūsī, Muḥammad b. Ḥasan. *al-Istibṣār fīmā ukhtulifa min al-akhbār*. Ed. by H. M. al-Kharsān. 4 vols. Najaf: Dār al-Kutub al-Islāmiyya, 1375–76/1956–57.
‹P. 23›

———. *Tahdhīb al-aḥkām fī sharḥ al-muqniʿa li'l-Shaykh al-Mufīd*. Ed. by H. M. al-Kharsān. 10 vols. Najaf: Dār al-Kutub al-Islāmiyya, 1958–62.
‹P. 23›

Tyan, Émile. *Le notariat et le régime de la preuve par écrit dans la pratique du droit musulman*. Beirut: Annales de l'École Française de Droit de Beyrouth, ii (1945).
‹P. 222›

———. *Le califat. Institutions de droit public musulman*, t. 1. Paris: Recueil Sirey, 1954.

———. *Sultanat et califat. Institutions de droit public musulman*, t. 2. Paris: Recueil Sirey, 1957.
‹P. 161›

———. *Histoire de l'organisation judiciaire en pays d'Islam*. 2 vols. Leiden: E. J. Brill, 1938–43. 2d rev. ed., in 1 vol., 1960.
‹P. 221›

al-Udfuwī, Kamāl al-Dīn Jaʿfar. *al-Ṭāliʿ al-saʿīd al-jāmiʿ li-asmāʾ al-fuḍalāʾ wa'l-ruwāt bi-aʿlā al-Ṣaʿīd.*
(a) Cairo, 1914.
(b) Ed. by S. M. Ḥasan. Cairo: Dār al-Miṣriyya lil-Taʾlīf wa'l-Tarjamah, 1966.
‹P. 204›

Udovitch, A. L. *Partnership and Profit in Medieval Islam*. Princeton, NJ: Princeton University Press, 1970.
‹P. 223›

———, ed. *The Islamic Middle East, 700–1900: Studies in Economic and Social History*. Princeton, NJ: Darwin Press, 1981. *See also* Baer, G.; Lapidus, I. M.; Morony, M.; Rabie, H.; Talbi, M.

———. "Time, the Sea, and Society: Duration of Commercial Voyages on the Southern Shores of the Mediterranean during the High Middle Ages." *Settimane di studio del Centro italiano di studi sull'alto medioevo*, XXV. *La navigazione mediterranea nell'alto medioevo*. Spoleto, 1978. Pp. 503–563.
‹P. 273›

———. "The Jews and Islam in the High Middle Ages: A Case of the Muslim View of Differences." *Settimane di studio del Centro italiano di studi sull'alto medioevo*, XXVI. *Gli Ebrei nell'Alto Medioevo*. Spoleto, 1980. Pp. 655–711.
‹P. 257›

ʿUmar, Fārūq. *See* Omar, Farouk.

al-ʿUmarī, Aḥmad b. Faḍlallāh. *al-Taʿrīf bi'l-muṣṭalaḥ al-sharīf.*
(a) Cairo, 1312/1894.
(b) Partial translation by R. Hartmann. "Politische Geographie des Mamlukenreichs: Kapitel 5 und 6 des Staatshandbuchs Ibn Fadlallah al-ʿOmari's." *ZDMG*, lxx (1916), 1–40, 477–511; lxxi (1917), 429–430.
‹P. 175›

———. *Masālik al-abṣār fī mamālik al-amṣār.*
(a) Partial edition by A. F. Sayyid. *l'Égypte, la Syrie, le Ḥiǧāz et le Yemen*. Cairo: Institut Français d'Archéologie Orientale, 1985.
(b) Partial translation by Maurice Gaudefroy-Demombynes as *L'Afrique moins l'Égypte*. Paris: P. Geuthner, 1927.
(c) Partial translation by Klaus Lech as *Das Mongolische Weltreich*. Wiesbaden: O. Harrassowitz, 1968. (Arabic text, with German resume and detailed commentary).
‹Pp. 174–175, 298›

University of Chicago. *Catalog of the Oriental Institute Library*. 16 vols. Boston: G. K. Hall, 1970.
‹P. 23›

———. *Catalog of the Middle East Collection. First Supplement.* Boston: G. K. Hall, 1977.
‹P. 24›

Urvoy, Dominique. *Le monde des ulemas andalous du v/xie au vii/xiiie siècle*. Geneva: Droz, 1978. *See also* Arié, Rachel.
‹Pp. 207–208›

al-ʿUṣfurī. *See* Khalīfa b. Khayyāṭ.

Vajda, Georges. *Répertoire des catalogues et inventaires de manuscrits arabes*. Paris: Centre National de la Recherche Scientifique, 1949.
‹P. 39›

———. *Les certificats de lecture et de transmission dans les manuscrits arabes de la Bibliothèque Nationale de Paris*. Paris: Centre Nationale de la Recherche Scientifique, 1956.
‹P. 35›

———. *Album de paléographie arabe*. Paris: A. Maisonneuve, 1958.
‹P. 33›

———. "Juifs et musulmans selon le ḥadīṯ." *JA*, ccxxix (1937), 57–127.
‹P. 260›

Valensi, Lucette. *Fellahs tunisiens: l'économie rurale et la vie des campagnes aux 18e et 19e siècles*. Paris and The Hague: Mouton, 1977. Trans. by Beth Archer as *Tunisian Peasants in the 18th and 19th Centuries*. New York: Cambridge University Press, 1985.
‹Pp. 286–287, 292, 304›

Vansina, Jan. *Oral Tradition: A Study in Historical Methodology*. Trans. by H. M. Wright. Chicago: Aldine Publishing Co., 1965.
‹Pp. 86–87›

———. *Oral Tradition as History*. Madison and London: University of Wisconsin Press, 1985.
‹P. 87›

Vaumas, Edmond de. "Études irakiennes (2eme serie): le contrôle et l'utilisation des eaux du Tigre et de l'Euphrate." *Revue de geographie alpine*, xlvi (1958), 235–331.
‹P. 295›

Verzeichnis der orientalischen Handschriften in Deutschland. Wiesbaden: F. Steiner, 1961–in progress.
‹Pp. 37, 39›

Vesely, R. "Trois certificats delivrés pour les fondations pieuses en Egypte au xvie siècle. Troisième contribution à la question des fondations pieuses Ottomanes d'Égypte et de la diplomatique judiciaire." *Oriens*, xxi–xxii (1968–69), 248–299.
‹P. 220›

Vloten, Gerlof van. *De Opkomst der Abbasiden in Chorasan*. Leiden: E. J. Brill, 1890. Reprinted Philadelphia: Porcupine Press, 1977.
‹Pp. 116, 117›

———. "Recherches sur la domination arabe, le chiitisme, et les croyances messianiques sous le Khalifat des Omayades." *Verhandelingen der Koninklijke Akademie van wetenschappen te Amsterdam; Afdeeling Letterkunde*. Deel I, no. 3 (Amsterdam: J. Muller, 1894).
‹Pp. 116, 117›

Vryonis, Speros. *The Decline of Medieval Hellenism in Asia Minor and the Process of Islamization from the Eleventh through the Fifteenth Century*. Berkeley and Los Angeles: University of California Press, 1971. *See also* Cahen, Claude (1973).
‹Pp. 279–281›

Waardenburg, Jean Jacques. *L'Islam dans le miroir de l'Occident.* Paris: Mouton, 1963.
‹P. 195›

Wahb b. Munabbih. *See* Khoury, R. G.

Wakin, Jeanette, ed. *The Function of Documents in Islamic Law: The Chapters on Sales from Ṭaḥāwī's Kitāb al-Shurūṭ al-Kabīr*. Albany, NY: State University of New York Press, 1972.
‹Pp. 218, 222›

Waldman, Marilyn R. *Toward a Theory of Historical Narrative: A Case Study in Perso-Islamicate Historiography*. Columbus, Ohio: Ohio State University Press, 1980.
‹P. 134›

Walker, John. *A Catalogue of the Muhammadan Coins in the British Museum*. 2 vols. London, 1941–56.
‹P. 50›

Wansbrough, John. *Qur'ānic Studies: Sources and Methods of Scriptural Interpretation*. Oxford: Oxford University Press, 1977.
‹P. 84›

———. *The Sectarian Milieu: Content and Composition of Islamic Salvation History*. Oxford and New York: Oxford University Press, 1978.
‹P. 84›

al-Wansharīsī, Aḥmad b. Yaḥyā. *Kitāb al-Wilāyaāt*. Trans. by H. Bruno and M. Gaudefroy-Demombynes as *Le livre des magistratures*. Rabat: F. Moncho, 1937.
‹P. 222›

———. *See also* Amar, Emile; Idris, H. R.
‹P. 218›

Watson, Andrew M. *Agricultural Innovation in the Early Islamic World: The Diffusion of Crops and Farming Techniques, 700–1100*. Cambridge: Cambridge University Press, 1983.
‹P. 294›

Watt, W. M. *Muhammad at Mecca*. Oxford: Clarendon Press, 1953.
‹P. 84›

———. *Muhammad at Medina*. Oxford: Clarendon Press, 1956.
‹Pp. 88, 93, 95–96, 97›

———. *The Formative Period of Islamic Thought*. Edinburgh: Edinburgh University Press, 1973.
‹P. 125›

———. "The Materials Used by Ibn Isḥāq." In Lewis and Holt, *Historians of the Middle East*, 23–34.
‹Pp. 79, 84›

Wehr, Hans. *A Dictionary of Modern Written Arabic*. 1st English edition. Ithaca, NY: Cornell University Press, 1961. 4th ed., revised and expanded. Wiesbaden: O. Harrassowitz, 1979.
‹P. 13›

Weisweiler, Max. "Das Amt des Mustamlī in der arabischen Wissenschaft." *Oriens*, iv (1951), 27–57.
‹P. 35›

Wellhausen, Julius. "Muhammads Gemeindeordnung von Medina." In Wellhausen, *Skizzen und Vorarbeiten* (6 vols. Berlin: G. Reimer, 1884–99). Vol. IV (1889), 65–83.
‹Pp. 92, 96, 97›

———. *Prolegomena zur ältesten Geschichte des Islams*. In Wellhausen, *Skizzen und Vorarbeiten* (6 vols. Berlin: G. Reimer, 1884–99). Vol. VI (1899).
‹Pp. 79, 82–83›

———. *Die religiös-politischen Oppositionsparteien im alten Islam*. In *Abhandlungen der Königlichen Gesellschaft der Wissenschaften zu Göttingen*, vol. V, no. 5 (1901). Trans. by R. C. Ostle and S. M. Walzer as *The Religio-Political Factions in Early Islam*. Amsterdam: North Holland, 1975.
‹P. 125›

———. *Das Arabische Reich und sein Sturz*. Berlin, 1902. Trans. by M. G. Weir as *The Arab Kingdom and Its Fall*. Calcutta: University of Calcutta, 1927. Reprinted, Beirut: Khayats, 1963.
‹Pp. 117, 118›

Wensinck, A. J. *A Handbook of Early Muhammadan Tradition, Alphabetically Arranged*. Leiden: E. J. Brill, 1927. Reprinted 1960; 1971.
‹Pp. 23, 259›

———. et al., eds. *Concordance et indices de la tradition musulmane*. 8 vols. Leiden: E. J. Brill, 1933–88.
‹Pp. 23, 260›

———. *Mohammed en de Joden te Medina*. Leiden: E. J. Brill, 1928. Ed. and trans. by Wolfgang Behn as *Muhammad and the Jews of Medina*. Freiburg im Breisgau: K. Schwarz, 1975.
‹Pp. 93, 97›

Weulersse, Jacques. *L'Oronte: étude de fleuve*. Tours: Arrault, 1940.
‹P. 297›

———. *Le pays des Alaouites*. 2 vols. Tours: Arrault, 1940.
‹P. 297›

———. *Paysans de Syrie et du Proche-Orient*. Paris: Gallimard, 1946.
‹Pp. 297, 305, 306›

White, K. D. *Agricultural Implements of the Roman World*. Cambridge: Cambridge University Press, 1967.
‹P. 300›

———. *Roman Farming*. Ithaca, NY: Cornell University Press, 1970.
‹P. 300›

Whyte, R. O. "Evolution of land use in south-western Asia." In Stamp, *History of Land Use in Arid Regions*, 57–118.
‹P. 291›

Widengren, Geo. "The Sacral Kingship of Iran." In *The Sacral Kingship*, 242–258.
‹P. 162›

Wiet, Gaston. *Catalogue général du Musée Arabe du Caire: lampes et bouteilles en verre émaillé*. Cairo: Institut Français d'Archéologie Orientale, 1929.
‹P. 62›

———. *Catalogue général du Musée Arabe du Caire: objets en cuivre*. Cairo: Institut Français d'Archéologie Orientale, 1932.
‹P. 62›

———. "Les inscriptions arabes de Damas." *Syria*, iii (1922), 153–163.
‹P. 243›

———. "Les secrétaires de la chancellerie (*kuttāb al-sirr*) en Égypte sous les Mamlouks circassiens (784–922/1382–1517)." In *Mélanges René Basset* (2 vols. Paris: E. Leroux, for the Institut des Hautes-Études Marocaines, 1923–25), i, 271–314.
‹P. 183›

———. "Notes d'épigraphie syro-musulmane: inscriptions de la citadelle de Damas." *Syria*, vii (1926), 46–66.
‹P. 243›

———. Les biographies du Manhal Safi. *MIE*, xix (1932).
‹Pp. 176, 206›

———. "Répertoire des décrets mamlouks de Syrie." In *Mélanges René Dussaud* (2 vols. Paris: P. Geuthner, 1939), ii, 521–537.
‹Pp. 172, 243›

Wilkinson, J. C. *Water and Tribal Settlement in South-east Arabia: A Study of the Aflāj of Oman*. Oxford: Clarendon Press, 1977.
‹P. 295›

Willcocks, William. *Egyptian Irrigation*. London: Spon Ltd., 1889. 3d ed., with J. I. Craig. 2 vols. London: Spon Ltd., 1913.
‹P. 299›

Williams, Caroline. "The Cult of ʿAlid Saints in the Fatimid Monuments of Cairo. Part I: The Mosque of al-Aqmar." *Muqarnas*, i (1983), 37–52.
‹P. 56›

———. "The Cult of the ʿAlid Saints in the Monuments of Fatimid Cairo, II: The Mausolea." *Muqarnas*, iii (1985), 39–60.
‹P. 56›

———. "The Qurʾānic Inscriptions on the *Tābūt* of al-Ḥusayn." *Islamic Art*, ii (1987), 3–13.
‹P. 56›

Winkler, Hans Alex. *Ägyptische Volkskunde*. Stuttgart: Kohlhammer, 1936.
‹P. 307›

Wirth, Eugen. *Agrargeographie des Irak*. Hamburger Geographische Studien, 13. Hamburg: Institut für Geographie und Wirtschaftsgeographie der Universität Hamburg, 1962.
‹Pp. 290, 295›

———. *Syrien: eine geographische Landeskunde*. In Wissenschaftliche Länderkunden, ed. Werner Storkebaum, vol. 4/5. Darmstadt: Wissenschaftliche Buchgesellschaft, 1971.
‹Pp. 290, 297›

———. "Zum Problem des Bazars (suq, çarşı). Versuch einer Begriffsbestimmung und Theorie des traditionellen Wirtschaftszentrum der orientalisch-islamischen Stadt." *Islam*, li (1974), 203–260; lii (1975), 6–46.
‹P. 230›

———. "Die orientalische Stadt. Ein Überblick aufgrund jüngerer Forschungen zur materiellen Kultur." *Saeculum*, xxvi (1975), 45–94.
‹P. 230›

Woods, J. E. *The Aqquyunlu: Clan, Confederation, Empire*. Minneapolis and Chicago: Bibliotheca Islamica, 1976.
‹P. 166›

Wörterbuch der klassischen arabischen Sprache. Wiesbaden: O. Harrassowitz, for the Deutsche Morgenländische Gesellschaft, 1957–in progress.
‹P. 13›

Wulff, Hans E. *The Traditional Crafts of Persia: Their Development, Technology, and Influence on Eastern and Western Civilizations*. Cambridge, MA: M.I.T. Press, 1966.
‹Pp. 63, 294›

Wulzinger, Karl, and Carl Watzinger. *Damaskus: die islamische Stadt*. Berlin and Leipzig: W. de Gruyter, 1924.
‹Pp. 244–245›

Wüstenfeld, Heinrich Ferdinand. *Geschichte der Fatimiden-Chalifen nach dem arabischen Quellen*. Gottingen: Dieterich, 1881.
‹P. 266›

Wüstenfeld, H. F., and E. Mahler. *Vergleichungs-Tabellen zur muslimischen und iranischen Zeitrechnung*. 3d edition, revised by J. Mayr and B. Spuler. Wiesbaden: F. Steiner, 1961.
‹P. 19›

Yaḥyā b. Ādam. *See* Ben-Shemesh, A.

Yaḥyā b. Saʿīd al-Anṭākī. *Annals*.
(a) Ed. by L. Cheikho, B. Carra de Vaux, H. Zayyat. *Eutychii Patriarchae Alexandrini Annales*. *CSCO*, 50–51 (*Scriptores Arabici*, ser. III, tt. vi–vii; 1906–1909).
(b) Partial edition and translation by I. Krachkovskii and A. Vasiliev, *Histoire de Yahya-ibn-Saʿid d'Antioche, continuateur de Saʿid-ibn-Bitriq*. *Patrologia Orientalis*, xviii (1924); xxiii (1932).
‹P. 277›

al-Yaʿqūbī, Aḥmad b. Abī Yaʿqūb b. Wāḍiḥ. *al-Taʾrīkh*. Ed. by M. T. Houtsma as *Ibn Wadhih qui dicitur al-Jaʿqubi Historiae*. 2 vols. Leiden: E. J. Brill, 1883; repr. 1969.
‹Pp. 72, 75, 102–103, 111›

———. *Kitāb al-Buldān*. Ed. by M. J. de Goeje. *BGA*, vii (1892). Trans. by Gaston Wiet as *Les pays*. Cairo: Institut Français d'Archéologie Orientale, 1937.
‹P. 18›

Yāqūt b. ʿAbdallāh al-Ḥamawī. *Muʿjam al-buldān*.
(a) Ed. by F. Wüstenfeld as *Jacut's Geographisches Wörterbuch*. 6 vols. Leipzig: F. A. Brockhaus for the Deutsche Morgenländische Gesellschaft, 1866–73.
(b) 5 vols. Beirut: Dār Ṣādir, 1955–57.
‹Pp. 17, 18›

Yūsuf Khāṣṣ Ḥājib. *Kutadgu Bilig*. Ed. by Rahmeti Arat. Istanbul, 1947. Trans. by Robert Dankoff as *Wisdom of Royal Glory: A Turko-Islamic Mirror for Princes*. Chicago and London: University of Chicago Press, 1983.
‹P. 166›

al-Ẓāhirī, Khalīl b. Shāhīn. *Zubdat kashf al-mamālik*. Ed. by Paul Ravaisse. Paris: E.

Leroux, 1894. Trans. by Venture de Paradis (1739–1799), ed. by Jean Gaulmier. Beirut: Institut Français de Damas, 1950.
‹Cf. pp. 173–176›

Zajączkowski, A. *See* Reychman, J.

Zambaur, Eduard von. *Manuel de généalogie et de chronologie pour l'histoire de l'Islam*. Hanover: H. Lafaire, 1927. 2d ed. Bad Pyrmont: H. Lafaire, 1955.
‹Pp. 20, 51›

———. *Die Münzprägungen des Islams, zeitlich und örtlich geordnet*. Ed. by Peter Jaeckel. Wiesbaden: F. Steiner, 1968.
‹P. 51›

al-Ziriklī, Khayr al-Dīn. *al-Aʿlām*. 1st ed. Cairo, 1927–28; 2d revised edition, 11 vols. plus supplement. Cairo, 1954–59; 3d revised edition, 8 vols. Beirut: Dār al-ʿIlm li'l-Malāyīn, 1979.
‹P. 28›

Zwettler, Michael. *The Oral Tradition of Classical Arabic Poetry*. Columbus: Ohio State University Press, 1978.
‹Pp. 87, 151›

INDEX OF TOPICS AND PROPER NAMES